MOON HANDBOOKS

HONDURAS

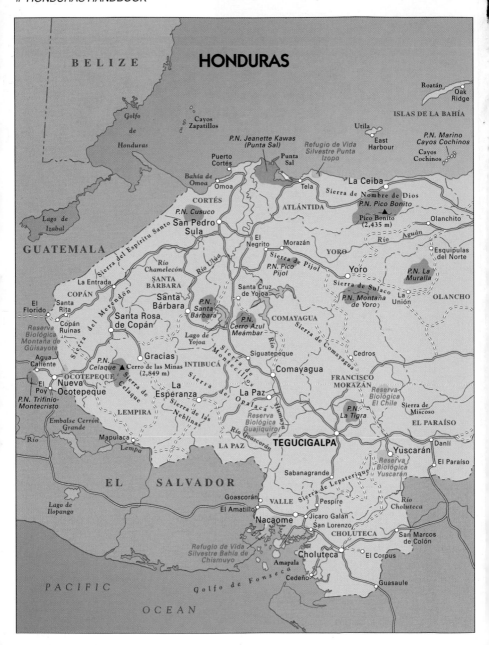

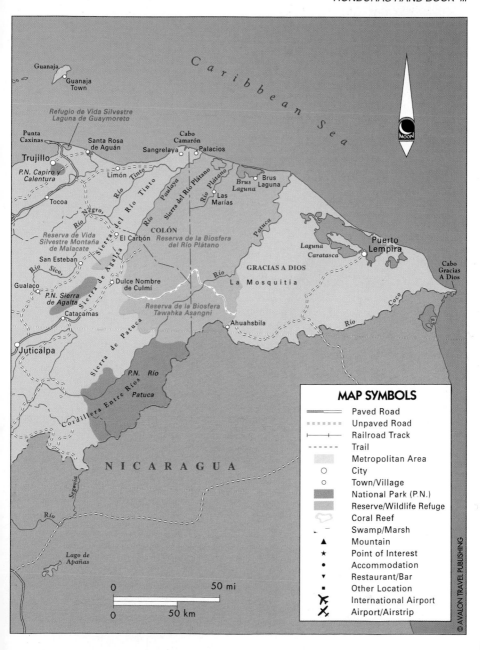

Caribbean Sea

Guanaja
Guanaja
Town

Refugio de Vida Silvestre
Laguna de Guaymoreto

Punta
Caxinas
Santa Rosa
de Aguán
Cabo
Camarón
Sangrelaya
Palacios

Trujillo

P.N. Capiro y
Calentura
Limón
Río Tinto
Río del Río Tinto
Paulaya
Sierra del Río Plátano
Río Plátano
Río Plátano
Brus
Laguna
Brus
Laguna
Las
Marías

Tocoa
Río Negro
Río

COLÓN
Patuca

Reserva de Vida
Silvestre Montaña
de Malacate
El Carbón
Reserva de la Biosfera
del Río Plátano
Laguna
Caratasca
Puerto
Lempira

San Esteban
Sierra de Agalta
GRACIAS A DIOS
Cabo
Gracias
A Dios

Gualaco
Río Sico
La Mosquitia

P.N. Sierra
de Agalta
Dulce Nombre
de Culmí
Río
Río Coco

Catacamas
Reserva de la Biosfera
Tawahka Asangni
Ahuahsbila
Río

Juticalpa
Sierra de Patuca

P.N. Río
Patuca

Cordillera Entre Ríos

N I C A R A G U A

Segovia
Río

Río

Lago de
Apañas

MAP SYMBOLS	
═══════	Paved Road
- - - - - -	Unpaved Road
├──┼──┤	Railroad Track
- - - - -	Trail
	Metropolitan Area
○	City
○	Town/Village
	National Park (P.N.)
	Reserve/Wildlife Refuge
	Coral Reef
	Swamp/Marsh
▲	Mountain
★	Point of Interest
●	Accommodation
▼	Restaurant/Bar
■	Other Location
✈	International Airport
✕	Airport/Airstrip

0   50 mi

0   50 km

MOON

MOON HANDBOOKS

HONDURAS

INCLUDING THE BAY ISLANDS AND COPÁN
SECOND EDITION

CHRIS HUMPHREY

AVALON
TRAVEL
publishing

MOON HANDBOOKS: HONDURAS
THIRD EDITION

Published by
  Avalon Travel Publishing, Inc.
  5855 Beaudry St.
  Emeryville, CA 94608, USA

Please send all comments,
corrections, additions,
amendments, and critiques to:

**MOON HANDBOOKS: HONDURAS
AVALON TRAVEL PUBLISHING, INC.
5855 BEAUDRY ST.
EMERYVILLE, CA 94608, USA
e-mail: info@travelmatters.com
www.moon.com**

Printing History
1st edition—1997
2nd edition—September, 2000
  5 4 3 2

ISBN: 1-56691-210-5
ISSN: 1094-4389

Editor: Marisa Solís
Map Editor: Mike Ferguson
Production & Design: Carey Wilson
Cartography: Brandon Taylor, Chris Folks, Rob Warner, and Mike Morgenfeld
Index: Sondra Nation

Front cover photo: Michael Durham/ENP Images © 2000

All photos by Chris Humphrey unless otherwise noted.
All illustrations by Bob Race unless otherwise noted.

Distributed in the United States and Canada by Publishers Group West
Printed in the United States by Publishers Press.

In memory of all those
who did not make it through
Hurricane Mitch, Oct. 26-Nov. 4, 1998

CONTENTS

ABBREVIATIONS AND ACRONYMS

a/c—air conditioning
cm—centimeters
CODEFFAGOLF—Comite para la Preservación de la Fauna y Flora en el Golfo de Fonseca
Cohdefor—Corporación Hondureño de Desarollo Forestal
d—double
Fucagua—Fundación para la Protección de Capiro, Calentura y Guaymoreto

Fucsa—Fundación Cuero y Salado
IHAH—Instituto Hondureño de Antropología e Historia
km—kilometers
Mopawi—Mosquitia Pawisa, or Mosquitia Development
NGO—non-governmental organization
pp—per person
Prolansate—Fundación para la Protección de Lancetilla, Punta Sal, y Toxiguat

s—single
tel.—telephone
t—triple
UNAH—Universidad Nacional Autonoma de Honduras
P.N.—Parque Nacional
NO—northwest (noroeste)
SO—southwest (sudoeste)
NE—northeast (noreste)
SE—southeast (sudeste)

HELP MAKE THIS A BETTER BOOK

W riting a guidebook is a lot like taking a snapshot: freezing the image of a place on a giant frame. At the same time, however, it's also like stopping progress: locking one version of ever-changing details into print. Although we make herculean efforts to check our facts, the task is an enormous one. You can help us keep up.

If something we mention no longer exists, if certain suggestions are misleading, if you've uncovered anything new, please write in. Although we try to make our maps as accurate as possible, we are always grateful when readers point out any omissions or inaccuracies. When writing, always be as specific and accurate as possible. Notes made on the spot are better than later recollections. Write your comments in your copy of Honduras Handbook as you travel about, then send us a summary when you get home. This book speaks for you, the independent traveler, so please help keep us up to date. Address your letters to:

Honduras Handbook
c/o Avalon Travel Publishing
5855 Beaudry St.
Emeryville, CA 94608
e-mail: info@travelmatters.com (please put "Honduras Handbook" in the subject line of your message)

HOTEL PRICE CATEGORIES

Shoestring . . . . under US$10
Budget . . . . US$10-20
Inexpensive . . . . US$20-40
Moderate . . . . US$40-60
Expensive . . . . US$60-100
Premium . . . . US$100+

MAPS

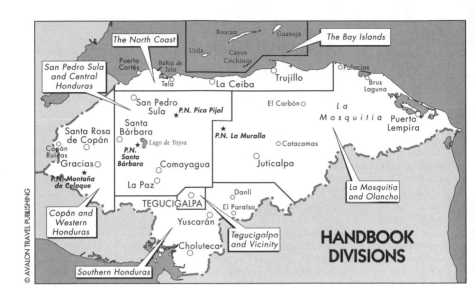

The North Coast

San Pedro Sula and Central Honduras

The Bay Islands

Roatán

Guanaja

Utila

Cayos Cochinos

Puerto Cortés

Bahía de Tela

Tela

La Ceiba

Trujillo

Palacios

Brus Laguna

San Pedro Sula

P.N. Pico Pijol

El Carbón

La Mosquitia

Puerto Lempira

Santa Rosa de Copán

Santa Bárbara

Lago de Yojoa

P.N. La Muralla

Copán Ruinas

P.N. Santa Bárbara

Catacamas

Gracias

Comayagua

Juticalpa

P.N. Montaña de Celaque

La Paz

La Mosquitia and Olancho

TEGUCIGALPA

Danlí

Copán and Western Honduras

El Paraíso

Yuscarán

HANDBOOK DIVISIONS

Choluteca

Tegucigalpa and Vicinity

Southern Honduras

ACKNOWLEDGMENTS

Of the many, many people I am indebted to for helping me out on this edition, first and foremost goes a collective huge thanks to Peace Corps volunteers past and present, who are my most faithful readers, best informants, and generally a good bunch of people. Among the volunteers whom I ran across and ruthlessly interrogated this time around are Tony and Caroline Teene in La Esperanza, Eric Wilson and Todd McCormick in Gualaco, Anat Shenkar at La Tigra, Aaron Hall and Alina Cushing in Dulce Nombre de Culmí, Clint in Teupasenti, Peter Weber, Mark Wolf in Colomancagua, Chelly Richards in Olancho, the three volunteers I met in El Corpus (whose names I unfortunately forgot to write down), and Paul White in Sabanagrande. Past volunteers I spoke with include Kent Forté, Roberto Gallardo, Erik Nielsen, and Mandy Thill. Mark Bonta and his lovely wife Luz get a special thanks for providing an incredible amount of information on their beloved Olancho and the birds of Honduras.

The list of "civilians" in Honduras who took the time to answer all my pesky questions would go on for pages. Those mentioned below went out of their way to help me in some way or another, and for that a heartfelt thanks to Phil, Carol, and Kaj at Ocean Divers in West End; Jennifer Keck at RIMS; Marion Seaman in Coxen Hole; Candace in Sandy Bay; both Hugo Cisneros at the Coral Cafe and Hansito of Manati Resort in Guanaja; Peggy Brinkley and Peter at Turtle Tours in Trujillo; Howard Rosenzweig and Dr. Oscar Cruz in Copán Ruinas; Alan Youngblood and family in La Ceiba; jungle adventurer par excellence Jorge Salaverri of La Moskitia Eco-Aventuras; Pierre Couture and French Freddie in Tela; Jorge Travieso; Alexis Oliva at Aldea Global in Siguatepeque; Tom Taylor (again—keep up the good work!) at Tobacco Road Tavern in Tegucigalpa; Gloria Zelaya and Jochen Leitz of the Proyecto de Manejo y Protección de la Biósfera del Río Plátano; Karl Borski at Ríos Honduras; George Bustillos in Yoro; Antonio Orellano and Israel López for helping me out of a serious fix in Morazán; "El Negro" for providing unexpected insights into life in Tegucigalpa; Enrique Campo and Richard Joint on Lago de Yojoa; César Sánchez Moreno; Don Cecilio Tatallón, Cely Lainez, and hoopster Tom Keogh in Puerto Lempira; and Digna Domínguez at the Instituto Hondureño de Turismo. John Dupuis and Peter Hughes of Honduras Tips, I owe you one for rescuing my truck and myself from an unpleasant evening in La Barca. Thanks to Guillermo Cobos and Vince Murphy for taking lots of lovely photos, a few of which grace the pages of this book, and for their useful suggestions and tips accumulated from years wandering the back roads and trails of Honduras.

Thanks to those who took the time to write me, either by snail mail or email, with their observations and comments about the book and Honduras in general: Mark Getzoff, Clayton & Merilee Reed, H. Wooler, Lil' Smiley, Hans & Carrie Levenson-Wahl, Birgit Arras, Dr. Mary Ann Danowitz Sagaria, Mark & Denise Brandon, Jenifer Neils, Sarah Robinson, Corien van Vliet, Don Meinders, Tomoko Arikawa, Ken Bradshaw, and Dan Moscow. And to Kendra McSweeney for passing along a very well-written article on the Tawahka, which I cribbed shamelessly.

To good friend Grant Raddon, thanks for doing an excellent job updating Utila, Tela, and parts of western Honduras—hope you've got some spare time in about three years.

And last but far from least, thanks to Pete, Kate, and Carmen, for keeping me company on parts of the journey.

INTRODUCTION

Well, it made no difference to him now. He had eaten of the lotus. He was happy and content in this land of perpetual afternoon. Those old days in the States seemed like an irritating dream . . . The climate was as balmy as that of distant Avalon; the fetterless, idyllic round of enchanted days; the life among this indolent, romantic people—a life full of music, flowers, and low laughter; the influence of the imminent sea and mountains, and the many shapes of love and magic and beauty that bloomed in the white tropical nights—with all he was more than content.

—O. HENRY,
CABBAGES AND KINGS

A growing number of foreigners are eating of the same lotus that so entranced short-story writer—and, at the time, fugitive from the law—O. Henry (William Sydney Porter) and his fictional consul Willard Geddie at the turn of the century. Long a forgotten Central American country—thought of, when at all, as the ultimate banana republic—Honduras is fast emerging as a favorite travel destination.

It's surprising that it didn't happen sooner. All the ingredients are here: powdery soft beach-es lined with palm trees and lapped by turquoise waves, superb coral reef, Mayan ruins, cobblestone colonial villages clinging to green hillsides, the untracked jungles of La Mosquitia, and mountaintop cloud forests teeming with colorful birds and chattering monkeys.

When foreigners return from Honduras, they invariably comment with surprise on the extent of the country's forests, the many possibilities for adventure traveling and visiting remote towns and countryside, and the remarkably low cost of food, transport, and accommodations.

But Honduras' greatest asset, and the most important reason travelers find the country a joy to explore, is the relaxed, friendly people. Foreign tourists are still uncommon in many parts of Honduras, especially out in the countryside, and visitors often feel they're being treated as equals. Anyone who spends any time at all in Honduras with an open mind and a friendly disposition will be amazed at how easily Hondurans open themselves up to strangers. They're curious to learn about your country and eager to tell you about theirs.

Devastating Hurricane Mitch, which struck in late October 1998, brought Honduras to front pages around the world for a couple of weeks, and the ensuing negative image left in foreign minds about the country put a severe dent in

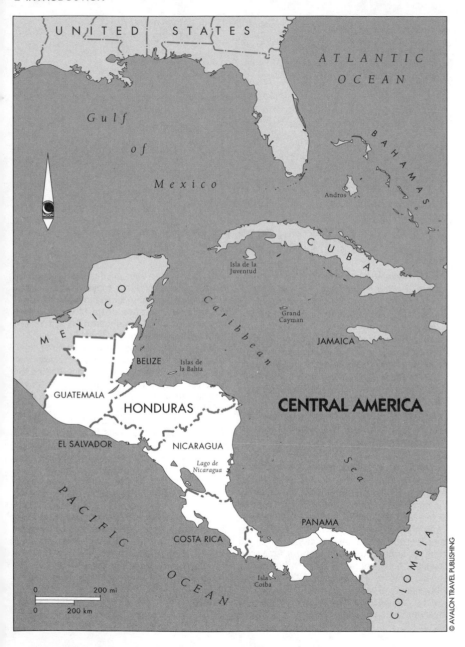

UNITED STATES

ATLANTIC OCEAN

Gulf

of

Mexico

BAHAMAS

Andros

MEXICO

CUBA

Isla de la Juventud

Caribbean

Grand Cayman

JAMAICA

MEXICO

BELIZE

Islas de la Bahía

GUATEMALA

HONDURAS

CENTRAL AMERICA

EL SALVADOR

NICARAGUA

Lago de Nicaragua

Sea

PACIFIC

PANAMA

COSTA RICA

Isla Coiba

COLOMBIA

OCEAN

0   200 mi

0   200 km

© AVALON TRAVEL PUBLISHING

tourism the following year. While a few roads are still pretty beaten up and several temporary bridges have yet to be replaced, the vast majority of tourist infrastructure was little touched by the storm, and Hondurans are eagerly hoping foreign visitors return in even greater numbers to help give their economy a much-needed boost.

THE LAND

Honduras is located at the great bend where Central America sweeps east into the Caribbean from the base of Mexico and then takes an abrupt 90-degree turn southward before trending eastward again to link with South America. The second-largest country in Central America, after Nicaragua, Honduras covers 112,491 square kilometers, an area about the size of England. While one imaginative geographer likened Honduras' shape to that of "a sleeping basilisk," the more prosaic-minded among us see an inverted triangle, the apex pointing due south into the Pacific Ocean, and the base (bulging on the eastern side) facing north into the Caribbean Sea.

The country's perimeter consists of a 342-km border with El Salvador, a 256-km border with Guatemala, a 922-km border with Nicaragua, 735 km of north-facing Caribbean coastline, and 153 km of southern, Pacific coastline. At its widest point—between Cerro Montecristo, on the border with El Salvador and Guatemala, and Cabo Gracias a Dios, bordering Nicaragua—Honduras extends 675 km.

The main landmass of Honduras sits roughly between latitude 16° N on the north coast and 13° N at the Gulf of Fonseca, and between longitude 83° 15" W at Cabo Gracias a Dios and 89° 20" W near Nueva Ocotepeque. Honduras'

HONDURAS HIGHLIGHTS

SUGGESTED ITINERARY (TWO-WEEK TRIP)

- Two days at the Mayan ruins of Copán
- Three days at the colonial town of Gracias, with side trips to colonial villages and/or a hike up to the cloud forests of Parque Nacional Celaque
- Four days at the beaches of Tela, with visits to nearby Garífuna villages and the nature reserves of Punta Sal, Lancetilla, or Punta Izopo
- Five days scuba diving or snorkeling on the Bay Island of your choice

THE BEST BEACHES, WITH ALL THE AMENITIES

- West Bay, Roatán
- Cayos Cochinos, Plantation Beach Resort
- Trujillo town beach
- Telamar beach in Tela

THE BEST BEACHES, WITH MINIMAL OR NO AMENITIES

- Water Cay, Utila
- Camp Bay Beach, Roatán
- Miami, near Tela
- Chachahuate, Cayos Cochinos
- Anywhere on the coast of La Mosquitia

BEST BIRDWATCHING SITES

- Lago de Yojoa
- Jardín Botánico Lancetilla, near Tela
- Parque Nacional La Tigra
- Parque Nacional Cusuco
- La Mosquitia

BEST ADVENTURE HIKING REGIONS

- Reserva de la Biosfera del Río Plátano
- Parque Nacional Sierra de Agalta
- Parque Nacional Pico Bonito
- Parque Nacional Celaque
- Sierra de la Botija, near Choluteca

BEST PLACES TO MEET OTHER TRAVELERS

- East Harbour, Utila
- West End, Roatán
- Copán Ruinas
- Hotel Granada, Tegucigalpa

BEST COLONIAL TOWNS AND VILLAGES

- Gracias a Dios, Lempira
- Belén Gualcho, Lempira
- Ojojona, Francisco Morazán
- Cedros, Francisco Morazán
- Yuscarán, El Paraíso

Caribbean possessions the Swan Islands lie at latitude 17° 30" N.

Approximately two-thirds of Honduras is covered by rugged mountain ranges, or *cordilleras*. These mountains are the country's principal defining geographic feature and have played an important role in Honduran history, isolating the country from its neighbors and limiting agricultural development.

Flat areas are found mainly along the narrow north and south coastal plains, the jungle-covered lowland plains of the Mosquitia, and a very few inland valleys.

GEOGRAPHY

Geological Setting

About 75 million years ago, in the mid-Cretaceous geological era, the tectonic plate on which Honduras sits constituted itself in the mid-Pacific Ocean and began drifting in a northeasterly direction. By the Miocene era, this plate—called the Caribbean Plate—had plugged itself neatly into an existing gap between the North American and South American Plates, forming a land bridge between the two continents. But as it happens, the gap wasn't as big as the landmass, so the Caribbean Plate has been gradually pinched by its two larger neighbors—a principal factor shaping Honduras' tumultuous topography. Although the pinching has slowed its

progress, the Caribbean Plate obstinately continues moving east and northeast at a rate of two to four centimeters a year. At that rate, Honduras should be nudging up against Cuba in 25 million years or so.

Crashing into the Caribbean Plate from behind is the Cocos Plate, the culprit in a great deal of seismic and volcanic activity in Mexico and on the western coast of Central America. The Cocos Plate, apparently propelled with a great deal of energy, is thrusting under the Caribbean and parts of the North American Plates, forcing these landmasses upward and creating the region's steep Pacific slope mountains. Tiny slips between these plates, pushing up against one another with unimaginable force, unleash regular earthquakes and volcanic activity.

Although plate tectonics are a prime factor in creating Honduras' tortured topography, the country is largely free of volcanoes and earthquakes. The most recent significant quake struck Amapala—on the Pacific and close to the Cocos Plate—on April 2, 1999, registering 5.0 on the Richter scale, causing minor damage but no serious injuries.

Situated on the northwestern part of the Caribbean Plate, Honduras forms part of the border (geologically speaking) against the North American Plate. The fault is clearly visible just over the border in Guatemala, in the form of the Río Motagua Valley. Offshore, the Bay Islands and, farther off, the Swan Islands are located

right at the edge of the fault—which at that point is a deep undersea trough called the Bartlett or Cayman Trench. Because the two plates are slipping past each other here, rather than meeting head-on, this fault is less prone to geological activity than the Cocos.

Mountain Ranges

After glancing at a topographical map of Honduras, one is tempted to say that the entire country is one big mountain range and leave it at that. In Mexico and other Central American countries, the *cordilleras* are long, parallel rows. But because Honduras is at the junction of the Caribbean, North American, and Cocos Plates, its landmass has been geologically squeezed, resulting in a jumble of small mountain ranges and isolated massifs zigzagging across the country in all different directions and in no apparent order.

In fact, however, the mountains are divided fairly clearly into two "groups." The first, caused by the pushing between the Caribbean and North American Plates, consists of several ranges roughly trending west to east or southwest to northeast. Forming the border with Guatemala, right on the south side of the Motagua Fault, is the ancient and well-worn range known variously, over the course of its run from the southwest corner of the country to its plunge into the Caribbean Sea by Omoa, as the **Cordillera del Merendón, Sierra del Espíritu Santo,** and **Sierra de Omoa.** The Bay Islands are actually an expression of this same range, where it pops its head up again offshore and forms the edge of Honduras' continental shelf in the Caribbean. In northern Honduras, the **Sierra Nombre de Dios** parallels the north coast between Tela and Trujillo, forming a narrow coastal plain and reaching an elevation of 2,480 meters at Montaña Corozal in Parque Nacional Pico Bonito. Farther east, **Sierra de Agalta** begins in the center of the Olancho department and extends northeast into La Mosquitia, though its name changes to **Sierra del Carbón** and **Sierra del Río Tinto** as it heads north. This range, along with the smaller **Sierra La Esperanza** to the west, forms the principal boundary on the western side of the Mosquitia, an isolated lowland region in northeastern Honduras. Branching off from the Agalta range just to the east is a jumbled cluster of mountains and high ridges known as the Mon-

tañas del Patuca, or Montaña de Punta Piedra. Beginning in the El Paraíso department is the aptly named **Cordillera Entre Ríos,** which runs northeasterly between the Patuca and Coco Rivers. Farther north into Mosquitia, this range is known as the Montañas de Colón.

The second group of mountains in Honduras is a series of short, rugged ranges running parallel to one another roughly northwest-southeast, extending from El Salvador into the center of the country. Closest to El Salvador is the tallest, **Sierra de Celaque,** topped by Cerro de las Minas, the highest peak in the country at 2,849 meters. Farther northeast are the **Cordillera Opalaca, Cordillera Montecillos, Montaña Meámber, Montaña de Comayagua,** and **Sierra de Sulaco** in Yoro. Beyond Sierra de Sulaco, these mountains run into conflicting geological formations, resulting in the crazy labyrinth of ridges and valleys in western and central Olancho.

Isolated ranges include Montaña de Santa Bárbara, at the edge of Lago de Yojoa—the country's second-highest peak at 2,744 meters—and several mountains in the vicinity of Tegucigalpa.

Except for a few eroded cones in the Golfo de Fonseca, none of the mountains in Honduras are volcanic—in sharp contrast to neighboring Guatemala, Nicaragua, and El Salvador.

Valleys and Rivers

Crisscrossing this mountainous countryside are several major river systems and countless smaller ones. Honduras shares the largest river in Central America, the Río Coco, with Nicaragua, but contains the second-largest, the Río Patuca, completely within its borders. Because the continental divide is quite far south in Honduras, most big rivers drain to the north, into the Caribbean Sea, though four sizable rivers do flow south to the Pacific.

In the western part of Honduras, long a center of human settlement and economic activity, is the broad **Valle de Sula,** through which flow the 200-km Río Chamelecón (born in the hills by the Guatemalan border near the ruins of Copán) and the much bigger Río Ulúa, draining a huge area of western Honduras in its 400-km course to the north coast. The flat, flood-prone lower part of the Valle de Sula, particularly around El Progreso and La Lima, is one of the principal banana regions of the country.

East of the Río Ulúa, several short but furiously intense rivers pour off the steep flanks of the coastal Sierra Nombre de Dios, notably the **Río Cangrejal**, near La Ceiba, a favorite among rafters and kayakers. Gathering the waters from the south side of the Sierra Nombre de Dios as well as the mountains of Yoro and western Olancho, the 200-km **Río Aguán** cuts its path in a northeasterly direction to the Caribbean. The banana companies maintain extensive plantations in the wide, rich Aguán Valley.

The wild Mosquitia region, in the far northeast corner of Honduras, is home to several large rivers, born in the mountains far to the south. The 215-km Río Tinto and its largest tributary, the Paulaya, both begin in the Sierra de Agalta of central Olancho, and pass through what was once rainforest but is now mostly pastures and small farms. Just east is the smaller Río Plátano, still blanketed by virgin jungle and protect-

ed as a biosphere reserve. The mighty Río Patuca, still farther east, courses over 500 km from as far south as the departments of El Paraíso and Francisco Morazán not far from Tegucigalpa, through Olancho and down to Mosquitia. Several of the Patuca's tributaries, including the Guayape, Guayambre, and Wampú, are known for producing gold. The Río Coco, even longer than the Patuca, forms a large part of the land border between Honduras and Nicaragua on its 550-km route to Cabo Gracias a Dios.

On the south side of the country, the largest river system is that of the Río Choluteca, which takes a convoluted horseshoe route starting off in a northerly direction through Tegucigalpa, then coming around in a sweeping 180-degree turn to empty into the Golfo de Fonseca. On the Pacific. West of the Choluteca are the smaller Río Nacaome and the Río Goascorán, the latter forming part of Honduras' border with El Salvador.

The so-called Honduran Depression cuts a lowland gap through the country, following the

THE SOCCER WAR AND OTHER BORDER DISPUTES

For over two centuries, Honduras and El Salvador have disputed portions of the border between them in a remote mountain region and in the Golfo de Fonseca. This conflict, along with land shortages and immigration pressures, contributed to the outbreak of the so-called "Soccer War" in 1969.

The war seemed to be sparked by a World Cup soccer match between the two countries. While sporting passions do run high in Central America, the real reasons behind the fighting were much more serious. For years, land-hungry *campesinos* from overpopulated El Salvador had been crossing the mountainous border and setting up small farms and businesses in Honduras. By the late 1960s, Salvadoran immigrants made up roughly 20% of Honduras' rural population—this at a time when Honduras had begun feeling land pressures of its own. Wealthy Honduran landowners began waging a cynical propaganda campaign that distracted from the country's internal problems and fueled a growing hatred for the Salvadorans.

In April 1969, the Honduran government gave Salvadoran settlers 30 days to return to their country; by June, some 20,000 had fled. (Others were victimized by irate Hondurans and the Mancha Brava, a National Party vigilante squad.) That same

month, the two countries faced one another in elimination matches to qualify for the 1970 World Cup.

The first match was held on 8 June in Tegucigalpa. As is common practice, loyal hometown fans gave the visiting team a sleepless night by screaming, honking horns, and setting off firecrackers in the streets below its hotel. The following day, the Salvadoran squad predictably lost, 1-0. A young Salvadoran girl shot herself in grief over the loss, furthering the drama and tension, and tens of thousands of Salvadorans—including the country's president and the soccer team—marched to her funeral.

A week later, for the second match, the Honduran team traveled to San Salvador. This time, of course, the Salvadoran fans kept the Honduran team awake all night; at the game, they booed the Honduran national anthem and ran a rag up the flagpole instead of the Honduran flag. Honduras lost the match 3-0, and violence erupted. The Honduran team had to be escorted to the airport by the military, and visiting Honduran fans were beaten (dozens were hospitalized, and two died).

Because of the violence, the deciding third match was postponed. A month later, on 14 July, the El Salvador military bombed several locations inside Honduras and launched a surprise land attack. The

Río Ulúa, up the Río Humaya into the Valle de Comayagua, over a low pass and down to the Pacific along the Río Goascorán. For many years successive Honduran governments hoped to build a transcontinental railway along this route, which at its highest point—on the continental divide—is only 870 meters. Another major tributary to the Ulúa, the Río Otoro, also almost meets the Pacific-flowing Río Lempa, separated by a pass of 1,050 meters.

Numerous intermontane basins of varying sizes, usually between 300 and 900 meters above sea level, are located throughout Honduras. The larger ones, like the Valle de Comayagua (Comayagua), Valle de Catacamas (Olancho), Valle de Jamastrán (El Paraíso), and Valle de Sensetí (Ocotepeque), are intensively worked for crops or cattle, or both.

Lakes and Lagoons

The only natural lake of any size in the country is **Lago de Yojoa,** 16 km long by eight km wide at an elevation of 635 meters. With the construction of El Cajón dam, a larger man-made lake has been created along the Río Humuya.

On the north coast, and particularly in Mosquitia, are many lagoons and freshwater wetlands, separated from the ocean by narrow sandbars. Among the larger lagoons are Laguna de Alvarado behind Puerto Cortés, Laguna de los Micos near Tela, Cuero y Salado just west of La Ceiba, and Laguna Guaymoreto outside of Trujillo.

In Mosquitia, farther east, these lagoon systems are much more extensive. The largest is **Laguna Caratasca,** measuring 66 km long by 14 km wide, and linked by waterways to the adjacent Tansin and Warunta lagoons. Other large lagoons in Mosquitia include **Laguna de Brus** and **Laguna de Ibans.** In fact, one could reasonably consider the entire Mosquitia coastal area one huge freshwater wetland system, as networks of canals and seasonal waterways extend basically from the Río Coco all the way to Palacios.

Salvadoran Army made it deep into Honduras, but, when the Honduran Air Force destroyed the Salvadorans' main fuel depot, was unable to advance. The war lasted 100 hours. Some 2,000 people, mostly Honduran *campesinos,* were killed, and 130,000 Salvadorans returned to their country. Apart from releasing nationalistic frustrations on both sides, the war accomplished nothing. The final soccer match was eventually held 26 June in Mexico City; El Salvador won 3-2.

A Tentative Peace

The two countries' governments signed a peace agreement formally terminating hostilities on 30 October 1980, but, unable to resolve their boundary dispute, submitted the problem to the International Court of Justice at the Hague. In September 1992, the ICJ handed down its ruling, awarding Honduras 300.6 square kilometers of the disputed 436.9 square kilometers. Of the six *bolsones* (pockets of land) in the mountains, Honduras was given control of one in its entirety and 80% of another; the remaining four were divided nearly equally with El Salvador.

In the Golfo de Fonseca, the islands of Meanguera and Meanguerita were granted to El Salvador, while Honduran ownership of Isla del Tigre was confirmed. The court also ruled that Honduras had the right to free passage in the Gulf—an important aspect of the dispute. According to the ruling, the Gulf is not international waters but is owned in a condominium arrangement between El Salvador, Honduras, and Nicaragua, each of which possesses gulf coastline.

In spite of the ruling, localized conflicts still occur in the *bolsones.* Honduran and Salvadoran *campesinos* occasionally attack one another in arguments over land. But both governments appear to be trying to calm tensions.

A Second Front

More recently, a second border conflict has caused turmoil between Honduras and another neighbor, Nicaragua. In the Caribbean, Hondurans draw the maritime border at the 15th parallel, while Nicaraguans claim their border extends to the 17th parallel (which would comprise the entirety of Honduras' Caribbean coastline, as well as a portion of Belize's). In December 1999, this long-simmering conflict blew up into mutual accusations, threats, and front-page news. It turns out that in passing a maritime treaty with Colombia, Honduras had stepped on Nicaraguan ambitions to expand its limited offshore territory in the Caribbean. After much saber rattling by the unabashedly populist Nicaraguan President Arnoldo Alemán, and the slapping of a 35% import tariff on Honduran imports, tempers cooled and the matter seemed destined to be settled in a lengthy court case at the International Court in the Hague. The expected result is that the border will remain at the 15th parallel.

Coastal Plains

Considered an inhospitable, malarial swamp by the Spaniards, Honduras' northern coastal plain has for the past century been the country's most intensively exploited region, mainly producing bananas and pineapple for foreign fruit companies. For most of its length the plain is quite narrow, in places only a couple of kilometers separating the ocean from the Cordillera Nombre de Dios.

The only places the plain extends inland a significant distance are the valleys of the Ulúa, Chamelecón, and Aguán Rivers, and in the broad expanse of La Mosquitia. The Mosquitia plain, in the northeast corner of the country, encompasses more flat land than the rest of the country combined, but because of its thin, acidic soil the region is unsuitable for agriculture.

The Pacific lowlands are on average only 25 km wide, composed mainly of heavily cultivated alluvial soils tapering into mangrove swamps at the edge of the Gulf of Fonseca. After years of deforestation and poor farming techniques, the once-rich soils of these plains have long since eroded.

Islands

In the Caribbean, the three main Bay Islands (Islas de la Bahía) of Utila, Roatán, and Guanaja, plus many smaller cays, are considered a continuation of the Sierra de Omoa, a northeast trending mountain range that meets the Caribbean west of Puerto Cortés. Farther north are the smaller Swan Islands (Islas del Cisne), also thought to be part of the same geological formation.

Honduras owns several small islands in the Gulf of Fonseca, the largest of which are Isla del Tigre and Isla Zacate Grande, both eroded volcanoes at the southern end of a mountain chain that begins in El Salvador.

CLIMATE

Temperatures

Honduras is situated completely within the tropics—south of the Tropic of Cancer and north of the Tropic of Capricorn—and like most tropical countries, temperature is defined more by altitude than by season. Generally, temperatures change little from month to month in the same location, apart from slight cooling during the rainy

season. January and February are the coolest months, while March and April are the hottest, although temperatures rarely vary more than 5° C on average throughout the year.

The Caribbean and Pacific lowland regions are both known as *tierra caliente* (hot land), where average daytime high temperatures hover between 28° and 32° C throughout the year. Rain and strong ocean breezes offer some relief and are often present on the north coast, the Bay Islands, and the islands of the Gulf of Fonseca. Interior lowland regions, such as the Valle de Ulúa or the Valle de Aguán, are often extremely hot and humid, and the Choluteca plains are downright scorching for much of the year, particularly during the dry season, with daytime temperatures occasionally hitting 40° C.

Much of central Honduras, between 500 and 1,800 meters, is *tierra templada* (temperate land). Here temperatures usually stay comfortable throughout the year, pleasantly warm but not overly hot during the day and cool in the evening. Tegucigalpa, in a sheltered valley at about 1,000 meters, is a classic example of such a climate zone; daytime highs average 24° C in January and 29° C in April, while lows in those months average 14° C and 18° C, respectively.

The mountain country, above 1,800 meters, is called *tierra fría* (cold land), where temperatures average 16-20° C during the day and can drop to freezing at night. Strong winds, mist, clouds, and tree cover help keep temperatures down. The highest, cloud forest-covered peaks are the coldest locations in Honduras. Hiking these forests can be pleasantly cool during the day, but be ready for the evening chill. Regions particularly known for their cold weather are in the departments of Intibucá, Lempira, or La Paz, in the mountains of southwest Honduras.

Precipitation

Relatively speaking, Honduras has a humid climate. The country averages around 82% humidity, with the dampest areas being the north coast and Mosquitia, and the driest on the Pacific coast.

In some regions, particularly in the south, center, and west of Honduras, the wet and dry seasons are quite well defined. Usually the rainy season *(invierno)* begins in May or June and continues to November or December. This wet period is often broken in August by a three- to four-week

THE PITILESS PATH OF HURRICANE MITCH

By late October, the 1998 Caribbean hurricane season was drawing to a close. The season had already been particularly ferocious, with several intense storms in September and early October, the most recent being Lisa, with winds up to 170 kph.

After a couple of quiet weeks following Lisa, the inhabitants of the Caribbean thought perhaps that would be it for 1998. But late in the day on Monday, 19 October, meteorologists monitoring the Caribbean Sea took note of a tropical low forming not far from the coasts of Colombia and Panama.

The system began to take proper shape as a low pressure zone by midday on Wednesday, 21 October, located some 600 km south of Jamaica. Revolving at a still-leisurely 50 kph but gathering speed rapidly, the low began moving north at about 15 kph. By the following day, with the barometer falling below 1,000 millibars, meteorologists dubbed the thirteenth tropical storm of the year Mitch. The eye of the storm, now surrounded by winds of almost 100 kph, was 700 km southeast of Bluefields, Nicaragua.

Predicting the course taken by a tropical storm is far from an exact science, but Caribbean hurricanes tend to follow certain routes. Meteorologists expected that Mitch, which had constituted itself in the southwestern Caribbean and moved off to the north-northwest, would continue northward. Shore-line residents in Mexico, Cuba, Jamaica, and along the U.S. Gulf of Mexico listened to the ominous weather reports and began to batten down and prepare for the worst.

But on 24 October, now with winds of 160 kph and classified as a category two hurricane on the Saffir-Simpson scale, Mitch ceased to follow a normal trajectory. Running up against a high pressure system in the Gulf of Mexico, the storm began to slow down, and veer off to the west, toward the coast of Belize and the southern Yucatán Peninsula.

On the 24th, the first heavy rains began falling on the Central American peninsula (starting, oddly enough, on the Pacific coasts of Costa Rica and Nicaragua) as Mitch's spiraling arms, spinning ever faster, interacted with a stationary low-pressure system west of Central America.

By Monday, 26 October, Mitch had progressed into a category five hurricane, with sustained winds of 290 kph, gusts over 350 kph, and a barometer reading of 906 millibars—the second-lowest reading recorded this century in the Atlantic (in 1969, Camille posted 905 millibars but only reached category four). The hurricane's eye passed over the Swan Islands, due north of Honduras, and kept moving very slowly to the west, roughly parallel to the north coast. Torrential rains began pummeling northern Honduras and northeastern Nicaragua.

(continued on next page)

the Río Choluteca swollen by Hurricane Mitch

GUILLERMO COBOS

THE PITILESS PATH OF HURRICANE MITCH

(continued)

Although the hurricane was only 50 km or so off of the coast, storm projections still did not foresee Mitch hitting Honduras; instead, estimates showed it moving west toward Belize or the Yucatán. But on the morning of 26 October, Mitch began turning yet again, this time to the south, appearing to come around the corner of Central America and take aim at Honduras.

The first inhabited land in the hurricane's path, and the only place to feel the storm's full category-five power, was the easternmost Bay Island of Guanaja. The effects were utterly devastating. The small fishing community of Mangrove Bight, built right on the water's edge on Guanaja's northeast shore, was completely wiped off the map by 10-meter waves and howling winds. Luckily, the locals were able to flee to higher ground before the storm struck, and no one in town died. Passing literally right over the top of Guanaja, the awesome winds of Mitch flattened just about all the vegetation on the island. Fully a year after the hurricane, although things are starting to regrow, the once-forested hills in the center of the island still looked like victims of a bombing run, with barely a tree left standing.

The main population of Guanaja, living in Bonacca Town on the somewhat sheltered south side of the island, spent the better part of 26 and 27 October huddled into the few cement buildings in town as the winds screamed around them. They emerged on 28 October to find many of their houses destroyed, and most of those left standing without roofs.

While the island's population was relatively unharmed, a crew of 31 sailors on a boat off Guanaja did not fare so well. The S.V. *Fantome*, a luxury cruise sailing ship owned by Windjammer Cruises, made the fateful decision to try to hide from the storm on the south side of Roatán, rather than docking. Believing Mitch to be moving west, the *Fantome* cruised east toward Guanaja, looking for sheltered waters. But just as the *Fantome* crossed into the open channel between Roatán and Guanaja, Mitch unexpectedly pounced to the south. Radio contact with the ship was lost on 27 October—it went down with all hands.

Leaving a dazed Guanaja behind, Mitch continued turning southward, making a beeline for the coastal town of Trujillo. Smacking right into the steep mountains lining the north coast of Honduras, the storm slowed its forward movement, although it continued spinning with furiously high winds of 250 kph. By 28 October, Mitch had been downgraded to a category four hurricane, and as it continued inching its way through the mountains of central Honduras on 29 October, it degraded to a category one.

One might suppose that with the lowering wind speeds, Honduras had seen the worst the storm had to offer. In reality, the destruction was just beginning. Unable to move quickly, Mitch began dumping immense volumes of rain on Honduras and parts of northern Nicaragua. Rivers flowing from the mountains down into the Caribbean flooded over their banks with a scary suddenness, swollen by the all the water pouring off the mountains. And the water was filled with thousands of trees uprooted from steep, sodden hillsides and swept downriver, lethal debris smashing into bridges, houses, and anything else in its path. The Río Bonito and Río Cangrejal, swollen with floodwaters and trees fallen from the slopes of Pico Bonito, smashed apart the bridges on either side of La Ceiba, cutting the city off from the rest of Honduras.

Just to the south and east, the floodwaters killed hundreds in broad, flat Río Aguán Valley and put entire towns under water. The Garífuna town of Santa Rosa de Aguán, perched on a sandbar right at the river mouth, was hit both by high seas and the flooding river, and several dozen people died. One local woman who was swept out to sea managed to grab hold of a piece of wood and was picked up several days later by a British ship near Guanaja.

Bridges fell throughout north-central Honduras, cutting off many coastal Garífuna villages and large areas in central Yoro, which had to be supplied by helicopter and boat for weeks after the storm. Mitch's floodwaters ruined the entire crop of the normally self-sufficient Mosquitia, leading to severe hunger in the remote region during 1999.

Finally forcing its way from the north coast through the mountains to the south, Mitch arrived in Tegucigalpa on the night of the 29th and morning of the 30th. Overnight, an incredible 55 cm of rain are estimated to have fallen in just a few short hours in the mountains around the capital. The rainwaters swelled the Río Choluteca and its tributary the Río

Chiquito, which join together right in downtown Tegucigalpa, and triggered mud slides in many neighborhoods perched on the steep hillsides around the city. One particularly bad slide dropped a huge amount of land, houses, and other debris right into the Río Choluteca gorge, just below the center of town. The mountain of rubble stopped up the river's outlet, and behind the dam the water levels swiftly rose, putting much of the city's riverfront under a raging flood of muddy water. The two main bridges connecting downtown Tegucigalpa to Comayagúela, which normally have about 13 meters of clearance between the river and the top of the arches, were completely covered during the night.

The next day the waters were still almost at the tops of the bridges, and residents on the riverfront watched with disbelief and horror as trucks, buses, houses, animals, trees, and human bodies floated right through the center of the city.

About 1,000 people are thought to have died in and around the capital city that night, many of them children who could not fight the torrents of water. The physical damage, more than a year later, seems to have barely begun being repaired. Tegucigalpa's riverfront was never a thing of beauty, but now it is truly ugly, with blocks of ruined buildings, empty lots, and streets still covered with mud. The riverbed remains filled with much rubble and dirt, which in turn worsened floods caused by the 1999 rainy season.

After leaving its wake of destruction in Tegucigalpa, Mitch continued southward toward the Golfo de Fonseca and the Pacific Ocean, dumping record amounts of rain as it went. The Río Choluteca, already at flood stage and carrying with it all manner of deadly debris, ripped a new valley for itself down the mountains toward the Pacific, sweeping several villages and hundreds of people with it. The downtown area of the city of Choluteca was completely underwater on 30 and 31 October.

Rather than heading off into the Pacific, Mitch once again took a sharp turn, heading back inland with the apparent intention of covering absolutely every square inch of Honduras before moving on. Now downgraded to a tropical storm and with little wind power, but still dumping incredible volumes of rain, Mitch moved slowly through western Honduras, parallel to the Salvadoran border, triggering floods on the Ulúa and Chamelecón Rivers downstream near San Pedro Sula.

Finally, by the night of 31 October, Mitch left Honduran territory for Guatemala, continuing as a tropical depression across Mexico and into the Gulf of Mexico. In the Gulf, Mitch renewed force and became a tropical storm again, racing northeast into Florida, where it kicked off tornadoes and violent rain storms. Mitch finally whirled off toward the Bahamas before disappearing on 5 November in the mid-Atlantic. The trajectory of Hurricane Mitch is, without question, one of the most erratic, bizarre, and destructive ever recorded for a Caribbean hurricane.

The Aftermath

The exact loss of life caused by Mitch will never be known, but experts say it was the most lethal storm to hit the Atlantic since the Great Hurricane of 1780. Suffice to say it was one of the worst natural disasters ever to hit Honduras, killing 7,007 people according to government estimates. The highest number of deaths were in the departments of Francisco Morazán (Tegucigalpa) and Choluteca, but deaths were recorded in every single department of the country, usually into the hundreds. A further 8,058 were reported missing, and 11,998 were injured.

Although Honduras faced the greatest death toll from the storm, another 4,000 people perished in Nicaragua and about 400 more in Guatemala and El Salvador. The worst single tragedy during Mitch occurred in northwestern Nicaragua on 30 October, when the crater of Volcán Casitas filled up with rainwater and burst its side, sweeping away several small towns and killing more than 2,000 people with devastating mud slides.

The amount of physical damage wrought by Mitch to Honduras' infrastructure is a matter of some debate. If we are to believe President Carlos Flores, some 70% of the country's infrastructure was destroyed, setting the country back 50 years. While one might wonder how he came up with the figure, no one can dispute that the damage was indeed extremely severe. For a start, an astounding 10% of the entire country's population—some 600,000 people—lost their homes. In Choluteca the number of inhabitants left homeless was nearly 40% of the population, while in parts of the north coast it hit 30%. As might be expected, the great majority of these people lived in rural areas near rivers. Rains rendered over 4,000 km of road unusable and washed away nearly a hundred bridges. The uncontrollable waters burst 85% of water pipes and 90% of the sewer pipes in Honduras. Hundreds of hospitals and schools throughout the country were destroyed.

(continued on next page)

THE PITILESS PATH OF HURRICANE MITCH
(continued)

Agricultural production took a heavy blow from the storm as well. The low-lying banana plantations along the Aguán, Chalemecón, and Ulúa Rivers got the worst of it, with over half of their cultivated fields washed away. Coffee, Honduras' number-one export crop, didn't fare as badly, with its smaller fields on higher ground. An estimated 24% of coffee fields were affected by Mitch, mostly due to mountain landslides. Because of the damages, banana exports fell by 80% in 1999, while coffee exports dropped 35%. In all, Mitch is thought to have directly and indirectly caused at least US$4 billion in damage.

The U.S. National Oceanic and Atmospheric Administration considers Hurricane Mitch the second-most-destructive storm ever witnessed in the Atlantic, a ranking, the report said, "likely to stand for a long, long time."

---

dry spell called *la canícula* or sometimes *el veranillo de San Juan.* During the rainy season, skies are often clear in the morning, and clouds start to build around midday leading to an afternoon shower, which usually passes by evening. But particularly later in the rainy season can come several days at a time when the drizzle doesn't stop and the world is gray and wet.

In much of the north of the country, the seasons are much less predictable, and rains can come at any time of year. On the north coast or in the Mosquitia, the season is not so much dry and wet, but rather wet and wetter still. The rainiest part of the year on the north coast is usually September to November, when the tropical storms and hurricanes developing over Atlantic rip through the Caribbean, and December to February, when *nortes,* northern cold fronts, make their way down from Canada and the United States, often bringing with them days of gray skies and rain. Because of the high humidity and the backing wall of the Sierra Nombre de Dios, the north coast is drenched by tropical storms just about every month of the year.

Hurricanes and Tropical Storms
Major tropical storms typically strike Honduras every decade or so, leaving thousands homeless and sometimes dead. The devastating Hurricane Mitch of 1998 will go down as the worst natural disaster of the 20th century to hit Honduras. Although not as powerful as Mitch, 1974's Hurricane Fifi in 1974 devastated the region around Choloma, in northwest Honduras.

In general, though, Honduras lies off the regular hurricane path in the Caribbean. Most storms come from the southeast and travel north-west, passing through the western Caribbean toward the Gulf of Mexico, to the north of Honduras. But it's best to try to avoid the north coast of Honduras during the August to November hurricane season. Even if the hurricanes themselves don't reach the shore, they bring heavy rains; flooding is an annual ritual and can seriously disrupt travel. Cases of cholera and other diseases are also more common during this time. Pacific hurricanes rarely strike Honduras.

Other Travel Considerations
During the rainy season, expect road conditions to deteriorate severely. Major highways are well maintained all year, but often the government will not bother patching other roads during the rains. As a result, many dirt roads become totally impassable, even with 4WD.

Also during the rains, water visibility for scuba diving is diminished on the Bay Islands. But because the islands don't have the high mountains like the mainland to catch precipitation, rainfall tends to be considerably lower than on the north coast. February to March and July to September are usually two good times of year for the islands. Divers can take comfort from the fact that, Mitch notwithstanding, the islands are not on the usual hurricane path.

Hiking in the mountains of central Honduras is possible year-round, but it's less muddy during the dry season, especially in the south part of the country. In places like Pico Bonito, Cusuco, or Sierra de Agalta, it rains all year, so just come prepared to get wet. If you're planning on rafting or river boating, the best time of year is after the rains, in December or January, when water levels are high.

FLORA AND FAUNA

FLORA

First-time visitors to Honduras may be surprised to find out that this modest-sized country houses a bewildering diversity of nearly 10,000 vascular plant species in a variety of different ecosystems. Although many nature-lovers aren't aware of it, Honduras has much more extensive intact cloud forest and rainforest than its more heralded neighbors, Costa Rica or Guatemala. Honduras also offers huge expanses of pine forest in the central highlands, kilometers of coastal mangrove forests, and even patches of rare dry tropical forests.

A mid-1990s estimate put Honduras at having just over five million hectares, or 46.1% of its territory, with forest cover. Of this total, 2.8 million hectares are pine forest and 2.3 million are broadleaf forest. This is by far the highest total amount of forest of any country in Central America. Next closest is Nicaragua, with 4.2 million hectares of forest, 32% of the country, followed by Guatemala, with 3.4 million hectares, 31% of its land. The much-ballyhooed Costa Rica is second to last on the list, with only 1.4 million hectares, beating out only tiny, overpopulated El Salvador.

The reason for this valuable natural patrimony is not, unfortunately, the result of any far-sighted planning on the part of the government, or a particularly enlightened eco-conciousness on the part of the inhabitants—far from it, in fact. Rather, it has been the country's daunting topography, lack of arable land, and comparatively low population density that have spared the forests.

But as with many other poor, underdeveloped countries, Honduras' population is now growing explosively, and the consequent pressures on the remaining forests are increasing hand in hand with it, at a vertiginously accelerating rate and in a variety of ways. Most obvious is logging, a notoriously inefficient and wasteful industry in Honduras. Modern forestry techniques are practically unheard of, and with lax, corrupt forestry officials and little police support, loggers

pretty much cut as they please. The government estimates that some 80,000 hectares of forest are lost each year, but the numbers are likely much higher. Formerly concentrated on the pine forests of central Honduras, loggers have in the last couple of decades mounted an invasion of the southern edges of the Mosquitia rainforests, where they destroy entire stands of forest just to get at a single mahogany, worth a pretty penny in wealthy western countries. A new forestry law expected to pass in 2000 will, depending on whom you talk to, either help the industry develop more moderate, eco-friendly practices, or open the country up to rapacious multi-national wood companies. The fact that the Callejas administration actually tried to concession off a large portion of the Mosquitia to a foreign pulp company in the early 1990s helps fuel suspicions of the new law and of governmental attitudes about the forests in general.

Close on the heels of the loggers, at least in Olancho and the Mosquitia, invariably come an army of *colonos,* invading peasants determined to hack out a small farm and later try to convince the government (often successfully) to regularize their de facto holdings. Large-scale cattle ranchers are often next in line, snapping up huge holdings from the *colonos.* Because Honduran ranchers use very elementary cattle raising techniques, their productivity is remarkably low, wasting huge amounts of land.

The 30-odd patches of cloud forest in highland Honduras face their own variety of threats. While the smaller trees don't attract loggers, their wood works just fine for the *carboneros,* who chop down whatever tree happens to be at hand to make charcoal. Even more ominous is the continual encroachment of coffee plantations into the lower reaches of the cloud forest, the perfect climate for high-quality *arabica* coffee beans. The mangrove wetlands on both coasts are a prime source of firewood, and in the Golfo de Fonseca are ceding to the expansion of coastal shrimp farms.

In the face of governmental apathy (not to say complicity), dozens of grass-roots environmental groups have sprung up across the coun-

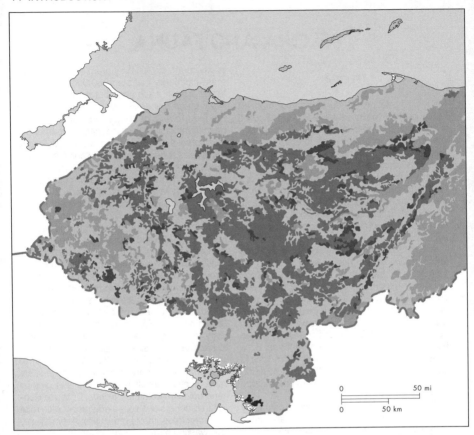

try, most dedicated to protecting a specific local natural area. True, many of these NGOs receive frequent criticism as being little more than sponges for foreign aide money. But others are well-organized, noisy defenders of the environment, not afraid of speaking up against the wealthy interests often behind environmental destruction. And this has not come without a cost, as these interests invariably have well-armed young thugs ready to make threats or carry them out. Just two of the better-publicized cases in the 1990s were the still-unsolved murders of activists Jeanette Kawas and Hector Rodrigo Pastor Fasquelle.

A more recent development in Honduras has been the increased participation of individuals, groups, and government missions from other countries in protecting the environment. Because suspicions of Honduran corruption run very high in other countries, many donors are paying close attention to environmental programs and even getting involved themselves. Two examples are Finnish foresters sent to help replant the island of Guanaja, which lost most of its vegetation when Hurricane Mitch ran over it, and the bi-national German-Honduran projects in the Río Plátano and at Celaque. Private foreign groups are involved also, like Proyecto Aldea Global from the U.S., to which the Honduran government has turned over administration of Parque Nacional Cerro Azul/Meámbar. One can hardly expect foreigners to be the miracle cure for Honduras'

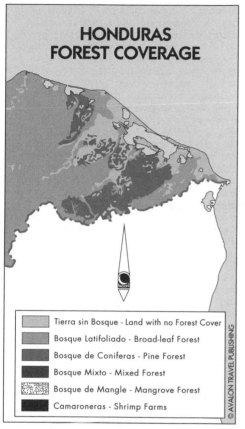

HONDURAS
FOREST COVERAGE

	Tierra sin Bosque - Land with no Forest Cover
	Bosque Latifoliado - Broad-leaf Forest
	Bosque de Coniferas - Pine Forest
	Bosque Mixto - Mixed Forest
	Bosque de Mangle - Mangrove Forest
	Camaroneras - Shrimp Farms

© AVALON TRAVEL PUBLISHING

*hairy green rope and clutching stems. . . .
This was more like a church, with pillars
and fans and hanging flowers and only the
slightest patches of white sky above the curved
roof of branches.*

Paul Theroux was a bit weak on Honduran geography in his popular novel *The Mosquito Coast*—the Río Aguán, which his fictional American family followed up into the jungle, actually leads into one of the most heavily cultivated valleys in Honduras. But his description of tropical rainforest certainly rings true. These forests, which once blanketed the entire north coast of Honduras, tend to move observers to religious metaphor, so awe-inspiring is their majestic beauty. Walking in a primary rainforest, one is indeed surprised with how little undergrowth exists between the immensely tall trees, sometimes over 60 meters high, with huge buttresses looking for the world like flanking supports on a medieval cathedral.

The annual average temperature in the forest hovers around 25° C, while rainfall averages between 200 and 400 cm a year, making it a natural hothouse, a perfect environment for plants to develop to their most efficient level. The evolutionary triumph of the rainforest is that almost all its nutrients are concentrated above ground—the forest has only a few centimeters of dirt. Under the dirt lies a mass of white threads, the rootlets of trees living in conjunction with a certain type of fungus, a sort of garbage collector of the forest that quickly decomposes any organic material and provides nutrients to the trees, which in turn supply the products of photosynthesis to the fungus. This is what plant biologists call a "mature system." As little as one-tenth of one percent of nutrients penetrate below the first five centimeters of the forest floor, meaning soil is one of the least important elements to the cycle.

The wealth of the rainforest is hidden from human observers, far above in upper stories of these great trees, where an entire world of plants and animals exist without ever coming down to the ground. Roaming around in this elevated ecosystem are all manner of vines and ferns, as well as snakes, monkeys, lizards, sloths, macaws, toucans, and literally thousands of species of insects, each living in their own particular niche. On the top is the canopy itself, an unbroken field of green leaves soaking up the

environmental problems, but they can use their aid money in a persuasive fashion, act as witnesses to what's happening in the countryside, and help curb some of the worst abuses.

Humid Tropical Forest (Rainforest)

This jungle, the start of the high forest, was tall and orderly. Each tree had found room to grow separately. The trees were arranged in various ways, according to slenderness of leaf size, the big-leafed ones on the jungle floor, the towering trees with tiny leaves rising to great heights, and the ferns in between. I had always pictured jungle as suffocating spaghetti tangles, drooping and crisscrossed, a mass of

deforestation in progress near El Carbón

generous sun and photosynthesizing for all they're worth. So complete is the canopy that practically no sun at all penetrates down to the jungle floor, unless a fallen tree opens a temporary gap. But the open space is invariably colonized in short order, with vines and new tree shoots moving in so fast you can practically watch it happen—the jungle is so vibrant it seems at times to be a single living creature rather than a forest.

The rainforest is composed of a dizzying variety of trees and plants, although to the untrained observer, many trees in the rainforest look strikingly similar. It is thought that at least 2,000 vascular plants, probably more, live in the rainforest, making it by far the most diverse ecosystem in Central America. Tree types include mahogany, cedar, laurel, rosewood, strangler fig, tamarind, oak, ceiba, almond, cacao, nance, and San Juan, to name just a few. Rarely are several trees of the same species grouped together, which makes identification all the more difficult. As naturalists Adrian Forsyth and Ken

Miyata put it in their 1984 book, *Tropical Nature,* "A naturalist in New England can easily learn all the species of native trees in the region in a single summer, but there are few people who, even after a lifetime of study, can confidently identify most of the trees in a patch of tropical American rainforest."

Because the rainforest offers so many lovely hiding places, trying to spot the abundant wildlife in it can be frustrating, especially on hikes. The jungles of the Mosquitia may support 80% of the mammal species in the country, but good luck finding all but a few of them. You won't have too much trouble running across the occasional troop of noisy monkeys, but most other creatures have excellent camouflage and stay well hidden. Many are nocturnal. Rainforest birds in particular are difficult to find, as their nests are extremely well hidden to avoid predators. One good way to look for birds and mammals in the jungle is along a river, where you can look into the upper stories of trees.

Until the beginning of the banana industry at the start of the 20th century, most of the entire north coast of Honduras was covered by rainforest. Most of the forest west of Trujillo has long since fallen victim to the machete, although healthy stretches of rainforest still exist in Parque Nacional Pico Bonito, near La Ceiba, and smaller ones in Parque Nacional Capiro y Calentura, near Trujillo. But farther east in the remote, isolated Mosquitia region is the largest chunk of remaining rainforest in Central America, protected by the biosphere reserves of the Río Plátano and Tawahka Asagni. For anyone who wants to experience a true rainforest in all its expansive, wild splendor, a trip out to the Mosquitia is mandatory.

Cloud Forest

A unique sort of high-altitude jungle atop the highest peaks in Honduras, the cloud forest is a fairy-tale world of oak and wild avocado covered in vines, huge ferns, orchids, and bromeliads. A perpetual mist creates a spooky stillness broken only by the plaintive call of a quetzal or the scurry of a fox. Walking up through the much drier pine forests below to the cloud forest, it seems nothing short of miraculous how much moisture the cloud forest retains. Although cloud-forested peaks do not receive significantly more rainfall than surrounding regions, temperatures (6-12° C on average) and subsequent evaporation levels are markedly lower, so the forest retains a great deal more water, much of it in the form of the near-permanent airborne mist.

The result is a dense, towering forest that appears similar to lowland rainforest in its exuberance but is totally different in composition. The number of tree species is quite low compared to the rainforest, but the profusion of epiphytes covering the trees to gather the moisture blowing through the forest is astounding. Although epiphytes passively live on the cloud forest trees and are not parasitic, they can sometimes colonize a tree so successfully it literally collapses under their weight.

Trees in the cloud forest don't reach the same heights as in the lowland rainforest, both because of the climate and because of the invariably steep slopes they grow on, and the undergrowth is often thick. But in a few places, for example the plateau atop Celaque, you'll find stately stands of towering oaks, spaced widely with few plants underneath. The cloud forest provides a home for many of the same mammals that live in the rainforest, such as jaguars, sloths, monkeys, and peccaries, but has a unique bird population not seen in lower, hotter forests. The quetzal is certainly the most famed of the cloud forest birds, and it is joined by other types of trogon as well as the odd-sounding three-watted bell bird and the emerald toucanet, among many others.

Two types of cloud forest exist in Honduras. In the southern and western part of the country, "true" cloud forest has developed. Here the geographic position of the mountains, in the prevailing wind patterns, has captured a constant cap of clouds, from which the forest sucks its moisture. The true cloud forest is located at elevations of roughly 1,800 to 2,800 meters and is isolated by a ring of drier pine or liquidambar (sweet gum) forest. Because these forests are biological islands, a variety of endemic plant and animal species are found within them.

In northern Honduras, another type of cloud forest is found at lower elevations. These forests receive more direct rain than those in the south and rise directly out of the tropical forest below them with only a small intervening band of pine, if any at all. These cloud forests are more accurately characterized as mountain rainforests and

are sometimes found as low as 1,000 meters. The forests of Pico Bonito are a prime example.

In a few places at the highest elevations, notably in the Sierra de Agalta, strong winds and high moisture levels have combined to create bizarre and rare **elfin forests.** Here gnarled, stunted pine trees only a couple of meters tall grow among a profusion of mosses, lichen, ferns, and shrubs.

A sort of transitional stage between the cloud forest and rainforest is the **subtropical wet forest,** which receives about the same amount of rainfall but hosts an intermediate mix of species. Because this climate is ideal for coffee growing, subtropical wet forests are under heavy pressure from small-scale plantations, especially in Olancho, Yoro, Santa Bárbara, and around Lago Yojoa. Were you to hike the very difficult route up the side of Pico Bonito just outside of La Ceiba, you'd walk up through, successively, tropical, subtropical, and montane wet forests—one of the few places in the Americas where this is possible.

Situated as they are at the sources of Honduras' rivers, cloud forests are vital to ensure the country's water supply. Unfortunately, they are also natural targets for *campesinos* who live in the valleys below, hungry for wild game, land, or wood. It was in recognition of cloud forests' critical importance that the Honduran government enacted the 1987 law creating the national park system, which was aimed primarily at protecting the cloud forests. While the laws have been of use in defending better-known parks like La Tigra, Cusuco, or Celaque, the destruction continues unabated in many remote, less-visited forests.

Highland Pine Forest

Probably the most extensive type of forest in the country is the pine forest of the central highlands, technically known as a Subtropical Moist Forest. The most common of the several pine species is the ocote *(Pinus montezumae),* but the Caribbean pine *(Pinus caribaea)* is common also. Ocotes generally occur between 600 and 1,400 meters, depending on the region. In wetter areas they grow in dense forests laced with epiphytes. In drier areas the ocotes are more widely spaced, often sharing the forest with *encino* or *roble* oak trees, particularly around water sources, and frequently with many broadleaf shrubs underneath.

Dry Forests

In lowland regions on both the Pacific and Atlantic coasts where rainfall levels are not high enough to support rainforest, deciduous tropical forests were once common but are now rarely found. Acacia and copa trees are common, often mixed in with tree cacti, agaves, and a variety of drought-resistent shrubs. A superb example of a deciduous tropical forest can be seen in the area around San Marcos de Colón and El Corpus, near Choluteca; other patches are found along the valleys of the Ulúa, Humaya, Otoro, Choluteca, and Goascorán Rivers, around Olanchito in the Río Aguán Valley, and in a few places on the Bay Islands.

Savanna

Surprising to casual tourists, as well as a few plant biologists, is the presence of grassland savanna over large portions of the Mosquitia. The grasslands, dotted with stands of Caribbean pine, receive the same amount of rainfall as the adjacent rainforest and are often submerged during the wettest parts of the year.

A drier type of savanna supporting grasses and occasional stands of acacia and cactus covers parts of Olancho and El Paraíso. Biologists believe these areas were originally forested.

Mangrove Wetland

Much of the Honduran coastline, both Pacific and Caribbean, was once fronted by marshy tidal wetlands supporting extensive mangrove swamps. While cultivation and ranching have wiped out much of the former wetlands, several sizable mangrove areas remain. An unusual tree able to withstand high levels of salt, the mangrove is able to thrive at the boundary between land and sea, where no other species can live. Most common close to the ocean are red mangroves, while farther inland, on drier ground, black and white mangroves appear more frequently.

Rather than having their root structure buried in dirt, as most trees do, the mangroves appear to be standing on tippy-toes in the water, supported by a network of roots. Amidst these root networks is a safe, nutrient-rich nursery of sorts for many fish and shellfish species. The mangroves are important in protecting many low-lying coastal areas from the worst ocean storms, and they also help filter sediment out of river runoff, thus actually helping to build new land. The mangrove swamp, and coastal tropical forest often behind it, provide a home to troops of monkeys, sea and land birds, manatees, and crocodiles.

Due to expanding fruit cultivation and cattle ranching on the Caribbean coast and shrimp farming on the Pacific, many of Honduras' mangroves have been wiped out. Patches remain in the protected areas of Punta Sal, Punta Izopo, Cuero y Salado, Laguna Guaymoreto, and the Bahía de Chismuyo in the Golfo de Fonseca. But by far the largest reserve of mangroves still largely unmodified by humans in the country is along the coastline of the Mosquitia, in far northeastern Honduras.

MAMMALS

According to reports surviving from the early colonial era, Honduras once abounded with all variety of game—from jaguars to deer to wild boar. Those days are long gone. In almost all settled areas, most mammals have been hunted out of existence, mainly to provide food or money to poor peasants.

Because of the country's rugged topography, however, a number of isolated regions remain refuges for species extinct elsewhere. The larger national parks, in particular Pico Bonito and Sierra de Agalta, and the rainforest of the Río Plátano reserve are the most likely places to encounter rare mammals.

Monkeys

Among the larger wild mammals in Honduras' forests, the three monkey species indigenous to the country—howler *(mono aulador),* white-faced *(mono cara blanca),* and spider *(mono araña)*—are unquestionably the easiest to spot. Noisy and very visible as they roam the upper stories of rainforests and cloud forests, the intelligent and social creatures hang out together in groups ranging from just three or four to over 25. Good places to scout for monkeys are Cuero y Salado and Pico Bonito, near La Ceiba; Punta Sal and Laguna los Micos, near Tela; Sierra de Agalta and La Muralla in Olancho; and all over the Mosquitia.

Howler monkeys are the largest and unquestionably the loudest of the three. A stocky beast with dark fur weighing as much as seven kilograms, the male howler is owner of an unusually large set of vocal cords, contained in the bulging sac in his neck. After warming up with a series of loud grunts, the male howler lets loose with an unearthly roar echoing out over the jungle, which can be heard for several kilometers. The howlers' favorite time to howl is in the early morning, and sometimes in the late afternoon also. Despite their intimidating cries, howlers are fairly passive and sedentary, and they live on a diet of fruits and plants.

Impressively acrobatic but shy and elusive, **spider monkeys** are named for their long, slinky limbs perfectly designed for cruising through the upper stories of tropical jungle. The tail of the spider monkey is astoundingly dexterous, equipped with sensitive pads like on the tips of fingers to better probe and grip with. Spider monkeys flee from human settlements and are much less frequently seen than other monkeys. But should you run across a group, for example out in the forests of the Mosquitia or in Sierra de Agalta, they will aggressively screech, fling twigs and nuts at you, rattle branches, and create a ruckus until you move on. Like the howler, spider monkeys subsist principally on fruits and leaves, though they may occasionally eat insects also.

Diminutive but remarkably intelligent, the **white-faced** or **capuchin monkey** stands only 40 cm tall or so, with a distinctive tuft of white hair around its head. Unlike the spider and howler, the white-faced monkey is an omnivore,

quite content to raid a bird's nest for its eggs or gobble a slow-footed lizard that happens by. If it finds a fruit too hard to gnaw into, a white-faced monkey will industriously bash the food against a tree or rock until it relinquishes its nourishment. Hikers are almost guaranteed to see white-faced monkeys in the forests of Sierra de la Botija, in southern Honduras near the Nicaraguan border.

Cats

Five different feline species still stalk the hills and forests of Honduras, though in a much-reduced habitat from former years. These animals are mainly nocturnal, so unless you go hiking at night or stumble across their den, it's very unlikely any of Honduras' cats will ever cross your path.

The king of cats is unquestionably the **jaguar,** called a *jaguar, tigre,* or *pantera* in Honduras. The largest cat in the Americas, jaguars measure up to two meters in length and can either be brown with black spots or flat black. These majestic, powerful animals are impressive hunters, known to drag off horses and cattle and even go fishing for crocodile or manatee. But their most common prey are jungle mammals like monkeys, wild boars, or deer.

Though certainly in grave danger from hunters and habitat loss (each jaguar needs 25 square km of territory to hunt), jaguars can show up in the oddest of places. In 1995, an evidently confused adult female wandered out of the forests of Pico Bonito, through pineapple plantations, across the La Ceiba-Tela highway, and into a

Jaguars live (largely unseen) in Honduras' rain and cloud forests.

VINCE MURPHY

house in the village of San Juan. The inhabitants, somewhat perturbed by their unwanted guest, left and closed up the house with the animal inside and called for help. After it had thoroughly trashed the inside of the house, local environmentalists eventually managed to get the jaguar into a wooden cage, which was then put into the back of a truck to drive back up to the forest. As the "rescuers" arrived at the edge of the forest, the enraged (or terrified) jaguar managed to destroy its cage and leap to freedom.

A bit smaller than jaguars and with an unspotted brown coat are **cougars,** also known as pumas or mountain lions *(león* in Spanish). While the jaguar sticks close to humid forests, cougars are quite happy in much more arid environments, like the mountains of southern and central Honduras. Cougars have unusually large back paws, which helps makes them gifted jumpers. Without much of a start, a cougar can easily clear seven or eight meters in a single leap, and they have been seen to jump from heights of up to 20 meters. Not standoffish when it comes to domestic animals, cougars are happy to raid the local farm for a tasty sheep, chicken, or pig to supplement their normal repast of wild pigs, raccoons, or other small wild mammals. Because of this proclivity, the rural folk of Honduras vilify cougars and hunt them down whenever they can.

Slightly smaller than the cougar, and often confused with it, is the **jaguarundi,** which can appear both in a rust color and in black. Smaller still, both about the size of a very large house cat and with spotted coats, are the **ocelot** *(tigrillo)* and **margay** (also called *tigrillo).*

Baird's Tapir
The largest mammal in the country, the tapir is an odd-looking creature related to the rhinoceros, measuring over two meters long and weighing up to 300 kg. Found in both lowland and highland forests, and even sometimes secondary forest, the tapir—called *danto* in Honduras—is a frequent target of hunters both human and feline for its meat. Tapir are invariably found near lakes and rivers, and if frightened it will beat a furious stampede straight to the water, flattening anything in its path and letting out an odd grunting sound as it runs. Living on a steady diet of leaves, the tapir stuffs its small mouth with an odd, elongated, mobile snout, a sort of proto-trunk.

Armadillos, Anteaters, and Sloths
With the common trait of having no teeth, these three foraging animals are united under the taxonomic order *Edentata.* The great anteater *(hormiguero),* up to a meter long, is the largest of Honduras' anteaters, followed by the more common lesser anteater *(tamandu)* and the smaller silky anteater, which rarely ventures out of trees and is seen infrequently. Anteaters spend much of their lives prowling the forests at a leisurely pace in search of ants and termites. After ripping up a termite or ant mound with its strong forearms and sharp claws, the anteater probes the mound with its most unusual tongue, a sticky appendage up to half a meter long that gathers up ants by the dozen. Biologists have estimated that anteaters can munch upwards of 30,000 ants a day. To defend themselves against the vicious stinging ants that live in Honduras' forests, anteaters have remarkably tough fur and hides, which local *campesinos* insist cannot be cut through by a machete. While not particularly agile or speedy, the anteater is known to defend itself so well with its vicious hooked claws that even jaguars prefer to look for easier prey.

Also subsisting on a steady diet of ants and termites, with a few other insects thrown in for variety, are two species of armadillo, the nine-banded *(cusuco)* and naked tailed *(pitero de uña).* Looking like baby dinosaurs, these curious creatures are equipped with calcified armor plates to defend themselves from attack as they waddle their ungainly way around the forest floor. A larger ancestor of the armadillo, the glyptodon, once lived in Honduras, as evidenced by fossils found near Gracias, Lempira.

If armadillos and anteaters seem unusual, the sloth is downright hilarious. Inching their way in slow motion along the undersides of tree branches in the perpetual quest for more leaves, the sloth is certainly the most relaxed mammal you're likely to run across in the forest. With an unusually slow metabolism, sloths simply don't have much get up and go. What stirs biologists to wonderment is that these proverbially lazy animals, seemingly so badly adapted to the pitiless wild, have managed to survive to the present day! Sloths are a favorite target of jaguars and harpy eagles, which literally pluck them out of trees. But with their algae-covered fur and slow movement, the animals are difficult for predators to spot. Perhaps to help keep an eye out for this constant threat, the sloth has an extra neck vertebra, allowing it to peer directly over its own back. Two species live in Honduras, the two-toed sloth *(perezoso de dos dedos)* and the three-toed sloth *(perezoso de tres dedos).* Despite the extra digit, the three-toed sloth is the slower of the two. Sloths come down from their tree homes every week or so to take their *toilette,* relieving themselves of some 30% of their body weight into a carefully prepared hole, which the sloth neatly covers with leaves before climbing back up for the rest of the week. While sloths are slow movers in the trees, on the ground they are practically invalids, barely capable of locomotion. A sloth clawing its way laboriously along the ground, over to a tree, and up the trunk to the safety of the branches looks like an actor in a really bad melodramatic movie, gravely wounded but still valiantly struggling across the ground. Because they are so easy to hunt, the inoffensive sloth has not fared well at the hands of man and is now seen only in more remote areas like Sierra de Agalta in Olancho or La Mosquitia.

Peccaries

If during a forest hike you should hear much grunting and furious activity nearby, you may have stumbled into a group of peccaries, called either *quequeo* or *chancho de monte* (mountain pig) in Honduras. A gregarious animal, peccaries forage in large groups of up to 30 of 40 animals, rummaging around in underbrush for plants, fruit, small animals, insects, or whatever else comes across their path. While peccaries have no interest in confronting humans, they are notoriously unobservant, not always seeing hikers just a few meters away on an open trail. The temperamental, aggressive animals are hunted by jaguar and cougar, but the cats have been known to come out on the losing end of a run-in with an irate band of peccaries.

The smaller collared peccary is extremely adaptable and is found in any type of forest, including lowland jungle, dry tropical forest, pine forest, cloud forest, and even secondary forest and farmland. The larger white-lipped peccary, which runs in larger groups across more territory and is much more sensitive to human presence, is less frequently seen in Honduras.

Bats

The mammal with by far the most representatives in Honduras is the bat, with 98 species registered at last count. Most common and one of the country's largest species is the **Jamaican fruit eating bat,** which lives on figs, bananas, and mangoes. More insidious is the **vampire bat,** loathed by *campesinos* in Central America not so much because the bat might suck their blood, but rather because it often kills off valuable livestock with paralytic rabies. An interesting sight is the **greater bulldog bat,** the only species in the Americas capable of catching fish, for which it is known as *murciélago pescador* in Honduras. These bats, with remarkably large wingspans and long claws, frequent the waterways on the north coast. They hunt by skimming over the water, locating their prey with a nifty little sonar system, and pouncing when the small fish or crustaceans near the surface. Other species include the **northern ghost bat** and the **Honduran white bat,** both with white coloring, and the **tent-making bat,** which, as its name suggests, builds itself a personal chalet of leaves and twigs to bed down.

Other Mammals

The adaptable **white-tailed deer** *(venado)* are seen in many different ecosystems throughout Honduras, despite being a favorite target for hunters for both its meat and valuable pelt. Considerably smaller, and with a reddish coat, is the **brocket deer** *(tilopo, venado colorado),* rarely seen and considered in danger of extinction. Both the **gray fox** and **coyote** still roam the mountain country in all parts of Honduras, particularly the west around Ocotepeque and the east in Olancho and El Paraíso.

The **kinkajou** *(mico de noche),* which looks like a cross between a cat and a small monkey with bulging eyes, is utterly unfazed by human presence and will come out for a look if you walk by in its cloud forest home. Found all over Honduras are the white-nosed coatis *(pizote),* a rat-like critter with razor sharp teeth; the bandit-faced, omnivorous raccoon *(mapache)*; porcupines *(zorro espín)*; rabbits *(conejo)*; squirrels *(ardilla)*; several species of skunk *(zorro* or *zorrillo)* and opossum *(guazalo)*; and a myriad of smaller rodents.

Marine Mammals

Otherwise known as the sea cow, the **West Indian manatee** (*manatí* or *vaca marina* in Spanish) is a huge, slow-moving, and gentle creature that resides in freshwater canals and lagoons near the ocean. The manatee, which can grow up to four meters long and weigh 700 kg, leads a lazy existence, resting for long periods with only its nose above water and nourishing itself with various aquatic plants. With their oversized lungs, manatee can stay under water for up to 15 or 20 minutes, propelling themselves with their single tail fluke and two slide flippers.

Once found all along the Caribbean coast of Central America, manatees are now in serious danger of extinction. The animal is hunted by both Miskito and Garífuna, who prize its meat (the Miskito claim it has seven distinct flavors in different parts of the body). Slow-moving as they are, manatees are also frequently hit by boats cruising around the coastal waterways, and they are often caught in fishing nets also. As a result of these depredations, manatees are no longer common on the north coast, and their slow birth rate (one calf every three or four years) is not helping replenish the population. The waterways of Punta Sal, Punta Izopo, and Cuero y Salado are thought to harbor only a few dozen manatees, while more live in the remote lagoons of La Mosquitia.

In the waters around the Bay Islands you might spy **spinner** and **Altantic bottle-nosed dolphins,** which often cruise through the surrounding waters in their patrols around the Gulf of Mexico and Atlantic Ocean. A dolphin program and research station at Anthony's Key Resort on Roatán can offer visitors an opportunity to scuba dive or snorkel with specially trained bottle-nosed dolphins. Much more rarely seen, sticking to the deeper waters of the Cayman Trench north of the Bay Islands, are **sperm, humpback, pilot,** and **killer whales.** Columbus spotted **tropical monk seals** during his stop at Guanaja in 1502, but the last confirmed sighting of a monk seal was on the Serranillas Islands (which now belong to Colombia) in 1952—the seal is thought to be extinct.

The **neotropical river otters,** called *nutria* or *perro de agua,* were once common in the rivers and lakes of mainland Honduras but seem to be going the way of their seal cousins due to excessive hunting and pollution in rivers and lakes. It's a shame, because these inoffensive creatures are extremely intelligent and even funny, prone to playing with one another. The otter can still be seen in the rivers of the Mosquitia and in a few protected areas on the north coast like Pico Bonito and Punta Sal.

manatee

ERIN DWYER

BIRDS, FISH, AND REPTILES

Fish

The greatest variety of fish in Honduras is undoubtedly found in the reefs and surrounding waters of the Bay Islands, which contain an estimated 96% of all the marine life found in the Caribbean. Fish of all sizes, from tiny chromides to barracudas to the whale shark, the world's largest fish, are found near the islands. In their 100-150 year lifespan, **whale sharks** can grow up to 15 meters long, with a weight of nearly 12 tons. Daunting though they may be, whale sharks are harmless to humans, living off plankton and tiny shrimp, which they filter through their gill rakers as they cruise the deep waters north of the Bay Islands. The blunt-snouted, speckled fish are equipped with two sets of dorsal fins toward the tail and a pair of larger pectoral fins. The Bay Islands is one of the few places in the world where whale sharks can be seen all year, although they are more common at certain times, particularly just after coral spawning in mid-August. Other **sharks,** such as hammerhead, nurse, and blacktip, frequent the deeper waters along the Caribbean coast of Honduras. The waters of La Mosquitia are particularly notorious for hammerheads, and more than a couple of Miskito lobster divers have stories to tell about unpleasantly close encounters with these aggressive sharks. Don't go swimming out beyond the waves! While sharks frequent the waters around the Bay Islands, there have been no reports of divers being attacked. A variety of other sharks live in the Pacific near Honduras, but they rarely make it into the Golfo de Fonseca. If they do, local fishermen promptly catch them and turn them into fillets.

A list of smaller fish species in the Caribbean waters off Honduras, with all the distinct species living on the reef, in deeper water, and along the coast, would go on for pages. A few of the colorful favorites on the reef include grouper, butterfly fish, barracuda, yellowtail snapper, jewfish, and angelfish. Other marine animals often seen on the reef are eagle and manta rays, green moray eels, sea horses, octopuses, and sea turtles, to name just a few of the more prominent residents. The deeper waters around the islands and off the north coast are patrolled by schools of wahoo, king and Spanish mackerel, bonito, blackfin tuna, kingfish, and marlin, while famed fighting fish snook and tarpon live in the lagoons along the coast, at the intersection of fresh and salt waters.

Several species of shellfish are found in Honduran waters, particularly lobster, shrimp, conch, and a kind of crayfish found in the lagoons and swamps of the north coast. Lobster and shrimp fishing is a major industry on the north coast and in the Bay Islands, and shrimp farming is also big business on the Golfo de Fonseca.

Resident freshwater fish include largemouth bass (found particularly in Lago de Yojoa), catfish, mollies, minnows, and mojarras. Mountain trout and related native species, like guapote, tepemechin, and the endangered cuyamel, still live in Honduran rivers. This last fish, very meaty and tasty, once abounded in the rivers all along the north coast but has been fished to near extinction everywhere except a few places in La Mosquitia and Olancho.

Reptiles and Amphibians
Honduras is home to some 20 species of **lizards,** including the common iguana and the larger and more intimidating basilisk lizard. On the sides of Honduran highways, you'll often see children carting around huge, hog-tied lizards, offering them for sale to passers-by. Two places especially well known for their huge and numerous lizards are the region around Brus Laguna, in La Mosquitia, and the Bay Islands. Several lizard species on the islands are found nowhere else in the world, though are in danger of extinction from overhunting.

Well over 100 species of **snakes** slither through the forests and pastures (and sometimes swim in the waterways) of rural Honduras, and almost all of them are harmless. Among the poisonous species are the dreaded fer-de-lance (called *barba amarilla,* yellow beard, for the bright yellow patch on its neck), coral snake *(coral)* with its distinct bands of red, black, and white, and the noisy rattler *(cascabel).* All of these species are common throughout the country, so watch out for them. When hiking in rural areas, it's always advisable to watch where you put your feet, particularly when walking amongst rocks, logs, or tall grass. Less dangerous but also frequently seen are **boas,** which can grow up to three meters long. Although not poisonous, boas have sharp teeth and don't hesitate to bite if threatened.

Crocodiles and their smaller relatives **caymans** inhabit the many lagoons, swamps, and waterways all along the Caribbean coast. So perfectly adapted to their environment that they have barely evolved since the age of the dinosaurs, crocodiles still maintain a healthy population in Honduras, despite the depredations of hunters after their meat and hide, or just avenging the loss of a pig or favorite hunting dog. One good place to see these ominous beasts on the north coast is at the crocodile farm at Hacienda Tumbador, just outside of Trujillo. Out in La Mosquitia, swapping legends of huge crocodiles is a favorite pastime among the Garífuna and Miskitos. A pilot flying a small plane over Laguna de Ibans not long ago thought he saw an abandoned canoe on one of the small islands in the middle of the lagoon. Swooping down for a closer look, he saw that it was in fact a monster of a crocodile, fully four meters long, basking placidly in the sun. Villagers living in Cocobila, Belén, Raista, and other communities nearby still insist on swimming and bathing in the lagoon, even though a croc will take someone's arm or carry off a baby every couple of years.

Sea turtles, especially hawksbill and green ridley but also loggerhead and leatherback, once

BIRDING IN HONDURAS

Honduras has its share of avian treasures—720 species and counting—many of which surprise and delight novice and veteran birdwatchers alike. Resplendent quetzals are not difficult to locate in more than 30 cloud forests, and rare harpy eagles and great green macaws still nest in the eastern rainforests. More experienced birders can look for dozens of more unusual species—and even have a good chance of adding new species to the country list, since Honduras remains one of the least-known countries, birdwise, in Central America.

The North Coast

The **Tela** area is with little doubt the best accessible place to birdwatch in Honduras—and one of the top spots in all of Central America. The tree plantations, brush, and a protected rainforest watershed of **Lancetilla Botanical Garden** is the best place in Honduras, outside the Mosquitia, to locate more obscure lowland rainforest species such as antbirds and ovenbirds, which need protected forest to thrive. Well over 300 species have been recorded here. The first-time tropical birder will be astonished by close views of toucans, trogons, motmots, tanagers, orioles, and parrots. More seasoned birders should investigate the brush and rainforest understory and canopy to find the great antshrike, cinnamon becard, lovely cotinga, keel-billed motmot, purple-crowned fairy, tawny-throated leaftosser, and many others.

Also near Tela is **Parque Nacional Jeanette Kawas (Punta Sal)**, excellent for lagoon and mangrove species, cane brakes, and shoreline. The less-known **Punta Izopo** reserve, east of Tela, has a similar environment. These coastal wetlands are havens for large numbers of pelicans (white and brown), roseate spoonbills, white ibis, magnificent frigatebirds, herons, egrets, gulls, terns, and sandpipers.

La Ceiba and Trujillo also have nearby protected rainforest reserves, notably **Parque Nacional Pico Bonito,** near La Ceiba, with trails through secondary forest and huge difficult-to-reach and, to this author's knowledge, unexplored stretches of old growth. Trujillo's **Parque Nacional Capiro y Calentura** is less diverse biologically, but the hike up Calentura along the road is good for spotting several species of tanagers, motmots, wrens, doves, and parrots.

Central and Western Honduras

Lago Yojoa is a must for all birders visiting Honduras, and the best place to observe birds is the Hotel Agua Azul, where one can see red-legged honeycreepers from the balcony during lunch and watch groups of fulvous and black-bellied whistling-ducks, as well as muscovy ducks, cruising over the water. In the pine and broadleaf woods around the hotel grounds, keel-billed toucans and blue-crowned motmots often nest. One can hire a boat to go to the nearby Isla del Venado, an excellent site containing secondary humid forest, with oropendulas, various tanagers and orioles, and other flashy tropical species. Accessed from the lakeside village of La Guama, **Parque Nacional Cerro Azul Meámbar** has a few trails from Los Pinos into a secondary forest frequented by many of the same bird species living around the lake.

From San Pedro Sula, it's easy to reach **Parque Nacional Cusuco**, which contains spectacular pine and oak forest (look for golden-cheeked warblers in oaks) and a fine trail system through mostly secondary cloud forest. For travelers restricted to the North Coast and Bay Islands, this cloud forest is a must-see, since it is the only easily accessible one in the area.

Parque Nacional La Tigra, right outside of Tegucigalpa, is the birder's best choice of Honduras' many central cloud forests. Its two approaches afford a sample of arid broadleaf forest and highland pine forest, while its lush cloud forest contains the majority of northern Central American highland endemics. In the cloud forest, quetzals are common, but the seasoned birder may be more attracted by specialties like the blue-and-white mockingbird, rufous-browed wren, wine-throated hummingbird, and green-breasted mountain gem.

In western Honduras, the **Copán Ruins** are wonderful for birds, because of the preserved tropical dry gallery forest in and around the Mayan ruin site. Motmot, toucanets, tanangers, and orioles are often seen in and around the ruins, while blue heron and other water birds frequent the Río Copán valley. Southeast of Copán Ruinas is **Parque Nacional Celaque**, the largest area of highland forest above 2500 meters in Honduras and the most likely spot to encounter extremely rare cloud forest specialties. The resplendent quetzal can be seen as low as the park visitors' center, though it is more commonly spotted in the higher reaches of the cloud forest. Highland guans, slate-colored solitaires, black robin, spotted nightingale thrush, mountain trogon, and numerous hummingbirds are among its avifauna, while the lucky birder may also encounter such scarce species as the blue-throated motmot, slaty finch, and maroon-chested ground dove. The dense pine forests around the visitors' center are home to brown creepers, red-faced warblers, and many neotropical migrants; American dippers frequent nearby streams.

Mosquitia and Olancho

Honduras' eastern rainforests in **La Mosquitia** are its greatest haven of biodiversity. Over 40 rainforest species, more prevalent farther south, are found here at the northern limits of their range. Some of the more spectacular and notable species found here and virtually nowhere else in the country include: the huge harpy eagle (the largest New World eagle); great green and scarlet macaws; herons; the very rare jabiru stork with its three-meter wing span; black-and-white hawk-eagle; rufous motmot; white-fronted nunbird; green-and-rufous kingfisher; chest-nut-mandible toucan; and yellow-eared toucanet, to name just a few.

The department of **Olancho,** by virtue of its size and biogeographic position, contains a rich avifauna of transition between arid interior valleys, piney highlands, cloud forest highlands, and eastern lowland rainforests. With at least 470 recorded species, making it the most diverse known place for birds in Honduras, **Parque Nacional Sierra de Agalta** offers the chance to bird in some of the wildest and most biodiverse habitat in montane Central America. The feature of the hike is the three-wattled bellbird; other sierran specialties include kites, hawk-eagles, king vultures, 12 woodcreeper species, crested and highland guan, great curassow, several motmots, and a host of cloud forest birds. **El Boquerón canyon** near Juticalpa is excellent for birding and easy to reach—look for the spectacular royal flycatcher, as well as motmots, toucans, and parrots. It is particularly rich in trogons and quetzals.

Southern Honduras

Honduras' south coast contains several specialties not found elsewhere in the country. Certain dense forests remaining in the Cerro Guanacaure near El Corpus are home to the long-tailed manakin and fan-tailed warbler. Wooded areas near the coast,

close to Nicaragua, are habitat for the Hoffmann's woodpecker, found only here, in western Nicaragua, and in northwestern Costa Rica. Scarcer Pacific Slope species include the ash-throated flycatcher, white-bellied chachalaca, and Pacific parakeet.

The wetlands around the Golfo de Fonseca, most notably the Jicarito reserve, are havens for many of the same water species found in the north coast wetlands, including white and brown pelicans, roseate spoonbills, white ibis, frigatebirds, wood storks, herons, egrets, terns, and plovers.

Guides

Although birding is not yet a major tourist activity in Honduras, it is possible to find guides to take you on a birdwatching trip in a couple different parts of the country. Jorge Barraza in Copán Ruinas, tel. 651-4435, is an excellent birding guide and knows the hills and valleys around Copán inside and out. On the north coast, Roberto Gallardo at the Butterfly Farm (no phone) near La Ceiba will lead tours in the forests on the edge of Pico Bonito. In Olancho, contact the environmental group Ecoambientes de Olancho, c/o Oscar Flores Pinot in Juticalpa, tel. 885-2460, to arrange birding tours. For La Picucha and other spots in northern Olancho, contact the birding expert Francisco Urbina at his house in La Venta, Gualaco, or during workdays at the Cohdefor office in the town of Gualaco. Contact tour groups such as La Moskitia Eco-Aventuras in La Ceiba, tel. 442-0104, to arrange trips or find contacts from birding in the Mosquitia.

A minimum of three **field guides** are recommended to assure the birder of complete coverage of the mainland in text and plates. Howell and Webb's 1995 *Field Guide to the Birds of Mexico and Northern Central America* contains the most accurate Honduran data, almost all species, and excellent plates, but lacks pictures of birds in eastern Honduras (c. 50 species) as well as neotropical migrant species. Bring a good North American guide for the migrants, and Ridgely and Gwynne's 1989 *Guide to the Birds of Panama,* with Costa Rica, Nicaragua, and Honduras, to cover eastern Honduras.

This special topic was written by Mark Bonta, who is compiling the soon-to-be-published Birder's Guide To Honduras, *with detailed information on each species and site. Contact Mark by email at talzopilotal@hotmail.com for details.*

regularly beached themselves on the north coast and in the Golfo de Fonseca to lay their eggs, but merciless hunting has devastated their populations. As a result of limited protection programs on a few beaches, for example Plaplaya in La Mosquitia, workers patrol beaches at night during the season when females come in, collect the eggs and protect them in incubators until they hatch, and then release them directly into the sea.

Spending almost their entire long lives at sea, only female turtles come to shore, and then only as long as it takes to laboriously dig a nest, deposit their eggs, and struggle back into the water. The turtles arrive at night, often shortly before dawn, and leave between 70 and 120 eggs, each about the size of a golf ball, with an odd leathery skin that feels fragile but is actually quite resilient. Left to their own devices, the eggs take about two months to hatch, sometimes less, at which point the tiny hatchlings struggle out of the sand and directly into the ocean. But rarely are eggs left alone these days, as they are considered a local delicacy and can fetch a good price. *Hueveros,* or "egg men," walk up and down the beaches at night during the season, raiding nests and frequently killing the defenseless mother for meat as well. While the number of turtles is but a fraction of what it was 30 years ago, protection programs in Honduras and other countries offer some hope that the populations can rebound.

green turtle

ERIN DWYER

HISTORY

All things considered, history has not been particularly kind to Honduras. It is thought of as the quintessential banana republic—the list of foreigners taking advantage of the country and its peoples begins at least as early as the incursion of Meso-american warriors shortly after the time of Christ, who would found the Mayan dynasty in Copán, and continues through the Spanish conquistadors down to the banana companies and *maquiladora* of today.

With its daunting mountainous topography, and lacking the fertile volcanic soils of its Central American neighbors, Honduras never spawned a "home grown" agricultural society of any significant size. During the colonial period, no elite class based on coffee or cattle, like those in neighboring Guatemala, Nicaragua, and El Salvador, developed in Honduras, and the wealth produced from the gold and silver mines was quickly shipped abroad. Instead Honduras remained a land of small-scale *milpa* farmers, who cultivated small patches of land planted with beans, corn, and vegetables to satisfy the immediate needs of their families.

Lacking any wealthy class of its own or a strong central government to defend itself, Honduras fell prey to the U.S. banana companies, who arrived at the beginning of the 20th century and in effect became the country's first land-based ruling class. These days, Honduras finds itself spending most of the little wealth it produces to pay interest on huge debts to private banks and international lending organizations.

Yet, despite this relentless cycle of underdevelopment and exploitation, Honduras somehow managed to maintain overall social peace for most of the 20th century, a remarkable feat considering the appallingly violent civil wars elsewhere in Central America. Some social disturbances did occur, most notably the Great Banana Strike of 1954 and, later, land-invasion movements by *campesinos*. But because Honduran authorities did not view their society through the prism of a rigid class divide, political and military leaders did not react with the blind opposition characteristic of their more repressive neighbors. Labor unions were legalized and limited demands met; the military even undertook a modest agrarian reform program when in power in the 1970s, which helped diffuse a potentially explosive situation in the countryside.

Apart from a brief interlude of militarization brought on by the U.S.-led Contra war against Nicaragua, the Honduran system has proved remarkably flexible in accommodating the needs of its people. The actual operation of government may be almost a caricature of incompetence and corruption, but somehow it's been enough to keep Hondurans from resorting to social revolt.

PRE-COLUMBIAN HISTORY

The First Hondurans

It remains a matter of conjecture whether the earliest settlers in Honduras arrived over land from Asia via the Bering Strait, as many believe, or on rafts from the South Pacific islands. Whatever route they took, the first people to live in what is now Honduras had arrived by about 10,000 B.C.

Next to nothing is known about these early Americans. Archaeologists hypothesize the earliest of them were hunters and gatherers who may have spent only a short time in the region before continuing on to South America.

Early Honduran Societies

Because of its position in the center of the Americas, Honduras was a crossroads for pre-Columbian indigenous cultures, a border zone of sorts where Mesoamerican and South American indigenous peoples met.

At some point between 3000 and 1000 B.C., three indigenous groups still found in Honduras today migrated into the region. From the northern rainforests of South America came the ancestors of today's Pech and Tawahka-Sumu. Both groups speak languages related to the Chibchan family and both settled in northeastern Honduras and in Nicaragua. From the north, possibly from as far away as the southwestern United States, came the forebears of the Tolupan, sometimes also called Jicaque, whose language appears related to Sioux. The Tolupan settled in north-central Honduras.

The earliest evidence of settled society in Honduras dates from 2000 to 1500 B.C. It appears localized cultures developed simultaneously in the Valle de Sula, at Yarumela in the Valle de Comayagua, and in Olancho near the village of Talgua in the Valle de Catacamas. The level of interaction between these different societies is a matter of debate, but judging from pottery remains, some intergroup trading took place.

Around or shortly after the time of Christ, several indigenous groups from Mexico and Guatemala migrated into Honduras. The Toltec-speaking Chorotega are thought to have first settled in western Honduras and later continued southward to the Choluteca Plain, where they were living at the time of the Spanish conquest. The Nahuatl-speaking Pipil migrated south from Mexico at about the same time.

Not long thereafter, another group moved into western Honduras from Mexico and Guatemala and set the foundations for an explosion of development. These people—who would become the Maya—went on to build one of the greatest civilizations ever known in the Americas.

The Maya

An unknown people thought to have links with the Teotihuacan culture in Mexico crossed the Sierra Espíritu Santo from Guatemala into the valley of Copán around A.D. 100, conquering the Mayan-speaking inhabitants of the region. After a slow beginning, these new rulers consolidated their local control over the next three centuries and began construction of the city of Copán by the fifth century.

The first glyph at Copán that can be positively dated was made in A.D. 426 to mark the accession of Yax K'uk'Mo' to the city's throne. Thus began the ruling dynasty of Copán, which spanned four centuries, ending sometime around A.D. 822.

For reasons not entirely clear, Copán was the greatest center for arts, astronomy, and science in the Mayan world. The elaborate stelae erected at Copán are unparalleled anywhere in Mesoamerica, and the city's royal astronomers calculated planetary movements, eclipses, and the yearly calendar with a precision equaled only by modern science.

Built gradually over the course of 400 years, with old temples buried and new ones built over them, the city of Copán is an impressive testament to the wealth and vision of the Mayan rulers, and their ability to marshal large numbers of laborers. At its height some 24,000 people are thought to have lived in and around Copán.

Mysteriously, classic Mayan civilization abruptly collapsed in the Yucatán, Guatemala, and Honduras around A.D. 900. The collapse is all the odder considering Mayan centers were independent city-states, not part of one great centralized empire. One widely accepted explanation for the demise of Mayan civilization is that the population simply grew too big for the surround-

detail of Copán altar relief

ing lands to support. This certainly seems to be the case at Copán, where recent studies confirm massive deforestation and soil erosion just before the city's collapse. Although Maya-speaking people continued to live in the Valle de Copán and still do so today, the city was abandoned entirely.

Honduras in 1502

After the decline of the Maya, and in regions outside of their control, Honduras was a complex mosaic of tribes, subtribes, and chiefdoms. There were only vague borders between them, and all were busy trading, bickering, and frequently warring among one another when Columbus first arrived on the scene in 1502.

Western and south-central Honduras in 1502 were dominated by the Lenca, a broad grouping composed of several different and often hostile subtribes, including the Potón, Guaquí, Cares, Chatos, Dules, Paracas, and Yaras. Although their language does not seem related to any South American group, the Lenca are theorized to have migrated up from Colombia.

The historical account of which languages were spoken by which Lenca tribes is extremely muddled. It's possible the same groups were given two different names by different witnesses, and that others were not Lenca at all. Some tribes were exclusively hunter-gatherers, while others cultivated maize and other crops in the mountain valleys of Comayagua and Sensetí, and around Lago de Yojoa.

In far western Honduras, the Chortí Maya held sway over the mountain region along the border with Guatemala as far west and south as El Salvador and were organized in local chiefdoms.

Throughout western, southern, and northern Honduras at the time of the conquest were trading outposts maintained by the Aztecs. Not far from present-day San Pedro Sula, the city of Naco—the largest urban center in the country when the Spanish conquest began—is thought to have been one such outpost, although others argue it was a Chortí Maya city.

Most of central and north-central Honduras was occupied by the Tolupan in 1502, while farther east in present-day Olancho and Mosquitia were the Pech and the Sumu. Each of these tribes survived by hunting, fishing, and practicing limited agriculture. Settlements were small and

frequently temporary, and groups moved often to find fresh game and rich soil for planting.

Unquestionably these various indigenous groups interacted with one another often, either through trade or warfare. In several places, they lived side by side in relative harmony, especially in the valleys of Comayagua, Catacamas, and Agalta, and around Lago de Yojoa. No group possessed the strength to exercise hegemony over the others, a fact that greatly helped Spanish invaders.

CONQUEST AND COLONIZATION

Columbus' Fourth Voyage

In July 1502, on the fourth and final voyage of Cristóbal Colón (Christopher Columbus), the famed admiral sailed from Hispaniola along the Caribbean coast of Central America and came upon the island of Guanaja, where he met with the local people and waylaid a trader's canoe laden with axes, copper goods, cacao, and pottery.

Despite the fact that the canoe was seen approaching from the west, Columbus continued east from Guanaja, which he named the Island of Pines. His first stop was at Punta Caxinas, near present-day Trujillo. The first Mass spoken on the mainland of the Americas was held at Punta Caxinas. A decrepit concrete cross now marks the site.

East of Trujillo Columbus stopped again at the mouth of a large river, which may have been either the Aguán, Sico, or Patuca. Because this was the place chosen to claim the lands for the Spanish crown, Columbus named the river Río de la Posesión.

Continuing farther east along the coast of the Mosquitia, Columbus's fleet was buffeted by severe storms until rounding the easternmost point of Honduras and reaching calmer waters off present-day Nicaragua. In honor of the better weather, the point was christened Cabo Gracias a Dios, a name it retains today.

The Conquest Begins

Following this uneventful first visit, Honduras was ignored for the next 20 years, apart from a possible scouting trip by explorers Juan Díaz Solís and Vicente Yáñez Pinzón in 1508. Occupied with consolidating their newfound possessions in the Caribbean, the Spaniards did not return to Honduras until 1522-23, when Gil González Dávila led an exploratory expedition up the Pacific coast from Panama, reaching the Gulf of Fonseca.

In the following couple of years, six Spanish expeditions converged on Honduras, each headed by ambitious soldiers after wealth and glory. Not an auspicious start to colonization, it presaged the trend of placing personal power over group interests—the rule in Honduran government ever since.

González Dávila, with the approval of the crown, was the first to land on Honduran shores, establishing a small town near the mouth of the Río Dulce, in what is now Guatemala. The explorer marched into the heart of Honduras toward Nicaragua in early 1524. Shortly thereafter, Mexican conqueror Hernán Cortés sent an expedition of his own led by Cristóbal de Olid, who arrived on the north coast in May and quickly set up a small town at Triunfo de la Cruz. It is said that the Aztecs told Cortés they received their gold from the mountains of Honduras. Thus it may have been no accident that the conquistadors made directly for the gold-rich rivers of Olancho.

Olid wasn't totally loyal to Cortés, and once on his own he tried to claim the province for himself. When word of this reached Cortés in Mexico, he promptly dispatched a second expedition, led by Francisco de las Casas, to ensure his authority. Further complications occurred from the incursions of Pedro de Alvarado and Hernando de Soto, who entered Honduras from Guatemala and Nicaragua, respectively. Amidst the bickering and fighting, in which Olid literally lost his head, the first permanent settlement was established in the country, at Trujillo.

Impatient with reports of fighting among these various factions, and not trusting anyone, Cortés personally led an expedition to Honduras. Beginning in late 1524, he undertook an incredible several-month overland trek through the jungles of the Yucatán and the Guatemalan Petén, reaching Honduras in the spring of 1525. Although Cortés briefly took control of the situation in Honduras, by the time of his departure in April 1526, his long absence from Mexico had undermined his position in the royal court, and he never again held a position of power.

Displeased with the turbulent course of conquest and wanting to ensure direct control over the new colony, the Spanish crown sent Diego López de Salcedo to act as royal governor of Honduras. López de Salcedo anchored off Trujillo on 24 October 1526, and after a few days of negotiations with suspicious colonists loyal to Cortés, he was allowed to land and take office.

Rebellion and Consolidation

The 15 years after López de Salcedo took over as governor were chaotic for the nascent colony and catastrophic for the indigenous people. Continued infighting, conflicting royal *cédulas* (orders giving authority to conquer and govern a given area), and repeated revolts by native peoples prevented the Spaniards from significantly extending their control across the country.

Several localized attacks against Spanish settlements took place around Trujillo and in the Valle de Sula in the early 1530s, but in 1536 mass rebellion broke out across most of western and central Honduras. Led by the Lenca warrior Lempira, for whom the national currency is named, thousands of Lenca and allied tribes took up arms against the Spaniards. The hostile tribes kept the colony in a precarious position until 1539, when Lempira was assassinated by the Spanish. Localized rebellions continued after Lempira's death, especially in the Valle de Comayagua, but the Spanish put them down easily.

Victory over the Lenca served the Spanish well, both eliminating further Indian resistance and uniting the conquistadors in the colonial project. Establishing the towns of Gracias a Dios, Comayagua, San Pedro Sula, Choluteca, and Tencoa in the late 1530s, the Spaniards laid the foundation for extending control throughout the region.

As always, gold and silver proved the main impetus for new Spanish settlements. Rich veins were discovered early near Gracias a Dios and Comayagua, and not long after in Olancho and in the hills above the Golfo de Fonseca.

In the early colonial era, the province was divided into two sections: Higueras, which comprised present-day western and central Honduras, and Honduras proper, which covered Trujillo, La Mosquitia, Olancho, the region around Tegucigalpa, and the Golfo de Fonseca.

Indian Decline

In the first decades after the conquest, the indigenous population of Honduras went into a precipitous decline, devastated by both the constant fighting and European plagues. Diseases for which the indigenous had no tolerance actually preceded the Spaniards, having been communicated by infected Indians coming to Honduras from Mexico and Caribbean islands. But when the conquistadors arrived in person, the plagues picked up force, ravaging local populations. An estimated 500,000 to 800,000 native people lived in Honduras before 1492, but by 1541 colonial reports put the number of Indians under Spanish control at just 8,000. Although this figure does not include the populations of Tolupan, Pech, and Tawahka *outside* Spanish influence, it still represents an almost unimaginable decline in population.

While this unintended biological weapon certainly facilitated the conquest, it also posed serious problems for the Spaniards, who needed laborers to work the mines and provide them with food. Indigenous populations would not recover from the plagues and begin to grow again for more than 50 years.

The Poorest Colony

Because of labor shortages and the rapid depletion of the richest veins of gold and silver by the end of the 16th century, Honduras quickly became a colonial backwater. Since the possibilities for getting rich were slim, able governors did their utmost to be stationed elsewhere, leaving Honduras with incompetent administrators who were eager to leave at the first opportunity.

Spain's control over Honduras, as with many other regions of Latin America, was through *encomiendas,* a method in which Spaniards received awards of land and the right to use the native people who lived on the land for labor in return for religious instruction.

Farming was difficult; Honduras lacked the rich volcanic soils of its neighbors and the rugged terrain made bringing produce to markets even harder. Because of these hardships, would-be colonists looked elsewhere for land. In the early years of the colony, the only industries of any importance were cattle ranching, often for local consumption, and gathering sarsaparilla, thought at the time to be a cure for venereal disease.

In addition, the developing colony was faced with the constant threat of pirate attacks against coastal towns on both the north and south coast, and later with actual British settlers in the Mosquitia and the Bay Islands. These raiders, helped by their Miskito allies, made living on the north coast a dangerous undertaking, effectively sealing off the Caribbean coast from Spanish control for the better part of two centuries.

Late in the colonial era, improved technology led to a renewed though short-lived boom in mining, particularly in the mines of Santa Lucía, above Tegucigalpa, and El Corpus, near Choluteca. Farmers in the region of Copán and Gracias also exported large quantities of high-quality tobacco to Europe and other colonies. Nonetheless these were mostly small-scale ventures compared to the wealthy coffee plantations of neighboring Guatemala and El Salvador, to say nothing of the fabulously rich mines of Mexico and Perú. Thus it comes as no surprise that Honduras did not attract significant migration or experience significant economic development during the colonial period.

INDEPENDENCE AND 19TH-CENTURY HONDURAS

Mexican Empire and Central American Federation

Rather than fighting for their independence from the Spanish empire, Central Americans had it handed to them without a struggle when colonial authority completely collapsed in the early 1820s. On 15 September 1821, representatives of the former colonies of Honduras, Costa Rica, Nicaragua, El Salvador, and Guatemala jointly declared independence from Spain in the government palace of Guatemala.

Brief struggles followed within the new countries over how to govern themselves. In Honduras, the two principal cities of Comayagua and Tegucigalpa split on the issue, the former opting to join with Mexico and the latter preferring a union of Central American republics.

By early 1822 the issue had been decided, and the countries declared themselves loyal to Iturbide, the new emperor of Mexico. This would-be empire lasted just over a year, at which point Iturbide was deposed and Central

FRANCISCO MORAZÁN: CENTRAL AMERICA'S GEORGE WASHINGTON

Honduras' national hero, Francisco Morazán is one of the most revered characters in Central American history, recognized as a visionary thinker and politician, a humane individual, and one of the finest soldiers ever to fight on American soil. Because of his appreciation for the American Revolution and his tireless efforts to promote Central American unity, Morazán is sometimes referred to as the George Washington of Central America.

Morazán was born 3 October 1789 to an upper-middle-class colonial family in Tegucigalpa. Gifted both physically and intellectually, and imbued with strong self-discipline, he was largely self-taught. He received his only formal education from a priest in the town of Texiguat, at that time the only school near Tegucigalpa. Morazán taught himself French so he could read Rousseau's *Social Contract,* and he continued with Tocqueville, Montesquieu, and the history of Europe.

When Central America declared independence from Spain in 1821, Morazán put himself under the orders of Liberal Dionisio de Herrera, then mayor of Tegucigalpa. Morazán's first command was at the head of a group of soldiers sent to Gracias in 1822 to transport a load of silver and mercury. He was captured by soldiers from Comayagua but managed to talk his way out of being detained by claiming he was traveling on business. After the Central American provinces broke away from Mexico and created their own union, Morazán took up arms for the Liberal side. He lost his first battle, defending Comayagua from Conservative troops, and was forced to flee to El Salvador to escape a prison term.

After this inauspicious start, Morazán's fortunes improved dramatically. In 1827 Morazán traveled to Nicaragua, where he gathered an army to invade El Salvador and fight off conservatives attacking from Guatemala, which he did the following year. In 1829 he continued by taking Guatemala; in elections the next year Morazán was voted president of the Central American Federation. With one brief interruption, Morazán held this post until 1838. Although the federation experienced constant strain from internal opposition, Morazán managed to institute farsighted reforms in bureaucracy, public education, taxation, freedom of religion, the judicial system, infrastructure, and the development, albeit temporary, of democratic institutions.

Morazán's Liberal policies antagonized the church and elite landowners in all five Central American countries. The forces pulling them apart proved stronger than those holding them together, and in spite of his best efforts, the union fell apart shortly after he left office.

Morazán was forced into exile in Peru in 1840, but he returned two years later. He led a coup in Costa Rica, with the idea of using that country as a base to reestablish the union. His forces were defeated by Conservatives in September of 1842, and on 15 September—ironically, the anniversary of Central American independence—Morazán was executed. He was given permission to order his own execution. After correcting the firing squad's aim, he called out, "¡Ahora bien, fuego!" ("Ready, fire!"). According to legend, he was heard to say, "¡Estoy vivo!" ("I'm alive!"), and a second volley killed him.

With Morazán's death died any real chance at Central American union, in spite of the obvious advantages of such an alliance. The idea has resurfaced repeatedly over the following century and a half and may be reappearing even today in the form of trade agreements among some Central American countries.

American nations joined together to become a separate federation.

The United Provinces of Central America was a fine idea in theory but in practice foundered on the unpleasant realities of local rivalries, suspicions, and the split between partisans of the Conservative and Liberal trains of political thought. Broadly, Conservatives favored the church, the land-owning elite, and a paternalistic attitude toward indigenous peoples and campesinos, while Liberals supported economic modernization, education, eradicating the power of the church, and a policy of erasing indigenous culture and homogenizing the population. By 1838, after 16 years of nonstop infighting among its members, the union was dead, and each province became a sovereign nation.

The Birth of Honduras

After a few months of vacillation, Honduras declared itself independent on 15 November 1838 and enacted the first of many constitutions in January 1839. Between this time and 1876, Honduras experienced a period of extreme instability and precious little economic or social development.

Rivalries between Liberals and Conservatives dominated the political landscape across Central America during this era, and when one side was in power in one country, rulers of the opposite persuasion organized invasions or coups from their territory. Being in the middle of Central America, Honduras was a frequent target of and participant in these schemes and aggressions.

As if the squabbles among its Central American neighbors weren't enough, Honduras also had to cope with the machinations of North Americans and British, both private citizens and government officials. American agent E. George Squier and British representative Frederick Chatfield abused their power to advance the interests of their respective countries, most particularly regarding a much-discussed but never realized transcontinental railroad or canal.

Even more ominous were the activities of private American and British citizens in Honduras. From the U.S. came the messianic, slightly lunatic "gray-eyed man of destiny," William Walker. Convinced he was the savior of Central America, and backed by wealthy U.S. financiers, Walker invaded Nicaragua and declared himself president in 1855. Although his rule was short-lived, Walker performed the heretofore impossible task of uniting all the Central American republics—at least for as long as it took them to defeat and expel the gringo. Undaunted, Walker returned to Honduras in 1860 with the idea of retaking Central America, only to be captured near Trujillo by the British, turned over to Honduran troops, and summarily executed.

Ever more subtle than North Americans, British power brokers contented themselves not with outright invasion but with contracting a series of debts with the Honduran government. This made a few British bankers and several corrupt Hondurans rich but crippled the country before it had a chance to get started in its modernization. In one of the shadier transactions in financial history, British bankers lent Honduras a bit less then six million pounds sterling to help construct a national railroad. The government eventually saw merely 75,000 of these pounds, the rest remaining in sticky fingers on both sides of the Atlantic. By 1871 only 92 km of track had been laid, and even that was shoddily built and soon collapsed. Unable to cope with even the interest on the loan, successive governments tried to forget it existed until 1916, by which time Honduras owed US$125 million and had to plead for the loans to be renegotiated.

The Liberal Years

One of the first forward-thinking governments in Honduran history began in 1876, with the inauguration of Liberal President Marco Aurelio Soto. A firm believer in modernization, Soto and his successor Luis Bográn did what they could to lay the foundations for development.

During the years between 1876 and 1891, when Bográn was deposed, state finances were regulated, free primary education was promoted, and the legal code was reformed. Convinced of the need for foreign capital to lift Honduras out of poverty, Soto also promoted mining among U.S. investors.

His campaign's most notable success, if it can be termed that, was the founding of the New York and Honduras Rosario Mining Company in 1880, which quickly became the most profitable and productive mine in the western hemisphere during that period. Although the company provided jobs for a thousand Honduran workers and was for a time the most important economic and political player in Honduras, all profits went directly to New York; in the long run Honduras saw little benefit for the concessions it offered.

The Banana Companies

The railroad and mining episodes gave merely a taste of the foreign domination that was to come, with the advent of the banana industry on the north coast. U.S.-bound freighters were buying bananas from local producers as early as 1860, but in 1899 the Vaccaro Brothers—later Standard Fruit, and now Castle and Cooke—set up the first foreign-controlled plantations on the mainland near La Ceiba. They were quickly followed by United Fruit and Cuyamel.

Once these foreign companies moved in, small-scale Honduran producers were forced out of business either through land buy-outs or crude threats. Thus, by the beginning of World War I, the three largest companies, all foreign-owned, controlled huge portions of land, the country's only railroads, and over 80% of the Honduran export trade. Large chunks of rich bottom land were literally given away to the companies in return for the construction of railroads, which for the most part were never built.

Along with economic domination, the banana companies showed no compunction about bribing and cajoling government officials and army officers. When quieter tactics proved unsuccessful, financing a revolution was not entirely out of the question, and disputes were often decided in the end by a U.S. invasion.

Reviewing this inglorious period, one historian observed that "North American power had become so encompassing that U.S. military forces and United Fruit could struggle against each other to see who was to control the Honduran government, then have the argument settled by the U.S. Department of State."

THE DEVELOPMENT
OF MODERN HONDURAS

The *Cariato*

The perennial instability proved a distraction to the banana companies and the U.S. government, and after the merger of United and Cuyamel in 1929, the political situation in Honduras changed.

Political strongman Tiburcio Carías Andino, who belonged to the newly born Partido Nacional (National Party), was able to seize power in 1932—and remained there for 16 years.

Carías, who began his career as a military cook, was a classic example of an uneducated yet extremely shrewd and ruthless *caudillo* (political boss). Social developments were minimal under his rule; the military was professionalized, the opposition and media suppressed, and the fruit companies—particularly United—given a free hand.

The *Cariato* was the kind of time when, in the words of historians Donald Schulz and Deborah Sundloff Schulz, "members of the opposition were forbidden to travel in automobiles, the First Lady sold tamales at the Presidential Palace, and the president of Congress justified Carías' long rule by noting that 'God, too, continues in power indefinitely.'"

Following the end of World War II, Central American dictators had become an unnecessary embarrassment to the U.S., and Carías was forced from office in 1948 in favor of protégé Juan Manuel Gálvez. Gálvez ruled for six years and began the long process of economic modernization by developing a central bank, starting a system of income tax, and expanding public works.

The Great Banana Strike

The landmark Banana Strike of 1954 represented the birth of Honduras' powerful and effective organized labor movement. Although sporadic strikes occurred on banana plantations and docks as early as 1916, the 1954 strike was the first large-scale labor action that could not be quickly bought off or put down with force.

Appropriately, the actions leading to the strike began on Labor Day, May 1, 1954. A group of dock workers in Puerto Cortés asked United officials for double pay for work on Sunday, which was mandated by law. Their request was put off for several days, and in the meantime United fired their designated spokesman.

In response, the dock workers went on strike. They were soon joined by all 25,000 United workers and 15,000 Standard Fruit workers, an expression of pent-up frustration at abysmal working conditions, low pay, and cavalier treatment by banana company officials.

The strike was supported by Hondurans throughout the country, and workers of several other industries struck out of solidarity. Lasting 69 days, the strike was eventually broken by a combination of limited concessions, payoffs to labor leaders, and the establishment of company-friendly unions in competition with the more militant ones. The American Federation of Labor (AFL) played a prominent role in setting up these "stooge" unions.

Although direct gains from the strike were minimal, it was a watershed for the nascent labor movement. By negotiating with the unions, both the government and the banana companies tacitly accepted their right to exist, and the following year laws were passed on union creation, collective bargaining, and the right to strike. While this may seem like a trivial gain, these rights were impossible to even contemplate in any of the countries neighboring Honduras.

Growth of Military Power

At the same time, a political watershed was taking place in Honduras. In the face of an incompetent and unpopular government, and partly spurred by the Banana Strike, a group of military officers organized a successful coup d'état on 21 October 1956.

Though elections were held the following year and the military duly turned power back over to civilians, the coup marked the beginning of military influence in the country's politics, a defining characteristic of Honduran government for the next four decades. One indicator of this influence was two clauses in the new constitution written by the military during its brief stay in power. One allowed the head of the military to disregard orders from the president that he considered unconstitutional, and the second gave him control over all military promotions.

Following the 1957 elections, the Constitutional Assembly chose Liberal Ramón Villeda Morales as president. He quickly instituted much-needed social reforms, such as literacy projects, public health care, road building, and agrarian reform. The agrarian reform, in particular, made Honduran land owners and fruit companies nervous (this all in the wake of the coup in Guatemala, triggered for similar reasons). When it appeared an even more radical Liberal would win elections after Villeda, the military again took control on 3 October 1963. Colonel Oswaldo López Arellano assumed leadership of the coun-

try, and apart from a democratic hiatus in 1971-72, the military stayed in formal power until 1978.

The first half of military rule, until the 1969 war with El Salvador, often called "The Soccer War," was characterized by a suppression of communist groups and *campesino* organizations, but at the same time it offered limited agrarian and social reform.

Following the war and the failed democratic experiment of 1971-72, López Arellano returned to power, this time convinced of the need for real agrarian reform. Between 1973 and 1976, 31,000 families received 144,000 hectares of land through the National Agrarian Institute (INA). Although it did not eliminate the problems of landless workers, it was a large step in the right direction and a reform that would have been completely unimaginable in El Salvador, Nicaragua, or Guatemala.

Following a scandal involving bribes paid by the banana companies to government officials, López Arellano was forced from power in March 1975. His replacement, Col. Juan Alberto Melgar Castro, slowed the pace of reform. Melgar Castro was ousted in 1978 by a junta led by Gen. Policarpo Paz García, who organized elections in 1981 that nominally returned civilian politicians to power.

Reagan and the Contras

Two external but related developments of extreme importance to Honduras took place shortly before the 1981 election of Liberal Roberto Suazo Córdova: the victory of the Sandinista revolution in Nicaragua, and the inauguration of U.S. President Ronald Reagan. Viewing the world through the paranoid prism of communist-capitalist conflict, President Reagan could not tolerate the presence of the socialist-leaning Sandinistas in "his" hemisphere, and Honduras proved the perfect launching pad for the U.S.-financed and -directed counterrevolution.

With the complicity of Suazo Córdova and the fascistic armed forces commander Gen. Gustavo Álvarez Martínez, the CIA at first overtly and later covertly directed a stream of training, funds, and weapons to an army of anti-Sandinista Nicaraguans living along the Honduras-Nicaragua border in Olancho and El Paraíso.

Along with the Contras, as the fighters were known, came U.S. military personnel by the hundreds and CIA agents by the dozen, using Honduras as a base not only for the Contra war but also to help the Salvadoran military in its own struggle against leftist rebels. The country had become a virtual appendage of the US military.

Concurrently, the Honduran military tightened its hold over society, although the country was still a formal democracy. Álvarez ruthlessly imprisoned, tortured, killed, or "disappeared" labor activists, peasant leaders, priests, and other opponents, often using the infamous hit squad Battalion 3-16. Though the repression never reached the heights it did in El Salvador or Guatemala—victims here numbered in the hundreds rather than thousands—these strong-arm tactics were unheard of in Honduras and created widespread discontent even within the military. In 1984 Álvarez was exiled by fellow officers, and his successor, Walter López Reyes, put an end to the blatantly unsavory acts of repression. Nevertheless, the military remained in firm control behind the scenes.

By 1988 the Contra war began winding down, due to U.S. congressional opposition, the Iran-Contra affair, the Central American peace process, and Honduras' growing unhappiness with having the Contras based inside its borders. The Contras were disbanded by early 1990, following the election of Violeta Chomorro in Nicaragua.

The 1990s

In the 1989 elections, National candidate Rafael Leonardo Callejas was swept into office by a large margin, promising a program of economic modernization.

Young, smooth Callejas believed the only way to pull Honduras out of the hole was a heavy dose of economic adjustment, that is, selling off public industries, laying off public employees, having a floating exchange rate, and encouraging foreign investment. A superbly gifted politician, Callejas managed to push these measures through and generally see them through to the end of his term in 1994, in spite of widespread public and political opposition.

The results were mixed, at best. Unemployment and absolute numbers of people living in poverty rose, but defenders claim it was a necessary price for putting the country's fiscal book in order. Critics retort that many of the privatiza-

tions were bought up by Callejas' cronies or members of the armed forces, which has since emerged as one of the strongest economic players in the country. Critics contend corruption was rife throughout Callejas' term, with the president himself accused of misappropriating a petroleum fund and benefitting from the sale of Honduran citizenship during his time in office.

The 1993 elections brought Liberal Carlos Roberto Reina to power, a long-time politician respected for his personal honesty. He took office in 1994 promising a "moral revolution" to clean up the corrupt political system. His success was limited. Corruption continued, of course, though perhaps at a lower level than before. While posting some impressive growth numbers during his term (mainly as a result of Callejas' policies), Reina made no significant moves to cope with his country's exploding debt.

Reina's one great success, which came to fruition under his successor, was beginning the process of placing the nation's then-autonomous military under civilian control.

The Flores Administration

Offering a "new agenda" of economic growth after years of neoliberal hardships, Liberal candidate Carlos Flores Facussé won the presidency on 20 November 1997, taking 53% of the vote to 42% for Nationalist candidate Nora Gúnera de Melgar, widow of one of the country's military rulers, Melgar Castro. Scion of an extremely wealthy Honduran family of Arab descent and brother of one of the country's top businessmen, 47-year-old Flores had been assiduously building his power base within the Liberal Party for nearly two decades. Flores was first elected deputy shortly after returning home from finishing his Masters degree in International Economics and Finance from Louisiana State University. He moved his way up to become the powerful Minister of the President under Suazo Córdova and later became president of Congress. Among Flores' many business interests is ownership of La Tribuna newspaper, which has long been his mouthpiece.

Flores took office in January 1998 and spent his first year negotiating with the many nations and organizations to which Honduras was indebted, trying to gain a reprieve on the country's seemingly impossible financial burdens. In part at the behest of the World Bank and IMF, Flores has accelerated plans for the sell-off of several notoriously inefficient state-run enterprises, like Hondutel, the electric utility company ENEE, four international airports, and the principal ports. And despite much campaign talk about easing the burden on the average citizen, Flores jacked up the sales tax from 7% to 12% in April 1998. At the same time, corporate income tax fell from 42% to 25%, and a range of other business taxes were eased or eliminated.

Clearly Flores was gambling that the combination of these measures, combined with expected debt relief, would be enough to reactivate the economy. But if anyone really thought these measures would succeed, Hurricane Mitch disillusioned them in short order. Since October 1998, the Honduran government has been in a near-permanent state of crisis management, unable to look beyond meeting immediate needs and trying to get the country back on its feet.

The record of Flores and his government in dealing with reconstruction is decidedly mixed. While damaged infrastructure and thousands of homeless people still abound, Flores claims with some justification that much promised aid has not yet actually been given to his government. International donors retort that past funds have been misused, and that they have no guarantees future money will be properly spent. If you can believe the newspapers, significantly more money and construction work is meant to be in the pipe for 2000.

One interesting political development, already underway before the hurricane but accelerated in its aftermath, is the increasing presence of international organizations, bilateral missions, and private foreign groups in everyday Honduran life. It seems that everywhere you turn in Honduras is a group of Finnish foresters, or German resource managers, or Japanese and Cuban doctors, or agriculture projects sponsored by the World Bank or US AID. The list is interminable. This international brigade seems to be supplanting, to a certain degree, the dominant role played by the United States in Honduran affairs until the mid-1990s. As if to architecturally express this new evolution of Honduras' international dependency, the United Nations has erected a new, imposing office building right in the center of Colonia Palmira in Tegucigalpa, rivaling the nearby U.S. Embassy building in size.

2001 Elections

Although little is certain in politics, conventional *catracho* wisdom has picked Nationalist Ricardo Maduro as the odds-on favorite to win the presidential elections in 2001. Charismatic and good-looking, Maduro has an air of sincerity (whether it's feigned is difficult to say) that other Honduran politicians lack. After two administrations out of power, the Nationalists put aside their bickering to rally behind Maduro, with only a token opposition by Elias Asfura for the party nomination.

The ruling Liberal Party is divided between two main contenders for the nomination: Jaime Rosenthal, an extremely wealthy banker and businessman (owner of, among many other things, the newspaper *Tiempo*), and Rafael Pineda Ponce, a septuagenerian old-school party stalwart and current president of Congress. A third candidate, up-and-coming *olanchano* Mel Zelaya, is ahead of Pineda Ponce in the polls but is considered likely to withdraw from the race in order to conserve himself for future elections.

As with almost all Honduran elections, differences in campaign platforms are likely to be minimal—and irrelevant anyway, since the vote will be decided chiefly by party loyalty and the personal popularity of the candidates.

GOVERNMENT

Political System

Remarkably, Honduras has the oldest two-party system in the western hemisphere (after the United States) in which power is exchanged through regular, peaceful general elections. Apart from brief interludes of direct military rule, presidents from either the Liberal or National parties have ruled the country since the beginning of the 20th century. Not that this means Honduras is any paragon of democracy. Rather, it points to the fact that both parties are cut from the same cloth and have managed to institutionalize a system permitting them to alternate turns skimming off a healthy slice of Honduras' national wealth. Venal though Honduran politics may be, the system has at least provided a surprising degree of stability in the desperately poor and underdeveloped country and avoided large-scale social revolts.

Since 1982, with the passage of its 16th constitution, Honduras has simultaneously elected a president, three vice-presidents, and the 128-member unicameral National Congress every four years. During the last election, some 2.9 million Hondurans were registered to vote, and only 26% failed to do so. This may not be great compared to some countries in Latin America, but it's quite a bit better than the United States. It's also worth noting that Honduran elections are a very peaceable affair, with violence and vote fraud almost unheard of.

The president—who cannot be re-elected—is by far the most powerful figure in the country. In theory the Congress has wide authority; in practice almost all policy initiatives come from the executive office. Congress, which is always controlled by the president's party, generally acts as a rubber stamp.

The system developed partly from the country's long tradition of *caudillo* rulers, and in part from the electoral system. Voters are allowed to choose only one party's slate for national elections and do not have the option of voting for a president from one party and a congressional deputy from another. Thus, deputies are merely loyal supporters of the president and do not answer to a local constituency.

The judicial system, supposedly independent, is in reality a completely politicized institution. Judges are changed every four years, from the Supreme Court down to local justices of the peace, according to political affiliation.

Honduras is divided into 18 departments: Altántida, Choluteca, Comayagua, Copán, Cortés, El

rural government office, San Antonio, Cortés

VINCE MURPHY

Paraíso, Francisco Morazán, Gracias a Dios, Intibucá, Islas de la Bahía, La Paz, Lempira, Ocotepeque, Olancho, Santa Bárbara, Valle, and Yoro. Each is ruled by a governor, who is appointed and removed at the discretion of the president.

Every four years, the country's 297 municipal governments hold votes for mayor *(alcalde)* and municipal council on the same day as the national elections. Until the 1993 elections, local officials were on the same ballot as national ones, but now voters may split the ticket between different parties. Rural *municipios* are further divided into *aldeas,* or villages, and *caseríos,* or hamlets.

Political Parties

For the better part of a century, Honduran politics has been formally dominated by two parties: the Liberals and the Nationals. The Liberal Party was created first, in an effort to institutionalize the modernizing liberal reforms of Marco Aurelio Soto and Luis Bográn. The Nationals were born as a splinter group of the Liberals in 1902 at the behest of Manuel Bonilla, who later became the party's first president.

Since their inception, little has distinguished the two parties in terms of policy. For many years the Nationals were linked closely to the military, but that was more an accident of circumstance than a true ideological stance, evidenced by the close cooperation of successive Liberal presidents Suazo Córdova and Azcona with the military in the 1980s.

For the most part, the parties have been vehicles for personal ambition, a fact never much disguised. Campaigns are invariably long on mudslinging and personal accusations and woefully short on political proposals.

Despite lacking clear ideological differences, each party has certain core areas of support—the Nationals in the rural departments of Copán, Lempira, Intibucá, and Gracias a Dios and in the southern departments of Valle and Choluteca, while the Liberals are more popular in the urban areas and the north coast. Political scientists have suggested that party allegiance is often merely passed down over generations, much like support for a favorite soccer club, rather than being a real assessment of the options.

Smaller parties have tried to break the grip of the big two, but with little success. Both the Christian Democrats (PDCH) and the reformist Innovation and Unity Party (PINU) constituted themselves in the late 1960s and received an initial burst of support after the Soccer War of 1969. While both parties began as very critical of the system, these days the PINU generally sides with the National Party, while the PDCH's support of the Liberals is so entrenched that the parties are considering a formal alliance.

The only truly unique political party on the scene is the beleaguered Democratic Unification Party (UDE), comprising land rights activists, leftists, and even a few ex-guerrillas. The UDE is particularly strong in conflictive areas like the Aguán Valley and faces regular repression from landowners and ranchers. UDE mayoral candidate Carlos Escaleras looked likely to win the November 1997 election in Tocoa, but he was shot dead on 18 October. Several other UDE members have been killed, and many more have been threatened into putting aside their activism to save their lives. In short, the party's chances of making significant changes in the established system are minimal, but one can only admire the members' courage for trying.

The Military

Until the mid-1990s it could be reasonably argued that Honduras' official political system was nothing more than window-dressing for the country's true power broker—the armed forces. Since taking direct power for the first time in 1956, the military has always maintained a watchful eye over civilian politicians, who, knowing the rules of the game, have been careful not to tread on any boots. While technically under civilian authority, the military was in reality fully independent, answering to no one. Changes in military leadership, the result of behind-the-scenes maneuvering, were presented to surprised politicians as fait accompli, and the Congress duly ratified the new leader without question.

Nonetheless, this independence did not automatically lead to military repression. The Honduran military is a curious animal. The officer corps is not made up of wealthy elites, as is the case in neighboring countries. It's much more egalitarian. In fact, in the absence of a strong homegrown elite, the military has become an elite class itself, with its own interests and agenda often quite different from the country's politicians, business leaders, and landowners. For this reason, the military has never been as rabidly conservative or repressive as other regimes in the region. When in direct power in the early 1970s under Colonel Oswaldo López Arellano, the military actually embarked on a far-ranging agricultural reform program, a far more radical measure for the countryside than those considered by civilian politicians.

During the height of the U.S.-sponsored Contra war, the military assumed a more sinister role, engaging in torture and disappearances similar to the abuses in neighboring El Salvador, Guatemala, and Nicaragua, but never on the same scale. Even opponents concede that fewer than 200 activists were killed by the authorities during the 1980s. But opposition to even these relatively few transgressions came from within the military itself, and with the winding down of the Contra war, complaints of military abuses declined.

The first steps taken to put civilians firmly in control of the Honduran military came from Pres. Reina, who began by abolishing mandatory service in 1995, and then transferred the police to civilian authorities in 1997. The transition was completed on 27 January 1999, when Pres. Flores relieved Gen. Mario Hung Pacheco of his command as Chief of the Armed Forces and appointed lawyer and journalist Edgardo Dumas Rodríguez as the new Defense Minister. While the position of Defense Minister had existed previously, changes in Article 15 of the Constitution gave the minister effective power to control the military leadership. Flores demonstrated his control shortly thereafter, by replacing Hung Pacheco with Col. Daniel López Carballo.

Although numbering only 13,000 soldiers, half the number as at the height of the 1980s buildup, the military is still a powerful force in Honduran society. To cope with falling military budgets and the curtailing of U.S. military aid, the military has started to develop its own financial base. It has been so successful that its investment arm, the Instituto de Previsión Militar (IPM), is one of the largest investors in the country. The IPM owns hotels, shrimp farms, a cement factory, and a range of other holdings thought to be worth US$100 million. However, many of these holding were put under civilian control in late 1999, and for the first time the Army now has a civilian paymaster also.

One ominous tendency in recent years is the increasing incidence of military personnel involved in drug trafficking, robberies, and other crime. Officers have been implicated in drug running, and in January 2000 a sergeant was caught red-handed holding up a taxi in Tegucigalpa. On the positive side, foreign countries are helping to fund the creation of special *batallones verdes,* or green battalions, to help combat natural disasters in Honduras.

ECONOMY

Honduras is an extremely poor country. For years it has been considered the second-poorest in the hemisphere, after Haiti, though due to the years of civil war Nicaragua is not far behind. Annual per capita income was US$650 in 1998, the unemployment rate is 40%, and a staggering 80% of the population lives below the poverty line.

The Honduran economy grew steadily throughout the 1960s and 1970s, following a policy of import-substitution and promotion of nontraditional exports, but the region's military conflicts during the 1980s sent investment and production into a tailspin. After the end of the Contra war and the implementation of fiscal reforms by President Callejas, Honduras became a favorite for foreign investors, particularly Asians building tax-free export factories, called *maquilas*. The growth in *maquila* exports, combined with steadily growing exports of coffee, bananas, sugar, and shrimp, fueled growth rates of three percent a year or better beginning in 1995.

Hurricane Mitch was a major setback for the Honduran economy, perhaps not setting the country back 50 years as Pres. Flores suggested, but extremely grave nonetheless. Growth for 1998 was projected at five percent, and even though the storm hit with only two months left in the year, damage pulled the number down to 3.9%. The following year, when the full effects of the destruction were felt, saw the economy shrink by an estimated 2.5%. With the *maquilas* exporting more than ever (the hurricane barely slowed them down) and agricultural production nearly back to normal, the government is somewhat fancifully predicting growth of five percent for 2000.

Agricultural products continue to be by far the most important export, led by coffee and bananas. With that dependency comes the often painful syndrome of having the national economy fluctuate in almost direct relation to the price of these goods in foreign markets, over which Hondurans have no influence.

Beyond the *maquilas,* precious little industry has sprung up in Honduras, and any ideas some motivated Honduran might have quickly falter in the face of a total lack of available bank financing. With interest rates too high to contemplate and a withered banking sector, the only people lending money to generate economic activity in Honduras are foreign countries or multilateral banks like the IMF, IADB, World Bank, and others. Another significant source of financing in Honduras, not much discussed but well known by all, is "dirty money," or the huge profits generated by the drug trade, looking for a place to hide.

Foreign Debt

One of many factors hampering the Honduran government's ability to stimulate growth and spend more on social programs is a massive load of debt, inherited from generations of improvident former governments. Honduras' debt hovered between US$3 billion and US$4 billion dollars for most of the 1990s, well over half of the tiny country's GDP. At the end of 1999, the total was around US$4.6 billion, not including several hurricane relief loans. Interest and service payments on the debt gobble up at least 30% of the annual budget, money that could be used to address many unfilled and critical needs.

Even before Hurricane Mitch struck, the creditor nations of the Paris Club—Canada, Denmark, France, Italy, Japan, Germany, Holland, Spain, Switzerland, and the U.S.—and the World Bank were considering including Honduras under the Highly Indebted Poor Countries initiative, which aims to forgive large portions of basically unpayable debt owed by poor countries. The proposal will likely include 41 countries, of which 33 are in Africa, four in Asia, and four in Latin America (Bolivia, Nicaragua, Guyana, and Honduras).

In the wake of the disastrous hurricane (and subsequent emergency loans to the tune of US$1.1 billion!), Honduras looks likely to be a shoe-in for the initiative, along with Nicaragua. Benefits will not be immediate, however. The first step is to restructure much of the Paris Club debt, followed by a sort of probationary period until 2003, during which the country is expected to exercise fiscal discipline.

If Honduras has been a good pupil and debt payments still take up an excessive portion of the budget (which is expected), major discounts on loans and payments will begin in 2003. If all goes as planned, Honduras could end up seeing a total of 80% of its debt forgiven.

AGRICULTURE

Agriculture, both for export and internal consumption, is the largest segment of the Honduran economy. Over half the population still survives by working the land, though it produces only a quarter of the nation's GDP. As in other parts of Latin America, an increasing number of people are leaving the countryside to look for work in the cities or emigrating to Mexico and the United States.

In spite of the large percentage of people living and working in the countryside, land ownership is dramatically skewed in Honduras. In 1993, over 60% of the country's arable land was in the hands of the Honduran government and the two largest foreign banana companies, Chiquita and Castle and Cooke. By contrast, 80% of the country's farmers owned less than 10 hectares of land, and the average parcel size is two and a half hectares.

Honduras has a complex system of land ownership and tenancy. While some farmers own their land outright, it's much more common to work the land under some other arrangement. An *arrendamiento,* or rental, is a straightforward rental of land for a pre-set amount. **Aparcería** is an arrangement whereby the farmer is obliged to give a part of the harvest—usually the famed *quinto,* or fifth part, dating from colonial times—to the property owner. A *colonato* is a mixed system, in which the farmer is required to work land for the *patron* for a wage, while having rights to work a piece of land for himself at the same time. Farmers working under this very common setup are called *colonos*. This term is also used to denote any small-scale farmer hacking out a homestead from virgin land, like the flood of migrants moving into the southern fringes of the Mosquitia rainforest. An *ejido* is a piece of land owned by the local municipal government but granted to a certain person or persons to use for a defined length of time. Communal land *(tierra comunal)* is also owned by a municipality and open for use by any of its inhabitants.

King among staple crops in Honduras is corn *(maiz)*, cultivated in just about every corner of the country. As the base of the *tortilla*, corn is considered the staff of life in Honduras, as in many other Latin American countries. If the weather gods are smiling, corn fields produce twice a year, first in May-August and then again in November-February. The exact time of harvest varies greatly depending on the region and that year's climate. Beans *(frijoles)*, yucca, potatoes, and rice are also common additions to the family plot, or *milpa*. Though technically a fruit, no discussion of staple crops would be complete without a mention of the ever-present *plátano*, or plantain, that bready version of a banana served fried with just about every Honduran meal.

A bewildering variety of luscious fruit grows in the tropical climates of Honduras, providing a reliable, healthy, and low-cost addition to the local diet. Among the most common fruits are the orange, watermelon, lemon, grapefruit, mango, banana, pineapple, guava, papaya, plum, and of course everyone's decadent favorite, avocado.

Agro-exports

Recently overtaking bananas as the country's top export cash crop, **coffee** is grown in many of the highland regions of central Honduras. The department of Santa Bárbara produces nearly a quarter of the country's coffee, followed by El Paraíso, Comayagua, La Paz, and Copán. The best coffee in Honduras is considered to be from Marcala, La Paz. Favored climates are between 1000 and 1600 meters in elevation, often right at the lower edges of cloud forests. Almost all coffee grown in Honduras is of the *arabica* variety, which is shade-grown, rather than the lower-quality *robusta* bean. Many coffee farmers are small-scale, over half with plots of two hectares of less. Around 70,000 people are employed in coffee production, many organized in local cooperatives. Coffee exports were worth over US$400 million in 1998, a record year, but because of plant damage caused by Hurricane Mitch, exports fell to US$256 million in 1999.

Coffee trees begin bearing fruit two or three years after planting, and they usually produce for at least 10 or 15 years, unless infected by bean bores or other plant diseases. Normally plants yield two harvests a year, one in February and the second in April or May. The harvest varies considerably from region to region.

ECONOMIC FIGURES

	1992	1993	1994	1995	1996	1997	1998	1999
GDP (% change)	5.6	7.1	-1.9	3.7	3.8	5.0	3.9	-2.5*
Exports (in millions of US$)	802	814	1,064	1,092	1,422	1,535	1,571	1,402*
Inflation (%)	8.8	10.7	23.1	29.5	24.0	12.8	15.6	10.9
Foreign Debt (in millions of US$)	3,539	3,904	4,152	4,372	4,073	4,095	4,408	4,545
Deficit (% of GDP)	2.7	10.6	11.0	3.6	3.8	2.8	3.6	8.0*

*estimates based on first semester figures

The fruit companies are still here, and bananas still play a major role in the Honduran economy.

Although much Honduran coffee is of high quality, the sorting and grading process is so lackadaisical that sacks of Honduran coffee beans are regularly discounted US$10 or US$15 on the international market. Fine quality coffee cannot have more than five percent of its beans off-grade, and many Honduran cooperatives run more like 10% or 15% off-grade. Nor do Honduran growers sort by altitude—a major factor in coffee quality. So, for the time being at least, Honduras remains well below El Salvador, Costa Rica, and the regional leader, Guatemala, in the coffee market.

The original "banana republic," Honduras still depends in large part on **bananas** as part of its export earnings. The two big banana companies, Chiquita (United) and Dole (Standard), still maintain large plantations in Honduras, though continued trade disputes with the Europeans and production problems after Hurricane Mitch have slowed business of late. Both companies—which together control half the world banana market—took major losses in 1999, as did the significant sector of independent producers, with total Honduran banana exports down almost 80% from the previous year. In an effort to placate unhappy stockholders, the big companies shed several thousand workers but hired some back after protests from unions and the government.

During normal years, each company exports around 15 million boxes (18 kilos each), out of a national total of 33 million boxes in 1998, worth US$212 million.

Other agricultural exports of note include African palm oil, pineapple, sugarcane, and a few nontraditional exports such as melon, black pepper, ornamental flowers, ginger, Chinese peas, and sweet onions. The **shrimp farm** industry on the Golfo de Fonseca has grown steadily since its inception in the 1980s, producing over US$100 million in 1998. In the Caribbean coast and the Bay Islands, lobster, conch, and shrimp fishing are a mainstay of the local economy.

Cattle and Lumber

In spite of taking up 30% of the country's arable land, much of it suitable for agriculture, the cattle industry plays a proportionally small part in the national economy. In part this is because ranchers rely on traditional cattle-raising methods dependent on rainfall and pasture feed, which result in unreliable, low yields. A few powerful landowners control most of the ranching.

The great majority of cattle in Honduras are descendents of the beasts brought by the Spaniards, the species *Bos taurus*. In more recent years, Hondurans have been busy cross-breeding these venerable cattle with other species, like the Brahman, also called Cebú in Honduras, and Santa Gertrudis from the United States. The latter is considered to produce better-quality meat. Milk cattle breeds introduced to Honduras include Holstein, Pardo-Suizo, and Jersey.

Considering the great wealth of forests in Honduras, judicious logging holds potential for providing jobs and good income. However, much of the country's forest wealth has been wasted through over-logging, corruption, and mismanagement. Nearly seven million hectares of land retained forest cover in 1964; by 1998 that figure had dropped to five million. Currently the forests are disappearing at an estimated rate of 3.6% each year.

The problems of erosion and desertification that go along with logging have hit most of the country but are particularly severe in the south. In search of valuable mahogany and other hardwoods, pirate loggers have even been cutting dirt roads into the periphery of the Río Plátano Biosphere Reserve.

Almost half the legal board-feet of wood cut in Honduras comes from Olancho, followed at a distance by Francisco Morazán, El Paraíso, Yoro, and Comayagua. Pine is still by far the biggest legal logging wood.

INDUSTRY AND TRADE

Maquiladoras

The nation's most dynamic economic sector is the maquila industry of San Pedro Sula and the north coast. The maquila boom began with the passage of the Puerto Cortes Free Zone law in 1976, which was extended to Amapala, Tela, Choloma, Omoa and La Ceiba three years later. By 1998, further legal modifications allowed for the creation of free zones (called ZIPS) anywhere in country.

Taking advantage of the favorable laws, as well as inexpensive labor and a strategic location close to the United States, some 180 factories have since opened, mainly clothing producers.

While the first factories were in Puerto Cortés and Choloma, with a few in La Ceiba, new ones have begun springing up in La Lima, Villanueva, Comayagua, and Naco, and more are planned. Growth has been explosive, with maquilas increasing their export value from US$646 million in 1994 to US$1.8 billion in 1998, and US$1.01 billion in the first six months of 1999. By the beginning of 1999, maquilas employed 110,000 workers (mostly women), and by the year's end the number was thought to be 125,000.

The broader benefits of maquilas to Honduras have been widely debated. Although they provide much-needed jobs, the jobs are invariably low-skilled and low-wage. The maquilas do nothing to increase the country's tax base, as they pay no tariffs except for minor infrastructure improvements. Also, the factories generally operate on a short-term basis; as soon as better conditions arise elsewhere or Honduran wages increase significantly, they can be expected to relocate. But judging from the steady increase in maquilas in Honduras, that doesn't seem to be a problem. Whether Honduras will move up the industrial ladder to garner more valuable work or remain stuck on the lowest rung remains to be seen.

The Lempira

Honduras' national currency, the lempira, has had a few brief periods of relative stability but has generally been dropping steadily in value over the past several years, due to the country's bleak economic outlook. Inflation put a severe strain on Hondurans, and those who can afford it took to buying dollars as a safeguard. At last report, the lempira was trading at 14.7 to the dollar.

SOCIETY

THE PEOPLE

Population

Honduras has a rapidly expanding population approaching seven million. The annual growth rate was 2.8% at last report, and 56% of the population is under 18 years old. Despite this growth, Honduras still has a relatively low population density, averaging around 50 people per square kilometer for the entire country and dropping as low as two per square kilometer in the wild Mosquitia region.

Although roughly half of the population still lives in rural areas, the country is experiencing the fastest urbanization rates in Central America. Most of the urbanization is centered on Tegucigalpa, the north coast cities, and San Pedro Sula, the fastest-growing city in Latin America.

Ethnic and Regional Diversity

Travelers coming south from Guatemala to Honduras may be surprised at the overwhelming non-indigenous nature of the population. More than 90% of Hondurans are mestizos, also called *ladinos,* (persons of mixed European and Central American Indian ancestry). Only five percent of the population, or about 300,000 people, claim to be pure-blooded Amerindian, while two percent are black and two percent are white.

Because it was only partially controlled by the Spanish during the colonial era, the north coast has a culture markedly different than that of the country's interior. English and North American influences have left their mark on the coast; English is spoken as often as Spanish, and the culture is more closely related to the Caribbean islands than the rest of Honduras.

The Bay Islands were settled first by pirates, then, in the early 19th century, by migrants from the Cayman Islands. Today the islands are inhabited by a unique pocket of English-speaking Anglo-Saxons. Due to their history and culture, the islanders have long disdained Honduran authority, preferring to consider the Bay Islands a separate mini-country. Another bastion of English colonists and pirates for much of the colonial era, the Mosquitia has only recently been brought under effective control by the Honduran government. The region is isolated from the rest of the country by swamps and rainforests, and its residents, like the Bay Islanders, have maintained a sense of separateness.

Amerindian Groups

While the number of minority ethnic groups in Honduras does not even reach 10% of the total population, certain regions of the country are strongly marked by these persistent pockets of ethnic and cultural diversity. The largest indigenous group in the country is the **Lenca,** who number around 100,000 people living in villages and towns throughout western and southern Honduras. Perhaps because they provided the stiffest defense to the Spanish invaders, the Lenca are, in a way, the emblematic tribe of the country, idealized in the national myth not unlike the Aztecs in Mexico. Nonethe-

HONDURAN ETHNIC GROUPS

NAME	ESTIMATED POPULATION	LOCATION
Lenca	100,000	Intibucá, Lempira, La Paz
Garífuna	98,000	Villages and towns on Caribbean Coast
Miskito	29,000	Gracias a Dios
Chortí Maya	4,200	Copán and Ocotepeque
Pech	2,500	Olancho, Gracias a Dios, and Colón
Tolupan	2,000	Yoro and Francisco Morazán
Tawahka	1,000	Río Patuca in Gracias a Dios and Olancho

PEACE CORPS VOLUNTEERS IN HONDURAS

Over 200 U.S. Peace Corps volunteers perform their two-year tour of duty in Honduras, one of the highest numbers of any country in the world. Peace Corps participation in the country began in 1962 and was boosted during the mid-1980s as part of a good-relations program intended to show Honduras' importance in U.S. regional policy. Although numbers have been scaled back recently, volunteers still work in most parts of the country, but particularly in western, central, and southern Honduras. Volunteers mainly concentrate on agriculture, public health, water quality, small business development, and tourist promotion, with an emphasis on the newly created national park system. After Hurricane Mitch, 53 former volunteers returned to Honduras to work with the new Crisis Corps emergency relief team. Peace Corps volunteers are invariably eager to talk about their sites and are excellent sources of information on their particular regions and the country as a whole.

less, the Lenca language is now lost entirely, and only a few traditions continue.

Tucked into the far western corner of the country along the Guatemalan border are an estimated 4,200 **Chortí Maya.** While Chortí traditions and language were on the decline for many years, in recent years the group appears to have reasserted itself, creating a strong and vocal Chortí organization.

Once living across large areas of central Honduras, the **Tolupan** have practically ceased to exist as a cultural group. Only one village in the mountains of northern Francisco Morazán still speak their language, though several thousand *campesinos* in rural Yoro call themselves *tribu* and organize their villages in a communal fashion.

Farther east in Olancho and Mosquitia are two former rainforest tribes now living in rural villages, the **Pech** and **Tawahka.** The Pech number around 2,500 people and are split into two regions, one around El Carbón along the highway from San Esteban to Tocoa, and the second northwest of Dulce Nombre de Culmí. The even smaller Tawahka, with a population of only about 1,000, live along the Río Patuca near the border of the Gracias a Dios and Olancho departments.

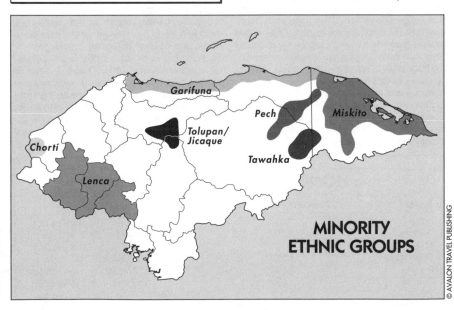

MINORITY ETHNIC GROUPS

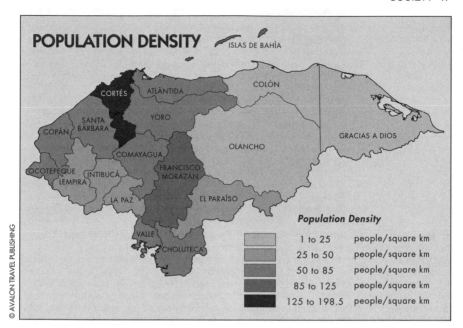

POPULATION DENSITY

ISLAS DE BAHÍA

CORTÉS · ATLÁNTIDA · COLÓN · SANTA BÁRBARA · COPÁN · YORO · GRACIAS A DIOS · COMAYAGUA · OLANCHO · OCOTEPEQUE · INTIBUCÁ · LEMPIRA · FRANCISCO MORAZÁN · LA PAZ · EL PARAÍSO · VALLE · CHOLUTECA

Population Density

1 to 25	people/square km
25 to 50	people/square km
50 to 85	people/square km
85 to 125	people/square km
125 to 198.5	people/square km

True to Honduras' propensity to join in collective action (which is perhaps in part derived from the communal tendencies of the indigenous groups), the Chortí Maya, Lenca, Tawahka, and Pech are in frequent contact with one another and with Garífuna and Miskito organizations to work together for their common cause, fighting against repression and governmental neglect. One recent example was a nationwide protest in October 1998, in which 2,000 Chortí Maya occupied the ruins at Copán, a large contingent of Garífuna took over the land reform office in La Ceiba, and Lenca protesters occupied three parties of large landowners in Ocotepeque, western Honduras. The Copán protest was particularly effective, prompting local hotel owners to ask the government to come to an agreement.

While this new collective action is a promising sign, Honduras has a long way to go. One of the reasons for the 1998 protest was to demand a more thorough investigation into the murders of two Chortí leaders, and other organizers face all manner of threats and pressure to quiet down. While governmental authorities generally refrain from open violence, preferring to make promises

that can later be conveniently modified, the annual Columbus Day protest on 12 October 1999 in Tegucigalpa ended with mounted police shooting and injuring several protesters.

Garífuna and Miskitos

Few ethnic groups in the world can trace their birth to historic events, but Honduras is home to two that can: the Garífuna of the north coast and the Miskito, in the northeast (see the special topic "Birth of a Race," in the La Mosquitia and Olancho chapter). These two unique ethnic groups were created from the mixing of African and indigenous peoples during the colonial era, and rather than fade in the face of modernization, both appear to have grown stronger.

The Garífuna, who populate the Caribbean coast from Belize as far south and east as the Mosquitia, are the product of a unique ethnic and historical odyssey. Most of the Garífuna's 50-odd villages are in Honduras, where the group first arrived in Central America in 1797. With their own language, customs, dances, and music, the Garífuna have maintained a distinctive lifestyle in the midst of the Honduran north coast

Miskito Indians pole a dugout canoe on the Río Plátano.

GUILLERMO COBOS

society. Colonial-era English and Spanish called the Garífuna "Black Caribs," an accurate description of the two ethnic strains that combined to create a new race.

For the first two centuries following Columbus, the Caribbean island of St. Vincent, in the Lesser Antilles, was left to the Island Carib Indians, who originated from the coast of South America, where Carib speakers still live today. During this time, the island became something of a refuge for black slaves, who were either shipwrecked in the area or escaped from plantations on nearby islands.

Details on the early encounters between the slaves and the Island Caribs are nonexistent, but it must have been a fascinating experience—two completely different cultures, one from Africa and the other from the rainforests of South America, meeting by chance on an island in the middle of the Caribbean. Not only did they get along, but they mixed their blood and their cultures, borrowing from each to develop a new language and new customs. One of many examples of the mixed culture is the *yancunu* Garífuna New Year's dance; it's very similar to dances of rainforest Indians in South America, while the music is clearly of West African origin. Possibly in an effort to distance themselves from their past as slaves, the Black Caribs on St. Vincent, and later the Garífuna in Central America, fiercely denied their African blood. In spite of their obviously African physiognomy, both groups insisted they were American Indians. In more recent times, though, the Garífuna have become much prouder of their African heritage.

In the beginning of the 18th century, French settlers from Martinique moved to Saint Vincent and began cultivating small-scale plantations of cotton, cacao, and indigo. They seem to have gotten along peacefully with the Caribs, both Black and "Yellow," as the pure-blooded Indians were called. The French were soon followed by the English, who abortively attempted to colonize the island in 1713. St. Vincent was officially recognized by both countries as neutral territory until 1763, when it was ceded to England in the Treaty of Paris. The English, intent on establishing large-scale sugar plantations, tried to cajole the Garífuna off their valuable island, with little success. When war broke out again between France and England in 1779, the Garífuna and French took the opportunity to seize control of St. Vincent.

The island was formally returned to the English in 1783, at which point the new settlers began pressuring the Garífuna to get off their land. Tensions finally broke out into open war in 1795, pitting the Garífuna and a few remaining Frenchmen against English troops. The Garífuna gained a reputation for uncommon ferocity and bravery during the war, which lasted two full years. The Garífuna were led by chief Chatoyer, or Satuyé, who remains a legendary figure among modern Garífuna. The British finally overcame Garífuna resistance by bringing in massive numbers of troops from Jamaica.

Having taken full measure of the Garífuna after years of battle, the British elected to deport the whole troublesome lot. Among the several sites considered were Africa, the Bahamas, or the island of Hispaniola. Eventually the British decided on Roatán, in the Bay Islands off Honduras, assuming the warlike Garífuna would become a headache for the Spanish.

On 3 March 1797 some 3,000 Garífuna were loaded onto a convoy of 10 boats; the fleet departed St. Vincent, stopping briefly in Jamaica before landing near Port Royal, Roatán, on 12 April. For reasons still unclear, the Garífuna did not like the looks of Roatán, which had literally been given to them by the British. A small group crossed to the north side of the island and started the village of Punta Gorda, the oldest continually inhabited Garífuna town, but most moved on to the mainland to Trujillo, probably with the help of the Spanish.

The first communities set up by the Garífuna on the mainland of Central America were at Río Negro and Cristales, on either side of Trujillo.

Garífuna drummer

The old port had recently been reconquered by the Spanish after 150 years of abandonment, and the Garífuna were welcomed as workers and mercenary soldiers. Over the next century, groups of Garífuna made their way up and down the Honduran coast, building villages as far north as Belize and as far east and south as the Nicaraguan Mosquito Coast. The Garífuna carved a niche for themselves on the north coast as boatmen, loggers, and superb soldiers. They fought defending coastal towns from pirates, and also in the wars of independence.

Although they gave up soldiering long ago and are no longer the first-class canoers of times past, the Garífuna have firmly established themselves as an integral part of the Honduran Caribbean coast. In keeping with their history, the Garífuna are known for their constant travel, either with fishing fleets, the merchant marines, or to Garífuna communities in New York and Los Angeles. In spite of this constant movement, the Garífuna have retained a strong sense of ethnic identity. Unlike other minority groups in Honduras, they show no signs of losing their culture. The Garífuna have a built-in resilience immediately apparent on the proud, strong faces and direct gazes that greet visitors to any Garífuna community.

RELIGION

Honduras is an overwhelmingly Roman Catholic country, although the secular Constitution guarantees freedom of religion. Yet Protestant churches have been on the rise in recent years. Traditional Amerindian religious practices have been all but forgotten, except for a few ceremonies still practiced in rural areas. Superstition and a belief in magic and witchcraft are common among Hondurans in both rural and urban areas.

The Catholic Church
The Catholic church in Honduras has traditionally been one of the poorest and most understaffed in Central America. Approximately 300 ordained priests minister to a population of just over six million, and most of the priests are from other countries. In the face of this difficulty, the church began a program called "Delegates of the Word,"

in which men and women of the laity are trained to be spiritual leaders of a given parish. Now some 10,000 Delegates of the Word live in Honduras, and the movement has spread through much of Central America. A small Jesuit mission continues in the central province of Yoro, run mainly by foreign missionaries.

Unlike other Catholic churches in the region, notably in El Salvador, the Honduran church has not been a major force for social activism. For a time during the 1960s and early '70s, church leadership allowed priests and delegates to pursue the "social option for the poor" and take an activist stance. But the massacre of 10 *campesinos,* two students, and two priests in Olancho in 1975 at the hands of wealthy landowners put a fast end to the campaign. Since the mid-1980s the church has once again begun to speak up on social issues but is not considered activist.

Protestants

Moravian missionaries were the first foreign religious group to come to Honduras, arriving in the Mosquitia region in the 1930s. Since the 1980s, evangelical groups, many sponsored by North Americans, have been growing rapidly. Denominations include the more traditional evangelical Baptist and Adventist churches, and Pentecostal churches such as the Assembly of God and the Church of God. An estimated 100,000 people in Honduras belong to Protestant churches.

LANGUAGE

Anyone visiting Honduras after Mexico or Guatemala will be immediately struck by the faster, softer cadences of Honduran Spanish, more similar to the Spanish spoken in Nicaragua and the Caribbean. Words are not as strongly enunciated and are often cut off at the end, with one word running into another. It takes a little getting used to, and you may find yourself saying *"más despacio, por favor"* (slower, please) or *"repita, por favor"* (repeat, please).

Generally, Honduran Spanish is similar to that spoken elsewhere in Latin America, with a few exceptions, particularly the use of *vos* instead of *tú* (see Appendix for more on this usage). Because of British and North American influence, broadly accented Caribbean English is the dom-

A FEW HONDUREÑISMOS

For a complete Spanish glossary, see the back section of this book. Below are a few words and phrases unique to Honduras, and a few others used in Central America only.

a todo mecate—really fast

adiós—literally, goodbye, but often used as a casual salutation when passing someone in the street, especially in small towns and villages

andar con filo—to be hungry

bolo—drunk

catrín—sharp dresser

chepos—"cops" or policemen

cususa—home-brew liquor, more commonly called *guaro*

buhoneros—street vendors

cachimbón—great, excellent

catracho—Honduran, used either as a noun or adjective, e.g., *comida catracha* means "Honduran food"

cheque—cool, alright, okay

guarizama—machete

juma—a drinking session, like a *borrachera*

Los United—the United States

macanudo—excellent

mata de . . .—field of (i.e., *mata de maiz* is a field of corn)

paja—literally, straw, but in slang meaning made-up stories, just hot air.

papa or *mama*—frequently used to refer to someone you don't know

¡que pinta!—an exclamation, like right on!

vaya pués—used after nearly every sentence, as an all-inclusive "okay" or "understood"

campesino family, Montaña de Celaque

inant language on the Bay Islands, although Spanish is increasing with the influx of Latinos from the mainland. English is also spoken along the north coast and in parts of La Mosquitia.

Garífunas and Miskitos mainly use their own languages amongst themselves, but almost all are bilingual or trilingual, speaking Spanish and/or English as well. Indigenous languages are fading, but some communities still speak Pech, Tolupan, Maya, and Tawahka. Lenca has fallen out of use entirely.

Language Study

After the raging success of language schools in neighboring Guatemala, it's no surprise several Hondurans have set up schools of their own. Language schools can be found in Copán Ruinas, La Ceiba, Trujillo, and Tegucigalpa. Generally the schools rate as fairly good to excellent, depending on the teacher. Prices are US$155-300 per week, including five days of one-on-one classes and room and board with a local family.

CUSTOMS AND CONDUCT

Typically Latino, Honduran society features customs and traditions similar to those in other countries in the region. Family is of paramount importance, although marriages are often informal due to the expense of weddings and the scarcity of priests. Most Hondurans are Catholic, though not necessarily strict ones.

For reasons far too complicated to enumerate here, but probably due in good measure to the country's history of foreign dominance and seemingly inescapable poverty, a strain of fatalism and apathy is prominent in Honduran society, especially in rural areas. This is not to say you won't meet motivated and energetic Hondurans. But a great many Hondurans simply do not see the point in hurrying or working harder to get ahead.

So, when traveling in Honduras, don't plan on being in a hurry to get anywhere. Things happen at a leisurely pace, and no one rushes. Trying to pressure people to act with haste will get little result other than laying the foundation for an ulcer. Take it easy.

Hondurans are fairly laid-back about clothes in general, but wearing shorts will certainly draw some odd looks in rural villages in the interior. Generally, beachwear should be left to the north coast and the Bay Islands. Public nudity, including swimming naked, is illegal in Honduras.

The litter level in Honduras is disturbingly high. Don't be surprised to see locals toss garbage on the street or out the bus window.

Sexual Politics

As in most of Latin America, Honduran women must cope with a host of sexist, macho attitudes from their menfolk, especially in rural society where women are expected to stay indoors and keep quiet when matters of business are being discussed. A budding feminist movement has taken root but has a long way to go to combat the ingrained machismo. According to government estimates, some 500,000 women suffer from physical abuse at the hands of men. Honduras has a large number of single mothers; it's very common for women to have one or two children by age 20. Many marriages are informal, and men have little compunction about leaving their wives for another woman. And men who do stay married are practically expected to sleep with prostitutes (legal in Honduras) or have affairs.

Despite the social obstacles, women have become more active in Honduran public life of late. Sick of watching men make a mess of things for so many years, women have began to play an increasingly important role in civil organizations in the last decades. Some of the most effective social organizers, labor leaders, and environmental activists in the country are women. Women play an ever-larger role in the country's labor force, as they account for nearly all the workers in the rapidly growing *maquila* factory sector. Several Honduran women also hold highly visible roles in Honduran politics, such as Tegucigalpa Mayor Vilma de Castellanos and the highly respected president of the Honduran Central Bank and the Minister of Finance in the current government.

For an excellent and at times harrowing account of life as a woman in rural Honduras, read Elvia Alvarado's *Don't Be Afraid, Gringo: A Honduran Woman Speaks From The Heart.*

Women Travelers

Foreign women will likely find themselves the object of a certain amount of unwanted attention while traveling in Honduras. Honduran men tend to view women as either pure, chaste mother figures or as objects of sexual attention. Unfortunately, due in part to representations of women in western media, most foreigners are viewed as the latter.

One way to cope with the situation is to dress and act conservatively. Tank tops, short skirts, and other skimpy garments do not help in this regard, though certainly on the north coast beach towns and in the Bay Islands these are accepted.

Also, avoid looking men in the eye—this is considered an invitation for the man to introduce himself and try to pick you up. Whether you handle forward men rudely or try to ignore them is up to you. Just remember, the more you talk to

them (regardless of what it is you're actually saying!), the more encouraged they will be. The flip side of these negative attitudes is that Honduran men have an ingrained consideration toward women and will often go to ridiculous lengths to do a favor for a lady. Since you have to put up with the bad side of *machismo* all the time, it seems perfectly legitimate to make use of its chivalrous tendencies when appropriate.

While men are often annoyingly persistent and need to be clearly told to go away, rarely do they present a real danger. Nonetheless, rape is certainly an issue to keep in mind in Honduras, as in most countries. The north coast beach towns are particular danger spots. Foreign women have been attacked while walking along isolated beaches near Tela and Trujillo.

These beaches are equally dangerous to men for assaults and should simply be avoided altogether. The main beaches in both of these towns are fairly safe, however. Other danger spots to watch for are discos in any town—if you go, better to go with male company or at least in a group of women. Best to stay away from cantinas and pool halls entirely.

Should you fall victim to an assault or rape in Honduras, you cannot expect a great deal of sympathy or help from the police. And needless to say, services like counseling and special health care for rape victims are nonexistent. The best bet for medical help is to go to one of the better private hospitals (not the government hospitals or the small clinics) in the cities of Tegucigalpa, San Pedro Sula, or La Ceiba. For legal help, contact your embassy in Tegucigalpa or consulate in San Pedro Sula.

On a more positive note, female travelers will, if they make the effort, find wonderful opportunities to get to know the many strong, worldly wise matrons who sometimes seem like the only sensible people in the country. And because women travelers are less threatening then men, Hondurans of both sexes frequently open up more to them. With a little looking around, interested travelers will find hundreds of grass-roots social organizations which, if not strictly feminist, are run mainly by women.

Male Travelers

Many Honduran women see foreign men with a combination of idealization of the *gringo* and a mercenary attitude about the possibilities of marrying one or getting some of their money. Thus, like foreign women, male travelers can expect plenty of attention from the opposite sex.

Most of this attention comes in the form of giggling from groups of women you happen to pass by. But often a single woman will catch your eye, or even boldly walk up to you and introduce herself, something women rarely do with Honduran men. If you stop to chat with a woman, even if she's a complete stranger, asking her out for a date is perfectly acceptable and indeed expected. And in the uncomplicated sexual culture of the Caribbean, if you go out on a date, it's just a very small step to go to bed together. What you wish to do about this state of affairs is of course entirely personal, but should you end up in bed with a *hondurena,* be sure to bring your own protection and use it, as AIDS is rife in Honduras. Honduran women rarely insist on a condom.

It's relatively common, especially in north coast beach towns, to see an older foreign man escorting around a young Honduran woman, which some find distasteful and others have no problem with. While hardly the sort of true love bond westerners idealize (the man is usually after some sort of sexual fantasy unattainable in his own country, while the woman invariably has dollar signs in her eyes), one can't be overly critical if both sides are happy. Another expression of this phenomenon is the many *hondurenas* listed with mail-order bride services in the United States and Europe.

ON THE ROAD
SPORTS AND RECREATION

HIKING AND BACKPACKING

Blessed as it is with more rugged mountain country and intact forest cover than anywhere else in Central America, Honduras offers more possibilities for wilderness adventuring than any other country in the region. Not that the country's natural areas have much in the way of tourist infrastructure. Apart from the national parks of Celaque, Cusuco, and La Tigra, hikers generally won't find sign-posted trails or informative visitors' centers. What they will find are dozens of unexplored patches of cloud forest across the mountains of central Honduras, huge areas of lowland tropical forest near the Caribbean coast, and several less extensive but unique ecosystems like mangrove wetlands, dry tropical forest, and thorn forest. Each of these environments is well stocked with its own varieties of vibrantly colorful tropical birds, stealthy predators, and a myriad of other creatures seen only by those who have the energy to get out into their habitat and the patience to wait quietly for them to appear.

Not only is hiking in Honduras the best (really the only) way to fully appreciate the country's natural beauty, but it also brings foreigners in contact with rural Hondurans, who are some of the most decent, open-hearted people you are likely to ever run across. The rule (replicated, no doubt, in most of the world) seems to be the farther one goes out into the woods, away from cities and roads, the friendlier people get. You may find yourself stopping repeatedly on the trail to share a cup of coffee at the friendly insistence of some *campesino* in his humble hut, talking with him and his family about yourself, the crops, the weather, or the state of the world. There are no hidden agendas here, no sly attempts to scam a foreign visitor, just curiosity and a firm, traditional belief in the importance of offering hospitality to strangers.

While most people logically prefer to head into the woods during the dry season (roughly Jan.-April, depending on which part of the country), hiking during the rains has its own appeal. The trails turn into muddy bogs, but the electric green brilliance of the forest often makes up for the discomforts.

Note: The role of foreign visitors is extremely important in helping protect Honduran natural areas. The concept of protected areas is new in Honduras and viewed with great skepticism, especially by the rural folk who live near (or sometimes actually within) these areas. Left to their own devices, the desperately poor, often literally starving *campesinos* use the wilderness to supplement their paltry income, by chopping wood for fuel, cutting out badly needed new farmland, or hunting wild game.

By leaving some form of economic benefit to the people who live nearby, foreigners can help encourage locals to view a natural area as a resource worth protecting, as it can attract tourists. This economic benefit can be from hiring a local guide, buying a meal from a family, or paying a few *lempiras* to pitch a tent outside a farmer's hut. Those going on a trip with a tour company are not exempt from this—you must be sure that the company you go with leaves some money behind, rather than using their own guides, transportation, food, etc. Just imagine how a self-sufficient trip must look to the locals—here come these unfathomably wealthy foreigners out enjoying themselves in our forest that we are no longer supposed to touch, and they don't leave us a *lempira!* And after that, they really expect us *not* to go hunting to feed our families?

Navigation

Hikers will find trails criss-crossing the hillsides all over rural Honduras, created and used for many centuries by local *campesinos*. Several principal trails, well-beaten and wide, act as "trunk roads" for an area, while smaller footpaths branch off in all directions. Once you arrive at the edges of farming and grazing land, wanting to enter the forest, trails are harder to find and often disappear entirely, used only by the occasional hunter. Sometimes forest trails can be found crossing from one side of the mountains to another, usually over a low pass rather than across the mountaintops, where the thickest forest is invariably found.

A few main trails are marked on the 1:50,000 topographical maps sold by the Instituto Geográfico Nacional. But when faced with the reality of dozens of trails, you will want to have a command of at least basic Spanish to ask directions from locals.

Most valleys, ridgelines, or other logical routes in rural Honduras have a path along them. If an apparently good route has no trail, that's probably for a good reason, like a impassable section out of sight ahead. Real trouble starts when you get off

the trail, thinking you know better. Bushwhackers should be fully prepared with topographical maps, a compass, and a sharp machete.

Hiring a local guide is an excellent idea when hiking in Honduras, for a variety of reasons. First and foremost, of course, he will relieve you of the difficult task of finding a good route. Also, guides are often very good at spotting wild animals (and killing them—they're usually hunters, which is why they know the forest so well), and if your Spanish is up to it they can tell you all sorts of interesting information about the forest and region. The best place to find a guide is invariably in the last village at the very end of the dirt road, near the edge of the forest. Sometimes you can ask the local Cohdefor forestry office for advice on guides, or just start asking around town. Rates are usually around US$7-10 per day, plus food for the guide.

Safety

The countryside of Honduras—areas accessible by foot only, not by vehicle—is quite safe from criminals. Which only stands to reason: what kind of thief is going to bother venturing out into the mountains to rob dirt-poor *campesinos?* Once you are on the trail, you can stop worrying about *banditos* and start paying attention to finding your way and enjoying the scenery.

It is true, however, that certain rural highways are known for holdups and assaults. Particularly bad spots include western Olancho, northeastern Olancho around Dulce Nombre de Culmí, and northern Francisco Morazán. I've tried to be extremely sensitive to such dangers and discuss them in more detail in the destination chapters, but suffice to say crime only affects a few areas (unfortunately lovely ones) and foreign visitors can easily avoid difficulties.

Natural dangers are always present when hiking and are no different in Honduras than most parts of the world. Bring sufficiently warm and dry clothes, enough food and water, a first aid kit, a good tent to protect you from the elements and bugs (or at least a jungle hammock), and—the basic rule of hiking—watch where you step!

Protected Areas

According to the government, the country's 107 actual or proposed protected areas—national parks *(parques nacionales),* wildlife refuges *(refugios de vida silvestre),* biological reserves *(reser-*

vas biológicas), and the two biosphere reserves *(reserva de la biosfera)*—make up 24% of Honduran territory. Though this may seem an astoundingly large percentage for such a poor, undeveloped country, the reality is that many of the "protected areas" are merely lines on a map in some bureaucrat's office. Faced with a chronic lack of staff and enforcement ability, the government department in charge of most reserves— Corporación Hondureña de Desarollo Forestal

PRINCIPAL PROTECTED AREAS IN HONDURAS

NAME	DEPARTMENT(S)	SIZE (SQUARE KM)	ECOSYSTEM
NATIONAL PARKS (PARQUE NACIONAL)			
Azul Meámber	Cortés and Comayagua	478	cloud and pine forest
Capiro-Calentura	Colón	49	tropical humid forest
Celaque	Lempira, Ocotepeque, Copán	247	cloud and pine forest
Cerro Azul	Copán	247	cloud and pine forest
Cusuco	Cortés	222	cloud and pine forest
La Tigra	Francisco Morazán	186	cloud and pine forest
La Muralla	Olancho	275	cloud and subtropical forest
Montaña de Comayagua	Comayagua	157	cloud and pine forest
Montaña de Yoro	Yoro and Francisco Morazán	125	cloud and pine forest
Montecristo-Triunfo	Ocotepeque	84	cloud and pine forest
Pico Bonito	Atlántida and Yoro	1,073	tropical and cloud forest
Pico Pijol	Yoro	252	cloud and pine forest
Punta Sal	Atlántida	782	tropical forest, mangrove, lagoons
Santa Bárbara	Santa Bárbara	190	cloud and pine forest
Sierra de Agalta	Olancho	655	cloud and pine forest
WILDLIFE REFUGES (REFUGIO DE VIDA SILVESTRE)			
Bahía de Chismuyo	Valle		mangrove
Cuero y Salado	Atlántida	132	mangrove, lagoons
Laguna de Guaymoreto	Colón	50	mangrove, lagoon
Punta Izopo	Atlántida	112	mangrove, lagoons, tropical forest
BIOLOGICAL RESERVES (RESERVA BIOLÓGICA)			
Guajiquíro	La Paz	67	cloud forest
Güisayote	Ocotepeque	128	cloud forest
Lancetilla	Atlántida	41	botanical garden, tropical forest
BIOSPHERE RESERVE (RESERVA DE LA BIOSFERA):			
Río Plátano	Olancho, Gracias a Dios	5,251	tropical rainforest, savanna
Tawahka-Asangni	Olancho, Gracias a Dios		tropical rainforest and savanna

(Cohdefor)—can do little to stop the invasion of land-hungry peasants, cattle herds, and loggers into protected areas. Luckily, Honduras' rugged mountains and relatively low population have helped where the authorities have come up short, but that won't work for many more years. NGOs have started to spring up to help protect specific reserves, and their very existence seems like a positive sign for the future of the parks.

Most of the natural reserves were established in 1987, when Congress passed a law declaring all land above 1,800 meters in elevation to be a national park. The reserves are composed of a central "core zone" *(zona nucleo)*, meant to be untouchable, and a surrounding "buffer zone" *(zona de amortiguamiento)* where some agriculture and hunting are allowed, depending on the area.

A number of the Peace Corps volunteers in Honduras—there are hordes of them—are involved with developing certain protected areas as tourist attractions. They have been hard at work drawing up maps, marking trails, building visitors' centers, and training guides. The volunteers are often the best sources of information on ways to get into a certain forest and on the flora, fauna, and other sights to look for there.

Cloud Forests

A dense mountaintop forest, with towering trees covered with lianas, vines, bromeliads, mosses, and ferns, all wrapped in mist and dripping wet most of the year, the cloud forest is a unique and magical ecosystem. Although the cloud forests of Costa Rica and Guatemala receive more publicity, Honduras has conserved considerably more virgin cloud forest than either of those countries.

Probably the most visited cloud forest parks in Honduras, because of the ease of access, are **Parque Nacional La Tigra**, just outside of Tegucigalpa, and **Parque Nacional Cusuco**, near San Pedro Sula. Both parks have visitors' centers and clearly marked trails, allowing even inexperienced hikers to enjoy the forest and look for birds without fear of getting lost. The forests at La Tigra and Cusuco are not the most pristine, having been logged earlier in the century. Nevertheless, patches of virgin forest remain, along with nearly 200 species of birds (including the popular quetzal), a variety of mammals, and countless reptiles and insects.

Two much more impressive cloud forest parks that can be visited without too much difficulty are **Parque Nacional Montaña de Celaque**, near Gracias, and **Parque Nacional Sierra de Agalta**, in central Olancho. Sierra de Agalta is Honduras' most extensive cloud forest, and, because of its remoteness, this truly spectacular forest and its animal inhabitants have been little disturbed by humanity. Celaque, though not as large as Sierra de Agalta, has a superb stretch of primary cloud forest on its high plateau and can be accessed by casual backpackers along a well-marked trail with two campsites on the way. The highest peak in the country, Cerro de las Minas (2,849 meters), is in Celaque.

Parque Nacional Santa Bárbara, with the second highest peak in the country, and neighboring **Parque Nacional Cerro Azul/Meámbar** loom up on either side of Lago de Yojoa—both have pristine cloud forests in their difficult-to-reach core zones, and surrounded by lower tropical forests. The lower reaches of Cerro Azul/Meámbar have several trails and cabins for visitors. Smaller reserves in central Honduras, like **Corralitos, El Chile, Yuscarán, Guajiquíro,** and **Montaña Verde** all harbor patches of little-visited cloud forest easily reached in an overnight hike.

In western Olancho, **Parque Nacional La Muralla** also has a large expanse of intact cloud forest covering its broad ridges. The park is a legendary place for birdwatching; it's an impatient tourist who doesn't catch a glimpse of a quetzal there. Unfortunately the highway out to La Muralla has become notorious for holdups in recent years, making La Muralla basically off limits for all but serious risk-takers (or the very well armed) for the time being.

On the lower edges of most cloud forest in Honduras, hikers will pass through stretches of pine and oak forest and small coffee plantations planted in the traditional style, amidst lots of wild fruit trees providing shade. Take the time to look around—patches of open area are often excellent places for spotting birds and small mammals.

La Mosquitia Reserves

The fabled jungles of La Mosquitia, the largest remaining broadleaf rainforest in Central America, is with no argument the most incredible adventure travel destination in Honduras. It is located in far northeastern Honduras, not con-

rainforest in the Tawahka Asangni Biosphere Reserve, along the upper Río Patuca

VINCE MURPHY

nected by road to the rest of the country. Most trips to the Mosquitia begin by flying into the region and then taking a boat trip upriver into the forest. Once in the rainforest, travelers will want to admire the incredible variety of plants and animals through a combination of cruising the river and taking side treks deeper into the forest.

Created in 1980, the **Reserva de la Biósfera del Río Plátano** covers 815,000 hectares of the densest, most inaccessible sections of tropical rainforest in the Mosquitia. The easiest way for visitors to get into the Río Plátano reserve is with one of the guide outfits leading tours into the Mosquitia. Trips can last anywhere from three days to two weeks; they include boating up the Río Plátano to the village of Las Marías and then into the rainforest beyond, often combined with short hiking forays into the forest. One company, La Moskitia Eco-Aventuras, runs rafting and hiking trips from the southern mountains of Olancho down the headwaters of the Río Plátano to the coast, an epic two-week trip.

Freelance trips into the reserve are possible for adventurous travelers who aren't on a tight schedule. The best way to get there is to fly to Palacios from La Ceiba and contract a boat up the Río Plátano to Las Marías, where guides can be found to take you farther upriver or into the jungle. Trying to cross over from Olancho into the reserve independently, with local guides, is a risky proposition both for the daunting natural obstacles and the rural violence prevalent in that part of northern Olancho.

East of the Río Plátano reserve, along two sections of the Río Patuca in the Mosquitia and Olancho, are the **Reserva de la Biósfera Tawahka Asangni,** covering 233,142 hectares of homeland for the small Tawahka indigenous group, and **Parque Nacional Río Patuca,** covering 375,584 hectares. Just created in December 1999, these new reserves are home to similar expanses of rainforest to the Río Plátano. The best place to go for guided trips into the rainforest on the Patuca is Krausirpe, the unofficial Tawahka capital, where you can find guides. Krausirpe can be reached either by a combination of plane to Ahuas and boat upstream from there, or downstream from Nueva Palestina in Olancho. Expensive charter flights into the Patuca region can also be arranged for those who have the cash.

Tropical Forest Reserves

Just behind La Ceiba is **Parque Nacional Pico Bonito,** the largest park in the country after the Río Plátano reserve. Towering Pico Bonito is blanketed with some of the densest tropical jungle in the country. Almost no trails exist in the park, making it serious adventure territory. The jagged terrain and thick jungle hide a wealth of wildlife rarely seen by tourists. A much smaller coastal mountain reserve with a similar type of forest is **Parque Nacional Capiro y Calentura** behind Trujillo.

Other patches of lowland tropical forest can be seen in the wonderful **Jardín Botánico Lancetil-**

la near Tela, around the shores of **Lago Yojoa,** and behind the north coast wetland reserves of **Parque Nacional Jeanette Kawas (Punta Sal), Refugio de Vida Silvestre Punto Izopo,** and **Refugio de Vida Silvestre Cuero y Salado,** though these last three are usually visited by boat, not by foot.

Infrequently visited by foreigners, the highlands on the south side of the country near the Golfo de Fonseca and the Nicaraguan border contain some of the best-preserved **dry tropical forests** in the region. **Sierra de la Botija,** near San Marcos de Colón, has seven peaks over 1,500 meters, each with a small patch of cloud forest on top, and primary dry tropical forest on the mountain flanks descending into Nicaragua. This almost totally unknown area, which may soon be declared a 10,000 hectare reserve, is the birthplace of the Río Coco, Central America's longest river, and is filled with waterfalls and wildlife.

Maps

Topographical maps of scale 1:50,000 covering the entire country are published by the **Instituto Geográfico Nacional.** Though accurate for terrain, the maps are not totally reliable when it comes to trails. The ones shown often (but not always) exist, but usually many more trails exist also.

The maps cost US$2 each and can be purchased at the Instituto's central office in Comayagüela (Tegucigalpa) at the Secretaría de Transporte (SECOPT) on 15 Calle, one block east of 1 Avenida, tel. 225-0752 or 225-3755. Some sheets are out of print, but the office staff will usually make a photocopy for you. The office is open Mon.-Fri. 8 a.m.-4 p.m. If your Spanish is up to it, you can write or call ahead for the maps; the staff will send you copies of the sheets you need (have the names handy) if you send advance payment for the cost of the maps and shipping. The IGN now has its own website where you can see its list of available maps: //ns.sdnhon.org.hn/~ignhon/.

It's also possible to get IGN topographical maps through **Omni Resources** in the U.S. for US$10-12 per sheet. Its stock of 1:50,000 topos is about as good as at the IGN—about half of the series is available. Omni is located at 1004 South Mebane St., P.O. Box 2096, Burlington, North Carolina 27216, tel. (800) 742-2677 or (336) 227-8300,

email: custserv@omnimap.com; website: www. omnimap.com/catalog/int/honduras.htm.

Equipment

Exploring the Mosquitia requires special gear suited to the jungle (see that chapter). But generally, no special equipment is needed for camping in the cloud forest reserves. Just keep in mind it rains more in cloud forests than in the surrounding lowlands, so come prepared with rain gear, heavy boots, and a change of warm clothes kept in a waterproof bag. Tents are more practical than hammocks for sleeping because of the frequent rain. Specially designed jungle hammocks with mosquito-netting and plastic roofs are fairly ingenious devices, however, and many jungle trekkers swear by them.

Machetes are not necessary for hiking the main trails in the more developed national parks, like Cusuco, Celaque, or Cerro Azul/Meámbar, but they are an invaluable tool to anyone really heading into the bush. You can pick one up in just about any hardware store *(ferretería)* for about US$3—and a *lima* (file) to keep your blade sharp for another 75 cents. Machetes are all fairly similar, with black plastic hand-grips, and vary somewhat in blade size.

Snakebite kits are a good idea, particularly in the coastal, tropical forests. Poisonous snakes are less of a danger in cloud forests. Mosquitoes are everywhere in Honduras, especially in the lowlands and on the coast, so come prepared with DEET or another repellent of preference.

Plenty of canned food, pasta, and dried soups are available in local *pulperías,* but carry a few freeze-dried meals if you're planning a long trip away from civilization. Running water in the upper reaches of cloud forests is often drinkable, as long as you're definitely above any settlements or cattle-grazing areas, but use a filter or purification tablets anyway to be safe. A couple of drops of bleach in each quart of water also works as a purifier.

White gas for camping stoves is difficult to come by in Honduras, so it's best to bring a stove that runs on gasoline or kerosene (like the excellent MSR XGK stove), or bring your own fuel.

Tour Operators

For real adventure traveling, it's hard to beat the superb trips run by **La Moskitia Eco-Aventuras** in La Ceiba, tel. 442-0104, run by veteran Honduras explorer Jorge Salaverri. Jorge offers rafting trips on the Cangrejal with his capable and amiable assistant boatmen for US$50 pp, and he will also organize just about any kind of trip you'd like to Parque Nacional Pico Bonito, the wetlands of Cuero y Salado near La Ceiba, the cloud forest of Parque Nacional Sierra de Agalta, or his famed longer trips to the Moskitia jungle. For more information, see the website: www.honduras.com/moskitia; or contact Jorge by email: moskitia@laceiba.com.

Another well-respected tour company is **MesoAmerica Travel** in Edif. Picadelli, between 2 and 3 Avenidas on 11 Calle SO, local 206, San Pedro Sula, tel. 557-0332, fax 557-6886, offering trips to Parque Nacional Cusuco, Parque Nacional Punta Sal in Tela, Montaña de Celaque, the Mosquitia, and elsewhere in Honduras. For more information on MesoAmerica Travel's extensive list of trips, send email to: mesoamerica@simon.intertel.hn, or check out its website: www.mesoamerica-travel.com.

Based in Trujillo, and offering very good trips to local reserves as well as into the Mosquitia, is **Turtle Tours,** tel. 434-4444, fax 434-4431, email: ttours@hondutel.hn, with offices in the Villa Brinkley Hotel.

The only full-scale adventure travel company exploring the beautiful mountain country of western Honduras is **Lenca Land Tours,** at the Hotel Elvir in Santa Rosa de Copán, tel./fax 662-0103, email: lenca@hondutel.hn. Run by Max Elvir, a relentless promoter of this little-known region, the company can take you on one-day or multiday trips up to the cloud forests of Parque Nacional Celaque or Cerro Azul, as well as to lovely Lenca villages like La Campa, Erandique, Belén Gualcho, and others.

BOATING

Wetland Reserves

In times past, almost the entire Pacific and Caribbean coasts of Honduras were lined with a maze of wetlands and mangrove forests, the majority of which have long since fallen victim to the machete. The remaining wetland areas are fantastic areas for water-bound exploration, providing habitat for howler monkeys, parrots, crocodiles, and myriad other creatures that hide in the tangle of vegetation along the waterways. Most tourists will want to take a guided boat trip, either with an organized tour outfit or just hiring a local boatman, but it's totally feasible to explore the reserves independently in sea kayaks or canoes. Only a couple of places on the north coast rent sea kayaks, but you should be able to find a local who will rent you his wooden cayuco for a nominal fee. And if you can bring your own craft down, all the better.

On the north coast, on each side of the wide bay around Tela, are Parque Nacional Jeanette Kawas (Punta Sal)and Refugio de Vida Silvestre Punta Izopo. Between Tela and La Ceiba is Refugio de Vida Silvestre Cuero y Salado, on land formerly owned by Standard Fruit Company. Though not protected as an official reserve, the wetlands farther east in the Mosquitia are immense and in much better condition than wetlands anywhere else in the country. Boat tours are easily arranged in Puerto Lempira or Palacios.

Tucked into the more isolated fingers of the Golfo de Fonseca is Refugio de Vida Silvestre Bahía de Chismuyo, protecting a singularly dense and tall mangrove forest, well worth a day trip to visit if you're in southern Honduras. Boats can be found in Coyolito, near Amapala.

Rafting and Kayaking

Several of Honduras' many rivers have extensive rapids ranging from class II to class V and above (i.e. unrunnable), tumbling through boulderstrewn gorges lined with tropical forest, excellent for whitewater adventuring. The best season for river running is right at the end of the rains, from November to February, but it's possible to raft just about any time on the north coast, which receives rain all year. Rafting and kayaking guide companies are all based in La Ceiba. While visiting kayakers can rent all the gear they need, they may wish to bring their own helmet or spray skirt along with them.

The best-known river in Honduras is the **Río Cangrejal,** right outside of La Ceiba, with four distinct rapids sections of varying difficulty and great beauty. Most rafters stick to the lower, "commercial" section, while kayakers head upriver to try their hand at the more treacherous and thrilling rapids, falls, and chutes of the other three sections.

Several other, smaller rivers pouring off the flanks of the Pico Bonito range near La Ceiba offer shorter but equally intense runs, like the **Río Coloradito,** just west of La Ceiba off the Tela highway. Getting to the put-in takes a bit of hiking, but it's well worth it for five tumultuous kilometers of class III-V rapids, suitable for kayaks only and with lots of scouting. East of La Ceiba, passing through the town of Jutiapa, is the **Río Papaloteca,** with several class IIIs and a couple of class Vs on its course toward the Caribbean.

Inland from La Ceiba, through the Río Aguán Valley and up a dirt road heading south into the Olancho mountains, is the **Río Mame,** requiring at least two full days and support with pack animals. The river has several sections on its long course down into the Aguán Valley, the upper ones with class III-V rapids, for kayakers only, while the class II-III lower stretch is okay for rafts. Roughly parallel to the Mame, some 40 kilometers to the west over the mountains in Yoro, is **Río Yaguala,** similar but with a heart-stopping subterraneo section, almost a full cave. Trips to the Yaguala take at least three days and are for kayakers only.

Farther east, in the jungle-clad Mosquitia region, four-day trips down the **Río Sico,** from the highway crossing at La Balsa all the way down to the town on Sico, and from there either back to Tocoa and La Ceiba by truck, or downstream farther to Palacios and back by plane. This is a good multi-day rafting trip, with some exciting but not too intense rapids and interesting scenery of homestead farms and cattle ranches amidst remnant sections of tropical rainforest. Deeper into the Mosquitia are the **Río Plátano, Río Patuca, Río Mocorón,** and **Río Coco,** to name just the main rivers. All of these are great for multi-day adventure rafting, through pristine tropical rainforest teeming with wildlife.

The Río Copán in western Honduras has quite a decent 12-km run of class III rapids running right past the Mayan ruins, a one-day rafting trip.

Yachts

Although not the top destination on the Caribbean boating circuit, Honduras has some won-

derful places accessible only by private boat, like kilometers of unexplored reef in more remote parts of the Bay Islands and dozens of little-known cays off Mosquitia.

Boaters will only find one full-on **marina** in all of Honduras, Lagoon Marina right outside of La Ceiba, tel. 440-0614, cell. 991-5401, radio channel 69. The German owner has 120 meters of jetty, with room for 20 to 25 sailing boats. Services include a fuel station, repair shop, and restaurant and bar on the weekends.

Out on the Bay Islands, yachts can tie up at the **Rock Bodega Marina,** tel. 455-1337 or 445-1127. There's a slip with electricity and water for US$150 a month. There's no gas here—boaters have to fill up in French Harbour or Coxon Hole.

Elsewhere on the Bay Islands or in the ports on the north coast, boaters are advised to tie up at the main dock and look for the capitanía del puerto (port captain's office) to inquire about where to moor and find boat services.

The only inland body of water worth sailing is **Lago Yojoa,** 16 km long by eight km wide and around 20 meters deep on average. Occasional regattas are held on the lake—contact Richard Joint at Honduyate, tel. 990-9386 or 990-9387, for more information.

SCUBA DIVING AND SNORKELING

Probably the most popular form of recreation with foreign visitors to Honduras, in terms of absolute numbers, is scuba diving and snorkeling on the Bay Island reef system. The diving around the three main islands and countless cays is unquestionably world class, rated by some as the finest in the western hemisphere.

Another advantage to diving the Bay Islands is the extremely low cost of certification courses and dive packages. Utila in particular has become a mecca for budget travelers looking for inexpensive explorations of the underwater world. Although divers in Mexico and Belize may hint that Honduras' low prices are due to inexperienced dive instructors and shoddy gear, the truth is competition among Bay

Islands dive shops keeps their standards at a top level, easily as good as, if not better than, elsewhere in the Americas.

BEACHES

Although it has two coastlines, Honduras' prime beaches are all on the north, Caribbean coast. Truly superb stretches of powdery sand lined by coconut palms can be found all along the coast, from Guatemala to the Mosquitia region near Nicaragua.

The best "urban" beaches, where tourists can stay at decent (not to say luxurious) hotels, are at Tela and Trujillo. Both have clean beaches right in town. The main beach in Trujillo, in particular, is excellent. La Ceiba and Puerto Cortés have city beaches, but they're dirty and not particularly attractive.

Visitors willing to take day trips or to rough it a bit in less-than-ideal accommodations will find the country's best beaches at villages between these four main towns. Many Garífuna villages are situated along idyllic beaches, including (from west to east) Bajamar, Miami, Tornabé, Triunfo de la Cruz, Sambo Creek, Río Esteban, Santa Fe, and Santa Rosa de Aguán. Basic hotel rooms are available in all these villages, and it's also usually possible to sling a hammock.

Much of the Mosquitia is lined with miles of wide open, deserted beach, though facilities are minimal. The Bay Islands also boast lovely stretches of beach. Guanaja in particular has fine stretches of powdery sand on the north side, with little development so far. And West Bay Beach in Roatán is about as fine a patch of tropical beach as you could hope to find.

GAME SPORTS

Fishing

Honduras boasts some of the finest deep-sea, flats, and lagoon fishing in all of Central America, rivaling its better-known neighbor Costa Rica. Not many tournaments are staged in Honduras, nor have world records been posted off its coasts, but some gargantuan tarpon are known to be lurking in the waterways around the Mosquitia in eastern Honduras, and hefty sailfish abound in the waters around the Bay Islands.

Fishing charters are easily arranged in the Bay Islands, either with outfits specifically catering to tourists, or less formal day trips (bring your own gear) arranged with local boatmen. Frequent catches include kingfish, marlin, king and Spanish mackerel, bonito, wahoo, blackfin tuna, red snapper, barracuda, and the occasional shark. Flats fishing is also excellent in shallow sandy areas around the islands, like south of Barbareta. Favorite targets are bonefish, two to four kilos of wily, recalcitrant muscle, and permit, as well as snapper and tarpon.

The dedicated sportsman out for really big fish many may want to consider a weeklong trip to La Mosquitia, and go for one of those 45 kilo tarpon frequently caught (and released) there. The best tarpon season is February through May. Snook are also common in the Mosquitia, and while not as big as tarpon, they put up quite a fight for their size. It's possible to bring your own gear and arrange freelance trips, or take charters out from the Bay Islands, but by far the best way to fish the Mosquitia is at **Cannon Island,** a personalized, high-quality fishing lodge on an island in Brus Laguna. The American-run resort offers eight-night, seven-day fishing packages for US$2275 pp, double occupancy, or four-night, three-day trips for US$1490 pp, double occupancy. The price includes transport to Mosquita from San Pedro Sula, lodging in one of three wooden cabins on the mosquito-free island, excellent homestyle cooking, and daily fishing trips aboard one of the lodge's six boats. The fishing excursions go to one of five rivers, the lagoon itself, or the open ocean in search of world-class snook, tarpon, snapper, barracuda, and shark, all catch-and-release. Guests are welcome to bring a favorite pole, but all equipment is provided. For information and reservations, call Pan Angling in the U.S. at (800) 533-4353, fax (317) 227-6803, or contact the resort at (504) 455-5460; e-mail: jdnovi@teleport.com, website: www.cannonisland.com.

The best inland fishing is at Lago de Yojoa, Honduras' largest natural lake. **Largemouth bass** were introduced to the lake years ago and a sizeable population took hold. Then the lake became a major fishing destination and overfishing depleted stocks. Because of stricter regulations, the population is reportedly on the rebound. The only place offering regular fishing trips on the lake is **Honduyate,** tel. 990-9386 or 990-9387, on the

San Pedro-Tegucigalpa highway right on the lake, at Km 162 near the village of Monte Verde. Honduyate has fishing gear available to use. Trips might also be arranged at the Hotel Agua Azul, tel. 991-7244 or 992-8928. Those with their own gear can negotiate trips with local boatmen in the village of Las Marías, on the west side of the lake.

Hunting

Hunting for game in Honduras is more a practice of survival for local *campesinos* than a sport, but foreigners are permitted to hunt in certain areas. National parks are off limits. The Pacific plains around Choluteca are legendary hunting grounds for white-winged dove, but dwindling populations of the birds have led to restrictions. Hunting is now allowed only for migrant doves and only in certain areas. Deer, quail, wild turkey, and boar are common game in other parts of the country, particularly the Olancho and El Paraíso departments. Hunting season normally runs from the end of November to 15 March.

For more information on hunting seasons, locations, and permits, check with the central Cohdefor office in Tegucigalpa, tel. 223-0324 or 223-4792, or with the Institute of Tourism, tel. 238-3974 or 222-2124 or in the U.S. (800) 410-9680.

SPECTATOR SPORTS

Fútbol

More of a national religion than merely a sport, *fútbol,* known to North Americans as soccer, is played just about everywhere in the country. Players range from shoeless young men whacking a half-deflated playground ball around a dirt lot to first-division professional teams and the beloved *bi-color,* the white-and-blue clad national team.

Honduras' league, composed of 10 teams, is one of the more competitive leagues in Central America, frequently sending players off to the Mexican league and, recently, even one to Italy's fabled *Calcio.* Going to a match is an inexpensive way to catch a glimpse of the fiery spirit lurking inside otherwise tranquil Hondurans. The league has two mini-seasons, from February to June and from August to October, with a championship determined through playoffs. The best teams perennially are Olympia and Motagua, from Tegucigalpa, and España, from San Pedro Sula.

When discussing the national team, watch out. Don't even think about making jokes about the team's ineptitude—this is no laughing matter. When the team lost to Jamaica in a 1996 World Cup qualifier, held on Independence Day no less, the country was in a tangible funk for days. The next weekend, when the team redeemed national honor by winning a sterling match against hated Mexico 2-1, the euphoria was positively unnerving—strangers hugged each other in the streets, even though the team was already out of World Cup contention.

Béisbol and Basquetbol

Both baseball and basketball are gaining popularity in Honduras. Bay Islanders are particularly fanatical about baseball and can be heard endlessly discussing the latest stats on major-league players in the United States. Surprisingly, a national basketball league was formed recently.

a hunter and his dog in Olancho

VINCE MURPHY

ARTS AND ENTERTAINMENT

FINE ARTS

Literature

Honduras may not be the most prolific country in Latin America's literary world, but it has produced two of the most famous early modernist writers in the region: poet and essayist Juan Ramón Molina and historian and journalist Rafael Heliodoro Valle.

Along with Nicaraguan Rubén Dario, Molina (1875-1908) was one of the founders of modernist Latin American poetry and is considered Honduras' national poet. Much of Molina's poetry expresses his existential anguish and a struggle with deep philosphical themes. Although he did not write extensive prose, what he did produce is beautifully lyrical. Shortly after Molina's death from a morphine overdose, his collected works were published in a volume titled, *Tierras, Mares, Y Cielos* (Lands, Seas, and Skies).

One of the most influential Latin American journalists of his era, Rafael Heliodoro Valle (1891-1959) was a prolific writer who published regularly in newspapers across the Americas and wrote extensive histories on the region. In one of his most famous professional coups, Valle in 1945 interviewed reformist Guatemalan president Juan José Arévalo in the Mexican newspaper *Excélsior*. Arévalo candidly discussed the backwardness of his country and the obstacles in the way of development. After Valle's death his most wide-ranging and reflective work, *Historia de las Ideas Contemporáneas en Centro-América (History of Contemporary Thought in Central America),* was published, a landmark in regional historical philosophy.

Modern Honduran literature of note is limited mainly to short stories. Three well-respected authors are Víctor Cáceres Lara, Marcos Carías, and Eduardo Bahr. The latter in particular is known for his politically oriented stories. One exceptional Honduran social novelist is Ramón Amaya Amador, who in 1950 wrote the famed *Prisión Verde (Green Prison),* a story about life as a banana plantation worker.

Visual Arts

Honduras has produced a number of top-quality visual artists, the most famous of which are the so-called "primitivists": Pablo Zelaya Sierra, Carlos Zuñiga Figueroa, and especially José Antonio Velásquez, who painted classic Honduran themes such as tile-roofed villages and rural scenes in a colorful and almost childlike style. Velásquez, a self-taught artist, spent much of his time painting the lovely colonial village of San Antonio de Oriente, near Tegucigalpa in the Valle de Zambrano.

More recent, innovative artists include Dante Lazzaroni, Arturo López Rodezno, Eziquiel Padilla, Anibel Cruz, and Eduardo "Mito" Galeano. Galeano, who works in the town of Gracias, is known for painting Lenca-oriented themes.

Architecture

Although modern Honduran architecture is unremarkable, a wealth of colonial buildings still stand, particularly in Tegucigalpa, Comayagua, Gracias, and in innumerable other small towns and villages.

Typically, the most visually interesting buildings are the cathedrals and churches. Most are built in a Central American style known as "earthquake baroque," which adapted the dominant styles of Spain to local conditions. Earthquake baroque is known for squat, ground-hugging structures built to resist frequent quakes. The buildings' solidity is relieved by intricate columns, sculptures, and decorations.

Churches built in the 16th and early 17th centuries, most of which have not survived, tended to be much simpler, while those erected in the late colonial period were much more elaborate. One particularly Honduran characteristic in colonial church architecture is the use of folded or pleated patterns on exterior columns.

The interiors of larger churches and cathedrals are invariably decorated with elaborate paintings and sculptures and are dominated by a carved and often gilded altarpiece *(retablo).* Smaller churches, especially in rural areas, are often painted in a more rustic style, sometimes with mud over plaster.

Catedral de San Miguel, Tegucigalpa

Large, airy wooden houses with porches are common in the north coast banana towns of Puerto Cortés, Tela, and La Ceiba, where North American influences predominated at the turn of the century.

Music

Honduran music consists primarily of Caribbean merengue, salsa, and *cumbia,* with a dash of American pop thrown in. Believe it or not, country music has also achieved some popularity in the discos of the north coast and the Bay Islands. Islanders and many of the Garífuna on the north coast also listen to a lot of Jamaican reggae.

The only native Honduran music of note is *punta,* the traditional music of the Garífuna. Original *punta* is a stripped-down music form based around a thumping drum accompanied by singing, blowing a conch shell, and dancers performing physics-defying miracles with their hips.

In recent years a modern version of *punta,* called *punta*-rock, has become the rage in Hon-

duras and has gained some recognition abroad. Three of the most popular groups playing *punta*-rock are the Grupo Kassave, Las Chicas Roland, and Garífuna Kids.

One recent development is the growth of rap in Honduras, and indeed all through the Caribbean. Of the several new groups scratching and rhyming in Spanish are Reggae Computo from La Ceiba and Baby Rasta y Gringo from San Pedro Sula.

The traditional music of the Lenca, Pech, Tolupan, and Maya Indians has, tragically, dwindled in importance over the centuries and is no longer played outside of special ceremonies. In many rural areas of Honduras, the venerable *conjunto de cuerda,* or string group, is always around to strike up a tune with their guitars, bass, and violin.

CRAFTS

Although not as well known as Guatemala for handicrafts, Honduras does offer several unique *artesanías* for tourists to purchase during their trips. Several villages near Tegucigalpa, especially Valle de Ángeles, are known for their woodcarvings and leatherwork, while others like Ojojona are good places to buy simple Lenca-style ceramics.

The region around Santa Bárbara is famed for producing *junco*-palm goods, from simple mats to baskets and hats. When buying *junco,* take a good look at the weave—the tighter the weave, the finer the quality and the higher the price.

On the north coast, you can buy traditional drums of the Garífuna, along with carvings, paintings, and recordings of *punta* music.

ENTERTAINMENT

Discos

It's a sorry town that doesn't have at least one disco where the locals can boogie until the daylight hours on Friday and Saturday. Larger towns and cities invariably have several, often near each other, and many are hopping from Wednesday to Sunday. The north coast towns of Tela and especially La Ceiba are famed for their nightlife, and any visitor with a partying spirit should be sure to go out at least one weekend to check out the scene.

The favored music in discos is salsa, merengue, *punta,* American pop, reggae, and the occasional slow country tune. Dancing is generally quite reserved—most couples seem more interested in looking cool than really cutting the rug.

Discos usually don't get cranking until midnight or later, though in some smaller towns festivities can start earlier. Fistfights and the occasional knifing are not uncommon but rarely involve foreigners, unless they do something exceptionally stupid like insult someone or try to pick up someone else's date.

Male travelers shouldn't be surprised if they're approached by some surprisingly friendly young women in the discos. Many are prostitutes. Foreign women can expect to get plenty of attention in a disco, even if accompanied by a man. As long as you keep your wits about you and fend off the overzealous men with good humor, all will be well. Going alone is not a great idea.

Pool Halls

Salones de billar, as pool halls are known, are common all over Honduras. They're not always the cleanest of places, and the players are a bit rough looking but are usually friendly to the occasional foreigner who stops in for a couple of games and beers.

In the most common game played, simply called "pool," players line up the 15 balls around the side of the table, potting them in numerical order. The shelves on the wall are for each player to keep track of the balls he has sunk, and at the end players add up their point total based on the face value of the balls. Any number of people can play. Eight-ball is common enough for most pool halls to have a triangle, but it is not the game of choice. Players from the U.S. will notice the unforgiving narrowness of the table pockets.

Generally, it's not recommended for women to visit pool halls. Even if you're accompanied by a man, expect at the very least to get a lot of looks. Going alone is an invitation to trouble.

ACCOMMODATIONS

Rooms in Honduras range from five-star luxury spreads in Tegucigalpa, San Pedro Sula, and the Bay Islands where you will be waited on hand and foot to a straw pallet in a *campesino's* hut in rural mountain areas. Camping is possible and safe in many rural areas, but designated campsites and RV hookups are nearly nonexistent.

HOSPEDAJES AND LOW-PRICED HOTELS

The vast majority of hotels in Honduras fall into the shoestring and budget categories, charging between US$1 and US$20 per night per person. In cities and large towns, these hotels—called *pensiones, hospedajes,* or simply *hoteles*—are often grouped near each other in the downtown area. In many smaller towns and villages, budget rooms are the only choice.

Rooms in cheaper hotels are extremely basic, often merely cement cubes with a fan, a light bulb dangling from a wire, and a bed of wildly varying quality. Take a look before you pay—key elements to check for are a good mattress, a

working fan, hot water if you're supposed to have it, a quiet location, and of course cleanliness. With heat and mosquitoes common in many parts of Honduras, especially the north coast, a fan can be a key component to a restful night. Overhead fans are preferable as they stir up the air in the entire room and keep the nasty bugs at bay.

Budget hotels frequently offer the choice of *baño privado* (private bathroom) or *sin baño* (without bathroom, that is, shared bathroom). Taking a room *sin baño* is a good way to save a few *lempira,* but be sure to wear sandals into the communal bathroom to avoid athlete's foot or other fungi.

The better quality low-priced hotels—usually at least one in every town—send maids out every day to scour the rooms and place fresh sheets on the beds. Many also have free purified drinking water in the lobby and provide pitchers for guests to fill up and bring to their rooms.

When a hot shower is offered, it's often in the form of an in-line water heater attached to the shower head, affectionately known among frequent travelers as "suicide showers." These con-

HOTEL PRICE CATEGORIES

Shoestring	under US$10
Budget	US$10-20
Inexpensive	US$20-40
Moderate	US$40-60
Expensive	US$60-100
Premium	US$100+

traptions usually (but not always) provide a stream of scalding water, and don't get too close to all those dangling wires unless you're looking for an unpleasant zap. The units can be so poorly wired they manage to electrify the entire showerhead. Beware.

Haggling over room price won't get you too far in the lower-end hotels, as prices are rock bottom as it is, but it's worth it to ask if there's anything less expensive (¿Hay algo más económico?) than the first price quoted, since owners often assume a foreigner wants the best room. The lower-end hotels rarely collect sales tax.

MID-RANGE HOTELS

Formerly limited to cities and major tourist destinations only, a growing number of good quality hotels falling into the inexpensive and moderate categories have been springing up in Honduras in recent years, charging between US$20 and US$60 per night. Most large towns have at least one moderately priced spot with air conditioning, TV with cable, clean bathrooms, decent mattresses, private parking, and a restaurant or cafeteria of some type.

Travelers won't have much luck trying to negotiate a better deal for one or two nights, but discounts are frequently available for stays of a week or longer. It's usually best to talk to the owner or manager, rather than a receptionist, in attempting such negotiations.

Apart from the standard hotels and motels, more cozy bed & breakfasts and apart-hotels can also be found, particularly in San Pedro Sula, Tegucigalpa, and La Ceiba.

Prices don't vary much throughout the year in most of the country, but during Semana Santa (Holy Week), rooms are more expensive in the

north coast beach towns of Trujillo, La Ceiba, Tela, and Puerto Cortés. In La Ceiba prices rise dramatically for the long weekend around the Feria de San Isidro, a famed carnival held each year in mid-May. On the Bay Islands, the high season for tourism is between late December and early April, with a mini-high season in July and August—hotel prices rise during these periods.

The 12% hotel tax and four percent tourist tax is usually, but not always, included in quoted room prices. It's always on the bill, though.

HIGH-END HOTELS AND RESORTS

Luxury Hotels

Full-service, top-class hotels are few and far between in most of Honduras, found only in Tegucigalpa, San Pedro Sula, Copán, the Bay Islands, and the north coast cities. In the capital and in San Pedro, well-heeled travelers have plenty of options to choose from, including brand-new Princess and Camino Real hotels in each city, as well as a couple of small, high-quality boutique hotels like Portal del Angel in Tegucigalpa. Rates run anywhere from US$80 to US$1300 for the finest suites. Rack rates are usually quite a bit higher than corporate rates, which are often available to ordinary travelers on request. Also, it's worth noting that many luxury hotels have weekend deals sometimes half the normal price, as many of the hotels' usual clients are businesspeople coming through during the week.

Dive Resorts

Some of the finest accommodations in Honduras are to be found in these often supremely tasteful and blissfully relaxed resorts on the Bay Islands. Most offer weeklong packages including three meals a day, two boat dives a day, and unlimited shore diving for US$600-900 pp. Rooms are often free-standing cabañas set next to the ocean to catch the sea breeze, making air-conditioning happily unnecessary. As these resorts are eager to attract repeat vacationers, service is frequently extremely attentive. There are several resorts on Roatán, Utila, and Guanaja, or those after a little privacy might consider the more secluded resorts of Plantation Beach on the Cayos Cochinos and Barbareta Beach Resort, on Barbareta Island off Roatán.

Beach Resorts

Although they've been talking about it for years, the north coast of Honduras facing the Caribbean Sea has yet to realize its promise as a tourist mecca. Very few high-quality resorts are to be found on the north coast, though this could change in the future. Probably the best options at the moment are Acantilados del Caribe, near Omoa, and the new Caribbean Sands, east of La Ceiba.

SLEEPING IN RURAL HONDURAS

Camping

Campsites and RV hookups have not yet made it to Honduras, so campers had best come prepared for primitive camping. In most areas in rural Honduras this is no problem. Generally speaking the countryside is the safest part of the country, and the worst hassle you can expect is to get pestered repeatedly by local *campesinos* to come have a cup of coffee and a chat with them.

When looking for a spot to pitch a tent, it's best to check around and see if you're about to set up on someone's farm. If so, ask permission, "¿Está bién acampar aquí?" Offering a few

lempiras is also polite, or perhaps inviting the owner over to your camp for a bite to eat.

The few campsites in the country can be found in some of the national parks, such as La Tigra, Cusuco, Celaque, Pico Bonito, La Muralla, and others. Camping is regulated in Cusuco and La Tigra but fairly laid-back in the other parks. If in doubt, stop in at the local Cohdefor office and ask.

No special gear is needed for camping in Honduras, just come prepared for the conditions. Tents are best to shelter yourself from the frequent rain and cold weather common in the mountains, though jungle hikers may prefer jungle hammocks.

"Dar Posada"

In many villages, like the central and western mountains, a few Garífuna beach villages, and in some parts of the Mosquitia, no hotels are available for travelers. No worries: just ask around to find a family willing to put you up for the night. The key phrase is *dar posada,* or "offer lodging." Often one family is known to have an extra room and is in the habit of renting it out to passersby for a few *lempiras* (US 50 cents-US$4).

FOOD

Honduras isn't known for its culinary specialties, but the discerning traveler will find plenty of ways to fill the belly and satisfy the taste buds at the same time. From the infinite variations of *plato típico,* the national dish, to the seafood of the north coast and the omnipresent and addictive *baleadas,* Honduran cooks do surprisingly well with limited resources.

Hondurans eat a light *desayuno* (breakfast) when they get up, a decent-sized *almuerzo* (midday meal) between noon and 2 p.m., and *cena* (supper) between 6 and 8 p.m.

WHERE TO EAT

Those restaurants in Honduras where you can expect table service and a menu are called *restaurantes.* In large towns and cities you'll find high-priced restaurants offering international-style food, or at least creatively prepared

Honduran standards. In smaller towns, hotel restaurants are often the best places to get a good meal.

Less pretentious places offering set meals at inexpensive prices are known as *comedores* ("eateries") or, less frequently, *merenderos.* The best way to judge a *comedor* is to check the number of locals eating there—the more, the better. Hamburger joints are very popular in Honduras—got to do something with all those cattle.

Most town markets have a section inside serving inexpensive and typically good-quality breakfasts and lunches. The quality of street food in Honduras is not as good as in Mexico, for example. Options are limited to snacks, fruit, and roasted corn.

Ordering and Paying

Most sit-down restaurants will have a menu, called *la carta* or *el menú,* but smaller establishments often just serve what they happen to

GUILLERMO COBOS

A Garífuna man demonstrates the proper technique for opening fruit with a machete.

cheese, and a dollop of sour cream. Possible variations might include saffron rice instead of plain rice, well-prepared beans instead of canned refrieds, or yucca instead of plantain. Tortillas, usually of corn, are served on the side.

A relative of the *plato típico* is the *comida corriente* or *plato del día,* also a set meal and usually a bit less expensive than the *plato típico.* The main course can be fish, chicken, pork, or steak, depending on whatever the cook got a good deal on that day. Fixings are similar to the *plato típico.*

In a country with a major cattle industry, it's no surprise that beef is a staple of the Honduran diet. Called *bistec* or *carne asada,* the country's grilled beef is not always the finest quality—as with many products, the best is reserved for export. The country's second-most-popular meat is *cerdo,* or pork. Although it may be dodgy if not cooked well, you'll often run across a pretty mean *chuleta de cerdo* (pork chop) in Honduran restaurants.

Pollo frito, fried chicken, is also one of the most common dishes in Honduras. It's a rare bus stop or small town that doesn't boast at least one restaurant specializing in fried chicken. One of the more creative and tasty Honduran meat dishes is *pinchos,* a sort of shish kebab typically made with skewered and grilled vegetables and chunks of marinated beef. *Pinchos* are invariably served with an *anafre,* an ingeniously heated clay pot holding refried beans with cheese and cream, to be eaten with *tostadas,* toasted tortilla chips.

A favorite Honduran soup is *tapado,* a vegetable stew often served with beef or sometimes fish. Another, which the squeamish will want to avoid, is *mondongo,* or tripe (intestine) stew served in beef broth with cilantro and potatoes or other vegetables.

When on the north coast, the Bay Islands, or near Lago de Yojoa, be sure to take advantage of the very tasty *pescado frito,* or fried fish. Some of the Garífuna villages on the north coast also whip up a superb grilled red snapper with rice and vegetables. On the Bay Islands locals are fond of skewering a variety of fish and making a stew called *bando* with yucca, other vegetables, and lots of spice.

Langosta (lobster), *camarones* (shrimp), and *caracol* (conch) are all commonly eaten on the north coast, though supply may be limited by the tight restrictions recently adopted to protect

have. To find out the day's pickings, ask *¿Qué hay para comer?* ("what is there to eat?).

When you are done eating, ask for *la cuenta* ("the bill"), or if the restaurant is a small eatery or food stand, ask *¿Cuánto es?* or *¿Cuánto le debo?* ("How much do I owe you?"). Tips are not common in most simple eateries, but 10% is expected at any mid-range or more expensive restaurant. Some of the better restaurants will add a 10% gratuity to the bill, so check before you leave another tip.

WHAT TO EAT

The main meal in any Honduran restaurant is without doubt the *plato típico,* a standard combination of ingredients which can vary dramatically in quality but is always relatively inexpensive.

The centerpiece of the *plato típico* is always a chunk of beef, accompanied by fried plantain, beans, marinated cabbage, rice, a chunk of salty the dwindling shellfish population. One superb north coast specialty is *sopa de caracol,* or conch stew, made with coconut milk, potatoes, and sometimes curry. Several restaurants in Tela make mouthwatering *sopa de caracol.*

Main meals are almost always served with a basket of warm tortillas, thin dough pancakes usually made from corn but sometimes from wheat flour. The unaccustomed palate often needs time to adjust to corn tortillas, but once converted the taste buds will crave the solid, earthy taste. Beans and rice are also frequent accompaniments to a meal.

On the north coast, North American and Garífuna influences have made tortillas less common, and you may find meals accompanied by *pan de coco* (coconut bread), a Garífuna specialty.

Breakfast
The standard Honduran breakfast consists of eggs *(huevos),* tortillas, a chunk of salty cheese, a slice of fried ham, and a cup of strong, sweet Honduran coffee. Eggs are normally cooked *revueltos* (scrambled) or *estrellados* (fried).

Western innovations like corn flakes and pancakes, frequently served with honey instead of syrup, are on the rise in Honduras but are not common in smaller towns.

Snacks
Travelers searching for the Honduran equivalent of the Mexican taco will be pleased to discover *baleadas,* the snack food of choice. *Baleadas* are flour tortillas filled with beans, crumbly cheese, and a dash of cream, then warmed briefly on a grill. Sometimes they throw in scrambled eggs and/or guacamole for a bit extra. Cheap and filling, *baleadas* make a good light midday meal.

Less frequently seen are *pupusas,* a snack of Salvadoran origin consisting of thick tortillas filled with sausage and/or cheese; and *nacatamales,* cornmeal stuffed with pork, olives, or other ingredients, then wrapped in a banana leaf and boiled. North American-style *hamburguesas* are extremely popular, especially on the north coast. And Mexican munchies like *tacos, tortas,* and *quesadillas* are common.

Rosquillas, crunchy bread rings, are popular for dunking in the omnipresent cup of strong black coffee. The town of Sabanagrande, between Tegucigalpa and Choluteca, is particularly known for *rosquillas.* And just about every town in Honduras has a *repostería,* a sweetbread bakery that also serves coffee and sodas, perfect for an afternoon break.

Often sold in street stands are *tajadas,* fried plantain chips served in a small bag with a slice of lime or a dash of salsa. *Tajadas* are also sometimes served in restaurants with a salad of cole slaw and salsa. Sliced fresh fruit such as pineapple and mango is commonly sold in street stands, along with bags of *nance,* a small fruit described by one expatriate journalist in Honduras as "cherry's evil twin."

Vegetarian Food
With a population of dedicated meat eaters, finding vegetarian food in Honduras is not an easy task, but not impossible unless you are vegan (in which case, plan on cooking a lot). *Quesadillas* and *baleadas* provide excellent snacks, as does fresh fruit sold cut up and ready to eat by street vendors (try to get just-cut pieces). For main meals, you can often request plates of rice, beans, and cooked vegetables. Most cooks are happy to cook without oil if you ask them—it just never occurs to them that people might like it

AZUCARRÓN PINEAPPLE

Those poor souls who have only tasted the pineapples imported to the United States and Europe are in for a taste sensation after slicing into their first fresh Honduran *azucarrón* pineapple.

The name—which roughly translates as "super-sugary"—hints at the mouthwatering pleasures to come. Many foreigners, long convinced they didn't like pineapple at all, have been known to become utterly addicted to the *azucarrón,* buying a fresh one at the market every morning and getting deliciously messy gobbling it down. The high sugar content that gives the *azucarrón* its succulent taste is also the reason it never makes it out of the country. The sugar content is so high that the fruit ripens quickly and can't survive the journey to foreign markets without going bad. Fruit companies have long tried to develop varieties that taste the same but won't ripen so fast, but have yet to succeed.

that way! *Sopa de verduras* (vegetable soup) is sometimes available, though more often you have to order a *sopa de res* (beef soup), take out the chunk of beef, and (if you can handle the broth) munch down the potatoes, yucca, corn, squash, onion, and other vegetables.

BUYING GROCERIES

The first word to learn when looking for groceries in most towns and villages in Honduras is *pulpería*. These all-purpose general stores might carry just a few canned goods, drinks, and candy, or might offer a full range of foodstuffs. Almost every population center of any size has a *pulpería*—in fact, if a village has any business establishment at all, it's always a *pulpería*.

Every town of size also has a market *(mercado)* where you can find a wide variety of fruits, vegetables, and meats—the squeamish should brace themselves for the sight of raw flesh covered with flies. Produce is sold in pounds *(libras)* just as often as in kilograms, if not more so; be sure you know the weight before buying. When buying food by the pound, don't just pick up a couple of pieces and ask how much it costs—that's simply an invitation to get ripped off. Check the price per pound or kilogram and watch it being weighed. It's often worth asking a couple of stalls their prices before buying. Although prices are normally standard, some vendors are not above trying to swindle a few extra *lempiras* out of a naive-looking foreigner.

Western-style supermarkets *(supermercados)* are found only in large towns and cities, and the produce here is often not as good as at the local market.

Tortillas can be bought in bulk at neighborhood *tortillerías*, which make them fresh daily. Good bread is not always easy to come by in Honduras; what there is can be found in *panaderías*. Sweet breads and cookies are more common than sandwich-style loaf breads, as most Hondurans eat tortillas.

BEVERAGES

Nonalcoholic Drinks
The coffee addict will be pleased to hear that Hondurans brew a mean cup of joe, most often served black with lots of sugar. In contrast to Guatemala, most of the coffee is actually brewed from beans; even in inexpensive *comedores* a fresh cup is more common than Nescafé. If you take milk, be sure to ask for it on the side as it is not normally served. Tea is much less common but can be found in better restaurants.

Blended fruit and milk drinks, called *licuados,* can be found all across the country and make a filling midday snack that could be substituted for lunch. Often they're served with a sprinkle of nutmeg or cinnamon on top, and a healthy dose of sugar. If you don't want either, be sure to advise the proprietor beforehand. Generally the milk is prepackaged and pasteurized, but you may want to check first to be sure.

Fresh fruit juices are also common, and in most establishments are mixed with purified water, but again check first. Two particularly tasty mixes are *agua de mora* (blackberry juice) and *agua de horchata,* a rice drink with cinnamon. Cartons of processed orange juice are available all over the country, but fresh-squeezed orange juice is surprisingly hard to find. Better to do what most Hondurans do—buy the cheap oranges sold everywhere on the street, cut in half and with most of the rind shaved off, to allow better squeezing as you suck out the contents. Oranges usually cost 50 centavos or a *lempira,* basically a few cents.

Tap water is rarely safe to drink in Honduras, outside of a few luxury hotels that have their own in-line purifiers. In rural areas, most towns chlorinate their water, meaning the majority of buglies are dead, but treatment seems to be haphazard. One Peace Corps volunteer working in water sanitation commented that sometimes the person in charge won't get enough money from the town for chlorine one month or just might not get around to using it. So while drinking the water might usually be safe, it hardly seems worth the risk, considering the nasty dysentery common in Honduras.

Many hotels, even less expensive ones, buy large bottles of purified water and keep them in the lobby for guests. Agua Azul is a popular brand of purified water sold in containers of various sizes. Be environmentally aware: don't buy lots of small plastic bottles and throw them away. Better to buy a gallon or liter jug and fill it up at your hotel. This saves you money and saves Honduras a lot of plastic garbage, of which it has plenty already.

Alcohol

All five brands of beers *(cervezas)* brewed in Honduras are made by the same company, Cervecería Nacional. Of the five, Nacional is the most universally consumed. It's thin and fairly tasteless, though not bad when the weather is hot and the beer is cold. Polar, mainly sold in cans, is similar. Much better are Port Royal, a lager sold in a green bottle with a colorful label, and the heavier Salvavida ("Lifesaver"), sold in a dark brown bottle. Brewed in Tegucigalpa, Imperial is the beer of choice for the cowboy country of central Honduras and Olancho. Going into a *cantina* in Olancho and asking for a Port Royal or Salvavida is like walking into a redneck bar in the western U.S. and asking for a wine cooler.

Several varieties of rum *(ron)* of reasonable quality are distilled in Honduras, but other local spirits such as gin and vodka are nauseatingly bad. The local rot-gut liquor is *aguardiente,* either made in local stills or bought in a bottle. The most popular variety is El Buen Gusto, also called Yuscarán for the town where it's made.

Local wines are not worth mentioning, but several foreign varieties can be found in better supermarkets and liquor stores. Avoid them on the north coast as they don't hold up well stored in the heat.

A word about drinking establishments: waiters in *cantinas* or inexpensive restaurants often leave the empty beer bottles on the table when you order more. This is merely a way to help with accounting at the end of the night.

HEALTH AND SAFETY

As an extremely poor, underdeveloped country, Honduras has its share of health and safety risks, and it doesn't have the best doctors and police to help its citizens or foreign visitors cope with them. Nonetheless, with a few basic precautions, travelers can greatly reduce their risk of falling ill or victim to crime.

Travelers might consider purchasing travel insurance before going to Honduras. Several types of insurance are available from many companies in the United States and Europe, covering different amounts of medical expenses and stolen luggage replacement.

COMMON AILMENTS

As in just about every country in Latin America, it's essential to watch carefully what you eat and drink. Tap water is absolutely never safe to drink; be sure to check that any water served at a restaurant or hotel is *agua purificada.* Be particularly aware of salads and uncooked vegetables, and make sure meat, especially pork, is well-cooked. Eating street food is standard practice for many veteran travelers, but someone just coming to Honduras for a short stay may want to avoid it and save themselves a possible case of **diarrhea.**

If you do develop diarrhea, two courses of action are available: eat as little as possible, drink a lot of water, and let the bug run its course (literally), or take medications such as Pepto-Bismol or Lomatil. Many travelers insist the drugs only prolong the problem, while others swear by them. They certainly are useful when you have to go on the move when sick.

Food poisoning is also relatively common. Although it may appear severe at first, with vomiting and uncontrollable bowels, the bug will pass in about a day. Hole up in a hotel room with a good book, a bottle of water, and maybe a few pieces of bread, and expect to feel a bit weak for a couple of days following the illness. If symptoms persist, see a doctor—you may have dysentery. It's extremely important to stay well hydrated if you've got either food poisoning or diarrhea.

DISEASE

Dysentery

Dysentery is a health risk for foreigners traveling in Honduras and other underdeveloped countries. The disease, which results from fecal-oral contamination, comes in two strains: bacillic (bacterial) and amoebic (parasitic). Bacillic dysentery hits like a sledgehammer, with a sudden onset of vomiting, severe diarrhea, and fever. It is easily treated with antibiotics.

Amoebic dysentery, caused by an infestation of amoebas, takes longer to develop and is also more difficult to get rid of. The most effective cure is a weeklong course of Flagyl, a very strong drug that wipes out all intestinal flora. During and after a course of Flagyl, it's important to eat easily digestible food until the body has a chance to re-build the necessary bacterias used for digestion. Yogurt is helpful. Weak cases of amoebas can sometimes be treated with a half-course of Flagyl or other less traumatic drugs.

Symptoms for either form of dysentery are not unlike those for malaria or dengue fever, so see a doctor and don't try to diagnose yourself. One of the greatest dangers with dysentery is dehydration, so be sure to drink plenty of water if you even suspect dysentery.

Malaria

The *vixa vivax* strain of malaria is present in most lowland regions of Honduras, and it is common on the north and south coasts, the coastal regions of La Mosquitia, and on the Bay Islands. If you're below 1,000 meters, malaria can be present. Thankfully, the Aralen-resistant *P. falciparum* strain has not yet made it north of Colombia.

Symptoms of malaria include high fever, headaches, fatigue, and chills. If these symptoms are present, see a doctor immediately, as medical treatment is effective.

Opinions on how to cope with malaria vary wildly. The most frequent recommendation from doctors is to take 500 mg of Aralen (chloroquine phosphate) weekly. Some people react negatively to Aralen, experiencing nausea, rashes, fever, or nightmares. Stop taking the drug if you have these side effects.

In high doses, well above 500 mg per week, Aralen has been linked to retina damage and hearing problems. It's not recommended to take the drug longer than six months. If you're on Aralen, continue the course for four weeks after leaving malaria-prone areas. Some travelers, leery of using strong drugs on a regular basis, prefer to carry one powerful dose of Aralen with them to use in case malaria strikes, rather than enough for weekly doses. Those who opt for this method should be very careful to avoid mosquito bites by applying repellent, wearing long-sleeved clothes, and using mosquito nets.

Other malaria preventatives include a daily dose of low-level antibiotics such as tetracycline or doxicycline. Antimalarial drugs are available in Honduras.

Other Diseases

Unfortunately, **cholera** is not uncommon in Honduras, particularly during the rainy season. The best way to avoid it is to be careful with your food and water, don't eat raw fish, and always wash your hands before eating.

The viral disease **dengue fever** is also a frequent health problem for Hondurans. There is no cure, but it is rarely fatal. The fever is contracted from the bite of an infected mosquito. Symptoms include fever, headache (especially behind the eyes), muscle and joint aches, skin rash, and swollen lymph glands. Usually the fever lasts 5-8 days, followed by about a week of the disease. Tylenol (not aspirin) will help cut the fever and relieve headaches.

A few uncomfirmed cases of hemorrhagic dengue, which are fatal, have been reported, particularly in the Mosquitia region. Symptoms appear similar to classic dengue at first, which makes it essential to seek medical attention immediately for any of the above symptoms. Hemorrhagic dengue is fully treatable if medical help is found within the first few days of the illness.

AIDS

After sub-Saharan Africa, the Caribbean Basin has the highest incidence of AIDS infections in the world. More relaxed, easygoing sexual practices and the frequent use of prostitutes by men are two prime causes for the quick spread of the disease.

AIDS is thought to have first arrived in Honduras in 1985, and since that time roughly 13,000 cases have been reported, with 2,723 cases registered in 1999. The actual number of cases is thought to be much higher, around 100,000 total cases in one estimate, one of the highest rates per capita in the Americas. San Pedro Sula, in particular, has been hard hit by the disease. The problem persists in part because of the lack of education about health risks and prevention, although the government has stepped up publicity campaigns in the past few years.

Many HIV-positive prostitutes continue working, either through ignorance or the need for money. Should you choose to sleep with a stranger or newfound friend anywhere in the country, *use a condom!*

Information

For more information on the health situation in Honduras, check the Centers For Disease Control and Prevention (CDC) Health Information for International Travel, tel. (404) 332-4565, website: www.cdc.gov; or the International Association for Medical Assistance to Travelers, 736 Center St., Lewiston, NY 14092, tel. (716) 754-4883.

MEDICAL ATTENTION

Doctors and Hospitals

As might be imagined, the quality of health care in most of Honduras is extremely low. Rural areas are particularly bad off, often with only a small, ill-equipped clinic to cope with several villages, usually staffed by a single doctor who was trained at the Universidad Nacional medical school in Tegucigalpa—not a paragon of higher learning. Sometimes out in rural regions you may happen across foreign medical brigades on temporary missions in Honduras, which often provide excellent medical help. Particularly good are teams of Cuban doctors sent to Honduras after Hurricane Mitch—in 1999, the newspapers were filled with stories of locals pleading with the Cubans to stay after their term was up.

In larger towns and cities, better clinics and hospitals can be found. Steer clear of the state-run clinics, which are inexpensive but also very crowded with poor service. Smaller clinics are sometimes staffed by doctors with training in Mexico or the United States, which is often a good sign. The three largest cities in the country—Tegucigalpa, San Pedro Sula, and La Ceiba—each have good quality private hospitals that can handle most ailments.

If you require special medical attention on a trip to Honduras, or want a doctor to come along with your group, contact **Emergency Medical Services** in San Pedro Sula on 5 Calle at 11 Av. NO, tel. 552-2255, email: ems@honduras.com.

Pharmacies

Most basic pharmaceutical drugs are available in Honduras, many without a prescription. Almost all are generic versions manufactured in Mexico and Guatemala. Nevertheless, it's always best to bring an adequate supply of any prescription medication you require, including blood pressure medicine, insulin, epilepsy drugs, birth control pills, and asthma medication. Keep in mind allergies may be triggered by unfamiliar allergens encountered in a new environment.

Pharmacies in Honduras normally operate on the *turno* system, in which one local shop stays open all night for emergencies on a rotating basis. Often the *turno* pharmacy of the night is posted on a sign in the downtown square. If not, ask at your hotel, or look for a listing in the local newspaper.

VACCINES

No vaccines are required to enter Honduras, but travelers should be up to date on their rabies, typhoid, measles-mumps-rubella (MMR), tetanus, and yellow fever shots. A Hepatitis vaccine is now on the market, taking the place of the questionable gamma gobulin shot. For Hepatitis A, two shots of Havrix six months apart is now recommended. For Hepatitis B, the recommendation is three shots of Engerix over the course of six months. Each course of Engerix shots is good for three years.

BITES AND STINGS

Mosquitoes and Sand Flies

Mosquitoes are found just about everywhere in Honduras and can be particularly bothersome during the rainy season. Everyone has a favorite method for dealing with the bloodsuckers. It's hard to beat a thick coat of DEET, but many travelers are loath to put on such a strong chemical day after day, especially on a long trip. According to some, eating lots of raw garlic is effective.

Sand flies, or *jejenes,* can be a plague on the Bay Islands, depending on the season and the wind level. Insect repellent will keep them away, and locals swear by Avon's Skin-So-Soft lotion, which is sold on the islands. The bites are annoying but will usually stop itching quickly if not scratched. As their name suggests, sand flies live on the sand and can be avoided by swimming, sunning yourself on a dock over the water, or just staying away from the beach. A few spots on the islands are known to be free of the pests. Thankfully sand flies are not a severe problem on mainland beaches.

Ticks

First, the good news: Lyme disease is not present in Honduras. However, incredibly itchy little ticks, known locally as *coloradillas,* inhabit pastures in rural areas of Honduras. They normally live off cows and donkeys but are in no way averse to infesting the flesh of an unsuspecting backpacker who decides to camp in a pasture, because it's the only clear land around for the tent (I write from personal experience). You will likely not see them at all, as the ticks are tiny—practically microscopic. If they get into you, the itching starts a day or two later and is usually concentrated around the ankles and the waist area, though they can spread everywhere if given a chance. The torture doesn't go away for at least a week, and sometimes lingers several weeks, long after the little buggers are dead. Some topical creams are helpful in alleviating the infestation and itching.

Larger ticks, called *garrapatas,* are sometimes found also. The best way to get rid of them is to pull out their heads with tweezers as soon as possible. Make sure you get the whole tick out, to avoid infection. Ticks favor warm, moist environments, like armpits, the scalp, and pubic hair.

Chagas' Disease

The chronic Chagas' disease, caused by the parasite *Trypanosoma cruzi,* is transmitted by the bite of certain bloodsucking insects (notably the assassin bug and conenose) found from southern Texas through South America. The disease is estimated to affect 12 million people in the Americas. The bugs prefer to bite while victims are asleep and usually bite the victim's face. While taking in blood the bugs often deposit feces, which transmits the disease to the victim's bloodstream. Such bug bites are common in Honduras, but before panicking note that only about two percent of those bitten will develop Chagas' disease. Young children are the most susceptible.

After an initial reaction of swollen glands and fever, one to two weeks after the bite, the disease goes into remission for anywhere from five to 30 years, with no symptoms apparent. It may, in fact, never reappear, but if it does, the disease

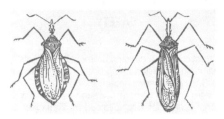

causes severe heart problems sometimes leading to death. There is no cure for Chagas' disease.

To avoid Chagas', avoid being bitten. The bugs are most prevalent in rural areas, often living amid dead palm fronds or piles of wood. If you are sleeping in a thatched-roof hut, try to cover your face with a cloth or put on a bug repellent containing DEET. A spray of pyrethrin insecticide will kill the bugs. If staying in an old hotel, check the room carefully for bugs, including under the mattress.

Chagas' is present in all departments of Honduras except the Bay Islands and Gracias a Dios (Mosquitia). Infestation is minimal in Atlántida, Colón, and Yoro, while it is a particular problem in Intibucá and parts of Olancho.

Snakes, Bees, and Scorpions

Honduras has its share of scorpions, wasps, bees (including the aggressive Africanized honey bee), and poisonous snakes. Most of the dangerous snakes live in the tropical forests of the Atlantic coast, particularly in the jungles of La Mosquitia, where pit vipers (including the deadly fer-de-lance) and coral snakes are common dangers.

The fer-de-lance is considered one of the most venomous snakes in the world. Bites are fatal unless the victim receives medical help within a few hours after being bitten. The fer-de-lance is easy to spot by the bright patch of yellow under its throat, a marking that earned it the nickname *barba amarilla* (yellow beard). Other poisonous snakes include the black-, red-, and white-striped *coral,* or coral snake, and the *cascabel,* or rattler.

When hiking in the jungle, wear boots and long pants. Watch where you put your feet, and if possible let a guide precede you. Be particularly careful around piles of dead wood or stones, which offer shade to snakes during the day. Jungle lore holds fer-de-lance are most frequently found near water holes and light gaps created by fallen trees.

SAFETY

Crime

Street crime is a growing problem in Honduras, although it is still nothing on the level of most U.S. cities, despite recent bad publicity. San Pedro Sula is without question the country's most dangerous city, followed by Tegucigalpa and the north coast cities. Tela is particularly bad, with *mareros* (young gang members) prowling the streets and nearby beaches, victimizing locals and tourists alike.

To avoid problems, simply take the same precautions any sensible traveler takes anywhere. Don't walk around with a lot of money in your pocket or flashy jewelry, keep copies of your passport somewhere safe, don't walk around at night in cities, and avoid seedy areas during the day. On the beach, don't bring a lot of stuff with you, to avoid tempting thieves while you're in the water. And, very importantly, don't walk isolated stretches of beach outside of the towns on the north coast. A great number of tourists have been mugged taking such walks. Bay Island beaches are quite safe.

The most high-profile crimes these days in Honduras are kidnappings, picking off family members of wealthy businessmen, cattle ranchers, and coffee growers, and holding them for ransom. Sometimes the victim is returned unharmed, other times not. Many Hondurans suspect former or even current military and police are involved in many kidnapping rings. Travelers are rarely, if ever, targets for kidnappers.

For the most part, rural Honduras is remarkably safe, considering the high poverty. Foreigners can generally wander around at will with little fear. The mountain country in western Honduras, in particular, is exceptionally safe and wonderful for trekking and backpacking.

There are a few exceptions to this, however. First and foremost are certain parts of western and northern Olancho, well known for their gunslingers and highway bandits. The two most important places to avoid are around Dulce Nombre de Culmí, near the edge of the Mosquitia rainforests; and the dirt highway between Limones, La Unión, and the Aguán Valley in western Olancho. Also notorious is the junction of the departments of Yoro, Olancho, and Francisco Morazán, a mountain region known as the Golden Triangle of Honduras because of the marijuana production.

Drugs

Though not a major drug-producing country itself, apart from small-scale marijuana growers supplying the domestic market, Honduras is becoming a favored conduit for South American cocaine on its way north to the United States. The deserted, unpatrolled expanse of the Mosquitia coast is a choice drop-off point for Colombian drug smugglers, as are the Bay Islands. From Mosquitia the cocaine is transported overland through Guatemala and Mexico to the United States, while from the Bay Islands the merchandise usually continues north by boat. But other parts of the country are used also—in September 1999, a helicopter ferried in a shipment of 369 kilos of cocaine to a village near Yoro. Low-paid police, customs, and military officials are easy targets for corruption, and in recent years many have been arrested for their involvement with drug trafficking.

The use of both cocaine and marijuana is illegal in Honduras, and the police will happily throw you in jail if they catch you. Drug-consuming travelers may assume they can easily bribe their way out of difficulties, and sometimes this is the case, but not always. As prison terms for drug use are stiff, it hardly seems worth the risk.

Police

Formerly known as Fusep (Fuerzas de Seguridad Pública), Honduras' police force was for many years a division of the armed forces, but in early 1997 it was finally placed under civilian leadership. It is now called the **Policia Preventiva Nacional.** A militaristic command structure remains in place, and the police still act more like a private army than public servants, but the situation seems to be improving slowly.

Police generally receive little formal training, are relatively incompetent, and are often corrupt. Despite this, if you are stopped for a traffic infraction or other minor offense, try to go through the proper channels. Do not immediately offer a bribe—this only encourages corruption.

If you are the victim of a crime, the police can sometimes be helpful, particularly in smaller towns where it's likely the culprit will be easily found. Police officers are usually happy to explain local laws or help tourists with directions.

IMMIGRATION AND CUSTOMS

VISAS

Tourist Requirements

Citizens of the U.S., western Europe, Canada, Argentina, and Chile are not required to have a visa and are issued a 30-day tourist card on arrival in Honduras. Citizens of all other countries are required to obtain visas before entering Honduras. Cost usually depends on what that country charges Hondurans for visas. Sometimes it's free, and sometimes it can cost up to US$20.

Tourist cards and visas must be renewed every month, up to a six-month maximum stay. Most large towns and cities have a *migración* office, where your card can be renewed quickly for a couple of dollars. Sometimes you may be asked to get a certain amount of *timbre* stamps, available at a local bank, as payment.

The one office in Honduras where renewing your card is a bit of a nightmare is, ironically, the central *migración* office in Tegucigalpa. Here you'll be made to wait in a couple of lines and then asked to leave your passport for one to three days. Best to take care of renewal elsewhere when possible.

Foreigners are required to carry their passport and tourist card with them at all times, but rarely if ever will it be checked. Be sure to keep photocopies in your hotel room, or better still just carry the photocopies.

CUSTOMS

Travelers entering Honduras are allowed to bring with them anything needed for a vacation, including any sports equipment, plus 200 cigarettes, 100 cigars, half a kilogram of tobacco, and two quarts of spirits. When leaving the country, be sure not to have any pre-Columbian artifacts, endangered animals, or coral, particularly black coral, as these could be confiscated either in Honduras or your home country; you could even wind up in jail.

Cars

Foreign cars are allowed into Honduras for a total of six months. Travelers overstaying the limit will be fined. When arriving at the border, be sure to have your title, license, and passport (with visa, if necessary). Insurance is not required.

Three-month permits are issued initially, for a US$20 fee. Sometimes you may be offered only a 30-day permit, but firmly request three months. Prices should be clearly posted on signs at border offices, and receipts should be given for every fee. If a border official will not give you a receipt, the fee is probably not required.

At border posts you will be pestered by *tramitadores* (people who help with official paperwork) offering their services. All *tramitadores* should have identification approved by the government—don't hire someone who is not wearing identification. If the border offices are crowded, or if you're not confident in Spanish, *tramitadores* can be quite useful in helping facilitate your way through the paperwork. But if you speak Spanish reasonably well, and there aren't too many people around, the procedures are not difficult to navigate alone. Basically, you first get your passport stamped by *migración,* then proceed to the *aduana,* or customs, where you must show your title, registration, driver's license, and passport. After filling out a form, go to one of usually two or three banks at the border, pay a fee, and return to the *aduana* receive your papers. As you leave the border entering Honduras, stop at the police station, where they will inspect your papers and register your car's presence in the country. You are under no obligation to leave through the same border post—leave wherever you like. The entire process usually takes an hour or so, on an average day.

If you'd like to renew your permit when the time expires, to a maximum of six months unless you receive a work visa in the country, go to the Dirección Ejecutiva de Ingresos just downhill from Parque Central on Ave. Cervantes, 9th floor, Tegucigalpa, tel. 238-6790, ext. 121. The cost was US$5 at last report, but you must go to the office first and check, because the fee is to be paid in *timbre* stamps, purchased for the exact amount at one of the nearby banks. Bring three photocopies of the front and back of the original permit, of your visa, and of every page in your passport (blank or not). Normally if your papers are in one day before noon, you can pick them up the next day by early afternoon.

BORDER CROSSINGS

Official border crossings into Honduras are: El Poy and El Amatillo from El Salvador; Aguas Calientes, El Florido, and Cuyamelito from Guatemala; Las Manos, El Espino, Guasaule, and Leimus (near Puerto Lempira) from Nicaragua. Several unofficial crossings are regularly used along the more remote reaches of Salvadoran border, and across the Río Coco to Nicaragua.

Entering and leaving Honduras by land is generally quick and easy. The best time to arrive is mid-morning, well before lunch break, but most border posts are open until 4 p.m. or 5 p.m. You may be asked to pay a small fee when crossing into Honduras. Technically you shouldn't have to pay anything, but it might be worth the few *lempiras* to avoid an argument with the border guards.

Those leaving Honduras by airplane are required to pay an exit fee of US$25.

MONEY, MEASUREMENTS, AND COMMUNICATIONS

CURRENCY

The national unit of currency is the *lempira*, often shortened to "lemp" by English-speaking Hondurans and expatriates. Bills come in denominations of one, two, five, 10, 20, 50, and 100 *lempira*, while coins are worth one, two, five, 10, 20, and 50 centavos. Coins are worth so little they're more of an annoyance than an asset. Fifty-centavo coins are known as *tostones*, and the slang word for cash is *pisto*. At last report, the exchange rate was roughly 14.7 *lempiras* to US$1.

EXCHANGE

Travelers to Honduras have the option of financing their trip either with U.S. dollars, traveler's checks (American Express preferred), expensive wire transfers, Visa or MasterCard cash advances, or through an ATM. The last is the best option, but at the moment only good with Visa debit cards.

Most banks in Honduras are open Mon.-Fri. 8 a.m.-noon and 1:30-4:30 p.m., Saturday 8 a.m.-noon.

Banks or Black Market?
Technically all currency exchange transactions must be done at a bank or in an authorized *casa de cambio* (exchange house), which are rare outside San Pedro Sula or Tegucigalpa. Exchanging money at banks is usually not an arduous affair, especially if you have cash.

Many travelers and Hondurans prefer the convenience of changing money on the black market, which, although illegal, is universally tolerated in the face of the steadily dropping *lempira*. The exchangers, who hang around the central square of Tegucigalpa and San Pedro Sula, wave around wads of dollars and *lempiras*. In other towns and cities, certain shop owners are often known to change dollars. The rates offered are marginally better than at the banks.

Although the black market may seem a bit shady, the changers are merely businesspeople

trying to make a living and are generally not out to rip you off. Nonetheless, make sure you understand the exchange numbers (borrow their calculator if you're not sure) and count your money carefully right in front of them to avoid any mistake. As you can tell from how openly the changers operate, there is no risk of getting into legal trouble, unless the government suddenly decides to crack down, which is extremely unlikely.

If you need to change *lempiras* into dollars, the black market changers are the source. Banks have strict limits on how many dollars they are allowed to sell.

Traveler's Checks
Any traveler on a long trip without means of accessing money on the road should bring traveler's checks. However, be aware that traveler's checks are not always easy to change in Honduras outside of cities and tourist areas like the Bay Islands or Copán. If you are planning to travel in rural areas, be sure to change enough to cover your time away from the cities.

American Express is by far the most recognized traveler's check—others such as Thomas Cook or Visa are more difficult to exchange. On rare occasions banks may require you to show your original purchase receipt to change checks, so keep it with you.

The American Express agent in Honduras is Mundirama Travel, with offices in Tegucigalpa, at Edificio Ciicsa, corner of Avenida República de Chile and Avenida República de Panamá, tel. 232-3943 or 232-3909, fax 232-0072, and in San Pedro Sula, next to the cathedral on 2 Calle SO, tel. 550-0490 or 550-1193, fax 557-9022. At these offices AmEx holders can purchase traveler's checks with a personal check, drawing funds from a bank account back home. They will not sell traveler's checks for cash.

Credit Cards and ATMs
Visa and MasterCard are often accepted at the more expensive hotels and restaurants in cities and some large towns, as well as with travel agents, tour groups, and car rental agencies.

American Express is much less commonly accepted. In small towns and villages credit cards won't get you much more than blank looks.

Visa holders can get cash advances from several banks, including many branches of Banco Atlántida, Bancahsa and Banco del Occidente. **Credomatic** will also offer advances on a Visa and is the only place to go for those using a MasterCard. In general, the banks don't charge excessive commissions, if at all, but they usually offer a poor exchange rate. Unless you have a debit card link, the advance is then posted to your credit card account, where it begins to compound interest daily, rather than monthly like any normal purchase. So if you plan to use this method, find some way to make payments by phone directly with Visa (if your account is linked to a bank account) or with the help of someone back home immediately after the advance, to avoid wasting money. For more information on Credomatic call its Miami, Florida, office at (305) 372-3027 or (305) 372-3015; card application requests tel. (800) 458-2733.

Finally, Banco Atlántida has hooked up its ATMs to the international network, offering the best way to get money in Honduras from banks back home. At the moment, a Visa debit card is the only link to non-Honduran banks. Fees are usually US$4 or so per transaction, and you may only be able to withdraw US$150 or so at a time, regardless of your account's limit, because of the *lempira* maximum withdrawal amount. The ATM machines say they work with the Plus network, but at last report this was false advertising. Perhaps Plus will work in the future. Most (but not all) Banco Atlántida branches in cities and large towns have an ATM.

Sending Money

It is possible to receive money wire transfers at both Bancahsa and Banco Atlántida in Honduras. The transfer normally takes three to four days, and charges are not excessive. The money comes in *lempiras*—often the bank will change some to dollars, but not much. Money can only be received in dollars if a dollar-denomination account is opened at the bank, which is usually not very difficult.

Western Union transfers are received at several branches of Banco Sogerin and Banco de Occidente, and at Western Union offices. Money can be sent and received at any Western Union representative—to retrieve the money all you need is the transfer number and a passport. Money is received in *lempira*. Western Union charges an exorbitant 10% service fee and offers a bad exchange rate.

MoneyGram, received through Bancahsa, is reported to offer a better exchange rate.

WEIGHTS AND MEASURES

Time
Honduras is six hours behind Greenwich Mean Time and equal to Central Standard Time in the United States. Daylight saving time is not practiced in Honduras.

Electricity
Almost all outlets in the country operate on 110 volts and are designed to fit two parallel flat blades. Sometimes a two-pronged round plug is required. A few outlets are 220 volts, but these are extremely rare. If in doubt, ask first.

Power outages and brownouts are frequent in Honduras, especially in the dry season when the El Cajón dam water level is low.

Measurements
Honduras has adopted a confusing mix of metric and nonmetric measurements. Old colonial *libras* (pounds) are more frequently used than kilograms as a unit of weight. Twenty-five *libras* equal one *arroba,* and four *arrobas* equal one *quintal.* One quintal equals 46 kilograms. U.S. gallons are used instead of liters for volume, but distance is measured in kilometers and meters rather than miles and feet or yards.

Land sizes are often quoted in *varas,* equal to 838 square meters, or *manzanas,* equal to 0.7 hectares.

COMMUNICATIONS AND MEDIA

Postal Service
Regular mail service *(Correos)* between Honduras and other countries is, at best, a lengthy process. Street numbers are almost nonexistent in Honduras, even in Tegucigalpa and San Pedro Sula. Addresses are usually given as on "X" Calle

between "Y" and "Z" Avenidas, or on "X" Calle next to the church, etc. Miraculously, mail does get delivered, though expect to wait anywhere from two to four weeks to receive mail or have it reach its destination. Airmail letters to the U.S. or Europe cost US 50 cents. Packages of up to two kilos can be sent regular mail, and cost US$3 for one kilo and US$6 for two to the U.S. or Europe.

Many post offices now have Express Mail Service (EMS), which reliably sends letters and documents of less than 250 grams to the U.S. in three to four days for US$10-15, depending on the destination, or to Europe in four to five days for US$20-25.

It's possible to receive mail general delivery in any post office in the country. The letters should be addressed to your name, Lista de Correos, town, department, Honduras. A couple of *lempiras* is charged when the mail is collected. Usually offices will hold letters a couple of months, or longer if you advise them ahead of time to await your arrival.

The best places to receive mail general delivery are in large towns—though mail may get lost in the chaos of *Correos* in San Pedro Sula or Tegucigalpa, it may *never* make it out to small towns or villages.

Three of the big international couriers, **UPS, Federal Express,** and **DHL** all have offices in the half-dozen largest cities in the country and charge a whopping US$30 or so to send documents to the U.S. in three days. Several low-priced courier services catering to Hondurans with relatives in the states, like **Urgente Express,** send letters to the U.S. in about the same amount of time, but for only US$3 or so, and are generally reliable. Within Honduras, packages can be sent quickly and reliably between most towns in one or two days for US$2-5 by **Expreco,** with offices all over the country.

Telephone Service

Hondutel, the notoriously inefficient national telecommunications company, has offices in every town. Hondutel was slated for privatization in mid-2000 and may be in private hands by the time you read this. Interested bidders at last report included France Telecom and Mexico's Telmex, among others. What will happen to rates after privatization is not certain, but at last check a three-minute call from Hondutel offices cost

---

TELEPHONE INFORMATION

The following numbers can be dialed from any coin or private telephone.

International Operators
8000-123—AT&T
8000-121—MCI

Public Service and Emergency Numbers
191—Long-distance national
192—Information
195—Red Cross ambulance
196—Official time
197—Long-distance international
198—Fire department
199—Police

Calling From Another Country
504—Honduras international area code

---

roughly US$8 to Miami, US$13 to New York, US$23 to France, US$28 to England, and US$23 to Australia. AT&T, MCI, and Sprint often have their own phone booths in Hondutel offices, where you just pick up the receiver and are automatically connected to an international operator with the respective company.

To place international collect calls from a pay phone, dial the international operator at 197. It is now possible to connect directly with an AT&T operator by dialing 8000-123, or an MCI operator by dialing 8000-121, which makes international calls simple for travelers who subscribe to those companies and carry one of their calling cards.

For local calls, pay phones use the tiny 20-centavo coins as the minimum, and 50-centavo coins for longer calls or a couple of short ones. Information within Honduras is 192.

Email

While certainly a new phenomenon, Internet cafes are springing up all over Honduras at an impressive rate. Destinations frequently visited by travelers like San Pedro Sula, Tegucigalpa, La Ceiba, Tela, the Bay Islands, and Copán Ruinas all have more than one place for travelers to check their email. Rates range from US 10 cents a minute with no minimum up to US$4 for a 30-minute minimum. Connection speeds vary dramatically but are usually more related to the time of day and system traffic than the quality of the hardware in different cafes.

Internet cafes are most easily found in large cities and tourist areas; they can also be found in towns like Santa Rosa de Copán, Comayagua, and Puerto Cortés. And in many smaller towns often someone will have a private connection in their house or business that they rent out—just start asking around.

Media

Newspaper reporting in Honduras is a simplistic affair, with little investigation beyond rewriting press releases, and often not even doing that accurately. Most stories are exceedingly short on hard facts and numbers and long on quoting the empty phrases of politicians. But local papers are nonetheless well worth reading to get a better feeling for the main events and trends of Honduran society. It's good practice for Spanish, too. The five main daily newspapers in Honduras are *La Prensa, La Tribuna, El Periódico, El Heraldo,* and *Tiempo.* All are owned by politicians (*La Tribuna* is owned by President Flores) and tend to favor one or the other of the two main political parties. Some articles can be incredibly slanted.

INTERNET RESOURCES

A number of web pages about Honduras have sprung up in recent years, many created by Hondurans living in other countries. As with just about any topic, the Internet can be an invaluable tool for learning about current conditions in Honduras and contacting other people interested in the country. Below are just a few suggestions to get people started—links from these sites will open a world of information on Honduras to the net surfer.

GENERAL INFORMATION

www.honduras-resources.com has links to newspapers, government organizations, businesses, foreign missions, tourist sites, chats, and more.

www.marrder.com/htw contains an excellent archive for the weekly English newspaper *Honduras this Week.*

www.projecthonduras.com has a wealth of socially oriented information, with many links to national and international social organizations working in Honduras.

TRAVEL

www.planeta.com is an award-winning website dedicated to eco-travels in Latin America, with a great deal of information on Honduras.

www.hondurastips.honduras.com contains useful up-to-date travel news.

DESTINATION-SPECIFIC SITES

www.roatan.com
www.roatanet.com
www.bayislands.com
www.utilainfo.com
www.tela-honduras.com

ECONOMIC AND SOCIAL STATISTICS AND INFORMATION

www.bch.hn—Banco Central de Honduras
www.iadb.org—InterAmerican Development Bank
www.eclac.org—Comisión Económica para América Latina y el Caribe

ISPS

www.datum.hn, contact at tel. 232-1190 or 552-1871, or by email: ceda@datum.hn
www.globalnet.hn, contact at tel. 566-1784 or 238-3630
www.caribe.hn, contact by email: webmaster@caribe.hn

Honduras' roads are used by all manner of transport.

La Prensa, which is published in San Pedro, has more of a business angle and comes the closest to balanced coverage of national news. This paper also has two or three pages of international news, including some international sports coverage. Although not as good as *La Prensa* on national news, *La Tribuna* also often features several pages of international wire copy.

Newspapers are usually sold on the street in small stands or merely on a designated street corner. *La Prensa* often sells out by midday. A welcome find for foreign travelers is the English-language weekly newspaper, *Honduras This Week.* Unlike many expatriate-oriented newspapers in the Americas, *Honduras This Week* actually covers issues of importance to the nation and doesn't shy away from touchy topics like corruption and the military. The paper also has valuable information for travelers and interesting features. It's sold at higher-priced hotels and tourist-oriented stores. The newspaper has an excellent website at http://www.marrder.com/htw/. Its email address is hontweek@hondutel.hn.

Eleven television and 176 radio stations operate in Honduras. Cable television is widely available.

MAPS AND INFORMATION

Maps
Finding totally accurate road maps of Honduras is, unfortunately, an impossible task. Several

decent maps correctly show the main highways but invariably mess up the placement of many rural dirt roads, while some incompetent cartographers go so far as to show main highways through tracts of virgin jungle and forest.

Formerly Texaco put out an excellent travel map of the country, but its recent edition is difficult to read because of the dark colors used. Nonetheless it's not too bad. Another good one is the ITMP Honduras Travel Reference, 2nd Edition 1998, available for US$9.95 through **World of Maps,** 1235 Wellington St., Ottawa, Canada K1Y3A3, tel. (800) 214-8524 or (613) 724-6776, website: www.worldofmaps.com.

The **Instituto Geográfico Nacional** publishes a tourist map for US$3, which shows the departments, main roads, and some geographic features. It can be purchased at the Instituto's main office in Comayagüela at the Secretaría de Transporte (SECOPT) on 15 Calle one block east of 1 Av., tel. 225-0752.

The Instituto also publishes a complete set of 1:50,000 topographical maps, several sheets of 1:250,000 topographical maps, geological, hydrographic, mineral, and official-boundary maps. The best map of the country available is the Instituto's large official map, which shows the latest border settlement with El Salvador. It costs US$11, but unfortunately the office was out at last check and awaiting a new printing.

If you need maps of Honduras before going to the country, it is possible to send the IGN money and they can send the maps to you, preferably by DHL or UPS. The office staff is friendly, competent, and knowledgeable, but you need to speak Spanish and know which maps you're looking for before calling. A list of maps can be seen at the IGN's website: //ns.sdnhon.org.hn/~ihnhon/.

It's usually easier to get IGN topographical maps through **Omni Resources** in the U.S. for US$10-12 per sheet. Their stock of 1:50,000 topos is about as good as the IGN's—about half of the series is available. Contact Omni at tel. (800) 742-2677 or (336) 227-8300, email: custserv@omnimap.com; website: www.omnimap.com/catalog/int/honduras.htm.

Tourist Information

The **Instituto Hondureño de Turismo** (Honduran Tourism Institute) is not the most professional outfit in the world, but it has been improving as the government wakes up to the lucrative possibilities of tourism. The Institute's central office in Honduras is in Edificio Europa, 5th floor, on Avenida Ramon Ernesto Cruz, behind the U.S. Embassy, tel. 238-3974 or 222-2124, fax 222-6621.

The Institute recently opened an office in the U.S. that can answer basic questions about traveling in Honduras. Contact this office at P.O.

PUBLIC HOLIDAYS

1 January—New Year's Day
Week leading up to Easter Sunday—Semana Santa
14 April—Día de las Américas
1 May—Labor Day
15 September—Independence Day
3 October—Morazán's Birthday
12 October—Día de la Raza (Columbus Day)
21 October—Armed Forces Day
25 December—Christmas

Box 140458, Coral Gables, Florida 33114-0458, tel. (800) 410-9608.

The English-language weekly newspaper *Honduras This Week* is a good source of general news and cultural information on the country, as well as specific travel hints.

The quarterly, free magazine *Honduras Tips* has excellent, up-to-date hotel, restaurant, and travel information on some of the more popular tourist destinations, such as Copán, the north coast, and the Bay Islands. It can be found at many travel agents and better hotels.

GETTING THERE

BY AIR

Several airlines fly direct to Honduras from other countries. From the U.S., **Continental, American, Taca,** and **Iberia** all fly direct to Honduras from either Houston or Miami, either into Tegucigalpa, San Pedro Sula, or both. Taca also flies from Belize City, San José, Cancún, and San Salvador, while Copa flies from Mexico City and Panama City, and Iberia flies from Madrid via Miami. AeroCaribe, a division of Mexicana, just initiated a flight from Cancún to San Pedro Sula for just over US$300 roundtrip. With all the cheap charter flights to Cancún from Europe, this makes a good new way to get to Honduras from across the Atlantic. At last check, no airlines had a direct flight from the United States to the Bay Islands, but Taca has daily connections via San Pedro Sula.

Standard roundtrip airfare between Houston or Miami and San Pedro Sula is roughly US$550, though better deals can sometimes be found in advance through travel agents, or even better, the many airline ticket web pages in the Internet.

BY LAND

If you're planning to visit just Honduras and not spend time touring nearby countries, getting there by land isn't the most practical way to go. From the U.S. border, it takes at least three days on buses through Mexico and Guatemala to reach the closest Honduran border post at Aguas Calientes. Those who are on longer trips, however, and have some interest in spending time in Mexico or Guatemala should certainly consider getting there by bus or car. If you're on your way directly to San Pedro, the north coast, or the

Bay Islands, the quickest route from Guatemala is via Esquipulas to Aguas Calientes, near Nuevo Ocotepeque. Many travelers opt for the longer ride through Chiquimula and El Florido, to incorporate a stop-off at the Mayan ruins at Copán on their way through. At last report the Guatemalans were finishing work improving their portion of the Chiquimula road, and the Hondurans were promising to do the same. If this road ever gets paved, it will be much quicker than the Ocotepeque route for getting to the north coast of Honduras.

If you're coming from or are on your way to Managua, Nicaragua, or farther south, the quickest border crossing is through Las Manos, beyond Danlí.

Depending on your destination in Honduras, travelers coming from El Salvador will want to cross at El Poy, near Nueva Ocotepeque, or at El Amatillo on the Pacific coast. El Poy is the fastest way to get to the north coast, while El Amatillo is the quickest for Tegucigalpa.

A new route has opened up between Omoa, near Puerto Cortés, and Puerto Barrios, Guatemala. While this crossing once entailed a few hours of hiking through the jungle, it can now be accomplished in either direction in one day, by a combination of buses and pickup truck rides. Private vehicles can cross, but not when it has been raining heavily, as the Hondurans still have not managed to put bridges across a couple of rivers near the border.

A slightly sketchier but still possible crossing is between Puerto Lempira, in the Gracias a Dios department (La Mosquitia) through the border town of Leimus to Puerto Cabezas, Nicaragua. No firsthand information is available on the crossing, but *migración* officials in Puerto Lempira say they have a post at Leimus.

With Car
Coming down from the United States with your own vehicle is not unduly difficult, though it's a long way. Get through the huge expanse of Mexico on the quickest route possible to get to Tapachula, Chiapas, and cross into Guatemala at Tecún Umán. Driving through Guatemala via Escuintla and Guatemala City to the Honduran border at either El Florido or Aguas Calientes takes approximately eight or nine hours. Alter-

natively, those with time on their hands can take the more scenic but considerably slower route through San Cristóbal de las Casas, Mexico, through the highlands of Guatemala and on to Honduras.

The car permit situation in Mexico was in flux at last report, possibly changing from the old credit card voucher system to something much more expensive. It remained unclear at press time whether less expensive transit permits would be available to those on their way through—contact Mexican embassies or consulates in the U.S. or elsewhere for the latest details. Guatemalan car formalities are quite simple, dispensed with in an hour or so for about US$30, as long as you've got your title, registration, and driver's license.

International Buses
Tica Bus has buses daily to and from Managua, Nicaragua (US$20, 8 hours); San José, Costa Rica (US$35, 15 hours); and Panama City, Panama (US$60, 31 hours). The Tegucigalpa office is in Comayagüela at 16 Calle between 6 and 5 Avenidas, tel. 220-0579 or 220-0590. The company also has offices in Managua, Nicaragua, two blocks behind the Antiguo Cine Dorado, tel. (505) 222-6094 or 222-3031; in **San José, Costa Rica,** Costado Norte Iglesia de la Soledad, between 9 and 11 Calles, Av. 4, tel. (506) 221-8954 or 255-4771; and in **Panamá,** Bajos del Hotel Ideal, Calle 18 Central, tel. (507) 262-2084.

King Quality/Cruceros del Golfo has one *ejecutivo*-class bus, with breakfast, television, and paperwork help at the border, between Tegucigalpa and San Salvador, El Salvador (US$25, 8 hours); and Guatemala City, Guatemala (US$45, 14 hours). A second, regular bus drives to San Salvador only, US$22. To Managua, Nicaragua (US$23, 9.5 hours), take the *ejecutivo* bus going to San Salvador and transfer to a second bus at El Amatillo. From San Pedro, buses take 7.5 hours to drive to San Salvador via Nueva Ocotepeque, for US$23. The Tegucigalpa terminal is located on Blvd. Comunidad Económica Europea, in Barrio La Granja, south of Comayagüela, tel. 225-5415 or 225-2600; the San Pedro terminal is on 6 Calle beween 7 and 8 Avenidas SO, tel. 553-

3443 or 552-9519. The company has offices in Guatemala City, tel. (502) 333-4735 or 368-0138; San Salvador, tel. (503) 271-1361 or 279-0060, Alameda Juan Pablo II 19 Av. Nte.; and Managua, tel. (505) 228-1454 or 228-2046, by Antiguo Cine Dorado.

Atitrans runs a van service between Copán Ruinas and either Antigua or Guatemala City for US$25 pp, with connections available to or from other destinations in Guatemala. The bus leaves usually three times a week, on Monday, Wednesday, and Saturday, but other trips can be arranged if enough people want to go. Contact the Atitrans office in Copán Ruinas, tel. 651-4390; in Antigua at 6 Av. Sur #7, tel. (502) 832-3371 or 832-1381; and in Guatemala City at 13 Calle 1-51, Zona 10, Edificio Santa Clara II, Local 22, tel. (502) 332-5788 or 331-8181.

BY SEA

From Belize
One boat a week plies the waters between Dangriga, Belize, and Puerto Cortés, charging US$35 for the two- or three-hour trip, and a second one goes to Belize City for US$40.

From Guatemala
Once or twice a week, boats ferry passengers between Livingston, Guatemala, and Omoa, near Puerto Cortés, for US$25-30.

GETTING AROUND

BY PLANE

Because Honduras is fairly small, flying between destinations in most of the country is not really necessary, with a few exceptions. If you're in a rush or absolutely hate buses, flights between the two main cities, San Pedro Sula and Tegucigalpa, cost US$30 one-way on either Isleña or Taca.

Two areas where it's not a bad idea to arrive by plane are the Bay Islands and the Mosquitia. The islands are serviced by an inexpensive and comfortable ferry, but plane flights from La Ceiba are also inexpensive and quick. Isleña, Rollins, and Sosa all fly to the islands daily, charging US$17 to Utila, US$17 to Roatán, and US$36 to Guanaja, one-way.

Flying is really the only way to get into La Mosquitia, unless you feel like spending a few days on the deck of a tramp freighter or walking up the coast for a week or so. Flights from La Ceiba with Isleña, Sosa, or Rollins go most days to Palacios for US$39, Puerto Lempira for US$58, and Brus Laguna for US$48.

Between towns and villages in La Mosquitia, travelers may also want to fly, as boat rides are long and often remarkably expensive. The most reliable option is Sami, a rattle-trap little Cessna flying daily between Palacios, Brus Laguna, Ahuas, Puerto Lempira, and occasionally other villages in the Mosquitia. On occasion, it's possible to get a ride with the Alas de Soccoro mission airplane, if it's going in your direction.

Airfares within Honduras are regulated by the government, so all airlines charge the same amount.

BY BUS

Buses are the most widely used means of transportation for Hondurans. Buses are often essential to visit the more out-of-the-way destinations, and budget travelers will be happy to hear most buses are relatively comfortable and remarkably inexpensive. For example, the four-hour bus ride between San Pedro Sula and Tegucigalpa costs only US$3.50.

Direct, first-class bus service is available between main cities like San Pedro Sula, Tegucigalpa, and La Ceiba, but elsewhere don't expect luxury. Many buses are converted U.S. school buses, with bench seating designed for children, so if you're tall, expect a bit of discomfort.

Apart from San Pedro Sula, Tegucigalpa, and Comayagua, the designated bus station in most towns is called simply the *terminal de buses*. In the above-mentioned cities, each company runs its own terminal, and unfortunately they're not centrally located. San Pedro Sula may soon get a new central terminal, but it was still in the planning stages at last report.

Determining bus departure times can be a bit of a guessing game. Some buses leave only when full, which means you should get there early, while others leave at the appointed time, full or not. Generally, long-distance buses leave on a regular schedule.

When you arrive at a station to catch a bus, expect to be accosted by *ayudantes,* or helpers, who will tell you in urgent tones that the bus you want is just out the door and you must buy a ticket immediately. You may then get on the bus and wait another hour before leaving. Another common trick is to tell you the bus is a direct *(directo)* when in reality it stops whenever it sees another potential passenger.

In some buses you are expected to buy a ticket at the station beforehand, while in others the *ayudante* will come around and collect the fare after the trip has begun. If the latter is the case, you will be asked how far you are going, and your fare will change accordingly. Hold on to ticket stubs, as the drivers sometimes collect them at the end of the ride.

In the converted school buses, backpacks and other luggage that does not fit in the overhead racks is stowed in the back, where a couple of seats are normally removed to add space. More expensive buses have compartments below, but if your bag is stashed there by an *ayudante* keep a close eye on the door until the bus pulls out. Bus stations in San Pedro Sula in particular are notorious for having bags ripped off while the unsuspecting victims are on board, awaiting departure.

Apart from the rare express buses, it's customary to flag down a passing bus anywhere along the route—extremely convenient for those traveling in rural areas. Don't bother trying to look for a designated bus stop, just get out on the road and stick out your hand when a bus comes by.

On rare occasion buses will be stopped by police and all men will be forced to get off and line up to be cursorily frisked and have their identifications checked.

HITCHHIKING

Travelers looking to get out into the backcountry of Honduras should be sure to learn the crucial word *jalón.* This literally translates to "a big pull," but in Honduras it means hitching a ride. In many rural areas hitchhiking is the only way to get around, and pickup trucks with room invariably stop to let another passenger pile into the back. When you get dropped off, ask how much you owe for the ride—there's usually a set price.

Not only is hitching safe and convenient in Honduras, but riding in the open air in the back of a pickup beats being crammed into a hot bus for a few hours. Many budget travelers and Peace Corps workers prefer hitching even when buses are available. Women, however, will want to think twice about hitching alone.

Hitchhiking is common only out on back roads, not on main highways. Some budget travelers in-

Hitching a ride in a passing pickup is one of the best ways to travel around rural Honduras.

sist on hitching everywhere, and it's usually possible, but hitching on main highways is both less common and less safe than in rural areas.

BY TAXI

Taxis are omnipresent in most towns and cities. Meters aren't used, and there's usually a going rate within a certain area. It may be tricky figuring out the going rate. US 75 cents usually gets you around within the downtown area of most towns, while taxis in Tegucigalpa and San Pedro Sula charge closer to US$2. For rides farther afield, expect to negotiate.

One risky technique is to get in, don't ask the price, and once at your destination hand the driver a 20- or 50-lempira bill, look like you know what the price is, and hope he gives you the right change. A better plan is to ask a local the prices before hailing a cab.

Taxis are generally collective in Honduras, meaning they stop and pick up passengers along the way and drop them off according to whichever destination is closer. If you're in a hurry and want a nonstop trip, tell the driver and expect to pay extra.

In San Pedro and Tegucigalpa, several *colectivo* taxis run fixed routes from a certain point downtown to the outskirts of the city, usually charging US 35 cents or so for the pleasure of being crammed in with four passengers and the driver.

Taxis are invariably found at the downtown square of any town or city, or at the bus station. If you hear someone honking at you as you walk through a town, more than likely it's a taxi—the driver's letting you know he's free if you're looking for a ride.

BY BOAT

To the Bay Islands
The ferry MV *Galaxy* runs regularly scheduled trips throughout the week to the islands of Roatán and Utila from the Cabotaje dock outside of La Ceiba. If you're really pinching your *lempiras* or just want the experience, a couple of small freighters leave Cabotaje for the islands every week and will take passengers. The only

way to find out about them is to go out to the docks and ask, and the money you spend getting to the docks would probably cover the difference to take the Galaxy.

Once on the islands, several outfits and resorts offer a variety of cruises and fishing trips. It's also possible to hire local fishermen to take you on freelance trips.

La Mosquitia
Getting to La Mosquitia by tramp freighter has an undeniably romantic appeal, but the reality is somewhat uncomfortable and wet. Should you be after this sort of adventure, get out to the Cabotaje docks in La Ceiba and start asking around. Freighters usually stop in at Brus Laguna and Puerto Lempira.

In La Mosquitia, *tuk-tuks* (small, motorized canoes) and *pipantes* (dug-out canoes propelled by poles) are often the only transportation available for getting upriver from the coast into the rainforest.

BY CAR

Although it's a long way to drive from the U.S., those who take a car to Honduras can explore large areas of the country accessed only with difficulty by public transportation. Customs regulations for importing cars are not arduous (see above). Foreign drivers are required to have a license from their country or an International Driver's License, available from AAA. Pickup trucks are the most practical vehicles to bring into Honduras, in terms of both usefulness on the rough roads and finding spare parts.

Hyde Shipping/Naviera Hybur, with offices in Miami, at 10025 N.W. 116th Way, Suite 2, Medley, FL 33178, tel. (305) 913-4933, fax (305) 913-4900, and in French Harbour, Roatán, tel. 445-5543, will send a standard-size car from Miami to Roatán or La Ceiba for US$600, and US$60 from La Ceiba to Roatán.

Road Conditions
Until quite recently, driving in Honduras was a white-knuckle adventure on rutted dirt roads, but the situation has improved dramatically with a road-building binge by successive governments. Honduras now has 2,543 km of paved highways,

9,830 km of all-season dirt roads, and 1,972 km of dirt roads passable in the dry season only. Hurricane Mitch was a serious setback, but as of early 2000, most (but not all) roads had been at least partly reconditioned. Several waterways with damaged bridges were still spanned by temporary Bailey bridges, installed by foreign emergency crews after the storm. Funds are in the pipe to permanently rebuild at least some of these bridges in the next few years. Major roads still in rough shape, but passable, include the stretch between Tocoa and Trujillo, and between Santa Rita and Yoro. The dirt road between Olanchito and La Unión, in Olancho, was still closed at last check, and the one out to Limón near the Mosquitia is practically impassable.

Well-maintained paved highways include: Tegucigalpa-San Pedro Sula, Tegucigalpa-Choluteca, Tegucigalpa-Danlí, Nueva Ocotepeque-San Pedro Sula, San Pedro Sula-Puerto Cortés, San Pedro Sula-Tela, and El Amatillo-Guasaule. The north coast highway is in good condition from Tela through La Ceiba to Tocoa but deteriorates severely in the last stretch to Trujillo.

Although some older maps don't show them, two all-weather dirt highways cut from Olancho through to the north coast, one via San Esteban and Bonito Oriental, and the other passing La Unión. These are both beautiful drives passing through interesting and rarely visited mountainous regions. The western road, via La Unión, is unfortunately off limits these days due to highway banditry. The easterly road, via San Esteban, is more populated and consequently not as risky, but nevertheless it's always best to avoid driving at night or even late afternoon.

When driving in cities, keep a close eye on signs indicating one-way streets. Most large towns and cities are not difficult to navigate, except Tegucigalpa. The traffic in downtown and in the Comayagüela district is horrific and the streets confusing. Better to leave your car at a hotel and get around downtown by taxi or on foot during your stay.

It's absolutely essential that foreign drivers drive very defensively, not expecting anyone else on the road to obey the laws or even act logically. Trucks in particular take positive glee in passing around blind curves on Honduras' many mountain highways, so don't take your eyes off the road and always be ready to dodge out of the

way. Keep a close eye on pedestrians and bicyclists, as they seem to be so fatalistic as to actually take delight in meandering around in the road and forcing cars to get out of their way.

Driving at night is not recommended in any part of the country. As with Mexico and the rest of Central America, there are just too many potential hazards to make it worth risking. The complete lack of other vehicles on the road should clue you in quickly. If you absolutely must drive for some reason, watch closely for cattle, potholes, and other random obstacles in the road. Keep an eye out for signs warning of upcoming *túmulos* (speed bumps). Driving Honduran highways in the rain can be treacherous as well and is not for the faint of heart.

Police checkpoints are common throughout Honduras, little yellow and grey painted shacks on the side of the road, usually with a policeman sitting in a chair out front, watching the day pass by. Slow down as you pass—usually you will be waved through or ignored entirely. But sometimes he will make it clear he wants you to stop. Do so without hesitation, and break out your papers to show. Your car permit, driver's license (a foreign one will do), and passport must always, always be with you. If not, expect hassles and fines.

Rules of the Road

Traffic rules in Honduras are fairly self-explanatory and similar to rules in the United States. Speed limits are not obeyed, but if you want to be safe, follow them anyway. Seat belts are mandatory. Turning right on a red light is sometimes allowed, sometimes not, so don't risk it. One oddity is that no left turns are permitted at any stoplight that does not have a left turn arrow indicator. Another is that no smoking is allowed while driving.

If you are pulled over for a traffic offense, your license will be taken. You can try to pay a bribe to get it back, but remember the official fines are usually cheaper than a bribe. If you ask for a ticket, you will be given one, and then you have 72 hours to go to the Tránsito office to pay the fine and reclaim the license. In Tegucigalpa, the office is the Dirección General de Tránsito in Colonia Miraflores. Usually the policeman who takes your license will turn it in the same day, and by the next morning you can go to Tránsito, pay your fine, and pick up the license again—a remarkably painless process.

In Case of Accident

If you have an accident with another car, tell someone to go get *tránsito*, the traffic police. Don't leave the scene of an accident before *tránsito* arrives. While waiting, get all information possible about the other driver. When *tránsito* arrives, the officers will talk to both drivers separately, then write out a description of events for both to sign and date.

An appointment will then be assigned at the *Juzgado de Tránsito* (traffic court), where a monetary arrangement will be made. No one carries insurance in Honduras, so the judge will arbitrate between the two parties to arrive at an agreement. If no agreement is reached, either party can sue.

In the case of an accident involving a pedestrian, again call the police immediately and do not leave the scene. You may have to spend up to a week in jail, but no more. It's very likely you will be forced to pay a fine to the victim in case of injury, or to the family of the victim in case of death, regardless of who was at fault.

Do not even consider fleeing the scene of an accident. This only creates more serious trouble for you. It's best to follow the process through to its conclusion.

Fuel and Repairs

At last report gasoline in Honduras was US$2.20 per gallon regular unleaded and US$1.40 diesel. Regular (leaded) gas is no longer available in Honduras. Gas stations, including many U.S. chains like Texaco and Esso, are common throughout the country, and in places with no gas stations, gas is sometimes sold out of barrels. Be sure to fill up whenever you're planning a trip into rural Honduras, and bring a gas can. Texaco publishes a country map showing the location of its stations.

Mechanical help is relatively inexpensive, but parts can be costly depending on your vehicle. Toyota is the unquestioned king of the road here, particularly the four-door, 4WD diesel pickups. Nissan is the next most common, followed by other Japanese and a few old American pickups. Japanese imports also dominate the passenger car market.

Be sure to get your vehicle thoroughly checked before leaving for Honduras, and consider bringing a few basic spare parts such as filters (gas, air, and oil), fan belts, spark plugs and spark plug wires, two spare tires (instead of one), fuses, and radiator hoses. Recommended emergency gear for vehicles includes a tow rope, extra gas cans, water containers, and of course a jack and tire iron. According to Honduran law you are required to have a fire extinguisher and reflective triangles in your car at all times (though it's very unlikely that any policeman will ever check for them).

Insurance

Apart from policies offered by car rental agencies, auto insurance is virtually nonexistent in Honduras, so you drive at your own risk. This should encourage you to drive defensively, which you should be doing anyway. The English-language newspaper *Honduras This Week* sometimes advertises insurance agents, but policies are generally for a year minimum and thus not practical for most travelers.

The Club Automovilística de Honduras' Soccoro Vial, a service not unlike AAA, is worth contacting should you plan on driving extensively in Honduras. Its coverage provides towing service and mechanical help for US$70 a year, 24 hours a day within 80 km of Tegucigalpa, and 8 a.m.-4 p.m. within 30 km of San Pedro Sula, La Ceiba and Choluteca. For another US$10 medical insurance is available as well. The central office is in Tegucigalpa, Avenida República de Chile 202, tel. 232-9909 or 232-9414, emergency number 232-9410. Another similar service is **Alerta Movil Inmediata**, tel. 236-6146.

Car Rental

Renting a car in Honduras is not cheap. Expect to pay at least US$45 per day with unlimited mileage, more with insurance. About a dozen different agencies, including several international companies like Hertz, Budget, Avis, and Toyota, operate in Honduras.

BY BICYCLE

Bicycle Touring

Remarkably, cyclists rate Honduras as the best Central American country to tour by bicycle. The main highways are in decent condition and highway traffic is low. Because many Hondurans get around by bicycle themselves or walk along the highway, the government has considerably included extra space marked off that bikers can safely cruise on without fear of being run down.

Bicycle touring may seem specialized, but it's actually a wonderful way to really see a country. There's no need to race—determine a comfortable pace for your group and plan your journey accordingly. Drawbacks to biking in Honduras include the extremely mountainous terrain, which will wear you down, and the lack of good quality spare parts. Riding in a group is best.

Mountain Biking

Mountain biking is a nascent but growing sport among the wealthy in Honduras. Few trails have been developed, but there are plenty of rugged logging roads to explore. Both the Sierra Merendón right behind San Pedro Sula and the mountains north and west of Tegucigalpa are fantastic for mountain biking, criss-crossed with trails and dirt roads through pine, tropical, and cloud forests and rural farming country. **Planet Bike,** with shops in both San Pedro (on Av. Circunvalación at 11 Calle "A" NO, tel. 550-3840) and Tegucigalpa (in Col. Palmira on Av. República de Panamá, tel. 232-3840), is a great place to hook up with other riders, find out about trails, and rent wheels.

ETHICAL TOURISM

The North American Center for Responsible Tourism suggests that travelers keep the following guidelines in mind on their trip:

• Travel with a spirit of humility and a genuine desire to meet and talk with local people.

• Be aware of the feelings of others. Act respectfully and avoid offensive behavior, particularly when taking photographs.

• Cultivate the habit of actively listening and observing rather than merely hearing and seeing. Avoid the temptation to "know all the answers."

• Realize that others may have concepts of time and attitudes that are different from—not inferior to—those you inherited from your own culture.

• Instead of looking only for the exotic, discover the richness of another culture and way of life.

• Learn local customs and respect them.

• Remember that you are only one of many visitors. Do not expect special privileges.

• When bargaining with merchants, remember that the poorest one may give up a profit rather than his or her personal dignity. Don't take advantage of the desperately poor. Pay a fair price.

• Keep your promises to people you meet. If you cannot, do not make the promise.

• Spend time each day reflecting on your experiences in order to deepen your understanding. Is your enrichment beneficial for all involved?

• Be aware of why you are traveling in the first place. If you truly want a "home away from home," why travel?

THE NORTH COAST

More like an entirely different country than a region of Honduras, the steaming hot, banana tree-blanketed plains of the Caribbean coast are worlds away from the rest of the country. The north coast is a polyglot melting pot, closer to the Anglo-African Caribbean islands than the more reserved Hispanic culture of the interior. North coasters are more extroverted: they like to dance, to party, to get out and have a good time.

Settled by the black-Carib Garífuna, North American banana men, Honduran job seekers, and immigrants from across the globe, the north coast is so diverse one never knows whether to address a stranger in Spanish or English; chances are they know a bit of both. For the traveler, the north coast's most appealing aspect is certainly the perfect trio of sun, sand, and sea. Superb beaches, where you can sling a hammock between two palms and enjoy the gentle offshore breezes in peace, line the entire coast.

The area also contains several of the country's most important natural protected areas, including the mangrove wetlands and lowland jungles of Punta Sal, Punta Izopo, and Cuero y Salado, as well as the mountain jungles, cloud forests, and rivers of Pico Bonito.

Many visitors blow through the north coast on their way between Copán and the Bay Islands, but those who stay a while invariably find themselves entranced by the unique blend of culture and natural beauty. It's no surprise the north coast has the largest contingent of expatriates in the country outside of the Bay Islands.

THE LAND

Most of the north coast is a narrow plain extending roughly 350 km from the Guatemalan border west of Omoa to Cabo Camarón east of Trujillo. Backed by the rugged Sierra de Omoa, Nombre de Diós, and Colón mountain ranges, the plain is only a few kilometers wide for most of its length, extending farther inland only along

---

NORTH COAST HIGHLIGHTS

- Touring the wetland reserves of Cuero y Salado, Punta Sal, Punta Izopo, or Laguna Guaymoreto
- Whitewater rafting on the Río Cangrejal
- Exploring the dense jungles of Parque Nacional Pico Bonito
- Beach-bumming at Tela and Trujillo
- Visiting the Garífuna villages of Triunfo de la Cruz, Miami, Tornabé, or Santa Fe
- Partying at the Feria de San Isidro, La Ceiba

the deltas of the Chamelecón, Ulúa, Lean, and Aguán Rivers, which flow north out of the highlands to the sea.

Originally much of the coast was covered by humid tropical forests, but those have long since been converted to fruit and palm plantations. The most intensive cultivation, due to the rich alluvial soils, is along the river deltas. Coastal mangrove swamps were also once extensive but have been hemmed in to a few protected areas (Punta Sal, Punta Izopo, Cuero y Salado) by the steady growth of plantations and cattle ranching.

The coast is usually swelteringly hot, with mean annual temperatures ranging from 25 to 28° C. The prevailing easterlies of the western Caribbean Sea dump an average 200 centimeters of rain annually, with a short (sometimes nonexistent) dry season from February to May and August to September. Both the amount of rain and its timing vary dramatically from year to year, and wet weather can arrive at any time.

Tropical storms and, less frequently, hurricanes are an annual ritual, most often coming in October and November and frequently causing flooding, especially in the Valle de Sula. Hurricane Mitch ripped through the north coast in October 1998, cutting off large areas by taking out bridges on the coastal highway over many rivers. Many remote Garífuna communities, especially those between La Ceiba and Trujillo, were totally isolated and had to have food brought in by emergency boats. While Mitch was exceptionally severe, storms can be expected to lash the north coast at least a couple of times each fall.

HISTORY

Pre-Columbian Residents
Archaeological and historical evidence suggests at least three indigenous groups lived on the Honduran north coast in pre-Columbian times, but because of the hot climate and lack of easily cultivated land, habitation was sparse.

The Maya are believed to have extended their influence to western Honduras around A.D.

300, and although settlements were located mostly in the highlands around Copán and near the Guatemalan border, they did farm land in the lower Valle de Sula. On the coast itself, the Maya maintained several important trading posts, the farthest east at Punta Caxinas near Trujillo. Similarly, Nahuatl traders from central Mexico had outposts on the Honduran coast as far east as Trujillo.

Although Jicaque, or Tolupan, Indians inhabited the entire north coast region from the Guatemalan border to Mosquitia, their settlements were almost all in the mountains, and they apparently ventured down to the coast only to trade.

1502 to 1860
Following Columbus' first landing on the Honduran coast near Trujillo in 1502, two decades passed before Spanish explorers returned. But when they did, they converged on the country in three opposing factions led by Gil González Dávila, Cristóbal de Olid, and Francisco de las Casas. In the midst of their power struggle, the three factions' bands of soldiers managed to establish settlements by 1525 at Puerto Caballos, now Puerto Cortés, Triunfo de la Cruz, near present-day Tela, and at Trujillo.

Deposits of alluvial gold were found in rivers near Trujillo and at the mouth of the Río Ulúa, but they were quickly spent. By the mid-16th century, Spanish attention turned toward more promising mineral deposits inland. Since gold and silver were the conquistadors' main concern, the north coast slipped into a long decline. The nascent colony was briefly ruled from Trujillo, but by the 1540s the seat of government and most colonists had moved to western Honduras.

If the lack of gold and quality agricultural land, uncomfortable heat, and danger of disease didn't scare away most colonists, the pirates who appeared in the western Caribbean by the mid-16th century certainly did. The pirates sacked the relatively unprotected towns of Trujillo and Puerto Caballos with regularity. So severe was the danger even Spanish traders lived inland and only ventured to the ports when the Spanish fleets arrived. By

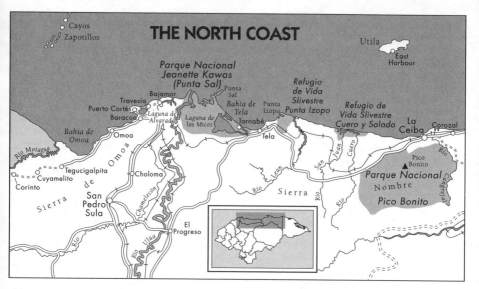

THE NORTH COAST

1643 Trujillo had been abandoned and only a small settlement remained at Omoa, near Puerto Caballos.

Having overextended themselves in their conquests, the Spanish essentially wrote off the Honduran north coast until the late 1700s, when expeditions ordered by the reformist Bourbon kings drove English settlers and pirates out of the Bay Islands and Mosquitia.

The Spanish regained control of the coast but still had no real incentive to populate it on a large scale. The first widespread settlement was undertaken by the Black Caribs, or Garífuna, who were forcibly deported to Honduras from the Caribbean island of San Vicente by the British in 1797. The Garífuna first established a community in Trujillo and then migrated up and down the coast, building villages from the edge of Mosquitia as far north and west as Belize. Apart from a few refugees from 19th-century violence elsewhere in Honduras, the north coast remained sparsely populated until North Americans and Europeans developed a taste for bananas.

The Banana Industry

The development of the modern north coast—and, some would say, of the entire country—is essentially the story of the growth of the banana industry. Two authoritative texts on the industry are Guillermo Yuscarán's *Gringos In Honduras: The Good, the Bad, and the Ugly* and *The Banana Men,* by Lester Langley and Thomas Schoonover. The historic information that follows owes much to both books.

Bananas were introduced to Central America by Spanish missionaries in the first years of colonization but were cultivated only on a small scale for local consumption. Banana exports began in the 1860s, when locally owned plantations on Roatán started to sell their fruit to passing tramp freighters, who in turn sold their loads in the United States and Europe at a tidy profit. When growers and boat captains realized the moneymaking potential of the trade, more plantations sprang up all along the north coast, particularly around La Ceiba, Tela, and Puerto Cortés.

For the first few decades, Hondurans owned and worked the banana fields, meaning local growers could sell to the highest bidder and make significant profits. By the turn of the century, however, North American exporters realized they could boost their earnings by running their own plantations and set about gaining control of as much of the Honduran north coast as possible.

This conversion of the north coast into a virtual North American colony was led by three com-

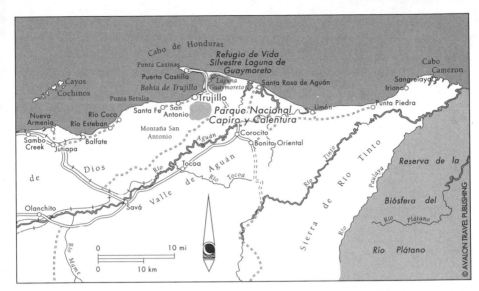

panies: United Fruit (now Chiquita), based first in Tela and now in La Lima; Cuyamel, which controlled lands west of Puerto Cortés; and Standard Fruit (now Dole, but still referred to as Standard), centered around La Ceiba.

Some land was actually purchased by the companies, but much more was awarded to them by the government in massive concessions, in return for railroad construction and jobs. Although the government was generally in favor of the concessions, wanting to modernize its backward country, the companies took no chances. To help their cause, company officials resorted to bribery and arm-twisting, even fomenting the occasional revolution to ensure a friendly, concession-generous administration.

By the second decade of the 20th century, the banana companies held almost one million acres of the country's most fertile land, were making huge profits, and unabashedly manipulated government officials to maintain the status quo. One historian writes: "If Honduras was dependent on the banana companies before 1912, it was virtually indistinguishable from them after 1912."

In the course of building their fiefdoms, the companies completely transformed the north coast. Puerto Cortés changed from a sleepy seaside village into one of the largest ports in Central America, and Tela and La Ceiba were essentially created out of nothing. The companies drained swamps to create plantations, constructed railroads between the plantations and newly built warehouses and docks, and drew migrants from across Honduras and around the world with the lure of quick money. Many of the country's first modern banks, breweries, hospitals, and a myriad of other services were built by the companies to suit their own needs.

Coastal development never strayed far from the direct interests of the banana companies, falling far short of what many Hondurans had envisioned. For example, railroads were built only between plantations and docks, and the companies preferred to pay token annual fines rather than fulfill their contractual promises to extend lines inland, connecting the coast to Tegucigalpa. To this day, the north coast has the country's only railway lines, and now that the companies use trucks, the lines have been allowed to fall into disrepair. The supposed original intention of the banana concessions, that the railroads would stimulate the Honduran economy, has long been forgotten.

The industry has fallen off steeply from the glory days between 1925 and 1939, when Honduras was the world's top producer and bananas constituted 88% of the country's exports. Still, Standard (now Dole) and United (now Chiquita, the biggest banana company in world) remain the top economic force on the north coast and have diversified into pineapple, African palm oil, and other fruit products. The two companies are still easily the largest landowners in the country, after the Honduran government, and almost all their holdings are on or near the north coast.

Since the beginning of the 20th century, the north coast has been the most dynamic economic sector of the country, and with the rise of San Pedro Sula as a major center for light industry and commerce, this trend has accelerated. Although San Pedro is not on the coast, its success is due to the short rail and highway connection to Puerto Cortés, and the city's growth has stimulated the entire north coast. In terms of population and economy, the four coastal departments comprise Honduras' fastest-growing region.

PUERTO CORTÉS AND VICINITY

INTRODUCTION

Situated on a deep natural harbor on the northwest corner of Honduras, only 60 kilometers from the industrial capital of San Pedro Sula, Puerto Cortés is perfectly located to serve as a transfer point for much of the country's trade. It handles the largest amount of boat traffic—though Puerto Castilla near Trujillo moves more total tonnage—and is considered to have one of the best port facilities in Central America. Since a duty-free zone was created in the port area in 1976, a sizable assembly industry has developed, mostly of clothing exported to the United States. More recently, international cruise ships have begun docking at Puerto Cortés for a day stop, while their tourist clients spend the day visiting the ruins at Copán. City officials have made much talk of cleaning up the docks and downtown area for the new tourists, but they've got a long way to go to make Puerto Cortés look attractive. And beware of downtown during a heavy rain, as the streets flood with regularity.

The thriving economy supports a population of 75,000. The city's annual festival day is 15 August.

History
The Spanish first settled west of present-day Puerto Cortés early in the colonial era, recognizing the value of the fine natural harbor. The first settlement was named Puerto Caballos (Port of Horses), after conquistador Gil González Dávila was caught in a fierce storm nearby in 1524 and

was forced to throw several horses overboard.

Puerto Caballos was repeatedly struck by epidemics and marauding pirates, and by the turn of the 17th century the Spanish relocated to the better-protected harbor of Omoa, to the west. Modern Puerto Cortés was established in 1870 on the other side of the bay from the old colonial port, at the terminus of a new railway line connecting San Pedro Sula to the coast.

In the late 19th century, Puerto Cortés was a favorite destination for all manner of shady characters, swindlers, and soldiers-of-fortune from the U.S. and Europe. Many were on the run from the law, as Honduras had no extradition treaties until 1912. For a time in the 1890s the Louisiana Lottery, banned in its home state, found refuge in Puerto Cortés and became one of the largest gambling concerns in the world.

Orientation and Getting Around
Although Puerto Cortés is a large city, the downtown area is compact and can easily be navigated on foot. Taxis around downtown should cost US$1, US$1.50 out to the dock where boats depart for Belize, or US$2 out to Playa El Faro. Buses all leave from within a couple of blocks of the shady *parque*. Beware of walking out on 1 Avenida at night, as muggings are common. For car drivers, the north-south "calles" are one-way streets, while the east-west "avenidas" are two-way (except for 1 Av., which runs east to west only). The state of Puerto Cortés' frequently flooded streets and the roads surrounding town are appalling—be prepared to go nowhere in a hurry while driving.

SIGHTS

It can be argued that the travel writer who once declared Puerto Cortés "the foulest blot on Central America's coastline" was overly unkind. The tropical seediness can be somewhat appealing, if one appreciates that sort of thing. But there's no doubt that the port city offers little draw for tourists.

The *parque*, punctuated by several towering Caribbean pines and few other trees and plants, is a shady, tranquil place to sit, but otherwise there's little to do in town except watch prostitutes and drunks stumble about their business on 1 Avenida. The bustling dockyards are off-limits without a special pass, though you can check them out from behind a tall fence.

Beaches

For a bit of sun and sand near town, **Playa Coca Cola** lies a couple of kilometers west of the city around the bay, a US$1.50 taxi ride or a long hot walk from downtown. Playa Coca Cola is neither clean nor particularly safe. East of down-

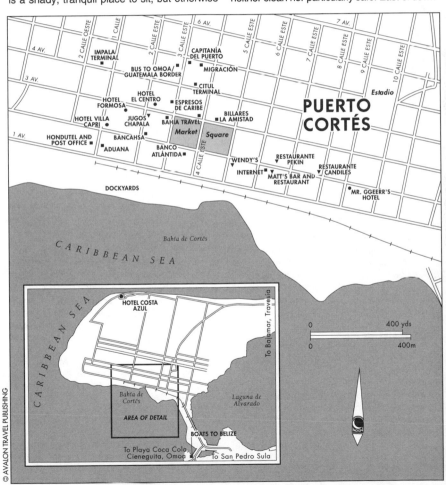

© AVALON TRAVEL PUBLISHING

town (go to the Texaco refinery, take a right and go to the end of the road) is **Playa El Faro** (Lighthouse Beach), which is not much better, though it does have a pleasingly windswept feel. Apart from the Costa Azul hotel, the only service for tourists on El Faro is Restaurante Vista Al Mar, with a small patio overlooking the beach.

Quieter and more attractive, though still nothing spectacular, is **Playa Cieneguita,** west of Playa Coca Cola and backed by three hotels and a row of private houses. Taxis to Cieneguita from Puerto Cortés cost US$4, or take the Ruta 1 bus from the corner of 2 Calle Este and 3 Avenida to the end of the line; it's a 10-minute walk up the road from there to the beach entrance. The hotels and beach at Cieneguita are usually packed on weekends with vacationers from San Pedro Sula and completely deserted during the week. All in all, unless one is pressed for time, better beaches can be found at Omoa to the west or Travesía and Bajamar to the east.

Next to the Hotel Playa at the far end of Playa Cieneguita is **Ancla Bar y Restaurante,** tel. 665-2331, with a good selection of fresh seafood at moderate prices (US$6-10 per entree, less for snacks). The owner, Manuel García, is a certified PADI scuba instructor and is fully equipped to give the open-water course in five or six days for US$200 pp. A favorite overnight trip is out to the idyllic Cayos Zapotillos, controlled by Belize but close to Honduras. Though not cheap at US$500 for four people, the trips come fully set with food, refreshments, camping and snorkeling gear, and permits for the Belize police station on the beautiful cays. Day-long fishing trips closer to Puerto Cortés with equipment and trips to look for howler monkeys in the lagoon cost US$25 pp, five person minimum.

Bajamar and Travesía
A 20-minute drive east of Puerto Cortés on the coast are the two Garífuna villages of Travesía and Bajamar, which can be reached by frequent local buses. Shortly before Travesía is the inexpensive **Hotel Fronteras del Caribe,** with minimal facilities. There are no hotels in Bajamar, but you can find a room or a space to sling a hammock by asking around.

Bajamar is the site of the annual National Garífuna Festival, normally held in late July, which draws Garífuna from Belize, Guatemala, and Honduras for a party of dancing and music.

Corozal also holds a lively party every January, with special masked dances over the course of the nine-day celebration.

ACCOMMODATIONS

Should you be unfortunate enough to have to spend the night in Puerto Cortés, you'll find at least one decent place to stay in each price range. Nicer hotels are out at Playa Cieneguita or in Omoa.

Shoestring
The best inexpensive rooms in town are at **Hotel El Centro,** on 3 Av. a half block west of the *parque,* tel. 665-1160, with no-frills rooms with fan and communal bathroom for US$5.50 s or US$8 d, or US$10 s and US$17 d for cable TV and a private bathroom.

The venerable **Hotel Formosa,** on 3 Av. between 1 and 2 Calles Este, tel. 665-0853, charges US$5.50 s or US$7 d for a basic room with a fan and private bath, US$12 d with a/c and private bath. The owners speak English.

Those with a penchant for cockroaches, drunks, and prostitutes can patronize any of several hotels on 1 Av., including the **Hotel Las Vegas.**

Budget
A few blocks east of the square is **Mr. Ggeerr's Hotel,** on 2 Av. at 9 Calle, tel. 665-0444, offering clean but somewhat claustrophobic rooms with semifunctional a/c and cable TV for US$17 s or d with one bed, US$23 for two beds. The hotel, on the second floor of a large building, has a pool table in the lobby and a bar and restaurant that aren't always open.

Moderate
Far and away the best place to stay in Puerto Cortés, a relative oasis in the dirty port town, is **Hotel Villa Capri,** at the corner of 2 Av. and 1 Calle, tel. 665-6136 or 665-6860, fax 665-6139, email: villa-capri@lemaco.hn. The converted house right near the entrance to the docks has only nine rooms renting for US$53 s, US$64 d, but each is spacious, comfortable, and equipped with hot water and a/c.

On the Beach

Mr. Ggeerr also owns **Hotel Costa Azul,** at Playa El Faro, tel. 665-2260, fax 665-2262. The large oceanfront complex, looking like a holdout from the 1950s (though certainly of a more recent vintage), has surprisingly decent if slightly threadbare rooms for US$28 s or d. The second-floor rooms have a breezy balcony. The beach in front of the hotel is nothing to rave about, but the hotel at least keeps it reasonably clean.

At Playa Cieneguita is the **Hotel Playa,** tel. 665-0453, fax 665-2287, email: hotelplaya@hotelplaya.hn, a motel-style arrangement with parking in front of the 12 wood-paneled rooms, each with a small porch, a/c, and TV. Service is very good, but the hotel is a bit pricey all in all at US$69 d during the week to US$85 d on weekends. Right next door is **Hotel Palmeras Beach,** tel. 665-3891, with seven rooms, two beds in each along with TV, a/c, and *electroducha,* US$44 for up to three people.

Past Hotel Playa is the **Club Náutico de Puerto Caballos,** tel. 665-1002, a somewhat more secluded beach hotel and restaurant with regular *cabañas* with a/c for US$32 for one double bed, or US$40 for a larger *cabaña* with a breezy second-floor patio and sitting area.

FOOD AND ENTERTAINMENT

Food

Puerto Cortés has a dearth of good low-priced food. The most popular place to eat is the new Wendy's on the *parque,* and a soon-to-open Pizza Hut will likely rival it in clientele.

The best restaurant in town is **Matt's Bar and Restaurant,** on 2 Av. between 6 and 7 Calle, tel. 665-0862, with hearty seafood entrees, including shrimp, fish fillets, and entire yellowtail or red snapper for US$6-10 per entree, and other dishes like burgers, salads, and chicken dishes for US$2.50-6. Matt's is open daily 11 a.m.-11 p.m. The owners speak English.

Also on 2 Av., a block up from Matt's on the opposite side, is **Restaurante Candiles,** offering well-prepared standard Honduran fare like *pinchos, anafres, queso fundidos,* fish dishes, steaks, and burgers in a *champa*-style building. Open daily 11 a.m.-11 p.m., with full bar service.

Travelers can find an acceptable, inexpensive plate of Honduran-Chinese at **Restaurante Pekin,** opposite Matt's on 2 Av. Este, with a large menu of different "chap sueys" in three different portion sizes. Open 9 a.m.-10 p.m. daily.

If you're after a juice or *licuado,* head for **Jugos Chapala,** opposite Hotel El Centro on 3 Av., open Mon.-Sat. 8 a.m.-10 p.m.

Entertainment

At 9 Calle and 4 Av., a few blocks east of the *parque,* is the local soccer stadium, home to **Platense,** usually a fairly competitive first division team. Tickets are always available for the weekend games, selling for US$3 sun, US$6 shade.

Should you have a perverse desire to consort with the local riff-raff, **Billiares La Amistad** on the *parque* offers beers and pool until midnight or later daily.

SERVICES

Bancahsa and Banco Atlántida in the center of town exchange dollars and travelers checks and also offer cash advances on Visa cards.

Correos and Hondutel are both on 1 Calle Oeste next to the main dock entrance. Hondutel is open 24 hours a day. Express Mail Service is available at the post office. UPS, on 2 Av. between 11 and 12 Calle, tel. 665-1427, is faster and more expensive.

Across the street from the post office and Hondutel is the **Aduana,** or Customs, open Mon.-Fri. 8 a.m.-noon and 1-4 p.m., tel. 665-0181 or 665-1209. This two-story building, filled with mini-branches of apparently all of Honduras' banks, is always a hive of bustling activity, everyone intent on getting their papers through the bureaucratic maze as quickly as possible.

PUERTO CORTÉS USEFUL TELEPHONE NUMBERS

Police: 665-0420, or dial 199
Fire Department: 665-0223, 665-0500, or dial 198
Cruz Roja Ambulance: dial 195
Hospital: 665-0562, 665-0787

A small Internet shop is open in the Plaza Marinakys building, on 2 Av. near Matt's Bar and Restaurant, open Mon.-Sat. 8 a.m.-6 p.m., US$2 for the 30-minute minimum.

The *migración* office, on 5 Av. between 3 and 4 Calle, tel. 665-0582, is open for most tourist business Mon.-Fri. 8 a.m.-noon and 1-5 p.m. There is a permanent on-call staff to deal with visiting sailors that also processes tourists coming in from Belize on the Saturday boat. Renewing tourist permits and registering after entering from Guatemala is usually quick and painless.

Two doors down is the **Capitanía del Puerto,** open Mon.-Fri. 8:30 a.m.-4:30 p.m., for dealing with any port business.

Bahia Travel Service, on 3 Av. between 2 and 3 Calle, tel. 665-2102 or 665-5803, fax 665-0218, can arrange airline tickets, rental cars, hotel rooms, and courier service, open Mon.-Sat. 8-noon and 2-6 p.m.

GETTING THERE AND AWAY

Bus

Expresos del Caribe and **Citul,** with terminals across from one another on 4 Av. Este, a block north of the *parque,* both operate frequent direct buses for the hour-long ride via Choloma to San Pedro Sula; fare is US$1 and the last bus leaves around 6 p.m. Local buses take twice as long.

Citral/Costeños runs buses via Omoa (US 20 cents) and Corinto (US$1.50), near the Guatemalan border, twice a day, usually early in the morning and around noon, from 3 Calle, half a block from the *parque.* Others going just to Omoa leave two or three times a day from the same location, the last usually in late afternoon. Buses to Bajamar and Travesía leave from next to the Citul terminal, on 2 Av. and 5 Calle Este, three buses a day for the 20-minute, US 35-cent ride, last bus at 4 p.m.

Car

The 60-km, four-lane highway between San Pedro Sula and Puerto Cortés is in good condition and takes under an hour to drive. A toll of US 15 cents is levied leaving San Pedro to Puerto Cortés, but not the other way. Side roads out to Omoa and Travesía were in extremely bad condition at last report, but passable by regular car.

Train

The only public train in Honduras runs between Puerto Cortés and Tela, a slow ride through an infrequently seen stretch of banana country. The four-hour trip in bare, often-crowded cars costs US$1. Some snacks and soft drinks are sold during the trip, and there is a stop at Baracoa, usually long enough to run into the track-side *pulpería.* The train departs Puerto Cortés Friday and Sunday at 7 a.m. The train does not depart from any official station—the best bet is to get out to the railyard near the mouth of Laguna Alvarado at 6:45 a.m. or so. Sometimes the train pulls all the way in to the center of town also.

Boat

At least two boats a week leave Puerto Cortés for Belize, from the old bridge over the mouth of the Laguna Alvarado. The old bridge, sorely abused by Hurricane Mitch, is due to be replaced, but the boats still leave from there. **Gulf Cruza,** tel. 665-1200 or 665-5556, runs a small, open boat every Monday to Big Creek, Placencia, and Belize City (US$40), all in Belize. The boat normally leaves Puerto Cortés at 10 a.m. and arrives in Belize City at 5 p.m. Gulf Cruza also has an office in Big Creek, tel. 20-24505 or 06-23236. On Tuesday a second boat reportedly sometimes goes in the late morning to Dangriga, Belize (US$35). The small *lanchas* make the two- to three-hour trip in good weather only, and be prepared to get wet regardless. Stop by one day before departure to put your name on the list.

NEAR PUERTO CORTÉS

Omoa

The sleepy fishing village of Omoa is built around a small bay 13 km west of Puerto Cortés, where the Sierra de Omoa mountains meet the Caribbean. The town itself was never a major population center, but for strategic purposes the Spanish built the largest colonial-era fort in Central America here.

Omoa's houses and shops are scattered along the two-km road between the Puerto Cortés highway and the sea. The main beach, lined with fishing boats and several small restaurants, is nothing spectacular, but it's a relaxing place to

THE GRAVEYARD OF HONDURAS: FUERTE SAN FERNANDO DE OMOA

The Caribbean coast of Honduras was sparsely populated throughout the colonial era, making it an easy target for attacks by pirates, marauding Miskito Indians, and, later, the British Navy. Although pirate assaults began just a couple of decades after the Spanish started to colonize Central America, it was not until the mid-18th century that colonial authorities made serious efforts to combat the marauders and fortify their positions on the coastline.

As early as 1685, the Spanish recognized Omoa as an ideal location for a fort—strategically situated on a deep, protected harbor between English settlements in Belize, the Bay Islands, and Mosquitia. But distractions elsewhere, a lack of funding, and bureaucratic inertia combined to delay actual construction until 1752, when royal engineer Luis Diez de Navarro arrived with a plan for a massive triangular bastion.

Work on the fort was painstakingly slow. For a start, there was no adequate stone in the area; it had to be cut and transported from as far as 150 kilometers away. Even more dire was the lack of workers; disease and heat took a brutal toll on the conscripted Indians. Omoa became known as the graveyard of Honduras among the highland Indians, and able-bodied males fled their villages when they heard that colonial officials were coming to look for workers. Eventually the Crown brought in black slaves to finish the fort.

Finally completed in 1773, the fort was an intimidating sight. Two of the three sides were 60 meters long, while the ocean-facing base measured 25 meters. The walls were six meters tall and two meters thick. The complex overflowed with 150 pieces of artillery and was surrounded by a moat. Despite its daunting appearance, the fort was never particularly successful.

A combined British-Miskito force of almost 1,000 men, led by Commodore John Luttrell, took it in 1779, just six years after construction had been completed. After that inauspicious first defeat, the fort at Omoa fell variously to Spanish royalists, Francisco Morazán's forces, and, later, Guatemalan soldiers. Easier to get into than out of, the fort was finally converted into a prison by the Honduran government in 1853.

In spite of its dismal record of defense, the fort is visually impressive, squatting ominously in the tropical heat a kilometer or so from the ocean. The Caribbean has receded in the years since its construction, leaving the fort standing amidst the fields and swamp between the Puerto Cortés highway and the beach.

Admission is US 10 cents for Central Americans and US 20 cents for all others. The fort is open Mon.-Fri. 8 a.m.-4 p.m., Sat.-Sun. 9 a.m.-5 p.m. Next to the fort is a museum with interesting descriptions (Spanish only) of the history of the colony and the construction of the fort.

SAM THE BANANA MAN

Of the many fascinating and colorful characters involved in Honduras' banana industry, few, if any, can top Sam Zemurray, better known as Sam the Banana Man. In an industry run mainly by cold-blooded bankers living in the U.S., Sam was famed throughout Honduras for traveling his plantations on a mule, speaking bad Russian-accented Spanish, and cultivating the loyalty of his workers by personally bringing Christmas presents and throwing parties.

Born Samuel Zmuri, a Bessarabian Jew, Sam immigrated to the U.S. in his youth and got his start in the banana business in Mobile, Alabama, in 1895. At the age of 18, Sam offered to buy $150 worth of ripe bananas that needed to be sold quickly. He fast cornered the market on selling "ripes" and within three years had $100,000 in the bank.

Heeding the call of the tropics, Sam headed to Puerto Cortés in 1905 as the owner of a formerly bankrupt steamship company, with United Fruit Company and a partner named Hubbard as temporary financial backers. By 1910, he made the daring move of buying 5,000 acres of land, all with borrowed money, and set up the first foreign-owned plantation in Honduras, along the Cuyamel River

southwest of Puerto Cortés. All the debt scared off both his partner and United Fruit, but Sam was happy to get rid of them anyway. Naming his new company the Cuyamel Fruit Company, Sam promptly sank even deeper into debt to acquire more land.

His small plantation could not produce enough bananas to pay off the debts quickly enough for his creditors. Sam needed more land. The usual acquisition method was to grease enough palms to ensure a large concession from the government, but conditions within Honduras made this an unlikely proposition. At the time, the U.S. government was considering taking over the country's customs receipts to cover bad debt, and it was unlikely the U.S. would look favorably on granting Sam a concession. Rather than panic, Sam decided a change of government was in order, so he organized his own revolution to install Manuel Bonilla, a personal friend and the former president of Honduras, who had himself recently been overthrown.

Sam's right-hand man in this adventure was one Lee Christmas, another larger-than-life character in the early years of the banana industry. A New Orleans railroad man who relocated to Honduras in the late 19th century, Christmas never missed a good fight, and when Sam contacted him in 1910 he was itching for a little "revolutin," as he liked to call it. Christmas, Bonilla, and Sam planned the revolt in New Orleans in December 1910, under the watchful eyes of federal agents who knew full well what was brewing and were determined to stop it. But Sam managed to dupe the agents with an unusual sleight of hand. The *Hornet*, a 160-foot ship recently bought by Sam and stuffed full of weaponry and eager mercenaries, sailed out to sea on the 20th, but as Christmas and Bonilla stayed in town the U.S. agents had no reason to stop it.

Christmas and Bonilla spent the evening in a famed New Orleans bordello, until the agents outside got tired of watching the fun and went home for the night. Whereupon Christmas declared to Bonilla, "Well, compadre, this is the first time I've ever heard of anybody going from a whorehouse to the White House. Let's be on our way!" Sam met the two on the docks with his own private yacht and ferried them out to the *Hornet,* which was waiting offshore. The drunken warriors sailed off to Honduras, which they took after a month of intermittent skirmishes.

With Bonilla safely installed in the presidency, the Banana Man received his concession.

The Cuyamel Company grew by leaps and bounds over the next two decades, making Sam a very wealthy man. In 1930, apparently succumbing to pressure from United Fruit, Sam sold Cuyamel to United for $30 million and returned to the United States. It was assumed Sam had tired of the banana business and was looking to enjoy his wealth, but that was not quite the case. Much of United's payment for Cuyamel was in the form of stock, and, unbeknownst to the company, Sam had proxies quietly buy up more shares over the years, ultimately giving him a controlling interest. By 1932, a combination of poor management and the Depression had caused stock prices to fall precipitously. Sam traveled to Boston and attended a board meeting, asking politely for an explanation.

In a condescending reference to Sam's accent, one director said, "Unfortunately, Mr. Zemurray, I can't understand a word you say." Sam reportedly looked at the directors a few seconds, muttered something under his breath, and walked out. He returned a few minutes later with all the papers demonstrating his control of the company, slapped them on the table, and said, very deliberately, "You gentlemen have been fucking up this business long enough. I'm going to straighten it out."

Thus began Sam's second coming in the banana industry. He was head of United Fruit for two decades. He quickly reorganized the management strategy of the company, handing responsibility to managers actually on the plantations rather than in U.S. boardrooms—a move fought by the Boston-based managers and cheered loudly by United Fruit workers in Central America.

The Banana Man had no compunction about manipulating local governments to suit his purposes—he is reputed to have uttered the famous quote, "In Honduras, a mule is worth more than a congressman"—but, unlike most banana men, he also actually cared for his adopted country and its people. Under his leadership, United began diversifying away from monocrop agriculture and developed other products such as pineapple, grapefruit, and African palm. Palm oil in particular has developed into a major industry in Honduras.

To help seek out more nontraditional products for Honduras and all of Central America, and to improve the region's agriculture, Sam funded the Lancetilla Botanical Research Station and the Escuela Agrícola de las Americas at Zamorano, both set up by William Popenoe. Zemurray stepped down as president of United in 1951 but just couldn't stay away from the fray. During the 1954 coup in Guatemala, which was due in large part to the interests of United Fruit, Sam directed the company's media efforts. He removed himself from the board of directors shortly thereafter, and he died in 1961.

---

spend a few hours after admiring the fort, located on the main road running between the highway and the beach. About a 45-minute walk south of the highway junction is a small waterfall in the woods—ask someone to point out the trail.

From Omoa a hiking trail winds up into the Sierra de Omoa and arrives at Parque Nacional Cusuco, above San Pedro Sula. This multi-day trek is normally done in the other direction, but Hurricane Mitch has temporarily closed off the upper stretch of the trail anyhow. The only way to get good information on the trail is to talk to the park guards at Cusuco.

Omoa celebrates its annual carnival on 30 May in honor of San Fernando.

Accommodations

Roli's & Bernie's Place, tel. 658-9082, email: RG@yaxpactours.com, is run by a Swiss traveler who rents four basic but clean rooms for US$5.50 s or US$8.50 d, with hot showers, a communal bathroom, and access to the Internet. Campers can pitch a tent for US$2 a night pp. The porch and yard at the hostel, a five-minute walk from the beach, is a friendly, easygoing spot. The owner also runs Yax Pac Tours, offering individually designed tours in Honduras and Guatemala.

On the beach, **Tatiana's,** tel. 658-9186; **Julita's,** tel. 658-9174; and **Aquí Pancha** tel. 658-9072, all have simple rooms with fans and shared bathrooms renting for US$8-10. Tatiana's is the best of the bunch.

More of a private house on the beach with guest rooms than a hotel per se, **Hotel Bahía de Omoa,** tel. 658-9076, is run by a European couple who rent three rooms with a/c and hot water for US$20-25 s or d. The owners have a boat and will organize sailing trips and excursions to the nearby Cayos Zapotillos. Reservations can be made by mail at P.O. Box 244, Puerto Cortés.

A couple of kilometers from Omoa on the highway to Puerto Cortés lies the best accommodations in the area, **Acantilados del Caribe Resort,** tel. 665-1461, fax 665-1403. The small resort is built on a private beach with a small marina and offers horseback riding, fishing tours, and other activities. The horseback riding trips, in a lush patch of tropical forest owned by the hotel in the hills behind the highway, cost US$20 pp for a three- to four-hour ride—same price for guests or non-guests. More expensive trips out to the Cayos Zapotillos can also be arranged. Each of the individual cabins at the hotel has two beds, a porch with hammocks, a/c, TV, and phone and costs US$48 s or d Mon.-Thurs., US$68 Fri.-Sun. More expensive apartments are also available.

Food and Services

Of the several beach restaurants in Omoa, **Champa Virginia** (recently being renovated) serves some of the better seafood in town for US$3-5 per plate, depending on the size of the fish. The restaurant stays open until 9 or 10 p.m., and the owners are friendly. Also with good seafood are **El Paraíso de Stanley** and **Los Cayuquitos,** both on the beach.

At the highway junction are a few *pulperías,* a burger joint, and, opposite the Texaco station, a **migración** office. The Banco de Occidente branch exchanges dollars, travelers' checks, and even Guatemalan quetzales, though Visa cardholders must go to Puerto Cortés for a cash advance.

Buses return to Puerto Cortés until 6 p.m. For those returning directly to San Pedro Sula from Omoa, ask the driver to stop at the highway junction outside of Puerto Cortés, where the direct San Pedro buses stop to fill up with passengers. The buses to and from Omoa are often tightly packed with passengers, and the horrific road makes the trip even less pleasant.

Boats From Omoa

Small, open boats run once or twice a week between Omoa and Livingston, Guatemala, usually on Tuesday and/or Thursday. The trip for the Guatemalan-based boatmen is usually already paid for, so your return ticket shouldn't cost more than US$25-30, or maybe less, depending on the boatman and your negotiating skills. Travelers need to be on the beach in the morning, on Tuesday in particular, and hope for good weather. The boats generally stay in Omoa an hour or less.

Trips to the Cayos Zapotillos can also be arranged at the beach in Omoa.

The Guatemalan Border

Formerly a long walk through the jungle, the border crossing to Puerto Barrios in Guatemala can now be accomplished by a combination of buses and truck rides taking three to five hours, depending on connections. Buses from Omoa or Puerto Cortés go as far as **Tegucigalpita,** 30 km from Omoa, where pickup trucks can be found 17 km farther up a terrible unpaved road to **Corinto,** where the Honduran immigration and customs offices are located. Ten kilometers farther, also by pickup on a bad road, is the Río Motagua bridge, with Guatemala and the settlement of **Arizona** on the far side. From here, the road is paved and in good condition to Puerto Barrios. If leaving for Guatemala, it's best to take care of exit formalities in Puerto Cortés. This route is possible by private vehicle, but high-clearance vehicles are recommended. Don't even try it in the rainy season, as four river crossings are required.

A quicker route is to take a boat to Livingston, Guatemala, which leaves Omoa Tuesday and Friday at about noon when the weather is good. The very wet trip costs US$27.

Cayos Zapotillos

Tucked into the Golfo de Amatique are the Cayos Zapotillos, a collection of beautiful patches of sand, palm trees, and reef whose ownership is unclear. The water around the cays is exceptionally clear and the reef is in good condition and teeming with marine life. The cays—Hunting Cay, Lime Cay, Nicholas Cay, Raggedy Cay, French Cay, and two others—are claimed by Honduras, Belize, and Guatemala. Belize has recently erected a police station on Hunting Cay, the largest of the islands, so it seems to have taken charge of the situation for the moment. All visitors must register at the station, show a *zarpe* paper, an international permit for a boat, available at the port captain's office in Omoa or Puerto Cortés, and pay US$10 for each visitor. Everyone must have a passport.

No facilities exist on the cays, so bring camping gear. Manuel García at the Anclas Restaurante on Playa Cienegüita runs overnight trips out for US$500 for four people, food and equipment included. Less expensive trips could also be negotiated with fishermen in Omoa. Keep in mind the *zarpe* paper costs around US$40, plus the US$10 pp cost, and gas is expensive. One boatman in Omoa quoted a price of US$350 for an overnight trip, or US$500 to drop a group off and return to get them several days later. Better deals are almost certainly available.

TELA AND VICINITY

INTRODUCTION

Honduras tourism officials, eyeing the wealthy beach resorts in Mexico with envy, tirelessly promote Tela Bay as Honduras' Cancún-to-be. Certainly all the elements appear to be in place: mile upon mile of pristine beaches, sleepy Garífuna villages, and three nearby natural reserves—Punta Sal, Lancetilla, and Punta Izopo—chock-full of exotic plants and wild animals. For the time being, however, the town remains a sleepy beachfront backwater, without even direct bus service from San Pedro Sula.

Reactions to present-day undeveloped Tela vary wildly. Some visitors are charmed by the town's relaxed seediness, while others take a look at the lowlife contingent hanging around the beachfront discos and hastily pack their bags. There's no doubt the downtown beach area is not pristine, but it would be a shame to let this put travelers off from seeing the tranquil Garífuna beach villages and natural beauty outside of town around the bay, especially the spectacular Parque Nacional Punta Sal.

Originally Tela (pop. 77,100) was built as a United Fruit Company town in the early years of the 20th century, but the banana business is now less important to the local economy since the Tela Railroad Company—United's Honduras division, also called Chiquita—moved its headquarters to La Lima, near San Pedro Sula, in 1965. Currently the town earns most of its money from African palm plantations, cattle ranching, and tourism.

One of the principal reasons tourists have kept clear of Tela is its well-deserved reputation for street crime. All sorts of young punks, known as *mareros,* hang around the beaches and streets of Tela, ready to relieve unsuspecting tourists of their possessions at knife point. Most muggings are limited to more remote stretches of beach outside of town, or on the streets near the beach, the market, and by the railroad tracks after dark. Visitors are advised to not wander around late at night, and to stick to the beach in front of Villa Telamar for sunbathing and swimming. The local business association has talked for years about hiring private tourist police, but no action had been taken at last check.

Though still fledgling, the Tela Chamber of Commerce actually has its own website in English for tourists: www.tela-honduras.com.

Orientation and Getting Around

A couple of kilometers off the El Progreso-La Ceiba highway, downtown Tela is a compact area bounded by the ocean, the Río Tela, and the railroad tracks. The square is two blocks from the beach. The Río Tela divides the main downtown area from "New Tela," a residential area built by the Tela Railroad Company for its U.S. officials. Apart from a couple of bars and restaurants, the only reason to go to New Tela is to enjoy the beaches in front of Villas Telamar. Taxis from anywhere around downtown to New Tela or out to the highway should cost US 50 cents pp.

SIGHTS

First stop for most visitors, the town's sweeping **beaches** are wide and fairly clean. The beach in front of the discos and restaurants, however, does not lend itself to peaceful sunbathing—there are just too many people wandering around, and leaving your possessions while taking a dip is an invitation to theft. A better spot is the beach in front of Villas Telamar, in New Tela past the river and the municipal dock, clean and constantly patrolled by the resort's guards. East and west of town, beware of the isolated beaches, which are known for muggings.

Dedicated to the Black Carib culture of Honduras' north coast is the two-story **Museo Garí-**

funa, tel. 448-2856. The museum was grievously mistreated by Hurricane Mitch but has been completely rebuilt and is open to the public Mon.-Sat. 9 a.m.-10 p.m..

Worth taking a look at on the way to Telamar beach, if only for historical value, is the ruined hulk of the **Tela Railroad Company headquarters,** near the dock in New Tela. It was formerly the command center for the United Fruit empire in Honduras, which is now based in La Lima, near San Pedro Sula.

Tour Operators

A couple of doors off the town square, **Garífuna Tours,** tel. 448-1069, fax 448-2904, offers popular, frequently recommended day trips to Punta Sal for US$17 pp, including a bilingual guide and boat transport. Sign up the day before the trip, and be prepared to get wet while riding in the boat. Tours to Punta Izopo (US$16) and to Laguna de los Micos and the Garífuna village of Miami (US$19) are also available. The company rents mountain bikes for US$4 half-day or US$6 full-day and has shuttle service to San Pedro Sula for US$13, La Ceiba for US$14, and Copán for US$30. For more information, contact www.garifuna.hn, or email: garifuna@hondutel.hn. There is now a second office at Villas Telamar, tel. 448-2196, ext. 702.

ACCOMMODATIONS

Shoestring

Boarding House Sara's near the beach is popular with the backpacker crowd, but the rooms are dirty and the street outside none too savory at night. Check your room first—some are quite dismal while others aren't too bad. Bring your own toilet paper for the shared bathrooms. This is the cheapest place near the beach, charging US$2.25 pp.

A block away from Sara's, right on the beach, is **Hotel Olas del Mar.** It's also a dive, but some rooms are large and breezy, with an ocean-facing balcony, for US$3.50 s or US$5.50 d, less for a longer stay. Be sure to get a room on the second floor facing the ocean, and if possible at the far end from the noisy (on the weekend) discos next door.

Probably the nicest of the bottom-end places is **Hotel Playa,** in an 80-year-old wooden house

clearly showing its years. The rooms, going for US$2.75 pp, are dimly lit, but the mattresses are good and the owners are a friendly bunch.

A significant step up is **Hotel Brisas del Mar,** tel. 448-2486, right near the market, a new place with good-sized rooms, new furniture, and spotless bathrooms, and even a small outdoor terrace around the second-story rooms. Rooms rent for US$7 d with a fan and private bathroom, US$8.50 with TV, or US$10 with a/c and TV.

About the best low-priced deal in town, and frequently full of travelers as a result, is **Hotel Marazul,** tel. 448-2313. It's a block from the beach, with clean and quiet rooms with fan and private bath for US$5 s or US$7 d, with a small

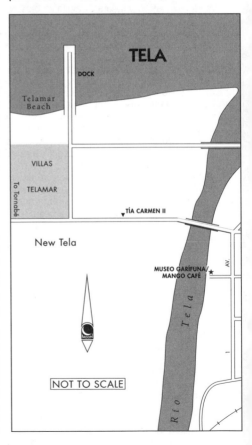

communal kitchen area.

At the other end of the same block is **Hotel Bella Vista,** tel. 448-1064, owned by Hotel Sherwood, with decent, modern rooms with fan and private bath for US$8 s or US$10 d.

A quiet place to stay in town, near the post office four blocks from the beach, is **Hotel Posada del Sol,** tel. 448-2111, run by an elderly couple who charges US$6 s or US$8.50 d for a simple room with fan and private bathroom around a small garden area. A couple of tiny singles with shared bathroom rent for US$4.50.

One cheapie on a quiet block near the bus station is **Hotel Preluna,** charging US$2 pp in a rickety old wooden house with shared bathroom.

Also near the bus is **Hotelito Mi Porvenir,** tel. 448-1459, with cell-like but clean and decent rooms for US$3.50 s with shared bathroom or US$5 s with private bathroom.

Budget

The venerable **Hotel Tela,** tel. 448-2150, two blocks west of the square, offers breezy, tile-floored rooms with high ceilings and ceiling fans for US$8 s or US$15 d, more with hot water. The hotel dining room is spacious and elegant.

Inexpensive

Clearly the realization of a personal vision of paradise is **Hotel Maya Vista,** tel./fax 448-1497,

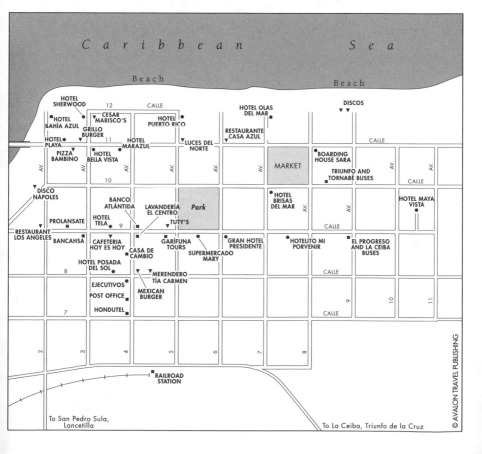

email: mayavista@mail.com, a massive pink structure perched high on a hill just east of the bus station, offering breathtaking views across the bay. Built by French-Canadian owner Pierre Couture, who it seems will keep adding on until the laws of physics rebel, the hotel currently has six double rooms for US$20-50, depending on the size of the room and whether it has kitchen facilities. Pierre and his wife are wonderful hosts, and the hotel restaurant offers excellent food. It's more like staying in a private house than in a hotel. Be sure to make reservations as they frequently have long-term guests.

On the square, the modern **Gran Hotel Presidente,** tel. 448-2821, fax 448-2992, has comfortable though small rooms with TV, hot water, telephones, and a/c for US$27 d, or US$40 d for a suite with a living room and refrigerator. Room service is available from the decent hotel cafeteria.

For those looking for self-contained apartments, **Ejecutivos,** tel./fax 448-2047, features eight spacious rooms with kitchens, a/c, and color TVs in a modern, gleaming white building a block from the post office; US$30 d.

Beach Hotels

Catering mainly to wealthy San Pedro Sula residents who flood in during the weekend are four hotels on the beach west of the discos. One favorite is **Hotel Cesar Mariscos,** tel./fax 448-2083, right on the beach above the superb seafood restaurant of the same name, with 10 lovely tile-floored rooms with hot water, cable TV, and a/c for US$31 d, with discounts available for rooms without a/c or for longer stays.

Next door is **Hotel Sherwood,** tel. 448-1065 or 448-1064, with elegant wood-trimmed rooms, some with private, ocean-facing balconies, for US$38-43 d. Owner Sherwood is a friendly character who speaks English and is happy to chat with tourists.

Less expensive, but not as nice as the above two, are **Hotel Bahía Azul,** tel. 448-2381, at the mouth of the Río Tela, charging US$23 d, and the large **Hotel Puerto Rico,** tel. 448-2413, with un-

exceptional rooms for US$19 d, or nicer ones with breezy, ocean-facing porches for US$27 d.

A sort of tropical suburb, certainly unlike any other resort on the Honduran coast, **Villas Telamar,** tel. 448-2196 or 448-2197, fax 448-2984, in U.S. (800) 742-4276, was built by the Tela Railroad Company in the 1920s to house its U.S. executives. The freestanding wooden houses, each with hardwood floors, wicker and mahogany furniture, a fully equipped kitchen, and perfectly maintained lawn, are located in a well-patrolled complex along a beautiful beach just west of the Río Tela. Facilities include a pool (which can be used by non-guests for US$3), a nine-hole golf course, tennis courts, sauna, jacuzzi, banquet and conference center, horseback riding, boating, and fishing. Villas go for US$110-350 a night with two to seven double beds, and single rooms and suites are also available for US$60-80. Some houses are in much better condition than others, so it's best to look at what's available before checking in.

FOOD

Inexpensive

Merendero Tía Carmen serves locally famed *baleadas* stuffed with various fixings, as well as tacos, simple meals, and fresh juices in a cafeteria a block south of the square. The first batch of *baleadas* usually sells out by 9 a.m. at the latest, but a second batch is made around 4 p.m. A second Tía Carmen location across the bridge in New Tela has *baleadas* all day until 10 or 11 p.m.

Opposite Garífuna Tours next to the square, **Tuty's** serves excellent *licuados* and juices, and decent breakfasts as well, Mon.-Sat. 6 a.m.-2 p.m. Be prepared to wait; service is terrible.

A popular spot for inexpensive meals and beers downtown is **Cafetería Hoy es Hoy,** on 9 Calle between 3 and 4 Avenidas, open daily 8 a.m.-10 p.m. For inexpensive burgers, *tortas,* and tacos, try **Mexican Burger** near the post office. **Grillos Burger,** near the beach on 11

Calle, cooks up a tasty burger.

Pizza Bambino, also on 11 Calle near the bridge, makes an acceptable and very inexpensive pizza, two-for-one on Tuesday nights.

Restaurant Los Angeles, 9 Calle between 1 and 2 Avenidas, serves up decent chop suey and other Chinese dishes daily for lunch and dinner.

Midrange

Luces del Norte, between the square and the beach, is a favorite among foreign visitors. Service can be painfully slow but it's worth the wait for the divine curried conch soup, lobster, grilled snapper, and very good breakfasts. The restaurant has a large second-hand book exchange. Open daily 7 a.m.-10 p.m.

Also serving a sublime conch soup and other seafood dishes is **Cesar Mariscos,** tel. 448-2083, with open-air seating facing the beach; open daily 7 a.m.-10 p.m.

If you've overdosed on seafood and are looking for a change of pace, try the expatriate-run **Restaurante Casa Azul,** 11 Calle and 6 Av., tel. 448-1443, for well-prepared Italian food. The small menu includes lasagna, fettuccini, garlic bread, and a wine selection (though the wines don't hold up well in the tropical heat) for US$3-5 per plate. The restaurant at the **Hotel Bahía Azul** serves a good breakfast at a reasonable price on the ocean-facing porch, but the other meals are not as good a value.

A bit on the expensive side, but not unreasonable considering the excellent quality, is **Hotel Maya Vista,** with seafood dishes (the lobster is superb) as well as a few non-seafood choices like lasagna or salads, for US$4-8 per entree. The breezy patio restaurant makes a relaxing spot to enjoy a leisurely dinner and a few drinks.

Right next to the Museo Garífuna on the banks of the Río Tela, **Mango Restaurante** whips up Garífuna dishes such as *tapado,* a goulash of fish, cassava, and coconut, and healthy-sized fresh fish. Open Mon.-Sat. 4-10 p.m.

ENTERTAINMENT

Tela is second only to La Ceiba for nightlife on the north coast. A cluster of discos on the beach on the east side of town are the center of the action, with large crowds meandering back and forth

between the dance halls until daybreak on weekends. The crowds can get violent, with shootings and knifings not uncommon, although mostly the violence stems from drunken brawls over girlfriends and is not aimed at foreign visitors. Expect to be propositioned by prostitutes and persistent drug dealers. A better (i.e. safer) bet for foreigners is **Disco Roy,** a block west of Hondutel on 7 Calle, considered to have the best dancing in Tela. **Villas Telamar** has a more upscale bar/disco on the beach, with occasional live bands. Across from the bus station is a nameless **pool hall** with relatively well-maintained tables and beer for sale. The bar and outside tables at **Casa Azul** make a relaxed place for a quiet drink.

INFORMATION AND SERVICES

Bancahsa and Banco Atlántida, both downtown, change traveler's checks and cash Mon.-Fri. and Saturday mornings. For quicker, hassle-free exchange, Casa de Cambio Teleña is open Mon.-Fri. 8-11:45 a.m. and 1-4:30 p.m., Saturday 8 a.m.-noon.

Hondutel, open daily 7 a.m.-9 p.m., fax 448-2942, and Correos, open Mon.-Fri. 8 a.m.-4 p.m., Saturday 8 a.m.-noon, are on the same block two blocks southwest of the square.

One block west of the square is **Lavandería El Centro,** open Mon.-Sat.; US$2 to wash and dry one load of laundry. **Supermercado Mary** on the square has an array of groceries and is open Mon.-Sat. 8 a.m.-8 p.m., Sunday 8 a.m.-noon.

Should you need a travel agent in Tela, contact **Agencia de Viajes Galaxia,** on 9 Calle just east of the bridge to New Tela, tel. 448-2152 or 448-2082.

Prolansate, tel./fax 448-2042, is a local environmental organization that helps manage nearby natural protected areas—a mission that

---

TELA USEFUL TELEPHONE NUMBERS

Police: 448-2079, or dial 199
Fire Department: 448-2350, or dial 198
Cruz Roja Ambulance: 448-2121, or dial 195
Hospital Rotario: 448-2073, 448-2051

does not always endear its staff to ranchers, developers, and land-hungry *campesinos*. The Prolansate office is downtown next to the cinema; open Mon.-Fri. 7 a.m.-noon and 2-5 p.m., Saturday until noon. Simple maps and some tourist information are available.

Internet

The best Internet access in town at last check is at **Orion Computer,** half a block off the park on 5 Av. in Edificio Abudayeh, tel. 448-1654, charging US$3.50 per hour on four relatively fast computers. The Garífuna Tours, tel. 448-1069, and the Mango Cafe, tel. 448-2856, also have Internet service.

GETTING THERE AND AWAY

Bus

Surprisingly, there are no direct buses from Tela to San Pedro Sula. Travelers must either take a bus to El Progreso from the downtown terminal and transfer to a San Pedro bus, or take a taxi out to the highway at Tío Jaime's Restaurant and flag down one of the La Ceiba or Trujillo buses going to San Pedro (US$3), which pass every hour or so. Those going to Tegucigalpa

can catch buses from La Ceiba with **Cristina,** tel. 448-2520, tickets sold at Tío Jaime's.

Those going via El Progreso would do well to wait for the twice-daily direct bus, which takes an hour to make the trip (US$1, Mon.-Fri. 7:30 a.m. and 8:45 a.m.; Saturday and Sunday 3 p.m. and 4:15 p.m.). The local bus to El Progreso (US 50 cents, every hour or so) takes at least twice as long. Buses to La Ceiba, none direct, take two to three hours (US$1, every half-hour or so until 6 p.m.).

Car

The 68-km, two-lane road to El Progreso through African palm and banana plantations is in good shape, and the additional 28 km to San Pedro Sula is a smooth four-lane highway. To the east, the 101-km, two-lane road to La Ceiba is in fair shape, but don't go very fast unless you want to break an axle slamming into a lurking pothole.

Train

The train to Puerto Cortés (four to five hours, US$1), which travels through coastal banana plantations, leaves from the decrepit train station several blocks south of the square Friday and Sunday at 1:45 p.m.

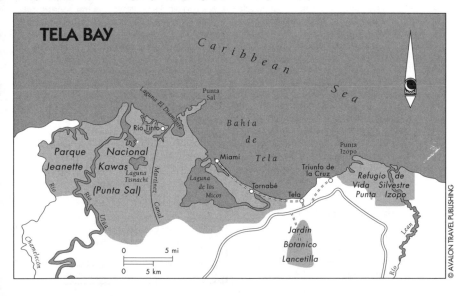

WEST OF TELA

Tornabé

Seven km west of Tela via a rough dirt road is the quiet Garífuna village of Tornabé. Lined along a dirt road parallel to the beach, it's a perfect place to relax and let the sun and waves lull you into a trance. Local fishermen will take visitors out to Punta Sal for a negotiable fee, either dropping them off for the day or acting as guides. Trips into Laguna de los Micos can also be arranged.

Near the center of town the Garífuna couple **Chola and Tritio** manage basic candlelit cabins, US$3 s or d, with home-cooked seafood and beers for sale.

The Last Resort, tel. 230-0491 or 996-3318, has the potential to be a superbly tranquil, low-key beach getaway, but at last check the cabins were a bit unkempt. The owners say a renovation is planned—worth looking into as the attractive cabins, each with a/c and hot water, are perfectly situated in a quiet part of town at the edge of the beach. The cabins rent for US$40 s or d. The hotel can arrange excursions to Punta Sal, Miama, or Laguna de los Micos. A few years ago this was a great place to stay, and hopefully it will be again soon.

Buses between Tornabé and Tela (US 30 cents) depart several times a day, the last in either direction usually at 5 p.m. Buses leave Tela from near the market. Trucks leave Tornabé heading west to Miami a couple of times a day (none on Sunday) at irregular hours, charging US 20 cents for the half-hour drive.

Miami

The idyllic Garífuna village of Miami rests on a narrow sand spit, backed by Laguna de los Micos and fronted by the Caribbean. Unlike Tornabé or Triunfo, Miami is almost totally undeveloped, with most families still living in the traditional Garífuna thatched huts. Facilities are minimal—if you want to spend more than the day here ask around for food and a room or a place to sling a hammock. One room with space for a hammock is usually available next to the only store in Miami.

Motorized and paddle canoes can be rented to explore the lagoon. More territory can be covered with the motor, but it scares wildlife away. Locals say camping on the inland side of the lagoon is possible, which would be excellent for early morning birdwatching.

Small boats are also available to take visitors to Punta Sal. For the budget camper, the absolute cheapest way to get out to Punta Sal from Tela is to get to Miami by bus and truck, then walk eight km on the beach out to the point.

Parque Nacional Jeanette Kawas (Punta Sal)

One of the most biologically diverse natural reserves in Honduras, the 782 square km of protected territory around Punta Sal includes humid tropical forest, mangrove swamp, coastal lagoons, rivers and canals, rocky and sandy coastline, coral reef, and ocean. Almost 500 types of plants have been identified within the park, as well as 232 animal species, including endangered marine turtles, manatees, jaguars, ocelots *(tigrillos),* caymans, white-faced and howler monkeys, wild pigs, pelicans, and toucans.

Most tours arrive by boat at the base of the point on the east side, offering visitors a chance to enjoy a beautiful beach before taking a half-hour hike over the point to the cove on the far side. This steep trail is a good opportunity to see the abundant and colorful birdlife, as well as noisy troops of howler and white-faced monkeys.

Apart from the rugged and beautiful 176-meter-high Punta Sal, most of the reserve's territory is flat, encompassing the Los Micos, Diamante, Río Tinto, and Tisnachí lagoons, the Martínez and Chambers canals, and the Río Ulúa. The Río Chamelecón forms the western boundary of the park. Traveling up these waterways by boat provides excellent opportunities for viewing wildlife—have binoculars and mosquito repellent at the ready.

No facilities are available in the park apart from one small *champa* on the point, which sells meals to tour groups. Camping on the beach is allowed and would be a superb way to spend a few days; come prepared with food, fresh water, and a tent or hammock. Although tour operators like to tout the great snorkeling, there's little in the way of interesting reef, and visibility is limited in the choppy water. Better to just enjoy the wonderful swimming and sunbathing.

A nominal entrance fee of US$1 is collected by a park *vigilante,* and the money goes to help the activities of Prolansate, a non-governmental

JEANETTE KAWAS

The national park at Punta Sal is named for Jeanette Kawas, former president of Prolansate, an environmental organization dedicated to protecting Punta Sal, Punta Izopo, Lancetilla, and Texiguat. In Honduras, as Kawas discovered, defending the environment is more than signing petitions and sending out leaflets like in the U.S. or Western Europe. It's a matter of life and death.

Several different groups and individuals—Honduran Colonel Mario "El Tigre" Amaya and an African palm cooperative run by the National Campesino Union, among others—have claimed ownership of Punta Sal land. But Kawas forcefully advocated the creation of a national park at Punta Sal. Although the effort was ultimately successful—national park status was granted in November 1994—she paid the price for her activism. Kawas was killed in April 1995, and her murder remains unsolved.

environmental organization working at Punta Sal. The Prolansate office, which has more information on the park, is in Tela on 9 Calle between 2 and 3 Av., tel./fax 448-2042.

EAST AND SOUTH OF TELA

Triunfo de la Cruz
Another Garífuna town similar to Tornabé, Triunfo is eight km east of Tela. The beach in town,

though lined by fishing boats and not kept conspicuously clean, is an excellent quiet place to sunbathe and swim in the warm waters. Locals are not bothered by visitors, and though they may not seem very friendly at first, neither do they hassle the few backpackers who come in search of a little peace and sun. Still, try not to sleep on the beach in Triunfo, as tourists have reported being robbed at gunpoint. The beaches are safe during the day, but at night it's best to stick to one of the hotels.

Tourism officials are reportedly helping organize a group of locals to perform a traditional *dugu* dance for visitors. Triunfo's annual festival is held on 3 May, the Day of the Cross.

Roughly in the center of town, on the beach, are a cluster of simple thatched cabanas run by **Panchi** that rent for US$3.50 d, and next door are concrete ones managed by **Margarito Colón** that rent for US$6 d. A friendly watchman keeps an eye on things so visitors can relax without fear of theft. Others in town rent out rooms for similar prices.

Jorge's Restaurant, just east of the hotels, serves up some of the meatiest and most succulent fried snapper this author has ever tasted, as well as a hearty, veggie-filled conch stew. Locals will come around the hotels to see if anyone wants breakfast cooked for them.

Several buses daily run to and from Tela (US 30 cents). The buses leave Tela from near the market, the last returning to Tela in mid-afternoon. A taxi to Triunfo costs about US$3, and sometimes one that has just dropped off passengers in Triunfo will offer a ride back to Tela for US 50 cents. Formerly, the two- to three-hour walk to Tela via the small village of **La Ensenada** was a pleasant way to return from Triunfo, but recently several muggings have been reported, so its best to take the bus or a car. Near La Ensenada is the site of Cristóbal de Olid's first landing on Honduras, marking the beginning of Spanish colonization. Triunfo was originally established as a settlement by Olid, but the colonists soon moved elsewhere and the area was not permanently occupied until the Garífuna moved there from Trujillo in the early 1800s.

Jardín Botánico Lancetilla
A small miracle of botanical science five km south of Tela, Lancetilla was first set up in 1925

by plant biologist William Popenoe of United Fruit Company, who is also responsible for starting the Escuela de Sciencias Agrícolas in the Valle de Zamorano, near Tegucigalpa. Initially Lancetilla was designed as a research station for testing different varieties of bananas, but Popenoe's endless inquisitiveness soon led to experiments with fruits and plants from all over the world. One of Honduras' most profitable agricultural products, the African palm, *Elaeis guineensis,* was first introduced by Popenoe in Lancetilla, and he did further work with coffee, cinchona (the source of quinine, for years the only treatment for malaria), cacao, rubber, mango, and a myriad of other plants.

Although Popenoe left Lancetilla in 1941 to go to Zamorano, United Fruit continued the work he began until 1974, when Lancetilla was turned over to the Honduran government. The garden has since become part of the Escuela de Sciencias Forestales and is still a fully functioning research station.

Lancetilla boasts one of the most preeminent collections of fruit trees, flowering trees, hardwoods, palm trees, bamboo, and other assorted medicinal and poisonous plants in Latin America. Named after the indigenous lancetilla palm, *Astrocaryum standleyanum,* Lancetilla contains 764 varieties of plants in 636 species, 392 genera, and 105 families on a mere 78 hectares in the William Popenoe Arboretum, and another 60 species of fruit and hardwood trees in the experimental research station.

The Lancetilla Biological Reserve, in the surrounding hillsides, contains both primary and secondary tropical humid and subtropical humid forest. Getting into the reserve requires some effort, as there are no trails designed for tourists. For the US$5 entrance fee, visitors are given an hour-long guided tour of a section of the arboretum and are then free to wander the paths for the rest of the day. Many plants are labeled to help identification. Labels are color-coded as follows: green indicates hardwood, red indicates fruit, yellow indicates ornamental, and most important, black indicates poisonous. Feel free to sample fallen fruit, but be sure not to try anything from a black-labeled tree! Keep an eye out for the mangosteen trees, *Garcinia mangostana,* a Malaysian native considered by some connoisseurs to produce the finest fruit on the plan-

et. Mosquitoes are often fierce in the arboretum, so come prepared.

Just under two km from the visitors' center, past groves of palms and bamboo, are two swimming holes along the Río Lancetilla. Though unspectacular, they're a good way to cool off after a hot walk.

You can arrange guides and purchase maps of the arboretum and a self-guided tour of one of the trails at the large, wooden visitors' center. There's also a cafeteria here, a pleasant place to write a letter or wait for a guide while sipping a cold drink.

Lancetilla is open Mon.-Fri. 7:30 a.m.-3 p.m., Sat.-Sun. 8 a.m.-3 p.m. Bunk beds are available in a hostel for US$4 a bed, but these are often taken by the many research and student groups who visit the gardens. Check with Prolansate in Tela, tel. 448-2042, to make reservations.

The highway turnoff to Lancetilla is just south of the power station outside of Tela. You could take an El Progreso bus, get off at the junction, and walk the 45 minutes into the gardens, or take a taxi from town for US$3.50. Another good option is to rent a bike at Garífuna Tours and pedal out at your own pace. The entrance fee is collected at a *caseta* at the highway junction, where there is also a small nursery selling fruit and palm-tree seedlings for US$1-2.

Refugio de Vida Silvestre Punta Izopo

Visible around the bay to the east of Triunfo is Punta Izopo, Tela Bay's second largest protected area, covering 112 square km, of which about half is a buffer zone and half is a supposedly untouchable nuclear zone. This refuge is much less frequently visited than Punta Sal but has similar ecosystems and wildlife; the swamps and waterways stretching into the jungle south of the point are superb for bird and animal watching.

Inside the reserve's boundaries are the small Río Plátano (not to be confused with the river of same name in Mosquitia) and Río Hicaque, and the larger Río Lean on the point's eastern side, as well as kilometers of swamps, lagoons, and estuaries. Several small settlements are also located inside the boundaries of the reserve, including Hicaque, Las Palmas, Coloradito, and the intimidatingly named Salsipuedes (Get Out If You Can). Near the base of Punta Izopo investors had planned a massive tourist development, but the project was on hold at last notice.

The easiest access to Punta Izopo is with a tour operator such as Garífuna Tours in Tela. Trips normally start by driving in on a dirt road east from Triunfo to the Río Plátano, where you put the boats in. A low-budget option is to hunt around Triunfo for a local willing to rent a dory (US$7 a day would be a reasonable amount for a two-person wooden boat with oars) and paddle out to the point with a companion. Don't try it alone, as it's a lot of work to fight the waves. Once at the point you can hang out on the beach or walk around the point (beware the hordes of sand flies), or cross the low sandbar into the Río Plátano or Hicaque and paddle up the waterways. Plastic sea kayaks would be ideal, but none are currently available for rent in Tela.

margay

LA CEIBA AND VICINITY

INTRODUCTION

The largest city on the north coast, with a population of just over 100,000 and growing, La Ceiba is not particularly attractive on first glance, but those who give it a chance may find themselves charmed. The beaches are dirty, there is no architecture of interest, and it's almost always steaming hot, but La Ceiba has a certain carefree Caribbean joie de vivre that has earned it the nickname "Honduras' girlfriend."

The most overt expression of this spirit is the unsurpassed nightlife and dancing scene centered on a strip of discos right along the beach, where you can boogie until all hours practically every night of the week. There's no doubt about it—ceibeños know how to party. As the saying goes, "Tegucigalpa piensa, San Pedro trabaja, y La Ceiba divierta" ("Tegucigalpa thinks, San Pedro works, and La Ceiba has fun"). The town's good times culminate in the annual Feria de San Isidro, or Carnaval, a weeklong bash of dancing and music held in May.

La Ceiba is a convenient base to explore nearby nature refuges such as Pico Bonito, the Cuero y Salado wetlands, and the rapid-filled Río Cangrejal, as well as the nearby beach towns of Corozal and Sambo Creek. It's also an inevitable stop-off point for travelers on their way to the Bay Islands, Trujillo, or Mosquitia, and it's a good place to take care of any business that needs attending to while on the road.

History
The area around La Ceiba was first settled by a few Garífuna families from Trujillo who built a village on the west side of the estuary in 1810. They were followed by Olancho immigrants fleeing violence in their homeland in the 1820s. One of these olanchanos, Manuel Hernández, built his house near a massive ceiba tree, which became the town's informal gathering place. The tree was cut down in 1917 to make way for the customs building, but the name stuck.

In the late 19th century, La Ceiba was in the midst of the booming banana industry. The first banana plantations on the mainland were planted near the mouth of the Río Cangrejal, and others soon followed in the vicinity. But the population of La Ceiba was still only about 2,000 when the Vaccaro brothers of New Orleans arrived in 1899, scouting for banana lands. They were awarded a concession at Porvenir, just west of La Ceiba, and quickly built a railroad track to transport their fruit to La Ceiba, where it could be shipped north. By 1905 the Vaccaros had moved their company headquarters to La Ceiba and began transforming the town.

The company offices and housing for American employees were built in what came to be known as the Mazapan district, unsubtly surrounded by high cyclone fencing. The Vaccaros—who by 1926 had named their operation the Standard Fruit and Steamship Company—built the city dock, managed the town port, supplied the city's electric power, set up the first bank, built the D'Antoni Hospital, and even brewed the first version of Salvavida, one of Honduras' most popular beers.

Standard's business quickly expanded to the Trujillo region and into the rich Aguán Valley, in the process attracting workers from across the globe and turning La Ceiba into one of the north coast's great cultural melting pots. Garífuna, Honduran campesinos, Jamaicans, Cayman Islanders, North Americans, Arabs, Italians, Spaniards, French, and Cubans, to name only the most prominent, all lived side by side in La Ceiba, and their mark can still be seen on the city today.

Standard Fruit—now Dole—is still La Ceiba's largest employer, although it has long since diversified into pineapple, African palm oil, and a myriad of other agricultural products. Most of its produce is now shipped out of Puerto Castilla, near Trujillo; the dock in La Ceiba is no longer used.

Orientation and Getting Around
Although La Ceiba is the largest city on the north coast, visitors usually spend most of their time in a relatively small area bounded by the square, the sea, and the strip of discos and beach to the east of the estuary, which divides the down-

town area from the La Isla and La Barra neighborhoods. Taxis within this area should only cost US 75 cents pp, but expect drivers to stop and pick up other passengers. The main drag in town is Av. San Isidro, running from the ocean south past the square all the way to the Burger King on 22 Calle.

SIGHTS AND RECREATION

La Ceiba is not bursting with tourist attractions. The town's beaches are downright filthy and not very safe, which is unfortunate since they could be attractive if cleaned up. The only halfway decent bit of sand and sea is **La Barra Beach,** east of downtown, between the Hotel Partenon and the mouth of the Río Cangrejal (hence the beach's name—"barra" is used in Honduras to designate a river mouth). As La Ceiba currently makes no effort to deal with its sewage beyond putting it out in the ocean raw, swimming in the beaches around town is ill-advised.

The downtown *parque* is nothing special, but take a look at the crocodile and turtle pen on the south side, where a dozen or so reptiles sit immobile for hours sunning themselves on their concrete pedestals, looking like statues. The nearby main commercial district, centered on Av. Atlántida and Av. 14 de Julio, between 4 and 6 Calles, is a lively and colorful scene. The central market is a 1931-vintage, weather-beaten wooden building at 6 Calle and Av. Atlántida.

Anyone with an entomological inclination should be sure not to miss the **Museo de Mariposas,** tel. 442-2874, email: rlehman@caribe. hn, displaying over 7,000 butterflies, of which 400 are from other countries. Included are examples of the two largest butterflies in the world, as well as over 1,000 other insects. Apart from

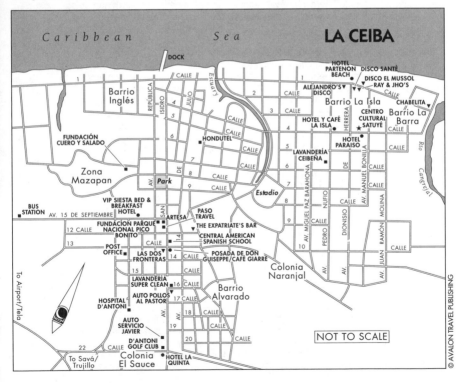

LA CEIBA'S OFFICIAL FIESTA:
LA FERIA DE SAN ISIDRO

In a town notorious for partying, la Feria de San Isidro is *the* party in La Ceiba—a several-day bash culminating in a blowout Saturday night that attracts some 200,000 revelers from across Honduras and the Caribbean. The country may have other national celebrations, but the Feria—held in mid-May—is Honduras' time to cut loose.

According to La Ceiba legend, three Spanish immigrants started the Feria. The Spaniards—supposedly named Norquer, Artuche, and Pallares—arrived in the village in 1846, bringing with them the tradition of honoring San Isidro Labrador, a patron saint of *campesinos.* According to custom they held a party in honor of the saint. The annual fiesta became a popular event with the Garífuna, who, although hardly *campesinos* themselves, are always ready for a reason to get out and dance. It quickly became a local institution. The Feria was declared La Ceiba's official annual fiesta in 1886, and in 1929 the tradition of parades and floats was added.

On the final Saturday of the Feria, floats bearing scantily clad women proceed down Av. San Isidro beginning in the late afternoon, headed by the Queen of the Carnaval. After the parade has passed, well-known Honduran and Central American bands on stages lined up and down the length of the avenue crank up, and the music keeps going until morning.

Many visitors, expecting to see crazed dancing in the streets, come away from Carnaval a bit disappointed. The only ones dancing, usually, are the fans at the rock stage who have a grand time head-banging and slam dancing, and the occasional group of gringos in front of one of the salsa or *punta* stages.

The secret, for those who really want to dance, is to enjoy the stage music on the avenue until midnight or 1 a.m. and then head out to the discos on 1 Calle. Normally packed anyway on weekends, the discos are bursting at the seams during the Feria

and should not be missed by the serious partier. When out on the streets during the Feria, beware of pickpockets in the crowds.

Saturday may be the official biggest party, but many locals insist the "real" bash is on Friday night in Barrio La Isla, with bands on 4 Calle on the east side of the estuary from downtown. Other mini-ferias take place the previous Sunday in Sitramacsa and Miramar colonias, Monday in Barrio Bellavista, Tuesday in Barrio Alvarado, Wednesday in Colonia Alhambra, and Thursday in Colonia El Sauce. La Ceiba on the Sunday following Carnaval is usually utterly and completely dead, with most people rousing themselves only if there's a decent soccer match on TV.

VINCE MURPHY

the displays are videos in English and Spanish, posters, maps, and all the gear needed to become an amateur butterfly collector, including traps and ultraviolet lights. The museum is in Colonia El Sauce just south of the golf course, Segunda Etapa, Casa G-12. Take the main entrance to El Sauce and turn left on the last paved road, and look for the museum two and a half blocks up on the right side. US$1 entrance for adults, US 75 cents for students. Open Mon.-Sat. 8 a.m.-noon and 2-5 p.m.; closed Wednesday afternoons.

At the southern end of Av. San Isidro is the **D'Antoni Golf Club,** tel. 443-0175, for the confirmed links addict only. Two rounds on the flat, nine-hole course cost US$14 for non-members; club rental is an additional US$7.50. The course is open daily 6 a.m.-4 p.m. The tennis courts, pool, restaurant, and bar are for members and their guests only.

Tour Operators

Several outfits run rafting trips on the Río Cangrejal just outside of La Ceiba, considered to have some of the best white water rafting in Central America. Trips are also available to other nearby destinations, such as Parque Nacional Pico Bonito.

Ríos Honduras, tel. 995-6925, website: www.roatan.com, runs very well-respected, safety-conscious rafting and kayaking trips on the Cangrejal, as well as longer trips to Olancho, Yoro, and elsewhere. A one-day raft trip on the Cangrejal, with lunch and transportation included, costs US$75, while the same trip including transportation from the Bay Islands costs

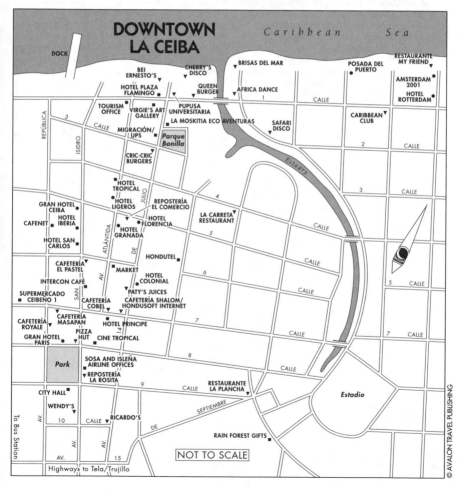

DOWNTOWN LA CEIBA

Caribbean Sea

DOCK

BEI ERNESTO'S
HOTEL PLAZA FLAMINGO
CHERRY'S DISCO
QUEEN BURGER
BRISAS DEL MAR
POSADA DEL PUERTO
RESTAURANTE MY FRIEND
AMSTERDAM 2001
HOTEL ROTTERDAM

TOURISM OFFICE
VIRGIE'S ART GALLERY
PUPUSA UNIVERSITARIA
LA MOSKITIA ECO AVENTURAS
AFRICA DANCE
SAFARI DISCO
CARIBBEAN CLUB

MIGRACIÓN/ LUPS
Parque Bonilla

REPÚBLICA
ISIDRO
CALLE

CRIC-CRIC BURGERS

HOTEL TROPICAL
HOTEL LIGEROS
REPOSTERÍA EL COMERCIO
LA CARRETA RESTAURANT

GRAN HOTEL CEIBA
CAFENET
HOTEL IBERIA
HOTEL FLORENCIA
HOTEL GRANADA

HOTEL SAN CARLOS

HONDUTEL

CAFETERÍA EL PASTEL
MARKET
HOTEL COLONIAL
INTERCON CAFÉ
PATY'S JUICES
SUPERMERCADO CEIBEÑO 1
CAFETERÍA COBEL
CAFETERÍA SHALOM/ HONDUSOFT INTERNET

CAFETERÍA ROYALE
CAFETERÍA MASAPAN
HOTEL PRINCIPE
GRAN HOTEL PARIS
PIZZA HUT
CINE TROPICAL

Park
SOSA AND ISLEÑA AIRLINE OFFICES
REPOSTERÍA LA ROSITA

CITY HALL
WENDY'S
RICARDO'S
RESTAURANTE LA PLANCHA

Estadio

SEPTIEMBRE

RAIN FOREST GIFTS

NOT TO SCALE

To Bus Station
Highways to Tela/Trujillo

Estuary

US$125. Kayak trips with boat rental and guide cost US$90 a day. Multi-day trips to the Río Sico or the Río Mame are also available.

Omega Tours, tel. 440-0334, email: omega-tours@laceiba.com, is a small outfit run by expat German and Swiss rafters who work out of a small lodge in the Río Cangrejal Valley, about 10 km upriver from the bridge at La Ceiba. Rafting costs US$50-70 pp for the day, everything included, and lodging costs an additional US$5-9 pp in the comfortable though simple lodge, with food and kitchen available. Backpackers could consider a very good package deal: transportation to the lodge, dinner, a bed, breakfast, and your choice of a half-day rafting, hiking, or horseback-riding tour in the Río Cangrejal Valley, all for US$50.

La Moskitia Eco-Aventuras, in a rambling old wooden house on Parque Bonilla in La Ceiba, tel. 442-0104, is run by veteran Honduras explorer Jorge Salaverri. Jorge offers rafting trips on the Cangrejal with his capable and amiable assistant boatmen for US$50 pp, and he will also organize just about any kind of trip you'd like to Pico Bonito, Cuero y Salado, or his famed trips to the Mosquitia jungles. The office, which is also Jorge's house, is open Mon.-Fri. 8 a.m.-noon or 1:30-5 p.m., but information on trips is available whenever Jorge or one of his employees is around. For more information, see the website: www.honduras.com/moskitia; or contact Eco-Aventuras by email: moskitia@laceiba.com.

Offering the best rates for rafting on the Río Cangrejal is **Jungle River Rafting,** located in Barrio La Isla on Av. Miguel Paz Barahona, tel. 440-1268, email: jungle@laceiba.com. The company charges US$35 pp for a rafting trip and can also arrange one-day trips to nearby a nearby lagoon or into Pico Bonito.

ACCOMMODATIONS

La Ceiba has dozens of hotels in all price ranges. With a little effort, visitors should have no trouble finding a room that suits exactly their taste and budget. During Carnaval week hotel owners raise prices considerably, sometimes as much as double, and rooms fill up fast. Usually it's possible to get a room as late as Wednesday during Carnaval week, but after that don't count on it. Many of the cheap hotels fill up on regular week-

ends, with people in town from the islands, Mosquitia, and elsewhere in Honduras.

Shoestring

Most inexpensive hotels are found between the square and the ocean, on or between Avenidas San Isidro, Atlántida, and 14 de Julio. For the real *lempira*-pincher, there are a string of not-recommended dives on Av. República, parallel to the railroad tracks, including Hotel Arias, Hotel Los Angeles, Hotel Mar Azul, and others.

The most acceptable low-budget deal, and often full of backpackers and Hondurans as a result, is **Hotel San Carlos,** in the middle of town on Av. San Isidro between 5 and 6 Calles, above a busy *comedor*. Lots of interesting characters populate the funky rooms, which go for US$4 s and US$5.50 d with private bath and fan. Some rooms are much better than others, but there usually aren't many choices available.

For a few more *lempira*, the popular **Hotel Tropical,** on Av. Atlántida between 4 and 5 Calles, tel. 442-2565, offers marginally cleaner and airier rooms, some with TV and a/c, for US$6 s or US$7.50 d with private bath and fans, more for the rooms with a/c and TV. The two-story cement-and-plaster building is often noisily filled with Bay Islanders and people in from Mosquitia, but there are usually a couple of rooms open each day.

Next door to the Tropical is **Hotel Ligeros,** tel. 443-0181, with similar rooms for slightly more money, and down a block toward the market on the opposite side of the street is **Hotel Granada,** tel. 443-2451, with relatively clean rooms around a dingy interior courtyard for US$5 s or US$8 d with private bath. Check the mattresses first, as some are terrible.

A favorite among backpackers for its location on the beach near the discos is **Amsterdam 2001,** a ramshackle little dive run by an old Dutch sailor. Beds in the communal room go for US$3. Behind the Amsterdam is the tidier two-story **Hotel Rotterdam,** tel. 440-0321, run by the same family but with nicer rooms with private bath and fans for US$7.50 s or US$9 d.

In case the above hotels are full, two other acceptable options are **Hotel Principe,** in the center of town on 7 Calle, tel. 443-0516, charging US$8 s or d for a modest, tile-floored rooms with private bath and fan, more with a/c and TV;

and **Hotel Florencia,** tel. 443-0679, with 15 functional, tile-floored rooms in the second floor of a corner building, near the market on Av. 14 de Julio, charging US$8 s or d with fan only, more with a/c and TV.

Budget

Two downtown hotels right next to each other on Av. San Isidro between 5 and 6 Calles, popular with middle-class Hondurans and tourists alike, are **Hotel Iberia,** tel. 443-0401, and **Gran Hotel Ceiba,** tel./fax 443-2737 or 443-0876. Each offers rooms with a/c, cable TV, hot water, and phones for US$17 s or d, US$20 d with two beds. The Iberia is the nicer of the two, often packed with Bay Islanders over the weekend. Both have parking lots.

Useful for those arriving late or departing early by bus is **Gran Hotel Libano,** tel. 441-2540, behind the bus station. It's not a bad deal at US$11 s or US$15 d with TV and a/c.

Rooms in Barrio La Isla

If you want to stay in the mainly Garífuna neighborhood of La Isla, east of downtown on the other side of the estuary, a decent option is **Hotel y Café La Isla,** on 4 Calle, tel. 443-2835, charging US$6 s and US$7 d for a room with fan and private bath.

A more upscale option—in fact a bit out of place on the dirt roads of La Isla—is **Hotel Paraíso,** a couple of blocks farther east on 4 Calle, tel. 443-3535, with clean rooms equipped with cable, a/c, and phones in a modern building with a parking lot and cafeteria. Rooms cost US$18 s or US$25 d.

Inexpensive

About the nicest place on La Ceiba's shorefront is **Posada del Puerto,** tel. 440-0030, a quiet, reasonably priced bed-and-breakfast charging US$20 pp. Each of the wood-roofed, tile-floored rooms has a/c, fan and TV. The bar is a relaxed place to have a few drinks whether you're staying in the hotel or not.

Farther up the shore toward the Río Cangrejal is the much more imposing **Hotel Partenon Beach,** tel. 443-1176, a large complex with three buildings and 110 rooms stretched across a large part of La Barra beach east of downtown. Prices range from US$23-38 d, depending on

the room's location and whether it has a fan or a/c. Facilities include a pool, outdoor bar, and screened-in patio restaurant.

A quiet, homey hotel a few blocks south of the square is **Posada de Don Giuseppe,** on Av. San Isidro at 13 Calle, tel./fax 442-2812, email: pgiusepe@caribe.hn. The 10 large rooms feature a/c, cable TV, and private baths for US$19 s or US$25 d. Less expensive rooms with use of the hallway bathroom cost US$16 s or US$22 d.

On 1 Calle at the corner of Av. 14 de Julio, **Hotel Plaza Flamingo,** tel. 443-2738, has 19 new, modern rooms with a/c, hot water, and cable TV for US$22 s or d, US$33 with king-sized bed.

First opened in 1912, the **Hotel Gran Paris** on the square is a La Ceiba landmark, and although it may have seen better days it is still a social center for the city, patronized by wealthy Hondurans and foreigners alike. It has 65 rooms, equipped with a/c, TV, and phones, and is set around an interior courtyard with a pool and bar. Rates run US$28 s, US$31 d, or US$50 suite. Downstairs is a restaurant and mellow patio bar next to a swimming pool, which non-guests may use for a fee. The restaurant has decent breakfasts and sandwiches.

A better value for the price downtown, but not well located in the market district, is **Hotel Colonial,** on Av. 14 de Julio between 6 and 7 Calles, tel. 443-1953, fax 43-1955. Classy but understated, the Colonial has 50 rooms with all the amenities for US$34 d, with a cafeteria, patio bar, parking lot, and a sauna (as if it's not hot enough outside).

Moderate

Hotel La Quinta, at the south end of Av. San Isidro, tel. 443-0223 or 443-0224, fax 443-0226, email: laquinta@psinet.hn, is the plushest spot in town, with 110 rooms spread out over a large area interspersed with grassy patios, two pools, and even a few slot machines. Rooms range US$40-90, depending on size and location. Inside is Maxim's Restaurant, serving excellent seafood and steaks for US$7-10 per plate and sporting an extensive wine selection.

The small and efficiently managed **VIP Siesta Bed and Breakfast Hotel,** south of downtown on Blvd. 15 de Septiembre, tel. 443-0968 or

443-6970, fax 443-0974, is a favorite with business travelers, offering modern, spacious, and tastefully decorated rooms for US$35 s, US$42 d, or US$47 t, breakfast included. The management can arrange a car and English-speaking driver on request.

Ecolodge

Fully deserving a category all by itself is the new **Lodge at Pico Bonito,** a taste of what tourist development can look like if done well. Nestled up against the emerald-green flanks of the Pico Bonito range are 22 wood and stone cabins, each with louvered wood windows and an overhead fan. Six rooms are in individual cabins, and the others are in eight two-room cabins. The location is really superlative—hundreds of species of birds as well as occasional troops of monkeys and other animals frequently venture down from Pico Bonito to sample the fruit trees around the lodge, making it a fine location for wildlife watching. Nearby and reached by trail is the Río Coloradito, a steep, narrow river pouring down a narrow, jungle-clad gorge. Just below the lodge is a new butterfly farm, worth a several-hour visit by itself. The lodge is reached by the highway from La Ceiba to Tela, turning off to the left (south) at the village of El Pino on a dirt road three kilometers up toward the mountain. Rooms are US$95 s or d a day ($125 in the Dec.-March high season), including transportation and daily activities. Meals are extra. Reservations can be made in the US with Terra Firma Adventures, tel. (888) 428-0221 (in the US and Canada) or (954) 572-1902, directly with the hotel at tel. 440-0388, or via the website www.picobonito.com.

FOOD

Eateries in La Ceiba consist of beer and burger joints or cafeterias, although a few better restaurants keep the discerning palate satisfied.

Cafeterias

For excellent breakfasts, *baleadas, pastelitos, platos del día* (daily specials), fresh juices, and other assorted goodies, **Cafetería El Pastel** is hard to beat. On the corner of Av. San Isidro and 6 Calle, with doors open to both streets, this is a great place to relax with a coffee and

ease into the day. With similar food and prices, though much more crowded (possibly because of the air-conditioning), is **Cafetería Cobel** on 7 Calle between Av. Atlántida and Av. 14 de Julio, open Mon.-Sat. 6 a.m.-6 p.m.

Around the corner from the Hotel Gran Paris on Av. República is **Cafetería Royale,** with quite a solid and inexpensive breakfast buffet, and average lunches and dinners. Open 6 a.m.-9 p.m. daily. **Cafetería Masapan,** on 7 Calle right behind the Hotel Gran Paris, is an extremely popular, cavernous buffet restaurant open 24 hours a day. The extensive buffet always has a lot of low-priced choices, including a few vegetarian plates.

A most unusual and welcome find on the ground floor of a mini-mall on 7 Calle between Av. Atlántida and Av. 14 de Julio is the Israeli-run **Cafetería Shalom,** with very tasty and inexpensive falafel, shawarma, chicken, *baleadas,* and a hearty, idiosyncratic *tamale,* steamed cabbage stuffed with chicken. Open daily 7 a.m.-7 p.m.

Bakeries and Juices

Repostería El Comercio on 5 Calle near Hotel Florencia, is a good spot near many hotels for a cup of coffee, sweet bread, or inexpensive breakfast. Open Mon.-Sat. 7 a.m.-7 p.m., Sunday until noon.

Facing the *parque* on Av. San Isidro is **Repostería Rosita,** open Mon.-Sat. 7 a.m.-6 p.m., with snacks and coffee.

Paty's Juices, with two locations, one on Av. 14 de Julio between 6 and 7 Calles and the second on 8 Calle a few blocks east of the *parque,* has *licuados* and fresh juices. Open Mon.-Sat. 7 a.m.-10 p.m., Sunday 7 a.m.-1 p.m.

Burgers, Chicken, and Snacks

Cric-Cric Burgers on Parque Bonilla cooks up a mean pepper steak sandwich, burgers, french fries, and other munchies and is a good place to people-watch if you can stand the full-volume music. Open Sun.-Thurs. 8 a.m.-11 p.m., Friday and Saturday 8 a.m.-1 a.m. **Queen's Burger** is similar, on 1 Av. just west of the *estero,* open 8 a.m.-3 a.m., burgers US$1.75-3, beers US 75 cents.

For well-prepared Mexican snacks like *carnitas* and tacos, as well as sandwiches and burgers, try **Las Dos Fronteras** on the corner of 13

Calle and Av. San Isidro, open Mon.-Sat. 8 a.m.-3 p.m. and 5-10 p.m., Sunday 5-10 p.m. Delivery available—call 443-0411.

Pupusa Universitaria, on 1 Av. right next to Queen's Burger, open until 11 p.m. daily, has *pupusas,* that ever-present Salvadoran snack food, a sort of fried tortilla stuffed with cheese and meat, as well as tacos.

A savory and plump piece of smoked chicken with a few tortillas and *salsa chimol* or *tajadas* will set you back US$2.25 at **Auto Pollos Al Pastor,** on Av. San Isidro at 16 Calle, open daily noon-9 p.m.

Pollitos La Cumbre near the highway turnoff toward Savá and Trujillo is open 24 hours, great for that late-night craving. The chicken, burgers, and *pinchos* run US$1.75-3.

Seafood

Chabelita, in a new building on 1 Calle past the Hotel Partenon, just short of the Río Cangrejal, tel. 440-0027, has some of the better seafood in town, though you may die of hunger before the food arrives. Don't go in a hurry and you'll enjoy yourself. Flavorful conch soup, fried snapper, and monster shrimp are served at reasonable prices (US$7 per entree). Open Tues.-Sun. 11 a.m.-10 p.m.

Restaurant My Friend, just in front of the Amsterdam 2001 hotel on the beach in La Isla, has a variety of different-sized fish to choose from, as well as shrimp, ceviche, and other dishes, served in a breezy patio restaurant. Open daily 11 a.m.-past midnight.

International

With little argument the best place to eat in town is **The Expatriate's Bar,** a favorite haunt, as the name suggests, of many foreign residents living in La Ceiba, and with good reason. The menu, including hearty, American-style burritos, barbecued chicken, stuffed baked potatoes, and *quesadillas* with chicken and guacamole, is of excellent quality and in hearty portions, not cheap but a good value. The large thatched-roof bar and patio is on the second story of a building on 12 Calle, two blocks east of Av. San Isidro. The Canadian owner is a cigar aficionado and keeps a selection of Honduran *puros* for sale at the bar. Doors open at 4 p.m., earlier during the U.S. football season; closed Tuesday and Wednesday.

Newly opened is the Italian-style **Café Giarre,** at the corner of Av. San Isidro and 13 Calle, in the same building as the Posada de Don Giuseppe, tel. 442-2812. Diners can sit out on the sidewalk or in the creatively decorated interior rooms. The steaks (US$7.50) are decent though unexceptional, but the different pasta dishes (US$4-6) are a better value. Open Mon.-Sat. 11 a.m.-11 p.m.

Bei Ernesto's, down on the waterfront behind Plaza Flamingo, is a bar/restaurant with a few dishes inspired by its German owner, including *frikadelle kartoffelsalat,* a ground meat dish, as well as seafood, burgers, and a full bar. Open 9 a.m.-10 p.m. or later on weekends.

A perennial favorite among foreigners for reliable pizza, lasagna, salad bar, and air-conditioning is **Pizza Hut** on the square, open daily until 10 p.m. In early 2000 a new **Wendy's** opened on Av. San Isidro, half a block south of the *parque,* which immediately rivaled Pizza Hut's popularity.

Honduran

Low-priced but unusually tasty *típica* food can be found at **Ray and Jho's.** The small patio restaurant, without a sign, is on 1 Calle in La Isla, on the south side of the street opposite Hotel Partenon. It's got a well-cooked pork chop, chicken, conch chowder, and fish for US$3-4 a plate. Open Tues.-Sun. 11:30 a.m.-11 p.m.

One of the better downtown restaurants is **La Carreta,** 4 Calle two blocks east of Av. 14 de Julio, tel. 443-0111, specializing in steaks but also serving decent seafood for US$5-10 per meal. Open daily 11:30 a.m.-2 p.m. and 5-11 p.m.

La Plancha, just off 9 Calle by the Esso gas station, near the stadium, tel. 443-2304, serves good-quality steaks, *pinchos,* and other hearty Honduran standards at US$5-9 per entree in a two-story converted house. Open daily 11 a.m.-2 p.m. and 5-11 p.m.

The classiest restaurant in town, along with Maxim's at the La Quinta Hotel, is **Ricardo's,** on Av. 14 de Julio at 10 Calle, tel. 443-0468. The atmosphere is upscale but not overly stuffy, with casual but neat attire recommended. The seafood and steaks are both excellent, and the conch soup is particularly good. Pastas and vegetarian dishes are available. Entrees cost US$7-20, and reservations are accepted. Open Mon.-Sat. 11 a.m.-1:30 p.m. and 5:30-10 p.m.

Groceries

Super Ceibeño supermarket has two branches in town, #1 (larger and better stocked) on 4 Calle just off Av. República, and #2 on 6 Calle near the market. Both are open Mon.-Sat. 7:30 a.m.-7 p.m., Sunday 7:30 a.m.-noon.

ENTERTAINMENT

Discos

As the party capital of Honduras, La Ceiba boasts a roaring nightlife, mainly centered around the discos on 1 Calle east of the estuary, the so-called *zona viva,* or live zone. Foreigners, mainly men, have been known to get addicted to the scene, spending days or weeks on end drinking, dancing, chasing local women, and consuming the odd illicit substance until all hours night after night.

The only slow nights are Monday and Tuesday, and even then the discos are open until at least midnight. On weekends the strip is quite an adventure, with large crowds in all the discos and milling around on the street until daybreak. The odd shooting or stabbing is not unheard of, and fistfights are considered just good fun. Generally, unless you do something stupid like try to pick up someone else's date, none of the violence is directed at foreigners. The crowd is totally mixed—*ladinos,* Garífuna, Bay Islanders, Miskito Indians, and gringos all enjoy themselves shoulder to shoulder.

One musical twist sure to amuse visiting foreigners who are expecting to hear only the hot rhythms of salsa, merengue, and *punta,* is the popularity of country and western music on the north coast. Don't be surprised to walk into a disco and see couples doing a slow two-step to the latest Garth Brooks hit.

Warning: While La Ceiba is not as dangerous as Tela for street crime, the area on 1 Calle around the discos, and in particular near Parque Bonilla, are not places to go wandering at night. If you do go out dancing, watch it on the way back to your hotel. Walk in groups and stick to the main avenues on the way home. Also, foreign women may be more relaxed if they go with a male companion or a couple of female friends. It's not the wisest plan for a female traveler to hit the discos alone.

Considered the most upscale (read: expensive and safe) of Ceiba's clubs is **El Mussol,** just east of Hotel Partenon, also on the beach side. The club is open daily starting at 7 p.m., women enter free on Thursday (US$1.75 for men), and everybody pays US$4.50 on Friday and Saturday. Open until dawn on weekends.

Also more upscale than most is **Alejandro's,** a green concrete block sitting by itself on the south side of 1 Av. in La Isla, just before the Hotel Partenon. A block farther east, across from the hotel, is the thatched-hut **Santé. Safari,** on 2 Calle right on the estuary, is a long-established disco with several small rooms, playing a good mix of country, techno, and Latino music. **Cherry's,** on the shore behind Queen's Burger, is favored by a younger crowd and considered unsafe.

Garífuna/*Punta* Clubs

Africa Dance, just east of the *estero* bridge, open Friday-Sunday only, plays live *punta* music to the mostly Garífuna crowd between 10 p.m. and midnight, and disco music from midnight until closing. US$1.50 cover.

Caribbean Club, on the south side of 1 Calle a couple of blocks east of the *estero,* is a Garífuna dance hall with almost no *ladinos* in sight, although no one seems to mind the occasional gringo patron. Occasionally, live music is featured. On 4 Calle in La Isla is **Centro Cultural Satuyé,** a Garífuna cultural center that also frequently hosts music and dance.

Bars

If the disco scene sounds a bit too energetic, but you'd still like to go out for a few drinks, you could go to the **Expatriate's Bar,** on 12 Calle, two blocks east of Av. San Isidro. The bar TV is invariably showing the sporting event of the moment. Down by the shorefront try **Brisas del Mar,** a restaurant/bar in a two-story *champa,* popular with some expats for inexpensive drinks and U.S.-southern-style cooking. Open early for breakfast until after midnight every day. **Bei Ernesto's,** behind the Hotel Plaza Flamingo, is also an expat hangout, particularly for Europeans.

Soccer

Two local first division teams are Victoria and Vida, the former generally much more successful than the latter. Vida fans are known for their perennial meager hopes, invariably dashed at the end of the season to the resignation of the long-suffering supporters. *Vida sufrido,* as the saying goes in La Ceiba.

Both teams play at the municipal stadium, on the east side of the *estero.* Tickets, easily acquired the day of the game, cost US$1.75-9, depending on the seat location.

Movies
Cine Tropical, a half-block east of the **parque** on 8 Calle, has two movies showing twice nightly for US$2.

INFORMATION AND SERVICES

Exchange
Several banks downtown will change dollars and traveler's checks, including Bancahsa, Banco Atlántida, and Banco de Occidente. The latter also receives Western Union wires. Credomatic, on Av. San Isidro between 5 and 6 Calles, tel. 443-3330, advances cash on Visa and Master-Card accounts with no commission, open Mon.-Fri. 9 a.m.-5:30 p.m., Saturday 9 a.m.-noon.

Communications
Correos is on Av. Morazán between 13 and 14 Calles, several blocks southwest of the square, open Mon.-Fri. 8 a.m.-4 p.m., Saturday 8 a.m.-noon. Express Mail Service, tel. 442-0030, is available. UPS is in Edificio Recomar next to Parque Bonilla, adjacent to the Migración office, tel. 440-1024.

Hondutel, one block east of Avenida 14 de Julio between 5 and 6 Calles (look for the orange tower), is open 24 hours a day. Faxes are sent and received 8 a.m.-4 p.m. only.

Internet
Intercon Cafe, on the second floor of the Plaza del Sol shopping center on Av. San Isidro, two blocks north of the square, charges US$1.30 for the 20-minute minimum, by the minute after that. Open Mon.-Sat. 8 a.m.-8 p.m., Sunday 9 a.m.-7 p.m.

Around the corner on 7 Calle, also on the second floor of a mini-mall, is **Hondusoft Internet Cafe,** tel. 443-4152, the best-known of the town's three shops. Hondusoft charges US$2 for 30

LA CEIBA USEFUL TELEPHONE NUMBERS

Police: 441-0795, or dial 199
Fire Department: 442-2695, or dial 198
Cruz Roja Ambulance: 433-0707, or dial 195
Hospital D'Antoni: 443-0593, 443-2264

---

minutes and is open Mon.-Fri. 8 a.m.-8 p.m., Saturday 8 a.m.-6 p.m.

A third choice is **Cafenet,** on Av. República, three blocks north of the *parque* heading toward the old dock, tel. 441-0548. The fee is US$1.75 for the 30-minute minimum. Open Mon.-Sat. 8 a.m.-8 p.m., Sunday 9 a.m.-7 p.m.

Immigration
The *migración* office is in Edificio Recomar, in front of Parque Bonilla on the second floor, tel. 442-0638, open Mon.-Fri. 8 a.m.-noon and 2-4:30 p.m..

Laundry
Run by an English-speaking owner who spent some time in the U.S., **Lavamatic Ceibeña,** on Av. Pedro Nufio between 5 and 6 Calles in Barrio La Isla, not far from downtown, tel. 443-0246, has American-style self-service washers and dryers. Open daily 7 a.m.-10 p.m., US$2 for a wash and dry with soap.

Nearby, on the west side of the soccer stadium, is **Wash & Dry** (no phone), open Mon.-Sat. 8 a.m.-noon and 1-5 p.m., 10 lbs. washed and dried for US$3.25. South of the square toward the highway is **Lavandería Super Clean,** on 16 Calle just off Av. San Isidro, tel. 443-2418; open Mon.-Fri. 8 a.m.-noon and 1:30 p.m.-5:30 p.m.; Saturday 8 a.m.-noon; US$2.50 for a 10 lb. minimum.

Travel Agent
For airline tickets and other travel information, try **Paso Travel Service,** on Av. San Isidro between 11 and 12 Calles, tel. 443-3186, tel./fax 443-1990. Some English is spoken.

Spanish School
A new Spanish school has opened in La Ceiba, **Central American Spanish School,** on Av.

San Isidro between 12 and 13 Calles, tel. 440-1707, email: cass@laceiba.com. The bright, motivated small staff offers classes for US$220 per week for four hours a day of classes Mon.-Fri., as well as a home-stay with a local family. Classes without the home-stay runs US$170 per week. At least once a week classes are held outside of the classroom at a nearby destination like Pico Bonito or Sambo Creek. The same company also plans to open a school in Utila. More information is available at www. worldwide.edu/honduras/css/index.html.

Information
To its credit, the **Consejo Municipal de Turismo,** at 1 Calle between Av. San Isidro and Av. Atlántida, is the only municipal tourist office this travel writer has seen in many months of traveling Honduras. The information offered is limited, but the staff can answer some questions and provide a small map. Open Mon.-Fri. 8 a.m.-4 p.m., Saturday 8-11:30 a.m.
Mopawi, an organization working in Mosquitia, has an office on Av. República half a block south of the docks on the west side of the railroad tracks, tel. 443-0553. Little general information is available here, but sometimes workers know of boats leaving for Mosquitia.

Car Rental
Agencies include **Toyota,** at the airport, tel. 443-4047, fax 443-0642, or in town at the end of Av. San Isidro, tel. 443-1976 or 443-1975; **Maya,** at La Quinta Hotel, tel. 443-3071, fax 443-0226; and **Molinari,** at Hotel Gran Paris, tel./fax 443-0055. Most charge around US$50 a day for the least expensive vehicle with insurance and 200 km free mileage.

Shopping
Virgie's Art Gallery, on 1 Calle, tel. 440-0666, is run by well-known Honduran artist Virginia Castillo and has a tasteful selection of hand-painted cards, printed fabrics, interestingly designed T-shirts, and other good-quality handicrafts.
Near the stadium on 9 Calle is **The Rain Forest,** tel. 443-2917, owned by an American family who live in the same house as the shop, selling Honduran wood carvings, paintings, music instruments, masks from Guatemala, ceramics from El Salvador, and a large English-language

used book swap. Open Mon.-Sat. 9 a.m.-noon and 2-5:30 p.m.
Souvenir Artesa, on 11 Calle between Av. San Isidro and Av. República, has a fair collection of wood carvings, ceramics, paintings, T-shirts, and other handicrafts.

GETTING THERE AND AWAY

Because of its strategic location in the center of the north coast, La Ceiba is a major transportation hub for the Bay Islands, the Mosquitia, and other towns and villages on Honduras' Caribbean coast.

Air
As elsewhere in Honduras, all domestic airlines offer the same government-mandated ticket prices. Most planes are of the twin-propeller, dozen-seat, unpressurized variety. Arrive one hour before flight departure. At the airport are a small restaurant and a couple of snack stand/gift shops, one of which usually sells international magazines.
Golosón International Airport is 12 km from downtown La Ceiba on the highway toward Tela. Airport taxis parked at the terminal charge US$7.50 to town for one or two people, or US$2.75 pp for more. If you don't have much baggage and want to save a couple of bucks, you can also walk out to the highway and flag down a passing cab for US$3 to the *parque* or a downtown hotel.
Isleña Airlines has offices downtown on the square, tel. 443-0179 or 443-2344, open Mon.-Fri. 7 a.m.-5 p.m., Saturday 7-11 a.m., and at

SAMPLE ONE-WAY AIRFARES FROM LA CEIBA

Brus Laguna	US$48
Guanaja	US$36
Palacios	US$39
Puerto Lempira	US$58
Roatán	US$17
San Pedro Sula	US$36
Tegucigalpa	US$35
Trujillo	US$26
Utila	US$17

the airport. Isleña flies several times daily to Roatán, Tegucigalpa, and San Pedro Sula, and flies daily except Sunday to Utila and Guanaja. To the Mosquitia, Isleña flies daily except Sunday to Palacios via Trujillo, and to Puerto Lempira on Monday, Tuesday, Thursday, and Saturday. Isleña also has one flight a day Monday through Friday direct to Grand Cayman.

The **Aerolineas Sosa** office is right next to Isleña downtown on the *parque,* tel. 443-2519 or 443-1399, and at the airport, tel. 443-2512. Sosa flies to Tegucigalpa twice a day, to San Pedro Sula three times a day, to Utila three times a day Mon.-Sat., to Roatán four times daily, and to Guanaja once a day Monday-Saturday. To Mosquitia, Sosa flies to Brus Laguna and Ahuas (US$58 one-way) on Monday and Friday, to Puerto Lempira on Tuesday, Thursday, and Saturday, and to Kaukira on Tuesday and Saturday (US$61 one-way).

Rollins, in town on 7 Calle next to Hotel Principe, tel. 443-3206, and at the airport, tel. 441-2177, has daily flights to Utila, Roatán, Tegucigalpa, San Pedro Sula, Trujillo, and Palacios, and also flies to Brus Laguna and Grand Cayman twice a week (US$180 one-way).

Taca, tel. 443-1912, in the U.S. (800) 535-8780, has flights every day to Miami via San Pedro Sula.

Bus

All buses (except the Viana luxury bus) leave from the central terminal on Blvd. 15 de Septiembre west of downtown, just across the railroad tracks. Taxis to or from the terminal cost US 50 cents, though taxis parked in the terminal itself will charge more going into town. Walk out to the road for a less expensive one. Small meals and snacks can be bought at stands and eateries at the terminal. Destinations, times, prices, and bus companies are as follows:

San Pedro Sula: direct, three hours, 12 departures daily between 5:30 a.m. and 6:30 p.m., US$3, with Catisa and Tupsa, tel. 441-2539.

Tegucigalpa: direct, six and a half hours with a stop for food at Santa Rita, Yoro, US$7, six departures daily with Etrucsa, tel. 441-0340, or Cristina, tel. 441-2028, the first at 4 a.m. and the last at 3 p.m.

Tela: local, two hours, every hour between 4:30 a.m. and 6 p.m., US$1

Trujillo: local, four and a half hours, eight buses between 4 a.m. and 4 p.m. , US$2.25

Tocoa: local, three hours, many daily between 4:30 a.m. and 5:15 p.m., US$1.75

Olanchito: local, three hours, eight daily between 6:30 a.m. and 5:30 p.m., US$2

Nuevo Armenia and **Jutiapa:** 90 minutes, usually twice daily at irregular hours, US 80 cents.

Balfate, Río Esteban, and **Río Coco:** Three buses from La Ceiba each day, the last at 2 p.m.; US$1.30 to Río Esteban, US$1.50 to Río Coco (three hours).

Corozal and **Sambo Creek:** usually four daily with the last at 6 p.m. (times very vague), US 30 cents to Corozal, US 50 cents to Sambo Creek. To get to these villages you can also hop on any westbound bus to Tocoa, Trujillo, Jutiapa, or Olanchito, get off at the highway turnoff, and walk the short distance into town.

La Unión: (for Cuero y Salado) several daily, last at 5 p.m., US 40 cents.

Luxury Bus

Viana, tel. 441-2330, runs luxury, non-stop cruisers to Tegucigalpa with two movies, a meal and coffee, nice but not cheap at US$18. Two buses depart daily at 6:30 a.m. and 2:30 p.m., arriving six hours later. The ticket office and bus departure is from an Esso gas station, a few blocks up the road west of the regular bus terminal.

Car

The 101-km, two-lane highway west to Tela is currently in fairly decent condition and takes a bit over an hour to drive. East of La Ceiba the highway continues along the coastal plain to Jutiapa, where it cuts through a low point in the Cordillera Nombre de Dios into the Valle de Aguán at Savá.

DISTANCES FROM LA CEIBA

Jutiapa	33 km
Olanchito	123 km
San Pedro Sula	202 km
Savá	80 km
Tegucigalpa	445 km
Tela	101 km
Tocoa	108 km
Trujillo	166 km

This 80-km stretch is in relatively good shape until the Río Aguán, where the bridge was trashed by Hurricane Mitch and has only been temporarily repaired. Past Savá, the highway to Tocoa is in good condition, but past the Corocito turnoff, the road continuing to Trujillo (166 km from La Ceiba) is a mess. A couple of the bridges, badly damaged by Mitch, have remained open despite the danger to motorists, though they may be fixed in the near future.

Boat

The new municipal dock, called **Cabotaje,** is east of the Río Cangrejal, reached by a dirt road turning off the Trujillo highway two km past the Río Cangrejal bridge on the road toward Sambo Creek, on the left side. The side road is three km out to the dock, making it too far to walk, so it's best to take a taxi from town (US$3.50).

The **MV** *Galaxy* departs Cabotaje to Roatán (US$9, two hours) and Utila (US$8, one hour) daily on the following schedule: leave Roatán to La Ceiba at 7 a.m.; La Ceiba to Utila at 9:30 a.m.; Utila to La Ceiba at 10:30 a.m.; and La Ceiba to Roatán at 3 p.m. For more information, call the offices in Coxen Hole, tel. 445-1795 and 455-5056, or in La Ceiba, tel. 442-0780.

Boats frequently pull in and out of Cabotaje on the way to Mosquitia. If you want to catch a ride, get out to the docks and start asking around. Some boat captains welcome a few extra *lempira,* while others refuse to take passengers. The *Captain Rinel,* tel. 441-2247, which makes regular trips to Brus Laguna and Puerto Lempira, has an office in an old container on the side of the road out past the bus station. If you take this route into Mosquitia, which certainly has romantic value, be ready to sleep on deck no matter what the weather for two to four days and bring all the food and water you will need. These are not passenger boats, but small, rusty cargo freighters, and amenities are minimal or nonexistent.

The only marina in the entire north coast of Honduras, **Lagoon Marina,** tel. 440-0614, cell. 991-5401, radio channel 69, was recently opened just behind Cabotaje. The German owner has 120 meters of jetty, with room for 20 to 25 sailing boats. Services include a fuel station, repair shop, and restaurant and bar on the weekends. A local captain will happily take visitors out on short trips to the Cayos Cochinos on his 10-meter dory, which is stored at the marina.

Local surfers (there are a couple, and they dream of faraway waves) insist that a decent left breaks off the eastern rock jetty at the mouth of Cabotaje, though only when the swell is large and coming in at just the right angle.

WEST AND SOUTH OF LA CEIBA

Refugio de Vida Silvestre Cuero y Salado

Formed by the estuaries of the Cuero, Salado, and San Juan Rivers, which flow off the flanks of the Cordillera Nombre de Dios to the south, the Cuero y Salado Wildlife Refuge comprises 13,225 hectares of wetlands and coastline filled with plant and animal life endangered elsewhere in Honduras. Jaguars, howler and white-faced monkeys, manatees (the reserve's mascot), turtles, crocodiles, caymans, fishing eagles, hawks, and several species of parrots are among the 196 bird and 35 mammal species identified within the reserve's boundaries.

The swampy mangrove-covered wetlands perform several important ecological functions. The dense walls of mangrove roots in the water act as a nursery for marine animals such as shrimp and several fish species, who make their way out to the open ocean after they've had a chance to grow. The vegetation serves as a way station for many migratory birds and as a buffer zone protecting the surrounding area during ocean storms and floods coming down from the mountains.

Much of the north coast formerly was covered with similar wetlands, but most have since been converted to pasture or plantations—a process all too evident as Cuero y Salado is surrounded by encroaching cattle-grazing land. An estimated 40% of the reserve's wetlands have been drained since 1987, when the land was donated by Standard Fruit to become a reserve. Chemicals leaking in from nearby pineapple and African palm plantations also threaten the wetlands.

Visitors may take guided boat tours of the reserve, US$17 for up to eight people. The trips, taking about two hours, tour through different waterways, with frequent stops to listen and watch for monkeys, birds, crocodiles, and other wetland denizens. Early morning tours are by far the best for wildlife watching. The guides are usually volunteers at the reserve and are very knowledgeable about the ecosystems and wildlife in the area. They can usually help visitors get a good look at a troop of howler monkeys or some of the more colorful bird species in the reserve. Be sure to bring some repellent or wear long sleeves—the mosquitoes aren't too bad on the beach or the encampment but can be fierce in the swamp. A short walk from the visitors' center is a wide-open, deserted stretch of Caribbean beach, perfect for a cooling-off swim after your boat tour.

For tourists, the interior section of the reserve is accessible by boat only, but don't be surprised to see a couple of locals standing on the shore farther in the swamps, fishing for their dinner. They know all the paths to get into the reserve and don't mind getting munched by mosquitoes to catch a free meal for their families.

It's recommended visitors make reservations with Fundación Cuero y Salado (FUCSA) in La Ceiba for boat tours, as groups often visit the reserve. As the early morning trips are the best for wildlife viewing, some visitors may wish to spend the night. The reserve formerly had a small bunkhouse, but that is now out of service, so bring your own tent, or rent a tent at the reserve sleeping up to five people for US$7.50 a night.

A US$10 (for foreigners) or US$1 (for Hondurans) entrance fee is charged above the price

of the boat ride. You can camp free on the 12-km-long beach, but you'll still have to pay the entrance fee. Locals will cook up a meal for unprepared visitors, but it's best to come with food. The beach is a great spot for a bonfire cookout.

Cuero y Salado is 30 km from La Ceiba. To get there, take a bus or car from La Ceiba past the airport on the road to Tela, and turn right into pineapple fields shortly after crossing the Río Bonito bridge. This road continues to the village of La Unión, but stop where the railroad tracks cross the road. From here, the Ferrocarril Nacional now runs a small car for US$3-5 pp, depending on how many people are in the group. To make arrangements, call 443-3525 or ask at the FUCSA office when you make your tour reservations. Alternatively, a local will offer to take you in by *burra,* a few boards with train wheels underneath propelled by a pole (US$7). Although it may seem demeaning to the sweaty *burra* poler, the locals are all for it—this is the only way they earn any money from the tourists coming to the reserve. For the totally destitute or ridiculously cheap, it's a two-hour walk along the rails to reach the headquarters. When returning, keep in mind the last bus leaves for La Ceiba at 3 p.m. The Bar El Bambú at the end of the train line makes a fine place to sip a cold beer or soft drink while awaiting the bus.

For more information on the reserve, or to make boat trip reservations, contact FUCSA, Edificio Ferrocarril Nacional, Zona Mazapan, Apt. 674, La Ceiba, Atlántida, tel./fax 443-0329, email: fucsa@laceiba.com. The FUCSA office is in an old railroad building behind the Standard Fruit offices in La Ceiba, just a couple of blocks west of the square, open Mon.-Fri. 8-11:30 a.m. and 1:30-4:30 p.m., Saturday 8-11:30 a.m.

Parque Nacional Pico Bonito

Chances are the first thing you noticed when you arrived in La Ceiba, especially if you came in by plane, was that massive emerald green spike of a mountain looming beyond the airport. This is the 2,435-meter-high Pico Bonito, centerpiece of the national park of the same name. Covering 107,300 hectares in the departments of Atlánti-

da and Yoro, of which 49,000 hectares is a buffer zone, Pico Bonito is the largest protected area in Honduras apart from the Río Plátano Biosphere Reserve. It is also one of the least explored, a dense, trackless jungle, ranging from humid tropical broadleaf forest in the lower regions to cloud forest on the peaks.

Some 20 river systems pour off the park's mountains; the rivers display their fullest splendor during the fall rainy season. Because of its rugged, natural isolation, Pico Bonito is a refuge for animal life seen only rarely in other regions of the country. Still, getting in to a place where one might run across a jaguar or ocelot requires some serious effort.

The park's main access is via the Río Zacate, a river pouring off the southern flanks of the mountains to the west of La Ceiba. Here one can hike into the **La Ruidosa** waterfall, reached by fairly well-kept trails through lush jungle alive with birds and sometimes monkeys at the edge of the mountains. Continue upstream to explore additional falls and look for more wildlife. The entrance to Río Zacate is near the highway village of Los Pinos, several kilometers west of La Ceiba on the road to Tela. Along the river, just past the pineapple fields near the highway, is a small *rancho,* the owner of which will ask to see your receipt for the US$6 entry fee, to have been paid at the park office in La Ceiba (see below). He can also, for a nominal fee, serve as a guide up to the waterfall. La Ruidosa can easily be visited in a day trip, or you could find a place to pitch a tent, to better watch for birds and other wildlife in the early morning.

It's also possible to get into the park via the village Armenia Bonito, which is reached by turning down a dirt road south off the La Ceiba-Tela highway just west of the airport, before reaching the Río Bonito. Past Armenia Bonito, a rough dirt road continues to the Río Bonito, where footpaths—mostly used by hunters, not hikers—continue upriver into the park. During Hurricane Mitch, the Río Bonito ran amok, creating a new riverbed for itself right through the middle of Armenia Bonito. Because of this disaster, park of-

howler monkey

ficials have been steering casual visitors to the Río Zacate. The small visitors' center and nature trail on the Río Bonito were trashed by the hurricane and have not been rebuilt. Nonetheless it is perfectly possible to hike in this way for one or more days. Past Armenia Bonito, near the edge of the Río Bonito, lives **Germán Martínez,** who is more than happy to take hikers into the forest on trips of varying length. Guide service is around US$8 a day. The Río Bonito Valley is the best route near La Ceiba to venture deep into the park, but day trippers or overnighters might be better off at Río Zacate.

For the adventurer, it would be hard to find more of a challenge in Honduras than a trip to the top of Pico Bonito. It may look like a relatively short jaunt, but in fact it takes a solid 9-10 days of hacking through the jungle while clinging to a steep, muddy hillside, hoping there are no snakes nearby. Germán has taken a few expeditions to the top and will gladly take other fearless climbers for a mere US$10 a day. Jorge Salaverri of La Moskitia Eco-Aventuras has also climbed the summit and can organize a trip for those who want to try their luck.

For an even tougher challenge, the truly obsessed jungle freak can contemplate getting to the top of Montaña Corozal (2,480 meters), the park's highest peak. It's in the heart of the park, hidden from view by Pico Bonito. There have been no known expeditions to the top of Montaña Corozal.

It is also possible to enter the park on the south side, in the Yoro department near Olanchito, where the lower elevations are blanketed with pine forest instead of tropical jungle. The best access is via Santa Bárbara, 21 km west of Olanchito on the road to Yoro. From here, hike three hours or more up a well-beaten trail to San Rafael, a village up in the hills where guides can be found. Ask around for Carlos Ramos Meléndez or Adan Hernández, who work for Cohdefor and can help find guides. From San Rafael, one can hike through the southeastern section of the park, across to the Río Blanco and down the Río Cangrejal Valley to La Ceiba, in two days and one night. Other, more difficult routes from San Rafael continue north through the center of the park to Armenia Bonito. These hikes afford excellent opportunities to admire the incredibly dense, lush vegetation of Pico Bonito and look for some of the abundant wildlife. A

group of Zapotal Indians, related to the Tolupan, control 3,500 hectares of land on the south side of the park.

For more information about the park, to look for guides, and to pay the US$6 entrance fee, stop in at the offices of Fundación Parque Nacional Pico Bonito (FUPNAPIB), at the southern end of Av. República, in the same building as Jet Stereo, tel. 443-3824, email: fupnapib@laceiba.hn. The office is open Mon.-Fri. 8 a.m.-noon and 1:30-4 p.m., Saturday 8 a.m.-noon.

Río Cangrejal

Forming part of the eastern boundary of Parque Nacional Pico Bonito, the Río Cangrejal tumbles off the flanks of the jungle-covered mountains through a narrow boulder-strewn valley before reaching the Caribbean at La Ceiba. Anyone spending a couple of days in La Ceiba should be sure to visit the middle or upper reaches of the river, at least on a day trip, to enjoy the spectacular scenery, take a dip in one of the innumerable swimming holes, or raft some of the finest whitewater in Central America.

A dirt road winds upstream along the Río Cangrejal, turning off the La Ceiba-Trujillo highway just past the bridge outside of La Ceiba. The road follows the Cangrejal Valley through the villages of Las Mangas, Yaruca, and Toncontín, ending in Urraco.

Between the highway and Las Mangas is **Balneario Los Lobos,** signposted, charging US 20 cents for a swim in some pools on the river. There's no real reason to swim there—many other free spots can be found upriver—but take the trail from the *balneario* to the **Cascade El Bejuco,** a waterfall visible on the opposite mountainside.

Las Mangas, where the road crosses a bridge, is a particularly lovely spot to admire the emerald green mountainsides and go for a swim. The bridge was out for more than a year after Hurricane Mitch, and your guidebook writer had the honor of being the first private vehicle across the new one in November 1999. The twisted remains of the old bridge, strewn down the river valley below, are a testament to the strength of the waters unleashed by Mitch.

Beyond Las Mangas, the road follows the river valley upstream on the western bank to the *aldea* of El Pital. Upstream from here the river passes through a tight gorge, which the road bypasses by crossing over a low ridge, coming down the far side to meet the river again at the village of Río Viejo. The gorge between Río Viejo and El Pital is the likeliest site of the medium-sized dam (40-50 megawatts) planned for the Río Cangrejal. The dam's construction, still in the planning stages at last report but looking likely, will not necessarily spell the end of boating downstream, depending on how the dam is managed. Time will tell.

At Río Viejo, three smaller rivers join to form the Río Cangrejal: the Río Viejo, the Río Blanco, and the Río Yaruca. The main road crosses the river and continues up to Yaruca and Urraco, where it dead-ends. The stretch of road beyond Urraco, leading down to Olanchito in the Río Aguán Valley, has been allowed to deteriorate and makes for great mountain biking. The trip from La Ceiba can easily be accomplished in one day, and convincing a bus driver in Olanchito to put your wheels on a La Ceiba-bound bus is not that difficult.

Upstream from Río Viejo, along its namesake river but on the opposite bank, is the *aldea* La Colorada. Right past the collection of houses, in a field on the right (west) side of the dirt path, are a collection of **ruins** of unknown origin. A couple of dozen mounds cover the cow pasture belonging to a wealthy local rancher, between the footpath and the river. The largest mound is at least five meters high and shows evidence of looters, with piles of stones thrown down and a hole in the mound's side. Word has it in La Ceiba that Hurricane Mitch helped clean much of the dirt away from the mounds, and looters came shortly thereafter to carry away small statues and ceramics. The government has apparently done no investigation at La Colorada, which is likely related to a smaller mound site right at the beginning of the dirt road up the Río Cangrejal, less than a kilometer from the La Ceiba bridge. La Colorada is an hour's walk from Río Viejo, but fording the river can be a bit treacherous after heavy rains.

At the moment, the only place to stay on the river is with Omega Rafting, tel. 440-0334, email: omegatours@laceiba.com, a lodge run by a German rafting outfit. The inexpensive (US$5-9) rooms in the laid-back lodge, with kitchen available, do not require rafting, if you just want to enjoy the river valley without risking life and limb. The owner offers a good package deal, with

transport from the airport, bus station or boat dock to the lodge, dinner, a bed, breakfast, and choice of a rafting, hiking, or horseback riding tour, all for US$50. The lodge is located roughly 10 km up the dirt road from the highway, well before Las Mangas. Keep an eye out for a dirt road to the left, leading to the house after a couple of hundred meters.

Usually a couple of buses daily make the bouncy and uncomfortable run between La Ceiba and Urraco. Instead of trying to figure out when the bus leaves, you could take a taxi or city bus out to the highway turnoff past the bridge and hitchhike. By private car, the road is passable (as long as the rains haven't been too heavy) as far as Río Viejo, beyond which 4WD and high-clearance vehicles are required.

Rafting the Cangrejal

For rafters and kayakers, the Río Cangrejal is one of the premier destinations in Central America. Depending on the water level, the four distinct sections of the river can boast dozens of different rapids, ranging from Class II to Class V, offering stretches exciting enough for river-running enthusiasts of any skill level. Total novices can take a several-hour trip, in which they will be shown the very basics of boating skills and sent down an appropriate stretch of the river with a group of trained guides. More experienced rafters and kayakers can tackle the more daunting rapids.

Most rafters will go down the lower section of the river, also known as the "commercial" section. Although fairly safe all in all, the lower has a couple of long rapids, class III-IV depending on the water, which are enough to get your adrenaline flowing. Above the lower stretch is the middle, starting at the bridge at Las Mangas. This is considered the most complex stretch of the river, littered with boulders of all sizes, a veritable labyrinth of drop-offs, chutes, and all manner of problems. One particular drop-off is not overly difficult, but on the far side is an underwater hazard known as El Submarino, which can suck an unsuspecting boater under. Most boaters wisely portage around El Submarino. Although it is possible to raft the middle, usually only kayakers brave this stretch.

The top, between the gorge and El Pital, and the upper, between El Pital and Las Mangas, both have several class III-IV rapids, plenty of boulders and drop-offs, and stretches shooting through bare rock riverbed. Like the middle, these stretches are more suitable for kayaks than rafts.

Kayakers or rafters looking for guides should see "Tour Operators" under "Sights and Recreation" above. The class II-IV rapids can be enjoyed year-round but are best run during or just after the fall rains when the river is deep. September to March are considered the best months, with the most water in November and December.

The Butterfly Farm

On the northern flanks of the Pico Bonito range, right next to the new Lodge at Pico Bonito, is the **Tropical Butterfly Farm and Gardens,** a private butterfly farm currently under construction by former Peace Corps volunteer Roberto Gallardo, who both exports butterfly larvae to the United States and organizes tours for visitors at US$6 pp. The farm was formerly at a different, nearby site; it was in the process of relocation at last report and should be running by the time of publication. A large, screened-in "garden house," with many plants, some 40 species of butterfly, and even a small waterfall are planned. Access is via a three-km dirt road south from the village of El Pino, on the La Ceiba-Tela highway just a few minutes west of La Ceiba. To get there without a car, take any of the frequent buses from the La Ceiba terminal to Tela, San Francisco, or La Masica, and get off at El Pino. From the highway it's a relaxed 20-minute walk. The trees around the farm are alive with birds and the occasional white-faced or spider monkey. The farm will be open daily 9 a.m.-4 p.m. Call the Lodge at Pico Bonito, tel. 440-1902, to confirm the farm is open.

EAST OF LA CEIBA

Playa de Perú

One of the better beaches near La Ceiba, Playa de Perú is reached by a 1.5-km dirt road turning off the Tocoa highway between kilometer markers 205 and 206, about 10 km east of downtown La Ceiba. It's not possible to walk to this beach from town since the mouth of the Río Cangrejal is in the way. Better to catch a bus headed for Sambo Creek, Tocoa, or Olanchito, get off at the turn, and walk down to the beach.

Río María

A fine swimming hole is found on the Río María, which passes underneath the highway between kilometer markers 207 and 208, east of Playa de Perú. On the east side of the highway bridge a path follows the river up a short distance until the path forks, one branch crossing the river and another leading up a hill to the left. Head up the hill, away from the river, for 15 minutes or so until the path comes back toward the river, audible below. Keep an eye out for a small trail cutting down a steep hillside; after a short but treacherous stretch this path arrives at the river's edge at a lovely waterfall with a pool at its base. If you're in doubt about the route, ask a local kid to guide you to the falls for a few *lempira*.

This is just the first of a series of waterfalls and pools created by boulders along the river, all surrounded by jungle—a wonderful place to spend a relaxing afternoon picnicking, reading, or just lazing around. The area is supposedly an ecological reserve but apparently in name only.

It's best to go during the week as a crowd often shows up on weekends, but should there be too many people for your tastes, just head downriver a bit and find a quieter pool. There have been some reports of thievery here, so leave valuables at home.

Corozal

Not one of the more attractive Garífuna settlements on the Honduran coast, Corozal is a fairly dirty fishing village on the beach a couple of kilometers west of Río María. In town are a couple of basic *comedores* and the inexpensive **Hotel Hermanos Avila.** Nearby is **Playa de Zambrano,** a decent though unspectacular stretch of beach.

A few hundred meters uphill from the highway, near Km marker 209 and marked by a sign, is **Los Chorros,** another local swimming hole on a small river gushing off the tropical hillside, with many pools, boulders, and falls, similar to Río María.

On the highway just east of the Corozal turnoff is **Villa Rhina,** tel. 443-1222 or 443-1434, fax 443-3558, a resort-hotel set into the hillside with views out over the Caribbean. On the 10-acre grounds are three freshwater pools, a small waterfall, and a trail up into the forest above, where you can catch views of the Cayos Cochinos.

Each of the attractive wood-paneled, air-conditioned rooms costs US$30 d, or US$37 for a bungalow. The hotel is well run, but the location—above the highway and away from the beach—is not the best.

Sambo Creek

A few kilometers east of Corozal and somewhat more appealing is Sambo Creek, another Garífuna village at the mouth of a small river. **Hotel Avila,** located at the eastern end of town right on the beach (no phone), has basic rooms for US$5.50-7 per night. Two very good seafood restaurants, often filled with Ceibeños out for a meal, are **La Champa** and **Sambo Creek Restaurant.**

On the south side of the highway on Río Cuyamel is a reputedly excellent swimming hole. Just west of town, near the mouth of the Río Cuyamel, lies a stretch of clean and deserted beach that would make for good camping, if the local family living nearby doesn't mind. A bit farther west is **Playa Las Sirenas,** a deserted beach at the mouth of a small river, with a *campesino* family living nearby.

Past Sambo Creek toward Jutiapa, 22 km from La Ceiba, is a new, upscale beachfront hotel complex, **Caribbean Sands Resort,** tel. 445-0035, fax 443-1026, email: caribbeansands@ caribe.hn. The 42 modern rooms, each with a/c and cable TV, cost US$70 d, with use of a large pool and patio, private beach, and tennis courts. The hotel can arrange day trips to the Cayos Cochinos.

Jutiapa, Nuevo Armenia, and Farther East

Just before the highway turns inland through the hills toward Savá and the Valle de Aguán, 33 km from La Ceiba, is the small town of Jutiapa, where a dirt road (in horrible condition at last report) turns off 10 km down to Nuevo Armenia at the sea's edge. From here you can arrange a trip on a motorized *lancha* out to the nearby Cayos Cochinos for around US$25 roundtrip, or more to leave you and pick you up another day. Rene Arzu is one person in Nuevo Armenia who can help arrange a boat trip. A simple hotel in Nuevo Armenia offers inexpensive, very basic rooms.

East along the coast beyond Jutiapa are the Garífuna villages of Balfate, Río Esteban, and Río Coco, all connected by a rough dirt road. From Río Coco, adventurers could make their way by foot or boat around the point to Trujillo in a day or two.

VALLE DE AGUÁN

From Jutiapa, the highway turns south into the hills, crossing into the broad Río Aguán Valley. The Río Aguán winds out of the mountains of Yoro, to the west and south, and is also fed by tributaries flowing north out of Olancho. It meets the Caribbean east of Trujillo, at the Garífuna town of Santa Rosa de Aguán. One of the most fertile regions in the country, the Valle de Aguán is owned in large part by the Standard Fruit Company (now Dole), and is covered by a sea of banana, pineapple, and African palm plantations.

The wide, flat valley was badly hit by Hurricane Mitch, which swelled the Río Aguán into a ferocious torrent. Bridges all along the valley were still out over a year after the disaster, although foreign aid groups have pledged funds for their reconstruction. All the main roads in the region are open, though the stretch between Tocoa and Trujillo is in appalling shape.

The rich lands of the Valle de Aguán, once a region designated for agrarian reform, are a source of major tension in the region. *Campesino* activists and leftist politicians are gunned down with depressing regularity by hired gunmen.

SAVÁ

A hot agricultural town on the south side of the Río Aguán where the La Ceiba highway meets the Olanchito-Tocoa-Trujillo road, Savá is a common transfer point for bus travelers. The town holds a couple of nondescript *comedores* and a gas station. Should you for some odd reason need or want to spend the night in Savá, rooms are available at **Hospedaje Carmen,** half a block from the main highway junction.

On the road to Olanchito, on the west side of the Río Mamé 28 kilometers from Savá, a dirt road turns off south. This road leads to La Unión in Olancho—86 km away and the closest town to **La Muralla National Park**—and eventually on to

Juticalpa and Tegucigalpa. Due to the high incidence of highway holdups, particularly between La Unión and Salamá, this road is not recommended. For travelers on their way directly to Tegucigalpa and not interested in stopping at La Muralla, the road from Corocito (east of Tocoa) through San Esteban is quicker and safer.

OLANCHITO

The second-largest community in the Valle de Aguán after Tocoa, Olanchito sits in the heart of Standard Fruit Company (Dole) lands. The town was founded in the 17th century by migrants from San Jorge de Olancho, a colonial town near Catacamas that was destroyed by a natural disaster. The town church, set on a palm-lined square, holds a small statue of San Jorge, the town's patron saint. The statue was reputedly carried here from San Jorge de Olancho by the original migrants. The 23 April festival in the saint's honor is quite a bash, with some 20,000 people dancing in the streets.

Most of the year, though, Olanchito is hot, dusty, and altogether uninteresting to the casual traveler. For anyone curious to see what a classic company town looks like, take a taxi or bus to nearby **Coyoles,** where practically all the buildings were built and are still owned by Standard Fruit. Almost all Olanchito residents, apart from a few small-scale ranchers and farmers, derive their income either directly or indirectly from Standard. In the wake of Hurricane Mitch, Standard was planning on closing several fields around Coyoles but had held off due to protests by workers afraid of losing their livelihoods.

Just outside of Coyoles is the largest intact **thorn forest** in Honduras, a rare dry tropical ecosystem fast disappearing in the country. Several species of rare birds are found here, including an endemic green-backed sparrow, green jays, elegant trogons, and white-lored gnatcatchers. The forest is the only known habitat for the white-bellied wren in Honduras.

Accommodations
Should you have some business in Olanchito, or a perverse desire to overnight in this out-of-the-way agricultural town, several acceptable hotels lie within two blocks of the square. The best inexpensive accommodations are at **Hotel Colo-**nial, tel. 446-6972, offering clean, sparsely furnished rooms, each with fan and private bath, a good deal at US$5 s or d, more for rooms with TV or a/c. The rooms are set around a courtyard, and there's even room for parking.

A step up in quality is **Hotel Valle Aguán,** tel. 446-6718, where the modern, a/c- and TV-equipped rooms surround a quiet courtyard; not a bad deal at US$8.50 s or US$10 d, or less with fan only. On the courtyard is **Restaurante La Iguana,** one of the better eateries in town. The **Hotel Olimpic,** tel. 44-6324, is a somewhat better deal at US$8 s or d with a refrigerator or US$10 with a/c. More expensive, and not much better, is **Hotel Olanchito,** tel. 446-6385.

Food
Most restaurants in town are cheap and basic. **Multisabores** on the park has burgers, chicken, *licuados,* and other snacks.

The only upscale restaurant in town apart from La Iguana at the Hotel Valle Aguán is **Eso Tito,** on the western edge of town, open Mon.-Sat. 7 a.m.-8 p.m. **Cafeteria Manalica** in Hotel Olanchito has a large menu of well-cooked snacks and meals at moderate prices.

Services
Bancahorro and Bancahsa in the center of town change dollars and traveler's checks. Hondutel and Correos share a building five blocks south of the main street. Gas is available in town.

Getting Away
It's possible, but not easy, to continue west from Olanchito to Yoro. The road deteriorates beyond Olanchito; swollen rivers can flood the route, cutting it off entirely. Twice daily buses cross the mountains to Yoro when the road is in good condition, the last at noon (four and a half hours, US$3)

The last bus from Olanchito to La Ceiba leaves at 3:30 p.m., but it's usually possible to catch a later bus to Savá and there change to another bus continuing to La Ceiba or Trujillo.

TOCOA

A bustling agricultural town 29 kilometers east of Savá, Tocoa has nothing whatsoever to attract a tourist. Even the downtown square is ugly, although the bizarrely designed church, reportedly the work of a Peace Corps volunteer, is an unusual sight.

Though lacking in tourist attractions, Tocoa is a magnet for land-hungry migrants who use the rapidly growing city as a base to invade the Río Sico and Río Paulaya valleys on the western edge of the Río Plátano rainforest. Many of these homesteaders are moving in on protected land, but little can be done to stop them, even if the government wanted to, which it doesn't always—it's easier to sacrifice a remote stretch of jungle than deal with the thorny problem of land redistribution in the rest of the country.

Accommodations

Because of all the agricultural and business activity in Tocoa, several hotels offer rooms of varying quality. The super-basic **Hospedaje Rosa** on the main drag charges US$2.50 for a room with private bath and fan. **Hotel Victoria,** a block away, tel. 444-3031, costs US$10 s or d with a/c and TV—a good deal. Adjacent to Bancahorro, the more upscale **Hotel San Patricio,** tel. 444-3401, has simple rooms with fan and private bath for US$8 s or US$11 d, more with a/c and TV.

Two cheap, acceptable places near the market and buses are **Hotelito Rossil** and **Hotelito Yendy.**

Food

The classiest restaurant in town is **La Gran Villa,** on the northwest end of the square on the road to the bus station, tel. 444-3943. The restaurant offers shrimp, conch, and steak dishes at US$4-7 per entree, as well as sandwiches, breakfasts, and a full bar. It's open Mon.-Sat. 8 a.m.-9 p.m.

Next to Hotel San Patricio is the **Restaurante Aquarium,** serving Honduran standards, with a full bar. Across from Banco Sogerin on the main street is **Cafeteria Claudia,** open Mon.-Sat. 7 a.m.-6 p.m., Sunday 7 a.m.-noon, with snacks, breakfasts and inexpensive *típico* food.

Services

Bancahsa, Banco Atlántida, and Bancahorro in the center of town all change dollars and usually traveler's checks. The **bus station** is four blocks north of the square, next to the market. Last bus to Trujillo leaves at 6 p.m., and the last bus to La Ceiba leaves at 4 p.m. The 24-hour

Texaco station on the highway can provide a fill-up anytime.

Getting Away

From Tocoa it's 59 kilometers to Trujillo via a poorly maintained paved road passing Corocito, which is the turnoff to Bonito Oriental, San Esteban, and Olancho, as well as to Sangrelaya at the edge of Mosquitia. Between Tocoa and Trujillo, slow down when approaching bridges as the bumps can be bone-rattling. One bridge left open

---

GETTING TO MOSQUITIA THE HARD WAY

Flying into Palacios, Brus Laguna, or Puerto Lempira is by far the easiest way into la Mosquitia, but for those with a sense of adventure (or a fear of light aircraft) it is possible to get to Palacios by a combination of truck and boat.

Rigged-out six-wheel trucks leave the Tocoa market daily between 8 a.m. and noon for a grueling but fascinating seven-hour trip (US$9) to the Garífuna village of Sangrelaya, at the western edge of the Mosquitia. You have to just show up and wait for a truck to leave, and it's best to get there early to ensure a good seat. Inside the cab is best, but if that's been taken, try to get a bench seat with your back against the cab—that offers some support on the long and bumpy ride. The truck leaves the Trujillo highway at Corocito and passes Bonito Oriental, Limón, and Iriona before arriving at Punta Piedra, where the road ends. From there, the truck follows the beach—often half in the water and half on sand, and sometimes at heart-stoppingly steep angles—to Sangrelaya, passing several small villages along the way.

From Sangrelaya, *lanchas* can be hired to Plaplaya or Batalla for roughly US$35 per boat, and from here onward to Palacios. The boat trip from Sangrelaya can be very wet, so be prepared. All told, the trip is more expensive than the plane, but incomparably more adventuresome.

It's also possible to catch trucks from Tocoa for a brutal eight- to 10-hour drive to the town of Sico, on the Río Sico, where boats can be found downriver to Palacios. The trucks leave the market at 3 or 4 in the morning and charge US$18 for the trip.

since Mitch is skewed at remarkable angles and looks set to collapse. Gas is available at Corocito.

Frequent buses run back and forth all day to Olanchito, La Ceiba, Trujillo, and Limón. Five buses a day run between Tocoa and San Esteban, in Olancho, charging US$2.25.

Cotuc, tel. 444-2181, runs five buses to San Pedro Sula daily for US$5, a six-hour trip, the last at 2:30 p.m. Cotuc's terminal is on the highway, on the exit to Trujillo.

Those heading into Olancho via San Esteban should turn off the Tocoa-Trujillo highway at Corocito, with a police post and gas station, and continue east four and a half miles farther on a paved road to the unsavory **Bonito Oriental,** which has a couple of *comedores* and functional rooms at the **Hotel Milton.** It's better to wait for bus or *jalón* rides into Olancho at Corocito rather than in Bonito Oriental, which has a reputation for violence.

TRUJILLO AND VICINITY

INTRODUCTION

Coralio reclined, in the mid-day heat, like some vacuous beauty lounging in a guarded harem. The town lay at the sea's edge on a strip of alluvial coast. It was set like a little pearl in an emerald band. Behind it, and seeming almost to topple, imminent, above it, rose the sea-following range of the Cordilleras. In front the sea was spread, a smiling jailer, but even more incorruptible than the frowning mountains. The waves swished along the smooth beach; the parrots screamed in the orange and ceiba-trees; the palms waved their limber fronds foolishly like an awkward chorus at the prima donna's cue to enter.

—O. Henry,
Cabbages And Kings

One of many foreigners who have been waylaid by Trujillo's lotus-land vibes, American writer O. Henry renamed the town Coralio for his short story, but the description is as good as one could ask for. Although it is the country's oldest settlement, Trujillo still feels like a forgotten, sleepy corner of Honduras, where it seems no one is in a hurry to do anything.

Even the local tourist industry has failed to take off, despite the obvious attractions of a broad bay lined by a beach and palm trees, a national park close to town comprising jungle-covered mountains and mangrove lagoons, and several quiet Garífuna villages not far away. It doesn't help that Trujillo is four hours by crowded, bumpy bus from La Ceiba, and about twice that from Tegucigalpa.

The capital of the Colón Department, Trujillo has about 30,000 residents. Its annual patron festival is held on 24 June in honor of San Juan Bautista.

History

Though Trujillo was officially founded on 18 May 1525 by Juan de Medina, acting under orders

from Hernán Cortés, the natural bay had long before drawn other settlers. According to colonial testimony and archaeological evidence, Trujillo Bay had been occupied for many hundreds of years before the Spanish arrived. Trujillo was apparently something of a pre-Columbian crossroads, site of Pech and Tolupan villages as well as settlements of Mayan and Nahuatl traders from Mexico and Guatemala.

The early Spanish colonists established their new town on the site of an Indian village named Guaimura, amid approximately a dozen other villages totaling several thousand inhabitants. Trujillo was named for the Spanish hometown of Medina's superior officer Fernando de las Casas.

In the first years after conquest, Trujillo was the administrative center of the new colony, housing both the governor of Honduras and the only bishopric, established in 1545. But the lure

Juan de Medina, founder of the Spanish settlement at Trujillo, is honored with a monument overlooking the beach.

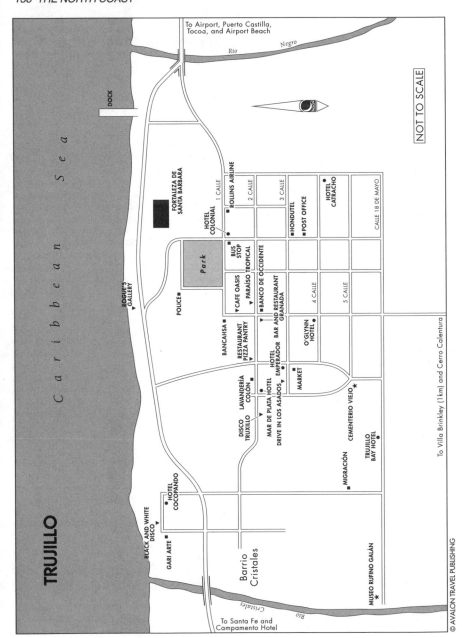

TRUJILLO

Caribbean Sea

To Airport, Puerto Castilla,
Tocoa, and Airport Beach

Río Negro

NOT TO SCALE

DOCK

ROGUE'S GALLERY

FORTALEZA DE SANTA BARBARA

HOTEL COLONIAL

ROLLINS AIRLINE

1 CALLE

2 CALLE

3 CALLE

HONDUTEL

POST OFFICE

HOTEL CATRACHO

CALLE 18 DE MAYO

Park

BUS STOP

POLICE

CAFE OASIS

PARAÍSO TROPICAL

BANCO DE OCCIDENTE

BAR AND RESTAURANT GRANADA

4 CALLE

5 CALLE

BANCAHSA

RESTAURANT PIZZA PANTRY

HOTEL EMPERADOR

O'GLYNN HOTEL

MARKET

LAVANDERÍA COLÓN

DISCO TRUXILLO

MAR DE PLATA HOTEL

DRIVE IN LOS ASADOS

CEMENTERIO VIEJO

MIGRACIÓN

TRUJILLO BAY HOTEL

HOTEL COCOPANDO

BLACK AND WHITE DISCO

GARI ARTE

Barrio Cristales

MUSEO RUFINO GALÁN

Río Cristales

To Santa Fe and
Campamento Hotel

To Villa Brinkley (1 km) and Cerro Calentura

© AVALON TRAVEL PUBLISHING

of gold in the mountains soon drew colonists to the interior towns of Gracias a Dios and Comayagua, which by the middle of the century had superseded Trujillo.

Trujillo faded into a backwater colonial port. The constant threat of pirate assault on the poorly guarded harbor was all the more reason for colonists to relocate. French corsairs first attacked in 1558, and others followed repeatedly from their bases on the Bay Islands and in Mosquitia. Since colonial authorities were unable to mount an effective defense, even the Spanish merchants who depended on the port took to living inland and came to the coast only when the Spanish fleet arrived.

In 1642 English pirate William Jackson led an assault on Trujillo with 1,500 men, almost entirely destroying the town. While Trujillo residents were still recovering from the blow, the next year Dutchman Jan Van Horn arrived and finished the work entirely. Those who hadn't been killed gave up the port as a lost cause, and the Spanish deserted Trujillo for almost 150 years, although British traders intermittently used the ruined town as a stop-off point.

In the late 18th century the Spanish began a major counteroffensive to turn back British settlements along Central America's Caribbean coast. As part of this effort, Trujillo was reoccupied by a contingent of soldiers in 1780. Although the Spanish colony was on its last legs, the new settlement took hold. It received a boost in 1799 after several hundred Garífuna, deported by the British from the island of San Vicente, built a village just west of Trujillo in what is now Barrio Cristales.

As with the rest of the north coast, Trujillo participated in the banana boom of the early 20th century. Both Standard and United Fruit acquired lands in the area. Standard still controls much land in the nearby Aguán Valley and ships most of its produce out of nearby Puerto Castilla. Trujillo's economy relies on the port, the departmental government, and the fledgling tourist industry.

The latest potential economic salvation for Trujillo is a rather outlandish project proposed by a most unusual U.S. developer. Norman Nixon has spent great energy and effort convincing all who will listen of the viability of his *Freedom Ship*. This gargantuan utopian floating structure,

expected to measure a kilometer in length, is intended to house 40,000 paying residents, plus a staff of 15,000. Nixon has chosen the deep harbor at Puerto Castilla as the most ideal place in the world to build his ship. Whether the plans get off the water, as it were, remains to be seen, but the job-hungry residents of Trujillo surely hope they do.

Despite being the first major population center on mainland Honduras to feel the effects of Hurricane Mitch, Trujillo fared relatively well during the storm. The main part of town, set on a bluff well above the ocean, was mostly untouched, though the beach *champas* were destroyed, and many of the trees on the surrounding hills were stripped of their leaves. Worse hit were lower-lying communities east of Trujillo along the coast, and south in the Aguán Valley.

Orientation and Getting Around
The center of Trujillo is on a rise above the beach and consists of a small square surrounded by government buildings, the church, and a few stores. The town continues several streets back up the hill, where the bulk of hotels and restaurants are located. To the west of downtown is Barrio Cristales, the first Garífuna settlement on mainland Honduras.

Robberies have been reported in the vicinity of Trujillo, but generally the downtown area, the main town beach, and the airport beach are safe. Less safe are the more deserted stretches of beach between Trujillo and Santa Fe and east of the airport beach toward Puerto Castilla.

Most visitors will find themselves easily able to walk between their hotel and the main beach in town. A taxi out to the airport beach costs about US 75 cents.

SIGHTS

First and foremost among Trujillo's attractions is the **beach** right below town—a wide, clean swath of sand lined with *champa* restaurants and lapped by the protected waters of the bay. Swimming and sunbathing here is safe, but don't tempt fate by leaving possessions lying around unguarded. The bay is not as clear as waters off the Bay Islands, but still it's warm, fairly clean, and calm. The **airport beach,** east of town in front of the airport and dominated by the Christopher Columbus Hotel, is an equally fine spot for relaxing, usually a bit quieter as it's farther from town. Sand flies are common enough on Trujillo's beaches, but they don't reach the plague proportions of elsewhere.

East of the airport, beaches continue all the way around the bay to Puerto Castilla, but robberies have been reported on these deserted stretches; stay at the two beaches mentioned above unless you go with a group.

For all its storied history, Trujillo retains little in the way of colonial monuments. The most interesting is the **Fortaleza de Santa Bárbara,** which was built piecemeal beginning in 1575. As was the fort at Omoa, Trujillo's fort was notably unsuccessful, falling continually to attackers over the course of the colonial era. Invaders were repelled with success only after the arrival of the Garífuna in 1799. The Garífuna were superb soldiers who gained experience from a half-century of guerrilla warfare against the British on San Vicente. The last real battle for the fort took place in 1910, when a Honduran general landed here in an unsuccessful attempt to launch a coup. The fort was closed in 1969 when its guard troops were

THE FALL OF WILLIAM WALKER

Filibuster William Walker—"the gray-eyed man of destiny," as he was called in his years of fame—was possessed by a burning desire to govern parts or all of Central America. He offered varied reasons, including a desire to expand slavery and to establish U.S. control over the fractious republics before England did. But the more important driving force behind his actions seems to have been a slightly crazed messianic fervor.

Walker invaded Nicaragua and ruled it from 1855 to 1857. His presence accomplished the heretofore impossible task of unifying El Salvador, Guatemala, Honduras, and Costa Rica in a common goal—namely, getting rid of the pesky gringo. After a series of bloody battles, Walker surrendered in Nicaragua on 1 May 1857 and returned to New Orleans. His hero's welcome there took the sting out of his defeat, and, convinced as ever of his destiny to rule Central America, he soon organized an expedition to conquer Nicaragua once again. It would be his last.

Walker departed New Orleans in June 1860, planning first to take control of the island of Roatán, then join forces with Honduran Liberal Party leader Trinidad Cabañas to overthrow the Honduran government. However, at the time, the British occupied Roatán. They had been about to turn the island over to Honduras, but on hearing of Walker's plan they postponed their departure. When Walker arrived off Roatán and saw the Union Jack still flying, he changed plans and decided instead to take Trujillo. Landing on the bay a few kilometers from town at night, Walker and his 200 men marched on the fort at dawn and took it in a 15-minute battle.

Walker quickly hoisted the flag of the Central American Republic over the fort and reassured the townspeople of his good intentions. However, he made the fatal mistake of taking over Trujillo's customs house—which, unbeknownst to him, was technically managed by the British. This gave British forces in Roatán the pretext they needed to help Honduras attack Walker. The British warship *Icarus*, commanded by Capt. Norvell Salmon, soon appeared in the harbor, and word came of a force of 700 Honduran soldiers just outside of town. Rather than give in to the inevitable, Walker chose to lead his men out of town during the night. They made their way east into Mosquitia in hopes of joining forces with Cabañas.

Walker eventually stopped to regroup on the banks of the Río Sico, where he and his men came under attack from Honduran soldiers. They fought off the attack for five days, but with many of his "Immortal" soldiers dead or wounded, and himself ill with a fever and shot in the cheek, Walker knew he was defeated. When the *Icarus* appeared near the scene of the battle, Walker surrendered to Salmon, figuring he and his men would at worst return in shame to the United States.

Walker's men were placed under the protection of the British flag, but Salmon had no sympathy for Walker; he turned him over to the Hondurans in Trujillo. At first Walker protested, but soon he resigned himself to his fate. On 12 September 1860, Walker was led to the outskirts of town—now the site of the town hospital—flanked by two priests and a crowd of heckling Hondurans, clearly relishing the sight of the famed invading gringo's execution. Walker remained calm, received his last sacraments from the priests, and stood straight in the face of a firing squad.

called into action against El Salvador in the "Soccer War." Shortly thereafter it was converted into a tourist attraction. Several colonial-era cannons are still set up on the fort's ramparts. Known locally as El Castillo, the fort is open daily 9 a.m.-noon and 1-4 p.m. Admission is US 10 cents for adults, US 5 cents for children, free for Hondurans.

Although Trujillo was the site of the first cathedral in Honduras, the original church was destroyed long ago. The unexceptional **Catedral de San Juan Bautista** was built in 1832 and remodeled 1930-39.

The **Museo Rufino Galán,** on the edge of the Río Cristales on a hillside above town, houses an eclectic collection of Trujillo bric-a-brac from across the centuries, given, bought, found, or fallen out of the sky—literally. Probably the most impressive display is the remains of a U.S. transport plane that crashed nearby in 1985. Don't expect any displays, signs, or other niceties: this is the life's work of a born packrat. Some pre-Columbian pieces are hidden amidst the junk. Entry to the museum costs US$1, and an additional 60 cents to swim in some murky pools. Don't bother swimming here; the ocean is much better.

The **cementerio viejo (old cemetery),** south of downtown, is worth a visit to see the grave of the "gray-eyed man of destiny," William Walker, whose filibustering days came to a violent end in Trujillo on 12 September 1860. Apart from Walker's grave, the cemetery also offers an interesting if decrepit assortment of grave monuments from across 300 years of Trujillo history.

ACCOMMODATIONS

With tourism still in first gear, and not much else going on in Trujillo either, hotel options in town are limited. But as long as you're not after real luxury, finding an acceptable room is not too difficult. Most accommodations are up in town, with only a couple of places near the beach. Apart from the hotels listed below, visitors could consider camping or renting a room at the homey beach resort at Campamento, a few kilometers west of Trujillo on the road to Santa Fe.

Shoestring
About the cheapest digs in town are at **Hotel Catracho,** a few blocks back from the center of town, with wooden rooms and porches round an unkempt grassy area for US$4 a night. Marginally better is **Mar de Plata,** tel. 434-4458, charging US$5.50 s or d for a simple room with shared bath, or US$7.50 s or d with private bath. Rooms are concrete cells with bad fans, and the shared bathrooms are not too clean.

A better deal is **Hotel Emperador,** opposite the market, tel. 434-4446, where a small courtyard is surrounded by 10 clean rooms with private bathroom, fan, and TV for US$7 s, US$8 d.

In Barrio Cristales is **Hotel Cocopando,** a three-story concrete structure on the beach charging US$5 s or US$6 d for a reasonably clean room with fans, popular with backpackers. The restaurant serves decent fish and *chuleta de cerdo* (pork chop), and the disco next door rages on weekends.

Budget
Apparently in perpetual construction, at least until the American owner runs out of room or gets bored, the **Villa Brinkley,** tel. 434-4444, fax 434-4269, in the US tel. (412) 791-2273, is an architectural oddity perched on a hillside above town. Currently 20 wood-and-plaster rooms of differing sizes, all tastefully decorated if a bit dark, are available for US$18-30. Some come with kitchenettes and sunken bathtubs. The food varies between good and excellent, depending on the current cook. Outside is a pool and expansive patio, with great views out over town and the bay. Less expensive rooms in a separate building rent for US$12-20 per night. The Turtle Tours office is in the hotel, and Internet access is available to guests. The owner is considering converting the building into a health spa of sorts, but at the moment the hotel business continues. Call for the latest.

The **O'Glynn Hotel,** three blocks uphill from the square, tel. 434-4592, rents modern, spacious rooms with a/c and hot water in a newly built annex for US$17 s or US$23.50 d, or older wooden rooms in the original hotel building for US$10 s or US$13.50 d. In the lobby of the hotel is a complete set of framed topographical maps of the region, an interesting collection of pre-Columbian jade figurines, and a copy of the testimony of the founding of Trujillo on 18 May 1525 in the name of Cortés, written by Capt. Francisco de las Casas.

Conveniently located on the corner of the square, but gloomy and unfriendly, is **Hotel Colonial,** tel. 434-4011, with a/c- and TV-equipped rooms for US$23 s or d. On the south side of the airstrip, opposite the Christopher Columbus Hotel, is the modern, two-story **Trujillo Bay Hotel,** tel./fax 434-4732. Well-maintained rooms with a/c, TV, hot water, and porches cost US$25 s, US$31 d, which is not a bad value, although the location is not the best.

Moderate-Expensive

A sprawling, lime green complex spread across the beach in front of the airport, the **Christopher Columbus Hotel,** tel. 434-4966 or 434-4249, fax 434-4971, may not be aesthetically elegant but it has all the amenities for a pampered vacation. The 70 air-conditioned rooms range from US$55 s to US$120 for a suite with views of the ocean and the mountains behind. Up to two children under 12 stay free. The private, patrolled beach is very safe, and the hotel supplies all manner of beach and water toys for guests. At last report the hotel was for sale, so best to call ahead and check.

FOOD

In Town

Apart from a couple of *merenderos* on the square, there is little in the way of inexpensive food in Trujillo. Almost all restaurants are midrange, usually US$3-6 for a full meal and a bit less for breakfast. If you're on a budget you may have to resign yourself to eating a lot of *baleadas* or hitting the market and cooking meals yourself. One decent low-priced spot is **Drive-in Los Asados,** a block west of the market, up the hill, which serves enchiladas, *pastelitos, tajadas,* burgers, and other snacks. The patio restaurant is a friendly place to have a few beers and chat with locals.

One of the oldest restaurants in Trujillo is **Bar and Restaurant Granada,** a block south of the square. The Garífuna owners serve a large selection of well-cooked meals, with heavy emphasis on seafood for US$4-10 per entree. Open Mon.-Sat. 8 a.m.-10:30 p.m., Sunday 5-10:30 p.m.

Similar is the **Restaurant Pizza Pantry,** which despite its name has a large menu including hearty breakfasts, shrimp, lobster, steak, sal-

ads, and a full bar; US$4-10 per entree. The pizza is not bad, but service can be slow. Open daily 7 a.m.-10 p.m.

Cafe Oasis, opposite Bancahsa downtown, serves reasonable but unexceptional fish dinners, sandwiches, and breakfasts. The food is mediocre, but the selection is good. Open 7 a.m.- 10 p.m. daily.

A welcome find on the block behind the church is **Paraíso Tropical,** with fruit drinks, fruit salads, licuados, and snacks; open Mon.-Sat. 8 a.m.-10 p.m., sometimes also open on Sunday afternoon.

On the Beach

Among the many restaurants lining the beach in front of town, **Rogue's Galería,** otherwise known as Jerry's, is the current favorite, popular with expats, travelers, and locals alike for the excellent seafood and relaxed atmosphere. Expect to enjoy a full meal; there is little in the way of snacks or light meals. Many travelers find themselves spending entire days here, lounging in the hammocks, chatting, drinking, and taking an occasional dip in the ocean. The kitchen is open daily until 9 or 10 p.m., but the bar often stays open later.

On the airport beach, just east of Christopher Columbus, is the **Gringo's Bar,** a restaurant and bar with tables and hammocks under *champas* out on the beach. Service can be painfully slow, but with the waves and sun to lull you into a daze, what's the rush? The seafood, chicken, sandwiches, and other munchies are all good and generously sized. Even if you're not hungry, this is a fine place to get a cold drink and relax on the beach. Open daily 8 a.m.-10 p.m., later on Friday and Saturday.

Right next door is **Bahía Bar,** similar in price and style to Gringo's but not quite as popular. The owners rent out sea kayaks for US$1.35 an hour, in which you could venture out into the bay or, for the industrious, into the Guaymoreto lagoon. **Chino's Bar and Grill,** farther east at the far end of the airport, has a full bar with a good music selection and lots of seafood.

ENTERTAINMENT

Rogue's Galería is a late-night hangout popular with travelers and a few locals. If you're after something a bit more energetic, the **Black and White Disco** next to the Hotel Cocopando on the beach in Barrio Cristales is popular on weekends, particularly Sunday nights. In town is **Truxillo,** just past Hotel Mar de Plata, always packed with sweaty dancers on Friday and Saturday nights.

INFORMATION AND SERVICES

Shopping
In Barrio Cristales, **Gari Arte,** tel. 434-4207, sells a variety of Garífuna *artesanías,* including drums, carvings, jewelry, paintings, *punta* cassettes, and T-shirts. The owner was at last report building a museum dedicated to Garífuna history and culture—check at the store for the latest.

The **Supermercado Popular** on the square has a large selection of groceries and is open Mon.-Sat. until 7 p.m. The public **market,** a couple of blocks south of the square, does not offer much variety but has a basic selection of staple fruits and vegetables at inexpensive prices.

Services
Just off the square, Bancahsa is the easiest place to exchange dollars and traveler's checks and get cash advances on a Visa card. Western Union wires are received at Banco de Occidente.

The **migración** office, tel. 434-4451, is in Barrio Cristales, a 15-minute walk from the park and renews tourist cards quickly and painlessly. Hondutel, a couple of blocks south of the square, is open daily 7 a.m.-9 p.m. Faxes are received at 434-4200. Correos is right next to Hondutel.

Tours
Turtle Tours, in the Villa Brinkley Hotel above town, tel. 434-4444, fax 434-4431, email: ttours@hondutel.hn, offers a variety of highly recommended, reasonably priced tours around Trujillo and into Mosquitia. Half-day canoe trips in Laguna Guaymoreto cost only US$15 pp, car-driven trips

---

---

out to the crocodile reserve at Hacienda Tumbador are US$20 pp, and hiking in Parque Nacional Capiro y Calentura is US$15 pp. Five-day trips out to Mosquitia, up the Río Plátano to Las Marías and upstream to visit the petroglyphs cost US$360 pp, everything included. The agency also rents 350cc and 650cc enduro motorcycles for US$35 a day. The *merendero* on the west side of the square acts as an agent and will drive you up to the hotel if you want to rent a cycle. Bicycles were once rented here as well and may be again in the near future. The soft-spoken, friendly owner speaks German, English, and Spanish.

Information
Fundación para la Protección de Capiro, Calentura y Guaymoreto, a.k.a. **Fucagua,** staffs an office on the second floor of the kiosk in the middle of the square, in the same room as the town library, tel./fax 434-4294. The office can provide you with a simple map and descriptive pamphlet of the surrounding natural areas.

Laundry
Lavandería Colón, almost opposite Hotel Mar de Plata, charges US$3 per load to wash and dry clothes and is closed on Sunday.

Language Schools
Trujillo would be a marvelous place to study Spanish—very relaxed, quiet, not a lot of distractions, fantastic location, and with prices comparable to or better than schools in Guatemala. Two Spanish schools in Trujillo both closed their

doors due to the tourist slump following Hurricane Mitch, but the new **Escuela de Idiomas Truxillo,** tel. 434-4135, opened in early 2000. The school, located past the old cemetery on the road leading to Museo Rufino Galán, charges US$130 per week for 20 hours of individual classes, or US$190 for classes along with food and lodging with a local family. For more information, check out their very groovin' website at www.spanishschool.hn.

GETTING THERE AND AWAY

Air
Both Isleña Airlines and Rollins send one plane a day Monday through Friday from La Ceiba to Trujillo, on to Palacios, and back again through Trujillo to La Ceiba. Both airlines charge US$26 to La Ceiba and US$28 to Palacios. Isleña sells tickets at the Christopher Columbus Hotel, which is owned by the airline, tel. 434-4966. The Rollins office, tel. 434-4140, is on the main street entering town, on the left a block before the Hotel Colonial.

Bus
Cotraipbal, tel. 434-4932, runs five direct buses to San Pedro Sula (US$5.50, five to six hours) between 2 a.m. and 8 a.m., and one to Tegucigalpa via San Esteban and Olancho (US$6, 9-10 hours) at 4:30 a.m. The buses leave from the terminal one block south of the square.

Regular buses to La Ceiba (US$2.50, four hours) leave from the square every two hours between 6 a.m. and 3 p.m. Tocoa buses (US 90 cents, two hours) leave every hour from the square until 4:30 p.m. Two buses daily go to Santa Rosa de Aguán (US$1, 90 minutes) usually around 10 a.m. and 2 p.m., though times frequently change.

To Limón, take a Tocoa bus to Corocito, then hitchhike from there. Buses to Santa Fe and San Antonio leave from opposite the Tiendo O'Glynn, Mon.-Sat. at irregular hours. Usually three buses daily run to Santa Fe for US 70 cents. A private *(especial)* taxi to Santa Fe would cost US$10, while a ride in a *colectivo* is about US$3.50.

Frequent buses run Mon.-Sat. between Trujillo and Puerto Castilla for US 50 cents.

Car
The stretch of highway between Trujillo and Tocoa was in an appalling state for over a year after Hurricane Mitch, which left its heavy mark on the Aguán Valley. One bridge incredibly left open to vehicles was skewed at a most ridiculous angle and doesn't look like it will last much longer. With luck the government will repair it before it collapses altogether. The road between Corocito, Tocoa, and Savá is in fine shape, while the main bridge at Savá over the Río Aguán was still provisional and pending reconstruction, though crossable. The remaining highway to La Ceiba past the Río Aguán is fine. The total drive to La Ceiba, barring any major road improvements, is about three hours.

If you're driving to Tegucigalpa from Trujillo, the dirt road turning off from Corocito and heading through the mountains of Olancho is faster and much more scenic than the route via La Ceiba and San Pedro Sula. The dirt road runs through isolated, mountainous country, so certainly drive only in the daytime and be prepared for a dusty, bumpy four or five hours before reaching the pavement near Juticalpa.

An extremely bad dirt road also leaves Corocito east to Limón and continues on as far as Punta Piedra, near the edge of La Mosquitia. There is no way to drive into La Mosquitia, other than trying to follow the beach past Punta Piedra.

NEAR TRUJILLO

Santa Fe and San Antonio
A large Garífuna town 10 km west of Trujillo, Santa Fe is strung along a sandy road parallel to a fairly cluttered beach. Cleaner patches of sand can be found nearby to the east and west of Santa Fe. At the western end of town are two very elemental concrete hotels, **Hotel Tres Orquídeas** and, just across the way, **Hotel Mar Atlántico,** each charging US$7 s or d with a fan and private bathroom.

Comedor Caballero, better known as Pete's Place, is worth making a trip to Santa Fe. The one-room restaurant, with the kitchen right next to the tables, serves up superb conch stew, lobster tail, shrimp in wine sauce, snapper, pork chops, and other dishes daily for lunch and dinner. Meals cost US$4-10, but it's well worth the splurge. Pete presides over the cooking with an eagle eye and is very knowledgeable about the Trujillo area.

There is said to be a small patch of reef known as **Cayo Blanco** lying offshore in front of Santa Fe; it could be reached with the help of a local fisherman.

Beyond Santa Fe the dirt road continues to the smaller villages of San Antonio and Guadalupe. Rooms can be found in San Antonio by asking around, and there is reportedly a small hotel in Guadalupe.

Thrice-daily buses ply the dirt road between San Antonio, Santa Fe, and Trujillo, leaving at irregular hours. The last bus normally returns to Trujillo around noon. From Guadalupe, in the dry season, walkers can follow trails around the point west past the settlements of Plan Grande and Manatí Creek to Río Coco, and from there get a bus onward to Jutiapa and La Ceiba. The river crossings are impassable in the rainy season. It would also be easy to arrange a boat ride out this way for a nominal fee with the fishermen who pull up daily near the dock in Trujillo.

Between Santa Fe and Trujillo, on its own private beach, is **Campamento Hotel and Restaurant,** fax via Hondutel in Trujillo at 434-4200, which rents five *cabañas* in a grassy area next to the beach for US$28 d or t, or a larger one on the beach sleeping four for US$40. Each room has a/c, hot water, and new furniture. The atmosphere is peaceful, the beach is clean, and the restaurant serves good seafood. Campers can pitch a tent on the grass for US$3 a night, with use of bathroom and showers—an excellent value. This is one of the best and safest place to camp on the northern coast.

Parque Nacional Capiro y Calentura

Comprising 4,537 hectares between 667 and 1,235 meters above sea level, Parque Nacional Capiro y Calentura is centered on the two jungle-clad peaks right behind Trujillo. The park has few trails or tourist facilities, as tourism was a secondary reason for establishing the reserve, the primary reason being to protect Trujillo's water supply. The easiest and most common access is via the dirt road past Villa Brinkley, which winds up the mountain to the radio towers just below the peak of Cerro Calentura. Formerly the U.S. Drug Enforcement Agency main-

tained a radar station here, but now the caretakers of a Hondutel tower and the Catholic radio station antenna are the only occupants. From the radio towers, a trail goes east a short distance to a lookout point with great views out over the bay and Laguna Guaymoreto. The peak of Cerro Calentura is a bit farther east, but no trails seem to exist. To get out there would require a machete. From the radio towers you can see out over the Valle de Aguán.

The two- to three-hour walk up to the towers from town is best done in the early morning, when it's cool and the birds are most active. Muggings have been reported on the road, so it might be wise to go in a group. A small wooden cabin at the bottom of the road is where the park *vigilante* stays—he will collect your US$3.50 entrance fee between 8 a.m. and 4 p.m. daily.

Another popular hike in the park is up the Río Negro, in a valley between Cerro Capiro and Cerro Calentura. The trail follows a water pipe along the river to a dam, above which are two small waterfalls.

Just outside the western edge of the park, a colonial-era stone road cuts over the mountains to the village of Higuerito on the south side of the mountains. The trail begins east of the village of Campamento, on the road to Santa Fe. Somewhere in the side of the mountains—good luck finding them—are the **Cuevas de Cuyamel,** which archaeologists say have been used as a ritual site since pre-Columbian times.

Puerto Castilla

The largest container port in Honduras in terms of total tonnage transferred (Puerto Cortés handles more ships), Puerto Castilla is 28 km from Trujillo, just inside Punta Caxinas. Most of the freight shipped out of Puerto Castilla is agricultural products and raw materials, much of it produced by Standard Fruit. Unless shipping is a personal fetish, there is little reason to go out to Puerto Castilla. The ocean-facing beaches nearby are lovely but not as safe for tourists as the beaches in Trujillo.

Fishing in Puerto Castilla's deep harbor is reputedly excellent. Waters drop straight down to 20 meters, allowing deep-water fish to be caught right off the docks. Boats can sometimes be found at Puerto Castilla going to La Mosquitia or the Bay Islands. Ask around the docks or talk to the port captain, tel. 434-4962, for more information.

Just before Puerto Castilla is the **Monumento a Colón,** a shoddy concrete cross marking the site of the first Mass celebrated on the mainland of the Americas, when Columbus landed here in 1502

Frequent buses run between Trujillo and Puerto Castilla, first arriving at the village of Castilla, then farther on arriving at a guarded gate at the entrance to the docks. Here tourists may pass, either on foot or in private car (park on the far side of the gate), and continue walking for a couple of hours to reach the windblown point.

A better option would be to look for a sandy road turning off the highway to the east, two km on the Trujillo side of the Columbus monument. A hundred yards or so farther on is a lovely windswept beach facing the open ocean, great for a swim, though the water is choppy. The sand flies and mosquitoes are ferocious back in the scrub away from the beach but are kept at bay near the water by the steady wind. Take care to go in a group and not bring many possessions out this way, as isolated beaches around Trujillo can be risky for muggings. This dirt road continues, winding between Laguna Guaymoreto and the ocean, eventually coming out at the crocodile farm at Hacienda Tumbador before looping back to the Trujillo-Tocoa highway.

Refugio de Vida Silvestre Guaymoreto

The Guaymoreto Wildlife Refuge, covering over 7,000 hectares, surrounds a broad lagoon formed by the Cabo de Honduras, east of Trujillo. The lagoon, canals, mangrove swamps, and a small island are excellent bird and monkey viewing areas. Getting into the reserve without guides is not easy—better to take an inexpensive day-trip with Turtle Tours, tel. 434-4444. If you want to freelance it, one option would be to hire a sea kayak at the Bahía Bar near the airport and paddle your way up to the mouth of the lagoon.

Near the back (south) side of the lagoon is **Hacienda Tumbador,** a crocodile farm where tourists can admire scads of these lethal, prehistoric-looking monsters slinking about in their native environs. If you have a car, take the highway toward Tocoa and look for a sign-posted turnoff between km markers 350 and 351. From here, the hacienda is a 30-minute drive on bumpy dirt roads. Turtle Tours also runs tours to Hacienda Tumbador.

Santa Rosa de Aguán

Situated on a sand spit at the mouth of the Río Aguán, about an hour east from Trujillo by car, is the large Garífuna town of Santa Rosa de Aguán. Until October 1998, Santa Rosa was a lovely, friendly place, dotted with many traditional thatched huts and great for foreigners to visit. But Hurricane Mitch was cruel to Santa Rosa, filling the Río Aguán to flood levels and spilling out onto the town. Dozens of residents were swept out to sea and drowned. Such a tragedy had never before hit Santa Rosa in its more than 200-year history, and the survivors still show the traumatic effects. The town has mainly been rebuilt, though with much more concrete construction than previously, but it understandably has lost, at least temporarily, the friendly vibe that made it such a fine town to visit. With luck the town will physically and emotionally recover soon. At the moment there is no lodging in Santa Rosa, though you could likely find a room by asking around. A couple of small *comedores* sell shrimp, fish, and chicken. Buses run several times a day between Santa Rosa and both Tocoa and Trujillo. If you're in a private vehicle, the turnoff to Dos Bocas and on to Santa Rosa de Aguán is exactly 22 km from the junction to Puerto Castilla, outside of Trujillo.

Limón

Another seaside Garífuna settlement, east of Santa Rosa and reached by a 34-km horrific dirt road, Limón is infrequently visited by outsiders and has a very remote, isolated feel, lost between the Mosquitia and the rest of Honduras. The condition of the road to Limón had reached epically bad proportions by early 2000, with locals holding protests about it at government offices in Tocoa. It may get repaired but likely not until after the paved roads in the area are fixed, which could take some time.

Beyond Limón, the "road" continues via Plan de Flores and Planes to Punta Piedra, where it hits the beach. If your vehicle is extraordinarily sturdy, it is possible to continue on the beach out to Sangrelaya, at the edge of the Mosquitia. Trucks from Tocoa run this route regularly. Five or six buses a day run between Tocoa and Limón, the first at 7:30 a.m. and the last at 1 p.m. If you're in Trujillo, get off at Corocito and wait for a Limón bus there.

THE BAY ISLANDS

For many travelers coming to Honduras, a visit to the Bay Islands is on the top of their vacation agenda. The three islands of Roatán, Utila, and Guanaja, plus some 60 smaller cays, are the country's prime tourist attraction—Caribbean jewels of sand, coconut palms swaying in the steady trade winds, green and blue waters, and one of the most spectacular coral-reef systems in the Americas, which attracts scuba divers from the world over.

For novice divers, finding a more convenient place to get a beginner's scuba certification or advanced training would be difficult. Eager instructors by the dozen are just waiting around for their next client, ready to take potential divers through the paces in calm, clear, 28° C waters, all at remarkably low prices.

Diving and snorkeling may be the activities of choice among Bay Island visitors, but life above the waves has its own appeal. Centuries of pirate raids, immigration, deportation, and conquest have left a fascinating cultural and racial gumbo of British, Spanish, African, and Native American influences that have combined to create the unique society of the Bay Islands. One trait that separates islanders from the mainlanders ("Spaniards," as the islanders like to say), and which many tourists will find comforting, is that English is the native tongue of the Bay Islands.

High season for Bay Islands tourism is from Christmas to Easter, with a mini-high season July September.

BAY ISLANDS HIGHLIGHTS

- Scuba diving anywhere!
- Snorkeling on West Bay Beach, Roatán
- Slinging a hammock on Water Cay, Utila
- Partying Saturday night on Utila
- Visiting the north side beaches on Guanaja
- Seeing the dolphin show at Anthony's Key, Roatán

THE LAND

The Bay Islands, arrayed in an arc between 29 and 56 km off the Caribbean coast of Honduras, are the above-water expression of the Bonacca Ridge, an extension of the mainland Sierra de Omoa mountain range that disappears into the ocean near Puerto Cortés. The Bonacca Ridge forms the edge of the Honduran continental shelf in the Caribbean. Thus, on the northern, ocean-facing side of the three main islands, shallow waters extend only just beyond the shore before disappearing over sheer underwater cliffs to the deep

THE BAY ISLANDS REEF SYSTEM

Coral reefs are one of the most complex ecosystems on the planet, comparable in diversity to tropical rainforests. The Bay Islands reef is particularly varied because of its location on the edge of the continental shelf, at the transition between shallow-water and deep-water habitats. Some 96% of all species of marine life known to inhabit the Caribbean—from tiny specks of glowing bioluminescence to the whale shark, the largest fish in the world—have been identified in the waters surrounding the Bay Islands. Divers and snorkelers flock here in droves to experience a dizzying assortment of fishes, sponges, anemones, worms, shellfish, rays, sea turtles, sharks, dolphins, and hard and soft corals.

What is Coral?

Contrary to what many people understandably assume, coral is a nonswimming animal, not a plant. Each "branch" of coral is made up of hundreds or thousands of tiny flowerlike polyps. Polyps, thin-membraned invertebrates, compensate for their flimsy bodies by extracting calcium carbonate from the seawater and converting it into a brittle limestone skeleton. Through this continual, tireless construction process, the bizarre and beautiful undersea forests seen by divers and snorkelers are created, at a rate of about a centimeter per year.

Tiny, extended tentacles bring in food drifting by in the water, but the anchored coral polyps must supplement their intake by housing minuscule algae cells; these cells in turn produce nutrients for the polyps through photosynthesis. Because of this symbiotic relationship, coral always grows in relatively shallow waters, where the sun can penetrate. Reduced water clarity due to pollution or erosion from construction, agriculture, or deforestation can be fatal for coral, robbing the algae of the light needed to photosynthesize.

The main reef-building coral in shallow areas is leafy lettuce coral (Agaricia tenuifolia). This species virtually excludes other corals from many spur tops, growing in some areas to within 10 cm of the surface. In areas with greater wave energy, such as along the north sides of the islands, forests of treelike elkhorn coral (Acropora palmata) are common. Star coral (Montastrea annularis), brain coral (Diploria spp.), boulder brain coral (Colpophylia natans), and elegant columns of pillar coral (Dendrogyra cylindrus) are often seen on the fore reef, at a depth of 10-15 meters. Black coral is still found around the Bay Islands, usually in deeper waters on reef walls. Many shallower patches have been destroyed by jewelry makers. In the water, black coral appears silver, only turning black when exposed to the air.

Fire coral, or hydrocoral, is not a true coral but a "battery of stinging nematocysts on tentacles of coral polyps," as Paul Humann, author of a good three-volume reference on reef systems, describes it. Learn what fire coral looks like right away, and keep well clear of it—even a light brush can be painful. Should you accidentally bump into it, remember never to rub the affected area or wash it with fresh water or soap, as this can cause untriggered nematocysts to release their barbs. Two recommended treatments are vinegar or meat tenderizer, both of which immobilize the nematocysts.

The Reef

It's often incorrectly claimed that the Bay Islands reef and the Belize reef system to the north together make up the second-longest reef in the world—after Australia's Great Barrier Reef. In truth, the Bay Islands reef is completely distinct from the Belize reef—not only does a 3,000-meter-deep undersea trench separate the two, but they are different kinds of reef. The Belize system is a barrier reef, with the coral wall separated from shore by a lagoon at least a mile wide, while the Bay Islands system is a fringing reef, essentially beginning right from the shore. Sections of the north side reef on the Bay Islands show characteristics of developing into a barrier reef in time but are still considered fringing reef.

Reef geography is generally the same on all three of the main islands. The north-side reef forms almost a complete wall, with only a few narrow passages allowing access to the shallow lagoon between the reef and the shore. The Guanaja north-side reef is much farther offshore (about a mile in places) than on Utila and Roatán. From the reef crest, which sometimes almost breaks the surface, the reef slopes to a plateau at around 10 meters, then falls off the wall. The south-side reef frequently starts literally at the water's edge and slopes down at a more gentle grade to a depth of around 10-12 meters, when it hits the sheer reef wall bottoming on sand at around 30-40 meters. The southern reef is generally more broken up than the north, with channels, chutes, headlands, and cays. Sea mounts—hills of coral rising up off the ocean floor—and spur-and-groove coral ridges are common and are often the best places to see diverse sealife.

The Cayos Cochinos reef system shares similar characteristics with the other islands, except it lacks steep dropoffs and lagoons on the north side.

The Health of the Reef

Generally speaking, the Bay Islands reef is in pretty good shape, although certain high-impact areas are showing signs of damage from over-diving and decreasing water quality. According to a recent study, the Roatán reef has 25-30% live coral cover (the rest covered by sand, sea grass, sponges, rubble, algae, dead coral, fire coral, etc.), a relatively healthy percentage compared to other Caribbean reefs.

Tourism development poses the most direct threat to the reef, since coastal and hillside construction generates runoff and other forms of water pollution. Degraded water quality leads to algae blooms, which steal sunlight, oxygen, and other nutrients from the coral, literally choking the reef to death. This threat is particularly severe on Roatán, where the island's long central ridge is being carved up on all sides for roads and houses, while coastal wetlands, which filter runoff, are being filled in for construction. The reef off West Bay in Roatán is particularly threatened, due to all the construction and tourist activity in the hills backing the beach. While Guanaja is quite hilly, construction on the main island is still limited, making runoff less serious. However, water pollution around Bonacca, Mangrove Bight, and Savanna Bight has damaged

most of the reef surrounding those towns. Utila, mostly flat and still retaining much of its wetlands, does not face much erosion at the moment, but water pollution is a problem around East Harbour and Pigeon Cay.

Coral bleaching occurs on the Bay Islands reef, as it does on reefs all over the world. During these usually temporary events, higher water temperatures than normal cause the coral to expel the zooxanthellae (algae cells) that give coral its color pigments. The cells return when the sea temperature returns to its normal level, ideally 23-30 degrees Celsius. 1998-99 saw a global bleaching event, in part as a result of the warming of the world's seas after the 1997-98 El Niño phenomenon. Ironically, Hurricane Mitch—so devastating above the water—helped spur the recovery of the Bay Islands reef from the prolonged bleaching episode, by bringing up colder water from deeper in the ocean and cooling off the waters near the surface by as much as three degrees Celsius.

The proliferation of divers is also beginning to take a toll on the reef; some oversaturated dive sites are closed off to allow for the coral to recover. These days dive boats more regularly tie off on buoys instead of anchoring on the reef, but divers continue to bump and grab coral in spite of frequent warnings. Each brush with a piece of coral wipes off a defensive film covering the polyps, allowing bacteria to penetrate. Just one small gap can compromise the defenses of an entire coral colony.

Black coral, formerly common around the Bay Islands, has been depleted in recent years by jewelry makers, whose work can be seen in several local gift shops. For those tempted to buy a piece, remember it is illegal to take black coral into the United States.

waters, while on the south side the waters fronting the Honduran mainland are much shallower. The height of the islands generally increases west to east, from the lowland swamps of Utila to the modest mid-island ridges of Roatán to two noteworthy peaks on Guanaja, the highest being 412 meters.

Flora and Fauna

Ecological zones in the Bay Islands include pine and oak savanna, arid tropical forest, beach vegetation, mangrove swamp, and iron shore, or fossilized, uplifted coral. Much of the once-dense native pine and oak forests have not survived centuries of sailors seeking masts, immigrants looking for building material, and hunters setting fires to scare game. The only forests left are on the privately owned island of Barbareta and in a few remote sections of Roatán, like by Brick Bay or around Port Royal. What was left of the famed forests of Guanaja was utterly flattened by Mitch's 290-kph winds—the island's vegetation has only begun to recover.

BAY ISLANDS DIVING

Upon arrival in the Bay Islands, divers can be overwhelmed by the number of dive shops and courses. Here's a primer to get you started, whether you're a first-time diver in need of certification or an old hand looking for the right shop for you.

Getting Certified

First, try to realistically decide if you are ready to go diving. Bay Islands dive instructors have many stories of would-be students who, believe it or not, could barely swim or were actually scared of the water. Although it's relatively cheap and other people seem to like it, if you just can't get rid of that lurking panic after a couple of shallow dives, accept the fact that diving is not for you. One of the best ways to find out how you will react to scuba diving is to try snorkeling a few times to see how you feel in the underwater world. Some people find they prefer the more relaxed shallow-water experience of snorkeling, which does not require all the gear, training, and expense of scuba diving.

Most divers getting certified in the Bay Islands follow a course created by Professional Association of Dive Instructors (PADI), the best-known scuba certification organization. Almost all dive shops on the islands work with PADI, but a couple of shops use National Association of Underwater Instructors (NAUI), Scuba Schools International (SSI), and Professional Diving Instructors Corporation (PDIC). While PADI is by far the most popular, almost all scuba shops around the world accept certifications from all of these organizations.

Novices ready to take the plunge into the world of scuba have a choice of either a resort course or open-water certification. A **resort course,** normally costing US$50-80, is an introductory dive for those who aren't sure if they'll like diving or not. It involves a half-day of instruction followed by a shallow, controlled dive.

The **open-water certification,** as taught in the Bay Islands, normally begins with two days of classroom instruction and shallow-water training, followed by two more days of open-water dives, gradually descending to a maximum depth of 15 meters. A 50-question multiple-choice test on material that has been drilled into your head is the last step to becoming a certified open-water diver. You are then allowed to dive without an instructor—but never without another diver. Diving alone can be deadly. While most courses are finished in four days, some shops will offer courses in three or three and a half days. Experienced divers warn against rushing the course, as the extra day with an instructor can be very helpful in making divers more comfortable in their new underwater world.

Dive shops will sometimes take **referrals,** wherein a person completes the academic and shallow-water training at home and finishes the open-water dives with the shop. Considering that the shallow-water training could be accomplished for less money in balmy, clear Caribbean waters instead of the local YMCA pool, there's not much attraction in using a referral unless your time on the islands is extremely limited.

Many newly certified divers come out of their open-water course feeling slightly uneasy about the idea of diving without that reassuring veteran instructor at their shoulder; they may want to immediately continue their controlled training with the **advanced open-water course.** The advanced course provides specific instruction in undersea navigation and multilevel diving—essential for planning your own dives—and includes two diving highlights: the night dive and the deep dive (to 40 meters). Although dive shops and PADI may imply otherwise (one of PADI's nicknames is Put Another Dollar In), divers are not required to have an advanced certification to do either deep or night dives. However, a shop is perfectly within its rights to only allow advanced divers to go on night or deep dives with their boats, to avoid potential risks caused by less-experienced divers.

Recreational divers are allowed to descend to a maximum depth of 40 meters. Going deeper puts divers in serious danger of both nitrogen narcosis and severe decompression problems when ascending. With a different mix of gases in the air tanks, however, it is possible with training to descend deeper and stay down longer than with a regular air tank. **Nitrox,** a mix of nitrogen and oxygen, allows divers to (depending on the mix) extend their time at depth by 20 or 30 minutes, increase depth to around 60 meters, or minimize the surface interval and allow more dives in a single day. Nitrox is very popular with live-aboard dive boats, which try to squeeze in as many dives as possible in a week. Nitrox diving requires certification and special equipment, which not every dive shop has. Two shops in West End, Roatán, that offer US$120, two-day Nitrox courses and have the gear are Ocean Divers and Bottom Time Divers.

Extreme depth freaks will be pleased to hear that another, even more specialized gas mix known as Trimix (nitrox plus helium) allows divers to go as deep as 150 meters, a truly spooky deep sea world. A Trimix instructor gives a course at the Bay Island Beach Resort in Sandy Bay, Roatán, every few months. Ocean Divers in West End has one complete Trimix set.

Many other specialty dive courses are available on the Bay Islands, including rescue diver, medic/first aid, reeflife identification, underwater photography, and divemaster, which certifies you to lead dives with a shop.

Course and Dive Prices (US dollars)
Open Water: $250 (Roatán), $160 (Utila)
Advanced: $200 (Roatán), $160 (Utila)
rescue: $225 (Roatán), $160 (Utila)
divemaster: $500 (Roatán), $500 (Utila)
single dive: $30 (Roatán), $15 (Utila)
10-dive package: $200 (Roatán), $125 (Utila)

Choosing a Shop
So you've decided you're ready to take a course or go on a series of dives—how to choose between all the different dive shops? Price is not much of a factor, as everyone pretty much charges the same amount. Minimum prices are set on both Utila and Roatán to avoid the brutal price wars that used to hit the islands. Prices at the different dive resorts on Guanaja are included as part of a weeklong package.

Perhaps the most important criteria for choosing a shop, especially for novice divers taking their first course, is the quality of the instructors. A good instructor can mean the difference between a fun, safe, and informative course, and one that just follows the book, or worse. Already-certified divers will also want to ensure their dive leader is competent, as they will be in part relying on that person's judgment and safety skills. Ask how many dives a divemaster has completed—100 is very few, 500 is a decent amount, 1,000 or more is a lot. Also, a divemaster with 100 or so dives is likely to have gone through all or most of his or her courses on the Bay Islands, where conditions are excellent almost all the time. Consequently, that divemaster will have less experience dealing with emergency situations than a diver trained in, for instance, the North Sea or the northern Pacific off California. Divemasters trained in commercial diving, mixed-gas diving, cave diving, or military diving tend to be more safety-conscious and cautious.

After talking to the divemasters, look closely at the gear you would be using. The newer, the better.

Especially crucial is having a well-maintained air compressor, to ensure clean air in your tank. Cast an eye over the hoses, regulator, and BCD air vest, which should all look new and be without signs of wear and tear. Most shops should and do replace their gear on a regular basis. Ensure fins and mask fit snugly and comfortably—this may seem like a trivial detail in the dive shop, but a tight fin or a leaky mask can be very distracting in the water and ruin a dive if annoying enough. A large dive boat is also a great bonus, much more stable and easier to get in and out of than the smaller launches used by many shops and giving a less choppy and wet ride to and from the dive sites. Those prone to seasickness should bring motion sickness pills, which are sold by many dive shops. Waters around the Bay Islands are usually a fairly balmy 28° C or so, but if the water temperatures get down to the low 20s C, as they sometimes do, you will want to make sure your shop has good wetsuits, full-length if you get cold easily.

Another factor to consider is the set-up and schedule of dives at the different shops. Most shops have one dive in the morning and another in the afternoon, at a fixed hour. While they choose the sites, clients should not be shy in requesting certain dives. Most dive shops are happy to accommodate, but some may put up resistance in going to a far-off site. And be sure the group you are going with will not be too large. An ideal group would be four to six divers, divemaster included. Certainly you don't want to go with more than eight divers, or it starts to feel a bit like an underwater procession.

Most Bay Island divers want to live on the islands to enjoy a taste of the quirky islander culture and have a chance to talk to islanders and other travelers alike, but single-minded divers without a lot of time might consider taking a week's vacation on a **live-aboard dive boat.** With Peter Hughes' boat having departed the Bay Islands, currently the only major live-aboard boat operating is the **Bay Aggressor,** of the Aggressor Fleet, information in the U.S. at P.O. Box 1470, Morgan City, LA 70381, tel. (800) 348-2628 or (504) 385-2628, fax (504) 384-0817, email: info@aggressor.com, web site: www. aggressor.com. The charge is US$1,600 for a one-week dive vacation living on the boat, everything included except transport to Honduras. A smaller, more personalized live-aboard option that gets rave reviews is the **Maid'en Dessert,** an 18-meter sailing ketch equipped for up to eight divers run by Roatán Charters, tel. 445-1620, website: www.roatan.com. Trips cost between US$1,750 pp with just two people to US$900 pp if there is a group of eight.

The Jamaica Tall coconut palms *(Cocos nucifera)* of the Bay Islands, normally a reliable source of liquid refreshment and shade, were struck in 1996 by Lethal Yellowing (LY), a mysterious plant disease responsible for the death of millions of palms in Florida, Jamaica, and Mexico. Despite programs to treat infested trees with antibiotics, the plague succeeded in wiping out most of the island's original trees. Early on when the disease hit, a few motivated islanders promoted replanting with LY resistant strains, such as the Malayasian Yellow and its hybrids with Panama Talls. Many first-time visitors, seeing the new palms, will not know the difference.

Many of the once-abundant animal species endemic to the Bay Islands have been hunted to extinction or to the brink of it: manatees, seals, fresh- and saltwater turtles, white-tailed deer, green iguanas, basilisk lizards, boa constrictors, yellow-crowned and red-lored Amazon parrots, frigate birds, brown pelicans, and roseate terns have all vanished or are now seen only rarely. As recently as 30 years ago, crocodiles were frequently seen crossing streets in Utila; when one was spotted (and promptly killed) in December 1995 the event was a major local news item.

In spite of the depredations of hunters, 15 species of lizard still survive on the island, along with 13 species of snake (including the poisonous but rarely seen coral), wild pigs, the small ratlike agouti, two species of opossum, and 13 species of bat. Over 120 bird species, most of which are migratory, have been spotted on the islands. Once at least 27 species of macaws, parrots, and parakeets lived on the islands; now the only macaws found are pets, and only about half the parrot species still survive in the wild. For those interested in birdlife on the islands, don't miss visiting Tropical Treasures Bird Park in Sandy Bay, Roatán.

The Bay Island Conservation Association (BICA), with offices on all three islands, coordinates efforts to protect different endangered species as well as the islands' remaining forests by overseeing reserves at Port Royal and Carambola in Roatán, Turtle Harbor in Utila, and, supposedly, the entire island of Guanaja. More funds are being made available for tighter environmental protection as part of a much-delayed Inter-American Development Bank program for the Bay Islands.

Climate

The Bay Islands have a superbly comfortable climate, with year-round air temperatures ranging between 25 and 29° C and east-southeast

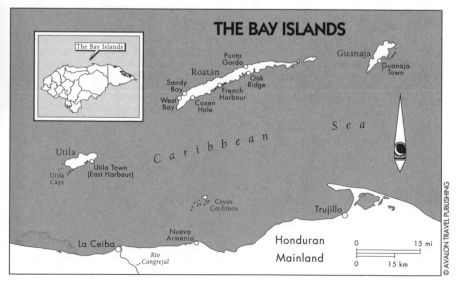

COPING WITH THE INSECTS

Sand flies and mosquitoes can be voracious on the Bay Islands, so come prepared. Sand flies (also called *jejenes* and "no-see-ums") can be a true nightmare on the beach, turning the arms and legs of an unsuspecting sunbather into pincushions of little red welts. DEET, Avon Skin-So-Soft lotion (sold locally, often with repellent included), and coconut oil are all good repellents, as of course are long, loose-fitting clothes. A good strategy for enjoying a sunbathing session without getting gobbled is to sit out on a dock over the water; sand flies don't stray far from the beach. A good stiff breeze will get rid of them entirely, so with luck the trade winds will be blowing during your trip.

trade winds blowing steadily most of the year. Daytime temperatures average 27° C, 21° C at night—hot but not stifling during the day and pleasant for sleeping at night.

Annual rainfall averages 220 cm, more than half of this coming in October and November, the height of the hurricane season. Water visibility is best when there is the least rain, usually March to September. Water temperature ranges from 26° C midwinter to 30° C in summer.

HISTORY

Pre-Columbian Residents

In spite of almost 50 identified archaeological sites, little is known of the early inhabitants of the Bay Islands. Most archaeologists now agree, after years of dispute, that pre-Columbian islanders were related to the mainland Pech, who prior to conquest lived close to the coast near Trujillo.

The first full-time residents are thought to have arrived no earlier than A.D. 600. After A.D. 1000 several major residential areas sprang up, such as Plan Grande in eastern Guanaja and the "80-Acre" site in eastern Utila. Because all the sites are located inland 10-20 meters above sea level, it is theorized that the first islanders hated sand flies even more than the current residents and fled the shoreline to escape the pests.

The island Pech grew manioc (cassava) and corn, hunted for deer and other game, fished from dugout canoes for reef fish and shark, and carried on a lively trade with the mainland Maya and Pech, as evidenced by discoveries of obsidian, flint, and ceramics with mainland designs.

Most pre-Columbian sites have long since been thoroughly sacked by fortune hunters both foreign and local. The best place to see examples of pottery and jade is in the museum at Anthony's Key Resort in Sandy Bay, Roatán. Locals may still try to sell visitors "yaba-ding-dings," as they call the artifacts, but after years of looting there aren't many pieces left to sell.

Conquest and Colonization

Believed to be the first European to visit the Bay Islands, Columbus landed near Soldado Beach on Guanaja in late July 1502 on his fourth voyage. After anchoring and sending his brother Bartholomew ashore for a look around, the Admiral named the island "Isla de los Pinos" (Island of the Pines) in honor of the impressive forests. He then commandeered a passing merchant canoe laden with goods from the mainland and forced its owner to accompany him to the Mosquitia Coast to serve as an interpreter. He remarked in his journal on a "very robust people who adore idols and live mostly from a certain white grain with which they make fine bread and the most perfect beer."

When the Spaniards returned on a slaving expedition in 1516, they made off with 300 Indians after a brief skirmish, only to have the would-be slaves take over the ship near Cuba and promptly set sail back to their home. But other ships looking for slaves soon followed, and not long after that, in 1530, the first *encomienda* was awarded on the Bay Islands. *Encomiendas* granted a conquistador rights to demand labor and tribute from the local inhabitants, supposedly in return for good governance and religious education.

This new economy had barely been established when European freebooters began appearing on the horizon, drooling at the thought of all the gold mined in the interior of Honduras passing through relatively isolated and unprotected Trujillo. French raiding boats appeared in 1536, followed by the English, who used the Bay Islands as a hideout for the first confirmed time in 1564 after capturing four Spanish frigates. By the early 17th century, the persistent use of the Bay Islands as a base for pirate assaults and, briefly, as a settlement area for the British Providence Company had become a serious threat to the Spanish, so colonial authorities decided to depopulate the islands. By 1650 all the native islanders had been removed, most ending up in the malarial lowlands on Guatemala's Caribbean coast. This only made the islands more appealing to the pirates, who pursued their ventures unabated.

The many pirates who found shelter on the islands before the British military occupation in 1742—including Henry Morgan, John Coxen, John Morris, Edward Mansfield, and a host of others—spent most of their time hunting, fishing, or fixing up their boats, never bothering to set up any buildings beyond temporary camps. Smaller groups preferred to anchor in the bay on the south side of Guanaja, with at least seven escape routes through the cays and reef, while larger fleets stayed at Port Royal, Roatán, with just one narrow, easily defensible entrance.

Following the declaration of war between England and Spain in 1739, British troops occupied Port Royal for several years, building two small forts and granting homesteads in Port Royal and

Sandy Bay. The Spanish were awarded the islands as part of the Treaty of Aix-la-Chapelle in 1748, and the last settlers were finally removed in 1751. The British returned in 1779 following another outbreak of war. In 1782 Spaniards attacked Port Royal with 12 ships and took the forts after two days of fierce fighting. The forts and surrounding town were destroyed, and Roatán was left uninhabited.

Development of the Modern Bay Islands

The earliest immigrant settlement in the Bay Islands that has survived to the present day is the Garífuna village at Punta Gorda, Roatán. Some 4,000 Garífuna were unceremoniously dumped on the deserted island on 12 April 1797 by the British near Port Royal.

The Garífuna were followed in the 1830s by a wave of immigrants, both white and black, leaving the Cayman Islands in the wake of the abolition of slavery there. Although some isolated settlers lived on the islands when the Cayman Islanders arrived, the newcomers laid the foundations for the present-day towns. They moved first to Suc-Suc Cay off Utila in 1831, and shortly thereafter to Coxen Hole, Flowers Bay, and

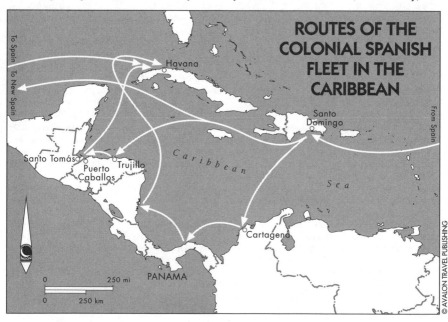

ROUTES OF THE COLONIAL SPANISH FLEET IN THE CARIBBEAN

To Spain
To New Spain

From Spain

Havana

Santo Domingo

Santo Tomás
Puerto Caballos
Trujillo

Caribbean   Sea

Cartagena

PANAMA

0   250 mi

0   250 km

© AVALON TRAVEL PUBLISHING

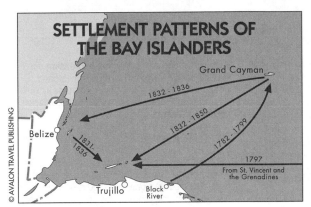

SETTLEMENT PATTERNS OF THE BAY ISLANDERS

Grand Cayman

1832 - 1836

1832 - 1850

1782 - 1799

Belize

1831 - 1836

1797
From St. Vincent and the Grenadines

Trujillo

Black River

Bonacca Town.

© AVALON TRAVEL PUBLISHING

Since the late 1980s, the pace has picked up dramatically. In 1990, an estimated 15,000 tourists came to the islands, by 1993 that number doubled to 30,000, and by 1996 it had doubled again. The accelerating development of Bay Island tourism took a blow from Hurricane Mitch and the ensuing bad publicity. But as memories of the hurricane fade (at least outside Honduras), tourists are starting to return to the islands in greater numbers, and further growth and development is expected. In early 2000 actor Christopher Lambert announced the construction of a new luxury resort on Guanaja, a sign that business is looking up again.

West End in Roatán and Sheen and Hog Cays off Guanaja, which would eventually become Bonacca Town.

The British government, seeing the Bay Islands as a useful geopolitical tool in its struggle with the United States for control over Central America, initially claimed ownership of the islands. In 1859, the British were forced to recognize Honduran sovereignty over the Bay Islands, but many islanders continued to think they were part of the British Empire until the early 20th century, when the Honduran government first began asserting its authority over the islands.

Current Society

The economy of the Bay Islands has long relied almost entirely on the ocean, despite brief forays into the banana and pineapple exportation business in the late 19th century. Fishing has always been and continues to be the mainstay of the economy, with a fleet of some 400 commercial boats on all three islands, fishing mainly for shrimp, lobster, and conch. Overfishing has led to bans *(vedas)* during certain months of the year, but with only two inspectors, the several plants on Roatán pretty much buy whatever comes their way, whatever time of year it is. A modest boat-building industry, based particularly in Oak Ridge, has declined in recent years. Islander men frequently join on with the merchant marine or work on international cruise ships for several months of the year.

This low-key existence began to change starting in the late 1960s, when tourists discovered the islands' reefs, beaches, and funky culture.

The changes wrought by tourism have benefited many islanders immensely, and most now live off the trade in one way or another. Even before the tourist boom, islanders had always maintained a better standard of living than their mainland countrymen (still called Spaniards by the islanders). Consequently a steadily growing stream of Latino immigrants have come over to get a piece of the good life, a trend that is changing the face of the islands—a trend some islanders are not too happy about. Recent estimates put the population at about 32,000 for all three islands, with an annual growth rate of nine percent, compared to just under three percent for the country as a whole.

The Inter-American Development Bank and the Honduran government are, after several years of delay, beginning to implement a US$24 million program of infrastructure and environmental projects on the Bay Islands—projects that aim to alleviate some of the harsh effects of tourism-related development on the marine and terrestrial ecosystems and on islander society. Strict regulations will be placed on construction and road building to safeguard against erosion, which, apart from being an unfortunate loss of scarce topsoil, also hurts the reef. A more complete sewage and water system is to be installed. Guanaja, Utila, and Roatán are supposed to benefit equally from the loan, but because of the heavy concentration of development on Roatán that island is expected to receive the most attention.

ROATÁN

Rattan-Island is about 30 miles long and 13 broad, about eight leagues distant from the coast of Honduras . . . The south side is very convenient for shipping, having many fine harbours. The north side is defended by a reef of rocks that extend from one end of the island to the other, having but few passages through, and those of but small note, being mostly made use of by the turtlers . . . It is likewise very healthy, the inhabitants hereabouts generally living to a great age.

—THOMAS JEFFERYS, GEOGRAPHER TO THE KING OF ENGLAND, 1762.

Jefferys may have been a bit off on the measurements—Roatán is actually about 40 miles long and only a little over two miles wide—but he did accurately describe the natural features that have long made Roatán the choice of Bay Island immigrants, from the first pirates 400 years ago to the resort builders and dive fanatics of today.

Theories on the source of the island's name vary wildly. The most popular explanation, supported by Jefferys and many other colonial-era chroniclers, is that Roatán is a derivation of rattan, the English word for a common vine found in the Caribbean. Another possibility is that it's a se-

vere corruption of the Nahuatl expression *coatl-tlan*, "place of women." A third, far-fetched hypothesis is that the name comes from the English expression "Rat-land," referring to the island's pirate inhabitants.

Tourists and retirees began arriving on Roatán in the 1960s, and in recent years the influx has increased dramatically. Roatán has been deemed respectable—enjoying fawning write-ups in travel publications and the limelight of frequent celebrity sightings—and is now home to a large expatriate community consisting mainly of Americans but also many Europeans.

After some 15 years of raging real-estate speculation and building fever, few nooks and crannies have escaped the scrutiny of developers. Remote sections of coastline on all sides of the island have been divided up in lots for development as private homes or resorts. Nevertheless, towns like West End and Sandy Bay remain relatively slow-paced and not outrageously expensive when compared to other Caribbean islands.

One recent change to the tourist profile in Roatán is the arrival in 1999 of international cruise ships. The monstrous crafts, dwarfing Coxen Hole at their dock site, normally come in twice a week (Tuesday and Thursday at last

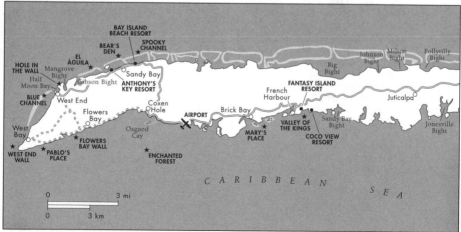

check) and disgorge hundreds of tourists for the day. It's a good idea to find out when the boats are coming, and avoid going snorkeling at West Bay that day. While the twice-weekly crowds can be a bit disconcerting for other foreign visitors, the islanders are all for the new business, especially since the tourists pay in dollars and only stay for the day.

Some 20,000 people, roughly two-thirds of the Bay Islands' population, live on Roatán. Coxen Hole, the island's largest town, is the department capital. Sand flies can be a plague here, so come prepared.

Real Estate

Roatán is well into a property speculation boom, with many foreigners and not a few Hondurans looking to pick up beachfront lots on the island, to build vacation homes or resorts or just hold on to for resale when prices rise. With the tourism slump after Hurricane Mitch, land prices temporarily halted their upward spiral, but it surely won't last.

While many of the best bargains in Roatán have long since been snapped up, there's still plenty of land for sale. Four of the better-known real estate agents on the island are: **J. Edwards,** tel. 455-5917 or 455-5725; **Island Properties** in Sandy Bay, tel. 445-1263; **Re/Max** in French Harbour, tel. 455-5379; and **Blue Moon Properties,** based in the U.S., tel. (516) 653-5848, with properties in both Roatán and Utila.

GETTING THERE

Air
As the most frequently visited of the three Bay Islands, Roatán has plenty of air service. Those flying out of Roatán to an international destination must pay a US$25 departure tax in the Roatán airport.

Sosa, tel. 445-1154, and **Rollins,** tel. 445-1967, offer several flights daily to and from La Ceiba (US$17), with connections to San Pedro Sula, Tegucigalpa, and the Mosquitia. **Taca/Isleña,** tel. 445-1387, offers flights once a week to San Salvador, daily to Belize City, daily to San Pedro Sula, and four times daily to La Ceiba. Flights to the U.S. include a stop in San Pedro Sula.

Apart from rental car stands and a couple of uninspired gift shops, there's not much to hold a traveler's attention at the airport. The **Banffaa** bank is open to exchange traveler's checks and U.S. dollars Mon.-Fri. 9 a.m.-4 p.m., Saturday 9 a.m.-noon.

The airport is three km from downtown Coxen Hole, on the highway toward French Harbour. Taxis to West End or Sandy Bay from the airport cost US$10. If you haven't got a whole lot of luggage or cash, it's possible to walk the short distance out to the highway and catch a bus to Coxen Hole, and from there on to West End. Buses run until about 4 p.m.

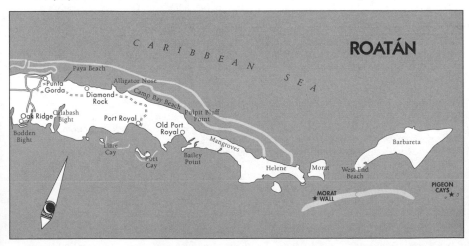

Boat

The **MV Galaxy** runs daily between La Ceiba and the municipal dock in Coxen Hole; the 90-minute ride costs US$9. Some snacks are available on the boat, and a movie is shown in the cabin. The Galaxy normally leaves Roatán at 7 a.m. and leaves La Ceiba at 3 p.m. for the return voyage. For more information, call the offices in Coxen Hole, tel. 445-1795 and 455-5056, or in La Ceiba, tel. 442-0780.

Coxen Hole's **Capitanía del Puerto** (Port Captain), tel. 445-1262, can be helpful (if you speak Spanish) in arranging rides to the other islands, La Mosquitia, Belize, or elsewhere. Better yet, prowl from dock to dock asking boat crews where they are going and when. Some boats refuse to take passengers, while others are happy to receive the extra cash.

GETTING AROUND

Roatán has the Bay Islands' only major highway; it runs east-west connecting various island settlements. While the majority of visitors are likely to stay put in West End, Sandy Bay, or the confines of their resort, the more adventurous may wish to explore Roatán's less accessible corners. Buses operate along the highway, and hitchhiking is a viable option for reaching places that get regular traffic but are off the main highway, such as Flowers Bay, Camp Bay Beach, or Port Royal.

Buses and Tours

Most of the island can be covered on Tica minibuses, which leave Coxen Hole frequently from 7 a.m. until late afternoon. The buses run to Sandy Bay (US 40 cents), West End (US 60 cents), French Harbour (US 40 cents), Punta Gorda (US 90 cents), and Oak Ridge (US 90 cents). All buses leave from the main street in Coxen Hole—the smaller minibuses to West End leave from the park next to the H.B. Warren Supermarket, while the larger (and less frequent) buses to French Harbour and points east depart from a little farther east up the street.

Librería Casi Todo in Coxen Hole, tel. 445-1944, email: casitodo@globalnet.hn, runs regular island tours for 8-10 people (you can join in with others or put your own group together) for US$32 pp for a three-and-a-half-hour trip out to the east side of the island to visit an islander farm, boat through mangroves, and see a Garífuna dance show in Punta Gorda. **Foncho's Tours,** tel. 445-1747 or 445-0392, offers similar excursions.

The Tica bus company also operates comfortable new vans and a 30-seater bus for island tours or excursions. Day rates or a set price for a trip can be negotiated. Those who have limited Spanish skills should request Matilde Zuñiga, the only English-speaking driver. It costs about US$100 for an eight-seat van on a full-day island tour. Call 445-1764, 445-2206, 445-1809 or 445-1290 for more information.

Car, Motorcycle, and Bicycle Rental

Several companies rent compact cars and small four-wheel-drives at rates ranging US$45-75 per day. All have stands in the airport, as well as central offices elsewhere on the island. **Toyota,** tel. 445-1729, and **Avis,** tel. 445-0122, both have offices across the highway from the airport. Two other companies are **Sandy Bay Rent-A-Car,** with offices in Sandy Bay, tel. 445-1710, fax 445-1711; and **Caribbean Rent A Car,** with an office in French Harbour, tel. 445-1430. **Roatán Rentals** in West End, tel. 445-1171 or 445-1150, has rickety Suzuki Samurais for US$45 a day.

Capt. Van's in West End rents 185cc motorcycles for US$35 a day, mopeds for US$25 a day, or pedal bikes for US$9 a day. There's no telephone, so go by to check out the vehicles and make arrangements, or send email to paradise@globalnet.hn, subject: Capt. Van's.

Jayes, near Foster's Bar in West End, tel. 445-1008, rents mopeds for US$30 full-day, US$20 half-day.

Bringing Your Car

For those who just can't do without their own set of wheels, it is possible to ship a car from either Miami or La Ceiba. One frequently used operator is **Hyde Shipping/Naviera Hybur,** with offices in Miami, at 10025 N.W. 116th Way, Suite 2, Medley, FL 33178, tel. (305) 913-4933, fax (305) 913-4900, and in French Harbour, Roatán, tel. 445-5543. Shipping a standard-size car to Roatán from La Ceiba costs US$60, from Miami US$600.

BOATING

Cruises and Charters

The clear, clean waters surrounding Roatán, stroked by steady trade winds most of the year and stocked with most of the known fish species in the Caribbean, are superb for sailing and fishing trips. Many boat owners offer half- and full-day cruises, snorkel trips, cocktail cruises, deep-sea and flats fishing, or combinations of the above.

Several boat captains offer cruises to the Cayos Cochinos, Barbareta, Morat, Guanaja, and elsewhere in the vicinity. The **Onaire III**, a 19-meter yacht, is available for half-day cruises with open bar, lobster salad and sandwich lunch, and use of snorkel gear for US$50 pp. Full-day trips are also available. For information stop in at Belvedere's Restaurant in West End, or email the owners: oceandivers@globalnet.hn, subject: "Onaire III." Islander Keven Wesley, tel. 445-1172, offers full-day, custom-designed island tours in his fast motor launch for US$200-225, up to six people. **TJ's** is a long-time favorite for an old-fashioned sunset "booze cruise," with tickets through Paradise Computers, Coconut Tree Store, or Twisted Toucan Bar, US$29 pp for a three-hour trip with open bar. TJ's also has longer trips to the Cayos Cochinos for US$55 pp. **Tabiyana Water Sports Club,** tel. 445-1805 (leave message), VHF Channel 16, also offers sunset cruises on a 12.5-meter Hunter sloop, as well as a variety of other custom cruises.

Roatán Sail and Dive Charters, tel. 445-1620, website: www.roatan.com, operates a 60-foot ketch equipped for six divers. Trips cost US$1750 pp with just two people or US$900 pp with up to eight people, including food and diving. Non-diving trips cost less. Destinations are worked out between guests and captain. This recommended charter is a favorite among honeymooners, with many annual repeat customers.

A most unusual excursion is a one- to two-hour trip in a miniature submarine hand built by an amiable American mad scientist who lives in West End. He will happily enumerate the attributes of his craft to allay safety fears. The submarine descends to a maximum depth of around 175 meters. Expect to see all manner of unusual deep-sea life, and occasionally even a shark. This jaunt is not for the claustrophobic. At last report the captain was considering closing up shop—ask at the Half Moon Bay Hotel if he's still open for business.

Fishing

Situated as it is at the division between the shallow waters toward the mainland on one side and the 3,000 meter-deep Cayman Channel on the other, Roatán and the other Bay Islands are ideally located to go after a variety of different shallow and deep-water species. Favorite game fish around Roatán are marlin, wahoo, tarpon, barracuda, kingfish, and jack, to name just a few. Waters around most major settlements are

DIVING RULES AND ETIQUETTE

- Don't dive alone.
- Know your limitations, and only dive if in good physical condition.
- Always follow the dive tables.
- Don't anchor anywhere in or near coral—use the buoys.
- Don't litter or discharge foreign substances into the water.
- When diving, always fly a diver-down flag and lower the flag when all divers are back on board. When passing moored boats, or boats flying a diving flag, always pass on seaward side at least 150 feet away, even in a small boat.
- Avoid contact with any living part of the reef.
- Always observe proper buoyancy techniques and secure dangling equipment.
- Never sit or stand on coral formations, or grab coral to steady yourself.
- Don't grab, poke, ride, or chase reef inhabitants.
- Don't feed the fish.
- Don't fish on the reef.
- Don't remove any marine organisms, alive or dead.
- Discourage reef degradation by refusing to buy black-coral jewelry, sea turtle products, shell ornaments, etc.
- If you find garbage on the reef, gently remove it and bring it back to shore.
- Take only photographs, leave only bubbles.

usually heavily fished by the locals, so more isolated spots, particularly on the north and east sides of the island, offer the best luck. The sand flats around Barbareta, on the eastern end of the island, are famed among local fishermen.

Capt. Steve Jazz, owner of Rick's American Café in Sandy Bay, tel. 445-1143, offers custom fly fishing trips in the flats around Roatán. Fishing trips can also be arranged with **Miller Fishing Charters,** run by the owner of Cindy's Place Restaurant in West End. The owners of **Happy Divers** in West End charge US$40 per hour pp for fishing trips, with gear and bait included. Other fishermen in West End, Sandy Bay, or elsewhere will also happily set up fishing trips for a negotiable fee.

Marina and Boat Services

With the French Harbour Yacht Club closed at last report, **Rock Bodega Marina** in Brick Bay, tel. 445-1337 or 445-1127, is the best place for yachties to tie up in Roatán. A berth in the 30-slip marina costs US$150 a month, with 24-hour electricity, water, and cable TV. No gasoline is available here—boaters have to fuel up elsewhere.

Dixon's Marina in French Harbour, tel. 455-5456 or 455-5458, can take care of boat repairs.

WEST END

Although it is the main tourist town of Roatán and lined with cabañas, restaurants, and dive shops, West End remains a slow-paced seaside village and an undeniably superb location to lose yourself in the relaxing rhythms of Caribbean life. Even during the high season (Dec.-April) people and events move at a languid pace up and down the sandy, oceanside road that

constitutes "town." It's a telling sign that the road has been left rutted and unpaved—cars and bicycles must slow to a snail's pace, bouncing along, while pedestrians are free to wander at leisure, stopping to browse for T-shirts or to admire yet another spectacular sunset right offshore.

Construction of new houses and cabañas continues, but in an unobtrusive way—new developments are tucked away amongst the palms and don't dominate the visual landscape. West End is not overwhelmed by wealthy tourists, as it has

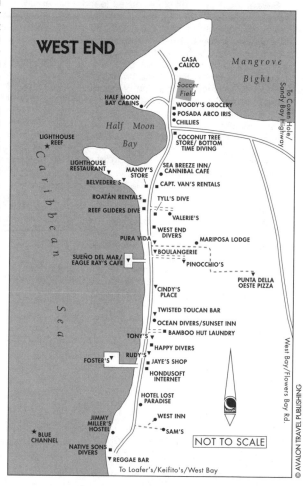

no luxury resorts. The roughly 500 local residents have not lost their easy friendliness and, fortunately, seem to be influencing the newcomers more than the newcomers are influencing them.

Sights

West End's main attractions are in plain view: beaches, 28° C bright blue water, and, a couple hundred yards offshore, the coral reef, marked by a chain of buoys. The waters around West End are kept very clean, and visitors can jump in pretty much wherever it's convenient. The best beach in town is **Half Moon Bay,** a swath of palm-lined sand right at the entrance to West End, bordered by points of iron shore (fossilized, raised coral) on either side forming the namesake shape. Another good place to swim and sunbathe is the dock in front of Jimmy Miller's hostel at the south end of town. Both of these spots happen to be near two of the best snorkeling sites off West End. The reef passes right across the mouth of Half Moon Bay, an easy swim from shore, with particularly fine reef near the more southern of the two points. Sea turtles and rays are often seen in the sand flats and shallower sections of reef here.

One of the buoys in front of Jimmy's hostel marks the entrance to **Blue Channel,** a spectacular channel cutting through the reef. It's a bit of a swim for snorkelers, so take your time heading out to conserve energy for exploring the reef and the trip back.

There are several other sites on the reef off West End, but in looking for them beware of boat traffic. Snorkel gear can be rented from any of the dive shops for US$7, or a bit less from stores in town, like **Jaye's Boutique** near Foster's Bar. A passport or US$10 deposit is usually required.

Dive Shops

Although not as numerous as on Utila, West End's fully equipped dive shops offer dives and courses for all levels and in several languages. Minimum standard prices have been set by the local government to avoid cutthroat competition, so courses and dive packages generally cost about the same everywhere: US$250 for a standard open-water certification, US$200 for the advanced open-water, US$75-80 for a resort course, US$30 per dive, and US$25 per dive

for five or more dives. Generally all shops have two dives daily, one morning and one afternoon, and start new certification courses every couple of days.

Divers must pay an extra US$1 on top of the price of each dive, which goes to fund the Northwest Marine Association, which helps organize patrols in the marine reserve.

Ocean Divers, tel. 445-1925 or 445-1005, in Europe 31-7114-1557, runs a hotel with its well-respected dive shop and offers package rates for diving and courses. Nitrox and other technical dive training is available also. An open-water certification package including five days accommodations, breakfast, and transport to and from the airport costs US$342-399. Weeklong dive packages, with room, breakfast, and 13 dives, tanks and weights included, cost US$510-573. Rooms alone are US$10-50 depending on occupancy and whether it has a/c or a fan, not a bad deal. For more information, check out Ocean Divers' web page at www.roatanet.com/sunset_inn; email: oceandivers@globalnet.hn

West End Divers, tel./fax 445-1531, one of the more popular shops in town as well as one of the oldest, has two dive boats and lots of new equipment. Go to the website: www.roatanet.com/wed or email: wedivers@hondutel.hn for more information.

Native Sons Divers, on the beach at the south end of town, tel. 445-1335, is a frequently recommended, locally run shop certified with PADI and providing experienced instructors. The shop can also arrange fishing trips and rents 10 rooms in three cabins for US$35 for two or three people.

Tyll's Dive, tel./fax 445-5322, email: tyllsdive@hotmail.com, is one of the oldest shops in West End and has a full range of courses and a friendly staff. Tyll's also organizes sailing trips on a 42-foot yacht.

Reef Gliders, opposite from Tyll's, is run by a German diver who worked with most of the shops in West End before finally opening up his own place. He's got everything for the PADI courses in a small shop on the edge of the water. Contact via email at: paradise@globalnet.hn, subject: Reef Divers.

Bottom Time Diving, in the same building as the Coconut Tree store in front of Half Moon Bay, tel. 445-1648, is one of the newer shops in town but has plenty of good gear and a large,

DIVING ROATÁN'S REEF

The reef topography in Roatán, as with Utila and Guanaja, is divided into a north side and a south side. On the north side of the island, the reef is separated from shore by a shallow lagoon, sometimes a kilometer wide but usually less. From the crest, which sometimes almost breaks the water's surface, the reef slopes down to a plateau or moat, followed by the reef wall. On the north side, sponges, sea fans, and elkhorn coral are common. The south-side reef slopes out gently until reaching the edge of the wall, normally dropping from 10 meters down to 30 meters, with a sandy bottom. Here grow a bewildering assortment of colorful soft corals. On the western end of the island, where the north- and south-end reefs meet, the reef shows characteristics of both formations.

The most popular dive sites in Roatán are in the Sandy Bay Marine Reserve, a protected water reserve between Sandy Bay and West Bay on the western end of the island, conveniently near the dive shops in West End. The reef on the eastern side of Roatán has many spectacular, infrequently visited sites—the best bet is to dive with two resorts in Oak Ridge that accept walk-ins.

Top Dive Sites

Hole in the Wall, a crack in the reef just around the bend from Half Moon Bay on the way to Sandy Bay, is justifiably one of the favorite dives near West End. Cruise down a steep sand chute from the upper reef, which leads downward through a cleft and pops out on the reef wall at around 40 meters. Below is very dark water—here is one of the places the Cayman Trench comes in closest to Roatán, and water depths just below Hole in the Wall are around 800 meters. Keep a close eye on that depth gauge. While the wall is the obvious highlight of the dive, leave time to explore around the labyrinth of sand chutes on the upper reef, where you might spot a barracuda or eagle ray.

Near Anthony's Key Resort is the wreck of *El Aguila,* a 71-meter freighter the resort bought and sank in sand flats at 34 meters, near the base of the reef wall, to create a dive site. Take good care not to catch yourself on any metal parts as you swim around the deck—and look for the green moray and large grouper that live at the site.

Just east of Anthony's Key, right in front of Sandy Bay, is **Bear's Den,** a cave system lit from above. The cave entrance, on the upper part of a steep reef wall decorated with much boulder and lettuce coral, is tight to get in, but widens out into a spacious cavern inside. Beautiful, shifting light from above illuminates schools of glassy-eyed sweepers that patrol the cave. The cave system continues farther, but only experienced cave divers should continue beyond the main cavern.

Spooky Channel, at the eastern end of Sandy Bay, is exactly what it sounds like, a channel through the reef almost completely closed over, and a bit unnerving to swim through for the dark water. The dive starts at 12 meters or so, and deepens as you go in to a maximum of 38 meters or so. While rock and fossilized coral predominate in the lower reaches of the channel, up higher on the reef barrel sponges, sea fans, and hard corals are common.

Right out front of West End is **Blue Channel,** a canyon with a narrow opening that gradually widens and deepens as you swim away from shore. A mellow dive, good for the afternoon, the channel has swim-throughs, interesting rock and coral formations, and plenty of fish to watch. Look for a green moray that hangs out near the entrance to the channel.

Off the southwest point of Roatán is **West End Wall.** Because of its location, strong currents flow past the site, meaning divers need to plan a drift dive. While the wall is worth seeing, it's also fun just to let the current zip you across the reef fields above the wall, which are invariably filled with hawksbill turtles, spotted eagle rays, and a dazzling array of colorful fish.

Considered one of the most dramatic dives on Roatán, **Mary's Place,** located just west of French Harbour on the south side, is a narrow cleft in the reef wall. Divers enter at around 25 meters, then zig-zag into the cleft, where you'll see plenty of large sponges and also lots of seahorses. Because of the tight channels, Mary's Place is for experienced divers only.

Right in front of Coco View Resort, east of French Harbour, is **Valley of the Kings,** an exceptionally lovely wall dive noted for the tall stands of pillar coral, several different types of sponge, and a profusion of marinelife tucked into crevasses and overhangs on the wall.

well-equipped dive boat. The shop keeps a flexible dive schedule to suit the needs of its clients. **Sueño del Mar,** tel. 445-1717, in US (800) 298-9009, email: suenodelmar@globalnet.hn, is housed in a large building out on its own private dock in the West End harbor, with the dive shop on the "ground" floor and a restaurant/bar above. The shop has two 10-meter dive boats and a boat kept at Brick Bay to dive on the south side. Sueño is about the best dive gear shop on the island.

Happy Divers, right next to Rudy's, tel. 445-1205, fax 445-0002, has been in operation for two years and has packages with Georphi's Tropical Hideaway Hotel.

At West Bay Beach is **Bananarama,** fax 445-1271, email: bananarama@globalnet.hn, run by another German dive instructor, this one with 10 years of experience. The owner also rents out cabins at West Bay for US$35-45 d (depending on the season) and offers package deals for divers.

Other Recreation

Sea kayaks are available for rent at the Sea Breeze Inn, tel. 445-0020, for US$4 an hour for a double. Half-day rentals cost US$12, and full-day rentals cost US$20. Full-day trips through the mangroves and to Gibson Bight, with lunch and snorkel gear included, cost US$55 per person. Bay Island Expeditions, tel. 445-1794, next to Rudy's, offers sea kayak tours, US$55 full-day or US$30 half-day, or rents kayaks for US$20 full-day, US$12 half-day.

Underwater Paradise, tel. 445-1075, runs **glass-bottomed boat tours** off the dock at Half Moon Bay Resort. You can find out about trips by calling 445-1075 or asking at the hotel reception desk. The one-hour ride costs US$20; group discounts are available. The Coral Explorer, tel. 445-1042, charges the same price for its daily trips from West Bay. Water taxi to West Bay from the Coconut Tree Store in West End is included in the ticket price.

Apart from renting bicycles and motorcycles, Capt. Van's can arrange **horseback riding** trips in the hills above West End, affording views over the surrounding coastline and a feel for the dry tropical forests native to the Bay Islands. This is a good option for folks looking for a break from all that diving. Jimmy Miller, erstwhile hostel owner and eternal local character of note, knows a few

interesting places in the hills near West End and may be able to take visitors on a horseback trip for a modest fee, perhaps US$8-10 pp.

Right at the large slip cut into the beach between West End and West Bay is Tabiyana Water Sports Club, tel. 445-1805 (leave message), VHF Channel 16, offering a slew of different **water diversions,** including jet ski tours, wind surfing, or sunset cruises on a 12.5-meter Hunter sloop. A variety of customized trips can be arranged, and prices are negotiable.

WEST END ACCOMMODATIONS

Hotels in West End mostly fall into the moderate range, US$20-60 for a double, generally in a cabin with ceiling fan, screened windows, and private bathroom. The budget traveler will be glad to hear, however, that less expensive digs are still available. There are no luxury resorts in West End. Keep in mind that during slower times of year, like June-Nov., prices are negotiable. Also note that the following prices were collected in early 2000, when tourism was still slow a year after Hurricane Mitch. Prices may increase if tourism comes back to former levels.

For those who become transfixed with diving and the mellow lifestyle in West End, locals rent many apartments and cabins of differing quality for about US$300-500 a month, more in the high season. Rents in nearby locations like Gibson Bight and Sandy Bay are lower.

Shoestring

Jimmy Miller's Hostel, at the south end of town right on the beach, was once a backpacker favorite, but the owner has currently suspended operations. Until Jimmy reopens, if he ever does, his brother Sam is picking up the slack at his place on the opposite side of the street from Jimmy's, a hundred meters or so back up in the trees. Sam rents a dormitory bed for US$3, a single room for US$4, or a double for US$8. All beds come with a much-needed though not always trustworthy mosquito net and use of the communal kitchen. The private rooms also have fans.

Budget

Valerie's is a comfortable, inexpensive, and somewhat ramshackle hotel/hostel behind Tyll's

Dive Shop, with dorm beds for US$5 with use of kitchen and comfortable patio, safe lock-up, mosquito nets, and bunk beds. Private rooms are US$10-20 d, some with porches and hammocks. Travelers are often found playing cards and socializing on the patio. The hotel has no phone, but the owner receives email: paradise@globalnet.hn, subject: Valerie's.

Chillies, facing Half Moon Bay, tel. 445-1214, is very popular with the low-budget crowd, who make good use of the clean dormitory beds for US$7.50 pp, the communal kitchen, and the front porch. Two private cabins in the back, each with a kitchen, rent for US$20 for one to three people.

Many local residents rent rooms out of their house for US$8-15 d—ask around. **Miss Edith** rents out three cabins near Tyll's Dive shop for US$10 s or US$15 d, a good deal and frequently patronized by divers on long stays.

Inexpensive

Two doors down from Chillies is **Posada Arco Iris,** tel./fax 445-1264, email: roberto@hondutel.hn, run by a friendly Argentinian couple. Rooms in the rambling wooden house run US$20-40 d, the more expensive with a/c and/or a kitchen. The top-floor rooms facing Half Moon Bay, with two large beds and a kitchen, cost US$60. There is also a travel agency here and telephone/fax service in the office.

The Sea Breeze Inn, tel. 445-0020, in the US (800) 298-9009, offers spacious, breezy rooms in a large, three-story wooden building set back off the road in the center of town. Rooms with hot water and refrigerator cost US$25 d, US$30 d with a/c, US$45 d with kitchenette. The owner offers good package deals for divers with the Sueños del Mar dive shop.

A calm, quiet place to stay is **Casa Calico,** fax 445-1241, email: paradise@globalnet.hn, subject: Casa Calico, web page: www.roatanet.com/casacalico. This two-story wooden house at the far end of the West End soccer field, north of town, offers three comfortable apartments on the second story, with full kitchen, a/c, and fan, easily sleeping four, for US$30-50 per room. A smaller room downstairs, next to where the American owners live but with a side entrance, rents for US$25 d a night. Sea kayaks are available for guests to use.

Right in the center of town next to West End Divers is **Pura Vida,** tel./fax 445-1141, email:

puravida@hondutel.hn, website: www.puravidaresort.com, with clean, airy, tile-floored rooms with hot water, fans, and two double beds for US$30 d or t, or US$65 with a/c and cable TV. The new hotel has 12 rooms.

In a three-story wooden house built atop a small hill a couple of hundred yards back off the main road, behind Pura Vida, is **Mariposa Lodge,** email: roatankid@hotmail.com, with four apartments with a homey feel, two with private kitchens and the other two with one common kitchen, with a breezy porch to relax on, for US$40 a night with up to three people.

The rooms for rent for US$35 d on the second floor above **Pinocchio's Restaurant,** tel. 445-1481, fax 445-1008, have received high marks from guests staying there, and the dinners downstairs are top-notch. Don't worry about noise from the restaurant, as it closes by 10 p.m. at the latest.

At the southern end of town is **West Inn,** tel. 445-1615, a large, two-story pink hotel with 18 bare rooms without much character, though it is clean. It's not an amazing value at US$25 s or US$35 d with a private bathroom and ceiling fan, although the owner is friendly enough. Prices are more flexible in the slow season.

Foster, owner of the popular bar bearing his name, rents rooms in West End for US$40 sleeping two to four people, on two large beds, with a/c and refrigerator. Reservations can be made at tel. 445-1124 or fax 445-1542. He also has rooms in West Bay.

Located 15 minutes from West End on the way to West Bay, **Keifito's Beach Plantation,** fax 445-1130, in the U.S. (888) 301-8047, has quiet, clean cabins for US$35-40 d that make for a great reasonably priced getaway. It's located on a tree-covered hillside sloping down to the water. Unfortunately, business has not been good since Hurricane Mitch, and the owner actually tried to convince the guidebook writer to buy it! So who knows if Keifito's will stay in business. If it does, it's a great place to stay, and the restaurant's food is tasty and a good value.

Moderate

Half Moon Bay Cabins, on the northern point of Half Moon Bay, tel. 445-1075, in the U.S. (800) 989-9970, fax (813) 933-1977, offers frequently recommended, spacious waterfront cabins for US$38 s or US$55 d with fan, more with a/c, all with hot water. The cabins closest to the water are the best, to enjoy views of Half Moon Bay from your porch hammock. Perks include free snorkel gear for guests, a small bay and reef right out front, and great seafood at the porch restaurant. The hotel staff is very friendly and quick to take care of their guests.

Right at the entrance to town, in fact a bit close to the road, are **Coconut Tree Cabins,** tel. 445-1648, email: coconuttree@globalnet.hn, website: www.coconuttree.com, all equipped with a/c and some with a small kitchen, ranging in price between US$35 and US$50. Hotel owner Vincent Bush also has rooms on West Bay and can help set up excursions for guests. More information is available at the Coconut Tree Store.

A long-time resident of West End, **Hotel Lost Paradise,** tel. 445-1306, fax 445-1388, rents newly renovated rooms in well-made wooden cabins on stilts right on the beach in the south end of town. Rooms cost US$56 s or d with fan, US$68 with a/c, all with a small refrigerator and some with small patios. Meal plans are available, as are better rates for multi-day stays. A new restaurant with second-floor deck was under construction at last check.

WEST END FOOD AND ENTERTAINMENT

Breakfast
The choice breakfast spot in town is unquestionably **Rudy's,** where the owner will serve you up a steaming cup of coffee and invariably reply heartily "Still alive!" when you ask how he's doing. The response is so famous it appears on a specially made T-shirt. Rudy whips up superlative, filling banana pancakes, excellent omelets (you pick the fixings), and fresh juices (the mango is nectar of the gods) for US$2-4. He also receives and sends faxes for a fee (fax 445-1205) and has cabins for rent.

For a fresh croissant, baguette, fruit salad, light sandwich, or a cup of good coffee, go to the **Boulangerie,** open Mon.-Sat. 7 a.m.-4 p.m., opposite the Sueno del Mar Dive Shop.

Papagayo's, next to Ocean Divers, whips up a solid American-style breakfast, and the open-air porch is a mellow place to greet the day.

Inexpensive Lunch and Dinner
Finding low-priced food in West End isn't easy, but luckily a couple of restaurants catering to the budget crowd serve excellent homestyle islander food at reasonable prices. **Cindy's Place** serves up hearty plates of chicken, steaks, or fresh fish caught daily by the fisherman owner. Entrees come with mashed potatoes, salad, cooked vegetables, or other fixings for US$5-8. The fish or chicken sandwiches and fries cost US$3-4. Run by friendly islanders, Cindy's is a relaxed place to talk, have a few beers, and hang out at one of the picnic benches on the lawn. Open Mon.-Sat. 11 a.m.-9 p.m. (sometimes 10 p.m.).

Another small local restaurant specializing in wholesome islander food is **The Lighthouse Restaurant,** located on the south side of the point dividing the main part of West End from Half Moon Bay. A sign on the main road points the way to the rickety wooden house and patio, right on the water. Fresh fish or shrimp are served a variety of ways, including the fiery and tasty *escabey* sauce made with lots of hot island peppers, US$8-10. The veggies are very well cooked, and a vegetarian plate with rice, potatoes, and beans is a meal in itself for only US$2.25. The menu is extensive, and it's all good. Open 7:30 a.m.-10 p.m. daily.

Midrange Lunch and Dinner
Pinocchio's Restaurant is tucked a hundred yards or so off the main road in West End, but well worth seeking out for the excellent, unusual dishes such as lobster in gorgonzola cheese, chicken with garlic and smoked cheese, vegetable stir-fry, bountiful salads, and crepes. Prices are not cheap (US$7-15 per plate), but the meals are generous in both taste and size. Open Thurs.-Tues. 6-9:30 p.m.

The waterfront porch at **Half Moon Bay Cabins** is a fine location to enjoy mouthwatering fish fillets, lobster, shrimp, and other seafood prepared in a variety of ways but invariably cooked to perfection. Dinners run US$6-10 and are worth every penny. Large chicken or fish sandwiches with fries cost US$4. The kitchen is open daily until 10 p.m.

Papagayo's Tropical Café offers a variety of creative dishes, like mango-stuffed chicken and grouper in a jalapeño-cream sauce for

US$8-11, as well as decent breakfasts. Open 7 a.m.-11 p.m. daily; it's next to Ocean Divers.

Italian
Tony's Restaurante Italiano, next to Ocean Divers, whips up a decent pizza pie for US$8-12. Tony's also has a good lobster-and-tomato pasta. The slices served in the stand on the street are not as good as the pizza in the main restaurant, open 5:30-10 or 11 p.m. daily.

An American couple operates **Belvedere's,** an Italian restaurant and bar near the Lighthouse Restaurant, on the point between Half Moon Bay and West End, with a rotating menu including eggplant parmesan, spaghetti, lobster, lasagna, and chicken for US$4-7. Open Sun.-Thurs. for dinner only.

Punta della Oeste, a brick-oven pizza restaurant located about half a kilometer's walk up the path behind Pura Vida and past the Mariposa Lodge, makes a good, crispy, thin-crust pizza and shows movies sometimes as well. Perhaps because of the long walk required to get there, business was not good at last check—if the sign is still up by Pura Vida, it's still open.

Entertainment
In addition to his many cabins, Foster Díaz is the owner of **Foster's,** one of the social centers of West End. The restaurant/bar is a two-story wooden contraption (recently grown even larger) built on a dock over the water, with a couple of hammocks swinging between the wood beams and always a few people hanging about drinking beers. The Friday night disco (or occasionally live band) at Foster's is obligatory for most locals and foreign visitors alike. Open daily 10 a.m.-10 p.m.; until 2 a.m. on Friday. For those who want to chase the island party scene, on Saturdays the place to be is **Bolongo's Disco** in French Harbour.

Pretty much every night the **Twisted Toucan Bar,** a small hut ringed with stools right in front of Ocean Divers, is swinging away with well-lubricated divers and travelers until a non-predetermined hour, usually around 11 p.m. Happy hour is 4-7 p.m.

The second-floor bar at Sueño del Mar dive shop, the only other large building over the water apart from Foster's, is a fine place to nurse a drink and watch the sun take its invariably sublime daily plunge into the Caribbean.

Farther down the beach, just south of town, is **Loafers,** a deck-bar on the second floor of what looks like a large shed, a very popular and chill spot to hang out, listen to good tunes, shoot a game of pool (if you can get in on the table), or join in the frequent beach volleyball games in front. While the volleyball is fairly relaxed during the week, the Sunday afternoon and evening games, when a lot of the islander boys come out to play, are more competitive and great fun to watch. The bar is open daily except Wednesday starting at 5 p.m., no set closing time, happy hour 6-9 p.m.

Restaurant, bar, and local institution Foster's is a West End social gathering spot.

Punta della Oeste, the brick-oven pizza restaurant up in the bush behind Pura Vida, occasionally shows free movies—keep an eye out for signs posted along the main road.

MORE WEST END PRACTICALITIES

Shopping
Mandy's Gift Shop and Grocery sells T-shirts, sunscreen, Avon Skin-So-Soft lotion, postcards, and a few groceries. You can place local calls there for a fee. Open Mon.-Sat. 8 a.m.-5:30 p.m.

Jaye's Boutique, opposite Foster's dock, tel. 445-1008, sells a variety of tourist bric-a-brac and rents snorkel and fins for US$6 a day or mopeds for US$30 for a full day, US$20 for a half day. Open daily 8 a.m.-6 p.m.

The best, and really only, grocery store in West End is **Woody's,** with a decent selection of packaged goods and the occasional slightly limp-looking vegetable. Open Sun.-Thurs. 7 a.m.-7 p.m., Friday 7 a.m.-5:30 p.m. H.B. Warren in Coxen Hole or Eldon's in French Harbour are far superior grocery stores. The **Coconut Tree Store** at the entrance to town has a good selection of packaged food and supplies and is open 7 a.m.-8 p.m. daily.

Internet
At last report, the small office of **Hondusoft,** opposite Foster's dock, tel. 443-1548, did not have a great reputation for its connection speed, but the situation may have improved. Open Mon.-Sat. 10 a.m.-6 p.m.; rates are US$5 for the 15-minute minimum, US$8 per half-hour, and US$15 per hour. Most regular Internet users prefer to go to Paradise Computers in Coxen Hole, as much for its coffee as for the excellent computer service.

Laundry
Bamboo Hut Laundry, behind Tony's Restaurante Italiano on the bottom floor of the owners' house, efficiently washes and dries 6-10 lbs. of dirty duds for US$4. Open daily.

Exchange
Several stores and dive shops will change dollars, and sometimes traveler's checks, but never at a good rate. Take care of exchanging money in Coxen Hole whenever possible.

Getting There and Away
Minibuses to and from Coxen Hole (14 km) leave frequently between 7 a.m. and 5 p.m., US 60 cents each way. Collective taxis cost US$1.30. The ride to and from Sandy Bay is US 30 cents in a minibus or US 75 cents in a collective taxi. After dark, rides can get progressively scarcer, with the last taxis leaving toward Coxen Hole at around 10 p.m., or later on weekends (especially Friday, when Foster's is raging). Most taxis come into town as far as Ocean Divers, where they await passengers. You can also wait for taxis at the highway exit by the Coconut Tree Store. After dark, hitching a lift in a passing pickup is often possible.

Water taxis to West Bay leave frequently during the day; they fill up from Foster's dock and cost US$1.50. Arrangements can be made with the captain to get picked up for the return trip later on, even after dark if you like. You can walk to West Bay along the beach in about 20 minutes.

WEST BAY

Around a couple of rocky points about two kilometers south of West End is one of Roatán's greatest natural treasures—West Bay Beach, one and a half km of powdery, palm-lined sand lapped by exquisite turquoise-blue water. At the south end of the beach, where a wall of iron shore juts out into the water, the coral reef meets the shore. For anyone who wants a low-key encounter with an exceptionally fine reef without a long swim or any scuba gear, this is *the* place. It's almost too beautiful—more like an aquarium than a section of live reef, with brilliantly colored fish dodging about, the odd barracuda lurking, and gently waving sponges and sea fans, just a few feet from the beach.

The reef comes closest to shore at the beach's south end, but for anyone willing to swim out a bit the entire bay is lined by excellent reef. Keep an eye out for boats when in the water. The cruise ship day-trippers frequently descend in numbers on West Bay, so it's worth checking what days the ships are coming in. Even on those days, though, the beach is generally quiet in the early morning or late afternoon.

Until the early 1990s, West Bay—sometimes called Tabiyana Beach—was totally deserted, save a few bonfire-building partyers. But after a sudden flurry of real estate transactions and building, West Bay is now lined with houses and hotels, most thankfully built out of wood in a reserved, unobtrusive style.

But the construction boom on West Bay and in the hills behind has brought unfortunate consequences for the nearby reef. A large wetland area a few hundred yards behind the beach, at the base of the hills, formerly served as a buffer, to catch rain runoff and either filter it or let it evaporate in the sun. Developers promptly filled in the wetlands (annoying little swamp!) when construction began in West Bay. As a result, and coupled with the hillside construction and road building, the West Bay reef is coated with waves of silty water after every strong rain. As one might surmise, reefs do not take well to such sudden drops in water quality. The reef will still be lovely for several years to come, but it remains to be seen whether island authorities will take action to protect perhaps the single most important tourist attraction in Roatán for the future.

Near West Bay
West Bay was formerly connected by trail to Flowers Bay, a small and little-visited village on the south side of the island toward Coxen Hole. This trail still exists, but the new housing construction in the hills around West Bay makes it difficult to find. Ask around in the hotels on West Bay for someone to point the way. It's also possible to walk to Flowers Bay by dirt road in about an hour—start out on the dirt road back toward West End and take the only turnoff to the right. A dirt road also runs between Flowers Bay and Coxen Hole, along the island's south shore.

In the hills between West Bay and West End are the remains of several pre-Columbian Indian burial sites and settlements. Jimmy Miller in West End knows the whereabouts of a couple of them and will take visitors there on horseback for a fee, as will others in town. There's not much to see beyond a few mounds and potsherds, but it's an interesting excursion and a break from the water. Capt. Van's Rentals also offers horseback excursions up into the hills.

Accommodations
Hotels in West Bay are a decided step up in price from West End. Those who are really after

red-lored Amazon parrot

some peace and quiet, and some serious beach time, may enjoy staying in West Bay, although one drawback is the lack of restaurants (only two) and dive shops (just one, Bananarama), as of early 2000. Many people sleeping in West Bay find themselves taking frequent water taxis to and from West End to eat and dive. If you want to stay in West Bay, try to rent a place with a kitchen, at least to cook your own breakfast, as none is available in West Bay.

Foster Díaz owns several cabins and duplexes near the north end of West Bay beach (inquire at his restaurant in West End). They rent for US$25-40 d, including a small room built into the branches of a mango tree, complete with electricity and running water.

Next door is **Coconut Tree Cabins,** tel. 445-1648, website: www.coconuttree.com, with light, airy wooden cabins with tile floors, equipped with hot water and a/c for US$60 d. Ask for more information at the Coconut Tree Store in West End.

Cabañas Roatana, about midway up the beach set back slightly from the shore, tel./fax 445-1271, has eight well-equipped rooms for US$60-90 (depending on the season) in a large two-story house, some with kitchen facilities. The owners can be reached in the U.S. c/o Jackson Shipping, 5353 W. Tyson Ave., Tampa, FL 33611, tel. (888) 626-9531, website: www.roatanet.com/ROATANA. Right next to the Italian resort is **Hotel Mayan Princess,** tel. 455-5525 or 455-5535, in the U.S. (888) 253-0014, with comfortable suites sleeping up to four with wicker furniture, small kitchens, and satellite TV for US$120 a night, less in the low season.

Island Pearl, run by a French-Canadian couple, rents attractive apartments in four separate houses set among shady trees at the southern end of the beach, each beautifully decorated with artwork and furniture from around the world. The rooms rent for US$100 d, US$120 t. The hotel owners also run a small store, selling fine clothes principally from southeast Asia, Africa, and Guatemala.

Perfect for a family or group of friends looking for a vacation house, **Casa Carnival** is a spacious beach house renting for US$800 a week in low season and US$1500 in high season. It has a fully equipped kitchen, satellite TV and all manner of water and beach gear, such as snorkels, sea kayaks, and a windsurfer. With two full bedrooms and fold-out couches in the living room and sun room, this place can sleep up to eight. An extra fee is charged for a/c. Reservations can be made through Mid-America Marketing, 8249 W. 95 St., Suite 100, Overland Park, Kansas, 66212, tel. (913) 385-7755, fax (913) 385-3337, email: midam@swbell.net.

Other rental units are available on West Bay—contact one of the Roatán real estate agents listed above for more information.

Worth mentioning, if only for its ostentation, is the large Italian resort in the middle of West Bay. Visitors to West Bay will invariably see large crowds of guests frolicking around on the beach, all flying in from Italy on package tours to stay at the Club Med-esque resort. The hotel is not open to the general public and is the butt of many a joke among the islanders.

Food and Entertainment
Bite on the Beach is a superb spot to enjoy a snack, beer, or full meal on a large, breezy deck right on the edge of the glorious Caribbean. The savory, well-spiced chicken, fresh fish, shrimp, burritos, sandwiches of Cajun-style blackened fish or chicken, US$4-8 per plate, are well worth the trip (by water taxi) from West End. Open for lunch and dinner Wed-Sat., lunch only on Sunday, closed Monday and Tuesday.

Bite on the Beach has been pretty much alone in nourishing the starving bellies of West Bay, but at least one other option will be available by the time this book is in print. **Neptune's,** the restaurant to go along with Vincent Bush's new Coconut Tree Cabins, was in the last stages of construction at last check. The new restaurant, at the north end of West Bay shortly before Bite on the Beach, will focus on good-quality seafood at US$6-10 per entree.

Volcano's Bar, at the Hotel Mayan Princess, is a little thatched-hut watering hole located conveniently about halfway down the beach. It's open Thurs.-Sun. 9 a.m.-6 p.m., with hot dogs and chicken wings to chase down with a beer or soft drink.

Getting There and Away
From West End you can walk to West Bay (25 minutes along the beach, past the boat slip on the point), or take a water taxi (US$1.50 from Foster's) or car (a four-km dirt road turns off the Coxen Hole highway near the entrance to West End). Water taxi captains are happy to arrange a return trip to pick up weary but content sun-fried beach bums at the end of the day.

SANDY BAY

With a full-time population of about 1,200, Sandy Bay is considerably larger than West End, but somehow it doesn't feel like it. The town is a collection of weather-beaten wooden houses, most built on stilts among patches of shady trees a hundred yards or so from the edge of the sea, strung out over three or more kilometers of shoreline. Development has arrived in Sandy Bay, but it's mostly limited to private houses and a couple of low-key resorts tucked away in the corners of town. Anthony's Key Resort (AKR), which literally splits Sandy Bay in two, is a large complex, but most guests don't venture off the grounds into town, so it doesn't much disturb the placid lifestyle of the local islanders. Sandy Bay is a popular place for foreigners living in Roatán to rent inexpensive houses or apartments.

Recreation

As its name would suggest, Sandy Bay has got plenty of beach right in front of town, but it's somewhat muddy and not totally clean, making it not as nice for sunbathing as West End or West Bay. The waters around Sandy Bay and Anthony's Key Resort were the first-established section of the Roatán Marine Reserve, created in 1989, and the snorkeling and diving are superb. Snorkelers can paddle out anywhere that's convenient across a couple hundred meters of shallow water, much of it blanketed in sea grass, to the edge of the reef. Finding a passage out across the shallow reef can be tricky—the best plan is to ask locals to point out the channels used by boats, marked by buoys. The steep coral and rock cliffs and formations on the ocean side of the reef are dramatic and great fun to explore with a snorkel and fins. When swimming, keep a sharp eye out for boat traffic.

The only dive shops in town are at AKR or Bay Island Beach Resort. Both will take non-guest divers, for slightly higher rates than at West End. Most West End shops will set up trips out to Sandy Bay dive sites on request.

Sights

In one of the few programs of its kind in the Caribbean, **The Institute for Marine Sciences** at AKR lets spectators watch a dolphin show, with information about the animals, at 10 a.m. and 4 p.m. every day except Wednesday for US$4, and certified scuba divers enjoy 35-40 minutes of controlled but unstructured swimming with dolphins over open-water sand flats (US$100, extra to rent equipment. You can also snorkel for 30 minutes with the dolphins for US$75. An Institute trainer accompanies all diving and snorkeling expeditions. Those interested in more detailed information on the dolphins can take a specialty course, with three days of lessons and activities for US$180 per person.

The IMS has several exhibits on invertebrates, reptiles, birds, fish, coral-reef life, and the geology of the Bay Islands, as well as a small but worthwhile bilingual museum on local archaeology and history. Admission to the IMS and museum only, excluding the dolphin show, is US$3; the facility is open daily 8 a.m.-5 p.m.

One of the few above-water Bay Island sights rivaling the reef in visual beauty, **Tropical Treasures Bird Park,** tel. 445-1314, has a collection of 80-odd tropical birds, including several species of green and scarlet macaws, parrots, and toucans. Most of the birds were donated to the park, either because they were injured, homeless, or owned by a foreigner who left the island. Almost all the animals are from Honduras, mainly the Mosquitia, though a couple of the macaws are from South America. While the extraordinarily colorful birds are usually left in their large cages, several at a time are allowed to roam around free when visitors walk through. Some of them can be handled. While all the birds are brilliantly eye-catching, the toucan, vividly painted in cartoon-character primary colors, is especially fun to watch. Visitors are taken on informative guided tours (in English or Spanish), with details on the different bird species, their habits, basic care, and current status in the wild. The park, privately owned but officially registered with the Honduran wildlife authorities, is open Mon.-Sat. 10 a.m.-5 p.m. and costs US$5 for adults or US$3 for children. Inside the main house is a small gift shop with *junco* palm woven baskets, local homemade jellies, island jewelry, and coffee.

Carambola Botanical Reserve, located off the highway opposite the entrance to AKR, is the only developed inland reserve on the Bay Islands. Well-built trails wind through forests of ferns, spices, orchids, flowering plants, fruit trees, and even a few mahogany trees on the way to the top of Carambola Mountain. Along the way is a turnoff to the fascinating Iguana Wall, a section of sheer cliff that serves as a protected breeding ground for iguanas and parrots. There are vestiges of pre-Columbian ruins in the reserve and great views from the peak over the surrounding reef and, in the distance, Utila. If manager Irma Brady is at the visitors' center, she can provide a great deal of information on the reserve's flora and fauna, but the other staffers in general are not very knowledgeable. For more information call Bill or Irma Brady at 445-1117. Entrance costs US$3; open daily 8 a.m.-5 p.m.

Accommodations

Sandy Bay's hotel selection tends to the middle and upper price categories. At last check, the only option for budget travelers was to ask around among the locals if anybody is renting out rooms.

The owners of Hotel El Paso in Coxen Hole were at last report building a few rooms on the hillside behind a *pulpería* right in the middle of Sandy Bay, by the school. The owner (who can be reached at tel. 445-1367) was tentatively planning to rent the rooms for US$25 s.

On a bluff just behind the main entrance to Sandy Bay from the highway is **The Pirate's Den,** tel./fax 445-1623, the oldest resort on the island and due to reopen in 2000. The new owners hope to charge US$50-70 for rather small though decent rooms with a/c, hot water, and wood floors, but perhaps the price will come down in time. Meals are expected to be available at the hotel restaurant.

The mellow **Oceanside Inn,** just west of AKR, tel. 445-1552, in the U.S. (407) 855-5517, email: oceanside@globalnet.hn, offers eight wood-paneled rooms, some with a/c, others with fan only, and all with a tiny bathroom, at US$60 s or d, or packages for US$50 per person per night with two meals a day for a week's stay. The hotel has a good restaurant and bar, and snorkeling equipment for guests to use.

Sunnyside Condominiums, on the beach at the eastern end of Sandy Bay, its entrance just past the Dance Hall Queen Disco, has rental options including a bed and breakfast room, a studio apartment with kitchen, a beach cottage, or a large house, ranging in cost from US$45 d to US$150 for the house, which has two bedrooms, a/c, and a fully equipped kitchen. Rates come down for longer stays. Snorkel gear and sea kayaks are available to guests. Contact Bill and Cathy Service at tel./fax 445-0006, email: sunnyside@globalnet.hn.

Ship's Inn, reached by a turnoff from the highway just as it comes into Sandy Bay from Coxen Hole, tel. 445-1661, in the U.S. 408-536-5360, has two wooden, two-story buildings on a secluded beach, with rooms renting for US$50 d.

Dive Resorts

One of the premier vacation resorts on Roatán and, for that matter, in all of Honduras, **Anthony's Key Resort,** tel. 445-1327, fax 445-1329, manages 56 cabins both on the small and serene Anthony's Key and on a tree-covered hillside on the mainland. Full-week diving and meal packages are available for US$600-675 pp for a couple—an excellent value, considering

the quality of the services. Prices include tanks, weights, transport to and from the airport, an excursion to West Bay beach, and a room with overhead fan and potable tap water. There's fantastic swimming and snorkeling on all sides and a fine sunbathing beach on the cay. Dive shop facilities are excellent, with several large boats, new equipment, and everything needed for a variety of PADI courses (at extra cost). The resort has its own underwater photo/video shop, tel. 445-1003, fax 445-1140, offering one-day slide processing and camera rentals (sometimes available to non-guests as well) for about US$60 a day for the Nikonos V system with strobe. For more information visit the website, www.anthonyskey.com, or email: akr@gate.net; the U.S. representative is Bahia Tours, tel. (800) 227-3483(954) 929-0090, fax (954) 922-7478.

For those looking to really get away from it all for a week, **The Inn of the Last Resort,** tel. 445-

The water in Roatán Marine Reserve around Sandy Bay and Anthony's Key Resort offer superb snorkeling and diving.

1838, in the U.S. tel. (888) 238-8266 or (305) 893-2436, fax 445-1848, email: lastresort@globalnet.hn, website: www.coral.net/innlast.html, might be the place for you. Set on a tree-covered, isolated peninsula, the Inn has no phones or TVs to disturb complete relaxation, only a huge selection of books, a breezy bar/restaurant, and the nearby reef. Rooms come with a/c and ceiling fans. Eight-day, seven-night dive vacations cost US$745 pp for a couple, US$645 pp for five days, with three meals daily, three boat dives, and one night dive during the week. Open-water, advanced, and Nitrox courses are available and cost extra. The dive shop is well equipped, and the dive boats are large and comfortable.

Just in front of the famed Spooky Channel dive site, at the east end of Sandy Bay, is the **Bay Island Beach Dive Resort,** tel. 445-1425, fax 445-1855, email: bisland@hondutel.hn, website: www.bibr.com, with 15 double rooms spread out in different buildings near the shore. The better and more expensive rooms are in a large wooden cabin of sorts on the beach, with high ceilings, tasteful furniture, a/c, and fans. The two rooms in the middle building are not quite as nice but not bad either, while the rooms in the main building, below the restaurant, are dark and cramped—make sure you don't end up there. Regular rates are US$775 for a full week with two boat dives, unlimited shore diving, and three meals a day, double occupancy. Group rates are available. Reservations in the U.S. at tel. (800) 476-2826 or (561) 624-5774, fax (561) 624-7751, email: BIBRUSA@aol.com.

Food and Entertainment
Those staying in Sandy Bay will likely be eating in their resort restaurant, but a couple of other places serve good meals at midrange prices.

Rick's American Cafe, set up on a hillside above the highway, is something of an island institution among Roatán expats. After climbing up the precipitous staircase patrons can relax with a beer on the large wooden deck and watch the ball game on cable TV, while awaiting an order of steak, baby-back ribs, nachos, chicken, or a burger (US$5-10 a plate). Rick's is open daily for dinner and also for brunch on Sunday.

The **Monkey Lala** is a new place out on the highway in Sandy Bay, just west of Rick's. The

very friendly owner presides over the little patio restaurant, serving very good seafood, including a mean lobster, for US$6-10 per entree. In season, the cook makes a mango cheesecake to die for. Open daily noon-10 p.m.

A new edition to the Roatán disco scene is **Dance Hall Queen,** a small disco on the highway. Opinions on the crowd vary—some say it's a good time, while others claim it's a shady place. Either way, the cramped dance floor and lack of air-conditioning make it a sweaty experience. Open weekends only.

Services
On the grounds of AKR is the **Cornerstone Medical Center,** tel. 445-1049, VHF channel 26, home to the only recompression tank on the Bay Islands, where divers who don't follow the tables end up spending uncomfortable hours wondering if they will avoid permanent damage. There are no X-ray facilities, but the doctors can treat ailments resulting from diving and other illnesses as well. Open daily 8 a.m.-5 p.m.

Sandy Bay is just off the West End-Coxen Hole highway; minibuses and taxis pass frequently in both directions. Shared taxis to Coxen Hole cost US 90 cents, US 75 cents to West End.

COXEN HOLE

A dusty, unremarkable town of weather-beaten wooden houses and shops, Coxen Hole is visited most frequently to change money, buy groceries, or take care of other business. All buses across the island are based out of Coxen Hole, and the airport is three km east of town, on the road to French Harbour.

Named for pirate captain John Coxen, who lived on Roatán 1687-1697, the town was founded in 1835, when several families arrived from the Cayman Islands and settled on the harbor.

Accommodations
Though most sun- and sand-seekers proceed directly from the docks and airport to West End, Sandy Bay, or elsewhere, there are a few hotels in Coxen Hole should you need to spend the night there for some reason.

The inexpensive **Hotel Noemi Allen,** just over the bridge at the western end of Main Street, tel. 445-1234, has rooms for US$6 s or d with fan in a large wooden house. It's in a slightly seedy neighborhood, but the owner is friendly and overall the hotel is a good budget value.

Hotel Coral (no phone), on the second story of a large Victorian in the center of town on Main Street, is a bit pricey at US$6 for a dingy single with shared bathroom or US$11 for a double. If no one is around in the hotel ask for assistance at the pharmacy across the street. A better value is the **Hotel El Paso,** on the eastern side of town near the ferry dock, tel. 445-1367, fax 445-1442, with clean rooms for US$10 s or US$15 d with fans and shared bath. The hotel also has long-distance phone and fax service, and a restaurant with a mean seafood soup.

Food and Entertainment
Excellent snacks, lunches, breakfasts, and espresso drinks are sold at the **Qué Tal Cafe,** inside the Librería Casi Todo, on the highway junction to West End. The balcony is a favorite spot for Roatán expats to meet up and have a coffee or try the daily lunch special. Open Mon.-Sat. 7 a.m.-3 p.m. The cafe at **Paradise Computers** has very good breakfasts and lunches.

Open Mon.-Fri. 7:30 a.m.-5 p.m., Saturday 7:30 a.m.-2 p.m.

Of the many inexpensive eateries in Coxen Hole, **R&R's,** otherwise known as **Roland's,** on Main Street next to Banco Atlántida, has decent breakfasts and lunches for US$1.75-2, and a good lunchtime *sopa de res* (beef soup) filled with veggies.

The restaurant at **Hotel El Paso** is famous for its delectable seafood soup and also makes a decent chicken sandwich. **H.B. Warren Supermarket** in the center of town has a 1950s-style cafeteria counter with good, inexpensive fried chicken and other light meals.

For a night of thumping *punta* and disco music, gyrating hips, and the occasional violent altercation, the **Harbour View Disco** near the ferry dock is the spot of choice. The other disco in town, **Paraguas,** near the bridge on the west side of town, has a worse reputation and is not recommended.

Shopping
Yaba Ding Ding—the islanders' nickname for pre-Columbian artifacts—carries paintings by well-known Honduran painters like Virginia Castillo, carvings, batik, woven *junco* baskets from Santa Bárbara, Honduran and Cuban cigars, T-shirts, and more. The store is located on the ground floor of a two-story building next to H.B. Warren supermarket, tel. 445-1683. **Coco Loco,** across from H.B. Warren, has a selection of clothing from Central America, mainly from Honduras, open Mon.-Sat. 10 a.m.-5 p.m.

Librería Casi Todo, on the highway to West End right by the Coxen Hole turnoff, tel. 445-1944, has a large array of used and new books, open Mon.-Fri. 9 a.m.-4:30 p.m. The shop has a frequently occupied computer to access the Internet. Adjacent to the bookstore is Qué Tal Cafe, serving coffee, breakfasts, and snacks, with a porch to relax with a coffee and a book. The store runs regular

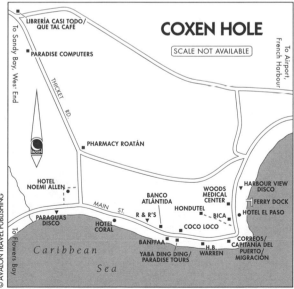

COXEN HOLE

SCALE NOT AVAILABLE

To Sandy Bay, West End

To Airport, French Harbour

To Flowers Bay

LIBRERÍA CASI TODO/ QUE TAL CAFÉ

PARADISE COMPUTERS

THICKET RD.

PHARMACY ROATÁN

HOTEL NOEMI ALLEN

MAIN ST.

BANCO ATLÁNTIDA

R & R'S

HONDUTEL

WOODS MEDICAL CENTER

HARBOUR VIEW DISCO

FERRY DOCK

HOTEL EL PASO

PARAGUAS DISCO

HOTEL CORAL

COCO LOCO

BICA

Caribbean

Sea

BANFFAA

YABA DING DING/ PARADISE TOURS

H.B. WARREN

CORREOS/ CAPITANÍA DEL PUERTO/ MIGRACIÓN

© AVALON TRAVEL PUBLISHING

half-day island tours for 8-10 people (you can join in with others or put your own group together) for US$32 pp.

In the center of town is **H.B. Warren,** the best supermarket on the western part of the island (Eldon's in French Harbour is considered the best on the island). Apart from groceries, Warren's has a low-priced cafeteria counter and a large post-up board with advertisements and messages. Open Mon.-Sat. 7 a.m.-6 p.m.

A small stand opposite the Hotel Coral has fruits and vegetables for sale.

Exchange

All the banks listed below are on Main Street in Coxen Hole and are open Mon.-Fri. until 4 p.m., Saturday until noon.

Banco Atlántida, tel. 445-1225, has a cash machine. It will advance *lempiras* on a Visa card, though at a poor exchange rate, and exchange a maximum of US$300 in U.S. dollars or traveler's checks. **Banffaa,** tel. 445-1091, cashes unlimited amounts of U.S. dollars and traveler's checks. **Bancahsa,** tel. 445-1232, exchanges unlimited amounts of dollars and traveler's checks and offers Visa cash advances at a reasonable

exchange rate. **Credomatic,** tel. 445-1703, offers cash advances on both Visa and MasterCards, but the exchange rate is not the best.

Internet

Paradise Computers in JC's Commercial Center, on the road leading out of town to West End, tel. 445-1241 or 445-1611, rents computers for US$15 per hour, or US 25 cents a minute, less to use a computer off-line. Many clients have an account with the store and use the off-line machines to write emails, which are sent at the end of the day. Received email messages are printed out and filed for clients. The attached café has superb coffee and Belgian-style omelets, yogurt, French toast, and homemade bread, which makes it easier to handle the frequent wait to use a computer. Roatán's residents can only hope the overworked but very friendly Belgian family that runs the place doesn't leave town, as they have been contemplating. Open Mon.-Fri. 7:30 a.m.-5 p.m. and Saturday 7:30 a.m.-2 p.m.

Librería Casi Todo, a couple hundred yards away at the highway junction, has a single on-line machine for rent, invariably with a wait to use it. But there is also a good cafe and porch on

---

SNORKELING

Many of us land-based creatures feel slightly ill at ease strapping on all that scuba gear and descending to the watery depths. We would much prefer to admire the undersea world wearing nothing more complicated than a mask, a snorkel, and fins. Snorkel gear is easily rented at any dive shop on the islands. When renting gear, be very careful to check that your mask fits snugly. Hold the mask against your face and suck in with your nose—it should stay held against your face without the help of your hand. Also, see that the snorkel has no obvious leaks (some shops are more conscientious than others) and fits in your mouth comfortably, and that your fins are neither too tight nor too loose. A constantly dripping mask or a painfully tight fin can ruin a good snorkel trip.

On both Roatán and Utila, snorkelers will find several good locations to paddle out to from shore. But more adventurous snorkelers, who are also confident swimmers, can often go out with scuba boats and snorkel the same site as the divers, but

from above. Ask around at different shops for appropriate dive sites, preferably shallow ones.

One of the great pleasures of snorkeling is to take in a great gulp of air and dive down amongst the reef and fish for as long as you can hold your breath, before shooting up to the surface and blowing the water out of the snorkel with your remaining air. Some gung-ho snorkelers, in an effort to improve their downtime, hyperventilate for two or three breaths before descending. If not done properly, this technique can be dangerous and can cause you to black out under water. In late 1999, an experienced snorkeler knocked himself out while hyperventilating off Roatán and, because he was alone, drowned. Hyperventilation should only be attempted by those with proper training, and if you should try it, certainly don't do it when you're alone.

But don't let such stories spook you—tragic accidents like this simply do not happen to casual, recreational snorkelers who just hold their breath normally.

which to enjoy a coffee or meal and wait your turn. Open Mon.-Fri. 9 a.m.-4:30 p.m.

Other Services
On the small square in the center of town are the Correos, *migración* office, and port captain, all open Mon.-Fri. 8 a.m.-noon and 2-5 p.m., Saturday 8 a.m.-noon. At last check *migración* had temporarily moved out to the airport, but officials said it would return to its old location by the end of 2000. Up the hill behind Bancahsa is Hondutel, fax 445-1206, open Mon.-Fri. 8 a.m.-noon and 12:30-4 p.m.

The **Bay Islands Conservation Association (BICA)** office is in the Cooper Building in downtown Coxen Hole, tel. 445-1424. Some pamphlets and maps are available, as well as *The Bay Islands: Nature and People,* an informative bilingual paperback by Susan Jacobson.

Paradise Tours Travel Agency, tel. 445-0392 or 445-1747, fax 445-1267, with an office in Edificio Bonilla, next to H.B. Warren's Supermarket, can sell airline tickets and make other travel arrangements.

In case of emergency call the **police** at 445-1138, 445-1190, or 445-1199; or the **fire department** at 445-1198. The main police station on the island is outside of Coxen Hole on the highway toward West End, on the left-hand side about a kilometer outside of town.

Pharmacy Roatán, tel. 445-1260, on the road leading to the West End highway from downtown, is open Mon.-Fri. 8 a.m.-6 p.m., Saturday 8 a.m.-2 p.m.

Wood Medical Center in Coxen Hole, tel. 445-1080, is not the finest operation in existence—better to go to the medical center at AKR for most problems—but does have the only X-ray machine on the island.

Getting There and Away
For most visitors, collective taxis or minibuses are the best way to move between Coxen Hole and other parts of the island. Collective taxis gather in front of H.B. Warren's to pick up passengers to West End (US$1.30), Sandy Bay (US 90 cents), Brick Bay (US 85 cents), French Harbour (US$1.35), and Oak Ridge (US$2). Minibuses cost less than half what taxis charge. Private taxi rides are negotiable (always negotiate before getting in) and usually expensive, especially for foreign tourists.

FRENCH HARBOUR AND VICINITY

A large south-coast town set about one km off the highway on a wide peninsula 10 km east of Coxen Hole, French Harbour is home to one of the island's two major fishing fleets (the other is based in Oak Ridge). This is a working town, a world apart from the nearby resorts of Fantasy Island and Coco View. Watching the activity on the docks is interesting, but otherwise French Harbour is not particularly visually attractive. Nevertheless, the town has a cheerful character that Coxen Hole lacks. There isn't much of a beach or dive-worthy reef around French Harbour—better to go farther east or west up the coast.

French Harbour is thought to be named for a Frenchman who had one of the first homesteads in the area during the British military occupation in the 1740s.

Accommodations
The basic **Hotel Brooks** occupies the second floor of a rickety wooden house between the bus stop and the docks, on the left side above a photo shop. With a small room and shared bathroom, it's about the cheapest place in town at US$8. A step up is **Hotel Gabriela,** a bit farther up the same road, tel. 455-5365, with double bed, a/c, and bathroom for US$17 s or d, or US$10 s or d with shared bathroom. Right next door is **Hotel Joe** (no phone), about the same as the Gabriela, while across the street is the nicer **Harbour View Hotel,** tel. 455-5390, charging US$19 s or US$23 d for rooms with with a/c and cable TV, or US$15 s and US$19 d for fan.

On the water's edge facing the open ocean, around the point from the harbor, **The Buccaneer,** tel. (and fax) 455-5032, was built in 1967 and at last report was under renovation. The owner expects the ocean-facing rooms to be equipped with a/c and rent for US$30 s, US$40 d. Rooms with TV or kitchenette will cost extra.

Upstairs from Gio's Restaurant and run by the same owners is **The Faro Inn,** tel. 445-1536, with eight rooms renting for US$45 s or US$50 d, each with cable TV, a/c and hot water.

For the best rooms in town, try **Casa Romeo,** tel. 455-1518, fax 455-5645, email: casarome@ hondutel.hn, website: www.casaromeos.com, a large stylish wooden house built on the dock, with a cool and quiet restaurant downstairs serving excellent seafood (the prices reflect the quality). Seven bright, whitewashed, and breezy rooms with wood floors, a/c, fans, and harbor views cost US$56 s, US$75 d, less per night for weeklong stays. Dive and meal packages are also available.

Food and Entertainment

Famed for its legendary king crab *al ajillo*, (cooked in garlic) **Gio's,** tel. 455-5214, across from the Banffaa Bank, also serves shrimp and a decent cut of beef at US$9-20 an entree. Open Mon.-Sat. 10 a.m.-2 p.m. and 5-10 p.m.

Casa Romeo's, just up the street, tel. 455-5518, also has superb seafood including lobster, shrimp, fish, squid, and conch chowder at US$8-15 per entree, served in a classy dining room on the edge of the harbor. Open Mon.-Sat. 10 a.m.-2:30 p.m. and 5-10 p.m.

Except for Gio's and Casa Romeo's, French Harbour has little in the way of decent food. **Snacks and Chicken,** just before Gio's, is one of the better low-priced eateries in town, serving *baleadas, pastelitos, comida corridas* and chicken at low prices. Open daily 7 a.m.-10 p.m.

Former local favorites among the expat crowd were the Daily Grind breakfast and lunch restaurant on the highway, and the French Harbour Yacht Club Bar and Restaurant, at the entrance to town. Both were closed at last report but may reopen in the future.

Eldon's, at the French Harbour turnoff, is considered by some to be the best supermarket on the island and certainly has the best fresh vegetables. Open Mon.-Fri. 8 a.m.-6 p.m., Saturday 9 a.m.-5 p.m., Sunday 9 a.m.-1 p.m.

Two discos get the locals hopping in town on weekends: **Al's** and **Bolongo's.** The former has a better DJ favoring merengue and salsa, while the latter has a slightly more upscale (read: safer) atmosphere. The air-conditioned Bolongo's is considered the place to be on the island on Saturday night, while Foster's in West End is the undisputed king of Friday night.

Other Practicalities

Bancahsa, just past Casa Romeo's on the left, will exchange U.S. dollars and traveler's checks, as well as advance cash on a Visa card. Farther down the road, near Gio's, is **Banffaa,** exchanging dollars and traveler's checks.

The Coxen Hole-Oak Ridge buses, which run until late afternoon, pull all the way into town so there's no need to slog out to the highway. The fare to Coxen Hole is US 70 cents. A collective taxi to Coxen Hole costs US$1.50.

The French Harbour **police station** is on the main road, up from the Harbour near the bus station, tel. 455-5099

Brick Bay

Formerly called Brig Bay, Brick Bay is a small cove on the south side of the island just off the Coxen Hole highway not far west of French Harbour. A secluded little dive resort and marina, **Brick Bay Resort,** tel. 445-1337 or 445-1127, fax 445-1594, charges around US$700 per week for a full dive and meal package, or US$100 a night. Rooms downstairs have a/c, while the breezy upstairs rooms have fan only. Non-divers pay US$50 s or d. Formerly Romeo's Resort, the hotel changed hands recently, and we've heard no reports yet on service quality, but dive sites nearby like Mary's Place and Valley of Kings are superb.

The resort runs a 30-slip marina, offering a berth with 24-hour electricity, water, and cable TV (if you want it) for US$150 a month. There is no gasoline here—fuel up elsewhere.

East of French Harbour

The narrow, two-lane highway (bicyclists beware) running east of French Harbour to Oak Ridge winds for most of its length along the ridge in the center of the island, affording superb views of both coasts and the reef, visible under the clear water. Between French Harbour and the Punta Gorda turnoff, the highway passes Juticalpa, a small Latino community and the only sizable inland settlement anywhere on the Bay Islands. Once heavily forested, these central island mountain slopes have been almost entirely denuded of their original cover and now support secondary scrub growth, pasture, or farmland.

Not far east of French Harbour on the south side of the island, are two of the best-known luxury dive resorts on Roatán: Coco View and Fantasy Island.

The Coco View Resort is, along with Anthony's Key, one of the oldest and most popular dive resorts in the Bay Islands. The hotel offers several room options, including homey wooden ocean bungalows and larger apartments, built right over the water with lovely porches facing the water and sunset. Those who insist on a/c (quite unnecessary in the breezy ocean rooms) can take a room in a larger, two-story unit on shore. Seven privately owned beach houses nearby, not used by their owners most of the year, can be rented through the resort, which is accessible by boat only. Diving is excellent right offshore—the reef wall starts 30 meters from the hotel and the wreck of the 42-meter *Prince Albert* is entombed in 20 meters of water nearby. Close by is the famed diving site Mary's Place, usually the culmination of the weeklong schedule of dives. The dive crew is extremely professional and friendly, and Coco View has a fleet of large, well-equipped dive boats, even with a hatch to come up from underneath directly into the boat in rough weather. Five- to seven-night packages cost US$650-750, slightly less during the Sept.-Jan. off-season. Contact the resort in Roatán at tel. 455-1011, fax 45-1013, in the U.S. at tel. (800) 282-8932 or (352) 588-4132, fax (352) 588-4158, email: info@roatan.com, website: www.roatan.com/cocoview.htm.

Situated on its own isolated 15-acre island complete with two man-made beaches, nearby reef, full dive shop, four dive boats, jet skis, tennis courts, sailboards, and myriad other services and recreation equipment, **Fantasy Island Resort,** tel. 455-5262, fax 455-5268, offers the complete get-away-from-it-all vacation. One-week packages including diving, lodging, and meals cost US$869-1050 pp for a couple, depending on the room. Four-night packages go for US$600-640. Each of the 83 rooms is decorated in tropical style with a/c, fan, TV, refrigerator, and balcony with ocean view. Local environmentalists are not great fans of the hotel for its allegedly heavy-handed construction methods, and one reader made a point of writing in to complain of poor service, making it probably not the top choice for a resort vacation. Fantasy Island does have new management as of January 2000, so perhaps the situation will improve. Reserva-

tions can be made in the U.S. at Fantasy Island Travel Services, 3951 A West Kennedy Blvd., Tampa, FL 33611, tel. (800) 676-2826 or (813) 353-9414, fax (813) 353-0454, website: www. empg.com/fantasy-island

PUNTA GORDA

The oldest permanent settlement in Roatán, Punta Gorda ("fat point") was founded shortly after 12 April 1797, when some 3,000 Garífuna deportees from the Caribbean island of St. Vincent were stranded on Roatán by the British. After settling in Punta Gorda, many Garífuna continued on, migrating to Trujillo and from there up and down the Caribbean coasts of Honduras, Nicaragua, Guatemala, and Belize, but their first Honduran home remained. The anniversary marking their arrival is cause for great celebration in Punta Gorda. Garífuna from all over the coast attend the event. For most of the year, though, Punta Gorda is simply a sleepy seaside town— dozens of *cayucos* pulled up on the beach, a steady breeze blowing in the palms, and Garífuna residents moving at a very deliberate pace, usually happy to spend a few minutes or hours chatting with a visitor. The only visible evidence of the town's history is a modest statue of Satuyé, the revered Garífuna warrior on St. Vincent, located at the entrance to town from the highway.

The beaches in town are not the best, but not far up the coast you'll find fine patches of open sand, like Camp Bay Beach to the east. Local boat owners will take you there for a negotiable fee. There's great snorkeling and diving on the reef near Punta Gorda, but watch out for boat traffic if you swim across the bay to the reef, and remember the north side of Roatán is choppier than the south and west.

The coastline of Punta Gorda felt the full effects of Hurricane Mitch, and many buildings were destroyed, including Ben's Resort, a small scale dive resort. Honoring the event in a macabre sort of way, the building once housing Ben's is now Disco Mitch.

Practicalities

On the main road looping through town (both ends connect to the highway) are a couple of *pulperías* and *comedores,* a pool hall, and one hotel, **Los Cinco Hermanos** (no phone), with six rooms at US$5 s or d upstairs in a worn wooden house. Mediocre lunch and dinner are served in the hotel's *comedor,* or you could grab a piece of fried chicken or a *baleada* at the **Chicken Shack,** right on the main road.

At the western end of town is **Disco Mitch,** the happening spot in town on weekends. **Salon Flores** is the other dance hall. *Punta* bands put on shows for the cruise ship tours but are infrequently seen otherwise.

OAK RIDGE

From the highway coming downhill to the water's edge, it seems Oak Ridge is scattered all over the place, clinging to hillsides, cays, and peninsulas all around a large harbor, which is literally the center of town. The harbor has always been the town's entire reason for existence, first serving as a refuge for pirates fleeing Spanish warships, then as the center of a major boat-building industry, and now as home to a fishing fleet and processing plant. Oak Ridge is the capital of the José Santos Guardiola municipality, which covers eastern Roatán.

Perhaps because of its relative remoteness, more of Oak Ridge's 5,000 residents are obviously of English descent than elsewhere in Roatán. But Spanish-speaking immigrants are beginning to settle in Oak Ridge, particularly along the highway coming into town. Though not a major tourist destination, Oak Ridge is near plenty of pristine, little-known sites on the southern and eastern Roatán reef. Two local dive resorts welcome walk-in divers. Near town are extensive mangrove swamps, which can be visited by hiring local boatmen.

Practicalities

Buses stop at the mainland dock next to a Bancahsa (which changes cash and traveler's checks and advances money on Visa cards) and the fish-processing plant. From there a visitor can walk along the shore, past the fish plant all the way around the western end of the harbor, over a small bridge, and out to a narrow point facing the ocean.

Apart from a couple of stores and a weather-beaten wooden church, there's not much on the point, though it's interesting to check out the town and docks. The ocean-facing side of the point has no beach, only exposed, rocky coral which makes it difficult to get out to snorkel on the reef.

At last check no budget hotels were open in Oak Ridge, though you might find a room by asking around. Nor are there any official restaurants, apart from at the two resorts mentioned below.

From the dock by the bus stop, water taxis will take a visitor over to the cay ("cayside") for US 75 cents or so, though some drivers may try to charge you more. Cayside is much the same as the point; several houses sit amidst the trees behind the rocky, coral-covered shoreline.

Most cayside visitors are coming to the **Reef House Resort,** tel. 435-2297, in the U.S. at P.O. Box 40331, San Antonio, TX 78229, tel. (800) 328-8897 or (210) 681-2888, fax (210) 341-7942, one of the oldest dive resorts on the island. The owners dive many little-known south-side sites nearby, including an excellent wall right in front of the hotel. One week with lodging, meals, three boat dives daily, and unlimited shore diving goes for US$725 pp for a couple; five days costs US$550 pp for a couple. One-night stays with meals cost US$90 for non-divers, US$120 for divers. Walk-in divers are gladly accepted—rates are US$25 per tank.

Offering the lowest-priced dive packages in Roatán is **Oak Bay Resort,** tel. 435-2337, email: ah6pn@arrl.net, website: www.roatandiving.com, charging only US$400 for weeklong dive and meal packages with double occupancy, a very low price compared to the rest of the island. PADI Open Water courses cost only US$200, with four nights' lodging included! Rooms are in a two-story wooden beach house, with a breezy front porch on both floors, located on Lucy Point just a five-minute walk west of downtown Oak Ridge.

Near Oak Ridge

Not far from town in both directions, but especially east, are several beaches. Dory captains on the main dock near the bus stop will transport you there for US$5 or US$10 return. Longer trips to Barbareta (US$40), Pigeon Cay (off Barbareta), Helene (US$20), Port Royal, or through the mangrove canals are also possible. Bargain hard, and remember it's least expensive to go with a group of people and split the cost of the boat.

EASTERN ROATÁN

Paya Beach

Between Oak Ridge and Punta Gorda a dirt road turns off the highway to the east, marked by a sign for the Paya Beach Resort, tel. 435-2139, fax 435-2149, website: www.payabay.com; in the U.S., reservations can be made with a relative of the owner, tel. (504) 924-2220. This small dive hotel is set on a bluff above the ocean, at the south end of a lovely secluded bay. The four rooms facing the ocean are smaller but have a balcony, while those in back are more spacious and have a refrigerator. The steady breezes keep the rooms cool day and night. Rooms cost US$75 pp with three meals a day or US$48 pp without meals, but there's nowhere else to eat. The dive shop has gear for 12 people and offers SSI certification; guests can dive many infrequently visited sites on the north side and around Barbareta.

Camp Bay Beach

Just east of Paya Beach along the same road, past the village of Diamond Rock, is Camp Bay Beach. The largest undeveloped beach left on Roatán, it's a veritable tropical daydream lined with nothing but coconut palms swaying in the steady breeze. This idyllic state will soon change, though, as property lots on the beach are frequently advertised for sale in local magazines and real-estate listings; enjoy it while you can. For the time being, this is still the sort of place you could find a secluded spot to pitch a tent or sling a hammock, if you've got a car or can manage to get out there on your own. No buses go out to Camp Bay, but rides from the highway can often be found in the morning and early afternoon. Also, a pickup drives every day from Oak Ridge to Diamond Rock in the early morning (6-7 a.m.). The beach is 13 km from the Oak Ridge highway turnoff.

Port Royal

The dirt road continues past Camp Bay over the hills to Port Royal, once the site of English pirate camps, now the site of luxury homes for retired expatriates. Named for the famous port in Jamaica, Port Royal was long the favorite anchorage for marauding pirates because of its protected, defensible harbor. It was chosen by the British military as its base in the 1740s for the same reasons. The British built two small forts to guard the harbor: Fort Frederick on the mainland, with one rampart and six cannons, and Fort George on the cay, with one rampart and 17 cannons. In spite of their heavy armaments, the forts didn't see much service before their destruction in 1782 by a Spanish expedition. The remains of Fort George can still be seen, while the foundations for Fort Frederick now hold a private home.

Currently no lodgings or restaurants exist in Port Royal, but rumor has it a resort will open there soon.

Old Port Royal, farther east, is thought to be the site of the ill-fated Providence Company settlement, dating from the 1630s and 1640s. This is the deepest harbor on the island, though it's no longer used for commerce.

The hills above Port Royal were declared the **Port Royal Park and Wildlife Refuge** in 1978 in an effort to protect the principal watershed for eastern Roatán and several species of endangered wildlife. The refuge has no developed trails for hikers.

East End Islands

East of Port Royal, Roatán peters out into a lowland mangrove swamp, impassable by foot or car, which connects to the island of **Helene,** sometimes called Santa Helena. Just east of Helene is the smaller island of **Morat,** and farther east is **Barbareta,** a two- by five-kilometer island home to pristine virgin island forest and several lovely beaches. All three islands are surrounded by spectacular reef.

On Barbareta is the **Barbareta Beach Club,** P.O. Box 72, Lemhi, Idaho, 83465, tel. (888) 450-3483, fax (208) 756-8246, a fully equipped resort set on 1,200 acres of thick forest and palm-lined beach. Rooms run US$220-280 pp with meals for three nights, and weeklong packages are also available. Rooms in the lodge are less expensive than in the beach bungalows. Each of the available activities for guests—diving, windsurfing, hiking, mountain biking, fishing—

costs extra, but prices are not outrageous. Reservations are required.

Southeast of Barbareta are the **Pigeon Cays,** a perfect spot for a relaxed day of picnicking and snorkeling with no one around. Boats to Barbareta, Morat, Helene, and the Pigeon Cays can be hired at the main dock in Oak Ridge.

Anthony's Key Resort often runs full-day dive tours out to Barbareta, with lunch included, for US$90, plus the cost of dive gear rental if you don't have your own stuff. Call ahead to find out when the next trip might be.

UTILA

Utila has the feeling of being lost in a tropical time warp. Listening to the broad, almost incomprehensible Caribbean English coming out of islanders with names like Morgan and Bodden, it seems pirates ran amok here just a few years back instead of three centuries ago. Life on Utila still moves at a sedate pace; local conversation is dominated by the weather, the state of the fishing industry, and spicy gossip about the affairs of the 2,000 or so inhabitants.

In the past few years, though, Utila has come face to face abruptly with the modern day. A steadily growing stream of budget travelers flow in from across the globe, all eager to get scuba certification for as little money as possible (about US$160 at last check) and to enjoy the balmy Caribbean waters and famed reef. With its semi-

official designation as the low-budget Bay Island, Utila has become one of those great backpacker hot spots like Kathmandu, Marrakesh, or Lake Atitlán—packed with young Europeans and Americans out for a good time in the sun. Utila is also well known among fish enthusiasts as one of the best places in the world to see the **whale shark,** the largest fish in the world. These monstrous creatures, getting as big as 15 meters, frequent the Cayman Channel right off Utila and can be spotted (with much patience and a good captain) most of the year.

Perhaps because backpackers are less put-off by natural disasters than other tourists (or maybe they just don't pay attention to the news), Utila saw its tourist business return much quicker after Hurricane Mitch than Roatán and Guanaja.

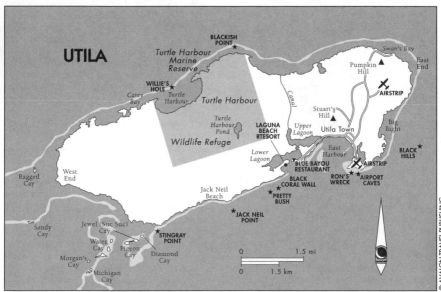

Crowds of young travelers throng the many dive shops, restaurants, bars, and cheap hotels. Most businesses are geared to low-budget travelers, and many offer excellent values for their services, be it a dive course, US$3 hotel room, or luscious fish dinner. While many Utila visitors will revel in the opportunity to meet other travelers and enjoy a taste of nightlife, don't forget to take the time to talk to the quirky, entertaining, and invariably friendly islanders.

Utila's name reputedly derives from a contraction of *ocotillo,* which in Nahuatl refers to a place with a lot of black smoke. The smoke is thought to have come from burning the resinous ocote pine, supposedly used by pre-Columbian islanders in a type of distilling process. The smallest of the three main Bay Islands, Utila is 11 kilometers long and five kilometers wide, with two-thirds of its area covered by swamp. Two small hills on the eastern part of the island, Pumpkin Hill and Stuart's Hill, are volcanic in origin. Sand flies can be voracious on Utila, so come prepared.

As in Roatán, the Utila reef is under threat from fishermen and careless divers, to say nothing of water pollution. But without the steep hillsides of Roatán and still plenty of undrained wetlands, Utila is not likely to face as serious a water quality problem, at least in the near future. The Bay Islands Conservation Association (BICA) in Utila is helping to fund more patrols of the Turtle Harbour Marine Reserve on the north side of the island, paying for environmental education in schools, and setting up more mooring buoys for dive boats.

The latest tourist development of note in Utila is word of a new **airport,** under construction in the bush north of town, off the road to Pumpkin Hill. It will reportedly be up and running, with a new road connecting it to town, by the end of 2000.

A website dedicated to information on Utila, with links, can be found at www.utilainfo.com.

UTILA TOWN (EAST HARBOUR)

Almost all Utilans live in East Harbour, on the south side of the island. Universally called Utila, the town wraps around a large harbor that's protected from the open ocean by an arm of reef. The town is divided into four parts: the point, between the old airport and downtown; Sandy Bay, between downtown and the western edge

of town; the Center, near the main intersection by Captain Morgan's Dive Shop, Bancahsa, and the municipal dock; and Monkey Tail Road, which cuts inland perpendicular to the shore. Connecting the old airport, downtown, and Sandy Bay is Main Street. Mamilane Road, leaving Main Street in Sandy Bay, also heads inland to the north, roughly parallel to Monkey Tail Road.

Although not a large town in total population, Utila's collection of wooden houses, dive shops, hotels, and restaurants is spread across a large area. To cover the ground between your hotel, dive shop, and favorite restaurants and bars, **Delco Bike Rentals,** just west of the dock on Main Street, rents out fairly sturdy **mountain bikes** at US$5 for a full 24 hours, or US$3 for the daytime only. Slightly more abused bikes are available for a bit less, and rates drop for multiday rentals. Another rental shop is **Utila Bike Rentals,** with similar prices.

Pedestrians should keep an eye or ear peeled for maniacal cyclists and three-wheeled motorcycle drivers. Locals appear to derive a secret thrill from whipping along the roads passing unsuspecting gringos as close as possible to scare them. Visitors may also notice that, unlike everywhere else in Honduras, baseball, not soccer, is the sport of choice on Utila. If you want one of those bonding sports conversations, a pertinent comment on the major leagues will help kick things off.

The town's generator runs 6 a.m.-midnight.

RECREATION

Dive Shops

If there's any complaint to be leveled against Utila, it's that all anyone ever talks about is diving. All things considered, that's no surprise. Word has gotten out that Utila offers possibly the least expensive open-water scuba certifications in the world, and business has been booming ever since. Competition between shops is fierce, but under new rules employees are not allowed to pursue potential clients in the street, which was getting out of hand a few years back. Eleven shops were in business in Utila at last count. All the competition is wonderful news to the discerning would-be diver, who will wisely spend a day or two asking around among other travelers

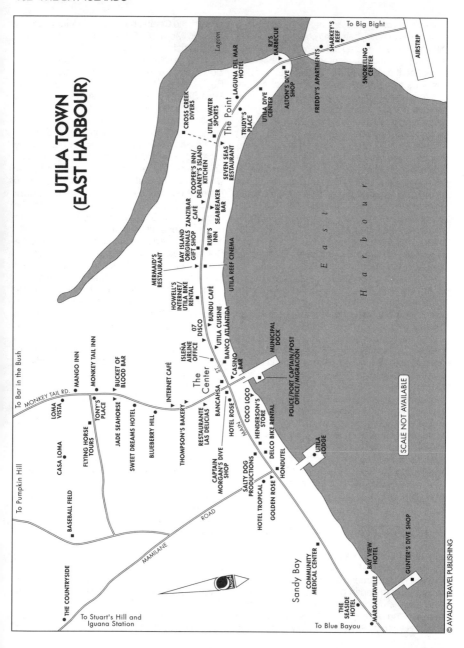

UTILA TOWN (EAST HARBOUR)

To Big Bight

Lagoon

AIRSTRIP

SHARKEY'S REEF

FREDDY'S APARTMENTS

SNORKELING CENTER

RJ'S BARBECUE

LAGUNA DEL MAR HOTEL

ALTON'S DIVE SHOP

CROSS CREEK DIVERS

UTILA WATER SPORTS

UTILA DIVE CENTER

TRUDY'S PLACE

The Point

COOPER'S INN/ DELANEY'S ISLAND KITCHEN

SEVEN SEAS RESTAURANT

ZANZIBAR CAFÉ

SEABREAKER BAR

BAY ISLAND ORIGINALS GIFT SHOP

RUBI'S INN

MERMAID'S RESTAURANT

UTILA REEF CINEMA

East Harbour

HOWELL'S INTERNET/ UTILA BIKE RENTAL

BUNDU CAFÉ

07 DISCO

UTILA CUISINE

ISLEÑA AIRLINE OFFICE

BANCO ATLÁNTIDA

Internet Café

The Center

CASINO BAR

MUNICIPAL DOCK

To Bar in the Bush

MONKEY TAIL RD.

MANGO INN

MONKEY TAIL INN

LOMA VISTA

CASA LOMA

FLYING HORSE TOURS

BUCKET OF BLOOD BAR

TONY'S PLACE

JADE SEAHORSE

SWEET DREAMS HOTEL

BLUEBERRY HILL

THOMPSON'S BAKERY

RESTAURANTE LAS DELICIAS

BANCAHSA

HOTEL ROSE

MAIN ST.

COCO LOCO

HENDERSON'S STORE

DELCO BIKE RENTAL

POLICE/PORT CAPTAIN/POST OFFICE/MIGRACIÓN

To Pumpkin Hill

BASEBALL FIELD

CAPTAIN MORGAN'S DIVE SHOP

SALTY DOG PRODUCTIONS

HONDUTEL

GOLDEN ROSE

HOTEL TROPICAL

ROAD

UTILA LODGE

SCALE NOT AVAILABLE

MAMILANE

COMMUNITY MEDICAL CENTER

Sandy Bay

BAY VIEW HOTEL

GUNTER'S DIVE SHOP

THE SEASIDE HOTEL

MARGARITAVILLE

THE COUNTRYSIDE

To Stuart's Hill and Iguana Station

To Blue Bayou

© AVALON TRAVEL PUBLISHING

RECOMMENDED UTILA DIVE SITES

SOUTH SIDE:

• Stingray Point
• Jack Neil Point
• Pretty Bush
• Black Coral Wall

NEAR THE AIRPORT:

• Ron's Wreck
• Airport Caves
• Black Hills

NORTH SIDE:

• Blackish Point
• Willie's Hole
• Ragged Cay

and investigating several dive shops before deciding where to go and what courses to take.

Note: Whispered comments may be heard about Utila shops cutting corners on safety, but most of the whispers come from Roatán shops and competing Utila shops. Diving accidents do occur occasionally in Utila, but invariably they are the result of a diver disregarding the diving tables, diving alone, or breaking some other rule. There have been no cases of a diver drowning or getting decompression sickness while in an open-water course.

Prices currently stand at US$159 for an open-water or advanced open-water course and US$30 for two-tank dives, plus US$3 a day for insurance and reef fee, or a package of 10 dives for US$125, plus US$3 a day. Most shops have open-water courses starting every other day, available in English, Spanish, German, French, Italian, Swedish, Hebrew, and probably a couple of other languages as well. Listed below are six of the more popular and responsible dive shops.

Utila Dive Center on the point, tel. 425-3326, fax 425-3327, email: shop@utiladivecentre.com,

steer clear of stinging fire coral

was the first dive shop opened on the island, in 1991, and is one of the better-respected shops in town. Frequent north-side trips on two 12-meter cabin cruisers are offered, as well as discount rooms at the Mango Inn.

Underwater Vision, also on the point, tel./fax 425-3103, email: tamara@psi.net.hn, has a lively social scene, weekly barbecues, and a large dive boat.

Alton's, right near the airport, tel. 425-3108, email: altons@hondutel.hn, is known for being very intense about safety.

Cross Creek Divers, on the point, tel. 425-3134, fax 425-3234, email: scooper@hondutel.hn, website: www.ccreek.com, offers US$2 rooms with its courses and has fax and Internet service at the office.

Gunter's/Ecomar, in Sandy Bay, tel. 425-3350, email: ecomar@hondutel.hn, has a good group of instructors with years of experience diving on Utila. The shop, on a dock in Sandy Bay at the western edge of town, also runs boats out to Water Cay.

Utila Water Sports, on the point, tel./fax 425-3239, has safety-conscious instructors and a large dive boat, when it's not in use by the Laguna Beach Resort (same owners).

Two shops selling dive gear are Cross Creek and Utila Water Sports. For more information on dive shops and diving in Utila, contact **Utila Dive Supporters,** tel. 425-3134.

Snorkeling

Basically all the dive shops rent out snorkel gear for around US$5 a day, or free if you are diving with them and just want to take a break from scuba. Many will also allow snorkelers to come out on appropriate dives to snorkel while the others scuba.

One shop dedicated entirely to snorkeling is the aptly named **Snorkeling Center,** on the point, offering a very good half-day tour of three snorkel sites with gear included for US$10. It rents gear for US$3 a day.

The most convenient places for visitors to go snorkeling on their own are at Blue Bayou, a 20-minute walk west of town along the shore,

THE DIVING HAZARD OF DECOMPRESSION SICKNESS

The thought of getting decompression sickness, better known as "the bends," sends a chill through every novice diver's spine. It's important to remember, though, that if a diver follows the tables, it won't be a problem. Divers who end up in trouble are invariably the ones who consider themselves exempt from the laws of physics and the averages used to create the diving tables.

Decompression sickness occurs when a diver returns to sea-level pressure too rapidly. While under increased pressure in the water, the nitrogen in a diver's breathing mixture is absorbed by blood tissues, where it can remain in solution with no ill effects. If a diver does not stay down too long (and hence did not absorb too much nitrogen) and goes up at a rate that allows for outgassing, all will be well. When the pressure is reduced too rapidly, the nitrogen returns to a gaseous form, producing bubbles in tissue and blood cells, causing severe pain and serious problems in the central nervous, peripheral nervous, or cardiopulmonary systems. One dive instructor compared it to shaking a bottled carbonated beverage and then opening it: the bubbles just want to explode out. When a diver ascends too fast, the same process is happening inside his or her tissues.

Due to this need to decompress, dive tables were developed to analyze how much gas the body has absorbed over different lengths of time. All recreational diving is non-decompression diving, intended to allow a diver to make a controlled ascent straight to the surface in the event of an emergency. When near the limits of the tables, a short three- to five-minute decompression stop in five meters of water is recommended.

If a diver is suspected of having decompression sickness, lay the person on his or her left side (in the hope that a bubble will not lodge in the heart) and administer 100% oxygen if possible. If the diver is not breathing, administer CPR. Keep the diver warm and get medical attention as soon as possible. Decompression symptoms may appear anywhere from three to 24 hours after diving. Symptoms include pain in the extremities, severe headache, impairment of speech or vision, seizure, shortness of breath or respiratory arrest, paralysis, or complete collapse.

All divers should wait a full day after their last dive before flying above 1,000 feet, as the altitude change can cause decompression difficulties right after diving.

The Cornerstone Medical Center at Anthony's Key Resort in Roatán, tel. 445-1049, which operates the only recompression chamber in the Bay Islands, offers **diving insurance** through all dive shops for US$2 a day. Although shops don't push it (so as not to seem more expensive), it is worth buying; emergency treatment, in the unlikely event of an accident, can be very pricey.

near the mouth of the canal, and around the airport (the old airport, should the new one open soon), on the southeastern corner of the island. It's also possible to get in the water at Big Bight, a half-hour's walk north of the airport on the east side of the island. You won't see as much colorful coral as on the south-side reef, but rather long ridges of rock and coral, with forests of elkhorn and staghorn coral. Getting into the water at the airport and Big Bight can be tricky, as the dead coral comes right up to the shore. It's easier off the dock at Blue Bayou.

Better still, take a day trip out to Water Cay or one of the other cays southwest of Utila. Talk with dive shops about which dive sites would be most suitable for snorkelers and consider tagging along a dive trip to snorkel.

Kayaking and Boating

Light sea kayaks make a fine way to explore the canals in the center of the island or to tie off at dive buoys and snorkel. Make sure to get detailed directions to find the southern mouth of the cross-island canal, as it can be tricky to locate.

Gunter's, tel. 425-3350, and **Cross Creek,** tel. 425-3134, both rent sea kayaks for US$5 half-day, US$8 full-day, slightly more for a double kayak. Capt. Morgan's Dive Shop in the center of town also rents kayaks.

Yacht skippers should call VHF channel 16 to request check-in and clearance-procedure information with Utila Harbour Authority (in Spanish), or go visit the port captain's office next to the police station. Anchoring is permitted in East Harbour and in the Utila Cays Channel for a

US$10 monthly fee; always use anchor lights, and do not empty bilges in the harbor or near land. Larger boats may dock at the municipal wharf for a daily docking fee.

Horseback Riding

If you'd like a break from water sports, consider going for a horseback ride in the bush-covered interior of the island. **Flying Horse Tours** owner JoJo takes visitors on three- to four-hour mounted trips out to **Aladdin's Cave,** with a large pool of fresh water inside for swimming, for US$10 per person. JoJo's office is just off Monkey Tail Road, a five-minute walk from the dock. Also recommended are the tours arranged at the **Internet Cafe,** charging US$20 for half-day trips out to Aladdin's Cave or elsewhere on the north side of the island.

ACCOMMODATIONS

In keeping with its status as the least expensive Bay Island, the majority of Utila rooms fall into the shoestring or budget categories, about US$4-12 d. A couple of hotels aim for travelers with a few more *lempiras* to spend on cleanliness and privacy, and two low-key resorts are competing to corner the well-heeled market. Except for the resorts, all hotels are in small, wooden buildings, often converted houses, so their proliferation is not overwhelming. Architecturally at least, Utila has not been greatly changed by the tourist influx.

One tip for divers: the different dive shops often offer rooms in their lodges for US$3 if you dive with them. While the regular hotel owners are none too happy about this, it suits budget travelers just fine.

When inquiring at hotels, one important question is whether the establishment has electricity all night. While most hotels do, some of the lower-priced ones do not. Also, while hot showers may not normally be a question of great importance to some travelers, they can be awfully pleasurable after a day of scuba diving.

Shoestring

Of the many cheap hotels in Utila, **Hotel Tropical** (no phone), near where Mamilane Road hits Main Street, is one of the best, charging US$5 s

or d for a simple, quiet room with fan and the use of a small kitchen.

The Countryside, tel. 425-3216 or 425-3206, is, as the name suggests, about a 15-minute walk outside of town on Mamilane Road, set amidst trees and fields. The US$5 d rooms are very basic but guests have kitchen rights, and there's usually a festive crowd of backpackers hanging out. The owners have apartments with kitchen and TV for rent at US$10 a day or US$200 a month.

One of the best deals in town (and often full as a result) is **Blueberry Hill** (no phone), an eclectic assortment of small wooden buildings on stilts built around the owner's house on Monkey Tail Road. Airy rooms each with kerosene stove, bathroom, and lots of character go for US$3.50 d. The same owners also have three houses for rent at US$150-200 per month.

Another cheapie on Monkey Tail Road is **Sweet Dreams,** tel. 425-3357, charging US$3.50 d with shared bathroom and 24-hour electricity. Farther up the road, past the Jade Seahorse Restaurant, is **Tony's Place,** tel. 425-3155, with simple rooms in a whitewashed house for US$2 s or US$4 d.

Past Tony's Place on the same side is **Loma Vista,** tel. 425-3243, with clean, sunny rooms with communal kitchen facilities and a porch for US$5 d, but it is usually full of long-term renters.

Cooper's Inn, on the point, tel. 425-3184, has clean rooms with fans and mosquito nets for US$5 d, with shared bathroom. The owners organize glass-bottomed boat trips, and excellent dinners are served downstairs at Delaney's Island Kitchen. The inn is conveniently close to several of the dive shops, for those out-of-bed-into-the-dive-boat mornings.

The Seaside Inn, near Gunter's Dive Shop in Sandy Bay, tel. 425-3150, has simple but acceptable rooms with shared bathroom for US$4 d or with private bathroom for US$7 d. The hotel also has good though small apartments with kitchenette for US$10 a night or US$250 a month. Next door is a small Internet business run by the hotel owners.

Rubi's Inn, tel. 425-3240, near Cooper's Inn on the ocean side of the road, offers clean rooms with fans for US$3 s or US$5 d. The inn sits right over the water on the point and has kitchen facilities and a breezy front porch.

Dive Shop Hotels

Many of the dive shops in town operate their own hotels, offering divers discounted rooms, sometimes as low as US$2-4 per person. Frequently recommended is **Cross Creek Hotel and Dive Shop,** and the **Mango Inn** with Utila Dive Center is also good. Others include **Alton's Hotel,** with Alton's Dive Shop; **Trudy's/Laguna del Mar,** with Underwater Visions; and **Harbor View Hotel,** with Parrot Dive Center. All rent out rooms to non-divers, usually for around US$10 per person, though the nicer upstairs rooms at Laguna del Mar with a/c are US$25.

Budget

Freddy's Apartments (no phone), near the old airport, rents very nice furnished rooms with fans and access to a communal kitchen for US$10 per person, or US$20 for an apartment with its own kitchen. Low-season and long-term rates are available. The building is located in a quiet part of town, with wrap-around deck facing the canal.

On the far western end of Main Street, in the tranquil Sandy Bay neighborhood, is **Margaritaville,** tel. 425-3366, with 16 breezy, spacious double rooms each with clean, tile-floor bathrooms for US$10. The hotel's deck affords views of both the harbor and lagoon.

A new hotel conveniently located right in the center of town is **Hotel Rose,** tel./fax 425-3127, a good deal at US$15 d with hot water, fan, and TV, more for a/c. The upstairs terrace has a fine view of the harbor and is a great place to relax in the afternoon and evening.

Next to the Utila Lodge, near Hondutel, is **Hotel Utila,** tel. 425-3340, email: annie@hondutel.hn, with a variety of rooms ranging US$15-45 d, depending on the room size and whether it has a/c or a fan. Rooms are clean and spacious.

The Mango Inn, out Monkey Tail Road, tel. 425-3335, email: mango@hondutel.hn, website: www.mango-inn.com, is affiliated with Utila Dive Center but rents out double rooms with shared bath for US$10 to non-divers.   In Sandy Bay is the **Bay View Hotel,** tel. 425-3114, with 11 neat, whitewashed rooms around a grassy lawn at the water's edge for US$10 s, US$15 d.

Inexpensive-Moderate

Out by the airport is **Sharky's Reef Hotel,** tel. 425-3212, email: hjackson@hondutel.hn, a wooden hotel with rooms more luxurious than most in Utila, with a/c, hot water, and cable TV for US$30 d, or US$45 with kitchen. The secluded, quiet hotel has a relaxing deck facing out over the lagoon.

Dive Resorts

Far and away the best hotel in East Harbour itself is **The Utila Lodge,** tel. 425-3143, fax 425-3209, in the U.S. tel. (800) 668-8452, email: ulodger@hondutel.hn. The lodge, run by Americans Jim and Kisty Engel, occupies the dark wood building behind Hondutel. It has its own dock for fishing boats and dive boats, as well as eight rooms with a/c and private balconies. Rates of US$725 a week include three all-you-can-eat meals and three boat dives daily. Non-divers pay US$625 a week. Daily rates are available, US$130 for a diver, and walk-ins are welcome. Jim is an avid fisherman and will arrange flats or deep-sea fishing trips for guests.

On the south side of the island and the west side of the canal is **Laguna Beach Resort,** tel./fax 425-3239 (Utila Water Sports), in the U.S. at tel. (800) 668-8452 or (318) 893-0013, fax (318) 893-5024, website: www.utila.com. The resort offers six bungalows (ceiling fans standard, a/c extra) set on a private sandy peninsula, accessible by boat only, wonderful if you're looking for a secluded place to forget about the world for a while. Swimming and snorkeling are fantastic right off the beach out front. One week with meals and two boat dives daily on a large dive boat goes for US$750 pp. Flats and deep-sea fishing, windsurfing, and sea-kayaking trips are available, and shore diving is unlimited.

Apartments

With so many travelers finding themselves transfixed by Utila's reefs and low-key lifestyle, plenty of apartments are up for rent. Prices can range anywhere from US$100 to US$400, depending on what kind of place you're looking for, but most basic ones with kitchenette average US$200 or US$250 a month. Apart from the many private individuals renting, who can only be found by asking around, several hotels offer longer-term rentals. They include Freddy's Apartments, the Countryside, the Seaside, Blueberry Hill, and the Mango Inn. Casa Loma, just off Monkey Tail Road, rents cabins for US$60 a week or US$250 a month.

FOOD

Breakfasts, Baked Goods, and Health Foods

Thompson's Bakery, on Monkey Tail Road not far from the main intersection, sells wildly popular and inexpensive breakfasts daily 6 a.m.-noon. It's always packed with divers stuffing themselves with pancakes, omelets, and the famous johnnycake (biscuits served plain or like a McDonald's Egg McMuffin) and washing it all down with a mug of coffee before running out to their 7:30 a.m. dive. Delectable chocolate chip cookies and cakes are sold to go.

Zanzibar Cafe on the point has excellent breakfasts, including top-notch omelets and pancakes with homemade syrup, as well as very good lunches, such as superb fish burgers and tuna sandwiches. The owner is also a professional masseuse who charges US$13 per massage. Open daily except Saturday, 6 a.m.-2 p.m.

Very popular with travelers is **Bundu Cafe,** on Main Street in the center of town, serving healthy breakfasts, crepes, fruit salad, bagels, sandwiches, fruit-yogurt milkshakes, and fresh juices. The food is of good quality, though portions are small for the price. The cafe shows great movies most nights, and the owner can help arrange trips to Water Cay. Closed on Thursday and Sunday, open other days 7 a.m.-3 p.m.

The **Green Ribbon Store** sells very tasty cinnamon rolls, chocolate cake, and inexpensive sandwiches (vegetarian and with meat). The **Internet Cafe** also has superb baked goods and sandwiches on homemade bread.

Inexpensive Snacks and Meals

Supremely addictive *baleadas* are sold by the **"baleada ladies,"** as they are affectionately known, for US 35 cents each at the intersection near Captain Morgan's dive shop. These very astute mainland immigrants saw a need for cheap eats and have filled the niche with raging success. Placidly whipping out fresh tortillas filled with beans, cheese, and soaked onions (a tasty twist on the traditional version), the ladies invariably attract a crowd to their outdoor stands during the lunch and dinner shifts. Sometimes they offer an inexpensive chicken-and-beans plate as well.

At the corner of Main Street and Mamilane Road is **The Golden Rose,** a lunch-and-dinner joint with a certain Brady Bunch charm, with both indoor and outdoor seating. The Golden Rose has rotating specials every day at US$2.50-4 per meal and very good pizza. Open daily 2:30-10 p.m.

In a large converted house is **Utila Cuisine,** opposite the 07 Disco, featuring burgers, steak, and fish for US$2.50-5. Meals here are cooked at a snail's pace, but there's plenty of cold beer and conversation to keep you occupied while you wait. This favored hangout for locals and travelers alike is open sporadically for lunch and dinner.

For the best fried chicken in town, as well as inexpensive *baleadas,* fried fish, burgers, and *comida corrientes,* try the **Seven Seas Restaurant** on the point, open 8 a.m.-10 p.m. every day except Monday.

Glady's Hamburgers, on a short path off Main Street marked with a hand-painted sign, serves tasty, inexpensive burgers and *comida corridas,* a good spot for a budget meal.

Midrange Meals

Certainly one of the more unusual finds in Utila is **Delany's Island Kitchen,** managed by a Danish chef cooking nightly dinner specials like Swedish meatballs, lasagna, veggie burgers, and superb pizza for a ravenous crowd of divers. It's best to arrive before 8 p.m. as Delany's frequently runs out of food due to high demand. Closed Sunday; US$3-5 per meal.

Also with a creative, rotating small menu is **Sting Ray Bar and Grill,** considered by some to have the best food in town. The dishes, invariably including at least one fresh-caught fish, are cooked with elegant simplicity, seasoned to perfection, and served with superb side fixings. It's open nightly for dinner only and is a popular spot for late-night conversation and beers.

Rivaling the above two restaurants in popularity is the newer **RJ's Barbecue,** offering superlative fresh fish, frequently snapper and tuna, thick steaks, and spicy chicken. Go early as the small restaurant fills up fast. Open daily 6-9:30 p.m.

The **Jade Seahorse,** opposite the Bucket of Blood Bar on Monkey Tail Road, serves healthy US$3-5 meals, *burrito-baleadas* (a unique concoction), large fruit shakes, salads, fish, and other dishes in a creatively decorated dining room filled with wooden furniture, backgammon and chess boards, and soft music in the background.

Always full of travelers hankering for the solid (though unspectacular) lasagna, pizza, salads, burgers, and daily specials for US$3-6 per meal is **Mermaid's Restaurant,** on the point. The lunch buffet is a good place for a hearty afternoon meal. Service can be fatally slow, but the tables, on a dimly lighted patio, make a pleasant place to chat. Open for lunch and dinner except Friday night and Saturday afternoon.

ENTERTAINMENT

With such an eclectic assortment of young travelers from around the globe, as well as a sizable population of fun-loving locals, it's no surprise that Utila has a flourishing nightlife. While the favored location varies depending on one's mood during the week, Friday night invariably sees a large crowd at the **Bar in the Bush,** literally in the bush at the end of Monkey Tail Road, a 15-minute walk from the waterfront. The sprawling cabaña complex, with an attached volleyball court, with an unusually loose, festive ambiance, with an odd mix of people wandering about with drinks in hand, enjoying the grooving music. It's open Wednesday through Sunday, but Friday is the big night. The road planned out to the new airport in Utila may somewhat change the bar's currently secluded feel.

Saturday night belongs, hands down, to the **07 Disco,** a scene of extreme debauchery late Saturday night into the wee hours of Sunday morning. A mixed crowd of progressively drunker travelers and locals bop to techno, funk, and Euro-disco sounds, while groups of people stand around in the street, looking for entertainment and on occasion finding it in the form of drunken, relatively harmless brawls. Cheap beer and rum and cokes are the only drinks available; there's no cover charge.

One of more *tranquilo* bars is **Coco Loco's,** a positively lethargic oceanfront place to chill out with some mellow tunes and a drink during the week. Often closed on weekends. Another good relaxed spot is the bar at **Cross Creek Restaurant,** on the edge of the lagoon.

German owner Hans keeps the clients happy with his fine music at **Las Delicias.** The wooden tables and open-air porch often have a crowd of divers and travelers having a couple of drinks after dinner.

One unusually located drinking establishment is **Treetanic Bar,** literally a treehouse bar, creatively designed and decorated in the canopy of a tree in front of the Jade Seahorse restaurant.

It's worth keeping an eye out for the many barbecues and parties held by dive shops, many of which are open to whoever wanders by.

Utila Reef Cinema has two or three movies a week in a well-designed theater, which is unfortunately often packed with noisy kids on Saturday (other nights are not as bad). It also rents videos.

Though its screen and sitting area is not as big, **Bundu Cafe** shows very good movies every night. Get there early to get a spot on the couches or floor cushions for a popular movie.

The Bucket of Blood Bar up Monkey Tail Road is an island institution. Although not as lively as it once was, it's still a good place for a late-night beer session. The colorful name has spawned a popular T-shirt, on sale at the bar.

The billiard aficionado need not fear: there is one small **pool hall** with three tables in Sandy Bay where you can get your fix until about 11 p.m. nightly. Beer is served.

After a late night at the bars, especially on Saturday night/Sunday morning after the discos, it's a good idea to walk home in a group. Muggings are not common but not unheard of either.

MORE UTILA TOWN PRACTICALITIES

Exchange
Both Bancahsa and Banco Atlántida change traveler's checks and will give a cash advance on a Visa card, but no cash machine is available. Open Mon.-Fri. 8-11:30 a.m. and 1:30-4 p.m., Saturday 8-11:30 a.m. Henderson's will also exchange traveler's checks and cash at a good rate.

Services
Hondutel is in Sandy Bay, next to the police station; faxes can be received at 425-3101. The *migración* office and post office are now out on the main dock in town. Visa renewal is usually hassle-free.

In an emergency contact the **police,** tel. 425-3255, or after hours at tel. 425-3187. For medical attention, the **Community Medical Center** opposite the church on Sandy Bay Road, charges US$4 per visit, Mon.-Fri. 8 a.m.-noon. For medical help after hours, contact Dr. Dan, the American expat who runs the center, at his home in the harbor on the yacht *Tabitha,* VHF channel 6.

Internet

Though Internet service is easily available in Utila, it's a lot pricier than on the mainland, costing around US$6 for a half-hour or US$12 an hour. Service is usually available by the minute. Three shops offering Internet access are: **Howell's Internet,** tel. 425-3317, on Main Street not far past the 07 Disco, open Mon.-Fri. 8 am.-5:30 p.m.; **Internet Cafe,** tel. 425-3124, where international phone service and addictive sweets are also available, open Mon.-Sat. 9 a.m.-5 p.m., and **Seaside Inn Internet,** tel. 425-3150, open daily until 5:30 p.m.

Information

The **BICA** office, tel. 425-3260, where travelers can find pamphlets, maps, and books on Utila and the Bay Islands, is in a small wooden building in front of Mermaid's Restaurant, open Mon.-Fri. 7 a.m.-7 p.m., Sat.-Sun. 6-8 p.m.

The Utila Times, tel. 425-3292, fax 425-3234, is the island's news and gossip sheet, an entertaining source of local information printed (usually) monthly and sold for US$1 at various locations.

Underwater Photography

Salty Dog Productions, tel./fax 425-3363, email: saltydog@hondutel.hn, can take care of all aspects of underwater photography for divers, including: renting out print cameras at US$25 for a half-day, videotaping a dive for US$80, plus US$20 per extra video copy, or giving courses in underwater photography or video for US$300.

Shopping

Several grocery stores in town sell fresh produce, cheese, milk, and other perishables, but they often run out over the weekend, before the next boat arrives. Most are open Monday-Saturday only.

Bay Island Originals sells locally designed T-shirts, Honduran coffee and cigars, and a variety of tourist collectibles. The expensive rolling papers are always a popular item with the backpacker crowd. **Hotel Utila** also has a small gift shop with handicrafts and T-shirts.

One place in town with a decent book exchange/book rental is the **Bundu Cafe.**

Getting There and Away

Monday through Saturday, several flights a day ferry passengers between Utila and La Ceiba. All flights on all airlines cost US$17 one way. Buy **Isleña** tickets at its office in the center of town, tel. 425-3368, tel./fax 425-3386; **Sosa** tickets are sold at Hunter and Morgan's Store, tel. 425-3161.

The **MV *Galaxy*** departs La Ceiba for Utila daily at 9 or 9:30 a.m., arrives at Utila at around 10:30 a.m., and departs again a half hour later. Travelers can spend the hour-long ride inside watching a video or outside on deck enjoying the breeze. Cost is US$10 per person.

The much less luxurious and slower **MV *Starfish*** leaves Utila for La Ceiba Monday at 5:30 a.m.; US$4.50. The advantage of taking the *Starfish* is arriving in La Ceiba early enough (8:30 a.m.) to make bus connections elsewhere. The trip also has undeniable ambient value—watching a hazy sunrise over the Caribbean from a rusty tramp freighter, admiring the views of Pico Bonito looming up on the mainland. No reservations are needed, just show up on the main dock at about 5 a.m. For those really counting their *lempira,* the owners of the *Starfish* are happy to let passengers sleep on deck the night before, saving one night's hotel rent and ensuring you don't oversleep.

In recent times a boat has run from Utila every Friday night to Livingston, Guatemala, arriving Saturday morning and charging US$98. At last report the boat was not running, but for the latest check with Gunter's Dive Shop in Sandy Bay, tel. 425-3350, email: ecomar@hondutel.hn.

For more information on local boating, stop in at the port captain's office by the dock or call 425-3116.

ELSEWHERE ON THE ISLAND

The **Iguana Research and Breeding Station** out Mamilane Road makes for an interesting expedition if you feel like taking a break from diving. Morning is the best time to see the bizarre-looking and surprisingly large iguanas feed and wander around. The station has several species of swamp iguana, *Ctenosaura baberi,* found only in the mangrove swamps of Utila and in danger of extinction due to overhunting and the cutting of the mangroves. To get to the farm, follow Mamilane Road past the Countryside Inn, and look for signs pointing out a path to the left. Open Monday through Saturday only.

The point at Blue Bayou, a 20-minute walk west of town, marks the southern entrance to the cross-island canal. About halfway up the canal by boat is a small dock, where a trail heads west to **Turtle Harbour Pond,** site of a small pre-Columbian ruin. On the north side of the island west of where the canal lets out are a couple of small, deserted beaches accessible by boat only.

From the end of Monkey Tail Road a five-km dirt road continues across the island to **Pumpkin Hill Beach** on the north side. Much of the coast here is covered with fossilized coral and rocks, but a few patches of sand provide good spots to put down a towel and relax in splendid isolation. Negotiating a safe passage into the water to swim and snorkel is no easy task, but in calm weather the determined will make it. Near the beach is **Pumpkin Hill,** 270 feet high and riddled with caves, one of which is the sizable **Brandon Hill Cave,** reputedly containing pirates' treasure. The smooth dirt road out to the beach makes a great 15-minute mountain-bike ride or an hour's walk.

Closer to town is **Stuart's Hill,** like Pumpkin Hill a former volcano. From the top are good views over town and the south side of the island, and nearby are the barely visible remnants of a pre-Columbian ceremonial site.

The **"Airport Beach,"** at the far end of the airstrip, is not exactly a sandy paradise, but there are a couple of good snorkeling sites just offshore. Getting in through the rocky shoreline is not easy. A path continues north past the airport to a small secluded cove, and farther on to a larger cove called **Big Bight,** which has a small patch of decent sand—a good locale for a lazy day of snorkeling and sunbathing. The coral reef ridges in the bay are not in the best health, but there are plenty of interesting formations and marinelife to admire with snorkel and fins. Big Bight is about two km north of the airport.

UTILA CAYS

The Utila Cays are a collection of 12 tiny islets located off the southwest corner of the main island. Some 400 people live on **Jewel (or Suc-Suc) Cay** and **Pigeon Cay,** which are connected by a narrow causeway and generally referred to jointly as Pigeon Cay. These islanders are descended from the first residents who came to Utila from the Cayman Islands in the 1830s. Originally the migrants settled on the main island but soon moved out to the cays, reputedly to avoid the sand flies, which are much less common than on the main island, especially when the easterly breeze is up. If you found Utila residents to be an odd Caribbean subculture, the Pigeon Cay population is odder still—a small, isolated group who tend to keep to themselves, but nevertheless welcome the occasional visitor with friendly smiles.

At the east end of the causeway on Jewel Cay is the small **Hotel Kayla** (no phone), with

---

PLAN A COOKOUT ON WATER CAY

With driftwood everywhere for bonfires and no one around to bother campers, Water Cay is the perfect spot for a fish cookout. Come prepared with all the fixings—foil, lemons, garlic, onions, and maybe a few sweet potatoes for good measure. When arriving from Utila, stop off at Pigeon Cay and go to Bessie's fish market to pick up a fish or three, depending on how many feasters are expected. If you ask nicely at the market, they might even fillet and season the fish for you. Once you've moved on to Water Cay and chosen an appropriate spot, build a roaring fire, wrap everything up in foil, and toss it into the coals for a few minutes.

If you're lucky, a group of islanders might be holding their own cookout and can show you how to whip up some *bando,* a spicy seafood and vegetable stew. Be sure not to forget liquid refreshments—one drink with an appealing tropical style is made by chopping open a coconut and spiking the milk with rum. As the milk dwindles the mix becomes progressively more potent and may lead to an early collapse in the hammock.

simple rooms for US$5-8 d. Another place next door has similar rooms. For food, **Susan's Restaurant** is famed for excellent fishcakes and conch stew. At **Bessie's Fish Factory,** visitors heading out to Water Cay and looking to make a cookout can buy a couple of fresh fish—and if you ask nicely, the proprietors will fillet and season the fish for you.

It's possible to rent a private island—Morgan and Sandy Cays are managed by George Jackson on Pigeon Cay, tel. 425-3161. A cabin is available on **Diamond Cay,** a tiny islet right in front of Jewel Cay. Ask around in Pigeon Cay for details.

If you were to conjure up the ideal tropical beach paradise, your picture might be something very close to **Water Cay.** Almost within shouting distance of Pigeon Cay, Water Cay is a patch of sand several hundred meters long, wide at one end and tapering to a point on the other; the only occupants are coconut palms and one small caretaker's shack. Piercingly blue, warm water and a coral reef just a few yards out ring the cay. There are no permanent residents on the island, and visitors are welcome to camp out with tents or hammocks for US$1 a night. The caretaker (who shows up most days but doesn't live on the island) rents hammocks for another US$1 a night, though they're not the finest quality—better to bring your own, or bring a tent. The attendant can motor you over to Pigeon Cay for a nominal fee. The best snorkeling is off the south side, though it can be a bit tricky finding an opening in the wall. Water Cay is a popular impromptu party spot for locals and travelers, especially on weekends and on the full moon.

To get to Water Cay, contact Steve at the Bundu Cafe, who helps put together groups for the trip. If you already have a group, you can get ahold of Fred at Freddy's Apartments, or Capt. Diamond at the Mango Cafe, who can find a boat for usually around US$23 roundtrip for the day, more if you get picked up another day.

GUANAJA

Guanaja has somehow ended up as the forgotten Bay Island, overlooked in the rush of travelers and migrants to Utila and Roatán. This oversight is surprising considering Guanaja's fantastic reef, wide-open north-side beaches, and quirky fishing towns.

But the days of Caribbean backwater status are fast coming to an end. Guanaja's real estate market is booming as more and more expatriates seek their own little chunk of paradise. While Roatán is a bastion of American immigrants, more Europeans seem to be buying up lots on the deserted beaches on Guanaja's north side. One of the latest Guanaja tourism news items was the announcement in early 2000 that actor Christopher Lambert had purchased property on the island and would soon begin construction of a US$12 million dive resort.

Contrary to conventional belief, it is possible to survive on the island on a budget, though not as easily as on Utila. But the few extra *lempiras* are worth it to catch a glimpse of what Utila and Roatán looked and felt like 30 years ago. And for those with a bit more to spend, dive resorts range from funky, homey little hotels to fully equipped luxury spreads.

The waters surrounding Guanaja constitute the only complete marine reserve in the Bay Islands, but until recently active conservation efforts have been minimal. Currently Texas A&M University is conducting a study on Guanaja's reef in conjunction with the Posada del Sol Resort.

Guanaja was the only inhabited land to feel the full force of Hurricane Mitch, when it struck on 26 October 1998. Coming in from the north, the hurricane utterly wiped out the fishing town of Mangrove Bight (miraculously with no deaths) and heavily damaged Savanna Bight and Bonacca Town. The 290-kph winds also knocked flat most of the island's once-famous trees, although reforestation projects got underway shortly after the storm passed. Although tourist infrastructure was temporarily out of commission, the hotels and dive resorts of Guanaja were mostly up and running by the end of 1999. Ferocious though it was above the waves, the storm appears to have had little effect on the reef in Guanaja or anywhere else on the Bay Islands.

BONACCA TOWN

Bonacca Town—sometimes just called Guanaja—is an architectural oddity built on rickety wooden causeways over a maze of canals, founded in the 1830s by immigrants from the Cayman Islands. They constructed their homes on what were then Hog and Sheen Cays. These two tiny little islets, with a total of one km of land space connected by a shoal, have since been built to cover 18 square km by generations tossing their garbage out the window and eventually covering it over with sand, shells, and coral.

Bonacca Town may look hopelessly defenseless in the face of a hurricane, but the fringing reef, sandbars, and islets ringing the town to the south protect it from all but the fiercest storms.

This of course came in 1998 in the form of Hurricane Mitch, which dealt roughly indeed with Bonacca Town. Many houses were destroyed, and most of those left standing lost their roofs. Reconstruction of the town was quick, and now little trace of the hurricane damage is visible.

With no beaches or other obvious attractions, Bonacca Town is worth a visit only to meet the islander townsfolk and take care of any business you might have. Anyone who spends a couple of days wandering the maze of causeways that comprise the island will soon make a few acquaintances and start to hear the endlessly entertaining local gossip and tall tales.

Recreation
At last report, Guanaja had no dive shops not attached to a hotel. Hugo Cisneros, owner of the

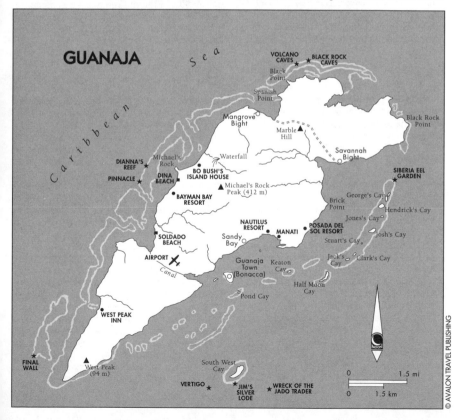

RECOMMENDED GUANAJA DIVE SITES

SOUTH SIDE

• Pond Cay Wrecks
• Wreck of the Jado Trader
• Jim's Silver Lode
• Vertigo

WEST, EAST, AND NORTH SIDES

• Final Wall
• Pinnacle
• Dianna's Reef
• Volcano Caves
• Black Rock Caves
• Siberia Eel Garden

Coral Cafe in Bonacca Town once ran a small shop but closed it with the drop in business after Mitch. It may reopen in the future. The Nautilus Resort in Sandy Bay, a short boat ride from Bonacca Town, takes non-guests out diving at US$40 per dive, as long as the dive crew is not occupied with their own guests. Similar arrangements can be made at Bayman Bay or Posada del Sol, though likely for a bit more money. Bo Bush, owner of the Island House on Guanaja's north side, will also take out day divers at reasonable prices.

Snorkeling right off Bonacca Town is an unpleasant affair, as the surrounding coral is dead and litter content in the water is high. Better to hire a boat and go to the northwest sides of either Southwest Cay or Half Moon Cay, where vibrant corals are found in shallow water.

Veteran Honduras fisherman Capt. J.C. Morgan, tel. 448-6402, or via the Nautilus Resort, website: www.captainjc.com, charges US$300 for a full day fishing excursion for up to six people, with drinks included. Wahoo, king mackerel, and barracuda are frequent catches.

Accommodations

Although not as grim as many travelers assume, the budget hotel selection is limited to the top end of the "budget" category, and even then only if there's two of you. Solo travelers can expect to pay for two beds regardless. The midrange options are scarce as well, and there are no resorts in Bonacca Town.

In the middle of town on the main street is **Hotel Miller,** tel. 453-4327, a large two-story house with rooms on the second floor. A not very attractive double room with overhead fan and small bathroom costs US$8, or more for a nicer room with TV. Similar is the **Carter Hotel,** toward the north end of the main street above Banco Atlántida, tel. 453-4303, US$17 s or d with fan and private bathroom—though water is not always reliable.

In a concrete building set back off the main street in the middle of town, the **Hotel Rosario,** tel. 453-4240, has rooms with a/c and TV for US$22 d. At the south end of the main street is the **Hotel Alexander,** tel. 453-4326, a large house on the water. Each of the 11 rooms has a sea-facing balcony and private bath; rates are US$35 s or US$45 d, more for a/c. A penthouse with three double beds, kitchenette, and TV is also available for US$150 a night.

If you're looking for something cheaper, you could ask around to see if anyone has a room for rent. At the south end of the main street, on the left side just before Hotel Alexander, **Jano** rents a couple of inexpensive rooms, but they're usually taken.

Next to the airstrip on the main island is the **Airport Hillton,** tel. 453-4299, where unexceptional rooms with private baths rent for US$28 d. There's no reason to stay here, aside from paranoia about missing a flight, though the owner is a colorful character who knows a lot about the island.

Food and Entertainment

One of the better restaurants in town is the cafeteria in back of the **Pirate's Den Bar,** on the main street, open daily until 9 p.m., with fried chicken, fish, pork chops, sandwiches, and breakfasts for US$2.50-5. A block away is **Mexitreats,** a new place owned by a Honduran and his Mexican wife, with inexpensive snacks and light meals like *chilaquiles, baleadas,* nachos, and burgers. It's open during the week for breakfast and closes at 9 p.m.

Across the street from Up and Down Bar a couple of blocks off the main street is **Joe's,** which has no sign but serves legendarily tasty chicken *guisado* (stewed) or *a la plancha* (fried), for US$3.25 a plate, or pork chops for US$5. Open daily 11 a.m.-3 p.m. and 6-11 p.m.

Zapata's, a small snack stand at the north

end of town, has a good soup of the day, burgers, cold sandwiches, and sweet treats, open Sun.-Fri. 8 a.m.-10 p.m.

Two doors away from Banco Atlántida on the same side of the main street is **Emma's** (no sign), serving decent and inexpensive breakfasts, burgers, *pastelitos,* and coffee.

The Coral Cafe in the center of town doesn't have much in the way of food apart from chicken *pastelitos,* but it serves as an informal town square, with everyone stopping in to chat and have a soft drink or beer. Cafe owner Hugo Cisneros is a friendly character always willing to help tourists find their way around or locate boats heading over to the big island. Usually open until 10 p.m., often closed on Sunday.

Groceries, and occasionally some acceptable vegetables, are sold at **HWB Supermarket,** open daily 7:30 a.m.-9 p.m.

The bars and discos of Guanaja are not for the faint of heart, filled as they are with rough characters who are always ready for a brawl, but they can be a good time if you know how to look after yourself. **Up and Down,** a couple of blocks behind the main street, is a fairly rowdy bar on the second floor of a wooden house, and next door is **Terraza Disco.** Just past the disco is a **pool hall** with six decent tables, usually open until around midnight.

Services

Banco Atlántida, tel. 453-4262, and Bancahsa, tel. 453-4178 or 453-4335, change both dollars and traveler's checks. **Guanaja Properties,** tel. 453-4276, tel./fax 4533-4299, is the largest real estate office on the island. **Hondutel,** at the south end of the main street, is open Mon.-Fri. 7 a.m.-9 p.m., Saturday 7 a.m.-4 p.m. Receive faxes there at 453-4146.

Police can be reached at tel. 453-4310. There is no fire department on Guanaja.

Getting There and Away

Sosa, tel. 453-4359, Isleña, tel. 453-4208, and Rollins, tel. 453-4202, fly once a day from La Ceiba to Guanaja for US$36. The airstrip is on the main island, with no terminal except a simple shelter. Boats always come out to meet the flights and charge US$3 for the 10-minute ride to town. All three airlines have offices in Guanaja where tickets can be purchased.

Although there is no regular ferry service between Guanaja and the mainland, ships frequently depart to various destinations up and down the Honduras coast and throughout the Caribbean. The port captain, tel. 453-4321, may be of some help in locating rides.

ELSEWHERE ON THE ISLAND

The favored lodgings for high-end vacationers on Guanaja have always been the several dive hotels scattered around the island—self-contained operations ranging from the luxurious Posada del Sol resort to the homey Island House. Resorts normally book weeklong meal-and-dive packages, including transport to and from the airport.

Budget travelers can seek out less expensive rooms in Mangrove Bight or Savannah Bight, or camp on one of the as-yet undeveloped northside beaches.

Private boats arrive and depart frequently each day, heading between Bonacca Town and various parts of the main island. Usually islanders arrive in town in the morning, shop or sell goods, and leave again at midday. Ask around, especially at the Coral Cafe, where owner Hugo Cisneros can often help arrange rides. A ride to Mangrove Bight, an hour or so away depending on the size of the outboard, normally costs about US$3 if the boatman is already going your way. Boats heading to Mangrove Bight can easily drop visitors off at Dina Beach or Michael's Rock, both superb beaches. Regular boats to Savannah Bight leave Guanaja Town daily at 7 a.m., returning immediately, for US$1. An express boat trip to Michael's Rock or elsewhere on the north side costs about US$25-35, depending on gas prices and your negotiating skills.

Hotels and Dive Resorts

One of the premier dive resorts in the Bay Islands, **Posada del Sol,** tel./fax 453-4186, in the U.S. at tel. (561) 852-8004 or (561) 624-3483, fax (561) 852-8979, email: posadadelsol@aol.com, has 23 Spanish-style rooms set on 70 acres of mountainside and beachfront property on the main island's south side. Among the many amenities are: freshwater pool, tennis court, two beaches, restaurant and bar, in-house massage therapist, Nautilus equipment, kayaks and snorkel gear, staff-organized trips to Barbareta, town tours, and archaeological hikes. Weeklong dive-and-meal packages cost US$756 pp for two people, US$917 for one; three-night packages are US$339 pp. Prices include three dives daily on one of three 42-foot dive boats, one night dive per week, and unlimited shore diving.

On the north side of the island is the **Bayman Bay Resort,** tel. 453-4191, fax 453-4179, in the U.S. at tel. (800) 524-1823 or (954) 572-1902, fax (954) 572-1907, featuring 18 wooden cottages distributed across 100 acres of wooded hillside fronted by a white-sand beach. Each cottage is decorated with local art and equipped with ceiling fans and louvered windows to let the trade winds blow through. Weeklong packages, including diving and three buffet-style meals daily, cost US$700-750.

Another option in the same price range is **The Nautilus Resort** in Sandy Bay, tel. 453-4389, in the U.S. at tel. (800) 224-3866 or (618) 985-2818, fax (618) 985-2841, with seven air-conditioned rooms on 25 acres of land, with a 1,000-foot sand beach and a nearby waterfall. Weeklong dive-and-meal packages cost US$700 pp double occupancy. The owner may soon open a new hotel on Dunbar Rock, the prominent rock with an oversized structure perched on it in the bay.

One of the more relaxed, friendly, and less expensive dive hotels in the Bay Islands is **Bo Bush's Island House,** fax (via Hondutel) 453-4146, built and managed by Bo and his wife. Bo is a bilingual, experienced island diver with over 5,000 dives under his belt and a fast boat, and he knows a whole world of north-side dive sites including caverns, walls, reef gardens, wrecks, and more. The comfortable stone-and-wood house set into the hillside can sleep 10, but Bo's boat can only handle six divers. Meals and room only costs US$50 a day, or US$80 with two boat dives and unlimited shore diving. The isolated hotel has a positively tranquilizing atmosphere, with wide stretches of deserted beach all around. Bo, a very friendly and laid-back host, will happily take guests on hiking trips and island tours.

For a less expensive, low-key hotel, check out **Manati,** fax (via Hondutel) 453-4146, a rambling wooden lodge built by the German owner in the eastern end of Sandy Bay. At the moment three spacious rooms with overhead fans are for rent at US$30 per room, s or d. Food can be arranged at extra cost. Diving is available through the nearby Nautilus Resort.

A new dive hotel on Guanaja, closed at last report but set to reopen soon, is **End of the World Resort,** with private wooden cabins on a leafy, secluded hillside on the main island. Weeklong dive-and-meal packages cost US$700 pp double occupancy. For more information, contact Terra Firma Adventures, 7481 West Oakland Park Blvd., Suite 308, Ft. Lauderdale, FL 33319, tel. (800) 524-1823 or (954) 572-1902, fax (954) 572-1907, website: www.guanaja.com.

Mangrove Bight

This small fishing village on the northeast corner of Guanaja, formerly perched over the shallow waters of a small bay, had the dubious distinction of being the first inhabited place to come in contact with Hurricane Mitch, at 10 a.m. on 26 October 1998. Luckily the storm hit in the morning, so the entire town had time to flee their houses and head up into the surrounding hills, watching as 10-meter waves swept their town away entirely. As of early 2000, the town had mostly been rebuilt, now located a safe distance away from the shoreline!

Mangrove Bight is populated by a mix of *ladino* and islander families, all dependent on the modest local fishing fleet. Electricity in town currently shuts off at 10 p.m., but the town generators may soon be replaced by 24-hour power lines. Mangrove Bight is usually stroked by a steady breeze, which keeps the sand flies and mosquitoes to a minimum. A couple of *comedores* in town serve up inexpensive eggs, burgers, and other basic meals. Before Mitch, rooms were often available for rent in town at around US$10 a night, and they may be again soon. Ask Hugo at the Coral Cafe in Bonacca Town if he knows of anybody renting rooms.

A few points of rock sticking up out in the bay in front of Mangrove Bight indicate the location of the reef. It's a fair swim out but doable for strong snorkelers who keep their eyes peeled for boat traffic. Once to the reef, poke around to find a sufficiently deep opening to pass through, and get ready for a heart-stopping drop-off into the blue depths below on the far side. Visibility is not fantastic and the water is a bit choppy, but it's worth the effort to snorkel around the drop-off.

Near Mangrove Bight

From Mangrove Bight a dirt road heads southeast past an unused airstrip and across a low point in the interior of the island to **Savannah Bight,** about an hour and a half away through mosquito-filled pasture land. Rooms are often available for rent in Savannah Bight, which has frequent boat service to Bonacca Town, especially in the mornings.

About halfway between Mangrove Bight and Savannah Bight you'll pass **Marble Hill,** an anomalous, tree-covered outcrop on the west side of the road. On the far side of the hill is the largest known pre-Columbian ceremonial site on the Bay Islands, **Plan Grande.** Thankfully the site was mapped in the 1930s before being completely pillaged of its pottery and jade artifacts and destroyed. Little remains of either the ceremonial site or a large residential complex nearby, but locals will take a visitor to poke around for a fee. An archeologist from the government's Instituto Hondureño de Antropologia e Historia (IHAH) is reportedly planning a serious excavation at the site in the near future. The road between Mangrove Bight and Savannah Bight offers good views of the mountains in the center of the island.

For the industrious, a trail leads from the western end of Mangrove Bight up a small valley, over a peak, and down the other side to Sandy Bay, on the south side of the island. The summit of the 412-meter peak is flat and reportedly a good spot for camping. Needless to say, the views from the top are stunning. Fresh water can sometimes be found but it's best to bring enough for the whole trip, which could be done in a long day. The walk is longer than it may look, due to several high valleys not visible from below which must be crossed.

About a 45-minute walk west of Mangrove Bight by trail begins a stretch of beautiful beach winding around to **Michael's Rock,** a rocky headland jutting into the ocean. The entire beach is lovely, but the best sections—two stretches of powdery sand and brilliant pale blue water separated by a grove of coconut palms—are right on either side of the headland. In its current state, this is a superb beach on which to sling a hammock or pitch a tent and enjoy a couple of days in isolation, but this may change soon if hotel construction plans come to pass. Small patches of reef around Michael's Rock offer snorkeling possibilities, but the main reef is about a mile offshore.

On the way to Michael's Rock is Bo Bush's Island House, a friendly, low-priced dive hotel that also makes a great place for non-divers to relax and enjoy the beach. Not far from Bo's place a small creek comes out of the hills, and a trail follows it a half-hour's walk uphill to a small waterfall surrounded by lush vegetation.

Don't forget to come prepared for sand flies; they can be fierce on the north-side beaches.

Elsewhere on the North Side

From Michael's Rock, **Dina Beach** is visible farther southwest, but walking is difficult as the trail passes through thick underbrush in order to bypass rocky coastline. It's better to get dropped off by boat and picked up later instead of trying to walk from Mangrove Bight. This is a great beach for camping, but there's no fresh water anywhere nearby so be sure to bring enough.

Southwest of Dina Beach is Bayman Bay Resort, separated by more rock headlands. Farther southwest still, near the mouth of the canal, is **Soldado Beach,** the reputed site of Columbus' landing in 1502. Nearby is a half-built monument marking the event—Spain donated money for a small museum, but somehow the money didn't go as far as expected.

Even larger unoccupied beaches are to be found on **West End Bay,** west past the canal on the north side of the island. So far the only facility in West End is the **West Peak Inn,** a small restaurant and lodgings charging US$75 a night with three meals included. Sea kayaks and snorkel gear are available, and a nearby trail ascends to the top of West Peak (94 meters) for views across Guanaja and over to Barbareta and Roatán. The hotel offers weeklong sea kayaks trips around the island, everything included, for US$1,095. Reservations and more information are available in the U.S. at tel. (408) 377-2714, email: wpi@vena.com

THE OTHER BAY ISLANDS

CAYOS COCHINOS (HOG ISLANDS)

The Hog Islands, called the Masaqueras by the early colonists, consist of two main islands and 13 small cays surrounded by pristine reef, 19 kilometers off the Honduran coast. The two larger islands are covered with thick tropical forest and ringed by excellent white-sand beaches. All in all, the Cayos are one of the most spectacular collections of islands, beach, and reef in the western Caribbean, yet they are infrequently visited by most tourists, who instead fly or boat right past on their way to Roatán and Utila.

The Cayos were declared a marine reserve in 1994. All marine and terrestrial flora and fauna within a 460-square-km area is protected from fishing, development, or any other harmful activity. From any point of land in the islands, the reserve extends eight kilometers in all directions. The cays were formerly managed by the Smith-sonian Tropical Research Institute, which had an office on Cayo Pequeño. At last report the institute had left the island, for unknown reasons, but the marine reserve continues.

The islands are all privately owned, except for Chachahuate, which holds a small community of a couple of dozen Garífuna families who survive by fishing.

Practicalities

The only "official" accommodations in the Cayos are at **Plantation Beach Resort,** Apto. Postal 114, La Ceiba, Atlántida, Honduras, tel. 442-0974, in the U.S. c/o A-1 Scuba and Travel, tel. (800) 628-3723, email: pbr@hondurashn.com, website: www.plantationbeachresort.com. The resort was included in the original management plan for the reserve. The hotel's mahogany and stone cottages with decks and hammocks are tucked into a small valley on the site of a former pineapple plantation on Cayo Grande. One week

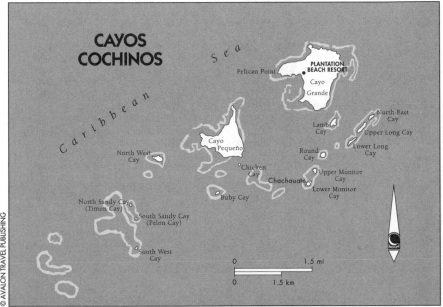

with meals and diving costs US$795; two PADI instructors provide certification courses. Traveler's checks and cash are accepted; credit cards and personal checks are not. Those looking for some hiking to complement their diving will find numerous trails over the 140-meter peak or around the shore to the north side, where there is a lighthouse and a small village. The resort boat, a twin 300hp 42-footer, comes to La Ceiba every Saturday and charges US$75 for the roundtrip.

Those who wish to appreciate a different side of the Cayos for considerably less money can take a boat from Nuevo Armenia, near Jutiapa on the mainland coast, to the Garífuna village of **Chachahuate,** on Lower Monitor Cay. This is the sort of place, as one visitor commented, where you should go with an open mind and heart. Because of its isolation, Chachahuate is one of the more traditional and friendly Garífuna villages in Honduras, so keep that in mind and try to be a relaxed and amiable guest. A couple of *pulperías* can supply minimal food, but there are no hotels or restaurants, so visitors will have to ask locals to cook food and help find a room to stay in (or at least for permission to sling a hammock). There's great snorkeling all around, but visitors should bring their own gear, as well as fresh drinking water and a few other supplies like fruit or crackers. Boats to the Cayos can be found in Nuevo Armenia for about US$30 roundtrip, or more if you wish to be dropped off and picked up later. Sometimes you can hitch a ride with a fisherman in Nuevo Armenia already going out to the Cayos, but this requires some effort.

A variety of one-day cruises to the Cayos Cochinos, with stops for snorkeling, can be arranged in Roatán and Utila, often for around US$50-70 pp, depending on how many people go, extra to bring scuba gear along. The Caribbean Sands Resort, on the coast west of Nuevo Armenia, tel. 445-0035, can arrange trips, and so can a boatman located through the Lagoon Marina in La Ceiba, tel. 440-0614.

SWAN ISLANDS

Three days by boat from Guanaja or Puerto Lempira are the tiny Swan Islands, the northernmost possession of Honduras in the Caribbean and an extension of the same geological formation that forms the Bay Islands. The Swan Islands lie some 160 km from the Honduran coast. Columbus landed on the islands in 1502, four days before arriving at Guanaja, and named them the Santa Anas in honor of the saint on whose day the islands were discovered. Because the islands are a good source of fresh water, they were frequently used as a way station by Caribbean voyagers over the centuries, and as a result their ownership has long been disputed. As late as 1893 a U.S. captain believed he had discovered them (not realizing he was 391 years too late) and so claimed them for the United States. The U.S. finally ceded ownership of the Swan Islands to Honduras in 1974, but the CIA continued to maintain a radio station there until the early 1990s.

Currently the islands are populated by Jamaican fishermen who have permission from the Honduran government to reside there on a temporary basis. The 14-mile reef surrounding the islands is reportedly in superb condition, and several Spanish galleons supposedly lurk in the waters below.

The Swan Islands—two small cays and many smaller islets—can be reached by private boat, helicopter, or plane (there is a small landing strip), or with one of the supply boats from Jamaica that bring in provisions for the fishermen.

COPÁN AND WESTERN HONDURAS

Along with the Bay Islands, the famed ruins of Copán are one of Honduras' top tourist attractions. But invariably travelers continue right on to the Caribbean coast from Copán without taking the time to explore other areas of the country's western highlands. It's their loss—this is one of the most naturally beautiful and least-explored areas in all of Central America. Here the adventurous can lose themselves for weeks, traveling the mountain roads and footpaths between isolated colonial villages like Erandique, La Campa, and Belén Gualcho, or climbing to the unsurpassed cloud forests of Montaña de Celaque, Honduras' highest peak.

Outside of Copán Ruinas, the colonial town of Gracias, and the region's unofficial capital of Santa Rosa de Copán, few tourist services exist in the western highlands. Yet the lack of creature comforts is more than compensated for by the thrill of visiting lovely villages seemingly lost in the mists of history, where locals may not know quite what to think of a passing foreigner but will invariably invite him or her in for a cup of strong black coffee and a chat.

Western Honduras is one area where the country's indigenous highland culture remains. This is Lenca territory, the land of Lempira, a famed Indian chief who battled the conquistadors to a standstill before being tricked and killed, and for whom the national currency is named. In the hills around Copán near the Guatemalan border are villages of Chortí Maya, a people related to their highland cousins to the northwest.

THE LAND

Western Honduras is an extremely mountainous region with little flat land apart from small, intermontane valleys. The mountain ranges, which include the Celaque, Opalaca, de las Neblinas, and Merendón, are the highest in the country, topping out at 2,849 meters at Cerro de las Minas on Montaña de Celaque. Unlike nearby El Salvador and Guatemala, the mountains of western Honduras are not volcanic but are formed of metamorphic rock overlain mostly with limestone. Soils in the region are generally thin and unproductive, apart from some of the intermontane valleys, which are covered with fertile topsoil.

The two major valleys in western Honduras are the Valle de Copán, along the Río Copán, and the Valle de Sensetí between Nueva Ocotepeque and Santa Rosa de Copán. Much of the re-

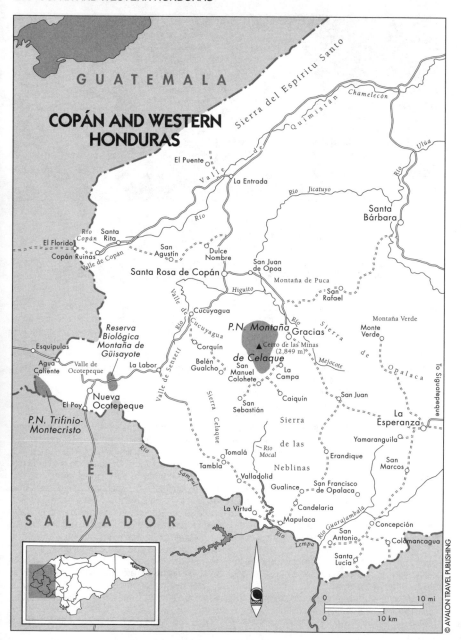

COPÁN AND WESTERN HONDURAS

GUATEMALA

Sierra del Espíritu Santo

Chamelecón

Quimistán

Sierra de

Río Ulúa

El Puente

Valle de

La Entrada

Río Jicatuyo

Río

Santa Bárbara

El Florido

Río Copán

Santa Rita

Copán Ruinas

Valle de Copán

San Agustín

Dulce Nombre

San Juan de Opoa

Santa Rosa de Copán

Montaña de Puca

San Rafael

Higuito

Cucuyagua

Montaña Verde

Reserva Biológica Montaña de Güisayote

Valle de Cucuyagua

Río

P.N. Montaña de Celaque

Gracias

Sierra

Monte Verde

Cerro de las Minas (2,849 m)

de

Esquipulas

Corquín

Opalaca

Agua Caliente

Valle de Ocotepeque

La Labor

Belén Gualcho

San Manuel Colohete

La Campa

Mejocote

To Siguatepeque

Nueva Ocotepeque

El Poy

Valle de Senseti

Caiquín

San Juan

La Esperanza

P.N. Trifinio-Montecristo

San Sebastián

Sierra

Yamaranguila

EL

Sierra Celaque

Río

de las

Erandique

San Marcos

Tomalá

Río Mocal

Neblinas

Tambla

Valladolid

Gualince

San Francisco de Opalaca

SALVADOR

Río Sampul

La Virtud

Candelaria

Mapulaca

Concepción

Río Guarajambala

San Antonio

Colomancagua

Río Lempa

Santa Lucía

0   10 mi

0   10 km

© AVALON TRAVEL PUBLISHING

COPÁN AND WESTERN
HONDURAS HIGHLIGHTS

• Admiring the Mayan ruins at Copán

• Visiting the colonial town of Gracias and hiking in the nearby cloud forest of Parque Nacional Celaque

• Touring the highland colonial villages of Belén Gualcho, La Campa, San Manuel Colohete, or Erandique

gion is still covered with *ocote* pine forest, mixed in with oak and liquidambar (sweet gum) at higher elevations, although deforestation is a serious problem in many areas as *campesinos* cut wood for fuel or to clear more farm or grazing land.

At elevations above 2,000 meters, dense cloud forest covers mountain peaks. Here, too, deforestation has taken a serious toll on the cloud forests. A classic example can be seen at Güisayote, near Nueva Ocotepeque, where a narrow strip of cloud forest covers the ridgeline but is surrounded by denuded slopes. But plenty of mountaintops in western Honduras still retain their original forest cover, spared by their isolation and the relatively low population of the region.

The rainy season in western Honduras is normally May through September, but wet weather can hit at any time in the mountains. If you're planning on camping, come prepared to get wet. Generally the area receives between 75 and 200 cm of precipitation a year, more in the mountains and less in the valleys. During the rains, the temperature ranges from cool to downright cold, while during the dry season it's normally quite comfortable—warm in the daytime and pleasantly cool at night.

HISTORY

Pre-Columbian Era

By all accounts western Honduras was densely populated by different indigenous groups, but archaeologists disagree on exactly which ones. Evidence from the Spanish suggests the Indians currently known as Lenca were at least a half-dozen distinct tribes during colonial times, including the Potón, Guaquí, Cares, Chatos, Dules, Paracas, and Yaras, who lived in an area stretching from Olancho to El Salvador.

At the time of conquest the Lenca were a relatively small group centered around the mountains near present-day Erandique. They had established villages but were essentially hunters and engaged in little agriculture. Loyalties existed only among those who spoke the same language, and tribes were constantly at war with their immediate neighbors.

Farther west, toward the Guatemalan border in the Copán and Chamelecón Valleys and in the department of Ocotepeque, the Chortí Maya dominated. The Chortí were the immediate descendants of the Classic Maya who had built Copán several centuries earlier. Although they were a relatively sedentary agricultural society, their political organization did not extend much beyond a group of neighboring villages at the time of the Spanish conquest.

Nahuatl-based place names, which have survived to the present day, suggest Mexican traders or immigrants also lived in western Honduras, though their numbers were not large.

Conquest and Colonization

Spanish conquistadors began their takeover of present-day Honduras in 1524, 22 years after Columbus first landed near Trujillo. The first forays into western Honduras came from Guatemala, when an expedition led by Juan Pérez Dardón took control of the Río Copán region under orders from Pedro de Alvarado.

By 1530 other expeditions from both the Honduran coast and from Guatemala converged on the mountainous region around Celaque. Alvarado sent Captain Juan de Chávez to establish a town, but he was forced to return to Guatemala when he found himself facing thousands of hostile Lenca warriors led by Lempira.

In addition to Chávez's report, other stories of fierce Indian resistance driven by Lenca leaders Tapica and Etempica along with Chortí Maya leaders Mota and Copán Galel flooded into Alvarado's office, convincing the notoriously cruel conquistador to personally lead an expedition into the region. In 1536 Alvarado cut a bloody swath through western Honduras, massacring Indians and burning houses in Laepera and Opoa.

Alvarado's actions only further enraged the Lenca, Maya, and other tribes, and his apparent

The best estimate of the date of origin of San Manuel Colohete's primitively elegant Iglesia de San Manuel places construction at the end of the 17th century.

victory over the region proved ephemeral. The town of Gracias a Dios was founded in late 1536 as a Spanish base, but early the following year the entire province was in open revolt, led by Lempira from his fortress at Peñol de Cerquin. Not until 1539, after two years of fierce warfare, was the revolt extinguished and Spanish control over the region consolidated.

Part of the Higueras province, western Honduras was extremely poor throughout the colonial period. The small mines of gold and silver found near Gracias a Dios were quickly spent, and treasure-seeking conquistadors headed for richer prospects in Peru and Mexico. After a few short years as the administrative center of Central America in the 1540s, western Honduras faded into a badly governed and sparsely populated region, surviving on the meager income from cattle production and the tobacco industry.

Independence to Present

Located between El Salvador, Guatemala, and the two main cities of Comayagua and Tegucigalpa, western Honduras was a major cross-roads during the wars of independence and the ensuing struggles between the Central American republics in the 19th century. Although many battles were fought in the region, there were no major prizes to be captured apart from Santa Rosa de Copán, which was at the time a major center for tobacco production.

Since the mid-19th century, western Honduras has steadily declined in importance to the national economy. The mining boom around Tegucigalpa and the burgeoning banana industry on the north coast at the turn of the century only drew workers eager to escape the region's poverty away from western Honduras.

To this day western Honduras is one of the poorest parts of the country, inhabited mainly by peasants, many of whom survive by subsistence farming supplemented by meager corn or coffee production. The booming *maquila* factories around San Pedro Sula draw a steady stream of job seekers from western Honduras. Much of the U.S. Peace Corps' work in Honduras has focused on encouraging nontraditional agricultural products and soil-conservation measures in the region.

COPÁN RUINAS TOWN

For many visitors, Copán Ruinas is the first Honduran town they see after crossing over from Guatemala, and it's hard not to be charmed by the relaxed friendliness of the place. In contrast to many Guatemalan mountain towns, Copán Ruinas evinces an overwhelming sense of safeness and a lack of resentful, tense vibes between locals and foreign visitors. Any afternoon and evening in the square, one can watch schoolchildren playing, elders leisurely passing the time of day, and a young man plucking a tune on his guitar under the admiring gaze of his girl.

A physically beautiful town with cobblestone streets, Copán Ruinas has an attractive locale amidst the green hills of the Río Copán Valley. The formerly low-key, shady little *parque* was at last report getting an ambitious facelift, involving large quantities of concrete. Hopefully it comes out well.

Copán Ruinas was originally a small village, an outlying settlement of the larger Santa Rita, before archaeology and tourism improved its fortunes and made it the largest town in the Copán Valley. Much of the agricultural land in the Copán Valley is dedicated to tobacco, as it has been since colonial times. For many years Copán tobacco was famed through the Americas and well known in Europe. In the 1960s other strains were introduced to the valley, and pests brought in by the foreign varieties quickly wiped out the Copán plant. Much of the tobacco is now used to make the national cigarettes, and some goes to the Flor de Copán cigar factory in Santa Rosa de Copán.

The biggest event of the year in Copán Ruinas is the annual festival in honor of the town's patron saint, San José. The festival takes place on 19 March.

SIGHTS

Although nothing on the level of the new Sculpture Museum at the ruins, the small **Museo Regional de Arqueología** on the square, tel. 651-4437, is worth a visit to admire its extensive collection of statuettes, jade sculptures, and the complete tomb of a shaman, laid out in a case just as it was found at the Las Sepulturas site. The museum is open daily 8 a.m.-noon and 1-4 p.m.; US$2 entrance fee.

The old **cuartel,** an old barracks building atop a hill five blocks north of the square, is a fine spot for views over the town and the Río Copán Valley.

ACCOMMODATIONS

Because Copán Ruinas is accustomed to tourists of all incomes from backpackers to luxury travelers, hotels are available in all price and quality ranges. The majority are located right in the center of town.

When arriving in town by bus, expect to be surrounded by a horde of young men who can help find a room for a couple of *lempiras* tip.

Shoestring
Hotel Los Gemelos, tel. 651-4077, is the favored backpacker spot in town, with good reason. This friendly, family-run hotel, down the hill northeast of the square, has a dozen neat plaster-and-tile rooms around a small courtyard for US$5 s or US$7.50 d, with communal bathrooms, a sink for washing clothes, and an attached souvenir shop with Internet access. The owners prefer that guests return to their rooms before 11 p.m. or so.

A few blocks west of the *parque* lies an exceptionally good deal, the **Iguana Azul,** tel. 651-4620, with dormitory beds for US$4.50, or US$7.50 s or US$10 d for a small private room, all in a clean, airy lodge. In the back are the communal showers, with hot water, and an area to wash clothes. The lodge is run by the Honduran-American owners of the Casa del Café, next door.

Budget
Across the street from Los Gemelos, a block below the square, is **Hotel California,** tel. 651-4314, with small bamboo-and-mat rooms with overhead fans and hammocks in front, in a grass

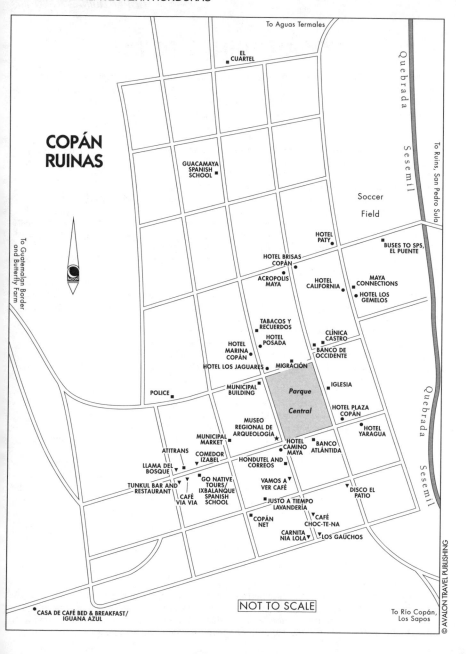

COPÁN
RUINAS

To Aguas Termales

EL CUARTEL

GUACAMAYA
SPANISH
SCHOOL

Quebrada

Sesemil

To Ruins, San Pedro Sula

Soccer

Field

HOTEL
PATY

BUSES TO SPS,
EL PUENTE

HOTEL BRISAS
COPÁN

ACROPOLIS
MAYA

HOTEL
CALIFORNIA

MAYA
CONNECTIONS

HOTEL LOS
GEMELOS

To Guatemalan Border
and Butterfly Farm

TABACOS Y
RECUERDOS

HOTEL
POSADA

CLÍNICA
CASTRO

HOTEL
MARINA
COPÁN

BANCO DE
OCCIDENTE

HOTEL LOS JAGUARES

MIGRACIÓN

POLICE

MUNICIPAL
BUILDING

Parque

Central

IGLESIA

HOTEL PLAZA
COPÁN

Quebrada

MUSEO
REGIONAL DE
ARQUEOLOGÍA

HOTEL
YARAGUA

MUNICIPAL
MARKET

HOTEL
CAMINO
MAYA

BANCO
ATLÁNTIDA

ATITRANS

COMEDOR
IZABEL

HONDUTEL AND
CORREOS

Sesemil

LLAMA DEL
BOSQUE

TUNKUL BAR AND
RESTAURANT

GO NATIVE
TOURS/
IXBALANQUE
SPANISH
SCHOOL

VAMOS A
VER CAFÉ

CAFÉ
VIA VIA

DISCO EL
PATIO

JUSTO A TIEMPO
LAVANDERÍA

COPÁN
NET

CAFÉ
CHOC-TE-NA

CARNITA
NIA LOLA

LOS GAUCHOS

CASA DE CAFÉ BED & BREAKFAST/
IGUANA AZUL

NOT TO SCALE

To Río Copán,
Los Sapos

© AVALON TRAVEL PUBLISHING

courtyard behind the bar, nicely decorated with handicrafts and art for US$7.50 s or US$10 d. The restaurant has pizzas, pastas, and salads. **Hotel Yaragua,** on the southeast corner of the square across from the Plaza Copán, tel. 651-4464, fax 651-4050, has 15 recently remodeled rooms with fans, hot water, and TV around a small leafy courtyard for US$10 s, US$17 d, US$3 pp discount with large groups, if arranged in advance.

Near the highway bridge leaving town toward the ruins is the two-story, motel-style **Hotel Paty,** tel. 651-4021, with a large parking lot and clean, sparse rooms US$11 s or US$13 d with fan and private bath. National newspapers are sold here around 9 or 10 a.m. every day.

Inexpensive

A block north of the square is **Hotel Brisas Copán,** tel. 651-4118, with quiet, clean rooms with hot water, fans, and TV for US$21 d or US$27 t. The owners live in the adjacent building, which is separated from the hotel by a small patio with chairs open to guests. The same family also runs the **Acropolis Maya** across the street, tel. 651-4634, with 10 larger rooms with a/c for US$30 d.

A unique set-up five blocks southwest of downtown is **Casa de Café Bed and Breakfast,** tel. 651-4620, fax 651-4623, email: casadecafe@mayanet.hn, website: www.todomundo.com/casadecafe, run by an American-Honduran couple. Behind their very lovely house are several wood-paneled guestrooms, tastefully decorated and featuring elegant wooden writing desks. From the hammocks on the patio, you'll enjoy unmatched views over the Río Copán Valley below. This secluded place is perfect for relaxing and soaking in the area's vibes. Rooms cost US$30 s or US$38 d with a hearty, home-cooked breakfast.

Moderate

Two similarly priced options on the square are **Hotel Camino Maya,** tel. 651-4578 or 651-4646, fax 651-4517, offering modern, comfortable rooms with TV, telephone, a/c, and fans for US$48 s or US$55 d, with breakfast; and **Plaza Copán,** an imposing new building on the *parque* next to the church, tel. 651-4274, fax 651-4039, email: hcopan@hondutel.hn, with 20 rooms, all

with tile floors, dark wood furniture, a/c, TV, and hot water, a decent value at US$40 s, US$45 d. The hotel also has a restaurant and a small pool.

Expensive

The best hotel in downtown Copán Ruinas is **Hotel Marina Copán,** tel. 651-4070, 651-4071, or 651-4072, fax 651-4477, email: hmarinac@netsys.hn. Rooms in the attractive one-level colonial-style building feature dark wood furniture and paneling, and a few have terraces and peaceful gardens out back—well worth requesting. Among the hotel amenities are a small pool on the main patio, a sauna and gym, a bar, and a recommended restaurant. Hotel service is very good. Prices range from US$75 d to US$105 suite.

Outside of Town

On the far side of the Río Copán from town, on a bluff just about opposite the ruins, is **Hacienda San Carlos,** tel. 651-4106, email: sanlucas@honduras.com, an old hacienda recently renovated and now equipped as a restaurant with a couple of rooms for rent. Prices are US$40 d for the rustic rooms, with hot water and a hearty breakfast included. All the food served is fresh produce right from farm. The old farmhouse is picturesque, and the well-maintained trails in the surrounding hillsides are lovely for walking. A small Mayan sculpture, Los Sapos, is on the hacienda property.

On the highway toward San Pedro Sula, past the village of Santa Rita, is the venerable **Hacienda El Jaral,** tel. 552-4457, tel./fax 552-4891 or 552-5067, founded as a working ranch in 1870. Now run as a stylish hotel by the great-grandson of the original owner, the hacienda is set on a private lagoon with a large heron population. The US$50 d rooms are in lovely rustic and cozy cabins, each with hot water, ceiling fan, TV, and a hammock on a small porch. Activities include horseback riding, hiking, mountain biking, and tubing on the nearby Río Copán. Run by the same owners as the hotel, just down the road, is a small shopping center and cinema.

Commandingly situated on a hillside above the San Pedro Sula highway at Km 164 is **Posada Real de Copán,** tel. 651-4480 through -4497, or in San Pedro tel. 556-8740, fax 556-8748, website: www.mayanet.hn/posadareal. A Best

Western hotel, it's equipped with a sizable patio swimming pool, two bars, a restaurant, and conference room. The 80 rooms each have a/c, cable TV, and purified tap water. Many offer views of the valley and ruins below. Perhaps because of its location outside of town, the hotel is often eerily empty. Rooms cost US$80 s, US$90 d.

FOOD

Inexpensive
Two blocks west of the square is **Comedor Izabel,** a local favorite for well-prepared, low-priced standards including beef and chicken dishes, vegetarian soup, *baleadas,* tacos, and breakfasts. Open daily 7 a.m.-9 p.m.

Next to Hotel Paty at the entrance to town are two similar *comedores,* El Jacal and El Sesteo, both with inexpensive and relatively clean *comida típica.*

Two unnamed eateries right next one another, near Copán Net, serve good and very cheap *pupusas,* a stuffed tortilla snack.

Cafes
Vamos a Ver Café, run by Dutch owners who know what travelers like, has a creative menu with vegetarian options, excellent sandwiches with imported cheese on homemade bread, a large selection of coffees, and pleasant indoor and outdoor dining areas. The restaurant is open daily 7 a.m.-10 p.m.

Another Euro-style café, this one run by Belgians and right next to the Tunkul Bar, is **Café Via Via,** tel. 651-4652, one of several in a chain of travelers' cafes around the world. They serve quite good, reasonably priced breakfasts and light meals, including *chile con carne,* vegetarian *baleadas,* a Greek salad, and Belgian waffles. There are also a couple of rooms for rent in the back with hot water, US$10 s or US$14 d. The restaurant is open Wed.-Mon. 7 a.m.-9 p.m.

Midrange Restaurants and Bars
Something of a Copán Ruinas institution, **Tunkul Bar and Restaurant** is a favorite gathering spot for expatriates and moneyed travelers; it often hosts tourist-oriented social events. Meal prices are reasonable, and the *baleadas* and burritos are notoriously huge. The garlic chicken is a specialty. The patio-bar is two blocks west of the square and has a billboard with tourist information. The kitchen is open daily 1 p.m.-10 p.m., happy hour 8-9 p.m., bar stays open until midnight if people stay.

In a similar style to the Tunkul, but with better food according to its many patrons, is **Carnitas Nia Lola,** with very tasty and filling nachos, *quesadillas,* huge *baleadas,* and of course the namesake *carnitas.* In the evening the grill is cranked up. Open daily 11 a.m.-10 p.m., this place is invariably packed for the 6:30-7:30 p.m. happy hour.

Across the street from the Tunkul is **Llama del Bosque,** tel. 651-4431, a more traditional and frequently recommended restaurant with a large menu and full bar service at slightly upscale prices. Entrees, including rice dishes, salads, shrimp, chicken in orange sauce, or pork chops, cost US$4-6. Open daily 7 a.m.-10 p.m.

An expatriate that couldn't escape Copán has opened **Pizza Rica,** three blocks from the *parque,* open 11 a.m.-11 p.m. daily. The small restaurant serves pizzas with a variety of ingredients for US$4-10, depending on size.

Entertainment
The two most popular bars in town among foreigners are **Tunkul** and **Nia Lola.** They conveniently have consecutive happy hours: Nia Lola 6:30-7:30 p.m. and Tunkul 8-9 p.m.

Several kilometers out of town on the road toward San Pedro Sula, Hacienda El Jaral has **movies** on Saturday and Sunday—look for signs in town with the current shows and times.

INFORMATION AND SERVICES

Services
Banco de Occidente and Banco Atlántida, both on the square, change dollars, *quetzales,* and traveler's checks and advance cash on Visa cards.

The local *migración* office is inside a large building on the north side of the *parque.* The word is that the official is a bit of a pain to deal with, and he was arbitrarily not around for three working days when I last passed. Best to deal with immigration at the border or in San Pedro Sula or Santa Rosa de Copán, which have hassle-free offices.

Correos, open Mon.-Fri. 8 a.m.-noon and 1-5

p.m., Saturday 8 a.m.-noon, is half a block west of the square. Hondutel, fax 651-4007, is just south of the square, near Vamos A Ver Café, open Mon.-Fri. 7 a.m.-9 p.m., weekends 7 a.m.-noon and 2-5 p.m.

Justo a Tiempo Lavandería, a block southwest of the square, will wash your grubby duds for US 60 cents per pound, Mon.-Sat. 7:30 a.m.-noon and 2-5:30 p.m. The American owner also runs a well-stocked paperback book exchange.

The most oft-used spot to check email is **Maya Connections,** tel. 651-4077, next to the popular backpacker digs, Hotel Los Gemelos. The minimum 10 minutes costs US$1, after that US 10 cents a minute. Open daily 8 a.m.-7 p.m.

A second Internet cafe is **Copán Net,** tel. 651-4460, managed by the friendly and computer-savvy Carlos, charging US 10 cents per minute, no minimum, open 9 a.m.-noon and 1-8 p.m. daily.

Emergency

Apart from dealing with crimes, the local **police,** tel. 651-4060, can also arrange ambulance service.

Clínica Castro, tel. 651-4504, is run by a competent doctor who speaks some English. His office, just up from Banco de Occidente, is open Mon.-Sat. 8 a.m.-noon and 2-4:30 p.m.

Shopping

As a major tourist destination, Copán Ruinas has its share of souvenir shops, many with Guatemalan and Salvadoran as well as Honduran crafts, including *junco* palm goods, leather, ceramics, jade and wood sculptures, and the ever-present T-shirts. Shops include Mahchi, Yax Pac, Honduras Es Amor (near the ruins), Sac Nic Te, and Copán Galel, all located within a couple of blocks of the square. Tabacos y Recuerdos opposite the Marina Copán Hotel has a decent selection of Honduran cigars.

Spanish School

For those who become hypnotized by the easy lifestyle of Copán Ruinas and want a reason to extend their stay, **Ixbalanque Spanish School,** tel./fax 651-4432, email: Ixbalan@hn2.com, offers five days of one-on-one classes and a week of housing with a local family for US$175, while five days of classes without lodging costs US$105.

Another school in Copán is **Guacamaya,** three blocks north of the *parque,* tel. 651-4360, email: guacamaya_@latinmail.com. Five days of classes, four hours daily, plus a week's room and board with a local family costs US$175, while five days of classes only costs US$110.

Spanish classes and family stays in Copán are generally very good—the families tend to be more interested in interacting with foreigners than similar set-ups in Guatemala.

GETTING THERE AND AWAY

To La Entrada, San Pedro Sula, and Santa Rosa de Copán

Etumi buses to La Entrada (one hour, US$2), where you can catch another bus to San Pedro (another two hours), leave every hour or so between 4 a.m. and 5 p.m. from the bridge at the north end of town. Both Casasola Express, tel. 651-4078, and Gama, tel. 651-4421, run "direct" buses to San Pedro, US$4, which often stop along the way anyhow. Usually one bus leaves early in the morning and the second in mid-afternoon. Buses straight through to Santa Rosa de Copán (three hours) leave daily at 6 a.m., but you can also take a bus to La Entrada and easily catch a San Pedro-Santa Rosa bus there. Best to double-check all bus departure times as they frequently change.

The 72-km road between Copán Ruinas and La Entrada is paved, but often in bad shape, especially during the rainy season.

To the Guatemalan Border

The Copán Ruinas-El Florido border crossing between Honduras and Guatemala is the crossing most frequently used by Central American travelers. Formerly a long, bouncy ride, the road from Chiquimula, Guatemala, to the border was in the process of being paved at last report. Work was underway on the short and much worse Honduran portion of the road also, though it was not clear if it was being paved or just graded. Either way, the trip is a lot faster than it used to be, just as quick as the other route via Esquipula, Guatemala, to Nueva Ocotepeque and Santa Rosa de Copán.

Buses to El Florido, at the border, leave Copán

Ruinas frequently and charge US 80 cents for the half-hour 12-km trip. Pickup trucks ply the same route and are often easier to find as they drive through town picking up passengers before leaving. The price should be the same, but be sure to ask before getting on as drivers might try to get more out of unsuspecting travelers. The last bus/pickups leave to the border around 3 p.m. and return around 4 p.m.

The border itself is in the middle of a field, with no services except a *pulpería* on the Honduran side and moneychangers offering bad rates. The border officials here are a fairly relaxed bunch, and crossing is not much of a hassle. More cargo traffic may congest El Florido if they pave both sides of the road, but for the time being all trucks go via Nueva Ocotepeque, and El Florido is almost always quiet. The border is supposedly open daily 6 a.m.-6 p.m., but this seems to fluctuate. The best time to arrive is midmorning, well before lunch.

From El Florido, buses continue on to Chiquimula, Guatemala, for US$2. The formerly bone-rattling two-and-a-half-hour ride now takes only about an hour, and it should be even less when they finish paving the road.

Direct Buses to Guatemala
Atitrans, with an office next to Restaurante Llamas del Bosque, tel. 651-4390, charges US$25 for a direct van ride to Guatemala City or Antigua, eliminating the hassles of changing buses and waiting at the border. The bus usually leaves Copán Ruinas three times a week, on Monday, Wednesday, and Saturday, but other trips can be arranged if enough people want to go.

NEAR COPÁN RUINAS

In addition to viewing the renowned Mayan ruins, many hikes and excursions can be made in the hills and valleys around Copán Ruinas. The countryside is very safe for wandering, and local *campesinos* are friendly and helpful to visitors who lose their way. In addition to the suggestions below, one can stroll along the Río Copán in any direction from town and enjoy the rural beauty of the valley. Most of the fields in the area are dedicated to tobacco; those odd-looking buildings all over the place are drying ovens for the leaves.

Eight kilometers northeast of Copán Ruinas on the highway to La Entrada is the lovely cobblestone village of **Santa Rita,** which was originally the main Spanish town in the area. Formerly the village was named Cashapa, which means "sweet tortilla" in Chortí Maya. The last buses back to Copán Ruinas pass at around 5:30 p.m.

About a half-hour walk from Santa Rita upstream along the small *quebrada* (stream) running through town into the Río Copán is **El Rubí,** a set of twin waterfalls pouring through a series of boulders. Another half-hour's walk farther upstream is a second set of falls, supposedly even nicer. After coming down from the hike, stop for a plate of tasty *tajadas* or *enchiladas* at a no-name but very good little eatery next to the gas station. On the far side of the Río Copán from Santa Rita, a rough dirt road winds up over the mountains to the southeast, ending up in **San Agustín,** where rides can be found to Dulce Nombre de Copán and on to Santa Rosa de Copán. The hike can be done in one day and passes along sections of the old Camino Real and near the cloud forest of Monte Quetzal. You can hitch part of the way with passing pickup trucks.

Spelunkers shouldn't miss the **El Boquerón cave,** 20 km northeast of Copán Ruinas on the highway to San Pedro Sula. To get there, follow the highway past Santa Rita up a hill called La Carichosa, then look for a dirt road turning left. Ask for El Boquerón, "The Big Mouth," about an hour's walk from the highway turn. The Río Amarillo runs through the cave, forcing those who want to explore the cave's many formations to go for a swim. Almost two km long, it's filled with stalactites, stalagmites, and bats. Guides to the cave (recommended) can be easily found in Copán Ruinas.

A fine afternoon trip from Copán Ruinas is out to the **aguas termales** (hot springs), 21 km and one hour northwest of town on a rough dirt road leaving town at the corner by Hotel Paty. The springs bubble out of a hillside just above a small river, out in a lovely area of Honduras countryside, dotted with coffee plantations and small farms. The owners of the springs have piped water across the river to a couple of manmade pools of different temperatures. But nicer, all in all, is to go down to the river and look for the spot where the spring water falls down the hillside. Rocks have been placed to catch the hot water and can be rearranged to change the water temperature. Take a short walk up the hillside to see the spot where the sulfur-smelling water pours out of the rock. If you have your own transportation, it's worth coming out in the late afternoon (to enjoy the scenery) and stay at the springs until after dark. If you don't have wheels, hitching out the dirt road for US$1-2 is not difficult, but make sure you head back toward Copán Ruinas by mid-afternoon to ensure a ride. Entrance to the springs is US$1.40 for men or US 75 cents for women. A small stand at the springs sells soft drinks and snacks, but if you want beer or other booze, bring your own.

Just outside of town on the road to El Florido is the new **Butterfly Garden,** set up by a former Peace Corps volunteer and his wife, with some 40 species of tropical butterflies in a screened-in garden. Visitors are given a laminated butterfly identification card with their US$6 entry fee. The deck and flagstone gardens make a relaxing place to hang out and write letters for a couple of hours.

Tours

Go Native Tours, tel. 651-4432, fax 651-4004, runs day trips to nearby hot springs, caves, villages, El Rubí waterfall, and other sites for US$25-45 pp, depending on the length of trip.

Travelers only in briefly from Guatemala might want to consider the multi-day trips to other Honduras destinations, like Punta Sal, Celaque, and La Mosquitia.

Yaragua Tours at Hotel Yaragua, tel. 651-4464, offers similarly priced local tours to a nearby coffee farm, Finca El Cisne, Los Sapos, and elsewhere. Horseback riding trips are also available.

Some 300 different species of vibrantly colorful **birds** live in the many micro-climates and ecosystems in the hills and valleys around Copán, and no one is more qualified to take you out to find them than **Jorge Barraza,** tel. 651-4435. A self-taught birder, Jorge is a genius at spotting feathered friends such as motmot, toucanets, tanangers, orioles, and blue herons along the Río Copán, even the occasional quetzal or trogon in remaining patches of cloud forest on nearby hilltops. Jorge also knows the countryside here like nobody's business and will happily take you stomping off into the mountains in any direction and probably introduce you to a few of his *campesino* friends on the way. Trips can be customized to fit energy level and types of birds you'd like to see, costing US$25-75 pp.

THE RUINS OF COPÁN

HISTORY OF THE MAYAN CITY OF COPÁN

Although not the largest Mayan city—at its height a population of 24,000 lived in the surrounding region, as compared to over 100,000 at Tikal—Copán was, as famed archaeologist Sylvanus Morley put it, "the Athens of the New World." For reasons that remain mysterious, Copán was the principal Mayan cultural center during the 400 years when the city was at the peak of its development, far ahead of other larger and more powerful Mayan cities in its development of sculpture, astronomy, and hieroglyphic writing.

The Early Years
The rich bottomland in the Río Copán Valley attracted farmers of unknown origin as early as 1000 B.C., but archaeological evidence indi-

cates the Maya did not settle the area until about the time of Christ. Construction on the city is thought to have begun around A.D. 100, and the recorded history of the city does not begin until 426, when Copán's royal dynasty began. Some archaeologists believe the dynasty began when outsiders, probably either from the then-dominant Teotihuacán empire in Mexico or allies of theirs, conquered the city and took over administration of the valley.

Detailed information on Copán's earliest rulers is difficult to obtain, in part due to the ancient Mayan tradition of destroying monuments built by past rulers or building over temples erected in their honor. Not until 1989 were references to Copán's first ruler discovered, in a chamber nicknamed the Founder's Room buried deep under the Hieroglyphic Stairway. Apparently built by Copán's second ruler, nicknamed Mat Head for the odd headdress he is always depicted wear-

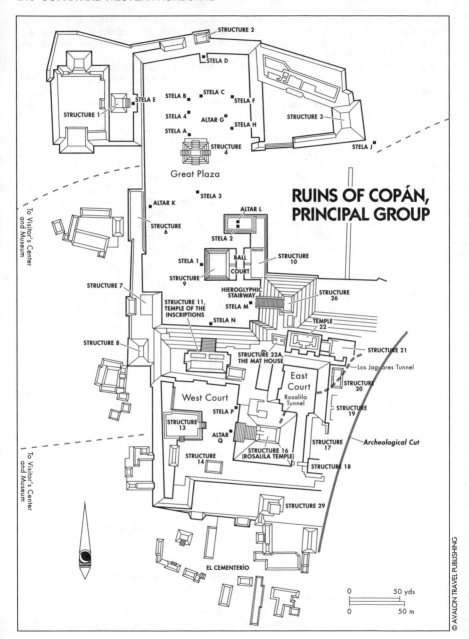

STRUCTURE 2

STELA D

STELA E

STRUCTURE 1

STELA B   STELA C

STELA 4   STELA F

ALTAR G   STELA H

STELA A

STRUCTURE 4

STRUCTURE 3

STELA J

Great Plaza

STELA 3

RUINS OF COPÁN, PRINCIPAL GROUP

ALTAR K

STRUCTURE 6

ALTAR L

STELA 2

To Visitor's Center and Museum

STELA 1   BALL COURT   STRUCTURE 10

STRUCTURE 9

STRUCTURE 7

HIEROGLYPHIC STAIRWAY

STRUCTURE 26

STRUCTURE 11, TEMPLE OF THE INSCRIPTIONS

STELA M

STELA N

TEMPLE 22

STRUCTURE 8

STRUCTURE 22A, THE MAT HOUSE

STRUCTURE 21

Los Jaguares Tunnel

STRUCTURE 20

East Court

West Court

STELA P

Rosalila Tunnel

STRUCTURE 19

STRUCTURE 13

ALTAR Q

STRUCTURE 17

Archeological Cut

To Visitor's Center and Museum

STRUCTURE 14

STRUCTURE 16 (ROSALILA TEMPLE)

STRUCTURE 18

STRUCTURE 29

MOON

EL CEMENTERÍO

0   50 yds

0   50 m

© AVALON TRAVEL PUBLISHING

ing, the room was dedicated in honor of his father, **Yax K'uk'Mo'**. According to a stela found inside, Yax K'uk'Mo', the city's first ruler, took the throne in A.D. 426 and governed until A.D. 435. In an astounding 1993 archeological find, the tomb of Yax K'uk'Mo' was discovered directly underneath the East Court of the Acropolis. Evidence indicates he was not a conquering warrior, but a powerful shaman who was revered by later rulers as semi-divine.

Little solid information is available on the next seven members of the dynasty, apart from a few names and dates. Apparently ruling only a small, provincial settlement at that time, these leaders created few lasting monuments or hieroglyphics telling of their deeds. At this time Copán's dynasty was thought to be consolidating control over its domain, as well as establishing trade links with other Maya cities in Guatemala, non-Maya groups farther south and east in Honduras, and even with civilizations as far off as Teotihuacán in Mexico, as evidenced by *teotihuacano*-style pottery in Copán tombs.

The Height of the Royal Dynasty
The period of greatest architectural construction, considered to be the height of Copán's dynasty, began on 26 May 553, with the accession of **Moon Jaguar** to the throne. Moon Jaguar, Copán's 10th leader, built the Rosalila Temple, which was discovered in 1989 buried under Structure 10L-16. A replica of the temple can now be seen in its full glory in the Copán Museum.

After Moon Jaguar, a series of rulers of unusual longevity governed Copán, providing the stability and continuity necessary for the city to flourish. **Smoke Imix,** the city's 12th ruler, took the throne 8 February 628 and ruled for 68 years, leaving more inscribed monuments and temples than any other ruler. Frequently depicted in full battle regalia and with representations of the jaguar god Tlaloc, Smoke Imix is thought to have been a great warrior. His successor, **18 Rabbit,** was also a prolific builder who gave final form to the Great Plaza and the Ball Court. He also encouraged the development of sculpture, from low-relief to the nearly full-round style of later years. Despite these achievements, 18 Rabbit's reign ended in tragedy; he was captured in battle by the nearby city of Quirigua, formerly a vassal state of Copán, and beheaded on 3 May 738.

The Decline
Possibly because of the devastating blow of 18 Rabbit's death, the 14th ruler, **Smoke Monkey,** erected no stelae in his own honor and built only one temple during his 11-year rule. He apparently conducted the city's affairs in a council with nobles, demonstrating the weakness of the regime. In what archaeologists consider an attempt to regain the dynasty's former glory, Smoke Monkey's successor, **Smoke Shell,** dedicated the impressive Hieroglyphic Stairway, the longest hieroglyphic inscription known in the Americas. The 2,500 glyphs narrate the glorious past of Copán, but the poor construction of the staircase itself reveals that Smoke Shell could not mimic the impressive work of his predecessors.

The final leader in Copán to complete his reign, **Yax Pac** governed the city 58 years and apparently attempted to legitimate his rule through the veneration of the Jaguar Tlaloc warrior-sacrificial cult. Depictions of the cult cover monuments built during his reign. One of the most important monuments left by Yax Pac is the famous Altar Q, a square bench illustrating all 15 prior rulers of the dynasty around its sides, with the first, Yax K'uk'Mo', passing the baton of leadership to Yax Pac. Although he may not have known it when he commissioned it, Yax Pac left on the small stone altar a brief résumé of the city's entire history.

A 17th leader, **U Cit Tok',** assumed the throne on 10 February 822. But for unknown reasons, his rule was never completed. The pathetic, half-completed Altar L, which he ordered built to commemorate his rule, suggests the dynasty ended with a single tragedy or defeat, rather than slowly fading from power.

The debate over the reason for the collapse of the Classic Maya kingdom has raged since serious archaeological work began at the end of the 19th century. The most accepted current explanation for Copán's collapse puts the blame on environmental factors and population growth. By the final decades of the 8th century, the city had grown to cover some of the best alluvial bottomland in the river valley; consequently, farmers were pushed farther up the hillsides, where land was not as productive. Recent investigations indicate that during this time the Río Copán Valley experienced droughts, deforestation, massive soil erosion, and sudden floods

REDISCOVERING COPÁN

... [W]orking our way through the thick woods, we came upon a square stone column, about fourteen feet high and three feet on each side, sculptured in very bold relief, and on all four of the sides, from the base to the top. The front was the figure of a man curiously and richly dressed, and the face, evidently a portrait, solemn, stern, and well fitted to excite terror. The back was of a different design, unlike anything we had ever seen before, and the sides were covered with hieroglyphics. ... The sight of this unexpected monument put at rest at once and forever, in our minds, all uncertainty in regard to the character of American antiquities, and gave us the assurance ... that the people who once occupied the Continent of America were not savages.

—JOHN LLOYD STEPHENS,
INCIDENTS OF TRAVEL IN CENTRAL AMERICA, CHIAPAS, AND YUCATÁN, 1841

L ikely because of its supremely beautiful artwork (unsurpassed by any other Mayan city), Copán has long attracted explorers and archaeologists and occupies a special place in the study of the ancient Maya. As a result of this long and close attention, the history of Copán is one of the best understood in the Mayan world.

The Colonial Years

After the great Mayan city collapsed and was overtaken by jungle in the 9th century, the outside world knew nothing of Copán until 1576, when Don Diego García de Palacio wrote an official report on the ruined city to King Philip II: "They [the ruins] are found on the banks of a beautiful river in an extensive and well-chosen plain, which is temperate in climate, fertile, and abounding in fish and game. Amongst the ruins are mounds which appear to have been made by the hand of man as well as many other remarkable things."

García's portrait of Copán, full of details and obviously the product of first-hand observation, would stand as the most informative for the next three centuries. In 1689 historian Francisco Antonio Fuentes y Guzmán unearthed García's report. Fuentes related the city to an incident that took place in the Chiquimula region in 1530, an Indian revolt led by one "Copán Galel, who had an army of 30,000 warriors" and fought the Spanish from a heavily fortified town surrounded by a moat. Fuentes concluded that this town and the ruins were one and the same, but modern historians and archaeologists reject the idea, placing Copán Galel's fortress farther south, in current-day Ocotepeque. Nevertheless, Copán Galel may have been the source for the ruins' name.

19th-Century Adventurers

Other historians after Fuentes rehashed García's initial description but apparently did not actually go to Copán. The next recorded visit came in April 1834, when the Guatemalan government commissioned Col. Juan Galindo, a naturalized Irishman whose real name was John Gallagher, to investigate the ruins. Galindo spent a couple of months at the site but added little useful information to what García wrote. He did, however, make the valuable observation that Copán bore striking similarities to Palenque, the Mexican ruins he had also visited. Galindo noted that the two sites seemed to be related.

Copán became known to the wider world through the work of John Lloyd Stephens and Frederich Catherwood, two uniquely talented men who visited the ruins in 1839—and then, as the story goes, bought them for US$50 from a *campesino*. An American diplomat, adventurer, and author, Stephens had already published the famous travelogue *Incidents of Travel in Arabia Petrea* before he convinced U.S. president Martin Van Buren to send him on a diplomatic mission to Central America. Stephens was accompanied on the expedition by his friend Catherwood, an English architect and artist.

The pair spent several weeks at the ruins, clearing underbrush, taking measurements, and sketching buildings, sculptures, and hieroglyphics. After many more adventures and explorations in Guatemala and the Yucatán, Stephens and Catherwood returned to the U.S. and published *Incidents of Travel in Central America, Chiapas, and Yucatán*, which was an immediate success and went on to become one of the most widely read books of the time, going through 10 editions in three months. It was just the sort of report needed to awaken a fascination with Mesoamerican civilization. While many educated people in Europe and North America had a vague knowledge that ruined cities existed somewhere in Central America, Stephens's detailed measurements and lively descriptions, accompanied by Catherwood's accurate and elegant drawings, captured the public's imagination.

The First Archaeologists

Largely because of *Incidents of Travel,* British archaeologist Alfred P. Maudsley made his way to Copán in 1881. Although he stayed for only three days, the enigmatic and beautiful Mayan artwork entranced Maudsley. He returned four years later to begin a full-scale project of mapping, drawing, photography, excavation, and reconstruction that would continue off and on until 1902. Maudsley's voluminous work on Copán and several other Mayan sites was compiled in the five-volume *Biología Centrali-Americana,* which was enhanced considerably by the superb drawings of Annie Hunter. Hunter's representations of glyphs are extraordinarily accurate and still used in research today.

Maudsley was followed by a long line of Mayanist scholars, who continued the work of excavation and reconstruction, gradually building a more accurate picture of what Copán originally looked like. Foremost among these scholars were Sylvanus Morley and J. Eric Thompson, who developed what has become known as the "traditional" model of Mayan civilization. Completely enamored with Mayan art and astronomical science, Morley and Thompson contributed more than any others to the prevailing view of the Classic Maya as peace-loving philosophers living in something akin to a New World Athens, minus the warfare. It was under the directorship of these archaeologists, and mostly with funding from the Carnegie Institute of the U.S., that the bulk of the reconstruction work at Copán was completed, allowing both specialists and the general public to appreciate the size and complexity of the Mayan city.

Digging Deeper

Beginning in the mid-1950s, the view of the Classic Maya as a miraculous, almost flawless society, began to break down. As archaeologists investigated smaller pre-Classic sites and the residences of ordinary ancient Maya, a more complex, richer picture of Mayan society began to emerge. New theories hold that Mayan society developed like many other ancient civilizations—amidst warfare, trading, agricultural innovation, and exploitation of the lower classes.

Probably the most stunning breakthrough in understanding the Maya came in 1959 and 1960, when archaeologists Heinrich Berlin and Tatiana Proskouriakoff began deciphering Mayan hieroglyphics—a process that continues to this day. Archaeologists had long presumed that hieroglyphics were a form of writing, but they could do little more than guess at the meanings.

The work of Berlin and Proskouriakoff has been taken up by noted linguists and archaeologists such as Yurii Knorosov, Linda Schele, David Kelley, Floyd Lounsbury, and others, with considerable success. It is now recognized that the glyphs are nothing less than a history of the cities where they are inscribed, recording in stone events such as battles and dynastic successions. Using clues provided by *Relaciones de las Cosas de Yucatán,* written by Bishop Diego de Landa, epigraphers can now translate some glyphs written in the ancient Mayan language.

Because of the abundant stelae and carvings at the site, Copán has been a major focus of the deciphering efforts, and the history of the city is perhaps better understood than that of any other ancient Maya center. According to veteran Copán archaeologist William Fash, "Our archaeological work shows there was no extensive rewriting of history on Copán's stone monuments. I view the inscribed monuments as concise and clear records of Copán's political history."

In 1975, the Peabody Museum of Harvard, which sponsored Maudsley's initial investigations, began a second major project at Copán, with a twofold aim. One group of archaeologists has undertaken more exhaustive investigations of sites overlooked by earlier efforts, including outlying, residential areas such as Las Sepulturas for clues into everyday life among the ancient Maya. The second target was to excavate the many layers of buildings buried underneath the Acropolis, to learn about the city's growth over time. Knowing that when successive Copán rulers erected new buildings, they generally carefully buried the previous structures intact, archaeologists undertook a project of tunneling under the Acropolis and, as it were, back into Copán's history. One of the first results of this fascinating work—which one investigator compared to arthroscopic surgery—was the 1989 discovery of the Rosalila Temple, with

(continued on next page)

REDISCOVERING COPÁN
(continued)

much of its brilliant original paint still visible, by Honduran archaeologist Ricardo Agurcia. The tunnel dug to Rosalila, now open to the public, offers a cramped view of the temple, while a full-scale replica of Rosalila is the centerpiece of the Sculpture Museum. Further tunneling under the East Court led archaeologists to a massive block of stone covered in glyphs, which appeared to be dedicated to the founder of Copán. Then, in 1992, some four meters directly under the East Court, workers clearing debris from an underground temple came upon the entrance to the tomb of a richly bejeweled noblewoman, who had clearly been venerated for many years after her death. And directly underneath her tomb, in 1993 archaeologist Robert Sharer of the University of Pennsylvania and his team opened up what they and many other archaeologists believe is the tomb of Yax K'uk'Mo', the noblewoman's husband and the founder of the Copán dynasty. The tomb was built at a time when the rest of the Acropolis did not exist and appears to form the axis for the construction of the rest of the city. Confirmation of the identity of the bones was provided by a jade pendant found near the skeleton's neck—identical to the one depicted on Yax K'uk'Mo' in the famed Altar Q. Medical tests determined the skeleton had a disfigured right forearm, which interestingly is hidden from view by a shield on Altar Q's portrait of Yax K'uk'Mo'. The University of Pennsylvania team continues work on the Yax K'uk'Mo' tomb, as well as other tombs and buildings under the Acropolis, to thoroughly evaluate the new discoveries, while other teams with Tulane and Harvard Universities continue work in other areas of Copán.

during the rainy season. It's likely Copán simply outgrew its environment.

Although the city center was abandoned, evidence suggests the population in the region did not drop drastically until about 1200, when the region reverted to the small village groups found by the Spanish when they entered the valley in 1524.

THE RUINS

The ruins of Copán are about a kilometer east of Copán Ruinas on the road toward San Pedro Sula, set off the road in a 15-acre wooded archaeological park along the edge of the Río Copán. After buying your US$10 entrance ticket, walk up the path from the visitors' center (where there is a small cafeteria and gift shop) through tall trees to the entrance gate, where a guard will take your ticket. If you'd like to enter the **archeological tunnels,** buy an additional ticket for that for US$12.

Much of the original sculpture work at Copán has been removed from the grounds and replaced by exact duplicates. Although this is a bit disappointing for visitors, it is essential if the city's artistic legacy is not to be lost forever, worn away by the elements and thousands of curious hands. Most of the finest stelae and carvings can now be seen in the Sculpture Museum.

Adjacent to the main ruins in the park is a kilometer-long nature trail with examples of ceiba, strangler fig, and other plants characteristic of the jungle originally covering the Copán Valley. Beware the *chichicaste* thorn shrub, which will give you a nasty sting if you touch it.

The Great Plaza
Past the gate, where colorful macaws hang out eyeing the visitors, the path continues through a forested area, with many uncovered mounds among the trees, before opening out onto the Great Plaza. In this expansive grassy area, which was graded and paved during the heyday of the city, are many of Copán's most famous stelae—free-standing sculptures carved on all four sides with pictures of past rulers, gods, and hieroglyphics. Red paint, traces of which can be seen on **Stela C**, built in 730, is thought to have once covered all the stelae. The paint is a mix of mercury sulfate and resins from certain trees found in the valley. Most of the stelae in the Great Plaza were erected during the reign of Smoke Imix (628-695) and 18 Rabbit (695-738), at the zenith of the city's power and wealth.

All of the stelae are fascinating works of art, but one of particular interest is **Stela H** (730), which appears to depict a woman wearing jewelry and a leopard skin under her dress. She may have been 18 Rabbit's wife.

At the south end of the Great Plaza is the **Ball Court,** probably the best-recognized and most-often-photographed piece of architecture at Copán. It is the third and final ball court erected on the site and was completed in 738. No exact information is available on how the game was played, but it is thought players bounced a hard rubber ball off the slanted walls of the court, keeping it in the air without using their hands. Atop the slanted walls are three intricate macaw heads on each side, as well as small compartments, which the players may have used as dressing rooms.

The Acropolis
South of the Great Plaza is the Acropolis, a massive architectural complex built over the course of the city's history and considered to be the central axis point of Copán, around which the rest of the city was focused. At its highest, the Acropolis is 30 meters above the Great Plaza, and the many large trees still standing atop the huge structure only add to its imposing grandeur. The current Acropolis—perhaps only two-thirds as big as it was during the city's heyday—is formed by at least two million cubic meters of fill. Some of the most fascinating archaeological finds in recent years have come from digging under buildings in the Acropolis and finding earlier temples which were carefully buried and built over.

Rising from the southeast corner of the Plaza up the side of Acropolis, and now unfortunately covered with a roof to protect it from the elements, is the famous **Hieroglyphic Stairway,** the longest hieroglyphic inscription found anywhere in the Americas. The 72 steps contain more than 2,500 glyphs. It was built in 753 by Smoke Shell to recount the history of Copán's previous rulers. Since the city was declining in prestige at that point, the stairway was shoddily made compared to other structures and collapsed at some point before archeologists began working at the ruins. In the 1940s, the stairs were assembled in the current, random order. It is thought that about 15 of the stairs, mainly on the lower section, are in their correct position. A group of archeologists have been using computer analysis of photographs to try to re-create the correct order of the stairway and thus read the long inscription left to us by Smoke Shell 1,250 years ago.

Underneath the Hieroglyphic Stairway a tomb was discovered in 1989. Laden with painted pottery and jade sculptures, it is thought to have held a scribe, possibly one of the sons of Smoke Imix. In 1993, farther down below the stairway, archaeologists found a subtemple they dubbed **Papagayo,** erected by the second ruler of Copán, Mat Head. Deeper still, under Papagayo, a room was unearthed dedicated to the founder of Copán's ruling dynasty, Yax K'uk'Mo', dubbed the **Founder's Room.** Archeologists believe the room was used as a place of reverence for Yax

Completed in 738, the Ball Court is one of the most recognizable highlights of the ruins of Copán.

K'uk'Mo' for over 300 years, possibly frequented by players from the adjacent ball court before or after their *pelota* matches.

A small, not visually arresting building called the **Mat House** occupies a corner of the Acropolis near the top of the Hieroglyphic Stairway. It was erected in 746 by Smoke Monkey, not long after the shocking capture and decapitation of his predecessor, 18 Rabbit. Decorated with carvings of mats all around its walls, the Mat House was evidently some sort of communal government house; the mat has always symbolized a community council in Mayan tradition. Following 18 Rabbit's death, the Copán dynasty weakened so much that Smoke Monkey was forced to govern with a council of lords, who were commemorated on the building according to their neighborhood.

Next to the Mat House is **Temple 22,** a "Sacred Mountain," the site of important rituals and sacrifices in which the ruler participated. South of Temple 22 is the **East Court,** Copán's original plaza. Deep underneath the floor of the plaza, found by archeologists in 1992 and 1993, are the tombs of Copán's founder Yax K'uk'Mo' and his wife, who were both venerated by later generations as semi-divine. The tombs were built at a time when none of the rest of the Acropolis existed and are thought to have formed the axis for the rest of Copán's growth. Studies are still underway on the tomb discoveries, which for the moment remain out of public eye.

On the eastern side of the East Court, the Acropolis drops off in an abrupt cliff down to where the Río Copán ran for a time, before it was diverted to its current course in 1935. Since the river ran alongside the Acropolis, it ate away at the structure, leaving a cross-section termed by Mayanist Sylvanus Morley, "the world's greatest archeological cut." A section of the southern part of the cut collapsed during Hurricane Mitch, and workers were busy shoring the wall up at last report.

Between the East Court and the nearby West Court is **Structure 16,** a temple dedicated to war, death, and the veneration of past rulers. Underneath the temple, in 1989 Honduran archaeologist Ricardo Agurcia found the most complete temple ever uncovered at Copán. It's called **Rosalila** (Rose-lilac) for its original paint, which can still be seen. Rosalila is considered the best-preserved temple anywhere in the Maya zone. The temple was erected by Copán's 10th ruler, Moon Jaguar, in 571. The **tunnel** accessing the front of Rosalila is now open to the public for a US$12 fee, paid at the museum entrance. The tunnel is very short, but the experience of seeing the lit-up facade of the original Rosalila, buried by its builders over 1000 years ago, is incomparable. A full-scale replica of Rosalila is in the Sculpture Museum.

The ticket price of the tunnel allows visitors to go inside a second, longer tunnel, which begins in the East Court and goes underneath Structure 20 to come out on the far northeast corner of the Acropolis. Both tunnels are well lit and have interesting written descriptions in English and Spanish explaining aspects of Copán archeology.

At the base of Structure 16 in the West Court is a square sculpture known as **Altar Q,** possibly the single most fascinating piece of art at Copán, depicting 16 seated men, carved around the four sides of a square stone altar. For many years, following the theory of archaeologist Herbert Joseph Spinden, it was believed the altar illustrated a gathering of Mayan astronomers in the 6th century. However, following breakthroughs in deciphering Mayan hieroglyphics, archeologists now know the altar is a history of the city's rulers. The 16 men are in fact all the rulers of the Copán dynasty, with the first ruler, Yax K'uk'Mo', shown passing the ruling baton— and the symbolic right to rule—on to the last, Yax Pac, who ordered the altar built in 776.

Las Sepulturas

Two km up the highway toward San Pedro Sula from the main ruins is the residential area of Las Sepulturas. Ignored by early archaeologists, Las Sepulturas has in recent years provided valuable information about the day-to-day lives of Copán's ruling elite. The area received its macabre name ("The Tombs") from local *campesinos,* who farmed in the area and in the course of their work uncovered many tombs of nobles who were buried next to their houses, as was the Maya custom.

Although these ruins have been rebuilt extensively, they are still not as visually interesting to the casual tourist as the principal group, and most of the sculpture has been removed. One piece that remains is the **Hieroglyphic Wall** on Structure 82, a group of 16 glyphs cut in 786, relating events from the reign of Yax Pac, Copán's last ruler. On the same structure is a portrait of **Puah Tun,** the patron of scribes, seated with a seashell ink holder in one hand and a writing tool in the other.

In **Plaza A** of Las Sepulturas the tomb of a powerful shaman who lived around 450 was discovered; it can be seen in its entirety in the Museo Regional in Copán Ruinas. In this same area traces of inhabitation dating from 1000 B.C. were found, long pre-dating the Copán dynasty.

Las Sepulturas is connected to the principal group of ruins by an elevated road, called a *sacbé*, which runs through the woods. The road is currently closed, meaning visitors must go around by the highway. Be sure to bring your ticket from the main ruins as you must show it to get in to Las Sepulturas.

Other Sites
In the hills on the far side of the Río Copán just opposite the ruins is the small site of **Los Sapos** (The Frogs). Formerly this rock outcrop carved in the form of a frog must have been quite impressive, but the years have worn down the sculpture considerably. Right near the frog carving, and

even harder to make out, is what looks to be the figure of a large woman with her legs spread, as if giving birth. Because of this second carving, archeologists believe the location was a birthing spot, where Mayan women would come to deliver children. Although the carvings are not dramatic, the hillside setting above the Río Copán Valley, across from the main ruins site, is lovely and makes a good two- to three-hour trip on foot or horseback. To get there, leave town heading south and follow the main road over the Río Copán bridge. On the far side turn left and follow the dirt road along the river's edge. A little farther on, the road forks—follow the right side uphill a couple hundred yards to **Rancho San Carlos.** The ranch owners have built a small network of trails for visitors to wander along and admire the views, thick vegetation, and noisy birdlife. Entrance is U$2. At the ranch is a small restaurant serving excellent traditional Honduran countryside food with products made by hand on the farm, like tasty fresh cheese.

Higher up in the mountains beyond Los Sapos is another site known as **La Pintada,** a single

VISITING THE RUINS: A LITTLE ADVICE

- The ruins are open 8 a.m.-4 p.m. every day. It's highly recommended to get in right when the gates open. In the early morning hours, you'll be able to enjoy the ruins in relative solitude, and you'll have good low-angle light for photographs. This is also the favorite time for a group of white-tailed deer that live in the woods to come out and wander through the ruins.

- When walking around the ruins, refrain from walking on stairways that have been roped off.

- Try not to lean on sculptures, stelae, or buildings—salts from your skin can corrode the stone, especially when multiplied by the 60,000 or so visitors who come to Copán each year.

- It should go without saying, but let it be said: it is illegal to remove any stones from the park.

- Two pamphlet-guides to the ruins are sold at the ticket office: *History Carved in Stone,* by William Fash and Ricardo Agurcia Fasquelle, and *Copán, Legendario y Monumental,* by J. Adan Cueva. The former, written in English, has an excellent interpretation of the growth of the city and advances in archaeology, but does not discuss each mon-

ument individually. The latter, in English and Spanish, is weak on recent advances in archaeology, and although it does give a description of many major sites, they are often incomplete and not entirely useful.

- Guides can be hired at the site for about US$10 for a two-hour tour. Some of these local men have worked at the ruins for many years and have a positively encyclopedic knowledge about the archaeology of Copán—not just the names of buildings, but explanations on how archaeological views changed, when certain discoveries were made and why they were important, and all sorts of other details. In addition to providing information on the ruins themselves, guides often relate interesting local legends and tall tales about the area. Casual tourists may find their brains spinning with the endless stories of temples, rulers, and altars, but if you're really curious to learn more about Copán, you are definitely encouraged to hire a guide.

- Although English-speaking guides are available, their language abilities vary. If your Spanish is nonexistent, check beforehand to make sure you and your guide can communicate well.

glyph-covered stela perched on the top of a mountain peak, still showing vestiges of its original red paint (hence its name). The views out over the Río Copán Valley and into the surrounding mountains are fantastic, particularly in the early morning. By foot or horseback La Pintada is about two to three hours from Copán Ruinas. Take the same road to Los Sapos, but stay left along the river instead of turning up to Rancho San Carlos. The road winds steadily up into the mountains, arriving at a gate. From here it's a 25-minute walk to the hilltop stela. It's best to hire one of the many guides for a negotiable fee in Copán Ruinas to take you there either by foot or on horseback to ensure you don't take a wrong turn.

On the far side of the Río Copán Valley is **Stela 10,** another mountaintop stela, which lines up with La Pintada during the spring and fall equinoxes. Covered with glyphs, some of them badly eroded, the stela stands about two and a half meters high. To get there, drive or walk four and a half kilometers from Copán Ruinas on the road to Guatemala, and look for a broad, well-beaten trail heading uphill to the right, which leads to the stela in a 10-minute hike. This stela can be easily found without a guide. For those without a car, catch a ride to the trail turnoff with one of the frequent pickup trucks to the Guatemalan border.

THE SCULPTURE MUSEUM

As of the summer of 1996, Copán has had a museum befitting the ruins' importance in the world of the ancient Maya. Designed by Honduran architect Angela Stassano, the museum is built into a hillside and illuminated by a massive, open-air skylight. Apart from the full-scale reconstruction of a buried temple, which is the centerpiece of the building, the museum contains some of the finest examples of Mayan sculptures ever found.

The museum's architecture was designed to depict different aspects of Mayan cosmology. Visitors enter through a tunnel, representing the mouth of the underworld in Mayan mythology, as well as the tunnels used by archaeologists in uncovering the buried temples, tombs, and buildings at Copán. The four sides of the building are aligned with the cardinal points of the compass, which were fundamental to the Maya, and also

the "Old Man" of Copán

represent the four sides of a cornfield. The two-story design symbolizes the Mayan concept of a lower underworld and the above-ground reality. The first floor contains sculptures of skulls, bats, and other images of death and violence, while the upper floor displays facades from buildings and many of the original stelae commemorating Copán's leaders.

Dominating the center of the museum is a full-scale replica of the Rosalila Temple found under Structure 16 in 1989; the temple was built in 571. The bright colors may be a bit of a shock at first, but all Mayan buildings were once covered with plaster and brightly painted. It will certainly change your attitude toward the Mayan aesthetic—not one of somber elegance but a more exuberant, technicolor style. With time, exposed to the elements from above, the temple's colors are expected to fade somewhat, replicating the process that must have taken place at the original temple.

A visit to the Sculpture Museum (US$5 entry) is a must to admire the dazzling sculpture of Copán. Apart from displaying the originals of some of the best-known stelae and sculpture in the Mayan world, the museum contains many pieces never before seen by the public. These pieces give a full view of the prodigious abilities of the Mayan craftsmen. The informative signs are in English and Spanish. Take the time to read them all—it's a short course in Mayan history and archaeology.

LA ENTRADA AND THE RUINS OF EL PUENTE

LA ENTRADA

Nothing more than a highway junction with a town built around it, La Entrada is worth stopping at only to transfer buses, or to visit the nearby ruins of El Puente, the second-most-developed Mayan site in Honduras after Copán.

Should it be necessary to spend the night in La Entrada, the three-story **Hotel San Carlos,** right at the highway junction, tel. 661-2228 or 661-2187, charges US$11 s or d with fan and TV, or US$20 s or d with a/c. The hotel also has the best restaurant in town.

While waiting for a bus to Copán (72 km), Santa Rosa de Copán (44 km), or San Pedro Sula (126 km), fill up on *baleadas* and other cheap eats at El Triangulo store and lunch counter, next to the Texaco station. Buses to all these destinations frequently pass, the last usually around 5 or 6 p.m.

EL PUENTE

Located north of the Río Florida Valley on the banks of the Río Chinamito, two km north of the Río Chamelecón junction, the modest Mayan ruins at El Puente were first visited by an archaeologist in 1935, when Danish explorer Jens Yde drew a detailed map of the structures. El Puente then received little attention until 1984, when the Japanese Overseas International Cooperation Agency began work on the site in an effort to create a second archaeological attraction in Honduras. Of over 600 sites identified in the La Venta and Florida valleys, only El Puente has been thoroughly excavated and studied. It is thought to have originally been an independent Mayan city-state at the far southeastern periphery of the Mayan zone, trading both with the Maya of Guatemala and Copán, but also with other Mesoamerican groups farther south and east. By the time of the Classic Maya, 550-800 A.D., El Puente had become a satellite of the opulent, powerful dynasty at Copán.

Because it does not have the name recognition or the incredible artwork of Copán, El Puente does not see even a fraction of the tourists of its more famous neighbor. As a result, it makes for a very pleasant and relaxing side trip on a journey between Copán and the north coast, if you've got a couple of hours to spare.

The 210 known structures at El Puente cover two square km, but only the main group has been restored. Generally oriented east to west, the main group has five well-defined plazas and is dominated by **Structure 1,** an 11-meter pyramid with six platforms, thought to have been a funerary temple.

Other buildings of note include **Structure 10,** a long pyramid on the south side of Structure 1 that holds an ornate burial chamber, and **Structure 3,** a pyramid complex whose south staircase holds an example of an *alfarda,* an inclined plane of decorative stonework. Tunnels allow visitors access into both of these buildings.

At the entrance to the site is a small museum with displays on the site itself and on Mayan culture in general, with descriptions in Spanish only. The ruins entrance ticket, US$5 for foreigners, includes admission to the museum.

From the museum it's about a one-km walk down a shady dirt road to the ruins, which are set amidst grassy fields at the edge of a small river. Although the main buildings don't take long to admire, the location is a pleasant place to relax or have a picnic. A nature trail runs through a small wooded area, and you can also take a dip in the river to cool off.

El Puente is in the municipality of La Jigua, five km from the La Entrada-Copán Ruinas highway on a newly paved road. The turnoff is at La Laguna, where you can catch a ride with a passing pickup truck to the ruins for US 75 cents or so. This road continues past El Puente to a lonesome stretch of the Guatemalan border. Traffic is fairly regular but not always frequent—better in the morning. A return ride can often be found with trucks carrying workers from the site back to La Entrada. A taxi from La Entrada costs US$10-15 roundtrip with a couple of hours at the ruins.

SANTA ROSA DE COPÁN

INTRODUCTION

Situated on a hilltop with a commanding view over the surrounding mountainous countryside—including the country's highest peak, Montaña de Celaque, to the east—Santa Rosa de Copán is a perfect base for exploring the fascinating and beautiful western highlands. Save for a local cigar factory, Santa Rosa doesn't boast any specific tourist sights in itself, but visitors frequently find themselves staying longer than they planned in this overgrown village of 32,400 people. The climate is pleasantly cool, accommodations and food are inexpensive, and the residents are happy to see outsiders enjoying their town, of which they are justifiably proud.

Although technically only the capital of the Copán department, Santa Rosa functions as the unofficial capital for all of the western highlands. Almost all commerce in the region passes through Santa Rosa, and *campesinos* from rural areas often wander the city's streets looking for merchandise or selling produce.

While not as dramatically colonial as other towns like nearby Gracias, Santa Rosa takes pride in its colonial heritage. The central section of the town is a protected area, with restrictions on building and renovations, to preserve the remaining colonial architecture.

Semana Santa, or Easter Week, is quite a spectacle in Santa Rosa, with elaborate parades throughout the week. Locals create beautiful carpets of colored sawdust and flowers on the streets for the processions to walk on. The culminating parade is the Via Crucis on Friday morning, with "Jesus" carrying his cross through town in a solemn procession.

History

Little is known about the area surrounding Santa Rosa de Copán during pre-Columbian times. Ar-

SANTA ROSA DE COPÁN

NOT TO SCALE

© AVALON TRAVEL PUBLISHING

chaeologists generally agree the region was a transition zone between the Lenca tribes, centered farther east and south, and the Chortí Maya, who inhabited the hill country along the Guatemalan border. The remnants of indigenous villages have been discovered at several sites near Santa Rosa, such as El Pinal, Yarushin, and Zorosca, but none within the town limits.

Early in the colonial period the Spaniards established a major settlement nearby at Gracias a Dios, but Santa Rosa itself was not founded until 1705. Juan García de la Candelaria, a captain of the Gracias town militia, applied for and was granted an *encomienda* in the name of Santa Rosa de los Llanos, also known as La Sábana. The site was strategically chosen on a hill above a fertile valley, along the royal road between Guatemala City and Gracias; the town quickly prospered as a transport way station and a cattle-ranching area.

A major boost in the nascent town's fortunes came in 1793, when the Spanish crown chose to move the Royal Tobacco Factory from Gracias to Santa Rosa, as the young town was nearer to the producing regions of the Copán Valley. Santa Rosa grew steadily after this, with migrants coming from Guatemala and directly from Spain to establish their own small farms and businesses. In the late colonial period and well into the 20th century, the tobacco industry based in Santa Rosa was by far the most important economic activity in western Honduras, and as a result the city quickly eclipsed Gracias as the most important urban center in the region.

Santa Rosa, along with Comayagua and Tegucigalpa, was deeply involved in the independence wars and the resulting strife between the different Central American republics. Honduran president José Trinidad Cabañas briefly made Santa Rosa the country's seat of government in 1853, when Honduras was under constant threat from Guatemala. The importance of Santa Rosa was officially ratified in 1869, when the department of Copán was established and Santa Rosa designated as its capital.

Orientation and Getting Around

Santa Rosa's downtown is a compact area of several blocks, but the town extends in all directions. The central market is east of the square, near the Ocotepeque highway, which continues down around the edge of town before looping northwest on its way to San Pedro Sula. The bus station is on the highway down the hill about one km north of downtown. Taxis anywhere in Santa Rosa should cost US 50 cents.

SIGHTS

In addition to the relaxed ambiance, there's one actual attraction in Santa Rosa: the **Flor de Copán cigar factory**, tel. 662-0185, in its new, larger location next to the bus station, a block off the main highway. Boosted by the recent boom in U.S. and European cigar smoking, Flor de Copán now employs 240 workers rolling stogies for export as fast as they can, over 30,000 cigars a day on average.

Free tours of the factory (Spanish only) range 15 minutes to an hour in length, depending on the guide. Afterwards visitors are allowed into the bodega to buy a few cigars. Prices are generally about a third of U.S. prices. The Santa Rosa mark is considered the lightest, while the Don Melo is considerably stronger. Zino is the factory's top-of-the-line brand. The original Flor de Copán factory, between the park and Hotel Elvir on Ave. Centenario, now serves as the company offices.

The simple, whitewashed *catedral* on the square was first built in 1798, then rebuilt in 1880. In the middle of the square is a two-story kiosk built in 1900, which now houses a small snack stand.

A block south of the square is the **Casa de la Cultura,** which sells books and artwork but offers little information on the region.

Several high points near Santa Rosa offer fine views over the town and surrounding countryside on a clear day. One close point is **El Cer-**

rito, reached by following Ave. Centenario west until the cobblestones end, then following the stairs up to the hilltop. Farther off is the **Hondutel tower,** about 45 minutes' walk from town, starting south along 3 Ave. SO.

ACCOMMODATIONS

Almost all hotels in Santa Rosa fall into the budget range, with only two midrange options. Most hotels are within three blocks of the square.

Shoestring
If you feel like braving the cockroaches, you'll find plenty of rooms for rock-bottom prices in Santa Rosa's many *hospedajes,* catering to the *campesinos* who come to town regularly. About the best is **Hospedaje Maya** (no phone), two blocks east of the church next door to the Hotel Copán and run by the same owners. The charge is US$1.75 for a basic cell room with shared bathroom.

An unusual set-up, but one that may appeal to some travelers, is to crash at the **Peace Corps House** (no phone), a couple of blocks northwest of the square. Rented by different volunteers living in many communities around western Honduras, the house serves as a weekend getaway. Visitors are allowed to stay in the bunk beds for US$4 a night, space permitting. Ask around to find the house and knock before entering. If no one's there, you can get the key at the nearby Mini Market Selina. Leave payment in the marked envelopes. The house has a large selection of books for which you can exchange your old paperbacks. The volunteers are excellent sources of information on nearby places worth visiting.

Budget
Of the cheap hotels in town, **Hotel Copán,** two blocks east of the church, tel. 662-0265, is the nicest, with small, clean rooms for US$6 s, US$12 d, more for TV.

Another reasonable inexpensive option is **Hotel Rosario,** tel. 662-0211, half a block north of Hotel Copán, with clean and quiet rooms for US$5 s or US$10 d for private bathroom, or about US$1 less for shared bathroom.

A step up in comfort, though still nothing special, is **Hotel Continental,** located four blocks

northwest of the *parque,* tel. 662-0802, with clean, bare rooms with TV and hot water for US$13 s or US$19 d.

Inexpensive
Unquestionably the best hotel in town is **Hotel Elvir,** tel./fax 662-0103, with spotless, modern rooms equipped with TV, bathroom, and bountiful hot water for US$22 s, US$28 d, or US$34 t, credit cards accepted. The staff is very helpful and the cafeteria serves tasty and reasonably priced food. Room service is available. Max Elvir, a tireless promoter of tourism in the area, runs **Lenca Land Trails** out of the hotel, offering tours of surrounding villages and natural areas, including Celaque, Monte Quetzal, Belén Gualcho, San Manuel Colohete, and any other place you might want to visit. Rates depend on how many people want to go but are generally quite inexpensive, and Max is an excellent and affable guide. For more information, call the hotel or email Max at: lenca@hondutel.hn.

For travelers getting in late or leaving early, **Hotel Grand Mayaland,** across from the bus station on the highway below town, tel. 662-0233, has its own restaurant and modern rooms for US$17 s, US$24 d with TV, telephone, bathroom, and intermittent hot water. The rooms are somewhat overpriced by Honduran standards but are clean and quiet. The hotel parking lot has a night watchman.

FOOD AND ENTERTAINMENT

Inexpensive
One very good, clean little *comedor* is **La Fonda,** with inexpensive breakfasts, *comida corrientes, bolibaleadas,* this last a giant *baleada* served with or without avocado.

Pollito Dorado, a block west of Hotel Elvir, serves basic Honduran standards and good fried chicken in a relaxed, inexpensive restaurant. The egg and bean *baleadas,* in a large, crispy flour tortilla, are an excellent light meal for only US 50 cents. The restaurant serves a decent breakfast also. Open daily until 10 p.m. **On Fu,** a block down from Bancahsa on 1 Av. SO, has unexceptional but large plates of Honduran-Chinese, usually enough to feed two.

Chicky's, a good spot for inexpensive munchies and beer, has relocated to a new building two blocks down from the park. If you're hungry while waiting for the bus, the *comedor* at the terminal serves a hearty vegetable soup with everything in it but the kitchen sink.

Midrange

The American-owned **Pizza Pizza,** on Calle Centenario at 5 Ave. NE, tel. 662-1104, serves up a decent pie as well as grinders, spaghetti, and garlic bread, all at reasonable prices. It's open daily except Wednesday until 9 p.m., sells some books and the *Honduras This Week* English newspaper, and even has Internet access on one computer for US$2 per 15 minutes.

A bit harder to find, but with tasty pizzas made by a friendly Italian couple, is **Bella Italia,** on 3 Calle SE, five blocks east and three blocks south of the *parque,* tel. 662-1953. Pizzas cost US$2-3 for a small, US$5-6 for a medium, or US$7-8 for a large. Open Tues.-Sun. until 9 p.m.

Café y Restaurante Paris, on Calle Centenario a block west of the *parque,* serves chicken, steaks, and surprisingly good (for Santa Rosa) seafood dishes, in a beautiful open-air patio dotted with flowers and plants. Meals are not cheap at US$5-8 per entree, but the quality, service, and ambiance are all top-notch. Open Mon.-Sat. 11 a.m.-10 p.m.

For a good selection of well-cooked Honduran standards for US$2-4 per entree, try **Las Haciendas,** with two locations a couple of blocks away from each other, two blocks from the park. One good low-priced deal is the large sandwiches for US$1.50. Both are open until 10 p.m. and have bar service. In the same neighborhood is the similar **El Rodeo,** with a good *plato típico,* nachos, hamburgers, and inexpensive drinks.

Entertainment

Apart from going to the bars at **El Rodeo** or one of **Las Haciendas** for a few drinks until they close down at 11 p.m., the only nightlife in Santa Rosa is at **Port Royal Disco,** two blocks south of the *parque,* with a packed dance floor on Friday and Saturday nights. When Peace Corps volunteers are in town on break, they are often an entertaining group to party with.

INFORMATION AND SERVICES

Hondutel, open daily 7 a.m.-9 p.m., and Correos are next to each other on the west side of the square. The *migración* office is one block northwest of the square.

Banco de Occidente is the best for exchanging dollars and traveler's checks, while Banco Atlántida has a cash machine for the Plus network and Visa debit cards. Cash advances on a Visa card are available at Banco Atlántida and Bancahsa.

Super Lavandería Florencia, on Calle Centenario between 4 and 5 Calle SO, washes clothes Mon.-Sat. for US 75 cents per kilo, or US$1 per kilo including ironing.

For Internet access, **Pizza Pizza,** four and a half blocks east of the *parque,* has one computer for US$2 per 15 minute; and **Computec,** two blocks south and one block east of the *parque,* also has one computer for a bit less, US$1.50 for 15 minutes. Computec's owner may install more computers soon. Both connections are relatively slow.

An unexpected find out here in Santa Rosa is a good, inexpensive **gym** half a block north of the *parque,* run by the Central American Medical Outreach (CAMO), with free weights, stationary bicycles, stair climbers, and even a sauna for US$1 per hour for visitors. Open Mon.-Fri. 8:30 a.m.-8:30 p.m.

An English-speaking doctor in town is **Dr. Soheil Rajabiian,** half a block north of Hotel Elvir, tel. 662-0956.

A new Spanish school has opened in Santa Rosa, **Santa Rosa de Copán Language School,** tel. 662-1378, email: starosa@mailexcite.com. No reports are yet available on its qual-

---

SANTA ROSA DE COPÁN USEFUL TELEPHONE NUMBERS

Police: 662-0918, 662-0840, or dial 199
Fire Department: 662-0823, or dial 198
Cruz Roja Ambulance: 662-0045, or dial 195
Hospital: 662-0128, 662-0093

ity, though the town would be a lovely and friendly place to spend a few weeks or months studying, and unlike in Antigua, Guatemala, you wouldn't speak a whole lot of English in your free time unless you wanted to.

GETTING THERE AND AWAY

Bus

Unless otherwise noted, all buses depart from the main bus terminal on the San Pedro Sula highway north of town. Departures, times, and prices are as follows:

To **Gracias,** 10 buses daily between 7:15 a.m. and 5:30 p.m., US$1, about 90 minutes.

To **Nueva Ocotepeque** and on to the **Guatemalan border,** six buses daily between 6 a.m. and 4:30 p.m. with Toritos y Copanecos, tel. 662-0156, or Empresa Escobar, tel. 662-0840, US$2-2.25, two to two and a half hours.

To **Copán Ruinas,** normally two buses daily in the late morning and early afternoon, US$2, three hours. Travelers can also take a San Pedro bus, get off at La Entrada, and catch another bus on to Copán Ruinas.

To **San Pedro Sula,** three direct buses daily that take only two and a half hours instead of four (worth planning on) at 8 a.m., 9:30 a.m., 2 p.m., US$3.

To **Tegucigalpa,** four buses daily between 6 a.m. and 10:30 a.m., stopping at the Sultana office on the highway east of the Texaco station, tel. 662-0940 or 662-0151, US$5.50, six hours.

To **Corquín,** six buses daily between 8 a.m. and mid-afternoon, US$1, one hour.

To **Belén Gualcho,** two a day at 10:30 a.m. and 11:30 a.m. US$1.35, three to four hours.

To **San Agustín,** one bus daily at 3 p.m. From here hitchhike or walk over the recently graded **Camino Real** down to Santa Rita near Copán Ruinas, an easy day's walk.

Car

The highways to La Entrada (44 km), San Pedro Sula (170 km), Gracias (47 km), and Nueva Ocotepeque (92 km) are all paved and well-maintained, except at the height of the rainy season.

NEAR SANTA ROSA DE COPÁN

A portion of the old **Camino Real,** now a dirt road, passes near Santa Rosa, beginning in the village of San Agustín, beyond Dulce Nombre de Copán. From here you can walk over the crest of the mountains down to Santa Rita, near Copán Ruinas, in a day. It's also fairly easy to catch a *jalón* on a passing pickup truck along the scenic road, which comes out by Hacienda El Jaral, just north of Santa Rita.

Near the Camino Real, on the south side close to the highest point in the road, is the privately owned **Monte Quetzal,** a 1,900 meter mountain with dense cedar forest and plenty of its avian namesakes flitting amidst the trees. On the top of the mountain is a lush fern forest. An old mine, abandoned in 1965, can be explored up to 200 meters into the hillside. Max Elvir of Lenca Land Trails knows the owner and can arrange trips there for US$25 a day per person for a small group.

Between Santa Rosa and San Juan de Opoa, on the road to Gracias, is **Parque La Montañanita.** Although not much more than a weekend picnic area for Santa Rosa residents, it's a good place to camp out.

Sixteen kilometers from Santa Rosa on the San Pedro highway is a dirt road turnoff to the east leading to **Quezailica,** a small town centered around the beautiful **Santuario del Milagroso Cristo Negro,** built in 1660 and declared a national monument in 1987. In the church is a carved wooden Black Christ, made by an unknown artist who was apparently a student of famed sculptor Quirio Cataño, who made the Black Christ of Esquipulas. A major Chortí Maya community in pre-Columbian times, this area contains many relics of the Chortí Maya, including an odd rock monolith carved in the shape of a face, which was found hidden in the church's atrium and is now sitting outside the church.

NUEVA OCOTEPEQUE AND VICINITY

NUEVA OCOTEPEQUE

A classic dirty border town, Nueva Ocotepeque is at least blessed with a fine setting amid the beautiful mountains at the junction of Honduras, Guatemala, and El Salvador. The town's name derives from the words "ocote," a local pine tree, and "tepec," meaning hill. Most travelers who enter here understandably get on the first bus heading in whatever direction they're going, but the hiking aficionado may want to dawdle for a couple of days to see the nearby **Reserva Biológica Montaña de Güisayote,** on the crest of the mountains rising right behind town, or **Parque Nacional Trifinio-Montecristo,** which forms the border of the three countries. It's also possible, and quite safe according to the locals, to meander up any of the trails winding into the surrounding hills for a short hike.

Practicalities

Of the several low-priced hotels in town, **Hotel Turista** (no phone), on the main street next to the square, is a good value, with clean and spacious rooms for US$2 s, US$3 d, or US$4 s and US$8 d with private bathroom. If its 15 rooms are full, you can try the **Turista #2** (no phone), across the street, same prices and owners. Another cheapie, not as nice but still acceptable for budget travelers, is **Hotel San Antonio** (no phone), a few *lempiras* cheaper than the Turistas.

Two blocks up from the bus station is the remarkably nice **Hotel Maya Chortí,** tel. 653-3377, fax 653-2100, so nice it's positively out of place in Nuevo Ocotepeque. All rooms have hot water, a/c, cable TV, and small refrigerators and go for only US$11 s, US$17 d. The restaurant has very good breakfasts, and the staff even speaks some English. A great value all in all. Parking is available.

A bit more expensive but not any better than the Maya Chortí is **Hotel Sandoval,** tel. 653-3098, fax 653-3408. Rooms with fan only cost US$13 s, US$19 d, with a/c US$17 s or US$22 d. The hotel restaurant, open daily 7 a.m.-9 p.m., has the best food in town.

Other than the Sandoval and Maya Chortí restaurants, eating options are limited to a number of unremarkable *comedores* serving standard *plato típico,* eggs, chicken-and-rice plates, or *baleadas.* Better than most is **Servi-Rápido El Reno,** half a block from the bus station on the main street. **Pollero El Buen Gusto,** around the corner from Hotel Turista, has a good *plato típico* for US$2.

Hondutel is across from the Hotel Sandoval, open daily 7 a.m.-9 p.m., while Correos is near the square. Banco de Occidente exchanges dollars and traveler's checks, but changing Salvadoran *colones* or Guatemalan *quetzales* is best done with moneychangers at the border. The closest bank that will advance cash on a Visa card is in Santa Rosa de Copán.

Getting There And Away

From Nueva Ocotepeque, you can catch any of the Toritos y Copanecos or Empresa Escobar buses coming from the Guatemalan border at Aguas Calientes onward to San Pedro Sula for US$3, or take a midnight bus direct from Nueva Ocotepeque for US$4.

Buses depart every hour or two between Nueva Ocotepeque and Santa Rosa, charging US$1.20 for the two-and-a-half-hour ride.

Aguas Calientes/Guatemalan Border

Regular buses are also available from Nueva Ocotepeque to the Guatemalan border at Aguas Calientes (22 km, US 25 cents). Between the Honduran and Guatemalan border posts is about three km of lonely road—rides are infrequent, so make sure to get to the border by mid-afternoon at the latest. Travelers arriving from Esquipulas, Guatemala, will find frequent transportation to Nueva Ocotepeque until the border closes, at 6 p.m. daily. Moneychangers arrive at 9 a.m.; some offer decent rates while others are happy to rip you off if you don't know the rates. Beware.

At least six buses daily between 5 a.m. and 6 p.m. drive from the border directly to San Pedro Sula in six hours, US$4, with stops at Nueva Ocotepeque and Santa Rosa de Copán, with

Toritos y Copanecos or Empresa Escobar. Toritos y Copanecos also runs several buses a day direct to Tegucigalpa, six hours, US$5.

El Poy/Salvadoran Border
Buses run frequently between Nueva Ocotepeque and to El Poy at the Salvadoran border (7 km, US 25 cents) until 5 p.m. It's always best to get to the border early to ensure buses onward. The border itself, not much more than a roadside collection of buildings with a lot of semi rigs lined up waiting to cross, is open daily 6 a.m.-6 p.m.

NEAR NUEVA OCOTEPEQUE

Reserva Biológica Montaña de Güisayote
The Güisayote reserve is what you would call a last-ditch effort to save a patch of disappearing cloud forest. The reserve covers a ridge above Nueva Ocotepeque, and the remaining strip of forest looks for the world like a mohawk haircut, surrounded by denuded hillsides.

It may not be anything like Celaque or some of Honduras' other mountain reserves, but Güisayote has a number of endangered birds and mammals hanging on in the reserve, including quetzals, blue foxes, wild hogs, monkeys, and maybe even a couple of pumas. The views across three countries on a clear day are enough to make it worth a day trip from Nueva Ocotepeque, easily accomplished with or without a private vehicle.

One of the reasons the forest is so decimated is that the Honduran Army built a road along the ridge at the time of the 1969 war with El Salvador in order to patrol the frontier, which gave farmers and ranchers easy access into hills. That same road is now being allowed by environmental authorities to deteriorate into a trail, which can be used by hikers in the reserve.

To get to Güisayote, take any Santa Rosa-bound bus from Nueva Ocotepeque 18 km uphill to El Portillo ("The Pass")—at 2,000 meters, this is the highest point of any paved road in Honduras. El Portillo is a collection of huts at the pass, from which a dirt road turns south up into the hills, following the ridge to a Hondutel tower a few kilometers from the highway, inside the reserve. A half-hour walk past the Hondutel

tower, the road comes to a three-way junction. The left road turns into a path descending the hillside, while the middle and right-hand roads continue into the forest. The middle road continues around the mountain to the villages of Ocotlán and Plan de Rancho, from where one can catch a truck ride back to Nueva Ocotepeque. The right-hand branch leads to Cerro El Sillón ("Big Chair Mountain"), the massive wall behind Nueva Ocotepeque. At 2,310 meters, it's the highest peak in the vicinity.

Those visiting the park by car can drive up the entrance road as far as the junction and from there must walk. It might be best to leave the vehicle at the rancho near the Hondutel tower, and pay a few *lempiras* to have the owners watch over it while you hike.

In the southern section of the reserve is a large mountain lake called Laguna Verde; ask a local *campesino* to guide you there. North of El Portillo, on the other side of the highway, another dirt road follows the ridge through another, smaller patch of forest.

The topographical map covering Güisayote is Nueva Ocotepeque 2359 II. The government office on the north side of the square in Nueva Ocotepeque will give tourists free photocopies of a section of the topographical map with the reserve boundaries marked.

Parque Nacional Trifinio-Montecristo
This national park, jointly administered by Honduras, Guatemala, and El Salvador, comprises a cloud-forested mountain peak forming the boundary between the three countries. The park is accessible from the Honduran side, but only with difficulty. One local forestry officer's advice for accessing it was, "Take a bus into El Salvador, where buses go up to within a few minutes' walk of the peak." Clearly the concept of actually walking up the mountain is not big in Montecristo. If you are interested in hiking it from the Honduran side, go to the village of Santa Fe, and then on to El Mojonal, where trails continue up to the peak. Guides are essential, as trails are nothing more than vague footpaths. From the top, you can see the Pacific on a clear day.

The topographical map covering the Honduran portion of the park is Montecristo 2359 III.

GRACIAS AND THE LENCA HIGHLANDS

One of the undiscovered treasures of Honduras, the mountain country between Gracias, La Esperanza, and the Salvadoran border is a beautiful region of pine forest and infrequently visited colonial villages. Foreign tourists are beginning to make it to the town of Gracias, for a brief time the administrative center for Spain's Central American empire, and to the nearby Montaña de Celaque, the country's highest peak, blanketed with spectacular, lush cloud forest.

But for the more adventurous, willing to brave a few minor hardships and lots of walking, the area offers much more: the dirt roads and trails connecting the highland villages of Belén Gualcho, La Campa, San Manuel Colohete, Erandique, and beyond are lovely places to lose yourself for weeks at a time, admiring the colonial villages seemingly long-forgotten in their secluded corners of the rugged countryside. The Lenca *campesinos* populating the region are extremely friendly, and although they might wonder what you're doing out there, the worst that will happen is you'll be invited in for so many cups of coffee you'll never get anywhere.

For more information about this fascinating though very poor region, contact **Proyecto Lempira Sur,** a development organization with offices in Santa Rosa, tel. 662-0916, fax 662-0039. Travelers can obtain a lotl of useful information on transportation and facilities at this office.

Note: Traveling in this region is not for everyone. Few amenities are available, apart from a couple of decent hotels and restaurants in Gracias. Travel is mainly on foot or by hitching rides on pickup trucks bouncing over bad dirt roads, and food is almost exclusively rice, beans, tortillas, and coffee. But if you're not in a hurry (and you'd better not be), a ride, a meal, and a bed always seem to be found for very little money.

And beyond the practicalities, those who venture out this way should try to keep a certain sensitivity to the realities and customs of the humble *campesinos* who inhabit the countryside. One is expected to stop and greet others met on the trail, at least with a gentle handshake (none of those U.S. finger-breaking grips, please!) and a friendly hello. You are not of course required to stop, have coffee, and talk at every hut you pass, but it's worth accepting the invitation once in a while. You never know—a conversation with a *campesino* family out in the mountains of Honduras, asking them about their lives and telling them about yours, may end up being one of your most memorable travel experiences.

Tours

At least two companies specialize in tours around western Honduras, particularly to the villages near Gracias. **Lenca Land Trails,** at the Hotel Elvir in Santa Rosa de Copán, tel./fax 662-0103, email: lenca@hondutel.hn, offers highly recommended trips to many different destinations in western Honduras, with times and prices depending on where clients would like to go. Both one-day excursions and multi-day trips are available.

In Gracias, a new guide company run by Frenchman Christophe Condon can arrange trips at very reasonable prices to local villages or natural areas, on foot, horseback, or in a four-wheel drive vehicle. Unfortunately for monolingual English-speakers, the tours are in French, Spanish, or German only. For more information, contact Christophe at Hotel Guancascos in Gracias, tel. 656-1219.

GRACIAS

A sleepy colonial town, its days of glory as the colonial capital of Central America over four centuries in the past, Gracias serves as an informal capital for the highland villages in this beautiful region of western Honduras. Formerly just a destination for backpackers, Gracias is these days attracting more tourists of all varieties, drawn by the town's fine colonial architecture; the cloud forest atop Montaña de Celaque, southwest of town; and nearby Lenca villages including La Campa and San Manuel Colohete.

Fossil hunters will be interested to learn that in the vicinity of Gracias are Miocene-era **fossil beds.** Though picked over by major foreign expeditions in the 1940s, plenty of fossils remain to be discovered.

History

Founded in the earliest phase of the conquest of Honduras, Gracias a Dios was relocated twice before being established at its current location on 14 January 1539 by Bishop Cristóbal de Pedraza and Juan de Montejo under orders of Francisco de Montejo, then ruler of Honduras. In those early years, the would-be colonists were engaged in a fierce struggle against the Lenca leader Lempira, and the settlement was apparently moved for strategic reasons. The second location reportedly served as the main Spanish base for quelling the revolt, after which the town was moved farther south to its present location.

According to legend, the town received its name because one of the conquistadors had a heck of a time finding any land flat enough for a town in the mountainous region. When a suitable spot was located, the Spaniards reportedly gave the heartfelt cry, "Thank God we've finally found flat land!" Hence, Gracias a Dios.

With the establishment of the **Audiencia de los Confines** in Gracias on 16 May 1544, the town became the administrative center of Central America. The *Audiencia* was a royal court of sorts with power to impart civil and criminal justice, and a jurisdiction ranging from the Yucatán to Panama. Some of the larger towns in Guatemala and El Salvador quickly became jealous of the prestige accorded Gracias and forced the *Audiencia* to move to Antigua, Guatemala, in late 1548.

Following the removal of the *Audiencia,* Gracias fell into a long, slow slide that has continued to the present day. When the little gold and silver in the area was quickly worked within a couple of decades after the conquest, local colonists had little to fall back on beyond cattle ranching and tobacco production. Gracias remained an important administrative center for Honduras

throughout the colonial period, but by the early 19th century nearby Santa Rosa de Copán had taken over the tobacco industry and not long after also became the de facto regional capital.

Currently Gracias survives on providing services for surrounding villages, cattle ranching, and the nascent tourist industry.

Sights

Of the four churches in Gracias, **La Merced,** a block north of the *parque* (square) is by far the most attractive. Its ornate sculpted facade was built between 1610 and 1654. The main church on the *parque,* **La Iglesia de San Marcos,** was built in the late 19th century. Next door, being used as the *casa cural,* (priests' house) is the building that once housed the *Audiencia de los Confines.*

To Santa Rosa de Copán

TEXACO

HOSPITAL

GRACIAS

CONDEFOR OFFICE

Río Arcagual

HOTEL ERICK
EL HOGAR
IGLESIA LA MERCED

BUS TERMINAL
POSADA DE DON JUAN
BANCO DE OCCIDENTE
MIGRACIÓN

HOTEL FERNANDO
MARKET
Parque Central
POLICE

HELADOS TATIYANA
LA GALERA
HONDUTEL/CORREOS
LA IGLESIA DE SAN MARCOS

EL CASTILLO DE SAN CRISTÓBAL
GUANCASCOS
HOTEL PATRICIA
CASA CURAL, FORMERLY AUDIENCIA DE LOS CONFINES

GALEANO HOUSE
LA IGLESIA DE SAN SEBASTIÁN
RESTAURANTE AND DISCO IRIS

NOT TO SCALE

To Parque Nacional Montaña de Celaque

To La Campa, San Manuel Colohete

To Aguas Termales, Erandique, La Esperanza

In the center of a shady square a few blocks southwest of the main square is **La Iglesia de San Sebastián**, known locally as La Ermita. On the west side of La Ermita is the **Galeano House** (Casa Galeano), residence of a prominent long-time Gracias family. The elderly Señor Galeano is extremely knowledgeable on local history and is usually happy to speak to a polite visitor who speaks Spanish. Don't be put off by his throat speaker, just listen closely. His son Eduardo "Mito" Galeano is a respected Honduran painter who will sometimes show visitors samples of his work. His workshop is right next to the house, and the doors are usually open during the day. One mural in the workshop, depicting the history of Gracias, is particularly interesting. Many of Galeano's paintings take as their subject matter village life in western Honduras.

Near Restaurante Guancascos is the **Casa Museo**, a colonial-era Gracias house now badly in need of renovation but still interesting to see. The Zacapa family, who owns the house, sells handicrafts from the surrounding villages.

Perched on a hill just west of downtown, **El Castillo de San Cristóbal** was built in the mid-19th century to help defend Honduras against the turbulence raging across Central America at the time. In spite of its impressive construction, the fort never saw any action and now doubles as a local lovers' lane. The remains of Honduran and Salvadoran president Juan Lindo (he served 1847-52), who ordered the fort's construction, are entombed inside. In addition to admiring the two cannons, a good reason to visit the fort is to check out the views across Gracias, the surrounding countryside, and Montaña de Celaque looming up to the southwest. The fort's gates are open daily 7 a.m.-noon and 1-5 p.m.

Gracias' fourth church is **La Iglesia de Santa Lucia**, two km down the road toward the Celaque visitors' center.

Accommodations

All hotels in Gracias fall into either the shoe-string or budget categories, though quality varies. About the best digs in town is **Hotel Patricia,** tel. 656-1281, with five spacious rooms with tiled bathrooms, hot water, and cable TV for US$12 s, plus US$10 for each additional person. The hotel has one very comfortable suite for US$40, with five beds and a full kitchen.

Also very nice, and hugely popular with backpackers, is **Guancascos,** tel. 656-1219, with nine rooms tastefully built in a rustic style, with banana trees and other plants around the grounds, renting for US$9 s or US$17 d with hot water, cable TV, fan, and a large window. Three of the rooms have beautiful views. The restaurant is the best in town and the main travelers' meeting point in Gracias.

Yet another good deal is **Hotel Fernando,** tel. 656-1231, with seven quiet double rooms with hot water, fans, and cable TV around a leafy courtyard for US$8.50 s or US$12 d. The friendly owners also run a good little cafeteria.

La Posada de Don Juan, tel. 656-1020, is a bit more expensive and without as much character as the hotels listed above, with rooms starting at US$12 s with hot water and cable TV, but it's acceptable if the others are full.

Travelers looking to save their *lempiras* should head directly to **Hotel Erick,** one block north of the square, tel. 656-1066, with a range of different rooms to suit your pocketbook, from US$2.75 for a simple single with a private bathroom, up to US$8.50 d with TV and hot water. Rooms are all spotless. The owner offers rides up to the Celaque visitors' center for US$10. The attached store is a good place to stock up on food for camping trips to Celaque.

The less expensive *hospedajes* are all pretty grim, but if the Erick is full, you could try **Hotel San Antonio.**

Food and Entertainment

Restaurante Guancascos, three blocks west and one block south of the park, tel. 656-1219, also known as Los Lencas, has cornered the market on travelers, and it's easy to see why. The restaurant, with a fine view over Gracias and the surrounding countryside, is run by a friendly and knowledgeable Dutch woman who offers very good cooking at reasonable prices. A few vegetarian dishes are always available. The food might take a while to arrive, but it's a great place to relax with a couple of beers and talk with other travelers about the many places to see around Gracias. Books, artwork, and some topographical maps are for sale, and camping gear rental and rides up to the Celaque visitors' center are also available (US$8 per carload). Frenchman Christophe Condon has recently started a guide service out of the restaurant, with reasonably priced trips to Celaque and other nearby destinations. The restaurant is open Mon.-Sat. 7 a.m.-10 p.m., Sunday 7 a.m.-8 p.m.

Near the bus station is **Restaurante El Hogar,** a bit on the pricey side for Gracias at US$4-5 per entree, but with well-cooked Honduran standards. Locals rave about the fresh wheat bread made in the restaurant, which often sells out early. Open Mon.-Sat. noon-10 p.m.

A new Mexican-style joint is **La Galera,** a block west of the park, with a big and filling *burrito* for US$1.50, as well as other inexpensive snacks and *licuado* drinks. Open Mon.-Sat. noon-4 p.m. and 6-10 p.m. **Super Burger** on the park has a large and inexpensive burger, though not much else.

Of the many cheap eateries, **Comedor Graciano** is a good choice for its hearty helpings at low prices. The restaurant in the **Hotel Colonial,** just off the park, has decent breakfasts, though its other meals are nothing special. Breakfasts at the restaurant in **Posada de Don Juan,** open daily at 7 a.m., are also good.

Several other *comedores* within a couple of blocks of the square serve *plato típico* and chicken for around US$1.50 a plate. For *pastelitos, baleadas,* and other snacks, try **Helados Tatiyana,** two blocks north of the square.

Information and Services

Hondutel and Correos are a block south of the square. The town's telephone lines seem to go on the blink with regularity, so don't plan on having to call anyone.

Banco de Occidente, a block west of the square, is currently the only place to change dollars and traveler's checks. The *migración* office is just north of the square, near the police station.

Some information and a useful photocopy of a topographic map of Celaque, with the trail marked, are available at the Cohdefor forestry office, near the entrance to town from Santa Rosa de Copán. More information can be found at Restaurante Guancascos, or with Walter Murcia, a local who is very knowledgeable about Celaque and speaks excellent English.

Getting There and Away

Buses to Santa Rosa de Copán leave from near the market roughly every hour or so until 4 p.m.,

90 minutes, US$1.25. Not far up the highway toward Santa Rosa is a dirt-road turnoff north up the mountains to San Rafael, reached by hitchhiking only. From here you can catch a once-daily bus onward to Santa Bárbara through a little-seen and very beautiful region of central-western Honduras. Apparently one bus a day now goes to San Rafael, leaving from the turnoff on the Gracias-Santa Rosa highway at noon. It might be quicker and more comfortable to catch a *jalón.*

Looking at a map it may appear the quickest route from Santa Rosa de Copán to Tegucigalpa is via Gracias, but the 80-km dirt road from Gracias via San Juan to La Esperanza can take as long as four hours, depending on its condition. The road is sometimes impassable during heavy rains. Nonetheless the pine-forested countryside is exceptionally beautiful, and for those not in a hurry this is a great trip. One *busito* (minibus) leaves Gracias daily from the terminal at 6 a.m. for the four-hour drive to La Esperanza, US$2, but hitchhiking might be preferable. Another *busito* leaves at 11 a.m. for San Juan, where it turns off south to Erandique, also four hours and US$2.

A bus leaves Gracias daily at noon for the nearby villages of La Campa and San Manuel Colohete, on the southeast side of Montaña de Celaque. Again, hitchhiking is quicker and more comfortable.

Hot Springs

The perfect remedy for those aching limbs after slogging up to the top of Celaque is a visit to the *aguas termales,* about five km east of Gracias on the road to La Esperanza. Three stone pools—one at 40° C, the other two at 37° C—have been built around the springs, which are surrounded by large trees and thick vegetation. One of the pools is long enough to take a few swimming strokes across, a very pleasurable experience in the warm water. A small restaurant at the pools serves up soft drinks, beers, and very tasty snacks and meals, and a barbecue pit is available for rent. Entrance is US$1.50 pp; open daily 8 a.m.-8 p.m., bathing suit required. The pools are often fun to visit at night. To get there without a car, either hitch a ride up the La Esperanza road to the turnoff, or start walking up the road and keep an eye out for a path heading off to the right—a shortcut to the pools. It takes about 90 minutes walking by the road and about 50 minutes by the trail.

PARQUE NACIONAL MONTAÑA DE CELAQUE

One of the premier natural protected areas in Honduras, Celaque boasts the country's highest mountain at 2,849 meters, as well as a magnificent cloud forest on the high plateau. This is the real forest primeval—towering trees covered with vines, ferns, and moss forming a dense canopy completely blocking out the sun, very little undergrowth between the trees, and everything dripping wet even when it's not raining. Celaque means "box of water" in Lenca; eleven major rivers begin on Celaque's flanks, which gives an idea of how wet it is.

The park covers 266 square km, with 159 square km in the core zone above 1,800 meters. Although treacherously steep on its flanks,

Celaque levels off in a plateau at about 2,500 meters, which is where the true cloud forest begins. Up on the plateau you can spend hours or days admiring the astounding flora and quietly keeping an eye out for quetzals, trogons, toucans, hawks, or any of the other 150 bird species identified in the park, as well as for the rarer mountain mammals such as jaguars, armadillos, or tapir. An ever-popular goal for foreign visitors, quetzal sightings are commonplace on Celaque, particularly on the hillside leading up to the highest peak.

An added bonus to this natural wonderland is the well-developed trail leading to the peak, which passes a visitors' center and two encampments on the way. This makes Celaque accessible for the casual backpacker, who is after a good hike but doesn't want to hire a guide or try to navigate by compass and topographical map.

The Visitors' Center
The Celaque visitors' center, staffed by the affable guard Miguel, is a rustic yet cozy set-up

PARQUE NACIONAL MONTAÑA DE CELAQUE AREA

some nine km from Gracias at the base of the mountain. Several bunks are available for US$1 a night, in addition to the US$2 park entrance fee. Miguel's mother, a wonderful elderly lady, will cook meals upon request, and she will also on occasion whip up a few *empanadas* or sweet *tamales* for hikers to take with them on the trail. Miguel will act as a guide for US$15 a day, though it's not necessary for hiking up the trail to

the peak since it's well marked. The visitors' center, at the edge of the forest next to the Río Arcágual, is a very peaceful spot to relax, and plenty of easy day hiking is possible nearby, along the river. Bring a sleeping bag and candles or a flashlight. The kitchen has some utensils and is available for visitors to use.

To get to the visitors' center from Gracias, either arrange a ride at Guancascos or at Hotel Erick for

CELAQUE SUMMIT THE HARD WAY

For some people, the idea of getting to a cloud forest in Honduras simply by hiking up a well-marked trail is altogether too easy. Never fear—there are more adventurous routes to the peak. Before venturing off into the woods, however, beware: The terrain on Celaque is extremely rugged, confusing, and often blanketed with fog. Even locals who live within the boundaries of the park have been known to get lost. In 1996, one El Cedro resident wandered around the plateau for three days, hungry and half-frozen, before he eventually struck the Gracias trail and was helped out by a passing group of foreign hikers.

Apart from the clear trail up the Gracias side (which locals call "the gringo trail," *el sendero gringo*), the most common route begins in **Belén Gualcho,** reached via bus or truck from Santa Rosa de Copán. From Belén Gualcho, it's a several-hour hike up to the lovely village of Chimis Montaña, set on a hilltop at about 2,000 meters on the west side of the plateau. From Chimis, it would take another two to four hours to hike up to the Celaque plateau. There, if your guide knows what he's doing, you will meet up with the Gracias trail near the peak. Juan Alberto Martínez and José Alonso de Diós both guide visitors for US$10 a day. Both can sometimes be found in Belén, but more often at their homes in El Paraíso, an *aldea* about 20 minutes' walk from Belén. You could also hike up to the fairly well-beaten path from Belén to Chimis on your own, and find a guide there willing to take you up to the Gracias trail.

Another option is to go by road from Gracias to San Manuel Colohete, and from there hike up five or six hours to the village of **El Cedro,** where Julian Vázquez is one local who definitely knows the route to "El Castillo," as Cerro de las Minas is known. From El Cedro, it's a brutal three- or four-hour hike (at Julian's pace) straight up through thick forest to

the Gracias trail, which you reach shortly before the final ascent to the peak.

Before leading one wayward guidebook author from El Cedro to the peak, Julian's last guiding venture was taking up a group of U.S. Marines, who must have seemed like aliens from outer space when they landed their chopper on the local soccer field. Evidently they were looking for a thrill after all those slow days at the airbase outside Comayagua. According to Julian, they kept up with him a lot better than the woefully out-of-shape travel writer.

A third fairly well-established back route up Celaque starts in **El Naranjo,** an *aldea* about 30 minutes' walk from San Manuel Colohete up the mountain. Guides Hilario Mateo and Fucio Martínez will happily take hikers up to the top of Celaque and down the far side to Gracias, or via El Cedro to Belén Gualcho, for US$10 a day. Currently no lodging is available in El Naranjo, but you could easily pitch a tent or spend the night in San Manuel.

Guides usually charge US$7-10. If you take a trip across the mountain, also expect to cover transportation costs for the guide back to his home. Guides tend to be more expensive from the Gracias side, where they are more accustomed to dealing with tourists. One recommended guide is Candido Melgar, who lives in Villa Verde, near the road to the visitors' center. Although he is reputed to be an excellent guide who can arrange multi-day trips across to Belén Gualcho or elsewhere, his prices have been increasing vertiginously. At last report he was asking US$75 for a two-day trip to Belén from Gracias, though he will likely come down with negotiation.

The villages around Celaque are desperately poor, so any small gifts of food, pens, flashlights, or other useful items (please, not candy!) are greatly appreciated. Although visitors are extremely rare on this side of the mountain, locals are friendly and hospitable.

US$10 to the last gate blocking vehicles from entering the park, from which point the visitors' center is another half-hour's walk. Or you can start walking from Gracias and hope a pickup truck comes by. It's about a two-and-a-half-hour walk from Gracias to the center by the road, or a bit less by a trail leaving the road just outside Gracias, which follows along a stone wall and rejoins the dirt road to the visitors' center at Villa Verde.

On the Trail
The trail up Celaque follows the Río Arcágual upstream from the visitors' center for a short while, ascends a steep hillside, then parallels the mountain. It continues upward at a less steep grade to **Campamento Don Tomás** at 2,050 meters, about a three-hour walk from the visitors' center, where you'll find a tin shack with three rudimentary bunks inside and an outhouse. The shack is sometimes locked, so it's best to check with Miguel beforehand. You might prefer to pitch a tent rather than use the cabin, though it can be relief to have a roof overhead if it's raining.

Beyond the first camp, the trail heads straight up a steep hillside. This is the hardest stretch of trail by far, and climbing it often entails clinging to roots and tree trunks to pull yourself up the invariably muddy path. Descending this stretch of trail is particularly treacherous. After two to three hours of difficult hiking, the trail reaches **Campamento Naranjo,** nothing more than a couple of flat tent sites and a fire pit on the plateau's edge, at 2,560 meters. As you wipe the sweat and mud off your face as you climb, take a look around at the plants and trees. By the time the trail reaches the plateau, you will have entered the cloud forest.

From Campamento Naranjo it's another two hours or so to the peak, but it goes up and down over gentle hills instead of straight up. Keep a close eye out for the plastic tags tied to tree branches—the lack of undergrowth in the tall, spacious forest makes it easy to lose track of the trail. The final ascent to the top of **Cerro de las Minas** is a half-hour of fairly steep uphill climbing, but go slow and listen for the quetzals and trogons that live there. The peak is marked by a wooden cross, and if the clouds haven't moved in you'll have superb views over the valleys to the east. From the visitors' center to the peak is six km and about 1,500 meters in elevation gain. A trail branches off between the visitors' center and the first camp to a lookout point admiring a **waterfall,** which pours down the flanks of the mountain.

You could, theoretically, hike all the way from the visitors' center to the peak and back in a day, but it would be a brutal day and would leave no time for enjoying the cloud forest. A better plan for a short trip would be to spend the night in the shack at Campamento Don Tomás (bring sleeping bags), hike up to the plateau in the early morning, and either come back down to the camp or make it all the way out to the visitors' center that night. If you only want to go on a day hike, it is feasible to hike all the way up to Campamento Naranjo to see the cloud forest, then return to the visitors' center by the same afternoon, if you leave early enough. Be sure to leave the plateau not long after midday to ensure you get back to the visitors' center before dark. If you leave the trail, take good care to keep your bearings, as it's very easy to get lost on the plateau.

If you want to spend a bit more time in the cloud forest, the best option is to bring a tent and sleep a couple of nights at the upper camp, Campamento Naranjo. Whatever your plans for Celaque, remember it's often cold and always wet, so come prepared with proper clothing, including stiff boots, waterproof jacket, and a warm change of clothes kept in a plastic bag. Both campsites are next to running water. Many visitors drink the water untreated, as there is no human habitation above, but the cautious will want to treat the water first.

The Cohdefor office in Gracias sells photocopies of the relevant section of the Gracias topographical map, with the trail and camps marked, for US 30 cents. This is much more useful than the actual topo itself, which does not show the trail. A map is not really necessary if you're just planning to hike up the main trail, but it does give an idea of the lay of the land and is not bad to have just in case. The topographical maps covering the entire park are: Gracias 2459 I, La Campa 2459 II, San Marcos de Ocotepeque 2459 III, and Corquín 2459 IV. Camping gear is available for rent at Restaurante Guancascos.

For more information on Celaque, you could contact **Proyecto Celaque,** a major project funded partly by the German government to help protect the park and work with the area's inhabitants. The officials there are very knowledgeable on guides, possible climbing routes, and potential new visitors' centers planned for El Naranjo and El Paraíso. The central office of Proyecto Celaque is in Santa Rosa de Copán, tel. and fax 662-1459, email:celaque@hondutel.hn.

SOUTH AND EAST OF CELAQUE

La Campa

Sixteen kilometers from Gracias by a rough dirt road is the Lenca village of La Campa, famed in the region both for its earthenware pottery and its annual festival. Those who only have a short time to spend in this region should consider a day trip from Gracias to La Campa to get an idea of what village life is like in the rural mountains of western Honduras. With only about 400 residents tucked into a small valley, La Campa is one of those supremely calm, quiet, uncomplicated mountain villages where it seems nothing, not even visits from outlandish foreigners, disturbs the rhythm of everyday life.

The **Iglesia de San Matías** in the center of town was begun in 1690 and renovated in 1938. It's a fine example of the churches found in many nearby villages, complete with a carved altarpiece and painted saint statues. The local priest is very knowledgeable on the region and happy to talk with visitors. The smaller **La Ermita** church on a hill above town was built in 1890.

Apart from the churches, the town holds just a couple of *pulperías* and several houses selling pottery. A small *hospedaje* may soon be built across from the entrance to the church, but as yet there are no accommodations in La Campa.

During the week leading up to 22 February, La Campa transforms from a sleepy village into the bustling site of one of the best-known annual *ferias* in the region. Pilgrims from all over western Honduras and Guatemala flood the town to pay homage to the town's patron saint, San Matías, and participate in the celebrations, which include the traditional *guancascos* exchange of saints with other villages, music, and ritual costume dancing.

The canyon and dramatic hillsides behind town can be reached by trail. Several caves reputedly line the riverbank. On the hill behind the church a trail winds upward, leading to **Cruz**

Alta, four km away, a good day-hike through the forest. This hill has long been venerated by people throughout the region. According to local legend, long ago the valley was struck by a series of earthquakes, which terrified the populace. So strong were the quakes that a new mountain was created. In hopes peace would return, the local priest advised the people to carry crosses and sacred images to the top of the new mountain. When this was accomplished, the quakes ceased, and since then the hill has been considered sacred.

Caiquín

West of La Campa, the road to San Manuel Colohete deteriorates severely. Three kilometers from La Campa a dirt road turns off, leading another five km to Caiquín. A colonial chapel stands in the center of the village. Reportedly the Caiquín church holds some well-preserved paintings on the plaster walls and a fine wooden altar. From Caiquín, well-beaten trails head east over spectacular mountain countryside, past Lenca warrior Lempira's old fortress at Peñol de Cerquín, to Erandique. The hike is possible in one day or a more relaxed two days, and guides can be found in Caiquín by asking around.

San Manuel Colohete

From the crest of the last hill on the road from La Campa, the view down over San Manuel is exceptionally lovely. The village sits on a rise above the junction of three rivers pouring off the side of Celaque, which soars skyward in a sheer wall that dwarfs the whitewashed village. With clouds almost perpetually wreathing the hills above town, it feels as though San Manuel has been lost in the mists of time, utterly remote and disconnected from anything save the stunning landscape surrounding it.

Similar in design to La Merced church in Gracias, the plaster, tile-roofed *Iglesia de San Manuel* features an ornately sculptured facade, and remnants of centuries-old mud paintings are still visible around the beautiful painted wooden altar. Only the most insensitive won't be entranced by the church's primitive elegance. Locals don't seem to know when it was built, but the best guess is at the end of the 17th century.

One local *comedor,* near the entrance to town, supplies basic, inexpensive meals, while a super-basic *hospedaje* just off the square offers a US$1, grim bed. If the *hospedaje* is full, you could certainly rough it under the porch of the government building on the square, if you ask nicely.

Don't be surprised if San Manuel residents don't know quite what to make of a foreign visitor, especially if not accompanied by a Honduran. But the worst that will happen is everyone will stare wordlessly at you, and the children will pester you relentlessly. Keep a friendly smile on your face and all will be well.

San Manuel is 14 km by very rough dirt road west of La Campa.

Uphill From San Manuel

Straight up the eastern flanks of Celaque from San Manuel by trail are the *aldeas* of Miande and El Cedro—basically collections of huts clinging to the hillside. At El Cedro you can find guides to go up to the peak of Celaque and from there down to Gracias, or conversely, find trails continuing to Chimís Montaña or down to Belén Gualcho, on the southwestern side of Celaque. The main trails in this vicinity are accurately marked on the topographical maps, and if in doubt just ask passing *campesinos,* who are usually all too happy to stop and find out what a stranger is doing passing through these parts.

San Sebastián

If the dirt road to San Manuel seemed bad, check out the barely drivable stretch continuing on to San Sebastián, another attractive village farther west around Celaque, also with a simple *hospedaje.* If no ride is available the road can be walked in three to four hours, and from there you can continue walking several more hours on a remnant of the old Camino Real to Belén Gualcho, where you can spend the night and catch a ride the next day to Santa Rosa de Copán.

South of San Sebastián, the adventurous can hike down to Tomalá through lovely, little-visited, and safe countryside in southern Lempira, near the border with El Salvador. Locals say the mostly downhill route can be hiked in 10 hours, but more likely it would require camping out one night. From Tomalá, transportation is available to San Marcos and on to Santa Rosa de Copán or Nueva Ocotepeque. Guides can be found in San Sebastián who know the way.

Belén Gualcho

On the western flanks of Celaque, accessible by dirt road from Santa Rosa de Copán via Cucayagua and Corquín, or on the trail from San Sebastián, is the village of Belén Gualcho. Perched on the flanks of Celaque, Belén is dominated by an imposing triple-domed colonial-era church, considered to be among the most beautiful in the country. Great views of the church are had from the local grade school—the guard will usually let you pass if you ask nicely.

The town hosts a large **Sunday market,** which attracts *campesinos* from the mountains all around Celaque and is quite a colorful and lively event, well worth scheduling your trip to see.

A conjunto de cuerda
(string band) plays into
the wee hours in Santa
Cruz de Lempira.

GUILLERMO COBOS

Belén's annual festival is held 24 June in honor of San Juan. The story goes that in years past, a spirit was so impressed by Belén's festival that every year he arrived on a black mule and took part in the revelry himself, afterward disappearing into the hills. But one year a group of young men thought it would be amusing to attach a bunch of firecrackers to the mule's tail. Offended by this evident lack of respect for his otherworldliness, the spirit—known as *El Hombre de Belén Gualcho*—rode off in a huff and has never returned.

A fine, comfortable hotel in Belén is **Hotelito El Carmen** (no phone), with 20 clean rooms renting for US$2-4. Bathrooms are communal, and no hot water is available. Don't come out here expecting luxury! Another option, for the same price but not as nice, is **Hotel Belén** (no phone). Both hotels are often full on Saturday and Sunday nights, before and after Belén's Sunday market.

The favored local eatery is **Comedor Merry,** with very good, inexpensive *típico* food served in a friendly little dining room. Comedor Merry often has some of the unusual and remarkably palatable homemade wines for which Belén is famous, like *vino de papa* (potato wine) or *vino de zanahoria* (carrot wine).

Buses drive twice a day between Belén and Santa Rosa de Copán, via Cucayagua and Corquín. You can also catch more frequent buses to Corquín and try to hitch from there, though pickups are often full already. The 24-km stretch between Corquín and Belén is extremely bad and can take over two hours to drive. Buses back to Santa Rosa from Belén leave twice a day at 6 a.m. and 9 a.m., US$1.35. The turn to Corquín and Belén is off the Santa Rosa-Nueva Ocotepeque highway, 15.8 miles from Santa Rosa.

Near Belén
Two or three hours of stiff hiking from Belén, via the *aldea* of El Paraíso, takes a visitor to the spectacular, 50-meter **Santa María de Gualcho**

LEMPIRA: THE MAN IN THE MONEY

The name of Honduras' currency honors the country's first great hero, a Lenca warrior who led his people in a fierce but little-known war against the Spaniards during the first years of the conquest of Honduras.

Spaniards first penetrated the mountainous region of present-day western Honduras in the early 1530s. From the start, the native Lenca, led initially by a chief named Etempica, fiercely resisted the newcomers. By 1536 the situation in the province had grown so precarious that the Spanish leaders called on the bloodthirsty conqueror of Guatemala, Pedro de Alvarado, to lead an expedition from that country to pacify the region. Alvarado laid siege on a few indigenous villages in the Río Mejocote Valley, then sent Juan de Chávez farther south to found Gracias a Dios. But Chávez ran into thousands of Lenca warriors enraged by Alvarado's actions and spoiling for a fight.

Chávez wisely left the region without founding a town. Later in the same year, three colonists were on their way from the Spanish base at Siguatepeque to Guatemala when they were waylaid and killed by unknown Indians. On hearing of the event, Honduran governor Francisco de Montejo led a strong contingent of soldiers into the region and called a meet-ing of native chiefs. All but one of the chiefs showed up—and were promptly hanged by the Spaniards.

The only chief who did not attend the meeting was Lempira ("Man of the Mountain" in Lenca), described by the Spaniards as about 35-40 years old, "of medium stature, with strong arms, brave, and intelligent." Rather than being cowed by the Spanish brutality, Lempira gathered a large force of warriors at Peñol de Cerquín—a natural fortress—and at several other mountain redoubts near what is now Erandique, in southwestern Honduras. Through either intimidation or negotiation, Lempira convinced the Cares tribe, traditional enemies of the Lenca, to join the fight against the Spaniards. Legend has it that Lempira swayed wavering Cares by scorning them: "How is it so many brave men in their own land can be subjugated miserably by so few foreigners?"

At that time the Spaniards did indeed have very few men in Honduras—compared to the treasure-laden regions of Peru and Mexico, it was not a rich province. Just when Montejo thought he had subdued the region with his show of force, Lempira coordinated surprise attacks on several Spanish settlements in Honduras from his mountain fortress. When the conquistadors learned of his role in the at-

waterfall, up a narrow canyon on the Río Negro. A guide is necessary to find the trail, which was damaged by Hurricane Mitch and was treacherous at last report. Plans were afoot to clear it again. Cohdefor workers José Alonso de Diós and Juan Alberto Martínez, who live in El Paraíso, charge US$5 to guide the five- or six-hour trip. Adventurous hikers can find guides up into Montaña de Celaque from Belén.

Erandique

About halfway along the dirt road between Gracias and La Esperanza is San Juan, where a rough dirt road turns south 24 km to Erandique, an exceptionally beautiful rural colonial town set amidst the Sierra de las Neblinas. The mountains around Erandique were the old stomping grounds of Lenca warrior Lempira when he waged his guerrilla war against the Spanish conquistadors in the 16th century.

Erandique has three *parques* (squares), each fronted by a small but very fine colonial-era church. Formerly each of the squares had a massive ceiba tree in front, planted over a century ago, but now only two survive. One of these remaining two ceibas was nearly split in half when struck by lightning. The one intact tree is impressively huge, dwarfing the square and the church behind it. A large statue to Lempira now stands in the center of the main square.

Bemused visitors to Erandique may find themselves surrounded by men, women, and children asking if they would like to buy opals. As it turns out, the surrounding countryside is one of the most famous areas in the Americas for the precious stone. Several different grades of opals are mined nearby, including black, white, river, garden, rainbow, milk, and the valuable aurora opals. Honduran opals are considered particularly valuable because of the frequent presence of scarlet coloring. Local *campesinos* are also always turning up obsidian arrowheads and other objects from pre-Columbian and conquest times and often trying to sell them to visitors for very little money.

---

tacks, they assembled a force led by Capt. Alonso de Cáceres to take the fortress at Peñol de Cerquín.

Lempira had chosen his spot well. The steep, rugged Peñol did not allow the Spaniards to employ their horses, and they were unable to take the fortress by force. After six months of blockading the fortress, the Peñol still had not been taken, as Lenca warriors easily snuck past the Spanish soldiers in the forest and had no trouble keeping themselves provisioned. Other Indian groups, seeing Lempira's success in holding out against the Spaniards, began their own uprisings across the province.

History offers us at least three different versions of what happened next. In the classic version, the frustrated Cáceres, unable to take the fortress by direct attack or by siege, decided to trick Lempira. Calling on the Lenca chief to discuss peace terms, Cáceres hid a soldier amongst the Spanish horses. Just as Lempira was disdainfully rejecting any terms short of Spanish withdrawl from a rocky bluff several meters from the Spaniards, the hidden soldier shot and killed the chief with an arquebus.

Much of this history is derived from *Historia de América,* written by Spanish historian Antonio de Herrera almost 100 years after the event. More recently, Honduran and Canadian historians uncovered a document in Seville, Spain, from the *Audiencia de México.* In the report, dated 1558, Spanish soldier Rodrigo Ruíz states that *he* killed the Lenca leader, whom he called "Elempira," in single combat (not by ambush) and took his head back to Siguatepeque as proof of his actions.

Yet another version comes from the Lenca town of Gualcinse, not far from the Peñol, and at the time of the revolt one of Lempira's allies. Local tradition has long held that Lempira was indeed shot while listening to a peace proposal by the Spaniards, but that he was only wounded, and that his warriors carried him off to hiding. According to the Gualcinse account, a contingent of Spaniards heard of Lempira's whereabouts, came to the town, and killed him on his sickbed. They then cut off his head and brought it back to Siguatepeque. This sequence of events would explain why according to Honduran lore Lempira was killed at Piedra Parada, which although nearby is clearly not the same location as Peñol de Cerquín, by all accounts the location of his fortress.

From all the supporting witnesses reported in the Ruíz document, it's clear that the soldier played some essential role in killing Lempira, but whether through treachery or single combat remains a mystery. In some manner Lempira's uprising and death must have been a last gasp for the Lenca; the formerly fierce warriors never again threatened Spanish rule in the region.

Apart from the occasional opal-buyer, Erandique doesn't receive many foreign visitors, so you may be the recipient of a few curious but usually good-natured stares from town residents. The town's annual festival is held on 20 January in honor of San Sebastián.

Erandique has only one *hospedaje,* behind the store on the first *parque* in town, where the bus stops. There are no restaurants in town, but ask around for someone who will cook a meal, and expect something very basic.

One minibus runs between Gracias and Erandique daily, leaving Erandique early in the morning for the two-and-a-half-hour, US$2 trip. Finding a *jalón* on one of the regularly passing pickup trucks is not difficult.

Near Erandique
The pine-forested mountains around Erandique are excellent for hiking, with footpaths leading in all directions. For a short afternoon trip, ask the way to **Las Cuatro Chorreras,** a wide waterfall about a half-hour's walk south of town down the valley.

Those with an interest in history, or looking for a good long walk, may want to make a pilgrimage to **Peñol de Cerquín,** Lempira's unconquered fortress in his war against the Spanish. Ask a local for the path leaving Erandique up the southeast flank of Montaña Azacualpa to **San Antonio Montaña,** a collection of huts and a small primary school perched on the side of the mountain. The trail rounds the side of the mountain near the schoolhouse, and from that spot the rocky spire of the Peñol can be seen in the valley below. From the schoolhouse a trail continues down the mountain to the Peñol, or you can continue up the trail on the far side of Azacualpa, which eventually connects to the Erandique-Mapulaca road. This roundtrip can be done easily in a day, with plenty of time to admire the views, but a trip to the Peñol would probably require one night of camping.

Other nearby mountains such as **Coyucatena, Congolón,** and **Piedra Parada** (according to local lore, the site of Lempira's assassination) can also be hiked up—generally trails lead in all directions. Reportedly a monument to Lempira sits atop Cerro Congolón. From Erandique, you could walk northwest to Celaque and Gracias in a couple of days, if equipped with good maps and a compass or a local guide. Camping is

safe, but it's always best to check with a local *campesino* before pitching a tent.

South toward El Salvador
The road leaving Erandique to the south heads up over the mountain behind town and continues on to Mapulaca near the Salvadoran border. Little traffic passes on this road even in the dry season, but hitchhiking is possible if you're patient. It might be quicker to find a guide and walk by trails through the lovely countryside. From Mapulaca, a dirt road winds its way north via Valladolid and Tomalá to La Labor, where it meets the Nueva Ocotepeque-Santa Rosa de Copán highway. This is serious adventure-travel country—pickup trucks or hiking are the only means of transport all the way. Don't plan on getting anywhere quickly.

LA ESPERANZA

The capital of the Intibucá department, La Esperanza lies in the heart of the most traditional Lenca region in the country. Although the town itself only has a population of about 5,000, the market area often swarms with residents from surrounding villages coming in to trade their produce or buy goods. The market is especially lively on weekend mornings, when you can watch Lenca women wearing colorful dresses and head-scarves going about their business.

Set in a mountain valley surrounded by pine forest in the heart of the Sierra de Opalaca at 1,980 meters, La Esperanza has a cool climate with daytime temperatures normally hovering between 10 and 20° C. Originally the Lenca village of Eramaní, which means "Land of Pottery" in Lenca, La Villa de La Esperanza was officially founded on 23 September 1848. The Spanish name derives, according to local legend, from a priest who came to the area with his younger cousin during colonial times, to convert the Lenca. The young cousin became enamored with a local girl and fathered a child with her. The priest promptly sent his cousin away in anger, but the girl and her child never gave up hope *(esperanza)* that the young Spaniard would return.

The cave visible on a hill just above town has a small chapel inside known as **La Ermita,** which is the site of religious services during Semana

a Lenca mother and child

Santa and other special occasions. The main street running past the square turns into a stairway leading up to the cave.

Practicalities

Two of the better hotels in town are **Hotel Solis,** tel. 898-2080, and **Hotel La Esperanza,** tel. 898-2068, each with clean rooms and hot water for US$7 d, or more with private bathroom. Less expensive is **Hotel El Rey,** tel. 898-2078, charging US$1.70 s, or US$3 s and US$6 d with private bath.

Just off the square is the clean **Restaurante Opalacas,** about the best place to eat in town with inexpensive *comida típica* and a decent salad or burger, although you might starve before the food arrives. Across the street is **Mexicanos,** good for *tacos* and beer or soft drinks.

Hondutel and Correos are next to each other on the square. Banco de Occidente near the square can change dollars but usually won't take traveler's checks.

Getting There and Away

La Esperanza is connected by a well-maintained, 67-km paved road to Siguatepeque. The road heads down out of the mountains, across the Río Otoro Valley, past the town of Jesús de Otoro, and back up into the mountains to the junction with the San Pedro Sula-Tegucigalpa highway.

Buses to Siguatepeque leave roughly every two hours from the terminal near the market, charging US$1 for the 90-minute ride.

Buses to Tegucigalpa (four hours, US$2.20) leave the terminal five times daily between 5 a.m. and 1 p.m., while buses to San Pedro Sula (four hours, US$2.20) leave three times daily between 6:30 a.m. and 11 a.m.

A usually fairly well-maintained, 80-km dirt road connects La Esperanza to Gracias, passing through some lovely high mountain country. One minibus drives to Gracias each day, leaving at a variable hour in the morning, charging US$2 for the four-hour ride. Hitchhiking is also easy and safe. Get out to the junction early, and expect to pay a few *lempiras* for the ride.

South of La Esperanza dirt roads continue to the villages of Santa Lucía (87 km) and San Antonio (93 km), in the hotter canyon country near the border with El Salvador. There has been some conflict in this region recently between the two countries over the so-called *bolsones,* pockets of land disputed since the end of the 1969 Soccer War. What little violence that has taken place, however, has been in extremely remote settlements and would not affect passing travelers.

Near La Esperanza

Seven km from La Esperanza is one of the most traditional Lenca communities in the country, **Yamaranguila.** Although they don't see a lot of tourists, residents are accustomed to outsiders, as a Peace Corps agricultural training center is located nearby. On certain holidays, traditional dances like the *guancascos* can be seen, though it's hard to find out when and where the dance

GUANCASCOS: PEACE CEREMONIES OF THE WESTERN HIGHLANDS

The language and many of the traditions of the Lenca have been lost over the past four and a half centuries, for reasons not entirely clear to anthropologists. One Lenca ritual still celebrated on certain days in the southern and western highlands is the *guancascos*, a bilateral ceremony between two towns, often neighboring. The *guancascos* is a sort of peace ritual, marking the friendship between the two communities. Many *guancascos* are thought to commemorate a past agreement over the division of farming land or hunting grounds. In the colonial era, and up to the present day in more remote areas, the *guancascos* is the single most important event of the year, marking the time when new village leaders take office and a day of many weddings and baptisms. Although originally a pre-Columbian ritual, since colonial times the *guancascos* has incorporated elements of Catholicism, particularly the use of saints in the ritual exchange between the communities.

The specific dances and format of the *guancascos* varies widely from town to town, but the general outlines are usually similar. In the days running up to the principal celebration, the townsfolk hold several preliminary ceremonies, such as the *Traída de la Pólvora*, the bringing of the gunpowder, when the all-important fireworks bought with the communal money are brought into the village and divided up among the *mayordomo* (neighborhood leaders). In certain towns, locals hold the *Danza de las Escobas*, the Broom Dance, so named because the newly elected village leader hands a flowered broom to the previous leader and in return receives *la Vara Alta,* the Tall Staff. In colonial times the staff marked the individual responsible for mediating between the community and the Spanish authorities.

On the "big day" of the *guancascos,* festivities begin with the townsfolk parading their patron saint through the streets, and then out of town to a designated spot, where the procession meets a second parade from the partner community. Lengthy greetings ensue, punctuated with much fireworks and music, and the two saint icons are exchanged. The two groups then walk together to the church of the main town, which has been decorated with pine branches and filled with copal incense smoke. Representatives of both towns give special speeches in the church, followed by a party of dancing and drinking.

Formerly the culminating dance of the *guancascos* in many towns was the *La Danza del Gorrobo,* or Dance of the Black Iguana, performed with elaborate costumes, and with musical accompaniment

The ceremonial bringing of the fireworks (Traída de la Pólvora) *is part of the* guancascos.

GUILLERMO COBOS

provided by *chirimía,* a type of flute, *caramba,* a stringed bow, and *sacabuche,* a gourd drum. This dance is no longer widespread—these days the processions and saint exchange continue, but the elaborate dances have devolved into more unstructured parties.

The few anthropologists who have researched the *guancascos* believe that some three dozen communities in southern and western Honduras still hold the ceremony in one form or another. Both **La Campa,** in the department of Lempira, and **Yaramanguila,** in the department of Intibucá, are well known for their festivals, usually held on 24 February and 8 December, respectively. Other towns include Ojojona in Francisco Morazán, Santa Cruz in Lempira, Lejamani in Comayagua, and Ilama, Chinda, and Gualala in Santa Bárbara.

Although the *guancascos* are meant to be celebrated on certain days, trying to ascertain which day that might be is no easy task. It's not that locals are trying to keep foreigners away; rather, that the chosen day seems a bit flexible, and the festival may not be held at all on certain years, depending in large part on whether the townsfolk have enough money for the festivities or not. In a way it works out perfectly, as the only foreigners who ever get to the festivals are the rare ones who hang out in these villages and get to know the inhabitants, and thus find out. And all in all, those are the sorts of folks who should witness these ceremonies, rather than the video camera-toting package tour crowd. Almost all *guancascos* are held in January and February, during the dry season, but beyond that, you just have to head to the hills and start asking around.

will be held. You could try asking with the local *alcalde* (mayor) for more information on the festivals. Near Yamaranguila is an impressive waterfall, reached by footpath—just ask directions to **La Chorrera.** Yaramanguila can easily be reached by frequent buses from La Esperanza.

On the dirt road heading to San Francisco de Opalaca, just outside of La Esperanza, is **Laguna Chiligatoro,** a good place for a swim on a rare hot day.

There are four supposedly protected natural areas in Intibucá: Montaña Opalaca, Mixcure, Montecillos, and Montaña Verde. Unfortunately much of the forests have already been severely logged, leaving little of the original flora and fauna intact. Because of its isolated location, only **Refugio de Vida Silvestre Montaña Verde** (Montaña Verde Wildlife Refuge) is still worth visiting, but getting into the forest is no easy task. Located near the border of the Lempira department, in the San Francisco de Opalaca municipality, Montaña Verde can be reached by first getting by bus or *jalón* from La Esperanza to the village of Monte Verde, where a guide can be hired to explore the mountain. As yet no trails exist, and facilities in Monte Verde are limited, but the forest is reputed to be very beautiful and intact. Topographical maps covering the reserve are 1:50,000 La Iguala 2559 IV and La Unión 2560 III.

For those with an exploratory inclination, the high pine forested hill country around La Esperanza provides lovely hiking and mountain biking and is generally considered to be quite safe.

From La Esperanza To El Salvador
South of La Esperanza, a dirt highway (in good condition only during the January-May dry season) descends an escarpment down into the hotter lowlands near the Salvadoran border. Beginning from around the area of **San Marcos de Sierra,** on a clear day one can see the volcanos of San Vicente and San Miguel across the border in El Salvador. The road continues down into a small valley, in the middle of which is the town of **Concepción,** and then continues up again briefly. Beyond Concepción, the road forks three ways, the southeasterly road going through **Colomancagua,** the southern road through **Santa Lucia,** and the southwesterly road through **San Antonio.** All eventually go into El Salvador, but the road through Colomancagua is in the best condition. It first passes through the unmanned border crossing of San Fernando, then continues to the first major Salvadoran town, **Perquín,** where there is an interesting museum about the civil war. From Perquín, the road is paved farther into El Salvador, but you'd have to find an immigration post to register yourself.

SAN PEDRO SULA AND CENTRAL HONDURAS

A far-flung region comprising the country's economic capital (San Pedro Sula) and largest lake (Lago de Yojoa) as well as the mountainous landscapes of Santa Bárbara and Yoro, central Honduras has much to offer. Travelers can take care of business and enjoy city life in San Pedro Sula, fish and boat on Lago de Yojoa, admire the gushing waterfall at Pulhapanzak, buy handicrafts and visit colonial villages near Santa Bárbara, or hike and birdwatch in the cloud forests of Cusuco, Meámber, Santa Bárbara, and Pico Pijol.

SAN PEDRO SULA

Situated on the southwestern edge of the broad, fertile Valle de Sula, up against the flanks of the Sierra Merendón, San Pedro Sula (often shortened to San Pedro) is a bustling, hot, modern city. If Honduras' governmental capital is Tegucigalpa, its business and financial capital is San Pedro Sula. According to recent statistics, the 800,000 inhabitants of San Pedro produce 40% of the national GDP.

Unless they come to San Pedro on business, most foreign visitors stop in the city only briefly. In spite of its nearly five centuries of existence, San Pedro has virtually no remaining colonial architecture, and apart from one good museum, not much to attract tourists. If you need to take care of some errands while on the road, though, San Pedro is a good place to do them. The city is easy to get around in and has just about every sort of store or business you could

---

SAN PEDRO SULA AND CENTRAL HONDURAS HIGHLIGHTS

- Birdwatching and boating on Lago de Yojoa
- Touring the lovely villages and beautiful countryside near Santa Bárbara
- Visiting the colonial churches of Comayagua
- Hiking in the national parks of Cusuco or Cerro Azul/Meámbar

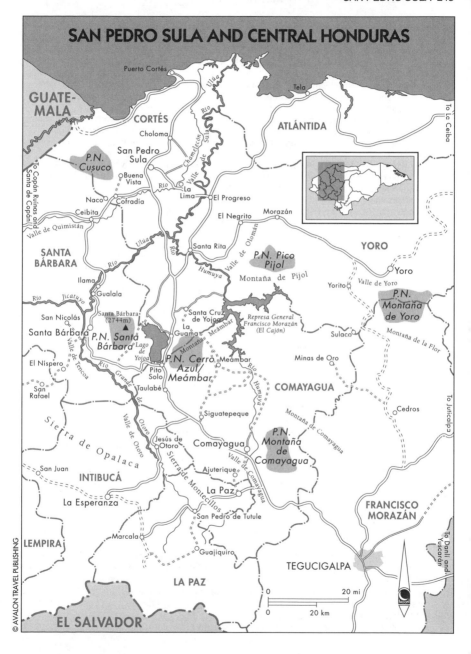

SAN PEDRO SULA AND CENTRAL HONDURAS

Puerto Cortés

Tela

GUATE-
MALA

To La Ceiba

CORTÉS

ATLÁNTIDA

Choloma

Río Chamelecón

Río Ulúa

San Pedro
Sula

P.N.
Cusuco

Buena
Vista

Río

La
Lima

Valle de Sula

El Progreso

Morazán

To Copán Ruinas and
Santa de Copán

Naco

Cofradía

Ceibita

El Negrito

YORO

Valle de Quimistán

Santa Rita

Río Ulúa

P.N. Pico
Pijol

Yoro

SANTA
BÁRBARA

Río Humuya

Valle de Olomán

Montaña de Pijol

Yorito

Valle de Yoro

Ilama

Río Jicatuyo

Gualala

Santa Bárbara
(2744m)

Santa Cruz
de Yojoa

Represa General
Francisco Morazán
(El Cajón)

P.N.
Montaña
de Yoro

San Nicolás

Montaña de la Flor

Santa Bárbara

P.N. Santa
Bárbara

La
Guama

Montaña Meámbar

Sulaco

El Níspero

Lago
de
Yojoa

P.N. Cerro
Azul
Meámbar

Meámbar

Minas de Oro

Río Grande

Río Humuya

Pito
Solo

COMAYAGUA

San
Rafael

Taulabé

Sierra de Opalaca

Valle de Otoro

Siguatepeque

Montaña de Comayagua

Cedros

To Juticalpa

Valle de Tencoa

Jesús de
Otoro

Comayagua

P.N.
Montaña
de
Comayagua

San Juan

Sierra de Montecillos

Ajuterique

INTIBUCÁ

Valle de Comayagua

La Paz

FRANCISCO
MORAZÁN

La Esperanza

San Pedro de Tutule

LEMPIRA

Marcala

LA PAZ

Guajiquiro

TEGUCIGALPA

To Danlí and
Yuscarán

EL SALVADOR

0   20 mi

0   20 km

MOON

MAQUILAS: GOLDEN OPPORTUNITY OR CONTEMPORARY SLAVERY?

The driving force behind San Pedro Sula's annual economic growth of five to six percent, and its status as one of the top earners in the national economy, is the 180-odd export-oriented *maquila* factories in the region. The *maquilas* mainly assemble clothes from fabrics imported tax free to Honduras, then re-export the finished product (again with no taxes) for sale in the United States. About a fifth of the plants are owned by Koreans, and the rest by Taiwanese, North Americans, Hondurans, and others.

Maquila factories, a concept first undertaken on a large scale along the Mexico-U.S. border, first arrived in Honduras in 1976, when the government passed the Puerto Cortés Free Zone law. Three years later, this was extended to Amapala, Tela, Choloma, Omoa, and La Ceiba. By 1998, further legal modifications allowed for the creation of free zones (called ZIPs) anywhere in country. By far the majority of *maquilas* in Honduras are within a 50-km radius of San Pedro Sula.

To many labor organizers outside Honduras, especially in the United States, the low wages and less-than-ideal conditions translate into a sort of modern slavery. In July 1996, the New York-based National Labor Committee accused television celebrity Kathie Lee Gifford of exploiting Honduran workers in a factory producing clothes bearing her name. The case was publicized widely after the news program *Hard Copy* aired a story on the factory and the U.S. Congress heard testimony from one 15-year-old factory worker, Wendy Díaz.

Honduran labor organizers agree that conditions in many *maquilas* are far from perfect. Verbal abuse, compulsory overtime, unreachable production quotas, and dismissal for pregnancy are all common. Nonetheless, local union leaders say some *maquilas* treat their workers with respect, subsidize lunch, and offer free medical care. Many female workers have developed a refined knowledge of the national labor laws and are quick to speak up for themselves and organize if treated unfairly.

The clamor in the U.S. passed right over like Honduras' annual tropical storms, and the *maquilas* continue attracting workers from all over the country. By the end of 1998, 110,000 Hondurans worked in *maquilas,* and a year later the number was up to 125,000. The local labor force continues its own struggle, without any help from U.S. journalists or anybody else, to improve conditions in the factories and gain wage increases, while the factory owners in turn do whatever they can to keep unions out of their shops and keep employee costs as low as possible.

hope to find in Honduras. The hotel and restaurant selection is excellent, covering all price ranges and tastes.

While San Pedro is much maligned by travelers as a place to get out of as quickly as possible, a large number of expatriates make their home in the city. Those who can afford to live in the wealthier, suburb-like neighborhoods on the west side of San Pedro at the edge of the mountains, who avoid going downtown if at all possible, find it a reasonably pleasant place to live.

A word of warning: San Pedro carries the dubious distinction of being the AIDS capital of Central America. Visitors who take it into their head to look for sexual relations here are strongly advised to take precautions. Further, the city has the highest crime rate in the country. Muggings are not unheard of, so pay attention to who's around you and where you are, especially after dark.

San Pedro is at about 40 meters elevation, and the climate is steaming hot most of the year, with daytime temperatures varying between 25 and 38° C. Rains in the Valle de Sula, which normally hit between July and November, can be torrential.

History

The Valle de Sula is one of the longest-inhabited regions of Honduras. A village site excavated in the early 1990s along the Río Ulúa was dated to 1100-900 B.C. Little is known about the site's builders other than they had some apparent contact with the Olmecs of central Mexico, suggesting a fairly high degree of development.

The Maya are believed to have maintained settlements along the Valle de Sula, but their

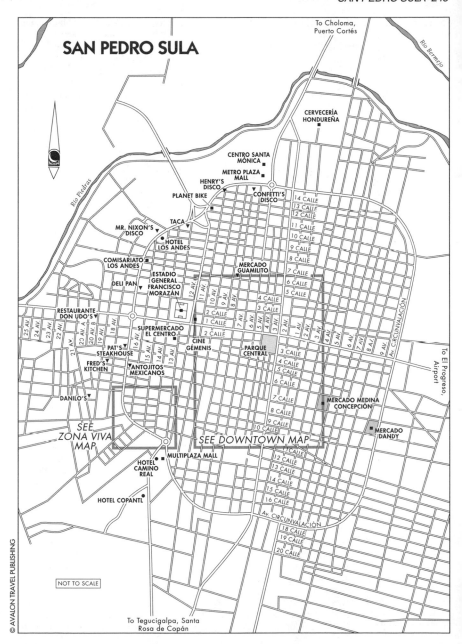

SAN PEDRO SULA

To Choloma,
Puerto Cortés

Rio Bermejo

Rio Piedras

CERVECERÍA
HONDUREÑA

CENTRO SANTA
MÓNICA

METRO PLAZA
MALL

HENRY'S
DISCO

CONFETTI'S
DISCO

PLANET BIKE

14 CALLE
13 CALLE
12 CALLE
11 CALLE
10 CALLE
9 CALLE
8 CALLE
7 CALLE
6 CALLE
5 CALLE
4 CALLE
3 CALLE

TACA

MR. NIXON'S
DISCO

HOTEL
LOS ANDES

COMISARIATO
LOS ANDES

MERCADO
GUAMILITO

DELI PAN

ESTADIO
GENERAL
FRANCISCO
MORAZÁN

RESTAURANTE
DON UDO'S

SUPERMERCADO
EL CENTRO

25 AV
24 AV
23 AV
22 AV
21 AV
20 AV A
20 AV
19 AV
18 AV
16 AV
15 AV
14 AV
13 AV
12 AV
11 AV
10 AV
9 AV
8 AV
7 AV
6 AV
5 AV
4 AV
3 AV
2 AV
1 AV
2 AV
3 AV
4 AV
5 AV
6 AV
7 AV
8 AV
9 AV

PAT'S
STEAKHOUSE

CINE
GÉMENIS

PARQUE
CENTRAL

FRED'S
KITCHEN

ANTOJITOS
MEXICANOS

2 CALLE
1 CALLE
2 CALLE
3 CALLE
4 CALLE
5 CALLE
6 CALLE

DANILO'S

7 CALLE
8 CALLE
9 CALLE

MERCADO MEDINA
CONCEPCIÓN

Av. CIRCUNVALACIÓN

To El Progreso,
Airport

SEE
ZONA VIVA
MAP

SEE DOWNTOWN MAP

MERCADO
DANDY

10 CALLE

HOTEL
CAMINO
REAL

MULTIPLAZA MALL

11 CALLE
12 CALLE
13 CALLE
14 CALLE
15 CALLE
16 CALLE

HOTEL COPANTL

18 CALLE
19 CALLE
20 CALLE

Av. CIRCUNVALACIÓN

NOT TO SCALE

To Tegucigalpa, Santa
Rosa de Copán

presence in what is modern-day Honduras was mainly limited to the region farther west and south near the present Guatemalan border. The largest Indian settlement in the region, which the Spanish saw when they first penetrated the interior of Honduras, was at Naco, in a small valley on the south side of the Sierra Merendón from San Pedro.

La Villa de San Pedro was founded on 27 June 1536 by Pedro de Alvarado, conqueror of Guatemala, on the flat area of the Valle de Sula, far enough from the edges of the Chamelecón and Ulúa rivers to protect the settlement from flooding. An early base of operations for the Spanish in their conquest of Honduras, San Pedro quickly faded in importance during the middle and late colonial period. After 1600 San Pedro was virtually abandoned, in part because of pirate and Indian attacks and also because colonists had moved on in the Spaniards' search for gold and silver in the highlands.

During the later part of the colonial era, San Pedro was a base for local cattle ranchers and a collection center for sarsaparilla, a root that grew wild in the region and at the time was considered a miracle drug by Europeans, who believed it cured venereal diseases.

In the mid-19th century San Pedro's fortunes took a turn for the better when commerce picked up at the port of Omoa, and San Pedro became a frequent stop-off point for goods on their way in or out of the country. But it was the growth of the banana industry and the reopening of Puerto Cortés in the late 19th century that jump-started San Pedro's economy, and it has continued growing steadily. Currently San Pedro is the fastest-growing city in all of Central America.

Orientation and Getting Around

San Pedro Sula is laid out in a straightforward grid pattern, divided into northern and southern sections by 1 Calle and into eastern and western sections by 1 Avenida. Avenues *(avenidas)* run north-south, streets *(calles)* east-west. The central part of the city is ringed by Av. Circunvalación. Addresses frequently refer to quadrants of the city: SO *(suroeste,* or southwest); SE *(sureste,* or southeast); NO *(noroeste,* or northwest), and NE *(noreste,* or northeast).

The casual visitor should not have much need to venture beyond Av. Circunvalación. Most ho-

tels, restaurants, businesses, and bus stations are within eight blocks of the downtown square. The western and southwestern section of Av. Circunvalación, sometimes referred to as the *zona viva,* is home to many upscale restaurants, hotels, and nightclubs. After dark, walking around is not recommended in parts of downtown, particularly around 1 Av. Sur and farther east toward the market district.

Most taxis charge US$1.75 for a ride anywhere within Circunvalación, more at night. Be sure to settle the price before you get in. *Colectivo* taxis charge only US 35 cents for the pleasure of being crammed into a cab following a set route with four other passengers and the driver. One useful *colectivo* leaves from 6 Av. at 3 Calle SO, and follows 6 Av. out to Av. Circunvalación to the highway exit to Puerto Cortés, in the northwest part of the city. Another, departing from 1 Av. at 8 Calle, takes a winding route south from downtown all the way out to the Tegucigalpa highway, past the turnoff to Santa Rosa de Copán. The local bus system is cheap, but routes are circuitous; unless you know the city well, it's easiest to take a taxi to destinations outside the center.

SIGHTS

Parque Central

San Pedro's downtown *parque central* (central square), always filled with a crowd of vendors, shoe shiners, moneychangers, evangelical preachers, and all manner of passersby, is a perfect spot to sit down and people-watch. The square often hosts impromptu music performances or other events. The adjacent *catedral* was built in 1949 and is not particularly interesting from an artistic standpoint. Running south from the center of the square is the *peatonal,* or pedestrian walkway, where moneychangers and a few jewelry sellers hang out.

Museo de Antropología e Historia

One of the better museums in the country, the Museo de Antropología e Historia, 3 Av. between 3 and 4 Calles NO, tel. 557-1496 or 557-1798, is the most interesting cultural site in San Pedro. Its two floors of exhibits outline the development of the Valle de Sula from 1500 B.C. to

DOWNTOWN SAN PEDRO SULA

NOT TO SCALE

© AVALON TRAVEL PUBLISHING

5 CALLE NO
9 AV. NO
8 AV. NO
7 AV. NO
6 AV. NO
5 AV. NO
4 AV. NO
3 AV. NO
2 AV. NO
1 AV. N
2 AV. NE

11 AV. NO
10 AV. NO
4 CALLE NO

MULTICINES PLAZA DE SULA

3 CALLE NO

HEDMAN ALAS BUS

SERVICIOS CULTURALES Y TURISTICOS ■

MUSEO DE ★ ANTROPOLOGÍA E HISTORIA

2 CALLE NO

CENTRO CULTURAL SAMPEDRANO ★

PLAZA CRISTAL SUITES ■

YUPI CHAT INTERNET ■

RESTAURANTE VICENTE

HOTEL BOLIVAR

HOLIDAY INN ●

1 CALLE O

PIZZERIA ITALIA AND CUSUCO PARK OFFICE ▼

DISCOVERY TRAVEL ■

GRAN HOTEL ● SULA

KODAK

HOTEL EJECUTIVO ■

SOSA ■ ISLEÑA ■

ESPRESSO AMERICANO/ ANTOJITOS MEXICANOS

3 AV. NE

2 CALLE SO

CINE TROPICANA ■

SUPER JUGOS ▼

Parque Central

CATEDRAL ■

1 CALLE E

COSTA'S BURGERS ▼

GRAN HOTEL CONQUISTADOR ●

HONDUSOFT INTERNET ■

CAFETERIA PAMPALONA ▼

MUNDIRAMA TRAVEL ■

4 CALLE SO

3 CALLE SO

CAFETERÍA EL BUEN SABOR ▼

MIGRACIÓN ■

SUPER DONUTS ■

SHAKES ▼

LA REPOSTERÍA ▼

PIZZA HUT ▼

HOTEL SAN ● PEDRO

5 CALLE SO

LAVANDERÍA ALMICH ■

HOTEL TERRAZA ●

CAFETERÍA MAYAN WAY ▼

HONDUTEL ■

SAENZ PRIMERA BUS ■

CAFETERÍA GRETCHEN ▼

CASA DE CAMBIO LEMPIRA ■

6 CALLE SO

EL REY BUS ■

HOTEL SAN JOSÉ ●

IMPALA BUS ■

COPÁN BUS ■

COMEDOR EL MERENDÓN ▼

EL MOCHITO BUS ■ HOTEL PORTO ALEGRE ●

KING QUALITY BUS ■

HOTEL PALMIRA ●

CATISA BUS ■

TRUJILLO AND SIGUATEPEQUE BUSES ■

7 CALLE SO

NORTEÑOS BUS ■

HOTEL SAN JUAN ●

4 AV. SE

HOTEL BRISAS DE OCCIDENTE ●

TUPSA BUS ■

8 CALLE SO

HOTEL AMBASSADOR ●

CITUL BUS ■

ANTOJITOS MEXICANOS ▼

EXPRESOS DEL ATLÁNTICO BUS ■

VANESSA/COTRAIPBAL BUS ■

9 CALLE SO

RIVERA BUS ■

EL REY EXPRESS BUS ■

TORITOS AND COPANECOS BUSES ■

10 CALLE SO

CONGOLÓN BUS ■

11 CALLE SO

SANTA BÁRBARA BUS ■

CORREOS ■

5 AV. SE

12 CALLE SO

3 AV. SO
1 AV. S

COFRADÍA BUS ■

13 CALLE SO

San Pedro Sula's cathedral

the present. The displays, mostly labeled in Spanish only, track Sula civilization from its earliest traces at the Playa de los Muertos site through the Lenca or Maya settlements at Los Naranjos, to the colonial and modern eras. It's interesting to note that the foreign-owned banana industry, a crucial part of the valley's economy, is barely mentioned, perhaps in concession to nationalist sentiment.

Noteworthy exhibits include the many different phases of Ulúa ceramics; sculptures from the Naranjo site reminiscent of the giant Olmec heads of La Venta, Mexico; examples of Spanish weaponry; details of the construction of the fortress at Omoa; and, oddly enough, a comprehensive history of beer production in Honduras.

Apart from the permanent historical exhibit, the museum has one gallery for rotating exhibits, and a gift shop well stocked with T-shirts, calendars, books, cards, and artwork. Outside is a small patio cafeteria. The museum is open Tues.-Sun. 10 a.m.-4:15 p.m. Admission is US 70 cents.

Centro Cultural Sampedrano

Around the corner from the museum, on 3 Calle between 3 and 4 Avenidas NO, is the Centro Cultural Sampedrano, which frequently holds concerts and dramatic performances, usually for US$3-4 per show. San Pedro's main drama group is **El Círculo Teatral Sampedrano.** For information on upcoming performances in the 420-seat theater, call 557-2575. The Centro also has a small library open to the public, stocked with books in Spanish.

RECREATION

Golf

The La Lima Golf Club, 20 minutes from San Pedro off the highway to El Progreso, tel. 668-1463, was originally built by United Fruit for its workers and guests but is now a private club open to anyone who will pay. Inscription costs US$2000, plus US$50 a month fees. Non-members may play the full 18-hole course for US$28, extra if you need to rent clubs. Generally no reservation is necessary, just ask for Nolan when you get to the clubhouse. The course is open every day. To get there, look for the Colonia Tela entrance from the El Progreso highway, just east of the Río Chamelecón.

In Choloma is the Las Lomas Golf Club, also open to non-members, tel. 553-3106.

Fútbol

For a taste of Honduras' national sporting passion, consider watching a soccer match at **Estadio General Francisco Morazán**, on 1 Calle O between 13 and 14 Avenidas. Tickets for regular season matches cost US$2-4, depending on seats; national team matches cost a bit more. Tickets can be bought in advance at the stadium, but usually it's no problem to get a ticket right before the match. If it's a sellout, scalpers will be offering tickets for not much more than face value, unless it's a league final. Crowds tend to be impassioned, but it's generally safe from hooligan-type violence, certainly not like watching a match in many European countries. Watch out for pickpockets.

ACCOMMODATIONS

San Pedro has a wide selection of hotels of all varieties and price ranges. Many of the less expensive hotels are in the southwest quadrant of the city, within 10 blocks of the square. The newer upscale hotels are generally located out on Av. Circunvalación, though the Holiday Inn and Gran Hotel Sula are both on 1 Calle Oeste in downtown.

Shoestring

The large, well-managed **Gran Hotel San Pedro**, on 3 Calle between 2 and 1 Av. SO, tel. 550-1513, fax 550-1655, is popular with foreigners and locals alike. Options range from US$7 s or US$9 d for a basic partitioned room with fan to US$16 s or US$19 d for a large room with TV and a/c, all cleaned daily. Free purified water is available, and there's a TV in the lobby. Check-out time is a relaxed 2 p.m. The hotel is close to many bus stations, particularly to destinations on the north coast.

Another low-priced good deal is **Hotel San José,** on 6 Av. between 5 and 6 Calles SO, tel. 557-1208, popular with Peace Corps volunteers. It's clean and offers tile-floor double rooms with fans and bathrooms for US$5. A step cheaper than the San José, but still not too bad, is **Hotel San Juan,** just around the corner on 5 Av. and 6 Calle SO, tel. 553-1488, with rooms as low as US$4.25 s or d with shared bathroom, or US$7.50 s or d with a private bath.

A five-story building, **Hotel Brisas de Occidente,** on 5 Av. between 6 and 7 Calles SO, tel. 552-2309, has huge, empty tile rooms looking like something out of a Paul Auster novel. Rooms are always available, and not a bad deal either if you like the slightly existential ambiance—US$4.25 for a double bed with fan, shared bath only.

Hotel Porto Alegre, east of 1 Av. on 5 Calle SE, tel. 557-2188, is a good deal, with quiet, clean, airy rooms for US$6 s or d with bathroom and fan, or US$8 with TV. Unfortunately the neighborhood is not so great, though it is centrally located near many bus stations.

Budget

Hotel Ambassador, on the second floor above some of the shops on 7 Calle between 5 and 6 Avenidas SO, tel. 557-6825, fax 557-5860, has 32 quiet rooms with a/c, TV, telephone, and hot water for US$17.50 s or d. Some rooms have balconies, and the hotel cafeteria offers room service.

Less expensive, and all in all just a better deal, is **Hotel Terraza,** on 6 Av. between 4 and 5 Calles, tel. 550-3108, fax 550-0798, charging US$14 for two beds with fan and TV, or US$15 with a/c. The restaurant in the Terraza has a large menu, acceptable food, and offers room service.

One of the lowest-priced hotels in San Pedro with a safe parking lot is **Hotel Palmira,** on 6 Calle between 6 and 7 Avenidas SO, right next to the buses to Copán, tel. 557-6522. The three-story building has 27 basic linoleum-floored rooms, all with private bathroom, with fan for US$12 s or US$15 d, or US$15 s and US$19 d with TV and air-conditioning.

Inexpensive

The **Gran Hotel Conquistador,** centrally located at 2 Calle between 7 and 8 Avenidas SO but on a quiet street, tel. 552-7605, has two floors of rooms around a narrow atrium, each with hot water, cable TV, and telephone, in a quiet, family-run hotel. Rooms cost US$23 s or US$28 d.

Hotel Ejecutivo, on 2 Calle and 10 Av. SO, tel. 552-4289, fax 552-5868, is patronized by expatriates who appreciate the quiet neighborhood, good service, and modern rooms with TV and hot water for US$31 s or US$35 d. Across the street is a second branch with 40 more rooms, a bit pricier at US$40 s or d.

In Colonia Trejo, southwest of Av. Circunvalación, is **Apart-Hotel El Almendral,** on 16 Av. B and 12 Calle B SO, tel. 556-8989, tel./fax 556-6476, a well-managed two-story hotel in a quiet, safe neighborhood. Each room has a/c, TV, telephone, hot water, a small stove, and a refrigerator stocked with drinks. Rooms cost US$38-50. Reservations are recommended as the hotel is often full. Nearby is **El Almendral II,** which does not have stoves but does have bathtubs and balconies. Both buildings have washers and dryers for guest use only and interior parking lots.

Right in the center of town, **Hotel Bolivar,** at 2 Calle and 2 Av. NO, tel. 553-3224 or 553-3218, fax 553-4823, is slightly overpriced at US$30 s or d, considering the 70 rooms are simple and dimly lit. But it does have a/c and TV, and it's quiet and centrally located.

Expensive

For years *the* hotel in San Pedro, the **Gran Hotel Sula,** facing the downtown square, tel. 552-9992 to -9999, fax 552-7000, in the U.S. (800) 223-6767, has been surpassed in quality by the newer high-end hotels, but it is still favored by many business travelers and tourists for its central location. The double rooms all have private balconies, telephone, TV, a/c, and throw rugs over tile floors and cost US$90 d or US$130 for a suite. Corporate rates are frequently available to regular travelers on request. The upscale **Granada Restaurant** serves lunch buffets and dinner à la carte, and the diner-style **Café Skandia** is open 24 hours, with a patio overlooking the small pool. The tobacco shop sells day-old U.S. newspapers and many magazines and books in English.

In the northwest part of the city at Av. Circunvalación and 15 Av. NO is **Hotel Suites Los Andes,** tel. 553-4425 or 553-2526, email: handes@mayanet.hn, a popular long-term residence for foreigners passing through San Pedro. Each of the 41 rooms has a clean kitchen, large beds, bedroom and living room areas, cable TV, a/c, and direct-line telephones. Prices are US$55 s, US$60 d, US$65 t (better rates are available for longer stays). Downstairs is **Caffe Latte,** a midrange cafe/restaurant open Mon.-Sat. 7 a.m.-10 p.m., Sunday 8 a.m.-2 p.m.

Similar to Hotel Los Andes, but closer to downtown and not quite as nice, is **Plaza Cristal Suites,** in Barrio Guamilito on 10 Av. between 1 and 2 Calles NO, tel. 550-8973, fax 550-9822. The converted apartment building rents 19 suites, each with a spacious living room, bedroom, modest-sized kitchen, a/c, color TV, and direct telephone line, US$60 s or US$70 d.

Premium

As in Tegucigalpa, San Pedro has seen a burst of high-end hotel construction, with new Princess, Camino Real, and Holiday Inn hotels springing up in 1998-99. The rates quoted below are the normal rack rates. Less expensive weekend or corporate rates are often available on request.

On 1 Calle between 10 and 11 Avenidas rises the 15-story grey tower of the new **Holiday Inn,** tel. 550-8080, fax 550-5353, in the U.S. (800) 465-4329, with 130 rooms, many with fine views and equipped with all the amenities, including a large-screen TV, two telephone lines (one for Internet), coffeemaker, iron and ironing board, and safe box. Non-smoking floors are available. The desk staff members are helpful and speak excellent English. The hotel has a cafeteria (good breakfast buffet), a small bar, and Antonio's Restaurant. Regular rooms go for US$160 s or d, up to US$1200 for the presidential suites. Corporate rates are available.

Right next to the new MultiPlaza Mall south of downtown, at the highway exit to Tegucigalpa, is the new **Camino Real,** tel. 553-0000, fax 550-6255, in the U.S. or Canada tel. (800) 327-0200, website: www.interconti.com. The hotel, with Honduran and foreign businesspeople always milling in its lobby, charges US$150-165 for most rooms, or as low as US$90 on weekends. The daily all-you-can-eat breakfast buffet at the Azulejos restaurant is not cheap at US$12, but you'd be hard-pressed to find a better breakfast in the city.

Hotel Princess, tel. 556-9600 or 556-9590, fax 550-6143, email: hotelprincess@globalnet.hn, is on Av. Circunvalación in the southwest part of the city. The hotel is not much to look at from the outside, but the rooms have all the amenities and service is top-notch. Rooms go for US$180 d, but less expensive corporate or weekend rates are often available.

An eight-story modern pink tower on the road heading out of town toward Tegucigalpa, **Hotel Copantl**, tel. 556-8900, fax 556-7890, has 200 modern, quietly tasteful rooms with TV, a/c, and direct telephone lines for US$170 d up to US$350 for a suite. Among the many facilities at the Copantl are a beauty parlor, a tobacco and gift shop selling many English-language publications, a travel center/information desk, a convention center, a casino, two bars, three restaurants, a health spa, and six tennis courts. While service at the Copantl was reputed to be slipping in recent years, the opening of three new competing high-end hotels may shape things up.

FOOD

Inexpensive

Ever popular with budget travelers and locals alike, **Cafeteria Mayan Way,** in a run-down building on 6 Av. between 4 and 5 Calles SO, has a distinctly funky yet somehow appealing atmosphere. The inexpensive meals are surprisingly tasty, considering the look of the place. Open Mon.-Sat. 6 a.m.-midnight, it's good for breakfasts, burgers, chicken, pork chops, and *plato del día*.

Cafetería Gretchen, on 5 Calle between 5 and 6 Avenidas SO, has inexpensive breakfasts, *baleadas,* burgers, and other light meals. Similar is **Comedor Merendón,** on 6 Av. between 5 and 6 Calles SO, open daily until 8 p.m.

Antojitos Mexicanos serves slightly greasy but very inexpensive Mexican-style *tortas, chilaquiles, huevos a la mexicana,* enchiladas, or tacos (US$1-2) and beer or soft drinks to wash them down. There are three locations: the *parque* above Espresso Americano, at 3 Av. between 7 and 8 Calles SO, and on Av. Circunvalación at 7 Calle SO. The *parque* branch is open Mon.-Sat. 8 a.m.-8 p.m., Sunday 9 a.m.-7 p.m., while the one on Av. Circunvalación is open daily 10 a.m.-midnight, sometimes later on weekends. Also on the *peatonal* is **Pupusería y Cafetería El Buen Sabor,** with inexpensive snacks and light meals.

Five blocks west of the square on 2 Av. O, **Costa's Burgers** is a popular lunch and snack spot serving burgers, sandwiches, and light meals. Open daily until 9 p.m. Across the street is the new addition, **Costa's Chicken and Burger.** Several clean *comedores* in **Mercado Guamilito,** between 8 and 9 Avenidas and 6 and 7 Calles NO, serve inexpensive *comidas corrientes.* Check out the handicrafts market before or after your meal.

Super Donuts, opposite the *catedral* on 2 Calle between 2 and 3 Av. SO, has an inexpensive and filling buffet breakfast.

Among the several juice stands downtown is **Super Jugos,** at the corner of 2 Calle and 6 Av. SO, open 8 a.m.-9 p.m. every day. Another is **Shakes,** on 3 Calle between 6 and 7 Avenidas SO, open Mon.-Sat. 8 a.m.-6 p.m.

Cafes

Cafetería Pamplona on the square always has a large crowd of cigarette-smoking, coffee-guzzling locals chatting or reading the newspaper at the Formica tables, and soft elevator music playing overhead. The Spanish owner, who oversees the place from behind the bar, has decorated the interior with blown-up photos of the famed running of the bulls. The espresso is very good, and the extensive menu is moderately priced at US$2.50-4 for a full entree. The breakfast—eggs, a chunk of cheese, a slice of ham, toast, coffee, and a small glass of fresh-squeezed orange juice—is a decent deal at US$1.75, though the eggs can be on the greasy side. Open daily 7 a.m.-8 p.m.

Espresso Americano on the *peatonal,* right on the corner of the *parque* and the *peatonal* pedestrian street, serves up a decent espresso in a modern, coffee-bar atmosphere. Open Mon.-Sat. 7 a.m.-7 p.m.

Café Skandia in the Gran Hotel Sula is a diner-style cafe conveniently open daily 24 hours, great for that late-night craving. The service is good, the menu is extensive, and the food reasonably priced.

Bakeries

On Av. Circunvalación between 3 and 4 Calle NO is **Deli Pan,** with a selection of tasty baked goods, as well as sandwiches and espresso coffee. Open Mon.-Sat. 7 a.m.-6 p.m., Sunday 9 a.m.-5:30 p.m.

In the center of town on 6 Ave at the corner of 3 Calle SO is **La Repostería,** an inexpensive bakery. Sweet bread and coffee there makes a good light breakfast. Open Mon.-Sat. 7 a.m.-6 p.m.

Italian

For an excellent pizza, don't miss **Pizzeria Italia,** on 1 Calle at 7 Av., west of the square, tel. 553-0094. Large pizzas, big enough for one person with a healthy appetite or two looking for a light meal, cost US$4-7 depending on ingredients. The lasagna, cannelloni, ravioli, and spaghetti are okay, but the pizza is the reason to come. The two small dining rooms are often full on weekends. Wine and beer are available. Open Tues.-Sun. 11 a.m.-10 p.m.

Nearby is **Restaurante Vicente,** on 7 Av. between 1 and 2 Calles, tel. 552-1335, owned by the same people as Pizzeria Italia. This is more of a formal restaurant, with many standard Italian dishes at reasonable prices.

In the Zona Viva is the restaurant/café **Italian Grill,** at 16 Av. and 8 Calle SO, tel. 552-1770, with a menu of well-cooked pastas and steaks at US$5-8 an entree, or US$3-6 for soups, salads, and sandwiches, served in an informal cafe atmosphere. Open Mon.-Sat. 10 a.m.-11 p.m.

Honduran

Restaurante Las Tejas, on Av. Circunvalación at 9 Calle SO, tel. 552-2705, offers well-prepared steaks, shrimp, seafood, *pinchos,* and chicken at midrange prices. Open Mon.-Fri. 10:30 a.m.-2:30 p.m. and 5-11 p.m., Sat.-Sun. 10 a.m.-10 p.m. At last report, the restaurant was undergoing renovations.

On the northwest part of Av. Circunvalación a block south of Hotel Los Andes is **La Espuela,** so popular it has replicated and now has two locations a block apart. Both offer steaks, *pinchos con anafre,* (shish kebab with hot bean dip as an appetizer), and a few other dishes for US$5-8.

Americana

Difficult to define, but definitely worth a visit, is **Fred's Kitchen,** on a block and a half west of Av. Circunvalación on 6 Calle SO in a converted house, tel. 553-1736. The restaurant, run by a U.S. native, has a friendly and attentive staff and such reasonable prices for its soups, salads, stuffed baked potatoes, nachos, and lasagna, that it attracts a lot more Honduran clients than the expatriates you might expect to see. Entrees are US$3-4. Open Mon.-Sat. 11 a.m.-11 p.m., Sunday 11 a.m.-9 p.m.

Chinese

Macau, tel. 553-4852, at the corner of 11 Calle and 14 Av. SO, is among the more popular Chinese restaurants in the *zona viva* for its menu of large, reasonably priced dishes, even if they are unexceptionally flavored. The place is clean and charges US$4-5 per large entree of *chap suey or chow min* with beef, chicken, pork, or shrimp. Open daily 11 a.m.-10:30 p.m. **Fujao,** nearby at 10 Calle between 15 and 16 Avs. SO, tel. 553-3157, is similar.

Mexican

El Mexiquense, in a residential neighborhood at 10 Calle and 14 Av. SO, tel. 557-3131, offers traditional Mexican dishes such as *mole, pierna adobada, carnitas, queso fundido, alambres,* and tacos *al pastor,* whipped up by a Mexican cook for US$3-6 per meal—very reasonable considering the quality of the food. Open daily 11 a.m.-11 p.m., later on Friday and Saturday.

Seafood

In a converted house in the *zona viva* district on 10 Calle near the corner of 16 Av. SO is **Arte Marino,** tel. 552-8046, serving excellent shrimp, ceviche, lobster, and fish filets for US$7-10 per entree. Open daily 11 a.m.-midnight.

A longtime San Pedro favorite for its well-prepared Garífuna-style seafood is **Chef Mariano,** in an eclectically decorated building on 10 Calle between 15 and 16 Av. SO, also in the *zona viva.* Open Mon.-Thurs. 11 a.m.-3 p.m. and 5-11 p.m., Friday and Saturday 10 a.m.-midnight, Sunday 10 a.m.-10 p.m.

International

Considered one of the classier spots in town, although you might not believe it looking at the fake windmill out front, **Restaurante Don Udo's,** in a residential neighborhood west of Av. Circunvalación on 1 Calle at 20 Av. O, tel. 553-3106, offers a variety of international dishes and a sizable wine list. The restaurant has indoor and patio seating and is open Mon.-Thurs. 5 p.m.-midnight, Fri.-Sat. 6 p.m.-1 a.m., and for brunch on Sunday 11:30 a.m.-2:30 p.m.

A favorite with the local jet set and business-people with expense accounts, **Pat's Steakhouse,** on Av. Circunvalación at 5 Calle SO, tel. 553-0939, is generally thought to have the best cuts of beef in town. A specialty is the *churrasco del rey* for US$13, with soup and a large salad. Quality fresh seafood is available also, and the wine list is extensive. The atmosphere is cool and casual yet elegant—proper attire and reservations recommended. Open daily noon-3 p.m. and 6 p.m.-11 p.m., until midnight on Friday and Saturday.

ENTERTAINMENT

Among the many discos in town, **Confetti's** on Av. Circunvalación, right near the Puerto Cortés exit, tel. 557-3033, is the current favorite. Cover charge ranges US$2-5, depending on the night, and ladies get in free on Thursdays. While the music is usually from a sound system, live bands sometimes play on Thursday nights. Confetti's stays open until 2 or 3 a.m. during the week and until 6 a.m. or later on weekends. The next most popular is **Henry's,** a few blocks away at Av. Circunvalación at the corner of 11 Av. NO.

For a more interesting experience, check out **Terraza's** on the corner of 15 Av. and 10 Calle SO, colorfully referred to by some locals as a "disco de la mala muerte" ("disco of the bad death") and known for its eclectic mix of artsy types, homosexuals, junkies, and hookers. Near Terraza's is the **Flamingo Night Club,** considered one of the less sleazy topless dance clubs in town. Clients pay for table dances, and pay a bit more to take the dancers home. If prostitutes are on your agenda, be sure to bring condoms, as San Pedro is the AIDS capital of Central America.

Cinemas showing first-run movies in San Pedro include **Cine Aquarius,** 10 Av. and 2 Calle NO; **Cine Gémenis,** 12 Av. and 1 Calle O; **Multicines Plaza de Sula,** 10 Av. and 4 Calle NO; and **Cine Tropicana,** 7 Av. and 2 Calle SO. The three main malls in San Pedro, the MetroPlaza Mall just north of Av. Circunvalación on the highway exit to Puerto Cortés; MultiPlaza by the exit to Tegucigalpa; and MegaPlaza by the exit to El Progreso, each have at least three screens and better sound systems than the older cinemas in the center of town. Check the *La Prensa* newspaper for the latest showings and times.

INFORMATION AND SERVICES

Exchange
Many banks in town can change dollars or traveler's checks, but the hordes of moneychangers on the square and along the *peatonal* are certainly a lot quicker and usually offer a better rate. It may seem shady to a foreigner, but there have been no reports of anyone getting robbed, nor of any problems with the authorities. Just be sensible: make sure you have the exchange rate clear in your head, and count the money. If you have doubts on the numbers, borrow the changer's calculator and check it yourself.

If the "black market" makes you nervous, try **Casa de Cambio Lempira** on 3 Av. between 4 and 5 Calles SO, open Mon.-Fri. 9 a.m.-5 p.m., Saturday 9 a.m.-noon. **Credomatic,** at Edificio Crefisa, 5 Av. and 2 Calle NO, tel. 57-4350 or 53-2404, advances cash on Visa and MasterCard with no commission.

The American Express agent in San Pedro Sula is **Mundirama Travel Service,** right next to the cathedral downtown on 2 Calle between 2 and 3 Av. SO, tel. 550-0490 or 550-1193, fax 557-9022. It's open Mon.-Fri. 8 a.m.-noon and 1-5 p.m., Saturday 8 a.m.-noon. Traveler's checks are available for sale to cardholders only, for a personal check drawn on a bank in a home country, with a 1% commission. Cardholders can also receive mail here.

Communications
The central Hondutel office, on the corner of 4 Av. and 4 Calle SO, fax 552-4923, is open 24 hours a day, but after 9 p.m. a guard lets you in. However, this is not the best neighborhood to

---

SAN PEDRO SULA USEFUL TELEPHONE NUMBERS

Police: 552-3128, 552-3171, or dial 199
Fire Department: 552-5841 or 556-7644, or dial 198
Cruz Roja Ambulance: 553-1283, or dial 195
Clinica Bendaña: 553-1618, 553-1614, 553-4437

be in at night, so try to take care of your phone calls during the day.

Correos, 9 Calle and 3 Av. SO, tel. 557-0707, is open Mon.-Fri. 7:30 a.m.-8 p.m., Saturday 7:30 a.m.-12:30 p.m., and has EMS express service. More reliable though significantly more expensive are **DHL**, in Edificio Aida, 2 Calle and 8 Av. NO, tel. 550-1000; and **UPS**, at the corner of 8 Av. and 9 Calle NO, Barrio Guamilito, tel. 557-8805, tel./fax 557-8921.

Internet

The most convenient and popular Internet shop in San Pedro is **Hondusoft**, on the first floor of a small mall on the *parque,* right behind Espresso Americano, tel. 550-4975. The half-hour minimum costs US$2. During the middle of the day there's often a wait for a computer. Open Mon.-Sat. 9 a.m.-7 p.m., Saturday 9 a.m.-6 p.m.

On 1 Calle at 10 Av. O, six blocks west of the *parque,* is **Yupi Chat,** charging US$3.50 for the half-hour minimum. Open Mon.-Fri. 10 a.m.-8 p.m., Saturday 10 a.m.-7 p.m.

Farthest from center of town, but with the best rates, is **Universal.com,** in the Santa Monica Mall behind Burger King, a few hundred yards past Av. Circunvalación at the exit toward Puerto Cortés, tel. 552-2716. It costs US$1 for the 15-minute minimum. Open Mon-Sat. 9 a.m.-8 p.m., Sunday noon-6 p.m.

Immigration

The *migración* office is half a block south of the square on the *peatonal,* on the east side of the street on the second floor, tel. 553-3728. Open Mon.-Fri. 8 a.m.-4 p.m., it offers hassle-free permit renewal.

Medical Attention

Clínica Bendaña, on Av. Circunvalación SO between 9 and 10 Calles, tel. 553-1618, 553-1614, or 553-4429, is a full-service private clinic capable of handling most medical emergencies and illnesses. Open 24 hours.

Laundry

You'll not find too many laundry shops near downtown, but one not too far away is **Dry Cleaning y Lavandería Almich,** on 5 Calle between 9 and 10 Avenidas SO, tel. 553-1687, charging US$3.50 for up to 10 lbs. of clothes, washed and dried in the same day.

CONSULATES IN SAN PEDRO SULA

Belize; Km 5 on highway to Puerto Cortés, tel. 551-0124 or 551-0707

Belgium; 4 Calle between 6 and 7 Avenidas SO, Edif. Camayaguey, tel. 550-2702 or 550-1896.

Chile; Colonia Bella Vista, 2 Calle between 33 and 34 Avenida, tel. 552-4223

Costa Rica; 3 Avenida and 13 Calle, Hotel Saint Anthony, tel. 558-0744 or 557-0790

Dominican Republic; Edif. Rivera, 6th floor, 3 Calle between 5 and 6 Avenida SO, tel. 553-0594

El Salvador; Edif. Rivera, int. 704, 3 Calle between 5 and 6 Avenida, SO tel. 553-3604

Finland; Almacén Lady Lee, exit to La Lima, tel. 553-2706 or 553-1642

France; 21 Avenida between 9 and 10 Calle NO, tel. 557-4187

Germany; 6 Av. at Circunvalación NO, tel. 553-1244 or 557-1832

Great Britain; 13 Avenida between 10 and 12 Calle SO, tel. 557-2046, fax 552-9764

Guatemala; 8 Calle between 5 and 6 Avenida NO, #38, tel. 553-3560

Haiti; Edificio Los Alpes, 8 Calle between 14 and 15 Calles NO, tel. 553-3944

Holland; Plaza Venecia, 14 Avenida between 7 and 8 Calles SO, tel. 552-9724 or 557-1815

Italy; Edificio La Constancia, 3rd floor, 5 Avenida between 1 and 2 Calles NO, tel. 553-3672

Mexico; 2 Calle and 20 Avenida SO, #205, Río Piedras, tel. 553-2604 or 553-2605

Nicaragua; 23 Avenida and 11 Calle, Col. Trejo, tel. 550-3394

Norway; Km 1 on the highway to El Cármen, tel. 557-0153 or 552-2458

Spain; 2 Avenida between 3 and 4 Calles NO, #318, Edificio Agencias Panamericanas, tel. 558-0708, fax 57-1680

In Barrio Los Andes, on the northwest part of town, near Hotel Los Andes at 7 Calle between 14 an 15 Avenidas NO, is **Lavandaría Blanco Azul,** charging US$3 per 10 lbs. for wash and dry. Open Mon.-Fri. 8 a.m.-6 p.m., Saturday 8 a.m.-1 p.m.

Tour Operators

One of the better-respected tour companies in Honduras is **MesoAmerica Travel** in Edificio Picadelli, between 2 and 3 Avenidas on 11 Calle SO, local 206, tel. 557-0332, fax 557-6886, email: mesoamerica@simon.intertel.hn, website: www.mesoamerica-travel.com. MesoAmerica offers trips to Parque Nacional Cusuco, Parque Nacional Punta Sal in Tela, Montaña de Celaque, the Mosquitia, and elsewhere in Honduras.

Explore Honduras Tours, Edificio Posada del Sol, 1 Calle and 2 Av. O, tel. 552-6242, fax 552-6239, also offers local tours and trips to Copán, the Bay Islands, and Lago de Yojoa. A day tour of a La Lima banana plantation costs US$35 pp.

Travel Agents

Two companies can arrange airline tickets. **Mundirama Travel Service,** next to the cathedral at 2 Calle SO, tel. 551-1192 or 550-0490, fax 557-9022, is also the American Express agent. **Discovery Travel,** Edificio Gold Brand, Apto. 786, on 1 Calle between 7 and 8 Calles O, tel. 550-0804, fax 550-0845, is the other local choice.

Car Rental

The several car rental agencies operating in San Pedro, all with offices in the city and at the airport, include: **Maya Rent A Car,** in town at 3 Av. between 7 and 8 Calles NO, tel. 552-2670 or 552-2671, at the airport tel. 668-3168; **Molinari Rent A Car,** at the Gran Hotel Sula, tel. 553-2639 or 552-2704, at the airport tel. 668-3178; **Toyota Rent A Car,** 3 Av. between 5 and 6 Calles NO, tel. 552-5498 or 557-2666; **Thrifty,** at the airport, tel. 668-3152 or 668-3153; **Hertz,** at the airport, tel. 668-3156 or 668-3157; and **Avis,** tel. 553-0888 or 552-2872, at the airport and in town, at 1 Calle and 6 Av. NE.

Should you for some reason be in need of a limousine while in San Pedro, **VIP Limo,** tel. 551-4998 or 992-8192, email: limo@honduras.com, provides classy and pricey service.

SHOPPING

Handicrafts

San Pedro has one of Honduras' best handicraft markets at **Mercado Guamilito,** between 8 and 9 Avenidas and 6 and 7 Calles NO. The several dozen *artesanía* stalls sell a wide variety of handicrafts from across the country, including woodwork, paintings, sculptures, weavings, and more. Also here you'll find a regular food market, many flower stalls, and several *comedores* serving light meals. It's a very pleasant place to shop—the salesfolk are all friendly, and the market is spacious and safe.

Two high-quality handicraft stores in San Pedro are **Mahchi,** on 1 Calle between 6 and 7 Avenidas O, tel. 552-9208, open Mon.-Fri. 8 a.m.-5 p.m., Saturday 8 a.m.-noon, and **Imapro,** on 1 Calle between 4 and 5 Avenidas E, tel. 557-3355, open Mon.-Fri. 8 a.m.-noon and 1-5 p.m., Saturday 8 a.m.-noon. Imapro sells mainly woodwork made in its El Progreso factory, along with T-shirts, postcards, maps, and books, while Mahchi features paintings, rugs, sculptures, and other artwork.

Danilo's is the premier store for leather goods in San Pedro, in Colonia Trejo at 19 Av. and 9 Calles SO, tel. 557-6855, open Mon.-Sat. 9 a.m.-5 p.m.

T-shirts and some artwork are often sold from stalls on the square and along the *peatonal,* though local authorities have been trying to move the vendors elsewhere.

Supermarket

One good supermarket near downtown is **Supermercado El Centro** on the corner of 2 Calle and 13 Av. SO, open Mon.-Sat. 8 a.m.-9 p.m., Sunday 8 a.m.-8 p.m. Larger and better-stocked is **Comisariato Los Andes,** in Barrio Los Andes on Av. Circunvalación at 6 Calle NO, open daily until 8:30 p.m.

Markets

The largest market in San Pedro is the **Mercado Medina-Concepción,** so named for the two neighborhoods in the southeast part of the city in which the sprawling market is located. The main market building is between 4 and 5 Avenidas and 6 and 7 Calles SE, but the surrounding streets are jammed with vendors of all variety. This is not an area all foreigners will feel comfortable walking around in and is definitely to be avoided after dark. Just up 7 Calle at 9 Av. SE is the smaller and newer **Mercado Dandy,** built in 1991 to ease the pressure on the main market.

Malls
U.S.-style malls are the latest retail rage to hit Honduras. Three large malls have sprung up in San Pedro in recent years, all with an array of high-end consumer goods, fast-food restaurants, and movie theaters. **MegaPlaza** is on the continuation of 1 Calle Este past Av. Circunvalación, heading toward the airport and El Progreso; **MetroPlaza** is just past Av. Circunvalación on the exit to Puerto Cortés; and **MultiPlaza** is at the intersection of Av. Circunvalación and the exit to Tegucigalpa, behind the Hotel Camino Real.

Books and Newspapers
The tobacco shop inside the Gran Hotel Sula carries the *Miami Herald, New York Times,* and *International Herald Tribune,* a day late for US$4. They also have a surprisingly good, though small, collection of books about Honduras, mainly in Spanish but with some in English.

Out in the Santa Monica Mall, behind Burger King on the exit toward Puerto Cortés, is **Metro Media de Sula,** tel. 552-1800, with a good selection of new English-language mysteries, classic novels, current fiction, romance novels, and a few used books, as well as a large magazine rack.

Photography Supplies
Film, including slide film, and other photography supplies are sold at **Foto Indio** on 7 Av. between 2 and 3 Calles SO; open Mon.-Sat. 7:30 a.m.-6 p.m. The **Kodak** shop on 1 Calle and 2 Av. O also sells some slide film and can develop slides, but reports say the quality is iffy. If you're desperate, **Foto Flash** on 2 Calle between 2 and 3 Avenidas NO can do basic camera repairs.

GETTING THERE AND AWAY

San Pedro is the central transportation hub for northern and western Honduras and is frequently the gateway to the country for foreign visitors on their way to the north coast or Bay Islands.

Most bus travelers in Honduras will eventually find themselves passing through San Pedro.

Air
Aeropuerto Internacional Ramón Villeda Morales, 13 km from downtown San Pedro, opened a terminal for international flights in late 1996; the old terminal now services domestic flights. At the terminal are Bancahorro and Banco Atlántida for exchanging money, Hondutel, Correos, a bookstore, duty-free shops, and a Danilo's leather store. Taxis from town to the airport cost about US$5, and there's no way to get there by bus. If you're leaving the country on an international flight, expect to pay a US$25 departure tax.

Isleña Airlines, city office at 7 Av. between 1 and 2 Calles SO, tel. 552-8335, tel./fax 552-8322, flies direct to La Ceiba twice daily (US$30 one-way) and Tegucigalpa once daily (US$30 one-way), with connections to the Bay Islands and La Mosquitia.

Sosa Airlines, tel. 668-3223 or 668-3128, flies daily to La Ceiba, with connections to Roatán and Utila. Sosa's office in town is at 8 Av. and 1 Calle SO, tel. 550-6545, open Mon.-Fri. 8 a.m.-noon, 1 p.m.-5 p.m., Saturday 8 a.m.-noon.

Taca Airlines at the airport, tel. 668-3333, flies daily to Belize City, Miami, and San Salvador. Taca has an office on Av. Cirvunvalación at 13 Av. NO in Barrio Los Andes, tel. 550-5262 or 550-5264.

American Airlines, office at Centro Comercial Firenze, 16 Av. between 2 and 3 Calles NO, tel. 558-0518 or 558-0519, at the airport tel. 668-3244, has one flight daily to Miami.

Continental, office at Edificio Shell on Av. Circunvalación at 7 Calle SO, tel. 557-4141, has a daily flight to Houston.

Iberia, office at Edificio Quiroz, 2nd floor, 2 Calle between 1 and 2 Av. SO, tel. 557-5311 or 553-4609, at the airport tel. 668-3218, flies Friday and Monday to Madrid by way of Miami.

Copa flew to Mexico City and Panama on Tuesday, Thursday, and Saturday, but at last report its flight was not stopping in Honduras. Check at the Copa office in the Gran Hotel Sula, tel. 550-5586 or 550-5583, for the latest.

AeroCaribe, tel. 557-1934, a division of Mexicana, recently inaugurated a new fight most days between San Pedro and Cancún, Mexico.

Bus

As in Tegucigalpa, bus stations in San Pedro are scattered across town. Plans are under way to build one or possibly two new central bus terminals, one in the south part of the city and the other in the north, but who knows how long it will take to get under operation. For the time being, each company maintains its own station, most of which are in the southwest (SO) quadrant of the city.

To **Puerto Cortés:** Three companies offer direct buses leaving between 6 a.m. and 5 p.m., US 90 cents, one hour. Expresos del Atlántico is on 8 Calle and 7 Av. SO; Impala is on 2 Av. between 4 and 5 Calles SO, tel. 553-3111; and Citul is on 6 Av. between 7 and 8 Calles.

To **La Ceiba:** Catisa, on 2 Av. between 5 and 6 Calles, runs 12 direct buses daily between 5:30 a.m. and 6 p.m., US$3, three hours. Buses stop at the turnoff to Tela. Buses to **El Progreso** leave from the same station frequently all day, US 60 cents, the last at 8 p.m. **Note:** This bus terminal is notorious for thieves—keep a close eye on your baggage at all times, particularly if it is stowed under the bus and you are awaiting departure. And beware of the foul restrooms, as at least one traveler was mugged inside. Those going to La Ceiba can also take the Cotuc buses to Trujillo (next listing) and get off at La Ceiba for US$2.75. Another La Ceiba company is **Tupsa,** terminal at 2 Av. between 6 and 7 Calles SO, tel. 550-5199, US$3.

To **Trujillo:** Cotuc, tel. 557-3175, runs semi-direct buses leaving six times a day between 6 a.m. and 4 p.m. from the Shell gas station on 1 Av. S between 5 and 6 Calles, US$5, six hours. Travelers can get off at Tela and La Ceiba. Cotraipbal, two blocks farther south on 1 Av., tel. 557-8470, runs the same route six times daily between 6:30 a.m. and 3 p.m. for the same price.

To **Tegucigalpa:** Companies running frequent regular buses include El Rey, on 9 Av. between 9 and 10 Calles SO, tel. 550-8355; Transportes Norteños, on 6 Calle between 6 and 7 Avenidas; Hedman Alas, at 3 Calle and 8 Av. NO, tel. 553-1316; and Saenz, on 8 Av. between 4 and 5 Calles SO, tel. 53-4969. Each offers departures usually every hour between 6 a.m. and 6 p.m., US$3.50, four hours. El Rey offers earlier departures starting at 3 a.m. Hedman Alas runs three **direct first-class buses** with a/c, TV, and

bathrooms daily from its terminal at 3 Calle and 8 Av. NO, at 5:45 a.m., 11:30 a.m., and 4:45 p.m., US$5. Saenz, at 8 Av. between 5 and 6 Calles SO, tel. 553-4969, operates six **luxury direct buses** leaving every two hours daily between a.m. and 6 p.m., US$8.

To **Siguatepeque:** Etul has local buses departing from the Shell gas station on 1 Av. S between 5 and 6 Calles every hour between 4:30 a.m. and 4:30 p.m., US$1.50, two and a half hours.

To **Comayagua:** Rivera, tel. 557-1134, and Vanessa, tel. 557-8470, next to each other on 1 Av. between 7 and 8 Calles S, both have buses frequently until 4 p.m., US$1.75, two and a half hours.

To **Santa Bárbara:** Cotisba on 4 Av. between 9 and 10 Calles SO, tel. 552-8889, runs regular buses roughly every hour between 5:20 a.m. and 6 p.m., US$1, two and a half hours, and two direct buses at 8 a.m. and 4 p.m., US$1.30, 90 minutes.

To **Lago de Yojoa:** To Pulhapanzak Falls, Peña Blanca, and La Guama, several buses leave between 10 a.m. and 4 p.m. daily from 5 Calle just east of 1 Av., US$1. Right across the street are other buses to El Mochito via Peña Blanca, every hour between 6 a.m. and 5 p.m., US$1.25.

To **Cofradia, for Parque Nacional Cusuco:** Frequent departures all day, US 25 cents, from a lot at the corner of 11 Calle and 4 Av. SO.

To **Gracias:** Gracianos has two buses a day, usually around noon and 2 p.m., US$2.50, five hours, from the same lot as the Copán buses on 6 Calle between 6 and 7 Avenidas SO, no office or telephone.

To **Santa Rosa de Copán:** Copanecos, at 6 Av. between 8 and 9 Calles SO, tel. 553-1954, runs six direct buses daily departing between 7 a.m. and 3:30 p.m., US$3, two and a half hours. Local buses, which leave frequently between 4 a.m. and 5 p.m. for US$1.75, take considerably longer—best to plan on getting a direct bus. It's also possible to ride the semi-direct buses to Nueva Ocotepeque, which stop at Santa Rosa.

To **Nueva Ocotepeque and the Guatemalan border:** Toritos at 6 Av. between 8 and 9 Calles SO, tel. 553-4930, and Congolón at 8 Av. between 9 and 10 Calles SO, tel. 553-1174, each have one direct bus a day at midnight to Aguas

DISTANCES FROM SAN PEDRO SULA

Copán Ruinas	198 km
El Progreso	28 km
La Ceiba	202 km
Nueva Ocotepeque	262 km
Puerto Cortés	57 km
Santa Bárbara	108 km
Santa Rosa de Copán	170 km
Tegucigalpa	246 km
Tela	90 km
Trujillo	440 km
Yoro	136 km

Calientes, US$7.50, four hours, as well as seven regular buses, US$4, five hours, between 7 a.m. and 3 p.m.

To **Copán Ruinas:** Casasola Express, tel. 558-1659, and Gamma both have a semi-direct bus a day at 2 and 3 p.m., respectively (US$4, three hours), and alternate local buses at 11 a.m. and 1 p.m. (US$3, four and a half hours), at 6 Calle between 6 and 7 Av.

International Bus
King Quality/Cruceros del Golfo, at 6 Calle between 7 and 8 Avenidas SO, tel. 553-3443 or 552-9519, runs one bus a day in the early morning to San Salvador via Nueva Ocotepeque. The bus is equipped with a bathroom, a/c, and TV (whether you like it or not) for the seven-and-a-half-hour drive, US$23 one-way or US$40 roundtrip.

Car
As the country's major industrial center, San Pedro Sula is well connected by paved road to the rest of the country. Highways to Santa Rosa de Copán, Nueva Ocotepeque, Copán Ruinas, Tela, La Ceiba, Trujillo, Yoro, and Tegucigalpa are all fairly well maintained and can be driven on safely year-round. During the height of the rainy season, however, road conditions tend to deteriorate.

Train
At last report, train service between San Pedro Sula and Puerto Cortés had been suspended, and officials don't think it will resume anytime

soon. For the latest information, check at the train station on 1 Av. and 1 Calle.

PARQUE NACIONAL CUSUCO

Situated on the highest reaches of the Sierra Merendón, a north-south-trending mountain range in northwestern Honduras, Cusuco covers 23,440 hectares, of which 7,690 hectares fall in the core zone above 1,800 meters. The park forms part of the watershed for the Río Motagua, on the north and west side, and for the Río Chamelecón, on the south and east. Cusuco encompasses the forests blanketing the highest peaks in the Merendón range, capped by Cerro Jilinco at 2,242 meters. Other peaks include Cusuco (2,000 meters), Cerro La Mina (1,782 meters), and La Torre (1,927 meters). In the 1950s, the forest around Cusuco was heavily logged by the Río Cusuco Company. Logging ended in 1959 when the region was declared a reserve on the recommendation of Venezuelan ecologist Geraldo Bukowski. The national park was established in 1987.

Cusuco is a popular park for both Hondurans and foreigners because of its proximity to San Pedro Sula and also for the great wealth of birdlife in the cloud, pine, and subtropical forests. Over 200 species have been identified in the park, and it's estimated that up to 300 species may actually live there. The best months for bird-watching are October to March, to see many of the migratory species as well as the permanent residents. The reserve is also inhabited by some endangered mammals, including the park's namesake, the armadillo *(cusuco)*, as well as white-faced and howler monkeys.

Getting To Cusuco
The main access to the Cusuco visitors' center is by car to Cofradía, a small town on the Santa Rosa highway 16 km from the turnoff outside of San Pedro Sula. From Cofradía continue 26 km up a dirt road through pine forests with lovely views to the village of Buenos Aires, perched on a high ridge, and then on to the visitors' center. The five kilometers between Buenos Aires and the visitors' center can be treacherous if it's been raining, and one stretch is almost too steep to drive even when it's dry, so you may want to leave your

wheels in Buenos Aires and walk the remainder. About half way up to the park from Buenos Aires, at the 1,800 meters mark and the edge of the core zone, is a gate *(tranca)* closing daily at 4 p.m., and on a few major holidays each year.

If you don't have a car, take one of the frequent buses from San Pedro to Cofradía. You can either get off at the town square and ask in the shops there for trucks heading up to Buenos Aires (they often leave in late morning or around noon), or stay on the bus to the end of the line, west of town, then walk a short distance to the start of the Buenos Aires road and hitch a ride with the first pickup to come by. From Buenos Aires, if no ride is available, it's a two-hour walk to the visitors' center.

It's possible to drive to the visitors' center straight up into the hills behind San Pedro Sula, although finding the dirt road leaving the city from the Primavera neighborhood southwest of downtown is no easy task. Ask for the road leading to Las Peñitas or El Gallito, which ends up in Buenos Aires, and from there on to Cusuco. This road is not in the best of shape but offers great views over the city and across the Sierra Merendón.

Hiking in the Park

An informative and interesting visitors' center at the end of the entrance road, with maps and displays on local flora and fauna, is the place to start your tour of the park. After looking at the displays and descriptions of the local flora and fauna, choose from a small network of four trails to hike around in the park. Ask the *vigilante* here to tell you where the three well-known birdwatching spots are. The trails—El Danto (two km), El Quetzal (one km), La Mina (two and a half km), and El Pizote (two km)—are well marked and not too steep or strenuous, but they can be muddy, so bring boots and watch your footing. Wildlife is very timid at Cusuco, so it takes patience, luck, and good binoculars to spot anything, but the forest is lovely to walk around regardless. At the northern end of Sendero El Danto is a small hut housing a local family who makes its living cultivating and selling cloud forest plants in a small outdoor nursery.

Right past the nursery begins a fifth trail, Sendero Cantiles, leading into the highest section of the park. The trail crosses the Río Cusuco and follows the river upstream on the eastern bank for a short distance, then crosses to the west side and begins a zig-zag climb up the ridge above the river. About an hour's hike from the river, the trail comes to a pass, just below Cerro Jilinco. On the far, north side, a trail once continued down the mountains to Tegucigalpita, near Omoa, in a full day's hike. Unfortunately, Hurricane Mitch triggered a major landslide just below the pass. Presumably the trail continues on the far side of the slide, but it appears to be little-used now and would be very difficult to find. So for the moment, only go as far as the pass and content yourself with exploring the forest around there. For some reason, the park organization discourages visitors from hiking out this trail, but the family running the nursery will be happy to point out the way and seems to think it's a fine place to go.

Although guides are not necessary to navigate the main trails, they can be of use in helping spot animals and birds. You can hire guides in the village of Buenos Aires, on the way to the visitors' center, or the park *vigilantes* themselves may be willing to guide for a negotiable fee. Early morning birdwatchers, or those who simply want to spend a night in the forest, may camp in one of four designated areas on the entrance road, just before the visitors' center. No camping is allowed in the park.

As at La Tigra near Tegucigalpa, entrance prices for Cusuco went up to US$10 for foreigners in 1996, a steep price to pay considering the fact that the forest is not in as pristine shape as several other parks in the country that don't cost as much. However, the location near San Pedro is certainly convenient, and the price is worth it for those who don't have the time or inclination to venture farther afield. The Fundación Hector Fasquelle in San Pedro Sula will sell you a ticket, or you can just pay the *vigilante* in the park.

For more information on the park, call or visit **Fundación Hector Rodrigo Pastor Fasquelle,** above Pizzeria Italia on the corner of 1 Calle and 7 Av. O, tel. 552-1014 or 557-6598; open Mon.-Fri. 8 a.m.-noon and 1-5 p.m., Saturday 8 a.m.-noon. Apart from a basic pamphlet and map, few practical hiking details are available, but the foundation library is an excellent source for ecological information on the park and Honduras in general. The topographical maps covering the park are the 1:50,000 Cuyamel-San Pedro Sula 2562 I, Valle de Naco 2562 II, Quimistán 2562 III, and Cuyamelito 2562 IV.

Mountain Biking in the Sierra Merendón
The Sierra Merendón is criss-crossed with dirt roads and trails that make for great mountain bike adventuring. From San Pedro, bikers can simply head west on 1 Calle past Av. Circunvalación, through La Primavera neighborhood

right into the forest, up steep dirt roads into the mountains. Some roads eventually end up in Buenos Aires and Parque Nacional Cusuco, while others branch off northward to Puerto Cortés. The best place to get details on rides is **Planet Bike,** on Av. Circunvalación at 11 Calle A NO, tel. 550-3840, open Mon.-Fri. 10 a.m.-noon, 1:30-7 p.m., Saturday 10-2 p.m. Group rides leave at 2 p.m. every Saturday after the shop closes, and newcomers are welcome to tag along. Sometimes the shop has bikes for rent.

emerald toucan

LAGO DE YOJOA AND VICINITY

Honduras' largest natural lake, Lago de Yojoa is roughly 16 km long by eight km wide, at an altitude of 635 meters, right along the San Pedro Sula-Tegucigalpa highway. Lake depth varies between about 18 and 25 meters, depending on season. The setting, backed by the majestic cloud-forested mountains of Santa Bárbara and Cerro Azul/Meámbar (both protected as national parks), is spectacular.

The extensive marshes and forests around Lago de Yojoa, located in the transition zone between the Valle de Sula and the central highlands, boasts the country's largest variety of bird species. One count put the number of species at 373. Whatever the exact number, the lake and surrounding forests are a birder's paradise. One particularly good spot is at Hotel Agua Azul or the nearby Isla del Venado.

The shores of the lake are dotted with innumerable ruins, mostly believed to be of Lenca or Maya origin, including Los Naranjos. Along with the Valle de Sula, Lago de Yojoa is thought to have been one of the most heavily populated areas in Honduras in pre-Columbian times, used as a home by the Lenca, Maya, and perhaps other groups.

Largemouth bass fishing in the lake was once legendary, attracting anglers from across the globe, but the bass population has declined due to overfishing. Much more common is nowadays is tilapia, a non-native species. Yacht and fishing trips can be arranged on the lake by contacting Richard Joint of **Honduyate,** tel. 990-9386 or 990-9387. Local fishermen, especially at Las Marías on the west side of the lake, will also be happy to arrange trips. If you go this route, it's best to come equipped with your own gear.

The lake is drained naturally on the south side by Río Tepemechín, which leads eventually into the Río Ulúa, and on the north by the Río Blanco, which has been partly channeled to power a hydroelectric plant at Cañaveral. Along the Río Lindo, a tributary to the Río Blanco, is Pulhapanzak Falls, an easily visited and very beautiful 43-meter waterfall.

Regular buses ply the roads around the lake, between Peña Blanca and El Mochito, La Guama, and Pulhapanzak Falls. If no buses are immediately apparent, just stick out your thumb—hitchhiking is fairly reliable.

LAGO DE YOJOA

Peña Blanca

Not much of a town itself, Peña Blanca lies at a major crossroads near the northwest corner of the lake. From here roads continue to El Mochito around the west side of the lake, to Agua Azul and La Guama along the north side, and along the Río Lindo past Pulhapanzak Falls to the San Pedro-Tegucigalpa highway to the north. Visitors will find no compelling reason to stop at Peña Blanca other than for transportation purposes or to grab a bite to eat.

Peña Blanca contains the only real budget-class hotel on the lake, **Hotel Maranata** (no phone), with rooms ranging from US$4 s with shared bathroom to US$10 s or d with TV and private bathroom.

Of the several low-priced *comedores,* **Cafetería y Repostería Candy,** just across the canal heading toward Agua Azul, is about the best. It offers a clean and tasty buffet for US$1.75 per meal until 7 p.m. every day. The restaurant also doubles as the local Hondutel office.

Buses leave Peña Blanca daily in late morning to San Luis Planes, a village set high on the northern flanks of Montaña de Santa Bárbara, where you can find guides to take you into the cloud forest. The road to San Luis turns off just north of Peña Blanca and takes a bit under an hour to drive in a private vehicle.

Pulhapanzak Falls

Of the several *balnearios* along the Río Lindo, a tributary of the Río Blanco north of Peña Blanca, by far the most popular is the 43-meter-high **Pulhapanzak Falls.** The falls are located just off the road leaving Peña Blanca to the north, connecting to the San Pedro Sula highway. To get to the falls, take a bus from either Peña Blanca or San Pedro Sula, and get off at San Buenaventura, which is 12.5 km from the San Pedro-Tegucigalpa highway and 10 km from Peña Blanca. From San Buenaventura, walk one km to the sign-posted turnoff to the falls. If in doubt, ask a local to point the way.

The dirt road dead-ends at a gate, where visitors pay an entrance fee of US 75 cents. Beyond is a parking lot and a few small changing rooms to put on bathing suits. Just past the changing rooms is a broad pool along the Río Lindo, just above the falls, which is great for a swim—just don't swim too close to the drop-off! On both sides of the river are plenty of shady places to take a rest.

To properly admire the falls, follow the steps down along the edge of the river to a viewpoint below. Take care to stay on the steps, as the short-cut pathway is slippery and steep. The land around this part of the river is private property and is still covered with dense forest, a visually pleasing background for the falls. A horde of local boys, some of whom speak smatterings of more than three languages, will offer their services to guide visitors to a cave behind the falls, where

Mayan artifacts are reputed to have been found. The boys will also show you a couple of great places to (safely) jump out into the water.

Back up by the gate is a restaurant and large open field, in the center of which are a few mounds covering what are thought to be Mayan-era ruins. The owners are happy to have people camp out for a nominal fee, either with a tent on the lawn or in a hammock amongst the trees. The area is usually packed on weekends and deserted during the week.

Between San Buenaventura and Peña Blanca is the hydroelectric power plant at **Cañaveral.** In front of the office are two sculptures from the Los Naranjos site, one a headless statue and the other a large dish, which were unearthed during the construction of the Río Blanco canal in 1962. Next to them is an example of one of the turbines used in the power plant.

Ruins of Los Naranjos
Along the jungly northwestern shores of Lago de Yojoa, not far from the village of El Jaral, are

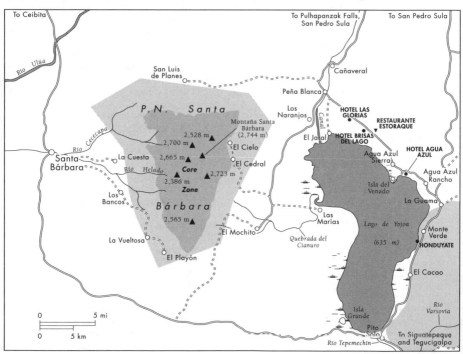

the unexcavated ruins of a pre-Hispanic settlement, thought to be of Mayan origin. The dirt road turn leading to El Jaral turns off the highway to Agua Azul just east of Cafetería Candy in Peña Blanca. Continue down about two km, where a second road branches to the right (west), which eventually dead-ends into the Río Blanco canal. In the area between this second dirt road and the shore of the lake, perhaps a kilometer to the south, several concrete and gravel pathways have been laid out through a patch of tropical forest along the lake and canal, apparently to attract tourists. Locals say the money ran out for further development of the site. The ruins themselves, buried in the bush and difficult for casual tourists to get to, are still unexcavated and sit on private property. Although the tourist project didn't quite come through, the pathways make a great place to go for a stroll in the exuberantly lush lakeside forest. Birdwatchers may find this area worth investigating, especially in the early morning, when dozens of very loud and visible bird species

Water plunges 43 meters from the lip of Pulhapanzak Falls.

make their presence known. Don't forget your binoculars or mosquito repellent.

El Mochito
On the south side of the lake, at the foot of Montaña de Santa Bárbara, is the mining town of El Mochito, currently extracting large quantities of lead and mercury from kilometers-long tunnels, some even burrowing under the lake. There's not much to interest tourists in El Mochito, but a couple of dirt roads lead from there up into the mountains via El Cielo.

Lake Shore Lodging and Food
The most popular accommodations on the lake are four km east toward La Guama from Brisas del Lago at **Hotel Agua Azul,** tel. 991-7244 or 992-8928. The rustic, slightly weather-beaten wooden cabins on a small rise above the lake cost only US$22 s or d, with fans and bathroom. The hotel has a great wooden porch restaurant offering unbeatable views out over the lake. The reasonably priced food is good, though service is slow. Pedal boats, motor launches, and fishing

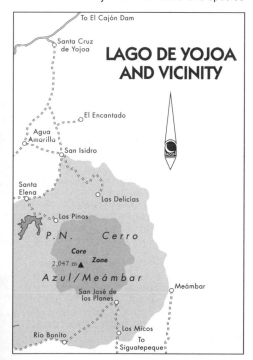

To El Cajón Dam

Santa Cruz de Yojoa

LAGO DE YOJOA AND VICINITY

El Encantado

Agua Amarilla

San Isidro

Santa Elena

Las Delicias

Los Pinos

P. N. Cerro

Core

2,047 m▲ Zone

Azul/Meámbar

Meámbar

San José de los Planes

Río Bonito

Los Micos

To Siguatepeque

trips are available. The nearby **Isla del Venado** and the rocks at **La Venta** are good places to birdwatch. Agua Azul may soon undergo a facelift and corresponding price increase, but the owner thinks they will likely keep a few lower-cost cabins for some time to come.

Also on the north shore of the lake, along the highway between Agua Azul and Peña Blanca, located one and a half km off the highway down by the lakeshore, is the more upscale **Finca Las Glorias,** tel. 566-0461 and 566-0462, renting very attractive cabins and apartments set on a grassy lawn by the water's edge, each with a/c, fans, TVs, and porch hammocks for US$45 s or d. The restaurant is a fine place to relax, and the hotel has its own small marina.

About a kilometer east of the Las Glorias entrance is **Brisas del Lago,** tel. 553-4884, with institutional-looking concrete buildings set on a hillside well away from the lakeshore. Although the rooms, which go for US$43 s or d, are actually quite nice, the buildings in which they are contained are decidedly unattractive.

Just past the entrance to Brisas on the highway heading toward Agua Azul, on the opposite side of the road, is the new **Restaurante Estoraque,** with a simple menu of burgers (US$1.75), fish dinners (US$5), and barbecued chicken (US$3.50), prepared with care in a spotlessly clean screened-in kitchen and dining room. Run by a Honduran-American couple, the restaurant is open Wed.-Mon. 8 a.m.-8 p.m.

At km 162 on the San Pedro-Tegucigalpa highway, near the village of Monte Verde on the east side of the lake, is **Honduyate,** tel. 990-9386 or 990-9387, a marina/restaurant/hotel managed by the amiable Brit Richard Joint and his Honduran wife Liliana. The small, relaxed restaurant has a variety of fish and seafood dishes (US$5-8), good breakfast omelets (US$3), and a few English specialties like shepherd's pie (US$4). The owners can arrange water ski and fishing trips, and they hire out their nine-meter yacht for full-day cruises with picnic lunch and bar service for US$120. Across the lake is a lovely, tranquil cottage at Gualiqueme owned by Honduyate, equipped to sleep up to eight people with maid service and ferry transportation for US$150 for the weekend, or US$50 for each additional night. It's a great place to go with a group of friends or family.

A couple of kilometers toward Tegucigalpa from Honduyate, also right on the lakeshore, is a strip of 20-odd fish restaurants crammed up against one another, all serving reasonably priced fresh fish and *comida típica.*

Pito Solo

At the southeast corner of the lake, where the Santa Bárbara road meets the San Pedro-Tegucigalpa highway, is the village of Pito Solo. The only rooms available are at **Los Remos,** tel. 552-0618, a one-level ranch-style place reminiscent of, in the words of one guest, the Bates Motel. Rooms are none too great and cost US$10 s or US$20 d.

From Pito Solo it's 157 km to Tegucigalpa, 97 km to San Pedro Sula, and 53 km to Santa Bárbara.

Cavernas de Taulabé

Approximately 17 km south of Pito Solo, at Km marker 140, are the Cavernas de Taulabé, which have been explored to a depth of 12 km without hitting the bottom. The first few hundred yards of the cave have been lit and have steps, but beyond that bring a flashlight and watch your footing. It might be best to hire a guide for exploring, as it's easy to get lost. Entrance costs US 40 cents, guides go for US$3-4 for a couple of hours. Ask about the legendary *bandito* who hid out in the caves for months. Locally made honey is frequently sold along the highway near Taulabé.

PARQUE NACIONAL CERRO AZUL/MEÁMBAR

Looming over the eastern side of Lago de Yojoa, and frequently shrouded in clouds, is a sheer-walled massif of mountain peaks cloaked in lush green forests, protected as Parque Nacional Cerro Azul/Meámbar. The park covers just over 400 square km ranging between 415 and 2,080 meters, supporting (from lower to upper elevations) coffee plantations, lowland humid forests, pine forest, and cloud forest. On one of the highest peaks in the center of the park is a rare elfin forest, similar to the one in Sierra de Agalta, Olancho, a bizarre ecosystem of stunted oak and pine trees, covered with moss and lichen.

Because of its location at the transition from the hot northern lowlands to the cooler, more arid mountain country of central Honduras, Cerro Azul/Meámbar supports an unusually diverse animal population, though the wildlife faces severe pressure from its human neighbors, who usually view animals either as pests or potential meals. But even in the coffee plantations on the lower stretches of the mountains, many of the park's 170 bird species can be seen screeching noisily and flitting about in the trees. And in the park's upper sections, reachable only by a multi-day hike, at least 50 (and possibly more) species of mammals make their homes.

Cerro Azul/Meámbar plays a vital role in Honduras' electric power generation, supplying some 80% of the water used by the huge El Cajón dam to the east, and 20% of the water to Lago de Yojoa, which in turn supplies the smaller hydroelectic plant at Cañaveral. No doubt recognizing the importance of the mountain's ecosystem to the national economy, the Honduran government has turned over administration of the park, temporarily at least, to Proyecto Aldea Global (Project Global Village), a non-profit organization linked to the Mercy Corps, a U.S.-based relief agency. Aldea Global began working in the area in 1984 and in 1992 signed a contract with the Honduran government to administer the park until 2002.

One of the best-respected of the dozens of NGOs operating in Honduras, Aldea Global funds a host of socially oriented projects in the 42 communities located within the park limits, in an effort to increase environmental awareness and protect the park as well as to improve the standard of living of the local residents. The group has also built a visitors' center, several cabins, and a few trails, making a one-day or an overnight trip to the park easily possible from either San Pedro Sula or Tegucigalpa. And for those looking to go on longer hikes, it's possible to find guides in several different communities around the edge of the park.

A new park center has been built at El Cacao, at km 160 of the San Pedro Sula-Tegucigalpa highway on the southeastern shore of Lago de Yojoa, though construction was not yet completed at last check. The center was due to open by the middle of 2000 and is expected to have several displays on the park's flora and fauna, as well as historical, archeological, and cultural information on the region.

Los Pinos

In Los Pinos, an *aldea* seven kilometers from La Guama via a dirt road (4WD only) passing through Santa Elena, Aldea Global operates three cabins for visitors who would like to spend the night in the park. The local caretaker will be happy to open up the cabins and let you sleep in a bunk for US$3 pp. A few wool blankets are available, but better to bring a sleeping bag anyway. While the cabins are usually empty, Aldea Global sometimes hosts large groups of visitors from other countries, so you may want to contact the office in Siguatepeque to be sure there will be space. Kitchen service can also be arranged through Aldea Global.

While a good portion of the forest around the cabins is secondary growth, it is in good condition and thriving with birds and other animal life. From the cabins, trails lead into the forest for exploration. The shorter trail, Sendero Venado, only a 20-minute walk, leads to a small waterfall, Cascada Los Bencejos. The longer Sendero Mirador trail loops across the top of a high ridge in a couple of kilometers, offering great views if the weather permits. It's possible to camp out on the high point of the trail, to enjoy a night in the forest and the views for sunset and sunrise. Climbing farther up into the mountains on this side is quite difficult, though not impossible if you hire a guide in Los Pinos.

Perched high on the side of the mountain overlooking Lago de Yojoa, the cabins at Los Pinos are a lovely place to go if you'd like to experience a Honduran mountain forest but don't have the gear, time, or inclination for a full-on camping trip. If you don't have a 4WD-vehicle or a ride with someone who does, hitch a ride or walk the three km from La Guama to Santa Elena, then walk the remaining four km through coffee fields, past a small dam, and up to Los Pinos.

Elsewhere in the Park

Los Pinos is by far the easiest entrance to the park, but it is also possible to hike in from several communities on the north, east, and south sides of the mountains. One route from the north side is via the village of San Isidro, six and a half km from the San Pedro Sula-Tegucigalpa highway on a rough dirt road. Look for the turnoff marked El Bambú, a couple of kilometers past Lago de Yojoa going toward San Pedro Sula. Southeast of San Isidro, an even rougher road continues about the same distance again to **Las Delicias,** where guides know the way up a several kilometer trail to the **Río Canchilla.** The steep river valley, lined with rocky bluffs and towering cliffs, is said to be very scenic.

Aldea Global has an office at San Isidro, which is generally not equipped to provide information to tourists but can help find reliable guides. North of San Isidro, another dirt road leads to Santa Cruz de Yojoa—follow this road one and a half km, take a right turn at a junction in a grove of orange trees, and continue another kilometer and a half to **El Encantado,** a visitors' cabin similar to the one in Los Pinos, but not in such a nice setting and without forest trails nearby. Nevertheless it may be convenient for those hiking on this side of the park. The cabin *vigilante,* Juan de la Cruz Turcios, can guide hikers into the mountains.

On the south side of the park, the *aldea* of **San José de los Planes,** right at the edge of the park's core zone, is a good base to find guides and start a hike. San José is reached by a rough dirt road from Siguatepeque. There are many forks along the way—just keep asking for the road to Los Micos, a village shortly before San José. Hitchhiking is possible from Siguatepeque, if you get out to the road early enough in the morning. You might ask at the Aldea Global office in Siguatepeque if they know of any rides heading out that way, or for recommendations on guides.

As you may have guessed, getting into the central, highest section of Cerro Azul/Meámbar is no small feat. The topography is daunting, to say the least, and there are no well-developed trails, only faint footpaths used by the occasional hunter. The determined, well-prepared hiker with a guide and sharp machete could probably make it in and back from Las Delicias or San José in three or four days. Typically guides earn US$7-10 per day, plus food.

Park Information
Although Aldea Global's central office is in Tegucigalpa, the office in charge of administering the park—the best place to get hiking information—is in Siguatepeque. The office is outside of town, on the old exit to La Esperanza (as op-posed to the main highway exit). The Aldea Global, tel. 773-0539, is a block behind the Iglesia Evangélica Betel, a yellow church with a pink bell tower on the right side of the road. The best person by far to talk to is Alexis Oliva, who has worked in the park for years and is an avid hiker himself.

Topographical maps covering the park are 1:50,000 Taulabé 2660 III and Santa Cruz de Yojoa 2660 IV.

El Cajón Dam
On the eastern side of Cerro Azul/Meámber, gathering a large part of the mountain's water, is the massive Represa General Francisco Morazán, otherwise known as El Cajón Dam. Completed in 1985, this huge dam on the Río Humuya supplies a good portion of the country's electric power. The watershed of El Cajón is severely deforested, a fact which gravely threatens the long-term viability of the dam. The absence of trees reduces the amount of water captured by the surrounding watershed and has also led to massive soil runoff from the deforested hillsides, which can destroy the dam machinery. Despite tree planting campaigns and the almost superhuman efforts of Aldea Global, the situation shows little sign of improving.

Though perhaps not on top of the list of most tourists, anyone with some time on their hands or a particular interest in monumental engineering may enjoy visiting the dam, an easy half-day trip from San Pedro Sula by private car or a full-day trip by bus. The dam administration offers tours of the dam's inner workings on weekends—get there by 10 a.m. on Saturday or Sunday, and ask the guard to call ahead for a tour. The tours, guided by young engineering students, are reportedly quite fascinating.

The easiest way to reach the dam is by private car, turning off the San Pedro Sula-Tegucigalpa highway 56 kilometers from San Pedro, toward Santa Cruz de Yojoa. Just before reaching Santa Cruz, a well-maintained side road turns toward the dam, 23.5 km farther on. After 12 km, at the crest of where the road crosses a ridge into the Río Humuya watershed, an Army gate is reached, where visitors must register and receive a written pass. Show the pass at a second Army post, three and a half km down the hill, and continue down to another gate, which the guard will open to let you pass. Just below the gate is a fork—turn to the right and wind up and around the edge of a hillside to the top of the dam, four km farther. Here you can park your car, wander out across the top of the massive structure, and peer over the side for heart-stopping views down to the dam's base, well over 200 meters straight down. At one side of the entrance to the walkway is a monument to 25 workers who died during the dam's five-year construction.

It is possible to reach the dam by bus from Santa Cruz de Yojoa, though visitors must stop to register themselves at the first Army post, then wait for another bus or a *jalón* farther on.

DEPARTMENT OF YORO

EL PROGRESO

An unattractive, hot agricultural city of 124,000 on the east bank of the Río Ulúa, El Progreso offers little to interest tourists. Most foreigners who find themselves in El Progreso are changing buses on their way between San Pedro Sula and Tela, a route that still does not have direct service. The only reason to delay your departure might be to check out two souvenir shops in town. The large **Imapro** shop, at the exit to Tela, tel. 666-2200 or 666-4949, has a large selection of Honduran handicrafts and tourist collectibles. **Mahchi,** a block from the main highway junction, tel. 647-0221, has some good quality Honduran paintings, folk art, and clothing.

Practicalities
Near the exit to Tela, a block behind the Dippsa gas station, is **Hotelito Max** (no phone), offering basic, concrete rooms with bathrooms for US$8 d for one bed, US$10 d two beds. The hotel has an interior parking lot. Better is **Hotel Las Vegas,** two blocks east of the main bus terminal, tel. 647-4667, with a range of rooms, from US$8.50 s or d with one bed and fan to US$14 for two beds, a/c, and TV. Downstairs is the **Restaurante Copa Dorada,** open 7 a.m.-midnight with room service available.

The best place in town is **Hotel Casa Blanca,** on the highway exit toward Tela, tel. 647-1926 or 647-1954, with 20 large and quiet rooms, each with telephone, a/c, and TV for US$20 s or d, more for a larger room.

El Pichón, across from the main bus terminal, is a good place to grab snacks and fresh juices while awaiting your bus. Next door is **Cafeteria La Cumbre,** with decent inexpensive meals.

Dollars and traveler's checks can be changed at Bancahorro and Banco Atlántida, both right in the center of town.

Buses to San Pedro Sula and Yoro depart from the main bus terminal, just off the square. San Pedro buses leave frequently all day long until 7 p.m., US 40 cents, 20 minutes; to Yoro every hour or so between 5 a.m. and 5 p.m., US$1.30, three and a half hours; to Morazán (for Pico Pijol), every hour between 6 a.m. and 6 p.m., US 70 cents, two hours. Transportes Ulúa, tel. 666-3270, runs four direct buses a day to Tegucigalpa, US$5, three hours.

Buses to Tela leave from a different stop, four blocks west of the main terminal. Direct buses leave Mon.-Fri. at 3 p.m. and 4:15 p.m., Sat.-Sun. 8 a.m. and 8:45 a.m., US$1, 45 minutes. Try to plan on the direct bus, as local buses take about two hours and seem to stop every kilometer.

El Progreso is connected to San Pedro by a new, 28-km, four-lane highway passing La Lima and the airport. Continuing north to Tela, the highway narrows to two lanes but is still in fairly good condition. East and south, a road cuts from El Progreso back to the San Pedro-Tegucigalpa highway at La Barca, passing Santa Rita. From Santa Rita another two-lane paved road winds up into the mountains to Morazán and Yoro. At Santa Rita, on the turn to Yoro, is the very good **Comedor El Triángulo,** a favorite stop for La Ceiba-Tegucigalpa buses for the inexpensive and hearty buffet. It even has scrambled eggs with spinach in the morning, for the Popeyes among us. Open daily 6 a.m.-6 p.m.

MORAZÁN AND PICO PIJOL

Morazán
Morazán, a dusty town of 8,500 set two km off the Yoro highway, is 45 km from Santa Rita in

the middle of the Valle de Cataguana, below the Sierra de Pijol. Morazán makes a good base for visiting Parque Nacional Pico Pijol, as it's the closest town with lodging and supplies. Located a kilometer or so off the highway, Morazán is strung along a bumpy east-west dirt road, with a Dippsa gas station in the middle to serve as a reference point.

The one place to stay in town is **Hotel Kike** (no phone), a block off the main street on the eastern side of town, charging US$7.50 s or d with one bed for a decent room with private bath in a large, two-story concrete building.

About the best food to be had is at **Marina Cafeteria,** on the main street two blocks east of the gas station, with a variety of breakfasts, snacks, and light meals, like burgers, beef and vegetable soup, and fried chicken at US$1.50-3 a plate. The thatched-hut patio, open until 9 p.m., is a good spot to relax with a beer. Across the street is **Comida Buffet,** a cafeteria-style restaurant with a buffet three meals daily.

A few blocks uphill from the gas station, next to the small *parque,* is the local Hondutel office. If it's closed, which seems to frequently be the case, the little snack stand in the center of the *parque* will allow customers to use its phone for national calls, for a fee.

The local Cohdefor office, one block uphill from the gas station, then one block to the left, has some limited information on Pico Pijol but on the whole is not geared for prospective campers and hikers. **EcoPijol,** a local environmental group with a small office next to Hondutel on the *parque,* may have more useful information but was closed at last check.

Campers will find several stores in town offering the usual assortment of packaged foods, while a good selection of fruits and vegetables can be found in the many stands lining the main street.

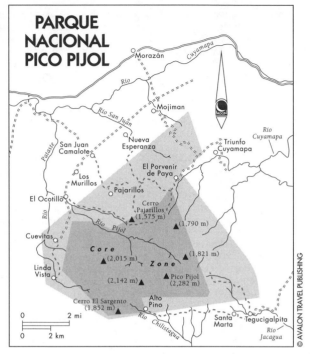

Parque Nacional Pico Pijol

A little-explored cloud forest reserve, the sheer-walled mountains of Pico Pijol are a major water source for the El Cajón reservoir and San Pedro Sula. The land has been set aside as a protected area more in the interests of resource conservation than tourism. No trails have been developed in the 11,206-hectare park, apart from those used by local hunters, but it is possible to explore the upper reaches of the forest with the help of guides and a machete. The imposing rock massif has several peaks, the highest being Pico Pijol, at 2,282 meters. On the western edge of the massif rises Cerro El Sargento, 1,852 meters, from where you can see San Pedro Sula on a clear day. Four major rivers flow off the mountains: Río Pijol, Río Pataste, Río Chilistagua, and Río Jacagua.

Much of the mountains' lower-elevation forest cover has been cut down to make room for coffee plantations, *milpas* (cornfields), or grazing land, but the core zone of the park, above 1,800 meters, is still in good shape. The south side of the Río Pijol Valley is particularly pristine, due to the precipitously steep mountain slopes.

Hikers aiming to get into the central, highest section of the park can choose between several potential access routes. From Morazán, the quickest way is from the village of Porvenir de Paya, reached by pickup truck or foot via Mojimán. In Porvenir, Cohdefor workers Lilian Torres or José María Hernández can help find a guide to take visitors into the park. Another option is to go in from the southeast side of the park, from the *aldea* of Alto Pino, the end of a dirt road turning off the Morazán-Yoro highway several kilometers east of Morazán. Near the village of Tegucigalpita, before Alto Pino, is a major cave system of unknown depth, with wide chambers and an underground waterfall near the cave mouth. It's also possible, though with a bit more difficulty, to hike up the steep slopes on the southwest side, near Cuevitas, into the center of the mountains.

Along the Río Pijol, reached from the village of El Ocotillo, is a triple waterfall called **Las Piratas,** an excellent swimming spot surrounded by forest, a short 20-minute walk from the road. Visitors can get out to Las Piratas and back to Morazán in the same day without any difficulty, catching rides on pickup trucks or walking from Morazán via San Juan Camalote. Buses do go out to some of the villages in the park from Morazán, but the schedule changes regularly, so you have to ask in Morazán for departure times.

With the bridge down near El Pataste after Hurricane Mitch, the best route to Porvenir de Paya or Las Piratas is via a dirt road leaving just west of the Morazán *desvío,* which fords the Río Cuyamapa at a relatively shallow spot, suitable for 4WD only and even then only if it hasn't been raining much. If the river is too high to cross here, walkers can get catch a ride to *desvío* La Regina, a turnoff from the Yoro highway between El Negrito and Morazán, between Km 37 and 38 near a Fusep police post. Here, where the old Pataste bridge was swept away by Mitch, a foot bridge provides the only "dry" connection across the river in the entire valley. From the far side of the bridge, a dirt road continues through Pataste to San Juan Camalote and Las Piratas waterfall.

For more information on Pico Pijol, contact the office of **EcoPijol** in Morazán. Ecopijol dis-

penses pamphlets and maps of the park. If the Peace Corps currently has volunteers in Morazán, they are often good sources of information on the park. The **Cohdefor** office in Morazán also has a large topographical wall map that can give you an idea of the park's geography. Topographical maps covering the park are 1:50,000 El Negrito 2661 I and Las Flores 2661 II.

YORO AND VICINITY

Yoro
Beyond Morazán, the highway winds up into the hills to the east before descending on the far side into the Valle de Yoro. At the eastern end of the valley is Yoro, a major market town for the region. This is the end of the paved road, some 110 kilometers from Santa Rita. The church in Yoro holds the remains of Padre Manuel de Jesús Subirana. Known as La Santa Misión, he was a tireless missionary and protector of the native Tolupan in Yoro; he died 27 November 1864. Subirana is still revered among the *campesinos* of central Honduras, many of whom consider him a saint.

There's not much for tourists in Yoro itself, but it serves as a base to visit the nearby **Parque Nacional Montaña de Yoro** and the colonial mission church of **Luquigüe.**

THE RAIN OF FISH

One and a half kilometers southeast of the town of Yoro, a swampy field called El Llano del Pántano is the site of a most unusual annual rainstorm, according to local legend. During the height of the rainy season, usually sometime in mid-June, a fierce storm will hit in the middle of the night, and in the morning residents find the fields full of flopping fish! The annual event has become known as the "Lluvia de Pesces," "Rain of Fish."

More skeptical minds have theorized that the fish come upriver from a tributary of the Río Aguán and use the inundation of heavy rain to reach the marsh, where they are accustomed to laying their eggs. Reportedly, some Japanese scientists traveled to Yoro not long ago to solve the mystery—and came away mystified.

Hotels in Yoro include the three-story **Hotel Nelson,** tel. 671-2269, US$6-10, depending on whether you get TV and a/c or not, and **Hotel Anibal** on the square, tel. 671-2228, US$7 s or US$10 d. Both hotels have decent restaurants, and the one at the Nelson is on the top floor of the four-story building, offering great views over the town and surrounding valley. A half-block down from Banco Atlántida on the square is **Restaurante Calle Real,** with well-prepared and inexpensive meals either from a buffet or off the menu, open daily 7 a.m.-9 p.m.

Banco Atlántida on the east side of the square can change dollars, and across the street is Hondutel and the post office. On the second floor of the kiosk in the middle of the square is **AMY,** or Asociación de Amigos de la Montaña de Yoro, where visitors can get some information on the nearby park.

Frequent buses depart Yoro for El Progreso until mid-afternoon (US$1.30), three and a half hours. Twice daily buses cross the mountains northeast to Olanchito when the road is in good condition, the last at noon (US$3, four and a half hours). Buses leave twice a day south to Sulaco, US$1.25, two and a half hours, with stops at Yorito, and San Antonio. Buses formerly ran east through the mountains to Minigüile and La Unión in Olancho, near Parque Nacional La Muralla, but these have been discontinued due to the deterioration of the road and occasional banditry. Private pickups still run the route and will take passengers on the three-hour ride, usually leaving by late morning at the latest. Ask at the market on the main street.

The scenic dirt mountain road to Olanchito (63 miles) via Jocon is generally in good condition and takes two hours in a private car. Be sure to check in Yoro on the current state of the road, as the rains sometimes cut off through traffic. The road to La Unión has exceptionally lovely scenery, but it is in very bad shape and has a reputation for not being safe, so it's best not to drive out that way.

Parque Nacional Montaña de Yoro
Just south of Yoro is this broad, forest-blanketed mountain, in theory reserved as a national park, though environmental protection and tourist infrastructure are pretty much nonexistent. The park covers 15,366 hectares, about one-third of which falls in the department of Yoro and the remainder in the department of Francisco Morazán. Although the cloud forest atop the mountain (2,282 meters) is fairly intact, wildlife is scarce what with the local *campesinos* frequently venturing up to hunt game.

The best access to the park is via the village of **San José Machigua.** To get there, catch a ride or walk three kilometers from Yoro to the Presa de Yoro, a small dam on the Río Machigua. From here it takes three hours to walk to San José, located at the transition between pine and broadleaf forest. In Machigua, visitors can hire a guide (US$7 a day, plus food for the guide) to take them up to the summit in a full day's walk. Ask for Lázaro Bueso Ramos in Machigua, who works for Cohdefor and can find guides. It's best to avoid the eastern and southern sides of the park, which are known for marijuana production.

For more information on the park, either stop in at the AMY office on the second floor of the kiosk on Yoro's central square, or go to Cohdefor's natural resources office outside of town, just off the El Progreso road, tel. 671-2355. At last check the Cohdefor office was manned by the friendly and helpful George Bustillo, who was happy to help tourists and even speaks a bit of English.

South of Yoro
Some 25 kilometers west of Yoro on the highway to Santa Rita, just before the village of Punta de Ocote, a dirt road turns southward to Yorito and Sulaco. At Yorito, 12.5 km down this road, a side road continues six km farther to **Luquigüe,** a colonial mission church established in 1751 by Franciscan missionaries in an effort to convert the Tolupan Indians who lived in the region at that time. The friars were generally unsuccessful; the Indians were kept there only by force and fled whenever possible. The mission was abandoned shortly after independence from Spain in 1821. The single-domed, whitewashed church, seemingly long forgotten in this isolated little village surrounded by pine-forested mountains, is worth seeing more for the atmosphere and surrounding countryside than the structure itself. Ask around for the *mayordoma,* who will give you the key to go inside to see two simple carved wooden *retablos* (altarpieces).

The next major town south of Yorito is San Antonio, known for a lovely natural bridge with a river cutting through it, called **Puente Natural de San Antonio.** The bridge, about six meters high and some 20 meters long, is a kilometer outside of San Antonio—ask anyone in town to point the way. Keep an eye out for a large ceiba tree, which marks the spot. Inside the cave are fine spots to swim in the Quebrada Los Anises, as well as thermal waters cascading down from the roof! It's a lovely spot to camp, and no one will bother you, except during Holy Week when locals come to enjoy the waters.

The mountains on either side of the Yoro-Sulaco road are the last bastion of the Tolupan, who once lived from the Guatemalan border to Olancho. In many of the mountain villages a few elders still speak the language, but it is fast disappearing except in a few isolated communities, particularly around Montaña de la Flor. The best way to get to the main settlement at Montaña de la Flor is via Cedros, north of Tegucigalpa.

Chalmeca

A tiny village on the banks of the Río Jalegua some 15 km northeast of Yoro, Chalmeca is home to a simple chapel containing a carved wooden black Christ statue, venerated by the many inhabitants of Yoro and surrounding parts of north-central Honduras. According to the local legend,

THE TOLUPAN OF MONTAÑA DE LA FLOR

Formerly one of the most widespread indigenous groups in Honduras, the Tolupan—or Jicaque, as they are called by *ladinos*—now number fewer than 1,000. Almost all of them live in one community, deep in the mountains forming the border between the Yoro and Francisco Morazán Departments.

In pre-conquest times, the Tolupan lived across a wide swath of present-day Honduras from northern Olancho almost all the way to the Guatemalan border. Unlike the Pech, a neighboring indigenous group who came originally from the jungles of South America, the Tolupan are thought to have migrated to Honduras from the southwestern United States, as their language is closely related to that of the Sioux.

Because the Tolupan refused to convert to Catholicism, opting to fight or retreat into the mountains rather than accept Spanish rule, they were a constant target of colonists needing laborers. Many thousands are thought to have died in the construction of the fortress at Omoa, and countless others were enslaved or perished working in dye factories or transporting sarsaparilla.

By the mid-19th century, only about 8,000 Tolupans still clung to their traditional ways in the mountains of Yoro, living in villages surrounded by wooden palisades deep in the forests and avoiding contact with outsiders whenever possible. Unfortunately for these remaining communities, they happened to live in an area rich in sarsaparilla; in the 1860s, the world market for this root boomed when adding it to beverages became all the rage. The governor of Yoro, Jesús Queróz, ordered his soldiers to force the Tolupans to gather the root year-round, even in the torrential rainy season, and march it to the coast at Trujillo or Tela.

This bleak period of slavery, which continued into the 20th century, is burned deep into the minds of the surviving Tolupans. They still speak of how, when an Indian died from exhaustion or disease while carrying sarsaparilla, the soldiers only stopped the column long enough to redistribute the dead man's load, but not long enough to bury him.

A group of three Tolupan families, desperate to flee the Yoro soldiers and live in peace, learned of an unpopulated forest on the far side of the Montaña de Yoro, out of the jurisdiction of the Yoro governor. They escaped there in 1864, just ahead of pursuing soldiers. The small group, led by men who had taken the names Juan Martínez, Francisco Martínez, Pedro Soto, and León Soto, settled in a region called Montaña de la Flor, at that time raw forest.

The village of Montaña de la Flor now has about 600 inhabitants, all descendants of those first three families, and it is the only Tolupan community retaining some of its original traditions. Most villagers still speak Tolupan, although all also speak Spanish. They do not drink alcohol, do not practice Catholicism, and for the most part disdain surrounding *ladino* villagers and their money-oriented ways.

How long their traditional ways will continue is uncertain, as Montaña de la Flor can now be reached by road from nearby *ladino* villages and towns, and some Tolupans have married with *ladinos*. One can hope they will fare better than their former compatriots in Yoro, who only vaguely remember their Tolupan past.

the statue miraculously appeared at the foot of an oak tree next to the river at an unknown date in the past and was found by José María Solórzano, who built the chapel to house the statue. By the time Padre Manuel de Jesús Subirana arrived to Yoro in the mid-19th century, the Cristo Negro was already famed in the region, and story has it the Padre paid a visit to Chalmeca to see the statue for himself. On the first of January each year, pilgrims from Yoro and nearby parts of Olancho come to Chalmeca to pay their respects and hold the annual festival for the Cristo Negro.

SANTA BÁRBARA AND VICINITY

SANTA BÁRBARA

At the foot of the towering Montaña de Santa Bárbara, cupped in the lush, hot lowlands not far from the Río Ulúa, Santa Bárbara is the capital of the department of the same name, and a major market town for surrounding countryside. There's not a lot to do in town except chat with the friendly locals, but the exceptionally beautiful mountain country around Santa Bárbara, dotted with lovely little villages, is well worth exploring. The region produces large quantities of coffee and is famed for making hats, baskets, and other crafts from the local *junco* palm.

History
Santa Bárbara was founded in 1761 by several families who moved to the region from Gracias, reportedly escaping usurious priests. Santa Bárbara remained relatively small until April 1815, when the nearby town of Tencoa, one of the first Spanish settlements in Honduras, was flooded by the Río Ulúa. Tencoa's surviving inhabitants moved to Santa Bárbara, and the combined population made it the biggest town in the area.

Sights
The 110-year-old **Catedral de Santa Bárbara** facing the town square (Parque Central) features an intricately carved wooden altar with painted statues of saints. Just outside of town are two *balnearios* in rivers coming off the mountain—**La Torre** and **Santa Lucía.**
   A visit to the long-abandoned **Castillo Bográn** in the hills above Santa Bárbara makes a great day trip. From the square, get someone to point out the castle, visible on a ridge southeast of town. The castle is four km from Santa Bárbara on a dirt road leading to the village of Las Crucitas. Pickups occasionally drive the road and will give you a lift for a few *lempiras,* or you can walk it in one or two sweaty hours, depending on your pace. Up close the deserted castle is not as impressive as it looks from below, but the views are majestic.

Accommodations
Most hotels in Santa Bárbara are on the lower end of the price scale, but comfortable rooms can be found without difficulty.
   Gran Hotel Colonial, one and a half blocks from the square going toward the hills, tel. 643-2665, features two floors of clean, tile-floored rooms around a small courtyard. Rates range from US$8 s or d with a communal bathroom to US$9 s or d with private bathroom and TV. All rooms have fans; a/c is available for a slightly higher price.
   One block southeast of the square is **Boarding House Moderno,** tel. 643-2203, a large, quiet building charging US$8 s with bathroom, US$9 with hot water, US$13 d with fan and hot water. The front desk sells sodas and fruit juices. For less money, **Hotel Santa Lucía,** two blocks north of the square, tel. 643-2531, is a good value at US$3 s with shared bath, US$5 s with private bath, US$7 d private bath. The tile rooms are clean and have fans.

A block east of the square is the ultra-cheap **Hospedaje Rodriguez** (no phone), for the real *lempira*-pincher at US$2 s, US$3 with private bath. The tiny rooms are often full.

Food and Entertainment

The best meals in town are at **Mesón Casa Blanca,** an unusual set-up. Food is served in the house of a middle-class Santa Bárbara family, two blocks southeast of the square. Decorated with paintings, old photographs, and sculptures, it feels a bit like eating in your grandmother's house. Three reasonably priced set meals are served daily during standard eating times (7-9 a.m., noon-2 p.m., and 6-8 p.m.).

Decent chicken, as well as burgers and *comida típica,* can be had at **Cafetería Pollo La Cesta,** half a block from the square on Av. Independencia; open daily until 9 p.m.

Charly's, on the northeast corner of the square, is a good spot for *baleadas,* tacos, pastries, juices, yogurt, and other snacks; open daily

8 a.m.-9 p.m. **Arco Iris,** on the southeast corner of the square, adjacent to the cathedral, has inexpensive fresh juices, *licuados,* and ice cream. Across the street from Hotel Colonial and down the street a bit is **Cafeteria Colonial,** with reasonable, inexpensive *comida típica.*

Weekend dance parties are held at **Disco Chalet El Tejado,** next to Hondutel. The town **cinema** is on the northwest corner of the square.

Information and Services

Hondutel, open Mon.-Fri. 7 a.m.-5 p.m., receives faxes at tel. 643-2550. Correos is right next door, a block south of the square. Banco de Occidente and Bancahsa will usually change dollars but not always traveler's checks.

Hammocks of fair quality are sold by inmates of the local penitentiary, who are always amused to see foreign visitors. The penitentiary is a block down the hill west of the square.

Estela de Zamora, on Av. Independencia, is one of the finer stores in town selling *junco*-palm

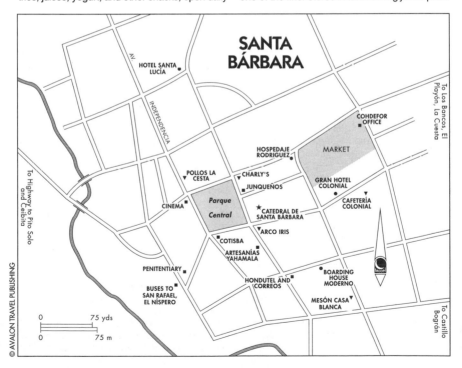

SANTA BÁRBARA

© AVALON TRAVEL PUBLISHING

goods. The owners have been in business for 30 years and are happy to explain the differences in quality of the various products. Another store is **Artesanías Yahamala,** just south of the *parque,* tel. 643-2905.

Getting There and Away

Junqueños, tel. 643-2113, runs buses twice daily to Tegucigalpa, leaving Mon.-Fri. at 7 a.m. and 2 p.m., Sat.-Sun. 9 a.m. and 2 p.m.; US$2.20, four and a half hours. The office, right next to the church on the square, also sells some handicrafts.

Cotisba, tel. 643-2387, runs buses roughly every hour between 4 a.m. and 5 p.m. to San Pedro Sula, US$1, three hours. No direct buses until the bridge at Ilama is back in operation—in the meantime, all buses run via Pito Solo, and all make stops along the way. Cotisba's office is on the southwest corner of the square, nearly opposite Junqueños.

Buses to San Rafael, a village in the mountains south of Santa Bárbara, leave from next to the penitentiary, a block below the square, at noon, US$1.50, three hours. From San Rafael, you can continue by hitching to Gracias. The bus returns from San Rafael at 4:30 a.m.

Buses to El Níspero leave at 11 a.m. from next to the penitentiary and return at 6 a.m., US 60 cents, one and a half hours.

From San Pedro Sula or Santa Rosa de Copán, the road to Santa Bárbara turns off at Ceibita, between Km 32 and 33. From Ceibita, where fruit is often for sale, it's another 61 km to Santa Bárbara. With the bridge at Ilama still down after Hurricane Mitch, at last report, buses were ferrying passengers across the river to a waiting bus on the far side to continue their journey to or from Santa Bárbara. Private cars may use a steel hammock bridge several kilometers downstream from Ilama (no trucks or buses, and only one at a time!) at Chinda, and drive up a dirt road on the far side of the river to Ilama. Beyond Chinda, the highway to Ceibita is in good shape and passes through very beautiful countryside.

East out of Santa Bárbara, the highway leads to Pito Solo, where it meets the San Pedro-Tegucigalpa highway. This 53-km stretch of road is not as frequently traveled as the one toward Ceibita (at least when the bridge is up), but it is also a scenic drive.

NEAR SANTA BÁRBARA

Villages Near Santa Bárbara

The department of Santa Bárbara is filled with colorful colonial villages infrequently visited by foreigners. Many, such as Gualjoto, El Níspero, Los Bancos, and San Vicente, are known for producing good quality *artesanías* (handicrafts). **Ilama,** on the road toward Ceibita and San Pedro Sula, is famous for its *junco* goods as well as its traditional colonial church. Also well known for handicrafts are La Arada and Nueva Celilac.

Set high on a mountain divide separating Santa Bárbara from the Gracias region is **San Rafael,** a scenic town dating from colonial times. A daily bus from Santa Bárbara travels past El Níspero up the dirt road to San Rafael, and the adventurous can continue onward to Gracias by hitchhiking down the far side of the mountains. No hotels exist in San Rafael, but locals will rent rooms for a night.

Parque Nacional Santa Bárbara

Surrounding the peak of Santa Bárbara, the second highest in the country at 2,744 meters, Parque Nacional Santa Bárbara covers about 13,000 hectares of cloud, pine, and semihumid tropical forest. Montaña de Santa Bárbara is not part of any major mountain range but an anomalous, solitary massif rising up between the town of Santa Bárbara and Lago de Yojoa. The inaccessible, rarely seen forest on top of the mountain is reputed to be dense and wild, full of weird rock formations and lots of wildlife.

As yet no sign-posted trails have been developed in the park, but it is possible to get into the forest from several of the villages around the edge of the mountain, if you're willing to make the effort. From Santa Bárbara, you can catch a ride on a truck or drive 20 minutes by dirt road to the villages of La Cuesta, Los Bancos, and El Playón and look for guides. In El Playón, Mario or Reino Orellano are usually willing to take visitors into the forest for a negotiable fee.

Another route into the forest is via **San Luis Planes,** a village set in a high valley on the north side of the park; you can get there by bus from Peña Blanca on Lago de Yojoa. The road from Peña Blanca is best negotiated by 4WD vehicle and takes about an hour to drive. The forest starts just beyond San Luis, though it would take more than a couple of days of hiking to get up to the peak, and you'd need a guide. Shorter hikes into the lower parts of the forest are easily possible here, and you could make a serviceable campsite not far from San Luis without difficulty.

From El Mochito, on the south shore of Lago de Yojoa, you can get a truck to El Cedral and continue on foot or horseback to El Cielo, where guides can be found to lead you up to the higher reaches of the park. The extremely determined could probably find a way over the top and back down the far side to Santa Bárbara. As with most places in Honduras, guides generally charge US$7-10 a day.

For more information on the park and access to it, stop in at the Santa Bárbara Cohdefor office. The topographical map covering the park is 1:50,000 Santa Bárbara 2560 I.

SIGUATEPEQUE

Set in a pine-forested highland valley midway between San Pedro Sula and Tegucigalpa, Siguatepeque (pop. 45,700) enjoys a cool and comfortable climate—a pleasant change for those coming from the steamy north coast. In spite of its long history—the town was one of the first bases for the Spanish in their conquest of Honduras—little colonial-era architecture remains in Siguatepeque. There are few attractions per se to interest foreign visitors, though the invigorating climate and fine countryside may inspire you to spend a couple of days hiking around the hillsides. Many highway drivers stop in Siguatepeque to eat at the ragingly popular Granja d'Elia buffet restaurant on the highway.

ORIENTATION AND SIGHTS

Unusual for a Honduran town, Siguatepeque has two main squares. The one with the church on it is known as the *"parque"* while the other, two blocks west, is called the "plaza." The center of town is about one and a half km off the San Pedro-Tegucigalpa highway.

At the highway intersection is the **Escuela de Ciencias Forestales,** the national forestry school. For those who read Spanish, the school library has useful books on the country and its natural resources; there are also some books for sale.

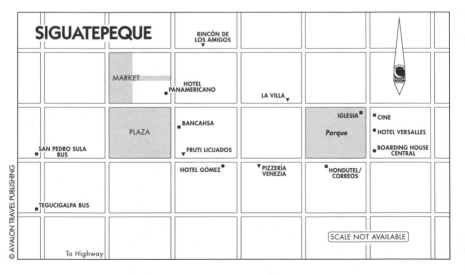

SIGUATEPEQUE

RINCÓN DE LOS AMIGOS ▼

MARKET

HOTEL PANAMERICANO ●

LA VILLA ▼

PLAZA

BANCAHSA ■

IGLESIA ■

Parque

■ CINE

● HOTEL VERSALLES

● BOARDING HOUSE CENTRAL

SAN PEDRO SULA BUS ■

FRUTI LICUADOS ▼

HOTEL GÓMEZ ●

▼ PIZZERÍA VENEZIA

■ HONDUTEL/ CORREOS

TEGUCIGALPA BUS ■

SCALE NOT AVAILABLE

© AVALON TRAVEL PUBLISHING

To Highway

About an hour's walk or a US$1.50 taxi ride outside of town is a small park at **Calanterique,** which means "mountain of water" in Lenca. The park has places to camp as well as picnic benches. About four km down the highway west to La Esperanza is the village of **El Porvenir,** a local center for Lenca pottery, sold out of several houses on the road.

PRACTICALITIES

Accommodations

The best all-around value in Siguatepeque is unquestionably **Hotel Panamericano,** tel. 773-0202, with three stories of clean (though small) rooms around an interior courtyard, each with cable TV and hot water for US$5.50 s or US$11 d.

Hotel Gómez, on the road between the two squares, tel. 773-0868, has similar rooms for a bit more money, and a large parking lot.

Boarding House Central on the southeast corner of the *parque,* tel. 773-2108, charges about the same as the Gómez. The rooms are not as nice, but it's not a bad choice if the others are full. Beware the less expensive rooms downstairs, which are dirty and unpleasant. The *comedor* in the Boarding House is not so great, but it's convenient for beers or soft drinks.

For the real penny-pincher, next to the cinema on the *parque* is the two-story **Hotel Versalles,** tel. 773-0157, with acceptable though unlovely rooms for as low as US$2 s, or US$4 d with private bath.

Food and Entertainment

A surprising find out here in the middle of Honduras is **Pizzeria Venezia,** run by an Italian expatriate who came to Siguatepeque for its cool climate. The unpretentious, popular restaurant between the two squares serves up a tasty, inexpensive pizza as well as pasta and sandwiches, daily 11 a.m.-9 p.m. Out on the highway, the owner has opened a new restaurant with more variety on the menu, catering to passing motorists.

La Villa, a Mexican-style restaurant next to the *parque,* has good fajitas, quesadillas, nachos, *tortas,* burritos, burgers, and breakfasts for US$2-3 per meal. Open daily 7 a.m.-8:30 p.m. A newer Mexican eatery is **Rincón de los Ami-**

gos, a small restaurant around the corner from the Hotel Panamericano, with chicken, *pinchos, tacos,* and other munchies for US$1.50-3. Open daily until 9 or 10 p.m.

Good low-priced breakfasts and lunches can be found in a string of *comedores* in an alley behind the market, which lets out next to the Hotel Panamericano. On the southeast corner of the plaza is **Fruti Licuados,** a good place to grab a fruit drink or *pupusas,* open until 9 p.m.

On the highway to San Pedro, at Km 118, a very good deli-supermarket, **Granja d'Elia.** All sorts of quality vegetables, meats, cheeses, and other goodies are available daily until 8 p.m. The adjacent restaurant, very popular with motorists driving between San Pedro and Tegucigalpa, serves an excellent buffet with a wide selection of breakfasts, appetizers, meat and vegetarian entrees, and salads, open 6 a.m.-9 p.m. daily

Cine Aeropuerto on the *parque* shows movies nightly.

Services

Hondutel on the *parque* is open daily 5:30 a.m.-9 p.m. and receives faxes at tel. 773-2008. Right next door is Correos, with EMS fast-mail service available. Tourist cards can be renewed hassle-free at the *migración* office, just off the *parque.*

Banco de Occidente and Banco Atlántida will change dollars and traveler's checks. The latter also has a cash machine.

Getting There and Away

Siguatepeque is 125 km from San Pedro and 117 km from Tegucigalpa, with well-maintained highway in both directions. Toward Tegucigalpa the steep, winding stretch of highway down into the Valle de Comayagua is known locally as Cuesta La Virgin. The easiest way to get to San Pedro or Tegucigalpa is to take a US 40-cent taxi ride out to the highway and catch the next bus that comes by in your direction. If you don't feel like waiting on the highway, however, both Transportes Maribel, tel. 773-0254, and Empresas Unidas, tel. 773-0149, run buses to Tegucigalpa from the plaza every two hours between 4 a.m. and 4 p.m.; US$1.50, a little over two hours. Etul has buses to San Pedro Sula at about the same schedule for US$1.50, two hours.

To get to La Esperanza, take a US 80-cent taxi ride to the highway turnoff, a couple of kilometers from the Siguatepeque turn on the way to San Pedro. From the gas station at the La Esperanza turn, buses leave roughly every two hours, charging US$1.30 for the 90-minute ride.

If you don't see any buses around, just stick out your thumb. The road to La Esperanza is 67 km, dropping down into the Río Otoro (upper Ulúa) Valley, past the town of Jesús de Otoro, and climbing back up into the mountains to La Esperanza.

COMAYAGUA

INTRODUCTION

Comayagua, Honduras' original capital city, is on the northwestern edge of the broad Valle de Comayagua, the largest flat region in central-western Honduras. The 390-square-kilometer valley lies roughly equidistant between the Caribbean and Pacific coasts. Comayagua (pop. 70,600) lies at the junction of the Río Chiquito and the Río Humuya.

After more than three centuries as the country's political and administrative center, Comayagua has a wealth of colonial monuments. City authorities have in the last couple of years begun promoting an ambitious project known as **Comayagua Colonial,** which is to entail renovating many old buildings, recobbling the streets, and enforcing strict building codes. While Comayagua is unlikely to become the next Antigua, Guatemala, the renovation projects would certainly be a welcome change, considering the state of some of the crumbling old structures.

Just outside of town, in the middle of the valley, is the Enrique Soto Cano Air Force Base, better known as Palmerola, used by the U.S. military. With the closing of the U.S. bases in Panama Canal Zone, activity at Palmerola has increased substantially. In another boost to the local economy, a new ZIP (free trade park) recently opened just outside of town. The surrounding region survives mainly on agriculture, particularly coffee grown around La Libertad, fruits like peaches and apricots, and many vegetable farms.

History
The fertile Valle de Comayagua attracted settlers long before the Spanish arrived in the region in 1537. For centuries, the valley had been a bastion of the Lenca, but during the years before

Columbus, Nahuatl-speaking migrants from central Mexico moved into the region, apparently coexisting peacefully with the original inhabitants. The attractions of the area were obvious and are further illustrated through the name Comayagua, which is thought to mean "abundance of food" in Maya.

It's unclear when the first conquistadors passed through the valley, but Alonso de Cáceres founded Santa María de Comayagua on 7 December 1537, under orders from Francisco Montejo. The first city was destroyed shortly thereafter by Indians in the region, who rose with Lempira in revolt against the Spaniards. In fact, the valley was the last bastion of Indian rebellion to be put down, holding out until the first months of 1539.

Comayagua was reestablished the same year, and by 1557 the crown recognized it as a city *(villa).* Not long after, veins of silver were found nearby, further encouraging Spaniards to settle there. By 1573 Comayagua was the most important city in the province, surpassing Gracias a Dios. It was made the administrative capital of the colony, which it remained through the rest of the colonial period.

Comayagua was a center for intrigue and a target for attack during the wars of independence and Central American union. The town was pillaged and burned several times in the mid-19th century, most notably in 1837 by Guatemalan General José Justo Milla. When Honduras was established as an independent country, Comayagua was declared the capital. The rise of Tegucigalpa in the late 19th century as a center for gold and silver production led to a bitter rivalry between the two cities, which was finally settled in 1880 when President Marco Aurelio Soto changed the seat of government to Tegucigalpa. The story goes that the decision was prompted by the snubbing of his indige-

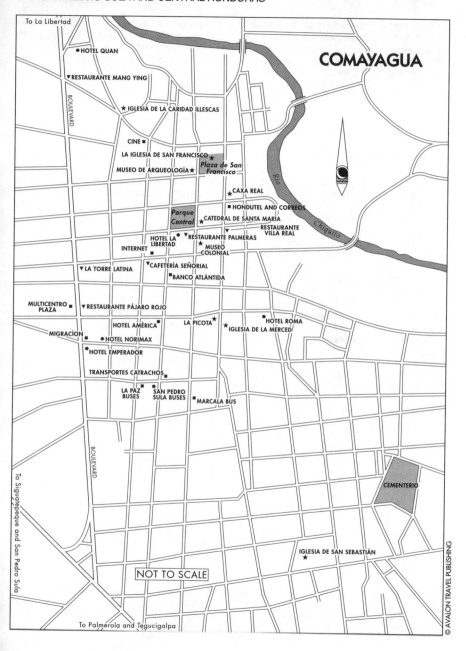

COMAYAGUA

To La Libertad

● HOTEL QUAN

▼ RESTAURANTE MANG YING

BOULEVARD

★ IGLESIA DE LA CARIDAD ILLESCAS

CINE ■

LA IGLESIA DE SAN FRANCISCO

MUSEO DE ARQUEOLOGÍA ★

Plaza de San Francisco

★ CAXA REAL

■ HONDUTEL AND CORREOS

Parque Central

★ CATEDRAL DE SANTA MARÍA

▼ RESTAURANTE PALMERAS

RESTAURANTE VILLA REAL ▼

HOTEL LA LIBERTAD ●

★ MUSEO COLONIAL

INTERNET ■

▼ CAFETERÍA SEÑORIAL

▼ LA TORRE LATINA

■ BANCO ATLÁNTIDA

MULTICENTRO PLAZA ■

▼ RESTAURANTE PÁJARO ROJO

HOTEL AMÉRICA ●

LA PICOTA ★

● HOTEL ROMA

MIGRACIÓN ■

★ IGLESIA DE LA MERCED

● HOTEL NORIMAX

● HOTEL EMPERADOR

TRANSPORTES CATRACHOS ■

LA PAZ BUSES ■

SAN PEDRO SULA BUSES ■

■ MARCALA BUS

BOULEVARD

Río Chiquito

CEMENTERIO

To Siguatepeque and San Pedro Sula

NOT TO SCALE

IGLESIA DE SAN SEBASTIÁN ★

To Palmerola and Tegucigalpa

© AVALON TRAVEL PUBLISHING

nous wife by the arrogant Comayagua elite.

Since then—a black day for every Comayagua resident—the city slid into a sort of genteel poverty, trying to retain the pretensions of a capital but without the economic or political power base. These days Comayagua mostly survives on the valley's agriculture and cattle industries, as well as on money derived from the nearby Palmerola Air Force Base and the new industrial park. The U.S. military presence in town is quite noticeable if you stick around for a couple of days; several ex-military personnel operate businesses in town.

Orientation

Downtown Comayagua is a couple of kilometers off the San Pedro-Tegucigalpa highway, connected by a divided avenue known as *El Bulevar*, "The Boulevard." Comayagua is centered around the broad downtown square (Parque Central), which was recently given a major facelift as part of the new Comayagua Colonial project. Unfortunately, the "improvements" included chopping down most of the trees and replacing them with large quantities of concrete. Locals point out that this was, in fact, how the *parque* looked during colonial years. One can only hope similar renovations don't hit the still-shady **Plaza San Francisco**, one block north of the *parque*. Four blocks south is the smaller **Plaza La Merced**. All the main sights in town are located within walking distance of the square, but a taxi might be desired to get out to the highway or to the bus stations.

SIGHTS

As the capital of Honduras for over 300 years, and the religious seat of the colony under Spanish rule, Comayagua boasts many colonial structures and works of art, though many are in disrepair.

Catedral de Santa María

The imposing Catedral de Santa María, also known as La Iglesia de la Inmaculada Concepción, was built on the site of the original Comayagua plaza over the course of more than a century, between 1580 and 1708. The prolonged construction stemmed from problems obtaining funds and the need to rebuild the church's foundation in the 17th century.

The church's facade is more complex than most in Honduras, decorated with sculpted columns and eight statues set in niches. The tower, built in 1650, holds one of the oldest known clocks in the world. The Reloj Arabe, as it is known, was made around 1100 and graced the side of La Alhambra in Granada, Spain, before it was donated to Comayagua by King Felipe II.

Inside the cathedral are three extraordinarily elaborate *retablos* in baroque style, with sculptures by Andrés y Francisco de Ocampo dating from the 1630s. Many colonial religious paintings hang on the walls inside. The cathedral is normally closed from 11:30 a.m. to 2 p.m. and shuts its doors for the day at 4 p.m.

Museo Colonial

A block south of the Catedral is the **Museo Colonial,** with an eclectic and occasionally fascinating collection of religious art from Comayagua's five churches, including paintings, chalices, statues, vestments, old documents, and an impressive wooden confessional. Many of the pieces were brought to the museum out of fear they would be stolen from the churches, a growing problem in recent years. The museum was moved into a more spacious setting with better displays in 1998. Entrance US 50 cents; open Mon.-Sat. 9:30-11:30 a.m. and 2-5 p.m., Sunday 10 a.m.-noon and 2-5 p.m.

Museo de Arqueología and La Iglesia de San Francisco

One block north of the square is the Museo de Arqueología, on one side of the Plaza San Francisco, in a building that was Honduras' seat of government for a short time in the 19th century. Many of the displays relate to digs made in the area of El Cajón dam, before the region was submerged in water. The museum is not extensive, but the collection of jade art, jewelry, painted pottery, and copies of petroglyph art are worth a look. Labels are in English and Spanish. US$1.35 entrance; open Tues.-Sun. 8:30 a.m.-4 p.m.

Next to the museum is the shady Plaza San Francisco, with the Iglesia de San Francisco on the north side. The church, originally called La Iglesia de San Antonio, was built in 1574 in a simple style and rebuilt completely between

1610 and 1620. An earthquake in 1784 badly damaged the structure, and the roof collapsed in 1806. Three years later another quake knocked down the bell tower. A second reconstruction was completed in 1819. No wonder the church attracts faithful worshipers—after all those disasters, it's a miracle it's still standing!

The church has an ornate carved *retablo* and a gory statue of Christ. Hours vary—ask around for the caretaker to let you in if it's closed. He may let you go up into the three-story bell tower, but watch out for the rotten wood planks if you go up.

Caxa Real

Around the corner from the Plaza de San Francisco are the crumbling remnants of the colonial Caxa Real, or tax-collection house, built between 1739 and 1741. Destroyed by the earthquake in 1809, only part of the front of the building remains standing, and that has a small garden growing on top and is leaning at a precipitous angle. The inscription above the door states the building was constructed under direction of Lt. Col. Don Francisco de Parga, under orders of Royal Field Marshal Don Pedro de Rivera Villalón, to serve as the Royal Treasury for King Felipe and Queen Isabel.

Iglesia de La Merced

Comayagua's first cathedral, La Merced was built in 1550 on the reputed site of the first Mass spoken in the valley. Its baroque facade is thought to date from the early years of the 18th century. Many of the paintings and sculptures in the church were made in the 16th century.

Across the street there's a small square with a pillar in the center, known locally as **La Picota.** It was erected in 1820 in honor of the liberal Spanish Constitution of 1812—illustrating Comayagua's loyal colonial sentiments when the rest of the country, and indeed the continent, was heading toward independence from the mother country.

Iglesia de San Sebastián

Some 10 blocks south of the square stands Iglesia de San Sebastián, built in 1581 as a site for blacks and Indians in the city to pray. The towers were added in later years and rebuilt in 1957 in a rather unattractive style. The church's architecture is fairly elemental, but the *retablo* inside, crafted by Blas de Mesa, is worth a look. The remains of Honduran president and general José Trinidad Cabañas are buried under the church floor, marked by an engraved stone.

Iglesia de La Caridad Illescas

Several blocks northeast of the square, La Caridad was also intended during the colonial era for the *mestizo,* black, and Indian populations in the neighborhood to use. Construction on the church began in 1629. Of the several religious artworks within, of particular note is the gold- and silver-lined *retablo* dedicated to Santa Lucía.

the remnants of the Caxa Real, the tax-collection house built between 1739 and 1741 (and destroyed by fire in 1809)

ACCOMMODATIONS

Shoestring

Centrally located right on the square, **Hotel La Libertad** (no phone) is certainly cheap at US$3 s or US$4 d, but the rooms are none too clean, the mattresses are in terrible shape, and the water supply is irregular. For the penny-pincher only. Better is **Hotel Roma,** behind La Merced church, tel. 772-1702, with simple, clean rooms for US$4 s or US$5 d with communal bathroom, US$7 d with private bath.

Budget-Inexpensive

Just off the Boulevard is **Hotel Norimax,** tel. 772-1210, a three-story building with small but comfortable rooms for US$10 s or d with TV and fan, US$14 d with a/c. The front-facing rooms have balconies, but the noise from the buses pulling past makes it worth requesting a room in the back. Parking available.

Similar to the Norimax and about the same price is **Hotel América,** tel./fax 772-0360, closer to the center of town.

Hotel Emperador, across from the Norimax, tel. 772-0332, has unexceptional rooms for US$8 s or d with one large bed and bathroom, US$10 d with two beds. TV and a/c are available for a few dollars more.

Hotel Quan, tel. 772-0070, has simple rooms with hot water and TV for US$10 s or d, less with a shared bathroom. Across the street the hotel has a motel-style building around a parking lot with nicer rooms, equipped with a/c, telephone, and refrigerator, for US$23 s or d. The hotel, popular with visiting Americans, is kept spotlessly clean, the management is very helpful, and the neighborhood northwest of downtown near La Iglesia de La Caridad is quiet.

Moderate

New, and a bit overpriced considering the so-so service, is the motel-style **Hotel Santa María** on the highway just outside of town, tel. 772-7872 or 772-8934, fax 772-7719. Charging US$50 s or d, its rooms have a/c, hot water, and cable TV.

FOOD AND ENTERTAINMENT

Inexpensive

Finding decent, inexpensive food in Comayagua can be difficult. One of the better places downtown is **Restaurante Palmeras,** a couple of doors down from Hotel La Libertad on the square, with low-priced breakfasts, *comida corriente, baleadas,* and other munchies. The modest, inexpensive **Cafetería Señorial,** a block southwest of the square, is popular with locals for the good set meals and breakfasts. Closed Sundays.

Midrange

Restaurante Pájaro Rojo, on the Boulevard, tel. 772-0690, has a good selection of well-cooked Honduran standards such as *pinchos,* steaks, and several seafood dishes for US$3-6 per meal, with patio seating. Open Tues.-Sat. 11 a.m.-10 p.m., Sunday 11 a.m.-9:30 p.m.

For a taste of Americana, check out **Dave's Burgers,** on the highway toward Tegucigalpa not far past the entrance to town. The fish burgers are excellent, though not huge, so you may want two if you're hungry. The burgers, club sandwiches, and BLTs aren't bad either; US$2-3 per sandwich. The place, run by an American ex-serviceman, is open Tues.-Thurs. noon-10 p.m., Fri.-Sat. noon-11 p.m., and Sunday noon-8 p.m.

Restaurante Mang Ying, on the Boulevard near Hotel Quan, tel. 772-0567, serves up heaping plates of chop suey, chow mein, and other dishes at reasonable prices. Open daily 9:30 a.m.-10 p.m., the restaurant is popular with American military personnel serving at Palmerola.

Upscale

Definitely the nicest place to eat in town, both for the setting and the food, is **Villa Real,** tel. 772-0101. Tables are set around a grassy courtyard garden, attractively lit up at night, in a restored colonial Comayagua house just off the *parque.* The restaurant owners are eager to show visitors around the different rooms of the house either before or after eating, to admire colonial furniture, decorations, and art. The kitchen makes very good traditional Honduran food, like an excellent *plato típico* with steak, rice, beans, avocado, cream, cheese, and tortillas, or a *sopa Villa Real* with chicken, toasted tortilla, tomato, cheese, and cream. Open daily 11 a.m.-10 p.m.

La Torre Latina, on the Boulevard, tel. 772-1193, is a quiet, small restaurant serving shrimp, lobster, steaks, chicken cordon bleu, and much else for US$5-10 per plate. Neat dress recommended. Open Mon.-Sat. 11 a.m.-3 p.m. and 5-11 p.m.

A favorite expat hangout in Comayagua is **Haneman's Bar and Grill,** on the second floor of the Multicentro Plaza Mall on the Boulevard, tel. 772-1746, with a full bar and a restaurant open Mon.-Sat. 6-10:30 p.m., Sunday 11:30 a.m.-2:30 p.m. and 5:30-10 p.m., closed Tuesday.

INFORMATION AND SERVICES

Betsy's Souvenirs in the Multicentro Plaza Mall on the Boulevard has a selection of *artesanías* from Honduras, including mahogany carvings, cigars, carpets, pottery, stone sculpture, and some paintings. Open Mon.-Sat. Across the way in the same mall is **Mr. T's,** with a similar selection, open Mon.-Fri. 9 a.m.-6 p.m. and Saturday 10 a.m.-9 p.m.

Hondutel is behind the Catedral de Santa Marí, open daily 7 a.m.-8:30 p.m. Next door is Correos, with EMS fast-mail service available, open Mon.-Fri. 8 a.m.-noon and 1-4 p.m., Saturday 8 a.m.-noon.

The *migración* office on the Boulevard near Hotel Emperador, tel. 772-2792, will renew visas with a minimum of fuss Mon.-Sat. 8:30 a.m.-noon and 2-5 p.m., Saturday 9-11 a.m.

A small Internet shop was open upstairs in the same mini-mall as the souvenir stores and Haneman's Bar, but it had closed at last check. Another option is **Centro Pedagógico de Edu-**

cación Virtual, tel. 772-0909, a computer school with Internet service a block southwest of the square in a shopping walkway called Pasaje Valladolid. Open Mon.-Fri. 8 a.m.-noon and 2-7 p.m.

Bancahsa, Banco de Occidente, Banco Atlántida, and others will exchange dollars or traveler's checks. Banco Atlántida has a cash machine.

For medical problems, **Centro Médico San Rafael,** tel. 772-0068, has a competent doctor and is not too expensive. Open 24 hours.

GETTING THERE AND AWAY

Bus
Buses to Tegucigalpa are offered by Transportes Catrachos, five blocks south of the square, tel. 772-0260. The buses run every half-hour between 5 a.m. and 5 p.m.; US$1.10, 90 minutes. Transportes Rivera, a block farther south on the same street, tel. 772-1208, has buses hourly to **San Pedro Sula** between 5 a.m. and 4 p.m.; US$2 for the two-and-a-half-hour ride. Alternatively, you can take a taxi out to the highway and flag down a bus headed in either direction with minimum hassle.

Empresa San Miguel (no phone), one block east of the other buses, runs buses to Marcala five times a day between 6:30 a.m. and 2 p.m.; US$1.35, two and a half hours, or less to La Paz or San Pedro Tutule (for Guajiquíro) six blocks south of the park. Next to the San Pedro Sula terminal, Emptreca (no phone) has regular buses to La Paz for US 35 cents until 6 p.m. daily. Minibuses, known as *rapiditos*, run frequently to La Paz from a small terminal a block south of Hotel Norimax, US 35 cents, last bus at 6 p.m.

Car
From Comayagua, the highway west to Siguatepeque (32 km) and San Pedro Sula (160 km) and east to Tegucigalpa (85 km) is kept in good condition all year. In either direction, the road ascends steeply into the mountains ringing the Comayagua Valley.

NEAR COMAYAGUA

Parque Nacional Montaña de Comayagua
Only seven km from Comayagua is the edge of Parque Nacional Montaña de Comayagua, cov-

ering 30,094 hectares, of which 6,600 hectares form the core zone. The highest point in the park is **El Portillo,** 2,407 meters. The forest is not one of the country's finest, certainly nothing compared to Celaque or Sierra de Agalta, but sizable patches of cloud forest remain, populated by quetzals, toucans, eagles, deer, monkeys, and a few pumas.

You can hike into the park from the villages of **Río Blanco** and **Río Negro,** both reached via dirt road from **San Jerónimo,** 12 km from Comayagua by dirt road. Near Río Negro is **Cascada En Sueños,** a waterfall hidden amidst the dense forest. Off the road to La Libertad, you can also enter through **Tres Pinos** or **Zona Helada.**

Some information on the park is available at **Ecosimco,** a small non-profit organization working to protect the mountain's forests. Its office, tel. 772-4681, is located on the outskirts of Comayagua, on the road to La Libertad on the right side, by the Cámara de Comercio. The **Cohdefor office,** on the highway leaving Comayagua to the west, has little information on hiking, but there is a useful full-size topographical map on the wall. Both Cohdefor and Ecosim-

co may have suggestions on possible guides living in mountain villages.

Topographical maps covering the park are 1:50,000 Comayagua 2659 II and Agalteca 2759 III.

Enrique Cano Soto
Air Force Base (Palmerola)
For much of the 1980s, Palmerola was essentially a U.S. military enclave, from where the Contra war against the Sandinista government in Nicaragua was directed. More recently the base has been used in the war against drugs.

Growing pressure from Honduran citizens and politicians against U.S. presence has led to a reduction in the number of personnel at the base. In 1995 over 2,000 U.S. military were housed here; that number dropped to 450 by 1996. After the bases in Panama were closed when the U.S. relinquished the canal, the number of military personnel at the base is reportedly on the upswing again. Despite de facto U.S. control, the base—a couple of kilometers southeast of Comayagua on the highway toward Tegucigalpa—is now officially under the Honduran flag.

LA PAZ AND VICINITY

The capital of the department of the same name, La Paz has little to interest the casual traveler. However, located on the southern edge of the Comayagua Valley, it's a good stop-off point for those visiting the mountain country south around Guajiquíro and toward the Salvadoran border. Near La Paz are the ruins of **Yarumela,** believed to be one of the oldest ruins sites in Honduras. Only a few mounds are visible.

Practicalities
One block from the market is **Hotel y Restaurante Alis,** tel. 774-2125, with decent accommodations and food. Rooms cost US$5 d, US$7.50 d with bathroom. **Merendero Criollos,** just off the square, has inexpensive *comida corriente* and snacks.

Bancahsa and Banco Atlántida will both change dollars but not traveler's checks.

Six buses daily leave to Marcala between 6:30 a.m. and 3:45 p.m.; US 80 cents, two hours on a paved road. To Guajiquíro, one bus leaves

daily at noon, US$1 takes the Marcala road for half an hour, then turns into the hills for another bumpy two and a half hours. Buses to Comayagua leave all day until late afternoon; US 30 cents, 30 minutes. All buses leave several blocks north of the square, between the market and the soldier statue.

San Pedro de Tutule and Guajiquíro
Roughly 20 km south of La Paz, set two km off the highway, is the town of San Pedro de Tutule, a market town for the villages in the surrounding mountains. San Pedro de Tutule is one of the last bastions of pure Lenca Indians in the country, along with the region around La Esperanza.

High in the mountains above Tutule, about two hours by rough dirt road, is Guajiquíro. The quiet Lenca village with a simple parish church is perched on the hillside with an impressive view across the valley below. From here you can hike up into the **Reserva Biológica Guajiquíro,** covering 67 square kilometers of pine and cloud forest, interspersed with patches of farmland and small ranches. The highest part of the reserve rests on a high mesa, with several small peaks of over 2,200 meters. While hardly in a pristine state, the park is nonetheless a scenic and relaxed mountain area for a couple of days of hiking, camping, and birdwatching. Plenty of small mammals, including foxes, wild pigs, deer, and even a few cats live in the thickest patches of forest. The forests of Guajiquíro are famed for having all the different pine species found in the Honduran highlands, sometimes even visible all on a single hillside. On clear days, from the more southerly peaks around Guajiquíro are dramatic views of the volcanoes across the border in El Salvador.

Topographical maps covering the reserve are 1:50,000 Opatoro 2658 III and San Pedro Tutule 2658 IV.

Toward El Salvador
South of Tutule, the highway winds up into the mountains to Marcala, the main town in an area that produces some of the finest coffee in Honduras. Five buses a day ply the road between Comayagua and Marcala, charging US$1.30 for the two-and-a-half-hour ride. Beyond Marcala, the road continues down into the lower, hotter canyon country near the Salvadoran border. Not far from the border is an impressive set of petroglyphs. To visit them, take a bus to Santa Elena, then continue by truck to the village of Azacualpa. From here it's two and a half hours by trail to the site, with a guide. Ask for the *"piedras pintadas."*

TEGUCIGALPA
AND VICINITY

Honduras' capital, a city of somewhere between 700,000 and one million people, depending on whom you ask, occupies a high mountain valley around 1,000 meters above sea level, with the Río Choluteca running right down the middle. The valley is ringed by mountains, with only a narrow valley to the north allowing the Río Choluteca to continue on its convoluted course to the Pacific Ocean.

Opinions of Tegucigalpa—called "Teguc" (Tegoose) by locals—vary wildly. Some visitors are uninspired and can't wait to catch the next bus out of town, while others are charmed by the mix of colonial and modern buildings, the mountain setting, and the relaxed atmosphere. Compared to San Salvador, Managua, or Guatemala City, it's definitely one of the most livable of Central America's capitals.

Visitors have no problem finding places and sites to see, including several colonial churches, three museums, a large market area, and plenty of handicraft stores, all in the downtown area. In the surrounding hills are the colonial mining villages of Santa Lucía, Valle de Ángeles, Ojojona, and Cedros, which make for great day trips. Parque Nacional La Tigra, just a dozen

kilometers from the city, has a network of trails through its cloud forest.

Because of its altitude, Tegucigalpa has a pleasant climate year-round, ranging from warm during the day to cool at night. The mean annual temperature is 28° C, although it can get considerably cooler during the rainy season.

History

Both archaeological work and historical records suggest the Tegucigalpa Valley was not a major population center, at least in the years shortly before the Spanish conquest. It's postulated that the mainly Lenca population was dependent on the larger settlements in the nearby Comayagua Valley. Many believe the city's name derives from the Lenca words meaning "land of silver," but the Lenca had no interest in silver and are not likely to have named a place because of it. Others have suggested "place of the painted rocks" and "place where the men meet." The ending "galpa," common in the region, means "place" or "land."

In the early 1540s at the latest, Spanish conquistador Alonso de Cáceres likely passed through the region on his way to Olancho under orders from Francisco Montejo, but he made no

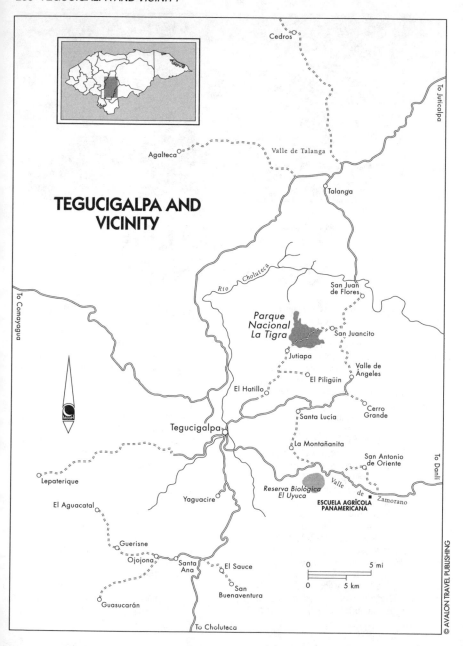

TEGUCIGALPA AND VICINITY

To Juticalpa

Cedros

Agalteca

Valle de Talanga

Talanga

To Comayagua

Río Choluteca

San Juan
de Flores

Parque
Nacional
La Tigra

San Juancito

Jutiapa

Valle de
Ángeles

El Piligüin

El Hatillo

Cerro
Grande

Santa Lucía

Tegucigalpa

La Montañanita

San Antonio
de Oriente

Lepaterique

To Danlí

Reserva Biológica
El Uyuca

Valle de Zamorano

El Aguacatal

Yaguacire

ESCUELA AGRÍCOLA
PANAMERICANA

Guerisne

Ojojona

Santa
Ana

El Sauce

0   5 mi

0   5 km

San
Buenaventura

Guasucarán

To Choluteca

report on the valley. It's probable that residents of Comayagua, who were combing the new colony for precious metals, found the first veins of silver near Santa Lucía by 1560. An official report to the Spanish authorities dated 1589 states silver was found in Tegucigalpa 12 to 15 years prior. According to local legend, the first strike was made on 29 September, Saint Michael's day; hence, San Miguel is the city's patron saint.

Whatever the exact date, by the late 16th century miners were building houses and mine operations along the Río Choluteca and in the hills above. Tegucigalpa had no formal founding, like Comayagua, Gracias, or Trujillo, but grew haphazardly and remained a small settlement of dispersed houses connected by trails for the first years of its existence. The original name for the settlement was Real de Minas de San Miguel de Tegucigalpa, but by 1768 the mines were producing enough wealth to merit the title "Villa."

By the end of the colonial period the city's mineral wealth allowed it to eclipse Comayagua in economic importance. Because of the rivalry between the two cities, the legislature of the short-lived Central American Republic alternated between the two, and in 1880 Pres. Marcos Aurelio Soto moved the capital definitively to Tegucigalpa. Some say Soto made the move out of anger toward the Comayagua aristocracy for snubbing his Indian wife, but more likely he was following his Liberal principles by locating the government where the economy was strongest.

In the early 20th century Honduras' economic expansion was centered on the north coast, and the lack of a cross-country railroad left Tegucigalpa behind in development. The mines at La Rosario provided some stimulus, but most of the profits went to New York rather than Tegucigalpa. To this day Tegucigalpa has no major industry to speak of and survives mainly through the government, the service industry, and a small financial community. In 1932 the Distrito Central was created, bringing neighboring Comayagüela and Tegucigalpa under a unified government.

During Hurricane Mitch, in the middle of the night of 29 October 1998, the Río Choluteca swelled quickly to over 10 meters above its normal height, completely covering the main bridges downtown, the floodwaters sweeping away entire neighborhoods. Over a year after this horrid tragedy, the riverfront area looks like the floods hit just a couple of weeks prior. Many buildings along the riverfront boulevard on the Tegucigalpa side are still in ruins, and parts of the street had still not even been fully cleared of mud. Not only is the river through Tegucigalpa unpleasant to look at and almost certainly a health hazard, but the rubble and trash still clogging the riverbed will only make the effects of future floods all the worse. City and federal officials insist ambitious plans are under way for a complete overhaul of the Tegucigalpa riverfront, if only foreign governments would release promised funding.

Orientation
Downtown Tegucigalpa is arranged around the *parque central* (central square), with the Parroquia de San Miguel Arcángel (known simply

the old Spanish bridge connecting Tegucigalpa with Comayagüela

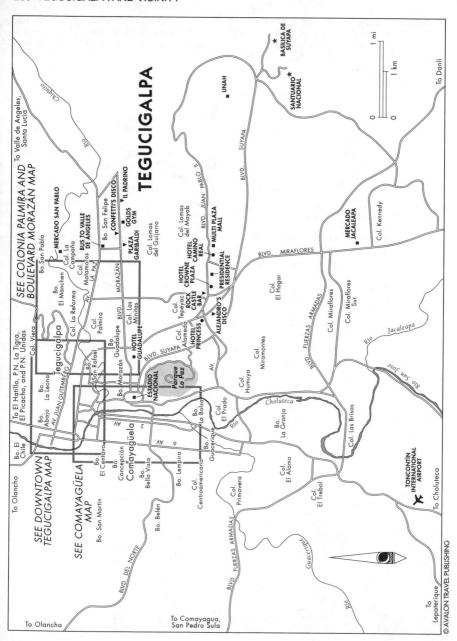

TEGUCIGALPA

SEE COLONIA PALMIRA AND BOULEVARD MORAZÁN MAP

SEE DOWNTOWN TEGUCIGALPA MAP

SEE COMAYAGÜELA MAP

BASILICA DE SUYAPA

SANTUARIO NACIONAL

UNAH

To Danlí

To Valle de Angeles, Santa Lucia

Río Chiquito

MERCADO SAN PABLO

BUS TO VALLE DE ANGELES

CONFETTI'S DISCO

IL PADRINO

PLAZA GARIBALDI

GOLDS GYM

Bo. San Pablo

Col. La Campaña

Bo. El Manchen

Bo. El Reforma

Bo. San Felipe

AV. Matamoros

AV. LA PAZ

Col. Lomas del Guijarro

Col. Lomas del Mayab

MULTI PLAZA MALL

MERCADO JACALEAPA

Col. Kennedy

HOTEL CAMINO REAL

BLVD. JUAN PABLO II

BLVD. MIRAFLORES

HOTEL CROWNE PLAZA

PRESIDENTIAL RESIDENCE

BLVD. SUYAPA

Col. La Reforma

Col. La Leona

Col. Palmira

Bo. Guadalupe

Col. Tepeyac

ROCK CASTLE BAR

ALEJANDRO'S DISCO

Col. El Hogar

Col. Miraflores Sur

Río Jacaleapa

Col. Viera

Col. Tegucigalpa

HOTEL GUADALUPE

BLVD. SUYAPA

HOTEL PRINCESS

Col. Alameda

Col. Humuya

Col. Miramontes

BLVD. FUERZAS ARMADAS

Río San José

To El Hatillo, P.N. La Tigra, El Picacho, and P.N. Unidas

Bo. La Leona

AV. JUAN GUTEMBERG

Bo. San Rafael

Bo. Morazán

ESTADIO NACIONAL

Parque La Paz

AV.

Col. El Prado

Río Choluteca

Col. Las Brisas

To Olancho

Bo. El Chile

Bo. Abajo

Bo. El Centavo

Bo. Concepción

Comayagüela

AV. 2

AV. 6

Bo. La Bolsa

Bo. Guacerique

Bo. La Granja

Col. El Alamo

TONCONTIN INTERNATIONAL AIRPORT

To Choluteca

Bo. Bella Vista

Bo. San Martin

Bo. Belén

Col. Centroamericana

Col. Primavera

Col. El Trebol

BLVD. DEL NORTE

BLVD. FUERZAS ARMADAS

To Lepaterique

To Olancho

To Comayagua, San Pedro Sula

Río Guacerique

1 mi

1 km

0

0

as *la Catedral*) on one side and many of the city's main businesses and government buildings in the surrounding blocks. Most of the sights of interest to tourists are in walking distance of downtown. Because of the city's broken geography and haphazard construction over the centuries, Tegucigalpa does not have an ordered street plan and can be a bit confusing to navigate at first.

East and uphill from downtown are Barrio San Rafael and Colonia Palmira, the first modern, wealthy neighborhoods developed in Tegucigalpa, home to many of the city's embassies, high-priced hotels, and nicer restaurants. Farther east continue Avenida La Paz, home to the imposing U.S. Embassy building, and the parallel Boulevard Morazán, with many shops, restaurants, and mini-malls. Southeast of downtown extends Avenida Juan Pablo II, where the new Princess and Inter-Continental Hotels and the Mega Plaza Mall are located, and Boulevard Suyapa, which leads to the Basilica de Suyapa and the National University. Cutting south across the city, connecting the San Pedro Sula exit to the highway leading east to Danlí, is the fast-moving Blvd. Fuerzas Armadas.

Across the Río Choluteca from downtown is Comayagüela, a noisier and poorer sister city to Tegucigalpa. The main city market and all of the long-distance bus stations are in Comayagüela. Some travelers may find it convenient and inexpensive to stay in Comayagüela, but take care walking around at night.

Getting Around
The main sights downtown can easily be covered on foot, but buses or taxis are needed to get to many of the bus stations and far-flung parts of the city. Taxis in Tegucigalpa are more expensive than in smaller towns, usually charging US$1.50-3 around town, depending on where you're going, or US$4 out to the airport.

THE *PATRONATOS* THAT HELP MAKE THE SLUMS LIVABLE

Like almost all cities in Latin America, Tegucigalpa has grown at an alarming rate over the past several decades, from about 200,000 people in 1950 to somewhere close to a million today. As any visitor to Tegucigalpa quickly notices, most of these newcomers have settled in the mountains ringing the city, in shanty villages crawling up the hillsides from the valley floor. Immigrants simply go to the edge of the existing city and build a home out of cardboard or tin, later improving it with wood or cement blocks when they've got the money. Basic social services have followed this explosive, unplanned growth at a much slower pace. As the Library of Congress's Area Handbook states matter-of-factly, "For the vast majority of Tegucigalpa's urban population, living conditions are dismal." Water, sewage systems, electricity, telephone lines, bus routes, and paved roads, not to mention health care and schools—all have been long in coming to the barrios. Most residents say these services wouldn't have come at all were it not for the pressure put on the government by the *patronatos*.

An example of Hondurans' propensity and ability to organize themselves collectively, the *patronatos* have their origin in religious festivals. Each barrio has traditionally had its own patron saint, and committees, called *patronatos*, were formed among residents to help organize and pay for the fiesta on their saint's day. When people realized they would have to fight to get any services from the government, the *patronatos* took on the task, collecting donations, organizing demonstrations, and meeting with officials. The *patronatos* are now a fixture in the social landscape across Honduras, one of the strongest civil networks in the country. They are particularly vociferous and powerful in the lower-class barrios of Tegucigalpa.

The *patronatos* are invariably dominated by women, and this has added to their effectiveness. Often the groups shame government bureaucrats into fulfilling their demands. One *patronato* member tells the story of how a group of 75 women tore down a fence around land they wanted to use to build a health center, and then went downtown to confront the official responsible for putting up the fence. After much yelling, he finally agreed to let them use the land, saying, "What can you do with these women who talk like battleships?"

TEGUCIGALPA HIGHLIGHTS

If you only have one day to tour Tegucigalpa, don't miss:

- The Parque Central and the Cathedral, to people-watch and admire colonial religious art
- The Galería Nacional de Arte, to see one of the finest art collections in Central America
- La Villa Roy, for a brief tour of the nation's history
- Parque La Leona, for views over the city and a visit to the colonial Buenos Aires neighborhood

If you have time for day trips, consider:

- Hiking in La Tigra cloud forest and to the Rosario mines
- Shopping for handicrafts at Valle de Ángeles
- Visiting the colonial village of Ojojona and the nearby petroglyphs at El Sauce

Colectivo taxis run set routes and charge only US 35 cents, but figuring out which taxis go where requires lots of questions and walking around. One useful *colectivo* drives between Puente La Isla near the stadium out to Colonia Kennedy for US 35 cents. Another departs from a block behind La Merced and the Galería Nacional de Arte and drives past the Honduras Maya out to Av. Juan Pablo II. A third *colectivo* leaves from the corner of Av. Cervantes and Calle Salvador Mendieta and crosses Comayagüela via 4 Avenida, going out to Carrizal, by the exit to San Pedro Sula and Olancho.

Most buses cross the city from the south or west, pass through Comayagüela, and continue through Tegucigalpa out to the north or east. Some pass right by the *parque central,* while others cross the river farther upstream and pass by the Penitenciaría or the Estadio Nacional. Two oft-used buses are the "21 Tiloarque-La Sosa," which runs from Mercado Mayoreo up 6 Avenida in Comayagüela, through downtown, and out Avenida La Paz to where the Valle de Ángeles and Santa Lucía buses leave, and the "32", which goes from Comayagüela out Boulevard Suyapa to the National University. All buses marked "Carrizal" go through Comaya-

güela to the highway exit to San Pedro Sula and Olancho, past Mercado Mayoreo. Buses for Universidad Nacional Autónoma de Honduras (UNAH) come from Carrizal and drive through Comayagüela, past the stadium, and out Avenida Suyapa.

If at all possible, avoid driving in downtown Tegucigalpa and in Comayagüela, as the traffic is hideous. Armed with a decent map the city is not all that difficult to navigate, but the endless wait, especially during rush hour, can be stressful. The eastern avenues like Morazán, Juan Pablo II, and Miraflores, as well as the southerly loop road Blvd. Fuerzas Armadas, all flow relatively smoothly throughout the day. Construction of a second stretch of "Períferico," across the eastern part of the city, was stalled at last report but should be completed ere long.

SIGHTS

Parque Central

Tegucigalpa's downtown square is a great place to relax and people-watch. It's invariably full of city folk walking around, buying newspapers, selling odds and ends, or just hanging out. Beware of sitting under the trees as you may find yourself the object of target practice from the pigeons above.

A *peatonal* (pedestrian street) extends several blocks west of the square and is lined with shops, restaurants, street vendors, and money changers. In early 2000, the city government cleaned out all the vendors (known as *buhoneros*) from the square and pedestrian street, but the feisty and well-organized vendors have sworn to return. Time will tell.

Parroquia de San Miguel Arcángel

Otherwise known as the Catedral, the Parroquia was built between 1765 and 1782 on the site of a simpler wooden church and is a fine example of late colonial architecture. Although the design is relatively simple, the vaulted ceiling and domed altar are impressive. The incredibly intricate gold-and-silver altarpiece sculpted by Guatemalan artist Vicente Gálvez is the church's artistic highlight. Presiding over the altar is a statue of San Miguel, the patron saint of Tegucigalpa. Several sculptures and paintings decorate the interior, including ones by famed colonial artist José Miguel Gómez.

The Catedral was damaged so badly in the earthquake of 1808 it was practically abandoned for almost 30 years before being reinforced. A 1975 earthquake caused further damage, which has since been repaired.

La Merced and Galería Nacional de Arte

A block south of the square is La Iglesia de La Merced, built in the mid-18th century and featuring a beautiful gilded altarpiece flanked by two smaller *retablos*. The building next door to the church, built in 1654, was originally a convent, then in 1847 became the Universidad Nacional. In 1996 the building changed again, this time into the Galería Nacional de Arte, tel. 237-9884, one of the finest art galleries in Central America.

The gallery traces the evolution of Honduran art, beginning downstairs with rooms dedicated to prehistoric pictographs and petroglyphs, stone

---

THAT STATUE~IS IT MORAZÁN OR IS IT NEY?

The statue in the center of the square in Tegucigalpa may not be exactly what it seems. Sometime around the turn of the century, a delegation of Honduran congressmen was sent to Paris to commission a statue of national hero Francisco Morazán. But in Paris, they wound up spending most of the commission money enjoying the pleasures of the City of Lights. When they realized that they had created a problem for themselves, the hung-over congressmen found in an art store a used statue of Michel Ney, one of Napoléon's famous generals and a marshal of France. Deciding that no one in Honduras would be the wiser, they had a new plaque inscribed for Ney's statue, and it suddenly became Morazán.

So goes a possibly apocryphal story, anyway, often used as a classic illustration of Honduran incompetence. More recently, a patriotic Honduran historian claims to have unearthed a receipt in the French National Archives from a Parisian sculptor contracting him to make a statue of Morazán. If the statue is indeed of Ney, then the Frenchman bore a remarkable resemblance to Honduras' national hero.

---

and ceramic art from the Mayan era, and a stunning collection of colonial paintings, sculptures, and gold and silver religious art. The pieces were all chosen for their visual beauty rather than historical importance. Upstairs, several rooms contain paintings from classic Honduran artists Pablo Zelaya Sierra, Carlos Zuñiga Figueroa, and José Antonio Velásquez, as well as lesser known painters and sculptors such as Eziquiel Padilla, Dante Lazzaroni, Arturo López Rodezno, and Anibel Cruz.

For such a small, economically deprived country, Honduras has produced an unusual number of fine visual artists, and the museum is an excellent tour of the country's artistic history. The artwork is laid out tastefully and with good lighting, and the historical progression allows visitors to appreciate the development of Honduran art. Art aficionados should not miss this museum. US$1 entrance fee; open Mon.-Fri. 9 a.m.-4 p.m., Saturdays 9 a.m.-noon.

Next to the church and art gallery is the Palacio Legislativo, or National Congress. It's known laconically by locals as El Sapo ("the frog") because the bizarre architecture makes it seem as though the building is about to hop away.

Museo Histórico de la República

A block west of the Congress building is the Museo Histórico de la República, housed in the old Presidential Palace. The neo-classical building, designed by Italian architect Augusto Bressani, took 10 years to build due to the political instability in Honduras at the turn of the 20th century. It served as the office and home of the president from 1916 to 1992, when Rafael Callejas declared it a museum and moved his offices to Colonia Miraflores.

The museum, now closed for renovations, formerly housed a collection of historical material, which is now at La Villa Roy. No word was available on when the old palace will reopen or what will be inside when it does.

Parroquia de San Francisco

Facing a small, shady park three blocks east of the square is the oldest extant church in the city, first erected in 1592 and rebuilt in 1740. Inside the church are a gilded altarpiece and several colonial-era religious paintings. The building next door, formerly the Franciscan monastery, is now used by the Army. At last report, the interior of the church was undergoing major renovations.

Museo del Hombre

Housed in the recently renovated building on Avenida Cervantes four blocks east of the *parque* is a quiet, modest museum dedicated to painting, principally by contemporary Honduran artists. Works of the revolving exhibits are hung in several spacious rooms around a small interior courtyard, in a house once owned by Indepen-dence hero Ramón Rosa. The house later served as the national Supreme Court. The museum has frequent receptions and events—for more information call 238-3198. Admission is free; open Mon.-Fri. 8:30-noon and 1:30-5 p.m. In the back of the museum is one of Honduras' principal art restoration workshops.

Parque Herrera and Teatro Bonilla

Six blocks west of the square is the shady, attractive Parque Herrera, in front of which stands

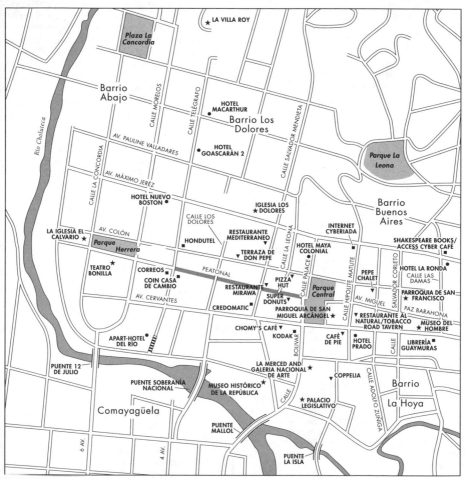

the Teatro Nacional Manuel Bonilla, built in 1915. The facade is nothing spectacular, but the ornate interior, designed in the style of the Athenée of Paris, is a sight to behold. The theater seats 600 in rows on the ground floor and in the compartments above. For information on upcoming performances, ask at the box office or call 222-4366.

On the west side of the park is **La Iglesia El Calvario,** dating from the mid-18th century and housing several *retablos* and an image of the Virgen de la Soledad.

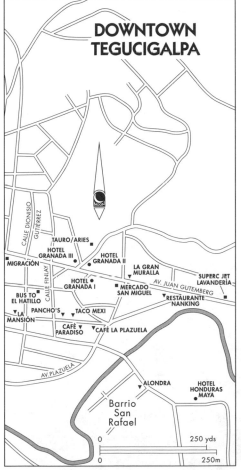

DOWNTOWN TEGUCIGALPA

Iglesia Los Dolores

Dominating a large square filled with vendors, Los Dolores is a large, bright white church with a relatively plain facade but featuring several attractive pieces of religious art inside, including relief paintings of the stations of the cross, a gilded, carved altarpiece, and the painted interior dome. The church, built in 1732, is several blocks northwest of the downtown square.

La Villa Roy

La Villa Roy, a mansion perched on a hillside just west of downtown Tegucigalpa, was donated to the public in 1974 by the wife of ex-president Julio Lozano Díaz. The gesture seems remarkably patriotic, considering her husband was deposed by a military coup in 1956. The mansion now houses the **Museo Nacional de Honduras,** tel. 222-3440 or 222-1468, the national history museum, tracing the development of the Honduran republic from its birth at the end of the Spanish colonial era to the present.

Though the museum is not particularly gripping, people with at least a passing interest in Honduran history will find several displays to hold their attention, especially if they can read the Spanish labels. The well-worn boots and trusty Eveready flashlight of great Honduran geographer and cultural historian Jesús Aguilar Paz, who created the first accurate map of Honduras in 1933 and compiled voluminous journals during his endless trips around the country on oral history, local legends, and observations on flora and fauna, are enshrined in a glass case. The rooms upstairs dedicated to the early part of the 20th century, complete with many old photographs and paraphernalia, are quite informative, but the history of the Carias era and the second half of the 20th century are bland.

On your way out, take a look at the fleet of black presidential vehicles parked in the garage, including a couple of wicked-looking Cadillacs. Unfortunately the museum staff doesn't seem to appreciate these beauties—one car's whitewall tire had a flat at last check.

Admission US$1.50; open Tues.-Sun. 8:30 a.m.-3:30 p.m.

Just below the museum, on the way back into downtown, is the small **Plaza La Concordia,** featuring several replicas of Mayan sculptures.

Parque La Leona

Set among the winding cobblestone streets and colonial houses of the picturesque Buenos Aires neighborhood just west and uphill from the square, Parque La Leona makes a pleasant spot to take a rest and admire the views over downtown and the valley. The park is a 15-minute walk from the square up a steep hill.

Parque La Paz

Atop Juana Laínez hill in the center of Tegucigalpa, near the National Stadium, is Parque La Paz, commemorating the peace treaty ending the so-called "Soccer War" between El Salvador and Honduras in 1969. The road winding up to the top starts next to the fire station behind the stadium. On top is a stone monument with a huge flag perpetually fluttering in the breeze, surrounded by trees that limit the views somewhat. The only way up if you don't have a car is on foot or in a taxi.

Basílica de Suyapa and Santuario Nacional

Honduras' patron saint, La Virgen de Suyapa, is venerated in a simple white plaster chapel set on a small square on the eastern outskirts of Tegucigalpa, near the National University (Universidad Nacional Autónoma de Honduras, or UNAH). The Basílica de Suyapa, built in 1749, houses the six-centimeter-tall statue of the virgin in a wooden case behind

HOLY WEEK IN TEGUCIGALPA

Although many of the capital's residents flee the city to the beach during Holy Week (Semana Santa) leading up to Easter Sunday, others stay behind to watch and participate in Tegucigalpa's traditional processions, which tell different parts of the biblical Easter story during the course of the week.

The series of parades begins with the Procession of the Triumphant Arrival, representing Christ coming into Jerusalem on a donkey, and is followed by the Lord of Humility Procession on Tuesday, the ominous male-only Procession of Chains on Thursday, the Holy Cross Procession on Good Friday, the late night Virgin of Solitude Procession, the Holy Burial Procession, and the festive Procession of the Empty Tomb on Easter Sunday, celebrating Christ's resurrection.

Each procession begins at the Catedral on the main square in Tegucigalpa and continues along Calle Real and Avenida Centenario (6 Avenida) in Comayagüela, ending at the Iglesia de la Inmaculada Concepción.

In former years, families along the procession path would set up *descansos,* or resting stops, for participants to stop and pray at small, home-built altars. Many city residents would also decorate elaborate carpets made of colored sawdust, or *alfombras,* to lay out along the road. *Descansos* and *alfombras* are still often seen, but not as frequently as in the past. Many smaller towns in central Honduras still hold these parades in all their glory.

the Santuario Nacional, in Tegucigalpa

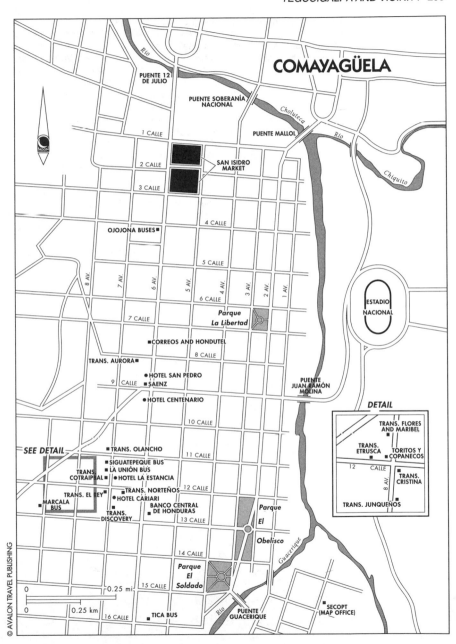

COMAYAGÜELA

PUENTE 12 DE JULIO
PUENTE SOBERANÍA NACIONAL
Río
Choluteca
PUENTE MALLOL
Río
Chiquito
1 CALLE
2 CALLE
SAN ISIDRO MARKET
3 CALLE
4 CALLE
OJOJONA BUSES ■
5 CALLE
8 AV.
7 AV.
6 AV.
5 AV.
4 AV.
3 AV.
2 AV.
1 AV.
6 CALLE
ESTADIO NACIONAL
7 CALLE
Parque La Libertad
■ CORREOS AND HONDUTEL
8 CALLE
TRANS. AURORA ■
9 CALLE
● HOTEL SAN PEDRO
■ SAENZ
PUENTE JUAN RAMÓN MOLINA
● HOTEL CENTENARIO
10 CALLE

DETAIL

SEE DETAIL
■ TRANS. OLANCHO
11 CALLE
■ SIGUATEPEQUE BUS
■ LA UNIÓN BUS
TRANS. COTRAIPBAL ■ ● HOTEL LA ESTANCIA
■ TRANS. NORTEÑOS
12 CALLE
TRANS. EL REY ■ ● HOTEL CARIARI
MARCALA BUS ■
BANCO CENTRAL DE HONDURAS
TRANS. ■ 13 CALLE
DISCOVERY
Parque El Obelisco
14 CALLE
Parque El Soldado
15 CALLE
Guacerique
TICA BUS ■
16 CALLE
PUENTE GUACERIQUE
Río
SECOPT (MAP OFFICE) ■

DETAIL
TRANS. FLORES AND MARIBEL ■
TRANS. ETRUSCA ■
TORITOS Y COPANECOS ■
12 CALLE
8 AV.
■ TRANS. CRISTINA
TRANS. JUNQUENOS ■

0   0.25 mi
0   0.25 km

© AVALON TRAVEL PUBLISHING

the altar. According to the story, the statue was discovered in a nearby cornfield in 1743. The church is often packed with worshippers from across the country praying to the diminutive virgin.

A short distance from the chapel, set on a hillside and dominating the skyline in the east part of the city, is the Santuario Nacional, a massive, cavernous church built in 1958. It's painted in bright colors and covered with pictographic stained-glass windows. Shortly after the church was built, the statue of La Virgen de Suyapa was placed here. Local legend has it that she didn't much care for her rather garish new sanctuary—shortly after moving in, she vanished and reappeared in the old chapel. Evidently she understands the problems of crowd control, however, and consents to be brought to the new church during the annual fiesta in her honor, 25 Jan.-4 Feb., when many thousands of worshippers travel to see her.

Parque Naciones Unidas
On the top of Montaña El Picacho off the road to El Hatillo, Parque Naciones Unidas commands views over the entire Tegucigalpa Valley. Opened in the 1940s, the pine-forested park is a fine place to escape the noise of the city for a while and breathe clean air. The park also features a frequently used soccer field, a small zoo, and (the most recent addition) the Cristo del Picacho, similar in style to the Christ statue over the harbor in Río de Janeiro. Buses to El Picacho leave from behind Los Dolores church on Sunday only—during the week take an El Hatillo bus, get off at the intersection, and walk one and a half km into the park, or take a cab. Entrance is US 20 cents; open daily 8 a.m.-5:30 p.m.

On the way to the park, just under a kilometer from the turnoff from Av. Jeréz, is the imposing white Universidad Católica de Honduras building, visible from around the city. The wide-open uni-

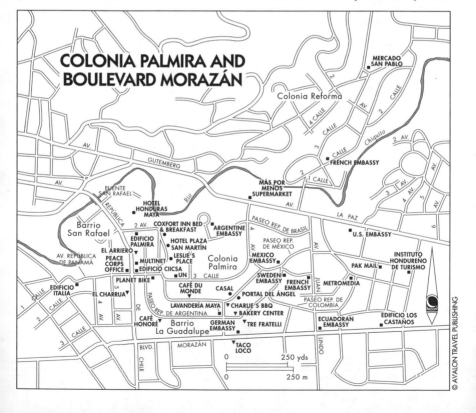

COLONIA PALMIRA AND BOULEVARD MORAZÁN

© AVALON TRAVEL PUBLISHING

versity parking lot makes a great place not too far from downtown to catch views over the city.

Sights in Comayagüela

The **San Isidro Market** just over the bridge in Comayagüela, between 5 and 7 Avenidas and 1 and 2 Calles, is worth a visit to check out the hustle and bustle—it's the city's largest market. Commerce is hardly confined by the actual market building, though, with thousands of vendors of all variety lining the surrounding streets, bridges, and sidewalks. Absolutely everything seems to be for sale: pencils, erasers, T-shirts, toothpaste, toilet paper, dried herbs still on the stem or ground in plastic bags, cheap silverware sets, pocket calculators, wristwatches, fresh slaughtered pork and beef, cheeses from Olancho, and myriad other sundries, really an astounding assortment of products. Most people in the market seem cheerfully amused by foreign visitors, but beware of pickpockets in crowds anyway. Take a chance and go inside the market building itself—it looks daunting from outside, but you'll generally find it a lot quieter and less hectic than the streets. It's even worth coming up with something to look for, just to go through the process of asking around and finally arriving at the one stall that has exactly what you're looking for.

ACCOMMODATIONS

As you would expect from a capital city, Tegucigalpa offers a wealth of hotel rooms in all price ranges. Most visitors will want to stay in the downtown area, which is where many hotels are located. More well-heeled travelers can choose from quality hotels in downtown, the Palmira area, and out on Blvd. Juan Pablo II, southeast of downtown. Comayagüela, across the Río Choluteca, also has plenty of hotels in the budget and mid-range categories—useful for travelers arriving late or departing early by bus, since most buses pull into Comayagüela.

Shoestring

Hotel Granada I, on Av. Juan Gutemberg in Barrio Guanacaste, tel. 237-2381, is something of a Tegucigalpa institution, attracting travelers, Peace Corps workers, and Hondurans with its three floors of clean, inexpensive tile-floored rooms; US$4 s, US$5 d with shared bath, or US$7 s, US$8 d with private bath. The communal bathroom on the second floor has an endless supply of hot water, drinking water is free, and the reception desk sells soft drinks. Around the corner from the Granada I are the Granada II, tel. 237-4004, and Granada III, tel. 222-0597, each charging US$7 s, US$9 d with private bath.

Half a block north of the square on Calle Palace, **Hotel Maya Colonial,** tel. 237-2643, offers high-ceilinged plaster-walled rooms around a courtyard in a colonial-era building for US$7 s or US$9 d. Some rooms have great old bathtubs, but unfortunately there's no hot water! Drinking water is free.

In an alley next to Iglesia Los Dolores are several very cheap but filthy *hospedajes,* only fit for the extremely poor willing to fight off the drunks who hang around the alley. Around the corner from Los Dolores is **Hotel Goascaran #2** (not to be confused with #1, one of the dives in the alley), a barely acceptable cheapie with double rooms for US$5 d.

Budget

A favorite among Peace Corps workers in town from their sites, **Hotel Guadalupe** is in Barrio Guadalupe near the start of Blvd. Morazán at Av. Tiburcio Carias Andino, Sendero Lamani No. 1501, tel. 232-8912 or 239-8745. Owned by the same people who own the Hotel Granada, the Guadalupe has very clean tile-floored rooms with cable TV, hot water, telephone, and a fan for US$10 s or US$12 d. For those hanging out downtown, the hotel is somewhat out of the way, but it's a good value otherwise.

For a bit of a splurge in the budget category, the American-owned **Hotel Nuevo Boston,** at Máximo Jeréz 321, just west of Los Dolores church, tel. 237-9411, offers very quiet rooms set around two small courtyards. The rooms have fans and hot water, and rent for US$15 s or US$20 d; more for the larger rooms facing the street. No TVs in the rooms, just the one in the comfortable sitting room next to the reception.

Inexpensive

Unique **Apart-Hotel Del Río,** tel./fax 22-1889 or 37-6678, rents 10 apartments of varying sizes in a converted modernist mansion above the Río Choluteca. Each apartment has a kitchenette, and some have balconies and telephones; US$25-40 per room, weekly and monthly rates available. The house has a large reading room, as well as a porch and garden overlooking the river. It's conveniently located just a couple of blocks from downtown, yet in a quiet neighborhood. Reservations are suggested as the bilingual owners often host groups.

Hotel MacArthur, in Colonia Dolores, a residential neighborhood close to downtown, tel. 237-9839 or 238-0414, fax 238-0294, email: homacart@datum.hn, features well-lit, airy modern rooms with hot water, telephone, and TV for US$28 s, US$33 d, or US$33 s and US$38 d with a/c. The well-managed hotel also has a reasonably priced cafeteria and an interior parking lot.

Bed & Breakfasts

Just above Hotel Honduras Maya, in the Colonial Palmira, are three comfortable, quiet bed & breakfasts falling into the moderate or expensive price ranges. **Coxfort Inn Bed and Breakfast,** tel./fax 239-1197 or 239-1254, email: coxfort@hondutel.hn, run by English-speaking owners who live on the premises, rents 14 very cozy, tastefully decorated rooms with TV and telephone for US$45 s or US$60 d, less for longer stays, a bit more for a larger room. Guests have use of a small pool and gym. Two rooms with kitchenettes are available for an extra charge. The B&B is right next to Hotel San Martín.

Leslie's Place, on the other side of Hotel San Martín, tel. 239-0641, fax 232-1687, email: services@dormir.com, website: www.dormir.com, in a converted house with a pleasant patio, offers eight rooms decorated with new furniture and equipped with TV and telephone for US$59 s, US$74 d.

A few blocks east of the other two B&Bs, at República de Perú 2116 in a quiet residential neighborhood, is a third: **Casal,** tel. 235-8891 or 235-8892. The small, well-managed hotel has only eight rooms, each spacious and comfortable, for US$55 s or US$70 d.

Expensive

A block up the hill from the Honduras Maya is the fortresslike **Hotel Plaza San Martín,** tel. 237-2928 or 237-2930, fax 231-1366, painted gleaming white with pastel accents, visible all over the city. Quieter than the Maya, the San Martín is fa-

vored by wealthier Hondurans and has 110 rooms with balconies for US$69 s, US$89 d, or US$147 suite. The hotel has a restaurant, bar, and a small gym with sauna on the 10th floor. At last report the same owners were building **Hotel Plaza del General** across the street, expected to be more upscale.

Opposite the San Martín is **Hotel Plaza del Libertador,** tel. 220-4141, fax 220-4242, email: libertad@netsys.hn, another high-rise hotel with similar prices. Each room has a small private balcony.

Hotel La Ronda, tel. 237-8151 to -8154, in the U.S. (800) 446-2747, is considered the finest hotel in the heart of downtown, with 72 modern, air-conditioned rooms going for US$62 s or US$74 d for one of the nicer, outdoor-facing rooms, less for an interior room, buffet breakfast included. The elegant dining room at Restaurante La Rondalla serves highly recommended food. Upstairs is a solarium dining room, and the bar often has a live combo playing.

Similar to La Ronda is **Hotel Prado,** adjacent to the Catedral on Av. Cervantes, tel. 237-0121 to -0127, fax 237-2221. Hotel Prado offers 70 rooms, each with a/c and refrigerator, some overlooking the square, for US$60 s, US$70 d, US$80 suite. Price includes breakfast at Restaurante La Posada. Live bands often play at the hotel's El Cabildo lounge.

Premium

For whatever reason (the influx of foreign aide workers, perhaps?), several new high-end hotels opened their doors in Tegucigalpa recently, including the Princess, Camino Real, and soon a Crowne Plaza. The rates quoted below are the normal rack rates. Less expensive weekend or corporate rates are often available on request.

On a hill overlooking downtown from the east, the **Honduras Maya,** tel. 220-5000, fax 220-6000, email: hondurasmaya@globalnet.hn, website: www.hondurasmaya.hn, has long been the hotel of choice for wealthy guests both foreign and local. The Maya has 189 rooms with all the amenities for US$140 s, US$155 d, or a special executive suite for US$230 with fax and direct phone lines. The downstairs cafeteria has a good breakfast but is otherwise nothing special, while the Restaurante La Veranda is better. Other services include an outdoor pool and ample patio; a souvenir shop selling English-language newspapers, magazines, and books; a travel agent; a hair stylist; and a large convention center. Next door, under different ownership, is the **Casino Royale,** the only casino in Tegucigalpa. Several blocks east of the Honduras Maya, in Colonia Palmira at Av. República de Perú 2115, is the very fine boutique hotel **Portal del Angel,** tel. 239-6538, fax 235-8839, email: hpangel@david.intertel.hn. Set in an attractive mansion, with a restful dining room/sitting area, the hotel has 14 rooms on two floors with tile and wood floors, carved wooden furniture, tasteful decorations and all the amenities. The hotel restaurant, El Portal, has an excellent menu, worth visiting even if you're not staying there. Rooms rent for US$101-131 s or d.

East of downtown are the two newest additions to Tegucigalpa's high-end market, the Intercontinental and the Princess. **Hotel Camino Real Intercontinental,** directly across from the MultiPlaza Mall on Av. Juan Pablo II, tel. 231-1300, fax 231-1400, in the U.S. (800) 462-6686, website: www.interconti.com, opened in December 1999. The sandstone-colored building, with a spacious atrium and adjacent outdoor patio, has 157 rooms, including suites and business-class rooms. Regular rates are US$180 s or d, though weekend prices go as low as US$90 and corporate rates are US$130. The Azulejos restaurant has a large and creative menu, with a pricey but hearty breakfast buffet (US$12), as well as a regular menu, and dinner entrees for US$9-12.

At the corner of Av. Juan Pablo II and Av. Juan Gálvez is **Hotel Princess,** tel. 220-4500, fax 220-5086, in U.S. and Canada 1-800-53 SUITE, email: princessteg@datum.hn. The boxy 10-story hotel may be architecturally uninspired, but facilities are top-notch, and the hotel service is attentive and efficient. Health spa, outdoor pool, business center, and meeting rooms are all available. Rates are US$160 s or US$180 d.

Comayagüela Accommodations

The four-story **Hotel San Pedro,** on 6 Av. between 8 and 9 Calles, tel. 222-8987, is popular for its ultra-cheap, clean rooms at US$4 s or d with one bed and communal bathroom, or US$8 s or d with private bath. **Hotel La Estancia,** near several bus terminals on 7 Av. between 11 and

12 Calles, tel. 237-3564, is a good value at US$8 s or d with private bathroom with hot water and overhead fans. The quiet rooms surround a small interior courtyard. The rooms also rent by two-hour periods, which is suspicious, but at least it's kept very clean.

Hotel Cariari, convenient to many bus stations at 7 Av. between 12 and 13 Calles, tel. 238-6285, features 12 clean, quiet rooms in a family-run hotel for US$5 s, US$8 d communal bath, or US$6 s, US$10 d private bath, all with overhead fans.

For a nicer room, check out **Hotel Centenario,** on 6 Av. between 9 and 10 Calles, tel. 222-7575 or 222-1050, charging US$11 s or US$14 d with one bed or US$21 with two beds. All rooms have TV and telephone.

FOOD

Tegucigalpa could hardly be considered a culinary mecca, but with a little poking around you'll find a variety of different cuisines and price ranges to suit all tastes. Apart from the restaurants described below, travelers will find many of their favorite fast-food joints, including Wendy's, McDonald's, Burger King, and Pizza Hut, most with branches downtown, in Comayagüela, Blvd. Morazán, and Av. Juan Pablo II, as well as in the food court at the MultiPlaza Mall.

Inexpensive

One relaxed, clean little eatery, five blocks east of the square on Av. Miguel Barahona, is **La Mansion,** with decent breakfasts (US$1.25) and a good lunch buffet (US$2-3). The restaurant, with tables in the courtyard of an old house, is open Mon.-Sat. 7:30 a.m.-2:30 p.m.

A good breakfast value is the large buffet at **Super Donuts** on the *peatonal,* just off the square. The servers invariably dish out a small mountain of scrambled eggs.

Pancho's, on Av. Miguel Barahona, east of Iglesia San Francisco in the Barrio Guanacaste, is a popular spot for excellent and low-priced *alambres, tortas, tacos al pastor, queso fundido,* and other Mexican-style meals. The music and relaxed atmosphere make it a good spot to hang out, drink some beers, and chat with friends. Open Mon.-Sat. 9 a.m.-10 p.m., later if there's business.

A few doors downhill from Pancho's on the same street is **TacoMexi,** selling very inexpensive and not overly greasy *tortas, tacos,* and other Mexican *antojitos,* open Mon.-Sat. until 8 p.m.

A perennial favorite among budget travelers for low-priced Honduran standards is **La Terraza de Don Pepe,** on the second floor of a building on Av. Colón, three blocks west of the *parque.* If you go to eat there, don't fail to take a look in the men's bathroom, where in 1986 the statue of the Virgen de Suyapa, Honduras' patron saint, appeared wrapped in newspaper, after being stolen some weeks earlier from its church. The bathroom has been converted into a colorful shrine. The restaurant is open daily until 9 p.m., and there's a second branch a block behind the Catedral on Av. Miguel Paz Barahona.

With similar food but a step up in quality from the other two Pepe's, and run by Pepe's son, is **Pepe Chalet,** at the corner of Av. Colón and Adolfo Zuñiga, tel. 238-1340. This mid-range place in a comfortable converted house serves better-than-average *plato típico* (US$4), *yucca al mojo* (US$2.25), fish (US$5) and a few other choices, open Mon.-Sat. 10 a.m.-9 p.m. A laughably bad pop band often plays tunes on a synthesizer during the lunch and dinner hour—be sure to sit well away so as not to spoil your digestion.

They call themselves **Restaurante Mediterraneo,** but their selection of Mediterranean food is limited to a Greek salad and "suflaky." No matter—the menu is extensive, prices are reasonable, and service is good. The diner-style restaurant is a popular place for office workers to have drinks and talk, and the waitresses will bring you an endless supply of *bocitas* (snacks) while you drink. The US$3 daily set meals are a good value. Open Mon.-Sat. 9:30 a.m.-10 p.m., on Calle Salvador Mendieta.

Should you find yourself looking for a low-priced meal out on Blvd. Morazán, check out **Taco Loco,** in a shopping center on the south side of the road, roughly opposite Calle Maipu. The small, clean taco joint serves a hearty *taco cazador,* with diced chicken in an oversized flour tortilla, with or without cheese, for US$2. Open 9 a.m.-11 p.m. daily. There is also a branch opposite the airport, in the south of the city.

Pastries, Coffee, and Snacks
The quiet **Café Paradiso,** on Av. Miguel Barahona in Barrio Guanacaste, tel. 22-3066, serves coffee and pastries amidst a small but interesting collection of Spanish-language books and *artesanías.* The cafe is popular with the local intelligentsia and frequently hosts poetry readings or other cultural events. Open Mon.-Fri. 9 a.m.-8 p.m., Saturday 9 a.m.-7 p.m. Soon to open just down the street, by the traffic circle, is **Café La Plazuela,** another espresso shop.

Tucked into a courtyard just off Av. Cervantes, half a block down from the park, is **Chomy's Café** with good espresso drinks and a variety of tasty pastries for US$1 a slice. It also has light meals, including a decent vegetarian quiche (US$1.15) and ham and cheese croissants (US$1.50). Open Mon.-Fri. 8 a.m.-6 p.m., Saturdays 8 a.m.-2 p.m.

Another small cafe in a pedestrian area off Av. Cervantes, this one near Hotel Prado, is **Café de Pie,** also with pastries and light meals, a good place for people-watching, open Mon.-Fri. 7:30 a.m.-6 p.m., Saturday 7:30 a.m.-1 p.m.

Salman's bakery chain, with several branches in town, including one on the *peatonal,* sells fresh sandwiches for only US 60 cents and has a few small tables where patrons can sit down and munch.

Anyone with a bagel craving should head post-haste to **Pan y Más,** in Bakery Center just off Blvd. Morazán in Colonia Palmira. Open Mon.-Sat. 7:30 a.m.-7:30 p.m.

Vegetarian
Behind the cathedral, **Restaurante Al Natural,** tel. 238-3422, is a shady enclave of quietness serving inexpensive, healthy dishes such as vegetable soups, Spanish tortillas, salads, juices, and breakfasts. Open Mon.-Sat. 8 a.m.-9 p.m.

Coppelia, on Calle La Isla a block behind La Merced church, prepares inexpensive, good-for-you *licuados* and fruit salads. Open Mon.-Sat. 7 a.m.-7 p.m.

Honduran
One of the more creative restaurants in Tegucigalpa is **Alondra,** in a converted house opposite the Honduras Maya on República de Chile, tel. 31-5909. Among the specialties are shrimp and

mushrooms soaked in whiskey, chicken in wine sauce, and steak *al jalapeño*. Neat attire and reservations are recommended. Open Mon.-Sat. noon-2 p.m. and 7-10 p.m.

Italian
The newest of several local Italian restaurants, and universally considered to be the current best, is **Tre Fratelli**, on Av. República de Argentina in Colonia Palmira, a block off Blvd. Morazán, tel. 232-1942. Of the many decadently rich and flavorful entrees is the *lasagna modo Fratello,* with mushrooms, spinach and bolognese sauce (US$5.50). Crispy pizzas cost US$4-5, and there have lots of pastas to choose from. Open Mon.-Sat. noon-3 p.m. and 6-11 p.m., Sunday 11-4:30 p.m.
At the far end of Blvd. Morazán, half a block in from the last stoplight right behind Pollo Campero, is **Il Padrino**, tel. 221-0198, one of the better Italian restaurants in town. An extensive selection of pastas, pizzas, paella, bacalao, and other Mediterranean specialties, US$5-10 per entree, are served in a slightly formal lounge with shades across the windows, straight out of a mafia flick. Open daily noon-11 p.m.

French
Café du Monde, tel. 239-0334, in a converted house in Colonia Palmira, appropriately close to the French Embassy, has a menu of quiche, sandwiches like brie over a croissant (US$4), salads for US$4-7, cheese and paté platters for US$7.50, and other light meals. A brunch is served Saturday until 2 p.m. Open Mon.-Sat. 10 a.m.-7 p.m.

Delicatessan/Gourmet Foods
Café Honoré, in Colonia Palmira on Av. República de Argentina, deserves a category all to itself. Though a bit pricey, the deli-style sandwiches, homemade soups, salads, and pastries are of truly excellent quality. Try the hearty corn chowder, with potatoes and bacon, or the artichoke dip. A hot or cold sandwich will set you back US$5-8 for a large or US$3-6 for a small, while soups cost US$3-5 for a bowl or US$1.75-3 for a cup. Lining shelves around the walls of the cafe are all sorts of gourmet crackers, jellies, spices, and other goodies, while imported cheeses and cold-cuts are for sale at the deli counter.

Chinese
Opposite Hotel Granada on Av. Juan Gutemberg, **La Gran Muralla** serves huge portions of chop suey and other dishes, big enough to feed two if you're not ravenous. Try the daily specials. Open 10 a.m.-9 p.m.
A couple of blocks farther east on the other side of the street is **Restaurante Nanking,** on the ground floor of the hotel of the same name, offering a monster chop suey for US$2.50 and other dishes in a spacious dining room. Open daily 11 a.m.-10 p.m.
Restaurante Mirawa, with dining rooms on Avenida Morazán and on the *peatonal* just off the square, has great wonton soup and inexpensive meals. It's open daily 10 a.m.-9 p.m.

Japanese
The new **Sushi Bar,** in the Bakery Center on Av. República de Argentina in Colonia Palmira, a block off Blvd. Morazán, tel. 239-3233, will fix the craving of traveler looking for a respectable (though not spectacular, but what can you expect?) tempura, teriyaki, and a variety of sushi. The sushi rolls run US$2-20. Open Mon.-Sat. noon-2 p.m. and 5:30-10 p.m.

Steaks
El Arriero, on Av. República de Chile just up from Hotel Honduras Maya, tel. 232-5431, serves pricey but excellent South American-style cuts of beef. Open Mon.-Sat. 11:30 a.m.-3 p.m. and 6-11 p.m., Sunday 11:30 a.m.-10 p.m.
Farther uphill on the same street, but on the opposite side, is **El Charrua,** tel. 232-3432, which bills itself as an Uruguayan-style steak house. The prices and quality are similar to El Arriero. Open daily 11 a.m.-11 p.m.

Out of the City
Far up on the mountainside above Tegucigalpa, on the road to El Hatillo, is **El Cumbre,** tel. 211-9000 or 211-9001, a restaurant that would be worth going to just for its spectacular views over the city but thankfully has excellent international food, including a couple of German specialties like *wienerschnitzel* and *jägerschnitzel*. Bring a sweater or jacket—you'll want to sit outside for the view, but it can be cool up in the hills. Open Tues.-Sat. noon-3 p.m. and 6-10 p.m., Sunday noon-3 p.m.; reservations recommended.

ENTERTAINMENT

Dancing

Plaza Garibaldi on Blvd. Morazán is a combination bar-restaurant-disco with a party ambiance that attracts locals and foreigners alike. The small dance floor gets packed with couples dancing until dawn on weekends, or until 2 or 3 a.m. during the week. The Mexican-style food is not outrageously expensive and fairly tasty, and it even has the *yarda loca,* an oversized glass of draft beer.

Of the several discos in town, **Rock Castle, Alejandro's,** and **Tropical Port,** on Avenida Juan Pablo II, and **Confetti's,** on Boulevard Morazán, are all lively and fairly safe. Rock Castle, still sometimes known by the name of its past incarnation, Back Streets, also has a couple of pool tables and is a good spot to party, whether you like dancing or not.

Bars

Tobacco Road Tavern, directly behind the Catedral in the same building as Restaurante Al Natural, tel. 237-3909, is the favorite expat/travelers' bar in town, a relaxing spot to tip a few quiet drinks on the patio or join in the international mix at the bar. American owner Tom Taylor sells a selection of Danlí cigars and is invariably glad to help steer travelers in the right direction. The bar is normally open Mon.-Sat. 1-11 p.m., or sometimes until midnight.

The lounge-bar at Hotel Prado is a mellow spot to go enjoy a few low-priced rum and cokes.

About halfway out Blvd. Morazán on the left-hand side is **Iguana Rana,** tel. 235-7644, a vaguely yuppie/sports bar, but not offensively so, favored by middle-class office workers. The Tex-Mex and U.S.-style bar food is very good and not expensive, and the porch bar is a relaxed spot to have a few beers with friends or watch a sports match on the TV. Open Mon.-Wed. until midnight, other days until the wee hours.

Billiards

Mr. Pool, a block north of the square on Av. Máximo Jeréz, is well lit and has many tables. Open daily 9 a.m.-11 p.m., the pool hall has a heavy male atmosphere, although women are allowed.

Cinemas

Movie theaters in Tegucigalpa showing first-run movies include **Tauro/Aries** in Barrio Guanacaste near the Hotel Granada; the **Multicines Plaza,** in Centro Comercial Plaza Miraflores; and the newest theaters at the MultiPlaza Mall. Check local newspapers for the latest showings and times.

Soccer

Two first-division soccer *(fútbol)* teams, Olimpia and Motagua, play their games in the Estadio Nacional near downtown. Matches are frequently held on weekends, with ticket prices running US$1.25-8 for normal league games and US$2-10 for national team matches. It's often possible to buy tickets at the box office right before the game, but for big matches it might be better to buy a day in advance. In the rare event that a game sells out, the *revendedores* will be out in front of the stadium, re-selling tickets at a mark-up.

After any victories by the national team, known variously as the *bicolor* or *el equipo de todos,* the favored place to cruise and celebrate is on Blvd. Morazán. Should either of the local teams win a national championship, victory celebrations can also be expected.

SHOPPING

Gifts and Handicrafts

A string of handicrafts stores are conveniently located next to one another on Av. Cervantes east of the square, including **Tikamaya, Regalo Maya, Don Quijote, Tesoros Maya,** and **Caoba.**

Cigars

Tabaco Fino, with branches next to Hotel Honduras Maya and at the new MultiPlaza Mall on Av. Juan Pablo II, has a good (though not cheap) selection of Honduran, Cuban, and Dominican cigars. **Casa Havana,** on Blvd. Morazán in Colonia Los Almendros, tel. 236-6632, sells a variety of high-quality cigars produced by its factory in Danlí.

Books

Metromedia, near the American Embassy in Edificio Casa Real, Av. San Carlos, tel. 221-0770 or 221-0771, sells a slew of English-language magazines, newspapers, and new and

pottery at Ojojona

used novels. Open Mon.-Sat. 10 a.m.-8 p.m., Sunday noon-5 p.m.

The small room of **Shakespeare and Co. Books,** on the second floor of a mini-mall on Av. Jeréz near Hotel La Ronda, is packed to the ceiling with shelves of used English-language books, with heavy emphasis on romance and adventure tales, but with a few high-brow novels, classics, and history books mixed in. The books sell at half-off cover price, and the store gives store credit of one-quarter cover price to sellers. Open Mon.-Fri. 9 a.m.-5 p.m., Saturday 9-noon.

Possibly the best Spanish-language bookstore in Honduras is **Librería Guaymuras,** on Av. Cervantes, tel. 237-5433 or 238-3401, which stocks an extensive collection of novels, poetry, and books on Honduran and Central American history, society, and politics. Open Mon.-Fri. 8:30 a.m.-noon and 1-6 p.m., Saturday 8:30 a.m.-noon.

Groceries

Más Por Menos, on Av. La Paz below the American Embassy, is a full-service grocery open Mon.-Sat. 8 a.m.-9 p.m., Sunday 8 a.m.-8 p.m. **Mercado San Miguel,** next to the Hotel Granada in Barrio Guanacaste, has a decent selection of fruits and vegetables and is considerably easier to navigate than the larger market in Comayagüela.

Maps

Topographical, road, mineral, resource, and other maps published by the Honduran government can be purchased at the **Instituto Geográfico Nacional,** at the Secretaría de Transporte (SECOPT) in Comayagüela, 15 Calle one block east of 1 Avenida, tel. 225-0752. The office stocks a large but not complete selection of 1:50,000 and 1:250,000 topographical maps, but the staff will often make a photocopy of ones not available for sale. Maps are inexpensive, bureaucratic hassles are nonexistent, and the staff is knowledgeable and friendly. Open Mon.-Fri. 8 a.m.-4 p.m.

INFORMATION AND SERVICES

Exchange

Any of the dozen or so banks downtown will change your dollars or traveler's checks, but it's easier to go to either a *casa de cambio* (try **Coin Casa de Cambio** at the end of the *peatonal,* open Mon.-Fri. 9 a.m.-5 p.m. and Saturday 9 a.m.-noon), or to one of the many men waving thick wads of *lempiras* and dollars along the *peatonal.* Though it may appear shady, the "black market" moneychangers are generally honest businesspeople. Still, it's always recommended you count your money right then and there.

EMBASSIES AND CONSULATES IN TEGUCIGALPA

Argentina; Colonia Rubén Darío, Avenida José María Medina 417, tel. 232-3376 or 232-3274

Belize; bottom floor of Hotel Honduras Maya, tel. 239-0134

Brazil; Colonia La Reforma, Calle La Salle 1309, tel. 236-6310 or 236-5873

Canada; Edificio Los Castaños, Boulevard Morazán, tel. 231-4538 or 231-4548

Colombia; Edificio Palmira, 4th floor, across from Honduras Maya, tel. 232-1709

Costa Rica; Residencia El Triángulo, 1 Calle 3451, tel. 232-1768 or 239-0787

Chile; Edificio La Interamericana, Boulevard Morazán, tel. 232-2114 or 232-4095

China; Col. Lomas de Guajiro, number 3705, tel. 232-4490 or 239-3062

Denmark; Boulevard Los Próceres, Edificio La Paz, tel. 236-6407 or 236-6645

Dominican Republic; Colonia Miramonte, in front of Banco Continental, tel. 239-0129

Ecuador; Avenida Juan Lindo 122, Colonia Palmira, tel. 236-5980, fax 236-6929

El Salvador; Colonia San Carlos 2A, #219, tel. 236-7344 or 236-8045

France; Colonia Palmira, Avenida Juan Lindo 3A, tel. 236-6800 or 236-6432

Germany; Edificio Paysen, 3rd floor, Boulevard Morazán, tel. 232-3161 or 232-3162

Great Britain; Edificio Palmira, 3rd floor, across from Honduras Maya, tel. 232-0612 or 232-0618

Guatemala; Colonia Las Minitas, 4 Calle, Arturo López Rodezno 2421, tel. 232-9704 or 232-5018

Holland; Rest. El Trapiche, Blvd. Suyapa, tel. 235-8090

Israel; Edificio Palmira, 5th floor, across from Honduras Maya, tel. 232-4232 or 232-5176

Italy; Colonia Reforma, Calle Principal 2602, tel. 236-6810 or 236-8027

Japan; Colonia San Carlos between 4 and 5 Calles, tel. 236-6828 or 236-6829

Mexico; Colonia Palmira, Avenida República de México, tel. 232-6471 or 232-4039

Nicaragua; Colonia Lomas del Tepeyac B-M-1, tel. 232-4290 or 232-9025

Panama; Edificio Palmira, 2nd floor, across from Honduras Maya, tel. 239-5508

Peru; Colonia La Reforma, Calle Principal, tel. 221-0596 or 221-0604

Portugal; Colonia Alameda, Avenida Principal, Edificio Festival, tel. 231-5007

Spain; Colonia Matamoros, Calle Santander 801, tel. 236-6875 or 236-6589

Sweden; Colonia Miramontes, Avenida Altiplano 2758, tel. 232-4935

Switzerland; Edificio Galerías, Boulevard Morazán, tel. 232-6239 or 232-9692

United States; Avenida La Paz, tel. 236-9320 to -9329

Venezuela; Colonia Rubén Darío, Calle Arturo López, tel. 232-1886 or 232-1879

If you need to change some money at the last minute before getting on a bus in Comayagüela, try Banco Atlántida, on the corner of 6 Av. and 11 Calle.

Credomatic, a block west of the square on Calle Salvador Mendieta, tel. 237-4596, advances any amount up to the limit of your Visa or MasterCard in *lempiras* for no fee. Open Mon.-Fri. 9 a.m.-5 p.m. and Saturday 8 a.m.-noon.

The American Express agent in Tegucigalpa is **Mundirama Travel,** Edificio Ciisca on the corner of Av. República de Chile and Av. República

de Panamá, tel. 232-3943 or 232-3909, fax 232-0072. They will sell checks to American Express cardholders with personal checks only—no cash. The office holds mail up to six months and is open Mon.-Fri. 8 a.m.-noon and 1-5 p.m., Saturday 8 a.m.-noon.

Communications

The main Hondutel office is on Av. Colón west of the square, open 24 hours a day. The office receives faxes at tel. 237-9715, Mon.-Fri. 8 a.m.-4 p.m. and Saturday 8 a.m.-noon. Other offices are in Comayagüela on 6 Avenida between 7 and 8 Calles, open daily 7 a.m.-8:30 p.m., and in Colonia Kennedy.

The downtown Correos occupies an attractive old building at the end of the *peatonal*. It's open Mon.-Fri. 8 a.m.-6 p.m., Saturday 8 a.m.-1 p.m. A small cafe inside offers tables to have a soft drink or coffee while you scribble out those postcards. In Comayagüela, the Correos is next to Hondutel on 6 Avenida; open the same hours. EMS express service is available at both offices.

DHL is on Av. República de Chile near the Honduras Maya, tel. 220-1800. **UPS** is in Edificio Palmira right across from the entrance of the Honduras Maya, tel. 232-7121.

Pak Mail, tel. 221-4366 or 236-8705, with both DHL and Federal Express service plus a host of packaging and services, is on Calle República de México, just off Blvd. Morazán, open Mon.-Fri. 8 a.m.-6 p.m. and Saturday 8 a.m.-2 p.m.

Internet

Internet Cyberiada, on the second floor of a large pink building on the corner of Av. Jeréz and Calle Hipolite Matute, charges US$2.10 per hour or US 5 cents a minute, no minimum time. The spacious room only has a few computers, but they may soon get more. And best of all, the store is open 24 hours a day, with a guard posted at the door downstairs.

Four blocks up Av. Jeréz, in a mini-mall across from Hotel La Ronda, is **Access Cyber Café**, tel. 220-5182, with six computers renting for US$1 for 15 minutes (the minimum), US$1.50 for 30 minutes, and US$2.75 for one hour. Open Mon.-Sat. 8 a.m.-7 p.m.

Just uphill from Hotel Honduras Maya on Av. República de Chile is **Multinet**, tel. 239-5237, with a half-dozen computers and a relatively fast connection renting for US$1 for the minimum 15 minutes, open Mon.-Sat. 9 a.m.-6 p.m. There is also a branch at the new MultiPlaza Mall on Av. Juan Pablo II, this one with two I-Macs to go along with the other PCs, open Mon.-Sat. 10 a.m.-9 p.m. and Sunday 10 a.m.-6 p.m.

Immigration and Car Papers

The central *migración* office is on Av. Máximo Jeréz, tel. 238-1957, ext. 24. Try to renew tourist

TEGUCIGALPA USEFUL TELEPHONE NUMBERS

Police: 237-1400, or dial 199
Fire Department: 232-1183, 232-5474, or dial 198
Cruz Roja Ambulance: 227-8023, 227-9344, or dial 195
Clinica Viera across from Alcaldia, 24 hours: 237-3156 through -3160

cards elsewhere, as doing it here requires waiting in line and leaving your passport at least one day. Offices in other cities and towns are usually much quicker, hassle-free, and less expensive. Open Mon.-Fri. 8:30 a.m.-4:30 p.m.

Should you have a foreign car in Honduras and need to renew the papers, the place to go is **Dirección Ejecutiva de Ingresos**, right next to the *parque* on Av. Cervantes, office on the 9th floor, tel. 238-6790, ext. 121, open Mon.-Fri. 8 a.m.-noon and 1:30-5 p.m.

Medical Help

The private **Clínica Viera**, Av. Colón just east of Calle Las Damas, tel. 237-3156 through -3160, stays open 24 hours and can take care of most health problems.

Laundry

The oddly named **Superc Jet Lavandería**, on Av. Juan Gutemberg just west of where it crosses a bridge and becomes Av. La Paz, charges US$2 to wash and dry seven lbs. of dirty duds the same day you drop them off; open Mon.-Sat. 8 a.m.-6:30 p.m.

In Colonia Palmira, just off Blvd. Morazán on Calle Maipu, is the more expensive **Dry Cleaning y Lavandería Maya**, charging US$4.50 to wash and dry up to 10 lbs. Open Mon.-Fri. 7 a.m.-6 p.m., Saturday 8 a.m.-4 p.m.

Peace Corps

The central Peace Corps office is in a large brick building on the corner of Av. República de Chile and Av. República de Panamá, tel. 232-1753 or 232-2451. Casual visitors are not allowed in, but if you're trying to get a message to a volunteer, this is the place to leave it.

Spanish Classes

At last report the only school in Tegucigalpa offering classes was **Conversa,** tel. 236-7420 or 236-5170, email: aerohond@david.intertel.hn, website: www.worldwide.edu/Honduras/conversa, with different levels of coursework to suit your needs. Classes cost US$4 per hour, and students can take either 10 or 20 hours of classes per week. Home stay with a Honduran family is available for US$285 a month, with two meals a day included.

Information

The **Instituto Hondureño de Turismo,** on the fifth floor of Edificio Europa, Av. Ramón Ernesto Cruz behind the U.S. Embassy, tel. 238-3974 or 222-2124, fax 222-6621, can be of some use if you have a specific query but is generally unaccustomed to dealing with individual travelers.

Travel Agents

Three travel agents in Tegucigalpa that can arrange plane tickets and take care of other basic services are: **Honduras Copán Tours,** across from the Honduras Maya, tel. 232-9736 or 232-9964, fax 232-6795; **Fiesta Americana,** on Boulevard Morazán next to Burger King in Edificio Castaños, tel. 232-4666 or 32-3766, email: fiesta@in-honduras.com; and **Mundirama,** in Edificio Ciisca on the corner of Av. República de Chile and Av. República de Panamá, tel. 232-3943 or 232-3909, fax 232-0072, open Mon.-Fri. 8 a.m.-noon and 1-5 p.m., Saturday 8 a.m.-noon.

Tour Operators

Greko Tours, on Av. República de Chile just past the Blvd. Morazán underpass, tel. 239-5998 or 239-5999, cell. 998-0304, runs recommended tours of Tegucigalpa, La Tigra, Valle de Ángeles and Santa Lucía, as well as farther afield to Comayagua, Amapala, Lago de Yojoa, and Copán at reasonable rates for two or more people.

Explore Honduras, in Edificio Medicast, Ste. 206, Boulevard Morazán, tel. 236-9003 or 236-7694, also runs tours around Tegucigalpa and other regions of Honduras.

Photography

The **Kodak** shop on the southwest corner of the square sells and develops slide and print film, although there have been some complaints about the quality of the slide developing.

If your camera's giving you problems, **Jorge Calderón** can handle basic repairs and will tell you if the problem is beyond his capabilities, rather than trying to take it apart anyhow. His office, cluttered with the corpses of cameras from times past, is on the first floor of Edificio Colonial, on the north side of the square, and is open Mon.-Fri. 9 a.m.-noon and 1-5 p.m.

Health Club

Those after a good workout in Tegucigalpa could try **Gold's Gym,** out Blvd. Morazán, tel. 236-7120 or 221-4212, with a full gym and a large outdoor pool. Regular membership is US$20 to join, then US$24 per month, but visitors can pay US$7.50 for a one-day visit. The small workout area and sauna on the 10th floor of the Hotel San Martin is open to non-guests for US$4.

GETTING THERE AND AWAY

While a great number of tourists fly in to San Pedro Sula because of its proximity to the north coast and the Bay Islands, Tegucigalpa remains one of Honduras' two principal transportation hubs. Bus travelers trying to find their way out of town will find themselves tracking down dozens of privately owned terminals scattered all over the city, mostly in Comayagüela.

Air

Toncontín International Airport, six km south of downtown on the highway leading out to Choluteca, is infamous among airline pilots for having an unforgivingly short runway. At the airport are several car rental agencies, Hondutel (open daily 6 a.m.-6 p.m.), a snack bar, and a souvenir shop. Bancahsa has a branch in the terminal, which will exchange dollars and traveler's checks, as well as advance money on a Visa card, Mon.-Fri. 9 a.m.-noon and 1:30-4:30 p.m. A crew of moneychangers also hangs around after just about every international arrival, if the bank is closed or you're in a hurry. Toyota, Budget, Thrifty, Hertz, Molinari, Avis, and National all have car rental booths at the airport.

Airport taxis cost US$8 to downtown, more with three people. If you don't have much luggage, it's cheaper to walk right out front to the main road and catch a bus there. All the buses passing in front of the airport to the north go to downtown.

If you're leaving the country on an international flight, expect to pay a US$25 departure tax.

Taca/Isleña, offices in town at both the Honduras Maya Hotel and on Blvd. Morazán, tel. 239-1841 or 239-0105, at the airport at tel. 233-6681 or 233-3566, has national flights on Isleña direct from Tegucigalpa to San Pedro Sula, La Ceiba, and Puerto Lempira, with connections to the Bay Islands and the Mosquitia, and international flights with Taca to San Salvador, Managua, Guatemala City, and the United States.

Continental, downtown office is in Edificio Palmira, opposite the Honduras Maya, tel. 232-1415 and 232-1421., at the airport tel. 233-7676 or 220-0999, flies to Houston daily. **American Airlines,** tel. 233-6919 or 233-9680, flies daily to Miami.

Rollins, tel. 234-2766 at the airport, or in town on Blvd. Morazán, tel. 221-0533 or 221-0544, flies daily except Saturday to La Ceiba and Puerto Lempira.

Sosa, tel. 233-7351 or 234-0137 at the airport, in town on Blvd. Morazán near the corner of Calle Maipu, tel. 239-0757, flies to San Pedro Sula and La Ceiba.

Buses to Central and Western Honduras
To **San Pedro Sula:** Offering direct hourly service between 6 a.m. and 6 p.m. are Hedman Alas, on 11 Av. between 13 and 14 Calles, tel. 237-7143; and Transportes El Rey, on 12 Calle and 7 Av., tel. 237-8561, US$4. Transportes Saenz, at 6 Av. and 9 Calle, tel. 237-6609, and Transportes Norteños on 12 Calle between 6 and 7 Avenidas, tel. 237-0706, both offer local service for US$2.50. **Saenz** runs six **premier** buses a day between 6 a.m. and 6 p.m. to San Pedro from a terminal opposite the airport, tel. 233-4249 or 233-4229, US$8. Three and a half hours.

To **Siguatepeque:** Transportes Maribel, at 8 Av. between 11 and 12 Calles, tel. 237-3032; and Empresas Unidas, on 7 Av. between 11 and 12 Calles, tel. 222-2071, both have frequent departures between 6 a.m. and 5 p.m.; US$1.50, two hours.

To **La Paz:** Under the same roof as Transportes Maribel, at 8 Av. between 11 and 12 Calles, is Transportes Flores, with buses every hour between 5 a.m. and 5 p.m.; US$1, 90 minutes.

To **Marcala:** Transportes Lila, at 9 Av. between 12 and 13 Calles, tel. 237-6870, has three buses a day, the last at 2 p.m., US$2, three hours.

To **Santa Bárbara:** Transportes Junqueños, at 8 Av. between 12 and 13 Calles, tel. 237-2921, has two buses a day, US$3, four hours, with a third bus on Monday and Friday. No direct buses at the moment—local service only.

To **Santa Rosa de Copán, Nuevo Ocotepeque** and **the Guatemalan border:** Toritos y Copanecos, at the corner of 8 Av. and 12 Calle, tel. 237-8101, has two buses daily all the way to the border at Aguascalientes, US$8, six hours, and more frequent buses to Santa Rosa de Copán, US$6.

Buses to the North Coast and Olancho
To **El Progreso:** Transportes Ulúa, tel. 238-1827, with four direct buses daily for US$5, three hours, the last in mid-afternoon, from its terminal at the corner of 6 Av. and 18 Calle.

To **La Ceiba:** Etrusca, on 12 Calle between 8 and 9 Av., tel. 222-6881, has two buses a day, at 10 a.m. and 4 p.m., US$7 and six hours to La Ceiba, the same price to Tela; Traliasa, also on 12 Calle between 8 and 9 Av., tel. 237-7538, and Cristina, on the corner of 12 Calle and 8 Av., tel. 220-0117, both have similar buses for the same price.

The **luxury** bus line Viana, tel. 239-8288 or 239-9988, runs luxury, non-stop cruisers to La Ceiba with two movies in English, a meal and coffee, nice but not cheap at US$18. Two buses depart daily at 6:30 a.m. and 2:30 p.m. from its terminal on Blvd. Fuerzas Armadas, just west of the exit to the airport and Choluteca, near the Supreme Court building.

To **Trujillo** via **Juticalpa** and **Tocoa:** Cotraipbal, tel. 237-1666, now has two buses a day to Trujillo leaving at 2 a.m. and noon, US$9, nine hours through spectacular scenery—first across the central highlands, then past the Sierra de Agalta in Olancho and down into the tropical department of Colón.

To **Juticalpa** and **Catacamas:** Transportes Discovery, on 7 Av. between 12 and 13 Calles, tel. 222-4256, offers three direct and nine local buses daily between 6 a.m. and 5 p.m.; US$2.50 to Juticalpa direct (two hours), US$1.50 local (three hours), and US$3 to Catacamas direct (three hours), US$1.90 local (four hours). Empresa Aurora, on 8 Calle between 6 and 7 Avenidas, tel. 237-3647, also runs local buses to Juticalpa and Catacamas between 4:30 a.m. and 5 p.m., US$1.50 to Juticalpa and US$1.90 to Catacamas.

To **San Francisco de la Paz, Gualaco,** and **San Esteban:** Transportes Olancho (no phone), in front of the Elektra store on 7 Av. near the corner of 11 Calle, runs two buses daily via Juticalpa at 5 a.m. and noon. The six-hour ride to the end of the run at San Esteban costs US$4.

To **La Unión** and **La Muralla:** The highway through western Olancho to La Unión has a well-deserved reputation for holdups. At the moment only one bus a day makes it out to La Unión, leaving at 6 a.m. from 7 Av. between 11 and 12 Calles, US$3. There's no office, so the only way to find out if the bus is currently running is to go to the pickup spot the day before and ask around. Formerly this route continued down the mountains and out to Tocoa, but buses no longer venture down the lower stretch of the highway beyond La Unión.

Buses to the East and South

To **Yuscarán, Danlí,** and **El Paraíso:** Discua, tel. 232-7939, operates buses to Danlí every 45 minutes between 6 a.m. and 6:30 p.m. from Mercado Jacaleapa in Colonia Kennedy. The two-hour ride to Danlí costs US$1.25, or US$2 for the direct bus; US$1.40 to El Paraíso. Some buses only go to Danlí, but from there frequent buses continue to El Paraíso. (*Colectivo* taxis run out past Mercado Jacaleapa from Puente La Isla, between downtown and the stadium, for US 30 cents.) Buses to Yuscarán leave from Mercado Jacaleapa three times daily, charging US$1. It's also possible to find buses leaving on an irregular schedule from the same market out to Nueva Palestina in Olancho, near the Río Patuca.

To **Choluteca** and **the South:** Mi Esperanza, tel. 225-1505, has direct service four times a day to Choluteca for US$2.25, the last at 6 p.m., from its terminal on 7 Av. at 23 Calle, a block from the Instituto de Seguro Social. Right around the corner on 7 Av. is Bonanza, tel. 225-2863, with several buses to Choluteca (US$1.65, two and a half hours), San Marcos Colón (US$2, four hours), and Guasaule (US$2, four hours) every day. Dandy, at 20 Calle between 6 and 7

Av., tel. 225-2596, has similar service at the same prices. Buses direct to El Amatillo (US$2.50, four hours) and El Salvador leave from Mercado Mayoreo, southwest of Comayagüela on the highway exit toward Olancho (reached by local buses marked "Carrizal").

Buses Near Tegucigalpa

To **Santa Lucía:** Buses leave from Mercado San Pablo, off Av. La Paz. Santa Lucía buses leave every US 45 minutes between 6 a.m. and 6 p.m. for US 30 cents, 30 minutes.

To **Valle de Ángeles:** Buses leave frequently between 6:30 a.m. and 7:30 p.m. from a small parking lot half a block in from an Esso station on Av. La Paz, across from the Hospital San Felipe, US 40 cents, 45 minutes.

To **San Juancito** and **La Tigra:** Catch a bus going to Cantarranas (also called San Juan de Flores) from the Esso gas station on Av. La Paz, right across from the Hospital General. Five buses a day make the one-and-a-half-hour trip to San Juancito between 10 a.m. and 5 p.m., US 80 cents all the way to Cantarranas.

Any of the Santa Lucía, San Juancito, or Valle de Ángeles buses can be caught at the Dippsa gas station at the end of Av. La Paz.

To **El Hatillo** and the west side of **Parque Nacional La Tigra**: Buses leave from Av. Colón just west of Calle Finlay, near the Hotel Granada,

---

TEGUCIGALPA CAR RENTAL AGENCIES

Budget: airport office, tel. 233-5161, fax 233-5170

Hertz: downtown, across from Hotel Honduras Maya, tel. 239-0772 or 239-0774, and at the airport, tel. 234-3784

Maya: Av. República de Chile 202, tel. 232-0682 or 232-0992

Molinari: at Hotel Honduras Maya, tel. 232-8691, and at the airport, tel. 233-1307

Avis: across from the Hotel Honduras Maya, tel. 239-5711 or 232-0088, fax 239-5710, and at the airport, tel. 233-9548

National: in Colonia El Prado, tel. 225-2653, and at the airport, tel. 233-4962

once a day to Jutiapa (US 40 cents, one hour), four times a day to Limones (US 30 cents, 45 minutes), and whenever they fill up to El Hatillo (US 20 cents, 30 minutes).

To **Ojojona:** Buses leave as soon as they fill up from the 6 Av. near the corner of 7 Calle, US 25 cents, 45 minutes, last leaves to Ojojona at 6 p.m.

To **Cedros** and **Minas de Oro:** three buses a day, the last in early afternoon, make the two-hour trip from Mercado Mayoreo, on the highway exit toward Olancho, for US$2.25.

International Buses

Tica Bus, at 16 Calle between 6 and 5 Avenidas, tel. 220-0579 or 220-0590, runs one bus a day to Managua, Nicaragua (US$20, eight hours); San José, Costa Rica (US$35, 15 hours); and Panama City, Panama (US$60, 31 hours). **King Quality/Cruceros del Golfo,** tel. 225-5415 or 225-2600, has one *ejecutivo*-class bus, with breakfast, television, and paperwork help at the border, to San Salvador, El Salvador (US$25, eight hours) or Guatemala City, Guatemala (US$45, 14 hours). A second, regular bus drives to San Salvador only, US$22. To Managua, Nicaragua, (US$23, nine and a half hours), take the *ejecutivo* bus going to San Salvador and transfer to a second bus at El Amatillo. The terminal is located on Blvd. Comunidad Económica Europea, in Barrio La Granja, south of Comayagüela.

By Car

Four principal highway exits lead out of Tegucigalpa. West to San Pedro Sula, the easiest route out of town is from the western end of Blvd. Fuerzas Armadas, while the exit to the east and

---

DISTANCES FROM TEGUCIGALPA

Catacamas	232 km
Choluteca	142 km
Comayagua	85 km
Danlí	93 km
Juticalpa	192 km
San Pedro Sula	246 km
Siguatepeque	117 km
Yuscarán	77 km

Danlí departs Tegucigalpa from the eastern end of the same boulevard. South to Choluteca, follow Blvd. Comunidad Económica Europea south from downtown, past the airport. To Olancho and the north, follow either 6 Av. through Comayagüela and out Blvd. del Norte, or (much faster) get to Barrio Abajo, northwest of downtown near Parque Concordia, and look for the road exit crossing a bridge and heading uphill to Cerro Grande, where it meets the Olancho highway.

If you're coming back into the city from the south or west and want to get to downtown, it's often quicker to loop around farther east along Blvd. Fuerzas Armadas and Blvd. Miraflores, and come into the downtown area via Juan Gálvez, rather than coming through crowded Comayagüela.

One secondary road leaves Tegucigalpa to the northeast along Av. La Paz to Santa Lucía and Valle de Ángeles, while another leaves Av. Juan Gutemberg in Barrio Guanacaste up to El Hatillo and villages on the west side of La Tigra.

NEAR TEGUCIGALPA

SANTA LUCÍA

A picturesque colonial village of red tile roofs and cobblestone streets perched on a hillside 13 km above Tegucigalpa, Santa Lucía is a growing destination for Hondurans and a few expatriates looking for a quiet, cool escape near Tegucigalpa. Along with nearby Valle de Ángeles, it's also a popular weekend day trip destination for city residents. For much of the colonial period Santa Lucía was home to some of the richest mines in Honduras. The town produced so much wealth for the crown, King Felipe II sent a wooden statue of Christ in appreciation, which can still be seen in the attractive white-washed church. Several other icons, including the town's patron saint, are also kept inside the church. You may notice a large number of young Americans in town—since the 1980s, Santa Lucía has served as the training center for the Peace Corps, where new volunteers spend their first few months in country before moving out to their sites around the country.

Apart from enjoying the views and admiring the colonial church, there's not much to do in Santa Lucía, but it's a pleasant place to spend an afternoon wandering around. A new Spanish school has reportedly opened in Santa Lucía, but no details were available and the telephone (237-5670) had not yet been connected at last report.

For those who want to stretch their legs, the dirt road continuing past the church and turning uphill into the forest offers a route to hike along for great views over the town, Tegucigalpa below, and La Tigra forest. The road continues across the mountaintop to the Danlí highway, reached in two to four hours walking, where you could hail a passing bus down to Tegucigalpa. This pine-forested mountain offers great scenery and clean air, and it is quite safe. The road would also be a great mountain bike ride.

A trail descends from Santa Lucía to Tegucigalpa, but it lets out into some tough shanty villages on the outskirts of the city, and robberies have been reported, so that walk is not recommended.

Practicalities

Restaurante Miluska, just above the center of town, near where the buses park, offers Czech- and Hungarian-style food Tues.-Sun. 10 a.m.-8 p.m.; US$3-6 per entree. Unfortunately the Czech owner may be leaving the town soon—pray she changes her mind. **Restaurant El Jorongo,** up by the lagoon at the entrance to town, has decent *comida típica* at mid-range prices.

To get to Santa Lucía by car, drive from downtown out Av. La Paz and continue straight uphill, following signs to Valle de Ángeles. The well-marked Santa Lucía turnoff is 11 kilometers from the edge of Tegucigalpa, and the town itself is two kilometers in from the highway. Frequent buses drive to Santa Lucía from the San Pablo market, US 30 cents. The last bus back down to Tegucigalpa leaves around 5:30 p.m.

Visitors will find no hotels in Santa Lucia, so plan on making a day trip. Anyone interested in a longer stay can find houses and rooms available for rent by week or month—just ask around.

VALLE DE ÁNGELES

Valle de Ángeles, 23 km east of Tegucigalpa, leads a sort of double life. It's part playground for wealthy Tegucigalpa residents and tourists, and part a rural Honduran mountain village. On weekends here you may feel a bit overwhelmed by the camera-toting, handicraft-buying crowd, but tough-looking cowboys still clomp around the cobblestone streets on horseback on their way into the surrounding pine forest.

As its name suggests, the town is beautifully set in a high mountain valley at 1,310 meters, surrounded by mountains on three sides and dropping off into a valley on the fourth. Apart from enjoying the atmosphere and breathing the clean mountain air, many visitors come to Valle de Ángeles to shop for handicrafts—particularly wooden carvings and furniture—in the dozen or so shops.

Practicalities

The only accommodations in town are at the **Posada del Ángel,** tel./fax 766-2233, offering 20 rooms around a large grassy courtyard with a pool in the middle. The rooms have hot water and cable TV, and they rent for a reasonable US$20 s or US$28 d. The hotel has its own restaurant, parking lot, and conference rooms. It's best to reserve rooms ahead of time as they often fill up.

Because of the high number of day-trippers coming through Valle, visitors will find several decent places to eat in different price ranges. Right on the square is **Carnes El Español,** named in honor of the owner, an amiable Andaluz who serves up a wide variety of different meats in the Spanish style, at reasonable prices. For the non-carnivore, he offers *tortilla Española* or mushrooms cooked *al ajillo* (with garlic). Formerly only open Thurs.-Sat. until 8 p.m., the restaurant may soon be open daily.

A few doors down on the corner of the park is *El Anafre,* serving a solid *plato típico* for US$4, or the namesake refried bean, cream, and chips munchie for US$3. El Anafre also offers *tacos* and several different spaghetti dishes. Open Wed.-Sun. 10 a.m.-7 p.m.

Restaurante Papagayo, one block below the square on the road leading out of town toward Tegucigalpa, serves well-prepared mid-range meals, including its famous *tortilla papagayo* stuffed with cheese, sausage, tomato, *chile,* onion, and beans. Other dishes on the menu include *pinchos,* chicken, and filet mignon; US$2-5 per plate. Open Tues.-Sunday 10 a.m.-6 p.m.

Set in a cozy old adobe house dating from the mid-19th century, restored by the new owners, is **La Casa de las Abuelas,** specializing in steaks and *pinchos* for US$5-8 per plate. Open daily until 9 p.m.

On the road out of town toward Tegucigalpa is **Restaurante La Florida,** tel. 766-2121, with hearty meat and poultry dishes, sandwiches, and a couple of good soups like the *tapado olanchano,* a thick stew with steamed pork, yucca, and plantain. Open daily 10 a.m.-8 p.m., later on weekends.

In addition to the many shops lining the streets around Valle de Ángeles, handicrafts are also sold in the **Mercado Municipal de Artesanías,** in the market building where the Tegucigalpa buses turn around. Among the handicrafts sold in town are woodcarvings, ceramics, pewter, tapestries, furniture, paintings, and much else.

To catch a bus to Valle, follow Av. La Paz past the U.S. Embassy, and take a right at the Esso station. The bus terminal for Valle is half a block in from the gas station. Buses leaving Valle back to Tegucigalpa leave daily until 5:30 p.m., charging US 40 cents.

Three kilometers from Valle toward Tegucigalpa on the left side of the highway is **Parque Turístico,** where you'll find picnic tables amidst the pine trees.

PARQUE NACIONAL LA TIGRA

The first protected area in Honduras, La Tigra was established as a reserve in 1952 and declared a national park in 1980. It covers 23,571 hectares across the top of the mountains above Tegucigalpa, of which 7,571 hectares form the core zone.

Because of the proximity to the La Rosario mines, the forests in La Tigra were heavily logged around the turn of the century, so only a few patches of primary cloud forest remain. The mining company cut a dirt road across the mountain from La Rosario to Tegucigalpa, which exposed the heart of the forest for the exploitation of its precious woods for use in mines and surrounding villages. In spite of the depredations, La Tigra still offers a good opportunity to admire the flora and fauna of a high-altitude cloud forest, especially for those who don't have the time or desire to venture farther afield to Celaque, Sierra de Agalta, or other, better-preserved forests. Being a drier cloud forest than many others in Honduras, La Tigra is also an opportunity for birdwatchers to view species not easily seen elsewhere in Honduras, such as the blue-and-white mockingbird, rufous-browed wren, garnet-throated hummingbird, and wine-throated hummingbird, as well as the ever-popular quetzal.

La Tigra has a well-developed trail system, enabling casual hikers to enjoy a day or two wandering about the woods at their leisure, without fear of getting lost—one of the principal reasons for the park's popularity. Three main trails run between the western entrance of the park near Jutiapa and the eastern entrance at La Rosario; two of these are actual footpaths and the third is the dirt road cut by the mining company, part of which is being allowed to deteriorate.

The two footpath trails unsurprisingly offer more opportunity to spot wildlife and enjoy the atmosphere of the forest. Though the dirt road does reach the highest accessible point in the park—Rancho Quemado at 2,185 meters—the views are limited by trees. The best spot to catch glimpses of the valleys below is next to the Hondutel towers on a ridge above the road. A newer path now makes a shorter loop near the Jutiapa visitors' center, good for children or those without a lot of mobility or energy.

Other peaks in the park include Cerro La Estrella (2,245 meters), Cerro La Peña de Andino (2,290 meters), and Cerro El Volcán (2,270 meters). Some of the most pristine stretches of cloud forest remain in the region south of the trails, around Cerro El Volcán, but unfortunately the area is off limits to visitors.

The entrance fee for the park is a tad high at US$10 per person, and plan on another US$10 to spend the night in La Rosario or US$3.50 to pitch a tent on the Jutiapa side. As with Cusuco near San Pedro Sula, you're paying for the proximity to a major city and a well-maintained, though modest-sized, network of trails. Some backpackers have had luck showing up a La Rosario, pleading poverty, and negotiating a discount, but don't count on it.

Spanish-language guides knowledgeable about the plants and animals of the park can be hired at the visitors' centers at either side of the park, for US$7.50 for a full day or less for shorter trips. Bilingual guides may soon be available—check with Amitigra in Tegucigalpa for the latest.

La Rosario

To get into the park from the east side, drive, hitch, or take a bus out to San Juancito from Valle de Ángeles. Buses to Cantarranas (San Juan de Flores) from Valle de Ángeles will drop you off at the *desvio* to San Juancito, from where you can walk 15 minutes into town. San Juancito holds several *pulperías* and restaurants, as well as a simple *hospedaje*. The steep canyon in which San Juancito sits became a raging river during Hurricane Mitch, sweeping away a great many buildings in the center of town, as well as a huge ceiba tree that was a town landmark.

From San Juancito a dirt road continues up the hill to La Rosario, the former mining complex. It's only a couple of kilometers up to the mines, but because of the steep grade it's a good hour-and-a-half walk, so hope one of the workers passes by in a truck to give you a lift.

La Rosario is a collection of turn-of-the-century mining buildings clinging to the precipitous hillside, some in ruins and others in good condition. The old cemetery is an interesting place, filled with the tombstones (all written in English) of the international vagabonds who worked in the mines in the 19th and 20th century. One of the old buildings houses the visitors' center, where you can pay your entrance fee, get a trail map, look at the displays on local wildlife and geography, and chat with caretaker Don Magín, who is very knowledgeable and speaks passable German and a few words of English.

Just above the visitors' center, in the old mine hospital, is the park *hospedaje,* with eight clean rooms with private bathroom, US$10 per person. Bring a sleeping bag, as no blankets are available and it's often chilly. A cafeteria can be opened when requested by guests, or you can bring your own food. As groups sometimes fill the place up, it would be wise to call ahead to Amitigra if you want to be sure of having a room. Camping out at La Rosario costs US$3.50 per person, with use of the bathroom facilities in the lodge.

Above La Rosario the dirt road continues across the top of the mountain to El Hatillo, on the far west side of the park. Several mines are along this road, some blocked off and others still open. If you want to go exploring, take good care and be advised the mines are usually full of water. Between the Hondutel towers and La Rosario the road has been allowed to deteriorate and is now no more than a wide footpath.

Jutiapa

Less visually dramatic than the mining complex at La Rosario, but easier to get to from Tegucigalpa, is the western entrance to the park, via the village of Jutiapa. The visitors' center on this side is not as good as at La Rosario, and trail maps are often unavailable. Those with a tent can spend the night next to the visitors' center on the Jutiapa side, with access to the bathroom facilities, for US$3.50 per person.

To get to the Jutiapa visitors' center without a car, catch a bus leaving from Av. Colón just west of Calle Finlay, near the Hotel Granada in Tegu-

LA ROSARIO: THE NEW YORK AND HONDURAS ROSARIO MINING COMPANY

High up on a mountainside above the town of San Juancito, on the far side of Parque Nacional La Tigra from Tegucigalpa, lie the vestiges of what was for a time the richest mine in the western hemisphere—the New York and Honduras Rosario Mining Company, better known as La Rosario.

With the active encouragement of Honduran president Marco Aurelio Soto, La Rosario was formed in 1880 by Julius J. Valentine and his four sons, Washington S., Ferdinand C., Louis F., and Lincoln. A firm believer in the need to develop the Honduran economy with foreign capital, Soto offered the Valentines tax breaks and incentives so generous that, for fear of nationalist backlash, he kept the details of the contract secret for 17 years. By 1888, La Rosario was far and away the most powerful economic concern in the country, exporting US$700,000 in bullion annually. To ensure a continued free hand to operate as they pleased, mine owners led by Washington Valentine assumed an increasingly important role in national politics, going so far as to engineer the reelection of Pres. Luis Bográn in the 1888 presidential vote. The company was so closely identified with the U.S. presence in Honduras that for a short time the U.S. embassy was located in the mine complex at La Rosario.

The political machinations paid off handsomely, as the government invariably sided with the company in disputes with local villagers and small-scale Honduran miners over land, water, timber, and limestone. The government also repeatedly helped round up reluctant workers for the chronically understaffed mines.

Over the course of its 74 years of operation, La Rosario produced some US$100 million of gold, silver, copper, and zinc from slightly less than 6.5 million tons of ore. In the process, the mine's U.S. owners and shareholders became extremely wealthy. The benefits, though, were less evident in Honduras. In spite of the relatively high wages paid to miners, abysmal working conditions led to constant labor shortages as workers fled to their homes—many only to be rounded up by local militia and brought back to the mines. The owners' cold-blooded view of Honduran workers is evident in a letter written to shareholders by Washington Valentine in 1915 about "the severe drought which occurred during the year past": "while undoubtedly a great hardship upon the country as a whole, for the Company it had its great advantages. . . [It] induced many people to seek work in San Juancito thus there was an abundance and even a surplus of labor."

In its insatiable thirst for timber, the company almost entirely denuded the forests on the San Juancito side of the mountain, and eventually punched an adit (horizontal mining tunnel) clear through the far side of the mountain to access virgin stands of wood. Much of the original cloud forest at La Tigra was destroyed by the mines, and almost all of the flora seen along the trails in the park today is secondary growth.

By 1954, the richest veins of ore were spent, and when the miners struck to support the banana workers' strike on the north coast, it was enough to convince the New York owners to shut down most of their operations. The deserted buildings of the mines, standing starkly empty on the bare hillside above San Juancito, are eerie reminders of the mine's boom years.

cigalpa, once a day to Jutiapa, or four times a day to Limones (seven km and two hours walking to the visitors' center in Jutiapa). Sometimes it's possible to hitch from Limones, but there's not much traffic, so it's better to try to catch the Jutiapa bus or plan on walking from Limones. The bus schedule varies, so check the day before to find out the exact hour for the Jutiapa bus.

If you're driving, take the paved road leaving Tegucigalpa from Av. Juan Gutemberg in Barrio Guanacaste uphill past Parque Naciones Unidas to the town of El Hatillo. Continue just under two km on the now-dirt road to a junction marked with a sign pointing to the right to Jutiapa and La Tigra, 10 km farther on.

Amatigra
For more information on the park, or if you want to make reservations for the La Rosario *hospedaje,* visit the office of Amatigra, Edificio Italia, Room 6, on Av. República de Panamá a couple of blocks down from Av. República de Chile, tel. 235-8494 or 235-8493, email: amitigra@sigmanet.hn. The office is quite well equipped—there is even a top-notch website, courtesy of the U.S. National Park Service: www.nps.gov/centralamerica/honduras/rosario/s html.

Mountain Biking
Although biking in the park itself is prohibited, the mountainsides around the park, especially in the vicinity of El Hatillo and farther north, are criss-crossed with hundreds of trails and dirt roads suitable for mountain bikers. One local rider declared, his eyes shining in quasi-religious rapture, that the region around Tegucigalpa *"es un paraíso"* for mountain biking.

One good place to go to get information on destinations and hook up with regular group rides is **Planet Bike,** in Col. Palmira on Av. República de Panamá, tel. 232-3840. The shop also sometimes has bikes for rent at US$10 a day. Open Mon.-Fri. 10 a.m.-5:30 p.m., Saturday 10 a.m.-1:30 p.m. Every Saturday a group of riders leave by car around 1 p.m. from the shop, and drive up to El Hatillo to start their ride. A possible longer ride would be from San Juancito to El Piligüin, on dirt roads around the northern side of the park.

OJOJONA

One of the loveliest of the many colonial villages near Tegucigalpa is Ojojona, 32 km from the capital on the crest of the mountains sloping down toward the Pacific Coast, at an altitude of 1,390 meters. Thought to have been settled by the Spanish in 1579 on the site of a Lenca village, Ojojona played a larger and more important role than Tegucigalpa for much of the colonial era, because of the rich mines of El Aguacatal, Guasucarán, El Plomo, and Las Quemazones in the nearby hills.

Among the many colonial buildings in the now-sleepy rural town are three churches, Iglesia San Juan Bautista (1824), Iglesia de Carmen (1819), and Iglesia del Calvario. In the Iglesia del Calvario, a few blocks from the square, hangs a colonial-era painting titled "Sangre de Cristo" (Blood of Christ). Quite a vision of gory religious symbolism, it depicts an agonized Christ on the cross, his blood gushing down onto a flock of sheep placidly grazing below. The house with the wooden pillars on the square is the oldest structure still standing in Ojojona, built in 1723. For a time the house was owned by the family of Honduran painter Pablo Zelaya Sierra, and it is now the local museum, although at last check it was closed for renovation.

Ojojona is known for the simple earthenware pottery made in surrounding villages and sold in several shops in town or, on weekends, at the outdoor market. A couple of kilometers from Ojojona is a viewpoint, **El Mirador,** from where you can enjoy views out toward the Pacific and into the interior of the country on a clear day.

Near Ojojona is **Cerro de Ula,** a traditional region known for its terraced hillside farming, a practice thought to date from pre-Columbian times.

Practicalities
The only hotel in town is **Posada Joxone** just off the square. The simple rooms around a garden courtyard go for US$4 pp, and the restaurant serves *carne asada, baleadas,* enchiladas, chicken, and other basic dishes at inexpensive prices.

A couple of other *comedores* serve up *plato típico.*

The last bus back to Tegucigalpa leaves at 5 p.m., charging US 25 cents for the 45-minute ride.

To get to Ojojona by car from Tegucigalpa, take the highway toward Choluteca until you reach a Dippsa gas station at a mountain crest, 24 km from the capital. From here a road turns right and leads eight km to Ojojona, passing through Santa Ana, where there is a colonial church with a lovely painted dome.

Guarisne and Guasucarán
The village of Guarisne, six km from Ojojona, is a traditional Lenca community and a center for ceramics. Near the town of Guasucarán, 16 km by rough dirt road from Ojojona, is one of the country's best examples of a ruined colonial mining complex. One worker with the Instituto Hondureño de Antropología e Historia reports that several of the large ovens *(hornos)* stand near the old mine, their chimneys still intact. To get there, drive or hitch a (rare) ride to Guasucarán, and from there hire a guide for the several-hour hike. A bus drives out to Guasucarán once a day from Ojojona. There's nowhere to stay in town, but you could probably find a bed without difficulty if you ask around, or you could camp. Bring your own food.

El Sauce Petroglyphs
Of the several prehistoric petroglyph sites in the vicinity of Tegucigalpa, one of the most impressive and easiest to visit is near El Sauce, a couple of kilometers east of the Choluteca highway. The turnoff is at the same gas station as the Ojojona turn, but on the opposite side of the highway. The dirt road, leading to San Buenaventura, heads across open fields, then winds down off the plateau to a valley below. At the bottom of the hill is El Sauce, and a 40-minute walk from there you'll find the petroglyphs. Once in the village, turn left off the main road at the only turn, and then left again through the first gate. Continue to the small rancho at the end of this road, and ask someone to point the way to "La Cueva Pintada" (The Painted Cave), as the site is known locally. The trail follows the edge of a small valley for about 15 minutes, reaching a point where another, smaller valley runs into it. At the junction is a small, usually deserted hut.

Another five minutes up the side valley, look for rock overhangs—facing upriver, there's one on the right side and three on the left. Each is filled with dozens of etched images and designs. Some modern graffiti has been added, but thankfully very little.

If you don't feel like spending too much time wandering around looking for the caves, ask one of the local kids to show you the way for a few *lempiras*. Apart from the caves, the valley is a beautiful place for a walk in the countryside. In this same valley are the remnants of a small colonial-era mine works, including a mill and canal.

VALLE DE ZAMORANO

The highway from Tegucigalpa east to Danlí winds up into the mountains above the city, crossing a pass before continuing down to the Valle de Zamorano. The highest peak on the south side of this mountain pass, quite close to the highway, is the **Reserva Biológica El Uyuca**, a small patch of cloud forest. Archie Carr, who worked at the school at Zamorano, described the forests of El Uyuca in vivid detail in his classic work, *High Jungles and Low.* The best way to get into the reserve is from the village of Tatumbla, reached via a dirt road turning off the highway about 10 kilometers from Tegucigalpa, before the pass, marked by a sign. Tatumbla is another five kilometers farther on; from there ask for advice on how to get up the mountain or look for a guide.

Past the turn to Tatumbla, the highway continues up and over the pass at **La Montañanita,** where a side road turns north to Santa Lucía. On the far side of the pass, the highway snakes down the mountains into the fertile Valle de Zamorano, one of the richest agricultural regions in central Honduras. In the center of the valley, along the edge of the highway, is the **Escuela Agrícola Pan Americana,** set up in the 1940s by the United Fruit Company under the directorship of William Popenoe. The school trains farmers from across Central America. Students receive hands-on experience in the fields and gardens around the attractive campus. Anyone interested in agricultural research may want to stop into the school's library or bookstore.

A dirt road turning off the highway opposite the school leads to **San Antonio de Oriente,** a colonial village that was the subject of many paintings by its most famous son, Honduran artist José Antonio Velásquez.

NORTH AND WEST OF TEGUCIGALPA

Cedros

Another fine colonial mining town near Tegucigalpa, less often visited than those described above, Cedros is a collection of whitewashed, tile-roofed houses clinging precariously to the edge of a pine-forested mountainside, 26 kilometers from the Olancho highway on an all-weather dirt road. The turn is some 60 kilometers north of Tegucigalpa on the road to Juticalpa, just past the town of Talanga. Cedros was founded in 1537 by Spanish conquistador Alonso de Cáceres Guzmán and has experienced several different gold mining booms throughout its history. Locals like to say it was the capital of the country for 24 hours, when Honduras' first national assembly met there on 28 August 1824. The building in which the historic meeting took place still stands, a block up from the *parque,* and it is marked with a small plaque. The town's main church, **San José de Cedros,** is a beautiful chapel with a gleaming white facade and bell tower, and two carved wooden *retablos* trimmed with gold inside. The church's roof was damaged during Hurricane Mitch, and the federal government is paying for major restorations, well under way during a visit in early 2000. A small **Casa de Cultura** on the *parque* next to the police station, with books on Cedros and general Honduran history, was also under renovation at last report. Don't fail to walk up the low hill called El Cerrito right behind the square, which offers fine views over the town and surrounding hills.

The lively local *feria,* now quite safe since liquor and gambling were banned in 1998, is held 15 January.

In the surrounding hills are many old mines, including two quite close to town that were in operation until recently, both run by small-scale foreign miners. The town residents, a singularly mellow and friendly bunch, seem to have little interest in striking it rich themselves, instead scraping out a living with coffee and other farm products.

If you'd like to spend a few days enjoying the bucolic atmosphere and bracing mountain air, **Doña Elinda** runs a *comedor* and *hospedaje,* a block uphill behind the church. She charges US$1.50 for a quite decent meal of chicken, rice, salad, potatoes, and tortillas, and if you stay for a while, she can accommodate reasonable culinary requests. Rooms are US$4 pp for a simple but acceptable concrete room with a bed and nothing else, and access to a shared bathroom.

Three buses a day ply the route between the Cedros *parque* and Tegucigalpa (at the Mayoreo market in Comayagüela), US$2.25, two

the colonial mining village of Cedros

hours, the last one leaving in both directions in the early afternoon. You can also catch one of the Minas de Oro buses from the same market in Tegucigalpa and walk the one and a half kilometers uphill to Cedros from the turnoff.

Northwest of Cedros, the dirt highway continues out to Minas de Oro, reportedly another attractive colonial mining town, with frequent buses from Tegucigalpa. Beyond Minas de Oro, the highway branches off to different lonely roads into the mountains toward Comayagua, Yoro, and Olancho. Though the towns and people out here are generally *tranquilo* and the mountain scenery superb, it's a bit risky to drive in your own car out past Minas de Oro, as highway holdups have been reported. The well-traveled road as far as Cedros and Minas de Oro is quite safe, however.

Reserva Biológica El Chile
A modest reserve of pine and cloud forest atop a broad mountain bordering the departments of Francisco Morazán and El Paraíso, El Chile covers 61 square km. Much of the forest on the lower flanks of the mountain has long since disappeared and been given over to coffee plantations, but good-sized patches of intact cloud forest can still be found in the highest part of the park, a plateau ringed with several peaks of around 2,100 m. The highest point in the park is Pico de Navaja (2,180 m).

Hikers can get to the reserve from either the north or the south, though the northern route is usually a bit quicker. Catch any Juticalpa bus as far as **Guaimaca,** a large town about an hour from Tegucigalpa set in a broad farming valley. From Guaimaca a side road in relatively good condition heads south into the hills to the village of **San Marcos,** an hour or so by pickup truck. In San Marcos is a small visitors' center with information about the park, and guides can be hired for trips of varying length into the forest and to nearby waterfalls. A half-day trip costs around US$3.50, more for a full day.

It's also possible to visit the south side of the park, by driving or catching a bus (from Mercado Jacaleapa in Tegucigalpa) to **Teupasenti,** a large coffee town with several hotels and restaurants located about 25 km north of the highway to Danlí. From Teupasenti catch a ride on a pickup

two and a half hours up to the village of El Chile, on the side of the mountain of the same name, and ask around for guides into the forest. Reportedly a lake is tucked into a high valley on the south side of reserve.

Zambrano
Some 35 kilometers west of Tegucigalpa on the way to Comayagua, in a high valley ringed with pine forest, is the roadside town of Zambrano. About one and a half km from Zambrano the dirt road to La Catarata Escondida (Hidden Waterfall) is **Casería Valuz,** tel. 898-6625 or 239-2328, email: caseriovaluz@hotmail.com, an attractive new lodge that was receiving its finishing touches at last report and was expected to open by the time this book is published. The large main house, built with lots of wood trim, has 15 rooms of varying sizes and a kitchen/dining room downstairs. Rooms, each with hot water and many with balconies and chimney, will rent for US$40-60 and sleep one to three people. Food packages will be around US$20 per person for three meals. Out back are two cabins, each equipped with two bedrooms, four beds, and a kitchen, to rent out as less expensive rooms to backpackers. The surrounding countryside is lovely and the air is pure. Owner Jorge E. Valle Aguiluz, an avid outdoorsman, can arrange horseback trips nearby or driving trips farther afield in the surrounding mountain country.

On the highway just past Zambrano going toward Comayagua, at Km 36, is **Parque Aurora,** a wooded area with fields and benches for picnicking, a small lake, and horses to rent. Open Tues.-Sun. during daylight hours, US 75 cents for adults, US 35 cents for children under 12.

Refugio de Vida Silvestre Corralitos
About 15 km north of Zambrano as the crow flies is this little-visited forest reserve similar in character to El Chile, covering 6,926 hectares of mountainside. While the pine and broadleaf forests are facing serious pressures from loggers, hunters, and farmers, plenty of intact forest still graces the upper slopes of Montaña de Corralitos (2,117 m), in the heart of the reserve. To get there, take a dirt road leaving the San Pedro highway just outside of Zambrano to the mountain town of **San Francisco Soroguara;** ask

around there for someone who could guide you into the forest, or at least give some directions on where to start hiking. This is a friendly and safe rural region, where the villagers have strong ideas on the importance of hospitality. You'll have no problems getting directions from families in their tidy, painted *ranchos* dotting the lovely mountain countryside.

For more information on Corralitos and suggestions on possible guides, contact **Fundación Educa,** in Tegucigalpa, Colonia Las Minitas, just off Blvd. Morazán, tel. 239-1793, 239-1642. Jorge Valle Aguiluz, owner of Casería Valuz in Zambrano, may also have ideas on how to get into the park. Topographical maps covering the reserve are Zambrano 2758 IV and Agalteca 2759 II.

LA MOSQUITIA AND OLANCHO

The two largest departments in the country, Gracias a Dios (La Mosquitia) and Olancho, combine to cover 36% of Honduras' territory but have a population density of only about seven people per square kilometer, far lower than any other part of Honduras. This is frontier country, populated by cowboys, loggers, and hunters—people accustomed to fending for themselves without anybody's help. If you came to Honduras tired of traveling the same well-beaten gringo trail through Latin America and in search of adventure, don't fail to leave a couple of weeks for the Mosquitia and Olancho. It's not the sort of region where you can expect to find a first-class hotel or haute cuisine, but if you're willing to rough it, unexplored expanses of tropical jungle and pine forest, raging rivers, and rugged mountains await.

LA MOSQUITIA

La Mosquitia, the fabled Mosquito Coast, is a huge swath of Caribbean coastline, lagoons, pine savanna, and the largest remaining expanse of virgin tropical jungle in Central America, all covering the northeastern corner of Honduras. Reached only by plane, boat, or foot, the Mosquitia has the feel of a separate country, cut off from the rest of Honduras and the world.

For the nature-lover, a river or hiking trip into the dense jungles of the Biosfera del Río Plátano is one of the most impressive trips available in Central America, a chance to see untamed rainforest teeming with wildlife. Both all-inclusive expeditions with tour companies or independent

LA MOSQUITIA AND OLANCHO HIGHLIGHTS

- Boating through the pristine rainforests along the Río Plátano and the Río Patuca
- Hiking to the dwarf forest on top of Sierra de Agalta
- Looking for quetzals and other tropical birds in El Boquerón, near Juticalpa
- For the real adventurer, hiking and/or rafting from Olancho through the Mosquitia jungle to the Caribbean coast.

trips using local guides are easily arranged, as long as you're prepared to rough it for a few days. Adventurers can seek out boats along the Río Patuca or the Río Coco, either up from the coast or downriver from Olancho, and also spend days or weeks exploring the Miskito villages lined along the region's endless, windswept beaches and inland waterways.

The Gracias a Dios department, which covers all of Honduran Mosquitia, is the second largest in the country, but has a population of only 51,772 people in a 1998 estimate. These inhabitants live in isolated villages and towns connected to each other mainly by boat or, less frequently, plane. The Mosquitia has no road connection to the rest of the country (despite what you might see on a few rather fanciful Honduras road maps), though a small, self-contained circuit of dirt tracks across the savanna connects Puerto Lempira, Rus Rus, and the Río Coco and Nicaraguan border at Leimus.

Unlike the rest of Honduras, most of the in-

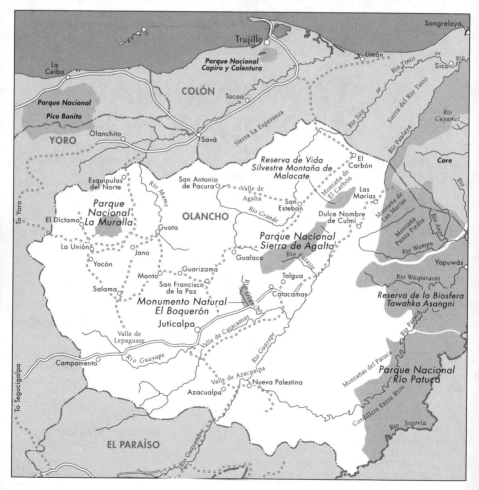

habitants of the Mosquitia belong to an indigenous group, either Miskito, Tawahka, Pech, or Garífuna. Indigenous is a relative term, though, since the ethnogenesis of both the Miskito and Garífuna people is a fairly recent historical event—for more on this, see the special topics "The Voyage of the Garífuna" and "The Birth of a Race."

Across the Río Coco and into eastern Nicaragua, the Mosquitia "cultural zone" continues down to the banks of the Río San Juan and contains a similar mix of ethnic groups, lush jungle, and coastal wetlands, and disconnectedness from the rest of Nicaragua. Many Miskito cross back and forth constantly to visit family and work in both countries with little regard for border formalities.

The rainforests of the Mosquitia, like its South American counterpart the Amazon, faces pressures on its edges by land-hungry peasants, cattle ranchers, and mahogany loggers who are chopping and burning the forest at a vertiginous rate. Most of the newcomers are immigrants

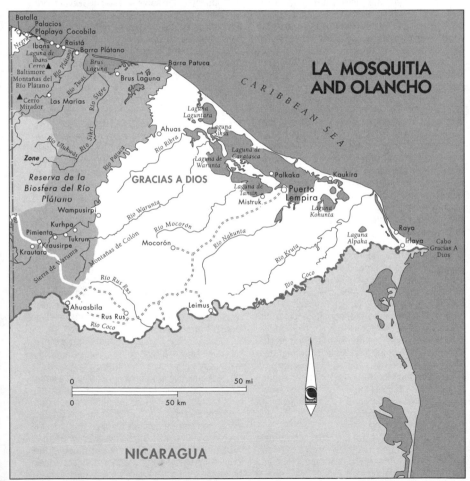

LA MOSQUITIA
AND OLANCHO

CARIBBEAN SEA

Batalla
Palacios
Plaplaya Cocobila
Ibans Raistá
Laguna de Barra Plátano
Ibans
Cerro Brus
Baltimore Laguna Barra Patuca
Montañas del Brus Laguna
Río Plátano
Cerro Las Marías
Mirador
Laguna
Zone Laguntara
Ahuas Laguna
Siksa
Reserva de la Laguna de
Biosfera del Río Caratasca
Plátano Laguna de Palkaka Kaukira
Wampusirpi Warunta Tansin Puerto
Mistruk Lempira
Kurhpa Laguna
Pimienta Kohunta
Tukrum Mocorón Laguna Raya
Krausirpe Alpaka Irlaya
Krautara Cabo
Ahuasbila Gracias A
Rus Rus Leimus Dios
Río Coco

GRACIAS A DIOS

Río Negro
Río Plátano
Río Twas
Río Sigre
Río Uluhwas
Río Patuca
Río Sikri
Río Ribra
Río Warunta
Río Mocorón
Río Nakunta
Río Kruta
Río Rus Rus
Montañas de Colón
Sierra de Warunta

0   50 mi
0   50 km

NICARAGUA

© AVALON TRAVEL PUBLISHING

from other parts of the country, particularly the extremely poor south, driven from their former homes by self-inflicted soil erosion and apparently intent on doing the same in Mosquitia.

In an effort to halt the tide of immigrants, or at least slow the destruction, in 1980 the Honduran government created the **Reserva de la Biosfera del Río Plátano** protecting 815,000 hectares of primary jungle and savanna in the center of the Mosquitia. After much debate, the government also finally approved the creation of Parque Nacional Río Patuca (375,584 hectares) and Reserva de la Biosfera Tawahka Asangni (233,142 hectares) on 21 December 1999, placing a huge region of the Mosquitia and northeastern Olancho all the way to the Nicaraguan border under nominal protection.

Exactly how effective these lines drawn on maps in Tegucigalpa are in actually stopping the destruction of the forests is another matter, but they are at least a step in the right direction. Environmentalists are pressuring the government and Army to place much-needed check points near Dulce Nombre de Culmí, at the mouth of the Río Patuca, and at the junction of the Río Paulaya and Río Sico. As most of the illegally logged wood is shipped out through one of these routes, the checkpoints could, if properly managed, help slow the logging, particularly in the severely threatened south part of the reserve near Culmí.

The Tawahka tribe on the upper Patuca appear to be learning how to organize themselves and take steps to defend their lands, though they continue to live in fear of more violent *ladinos* coming down from Olancho with lots of guns, looking out for grazing land and valuable hardwoods. The Tawahka—numbering about 1,000 in a dozen small villages—claim the amount of land allotted to the reserve falls far short of what they need to maintain their traditional lifestyle, a right guaranteed by a United Nations convention, which the Honduran government signed. A proposed dam on the Patuca, which would have seriously threatened Tawahka land, has finally been canceled due to the numerous protests raised by the plan.

In short, the jungles of the Mosquitia remain under serious, continual threat, victim of relentless economic and social pressures in Honduras and a thus-far almost total lack of government

control in the region. A recent sweep by an Army unit through the Mosquitia is a promising sign, though it should be noted that no loggers were arrested and the confiscated wood was promptly auctioned by the government at a tidy profit. One can only hope increased tourism, among many other factors, can play a positive role in the battle to keep the Mosquitia rainforests alive.

Traveling In Mosquitia

The Mosquitia may be remote and undeveloped, but that doesn't mean it's cheap to travel there. Airfare from La Ceiba to Palacios (for the Río Plátano) is US$39, or US$58 to Puerto Lempira. Flying between towns in the Mosquitia, particularly to get to the upper parts of the Patuca, is possible, but only by expensive (US$200-300) charters with Sosa, Rollins, or Sami (all contacted in Puerto Lempira or Palacios).

Boat trips can get expensive as well, especially if you hire a *viaje especial* (special trip), which is usually required for getting into the jungle. Prices for this sort of trip are always somewhat negotiable and require asking around to find a satisfactory captain. Your bargaining position will be improved if you can get a rough idea how many gallons of gas the trip will take, and what the current price per gallon is in Mosquitia. After that, you're just debating the cost of the boatman's time. Full day trips can easily run US$90-100 per boat.

Inexpensive *colectivo* motorized canoes ply routes around Palacios and Puerto Lempira for US$2.50-4 per trip but are less frequent elsewhere. With patience rides can be caught along the Río Coco, Río Patuca, and Río Plátano, for anywhere from US$7 to US$15 per ride, depending on where you're going. Be prepared for long, hot, cramped rides.

Because of the high transportation costs, travelers will find the Mosquitia pricier than they might have expected. For those on a budget, the best option is to visit the Mosquitia in a small group so you can split the costs of guides and boat transport. Often it's possible to hook up with other travelers in La Ceiba or the Bay Islands, and sometimes in Palacios.

Unless you're planning on flying everywhere in the Mosquitia (and you won't see much of the jungle that way), don't go on a tight schedule. Any trip to the Río Plátano or Río Patuca jungles

THE LAND OF MOSQUITOES?

One might, understandably, assume that La Mosquitia got its name from the voracious mosquitoes that thrive in some parts of the region. But as anyone who has been to the Mosquitia knows, mosquitoes are called *zancudos* there. So a couple of more creative explanations have been offered as to the name's origin. One suggests that the name is derived from the word musket, or rifle, with which the Miskito were well supplied by the British. Supposedly, the Spaniards took to calling the attacking Indians *mosqueteros* because of their weaponry, which none of the other Indian groups in Central America used. From this developed the name Mosquetos, which over the years became Miskito.

Another possible derivation, favored by Miskito nationalists, is from the name Miskut, a tribal chief of the Táwira Sumu. Miskut's people lived near Cabo Gracias a Dios and are thought to have been the original Sumu group that evolved into the Miskito.

But hard-headed realists like to point out that, although modern Hondurans generally call them *jejenes,* the Spaniards called sand flies *mosquitos* (little flies). Early in the conquest, Spanish explorers named several small islands just south of Cabo Gracias a Dios the Los Cayos Mosquitos, or the Mosquito Cays, for the clouds of pesky sand flies still found there today. Because the Miskitos frequented these and other cays in their oceangoing canoes, the Spaniards may have transferred the name to the raiders who, perhaps in the eyes of some metaphorically inclined colonist, plagued their settlements like sand flies.

realistically requires a week, or five days at minimum, though shorter trips to coastal areas are easily accomplished in three or four days. The only bank in Mosquitia that changes dollars is in Puerto Lempira, so be sure to bring plenty of *lempiras.* Locals will usually accept or change dollars in a pinch, but always at bad rates.

Malaria is rampant in the coastal and savanna areas of the Mosquitia, much less prevalent in the jungle. The Mosquitia may not have gotten its name from those little bloodsucking bugs, known locally as *zancudos,* but they certainly are well-known and prolific residents, particularly in the rainy season.

The Land

Much of the Mosquitia is a low-lying plain, by far the largest expanse of flat terrain in Honduras. The land holds practically no agricultural potential, though, as the region is covered either by coastal mangrove swamp, tropical jungle, or marshy savanna dotted with Caribbean pine. Land-hungry migrants from Olancho and other parts of Honduras have been eagerly chopping down the jungle for farming and cattle ranching, but as they have slowly been realizing, the rich exuberance of the tropical rainforest has little to do with the underlying soil, which is nutrient-poor, thin, and easily eroded.

Several major river systems zig-zag their way across the Mosquitia plains including, from west to east, the Sico, Paulaya, Plátano, Sigre, Patuca, and Coco (or Segovia); this last forms the border with Nicaragua. The only mountains near the coast are the Montañas del Río Plátano, which run southwest into Olancho, connecting to the Sierra de Agalta. Farther east and south, forming part of the watershed of the Río Patuca, is the Sierra de Warunta and the Montañas de Colón. In general, the land trends gently up from the coast to the mountains of Olancho, the source for the region's rivers.

The Mosquitia is the wettest part of the country, receiving 300-340 cm of rain on average annually. Rains regularly hit in May, June, and July, followed by a brief dry spell in August and September. Hurricane season is between September and November. February, March, and April are the most reliably dry months of the year, but wet weather can arrive at any time. Temperatures are invariably hot during the day, often reaching 35° C, but it can be surprisingly cool at night. The coast is usually stroked with ocean breezes, which keeps the heat down.

History

In the pre-Columbian times, the Pech populated much of western Mosquitia, living across a wide area delimited by present-day Trujillo, the Olancho and Agalta Valleys, and the Río Patuca. Farther east, several Sumu-Tawahka tribes inhabited the region from the Río Patuca to the Río Coco, and across into what is now

THE BIRTH OF A RACE

When Europeans first came to the Mosquitia, the region was inhabited by Pech Indians and several coastal and jungle subtribes of the Sumu. The Spaniards, intent on finding gold and quick riches, made few efforts to colonize the Mosquitia, and in the early 1600s the British began eyeing the region with interest.

In 1633, the British erected their first settlement, at Cabo Gracias a Dios. The colonists collected hardwood from the forests and traded peaceably with the Sumu, who were quickly smitten by British weaponry, manufactured goods, and rum. The coastal Sumu—possibly a group known as the Bawihkas—had always had a different physiognomy from their inland cousins, and in a few decades the differences became more dramatic. In part the Miskitos evolved from mixing with the English, but more so from several groups of slaves shipwrecked on the shores of eastern Honduras, the first in 1641. Unlike many other indigenous groups, the coastal Sumu tribes had an extremely open culture that allowed them to mix freely with outsiders, a trait that sped up the process of racial evolution.

The first written mention of the Miskitos appeared in 1672, when the pirate John Exquemelin said they numbered about 1,600 people. In 1699 an anonymous English traveler wrote that "the Mosquetomen inhabit the sea-shore, pretty close to the seaside, or on the sides of some lakes and lagunes hardby" between Cabo Camarón and Cabo Gracias a Dios.

It remains a mystery what process was under way in the latter part of the 17th century, which from the mixing of African, English, and Indian blood created a new race with a distinct language and culture, but by the turn of the century the Miskitos had been born. The English quickly saw the value of cultivating the Miskitos as allies against the Spanish, and in 1687 they invited the tribe's chief to Jamaica and crowned him Jeremy I, the first of the Miskito kings. In time the British also created governors, generals, and admirals at other Miskito settlements, who sometimes acted more like independent warlords than servants of the king. The chiefs were not recognized as legitimate by their subjects until they had made a ritual trip to Jamaica, or later Belize, to receive the British blessing. Reportedly the crowning ceremonies were amusing spectacles of bountiful speeches and much drunkenness.

The Miskitos needed little encouragement to fight the Spaniards, whom they detested. With a little training they became feared raiders with an insatiable thirst for attacking Spanish settlements. At first they joined pirate expeditions against Trujillo and Puerto Caballos, but soon took to launching their own attacks against León and Granada in Nicaragua, Juticalpa and San Pedro Sula, and any

a Miskito family
on the Río
Plátano

GUILLERMO COBOS

other poorly defended Spanish settlement they ran across in their forays.

During the course of the 18th century the Miskitos gained complete ascendancy over the Tawahka-Sumu and the Pech, demanding tribute and often raiding the communities for slaves to sell to the English. Unable to compete with the fierce and well-armed Miskitos, the Pech and Tawahka abandoned their former territories and fled into the jungle to escape attack, leaving the Miskitos the sole rulers of the shore. In fact the Miskitos invented the derogatory term "Sumu" to designate their former brethren the Tawahka.

With the Anglo-Hispanic Convention of 1786, the British agreed to evacuate the Mosquito Coast in return for Belize. The Miskitos, however, were not inclined to submit themselves to their erstwhile enemies, the Spanish. Some 1,300 immigrants from Spain arrived at Black River in 1788, but Miskitos attacked repeatedly and settlers were forced to flee to Trujillo, which became the eastern limit of Spanish control.

To this day, many Miskitos hold a special affection for the British, and for that matter any English-speaking white person, and fondly cherish the thought that they will return and kick out the *indios,* as they derisively call the Spanish. Only a few Miskitos speak English, but many still have Anglo names. The Miskitos were left alone by the Honduran government until the 1950s, when the government began building schools in the Mosquitia to spread the use of Spanish.

Since that time, Spanish has slowly replaced English as the *lingua franca* of the Mosquitia, and the government has gradually begun to assert its authority in the region. But, as with the English and the African slaves who ended up on the Mosquitia shores, the Miskitos seem to be incorporating the Spanish immigrants rather than vice versa. Their open culture, unafraid of change, has proved to be the Miskito's strongest tool in facing the brave new world.

Nicaragua. Little is known about the origin of these two groups or their society in pre-conquest times, other than that they are part of the Chibchan linguistic group and are thought to have migrated from the rainforests of Colombia to Central America. Joining the Pech and Sumu in around A.D. 1000 were groups of Nahuatl-speaking Pipiles who migrated down from Mexico. The ruins of what are believed to be either Pech or Pipil ceremonial centers have been located along both the Caribbean coast and farther inland as far as Olancho, but intensive archaeological work has yet to be undertaken.

Christopher Columbus was the first European to visit the Mosquitia. On his fourth voyage, after stopping at Guanaja and Trujillo Bay, Columbus sailed east along the coast until he came to the mouth of a major river, where he landed and spoke to the Indians living there through an interpreter he had brought from Guanaja. The river, which he named Río de la Posesión, could have been either the Aguán, Sico, or Patuca. Because some of the Indians apparently had large earlobes, Columbus named the region La Costa de las Orejas (The Coast of the Ears).

Following this landing, Columbus' fleet endured fierce weather for several weeks until the boats finally rounded Honduras' easternmost point and continued south along the coast of Nicaragua in calmer waters. In honor of the event, the point was named Cabo Gracias a Dios. After Columbus, in the 16th century the Spanish made a couple of abortive efforts to colonize the Mosquitia, but soon they gave up and chased their dreams of gold and riches in the more hospitable climate of central Honduras. This left the coast open for the pirates who flocked over from Europe beginning in the late 16th century to prey on the Spanish treasure fleets in the Caribbean. The pirates used the Bay Islands and the protected, isolated lagoons of the Mosquitia as their bases.

When war broke out between England and Spain in 1625, English captains based in Bermuda began exploring the Honduran and Nicaraguan coast in earnest, eager to gain a foothold on the mainland. In 1633, the first English settlement was established at Gracias a Dios, from where the English began trading and interacting with the coastal Sumu.

By 1700, the English had cemented a firm alliance with the coastal tribes of the Sumu-Tawahka—who had metamorphosed over the years into the Miskito—against their common enemy, the Spaniards. The Brits frequently launched raids from the Mosquitia against Trujillo and Puerto Caballos and even struck inland to Olancho and southward to Nicaragua. The attacks had a devastating destabilizing effect on the Spanish colonies.

William Pitt settled Black River (now Palacios) in 1699, and shortly afterward migrants moved into Brewer's Lagoon (now Brus Laguna). The Shoremen, as the new English settlers called themselves, were more interested in logging, collecting dyewood, and smuggling than in raiding the Spaniards, but the British had taught the Miskito too well and couldn't always contain their allies. The constant harassment by marauding Miskitos eventually prompted the Spaniards to action, and by 1780 a major offensive had been launched against the Mosquitia and the Bay Islands. In March 1782, the Spaniards led a two-pronged attack against Black River and Brewer's Lagoon, one contingent coming by sea and the other, incredibly, marching overland through the jungle from Olancho. The two settlements were taken with little struggle, but most of the Shoremen and Miskitos escaped through the canals, evading capture and soon retaking the towns.

By this point, the shore colonies had become a serious headache for the British government, which was more worried about the situation in Europe than about a few loggers on the remote coast of Central America. In the Anglo-Spanish Convention, signed 14 July 1786, the British ceded all Central American settlements to the Spanish in exchange for Belize. By August of the following year all Shoremen had been evacuated to Belize, except for a few stragglers in the woods, and the Spanish took possession of Black River.

Colonial authorities soon discovered, however, that ownership is one thing and settlement quite another. Several boatloads of would-be migrants shipped out to Mosquitia, but, faced with the steaming jungle and hostile, violent Miskitos, they most understandably fled at the first opportunity. Taking advantage of the general anarchy in Central America following independence from Spain in 1821, and in a bid to halt U.S. ascendancy in the region, the British government again officially recognized the Miskito Kingdom, but the U.S. forced England to back down in 1860 through diplomatic pressure.

Although Honduras gained undisputed control over the Mosquitia in 1860, the region continued to be populated solely by Miskitos, Tawahkas, Garífuna, Pech, and the occasional North American logger or gold miner, until the 1930s. Around this time Moravian missionaries from the U.S. began arriving in the area, setting up schools and eventually creating the first Miskito dictionary. Because of its years of work in the Mosquitia, the Moravian church remains very strong in the Mosquitia.

The Honduran government finally got around to setting up offices, building schools, and promoting the use of Spanish in the early 1950s. The department of Gracias a Dios was created in 1957, and since that time the government has promoted migration into the region, with limited success.

In the 1980s, the Miskitos again found themselves being used as proxies in a foreign war, armed and encouraged by the U.S. CIA to fight the Sandinista government in Nicaragua. Honduras' Puerto Lempira was the main base for the northern front of the so-called Contra War. The violence led to major immigration from Nicaragua into Honduras, a trend that only recently began reversing.

Most residents of the Mosquitia make a living by fishing or as small-scale farmers. The fishing season is technically only between September and February, but as locals have little other means of income, many fish illicitly all year. The lucrative lobster-diving trade, which exports to distributors and restaurants in the U.S., is particularly tempting to young Miskito men looking for cash. As might be expected, though, scuba training and the following of basic decompression rules are rare, resulting in frequent, often crippling diving accidents.

In recent years, cocaine has begun passing through the Mosquitia on its way north to the United States. Taking advantage of the huge stretches of unpatrolled coastline in this corner of Honduras, Colombian drug runners drop off major shipments of coke on the beaches of the Mosquitia, where it's taken north overland or by boat. Every once in a while a kilo or two will wash up on shore, and an entire village will be wired to the gills for a week or so.

As late as the mid-1990s, this scavenging was still a free-for-all industry, with many people out patrolling the beaches and seas for random packages, but the business is reputedly more organized now. Shipments usually come in by boat directly from Colombia to the Mosquitia coastline, then through the coastal waterways and by four-wheel-drive tracks out to Tocoa, where the product continues overland through Guatemala and Mexico to its final market. The government makes occasional noise about controlling the remote coastline, and even sent an Army patrol through in late 1999, but the traffic continues unabated. Tourists considering a trip out to Mosquitia should have no fear whatsoever about getting mixed up in any of this, as it all takes place far from prying eyes. About the only place to come in contact with the trade is in the disco in Puerto Lempira, where many of the nouveau-riche Miskitos like to flaunt their wealth.

PALACIOS

Situated on a spit of land near the mouth of the Río Sico, protected from the open ocean by a narrow sandbar, Palacios is a town of about 2,000, scattered across grassy pastures cut out of the jungle. Because planes fly daily between Palacios and La Ceiba, and because of the town's proximity to the Río Plátano, Palacios is a necessary stop-off point for visitors to the Biosphere Reserve. It's also a funky little town in its own right, worth visiting to experience the isolated life of the Mosquitia, and to check out nearby Garífuna and Miskito villages.

History

Black River, as the town was first called, was founded in 1699 by William Pitt, on the site of a Miskito village. A distant relative of the famed British prime minister of the same name, Pitt was instrumental in maintaining the Shoremen's alliance with the Miskitos; in the process he became extremely wealthy. He is said to have owned sugar plantations stretching up the Black River for 60 kilometers, 400 slaves, and a mansion built at the edge of the jungle.

Following the War of Jenkin's Ear between England and Spain in 1739, the British proclaimed sovereignty over Black River and sent military officers to build fortifications there and at Brewer's Lagoon. When the British finally relinquished the town in 1787, it fell to William Lawrie Pitt, grandson of the town's founder, to hand over Black River to the Spanish on 29 August. The Spanish renamed the town Río Tinto, but the

---

THE SCOTTISH CON MAN OF LA MOSQUITIA

Near Black River was the site of the ill-fated Poyais Colony, one of the more impressive swindles in Central American history. Scotsman Gregor MacGregor, a former British soldier and a mercenary general in Bolivar's South American wars of independence, ended up on the Mosquito Coast in 1820. He got along famously with Miskito King George Frederick. The king, predisposed to like any Englishman—especially one with a large supply of rum—awarded MacGregor enormous land concessions around the mouth of the Black River.

MacGregor returned to England proclaiming himself the representative of the fictitious nation of Poyais, looking for colonists. Calling himself His Highness Gregor I, Cazique of Poyais, MacGregor spent two years convincing politicians, financiers, and other dupes to back his scam. In 1822, he published *Sketch of the Mosquito Shore, Including the Territory of Poyais, Chiefly Intended for the Use of Settlers*, enumerating the many wonders of the region, though notably failing to mention that the region was an undeveloped jungle.

MacGregor convinced hundreds to financially back the would-be colony—and over 200 people, including teachers, clerks, shopkeepers, and a bankor, actually went to Honduras in late 1822. They arrived in the midst of heavy rains to find a patch of jungle on the Black River, totally unprepared to deal with their surroundings. In their anger at being duped, they alienated local Miskitos, who might have helped them, by refusing to swear allegiance to King George Frederick. The settlers were attacked by the Miskitos and devastated by disease. In the end, 50 bedraggled survivors were eventually picked up by a rescue ship from Belize.

Unperturbed by the fate of his "colony," MacGregor went on selling land to other Europeans for nine years before the situation got too hot, whence he bolted to Venezuela and lived, a wealthy man, until his death in 1845.

new name didn't protect it from repeated plunder by the Miskitos. The Spanish finally evacuated in September 1800.

The town, renamed Palacios, was not repopulated until the early part of the 20th century, when one of the U.S. banana companies made an abortive attempt to start a plantation in the vicinity. The remains of the company's railroad can still be seen, mostly covered over by jungle.

Although the jungle has long since claimed most of the remains of the old English settlement, some traces can still be seen. A few hundred yards east of Don Felix's hotel, along the waterfront road, is a large field on the right, where four old cannons from the British fort lie half-buried in the weeds. The owner of the land, who proudly claims British heritage though he speaks no English, said he understood that the mouth of the river, now farther to the east, was once right in front of his property. This would explain the location of the cannons, on a small rise in the land in front of the water.

On the west side of town, between the airstrip and the lagoon, just about opposite the Hospital Bayan, lives a Garífuna family, and in the front yard of their humble house is the grave of William Pitt, the town's founder. The worn stone is sometimes covered with dirt, but the amiable family will help you clear it off to see the still-legible inscription.

In memory of its English past, Palacios is still sometimes called La Criva, a corruption of Black River.

Practicalities

Options for eating and sleeping in Palacios are limited. Don Felix Marmol runs a *pulpería* in a ramshackle, two-story wooden building, which is also the Isleña office and the town's informal gathering place. Next to the store is **Don Felix's hotel,** a two-story motel-like affair with 10 simple rooms for US$9 s or d with private bathroom and a fan.

Between the store and the hotel is a small *comedor* with unexceptional meals for US$2. A bit farther east along the edge of the lagoon is **Comedor 8 Hermanos,** with similar fare.

West of Felix's, facing the airstrip on the edge of the lagoon, is the **Jungle Lodge,** a two-story house with a dock on the back. The upstairs rooms, going for US$10 s or d, are similar in

quality to Don Felix's hotel but more spacious.

The **Hospital Bayan** on the airstrip was first started by Bahai doctors in 1986. Recently the hospital was turned over to the Honduran government health system, meaning quality has fallen, but it is the largest clinic in the western Mosquitia.

Getting There and Away

Isleña flies from Palacios to Trujillo (US$28) and La Ceiba (US$39) every day except Sunday, leaving at 11:45 a.m. Don Felix sells tickets at his store.

Rollins flies out daily except Sunday to La Ceiba at 7:15 a.m. or so. Tickets are sold by a Catalán named Emilio Reyes, who presides over a small office at the eastern end of the airstrip.

Sami runs a rattletrap eight-seat, single-prop plane every day except Sunday from Belén (a 45-minute, US$5 boat ride from Palacios) to Brus Laguna (US$13), Ahuas (US$16), and Puerto Lempira (US$25), depending on where his passengers want to go. The plane usually leaves in the morning—ask Don Felix to check times and seat availability in advance on the radio. Sometimes Sami flies through Palacios also.

Boat prices from Palacios to Belén, Cocobila, Raistá, Sangrelaya, Batalla, and elsewhere in the vicinity of Palacios cost about US$3, sometimes more depending on how wealthy you look. Locals are invariably charged a bit less. Generally haggling won't get you too far, but it's worth a try.

Boats to the Biosphere

Boats from Palacios up to Las Marías on the Río Plátano, at last check, cost about US$100 roundtrip, including a couple of days at the village for a jungle trip. For each extra day in Las Marías, expect to pay a bit more for the captain to wait. In a *tuk-tuk,* or motorized canoe, the trip from Palacios takes 7-10 hours. Bring something soft to sit on (those wooden benches are a killer) and protection from the sun. A couple of outboard *lanchas* run the route in about half the time, but they charge upwards of US$150. Boats from Cocobila, Belén, or Raistá, on Laguna de Ibans, are about the same price.

Most travelers will likely hire a boat to Las Marías in Palacios, or in one of the villages on Laguna de Ibans, but if you're really broke and in no hurry whatsoever, you could walk three to four hours east of Belén on the coast to **Barra Plátano,** a Miskito village at the mouth of the Río Plátano. Here you can sometimes find a boat already going to Las Marías from the river mouth and pay just US$10 or so for the ride. Traffic is irregular, so unless you get lucky, come prepared to hang out a couple of days. Basic rooms and food are available in Barra Plátano.

NEAR PALACIOS

Facing the Caribbean Sea on a narrow, sandy peninsula backed by the Río Sico and, farther east, the Laguna de Ibans, are a string of Garífuna and Miskito villages home to much of the population of western Mosquitia.

Batalla and Plaplaya
Almost directly across the lagoon from Palacios, just a bit west along the coast, is the large Garífuna village of Batalla. Going west around Cabo Camarón from Batalla, walkable in a day on the beach, is Sangrelaya, another Garífuna village; trucks travel from here to Limón or Tocoa every day.

Several kilometers east of the mouth of the Río Sico, on the waterways about halfway to Laguna Ibans from Palacios, is **Plaplaya,** the easternmost Garífuna settlement in Honduras, a large collection of thatched and concrete huts on a sand bar facing the Caribbean. Plaplaya is home to the **Giant Leatherback Turtle Project,** run with the help of the Mopawi, a Mosquitia development organization, and a local Peace Corps volunteer. The project manages a protected nesting area for the turtles, which can grow to be 1,500 pounds and are the largest living turtle species. The turtles are most commonly seen between April and June, when they come in to the local beaches to lay their eggs. Being there to watch the mother turtles waddle in, laboriously dig a nest and lay their eggs, and struggle back out sea, is a magical experience.

A local women's group is more than happy—positively eager, in fact—to put on a very entertaining and lively Garífuna dance performance to visitors, for about US$25. Spectators are merrily encouraged to join in the dancing toward the

later part of the show, if they would like. At the end, the doll of a baby, wrapped in a blanket, is passed around to exchange payment, a pleasingly elegant way of dispensing with financial formalities.

Right next to the dock along the inland waterway is a simple *hospedaje* charging US$5 per person. A couple of other places offer rooms at the far end of town. Local ladies will gladly whip up a few simple Garífuna dishes, such as coconut-fish soup and cassava bread, for US$2 or so a meal.

Villages on Laguna Ibans
About two hours' walk east on the coast of Plaplaya, or half an hour by boat, is the Miskito village of Ibans, and beyond, in quick succession, Cocobila, Raistá, Belén, and Nuevo Jerusalem. Walking between these settlements, it's difficult to tell where one stops and the next begins—they all blend together, with houses and the occasional store and church scattered along grassy footpaths in the couple hundred meters of land between the ocean and Laguna de Ibans. The beach along this entire stretch is windswept and deserted. The swimming is great, but beware the strong shore currents.

Cold drinks and basic supplies are sold at *pulperías* in Ibans, Cocobila, and Belén, and you could probably find a room and a meal by asking around. At last report an American expat rented out several beds on the west side of Cocobila. Camping is allowed just about anywhere on the peninsula, but it's always best to ask first.

The best setup for travelers to spend the night is at the **Butterfly Farm (Finca Mariposa)** in Raistá, where you can rent a room for US$3 per person. The farm, started by a Peace Corps volunteer in 1996 and managed by a Miskito man, Eddie Bodden, raises and exports butterfly larvae to U.S. research institutes. An interesting tour of the farm by Eddie or one of the other workers costs US$2.50. Eddie's wife cooks up excellent meals for US$1.20 each—it's mainly rice, eggs, chicken, and beans, but somehow she has a knack for making it taste remarkably good. Occasionally you'll get a treat of *wabul,* a traditional Miskito drink made from bananas and coconut milk. The people at Raistá are a friendly bunch, and the Finca is a peaceful place to hang out for a day before or after a trip up the Río Plátano, if only to enjoy the broad beach. The locals prefer to swim in the lagoon, despite its resident crocodiles.

The office for Sami's eight-seater airplane is in Belén, a 10-minute walk east of Raistá. The Isleña office, where you can make reservations and buy tickets, is above a store in Cocobila. Boats back to Palacios usually cost US$3, and many leave very early in the morning, so it's best to arrange a ride a day ahead of time. *Lanchas* and *tuk-tuks* up the Río Plátano can be negotiated in any of these villages, for about the same prices as in Palacios. From the northeast corner of Laguna de Ibans, near Nuevo Jerusalem, locals have hacked out a canal to the Río Plátano, meaning boats don't have to go out to the open ocean to cut over to the river. The canal is sometimes closed when the water level is low.

Three hours' walk east of Nuevo Jerusalem along the beach is Barra Plátano, a village at the mouth of the Río Plátano where it's possible to find boats up to Las Marías.

Cerro Baltimore

Named by a U.S. missionary (from Maryland, one suspects), Cerro Baltimore rises 1,083 meters from the south side of Laguna de Ibans. The jungle-clad peak is on the inside edge of the Biosphere Reserve, but in spite of its protected status cattle ranchers and loggers have begun invading and cutting down the forest on the southwest side. The jungles across most of the mountain remain spectacular and stocked with all manner of birds and mammals. A guided, three-day trip to the peak makes a viable and less-expensive alternative to taking a boat up to Las Marías. Sergio Bodden lives on the south side of the lagoon and will guide travelers. Contact him through his brother Eddie, the manager of the Butterfly Farm in Raistá. On the eastern flank of Cerro Baltimore, a trail cuts from the lagoon through the forest to Las Marías, on the Río Plátano—a full day's hike, reputed to be superb for birdwatching. It can be difficult to find a boat ride back from Las Marías, unless you're willing to wait a few days.

WHAT TO BRING ON A JUNGLE HIKE

- light hiking boots
- lightweight long-sleeve clothes, shorts or bathing suit for swimming
- insect repellent and sunblock
- brimmed hat
- kerosene or gas stove
- survival knife
- compass
- flashlights
- waterproof matches and lighter
- sheet or light sleeping bag
- camera
- malaria pills
- water bottles
- water filter or purification tablets
- binoculars for bird and animal watching
- dry bags
- tent or hammock with built-in mosquito net
- first-aid kit with antiseptic, bandages, antibiotic, and snakebite kit

RESERVA DE LA BIÓSFERA DEL RÍO PLÁTANO

Created in 1980 and declared a UNESCO World Heritage site in 1992, the Río Plátano reserve encompasses a huge expanse of broadleaf tropical rainforest, mangrove swamp, sedge prairie, and gallery forest stretching across northeastern Honduras. This is one of the great jungles of the Americas, an untamed, emerald-green wilderness filled with an incalculable treasure of biological diversity in its plant and animal residents. Though much of the reserve is extremely difficult to get to and travel around, guided trips into the reserve along the Río Plátano from the Caribbean coast are easily accomplished, if you've got a week to spare, and are as incredible a travel experience as you could hope for.

By far the largest protected area in Honduras, the reserve covers 815,000 hectares, or about seven percent of the national territory, in the Gracias a Dios, Colón, and Olancho departments. Of this area, 215,000 hectares are delimited as an untouchable core zone. While the core zone can hardly be said to be "untouched," it nonetheless remains almost entirely virgin rainforest.

The reserve is bordered on the northwest by the Río Paulaya, on the north by the Caribbean Sea, on the east and south by the Río Patuca, and to the south and west by the Río Patuca and one of its tributaries, the Río Wampú. Other rivers within the reserve include the Río Sigre (Sikre) and the Río Twas, both of which empty into Laguna de Brus, and of course the Río Plátano itself. Notable mountains include Cerro Baltimore (1,083 meters), Pico Dama (840 meters), Cerro Mirador (1,200 meters), Cerro Antilope (1,075 meters), and Montaña Punta Piedra (1,326 meters).

Most foreigners come to the Río Plátano to admire the plants and animals of the largest remaining tropical forest in Central America, but several pre Columbian ruins near Las Marías and in the southern section of the park in Olancho are well worth exploring. The ancestors of the Pech, or of Pipil immigrants from Mexico, are the two likeliest candidates to have built the many ruins. Persistent rumor holds that a full-scale city called **Ciudad Blanca** lies in the middle of the jungle, waiting to be discovered.

Because of the critical deforestation problem with the reserve, the Honduran government has recently permitted the creation of a new project to oversee protection, funded in large part by the German government, called **Proyecto de Manejo y Protección de la Biósfera del Río Plátano,** main office at Av. República de Panamá 2043, Colonia Palmira, Tegucigalpa, tel. 232-8334 or 235-6251.

Visiting the Reserve

While there are numerous ways to get into the huge biosphere, the route used by the majority of independent travelers is to fly from La Ceiba or Trujillo to Palacios, and continue from there by boat up the Río Plátano to Las Marías, where trained guides can lead trips of varying length by boat farther upstream or hiking in the jungle.

Less frequently visited is the jungle-clad Río Sigre, parallel to the Plátano but farther east, letting out into Brus Laguna. You might find someone in Brus to guide you up the Río Sigre, but those who actually know the way are few and far between.

If you're really hankering for an epic voyage through the jungle, consider taking a guided trek into the southern part of the biosphere from Dulce Nombre de Culmí in Olancho, into the wild upper headwaters of the Río Plátano, and down along the river to the coast. Because of the natural dangers, combined with the high incidence of rural violence around Culmí, don't try this without a professional guide. An expedition of 12-14 days through one of the wildest regions in the Americas is not the sort of thing one should attempt on a whim.

Several tour outfitters in Honduras offer a range of different trips to the Río Plátano, if you prefer to avoid the hassles of organizing transportation and local guides. Apart from simplifying the logistics of the trip, professional guides are often able to give more detailed information and deeper insights about the reserve and its human and animal inhabitants than you might otherwise find on your own. When going with a guided tour, it's important that you leave some economic benefit with the people in the reserve. That is, buy local food, pay for lodging, or hire a boatman or local guide. Guide companies that earn money taking foreigners into the reserve, but that bring all their own food, gear, and guides, and don't let any of their profits trickle down to the local people, are very much disliked in the Mosquitia. The three companies below are all considered responsible in this regard and offer top-notch tours.

Generally considered the best guiding company in the Mosquitia is **La Moskitia Eco-Aventuras,** with its office in La Ceiba on Parque Bonilla, tel. 442-0104, email: moskitia@laceiba.com. Owner Jorge Salaverri, who grew up on the Río Coco, is an inveterate Mosquitia jungle hand and has an encyclopedic knowledge of the region and its peoples. Trips range anywhere from a three-day visit to the coastal waterways near Palacios for bird and animal watching, to the 12-14 day trip from Olancho down the Río Plátano. If you're considering the Olancho trip, Jorge is really the only guide to contact. Prices vary considerably depending on the length of the trip and how many people are going, but on average you can expect to spend US$200-300 pp for a shorter trip, US$1,300 pp or more for the longer trips from Olancho down the Río Plátano.

Also frequently recommended is **Turtle Tours,** run out of the Hotel Villa Brinkley in Trujillo, tel. 434-4444, fax 434-4431, email: ttours@hondutel.hn. Turtle Tours offers a five-day trip from

Trujillo to Palacios, then up the Río Plátano to Las Marías and a day upstream into the jungle for US$360 pp, everything included.

A newer tour outfit offering Mosquitia trips that has received good reviews is **Mesoamerica Tours** in San Pedro Sula, in Edificio Picadelli, between 1 and 3 Avenidas on 11 Calle So, local 206, tel. 557-0332, fax 557-6886, email: mesoamerica@simon.intertel.hn, website: www.mesoamerica-travel.com.

Las Marías

A mixed Miskito and Pech village of about 400 people, Las Marías is a collection of thatched huts spread over a large area on a rise above the Río Plátano, with no electricity and few amenities. Located just downriver from the edge of the primary forest, Las Marías is an ideal base for hiking and river trips, and local guides will lead visitors into the jungle.

Coming upstream from the coast to Las Marías, the Río Plátano is lined mostly with secondary forest and small riverside *ranchos,* hardly virgin jungle to be sure, but still teeming with birds and small wild mammals visible to the sharp-eyed, or better yet those equipped with binoculars. On the way, you're sure to see Miskito families cruising down or energetically poling their way up the river in their narrow dugout *pipantes.*

Once you've arrived in Las Marías and extricated your stiff limbs from the boat, get a bed in one of the two *hospedajes* in town, renting beds with mosquito nets for US$2.75 a night pp in comfortable, breezy buildings. One of the ho-

tels is closer to the river and the other a bit farther back, on the far side of the small airstrip. A third hostel rents similar rooms for similar prices at Puhlak, a sort of "suburb" just downstream from Las Marías. Each hostel serves three very basic meals a day. The food is generally not well prepared and expensive at US$1.50 for mostly rice and beans, but there's not much choice. As you will be bringing food for camping anyhow, it's worth bringing a bit extra to supplement your diet in Las Marías, too. Camping is not appreciated by locals, unless you offer to pay to pitch a tent in someone's yard.

The local water hole is a stream behind the medical center, away from the river. It's best to purify the water here, and most other places in Mosquitia. If you don't have purification tablets or a purifier, a couple of drops of bleach per quart will work. Don't drink the water from the river, as there are houses just upstream. Swimming in the river is considered safe; alligators and crocodiles are rare in the fast-moving water.

The small airstrip is used only by the Alas de Socorro mission plane, which comes for medical emergencies. If you really hate boats and have the money, Sami, Rollins, or Alas de Soccoro will fly a special charter to Las Marías from Palacios for US$200-250 for up to six people, more from La Ceiba or Tegucigalpa.

Hiking and Boating from Las Marías

The Las Marías guides work on a strict rotation among all 80 households in the village, as it's the only way to keep everyone reasonably happy.

A Pech man holds up a pre-Columbian artifact dug up in his yucca patch, in Las Marías, Olancho.

VINCE MURPHY

LAS MARÍAS:
A BICULTURAL RARITY

Las Marías is one of the few settlements in La Mosquitia where two ethnic groups—Miskito and Pech—live side by side. The locals have a story about how the two groups met. Supposedly in the early part of the last century, a group of Miskitos went up the Río Plátano from the coast in search of cuyamel fish. Above the present site of Las Marías, at a place where there is a small beach on the banks of the river, the fishermen surprised a group of Pech bathing in the river. These Pech were, at that time, still very much jungle people, and the Miskitos didn't know what to make of them.

The Pech fled immediately, and the Miskitos returned to the coast to tell the tale to their compatriots. Eventually another Miskito group went upriver, this time with clothes, which they left on the beach. Hiding in the jungle nearby, the Miskitos watched the Pech return to the beach, find the clothes, and start putting them on all wrong—shorts over their heads, shoes on their hands.

The Miskitos jumped out of their hiding spot and ran after the Pech, who fled into the jungle. One girl was too slow to escape, and the Miskitos captured her and brought her back to the coast, where they taught her Miskito and learned Pech. They returned upriver, and gradually the two groups began interacting and trading. Las Marías was founded about two generations ago, according to residents.

Whether the story is legend or fact, it says a lot about the two cultures. The coastal Miskitos have always been more worldly and domineering than the quieter, reserved Pech; these traits continue to the present day. The two still do not always get along with each other and live in separate parts of the village—the Pech upstream and the Miskitos downstream.

Don't try to mess with the system, or you will create problems. Quality varies dramatically from one guide to the next—some are quite shy and, although possibly knowledgeable, don't know what gringos want to hear. For best results, keep asking questions. No English is spoken. Generally the older guides are better, but trying to request a specific guide is generally fruitless. The rotation is managed by Martin Herrera, a young man who will make himself known to you when you arrive in Las Marías. At last report, guides cost US$5 per guide per day, extra on Sunday and holidays. For hiking trips with more than five people, two guides are required.

For trips upriver by *pipante,* narrow dugouts propelled by poles, travelers must pay for three guides per *pipante* (two polers and one guide) plus US$3.50 per boat. Each *pipante* can only fit two visitors, so if you have a group of three, two boats and six guides are required. Although the *pipante* trips are pricier than hiking, it's hard to beat a silent, unmotorized boat ride on the river, which acts as a sort of cross-section of the virgin jungle. Brilliantly colored parrots, toucans, and other birds cruise unmolested overhead from one side of the river to another, troops of noisy monkeys swing about in the trees, and mammals like tapir, anteaters, or *jaguarundi* frequent the river banks, looking for a drink of water or hunting other animals.

While visitors could content themselves with a one-day *pipante* trip, better to camp out on the edge of the river, both to experience at least one night out in the bush and to have enough time to see two sets of prehistoric rock carvings upstream from Las Marías, **Walp'ulban'sirpi** and **Walp'ulban'tara.** The first, on a large rock in the river, resembles a person/serpent, while the second depicts several different figures, including monkeys, birds, and human figures. Both can be visited in a two-day trip, with one night of camping. Between the two carvings is the class II-III Brokwell Rapids, so named for an American gold miner who lost all his gear here in the '50s. To avoid Brokwell's fate, the guides will portage around the rapids if the river is high.

If you've come as far as Walp'ulban'tara, it's worth going one more day upstream to the junction of the **Río Cuyamel,** deep in the jungle. Here you'll have a better chance of seeing the jungle wildlife, more plentiful here away from the hunters in Las Marías. At the mouth of the Cuyamel, a trail leads to **Cerro Mirador** (1,200 m), at least a week roundtrip from Las Marías, but an excellent opportunity to fully appreciate both a river trip and a several-day hike. Beyond Río Cuyamel are the wild headwaters of the **Río Plátano,** the very heart of the Biosphere Reserve. From Las Marías it takes a week to 10 days of boating and hiking to reach the region. All times upriver change dramatically depending on how fast the river is running. Another option for those wanting to get into the headwaters area is to take a two-week trip with Jorge Salaverri of La Moskitia Eco-Aventuras, from Dulce Nombre de Culmí across the mountains and down the Río Plátano.

Pico Dama (840 meters), the jagged peak looming up out of the jungle not far from Las Marías, can be climbed in four to five days roundtrip and offers great opportunities to see wildlife as well as stunning views over western Mosquitia. A ruler-flat ridge near the summit, clearly visible from below, makes a spectacular high camp (bring water). For those wanting just a taste of jungle hiking, a viewpoint known as **Cerro Zapote** is a two- to three-hour walk from Las Marías and offers vistas toward Cerro Baltimore and Laguna de Ibans. From Cerro Zapote you can see what a serpentine course the Río Plátano follows below Las Marías on the way to the coast.

A trail also leads from Las Marías past Cerro Baltimore to the southern edge of Laguna de Ibans. Reputed to be an excellent trail for bird-

MAMMALS IN THE RÍO PLÁTANO BIOSPHERE RESERVE

ENGLISH	SPANISH	MISKITO	PECH
opossum	tacuacín	Sikiski	maishí
three-toed sloth	perezoso de tres dedos	siwaiko	siwuá
two-toed sloth	perezoso de dos dedos	siwaiko	siwuá
pygmy anteater	perico ligero	likor	kuráhuwuista
giant anteater	oso caballo	wingkutara	kurah ujáh
tamandu anteater	oso hormiguero	winkusirpi	kuráh
white-faced monkey	mono cara blanca	waklin	guayá
howler monkey	mono aullador (or olingo)	kong kong	huquí
spider monkey	mono araña (or mico)	urus	hurus
white-nosed coati	pizote	wistan	tuská
kinkajou	mico de noche	uyuk	wuachác
northern raccoon	mapachin (or oso lavador)	skusku	n/a
striped skunk	zorrillo	piskrauat	wuahá
river otter	nutria (or perro de agua)	mamo	taoó
jaguarundi	jaguarundi	limi siksa	misto sonwá
ocelot	ocelot (or tigrillo)	krujuba	huc brú
mountain lion	león (or puma)	limi pauni	huc pawá
jaguar	tigre	limi bulni	huc cewáh
red brocket deer	tilopo	snapuka	ichaá pawua
white-tailed deer	venado cola blanca	sula waika pijini	ichaá kamazá
white-lipped peccary	jaguilla	wari	quitán
collared peccary	kekeo	buksa	wuareká
Baird's tapir	danto	tilba	chajú
squirrel	ardilla	buston	torenah
porcupine	eriso	haksuk	n/a
paca	tepiscuinte	ibijina	huaquí
agouti	guatuza	kiajki	barka
rabbit	conejo	bang bang	mi nih
nine-banded armadillo	cusuco	tayra	patuhá
naked-tailed armadillo	tumbo armadillo	takan-takan	yucrú
bat	murciélago	sankanki	tiquimi
vampire bat	murciélago vampiro	sankanki tara	tiquimi

watching, this route takes a full day to hike to the lagoon, where boats can take you across to Raistá or Palacios. While this is an alternative route back to Palacios, guides may be reluctant to take the trail, as the local boatmen are afraid it will cut into their lucrative business. Also, if you want to hike the trail back, you may have a hard time convincing a boatman to charge you less for a one-way trip up to Las Marías.

Río Sico and Río Paulaya
Until just 20 years ago, the upper reaches of the Río Sico Valley (also called the Río Tinto or the Río Negro) and all of the Río Paulaya Valley

DESTROYING A RAINFOREST~HONDURAN STYLE

In spite of the Río Plátano's nominal protection as a biosphere reserve backed by UNESCO, *campesinos,* cattle ranchers, and mahogany loggers have been steadily hacking away at the edges of the rainforest. The hardest-hit areas are along the Río Paulaya, in the southern mountains where roads cut into the forest from Olancho, and along the upper Río Patuca and its tributaries. In places depredations have hit not only the so-called "buffer zone" (not doing its job, apparently), but up to 30 km inside the supposedly untouchable "core zone" of the reserve. A recent survey found that 650 *colonos* live in the core zone, in five small but well-established settlements, and that 35 more *colonos* farm in the core zone but live outside it. Efforts are under way to relocate the invaders, but as authorities are loath to evict them by force, there they remain for the time being.

One 1991 environmental study estimated that 60% of the forest in the buffer zone had been logged, and the deforestation since then has actually accelerated. In December 1995 the Reina administration, under pressure from cattle ranchers and *campesino* unions, declared the Paulaya valley a region for "agrarian reform," a green light for migrants to move in from other parts of the country. The decree has since been rescinded, but the damage was done. The entire Sico and Paulaya region, seen as a mythically rich promised land in the rest of Honduras, is the great prize currently being fought for amongst cattle ranchers, loggers, and poor *campesinos* looking for land. The town of Sico holds great importance in the battle. If the town is declared a municipality, the new local authorities would have a much easier time putting through a good all-weather road to Tocoa and opening the whole region up for development. A road currently exists from Tocoa to Sico, but it's only passable part of the year. Whenever the road is improved enough to handle year-round traffic—which is only a matter of time—the flood of hardwood coming out of the western part of the reserve and the flood of *campesinos* and cattle coming in the other way will only increase. Spurred by the vertiginous deforestation of the Sico and Paulaya valleys, UNESCO placed the reserve on its list of World Heritage sites in danger. It can be expected that this will have roughly the same effect as the UNESCO declaration of the Río Plátano as a heritage site in the first place, which is to say, next to none.

According to those who've seen the process in action, the first wave of invaders is usually chainsaw-wielding loggers, probing into the periphery of the rainforest in search of valuable mahogany, ironwood, or other hardwoods. Next come poor peasants from other parts of Honduras, often from the south, which has been devastated by erosion. The *campesinos* usually work the land for a couple of years and get a title from the Agrarian Reform Institute. By this time the thin rainforest soil will have eroded under the poor farming techniques used by the *colonos,* who then sell the land to large-scale cattle ranchers. These ranchers have amassed huge expanses of former jungle, sometimes legally and sometimes through threats and outright murder.

Until recently, essentially no one has patrolled the frontiers of the reserve, apart from a few well-meaning but ineffective Miskito volunteers. In December 1999 the government finally ordered a sweep through the reserve by the Army, but with so many well-connected interests benefiting from the current lax control it's difficult to imagine dramatic action in the near future. One sign of hope is a new protection program for the reserve backed by the German government, which may prod the Honduran authorities into improving vigilance over the reserve's boundaries. It can't get any worse, that's for sure—the only thing that has protected the jungle so far is its immensity and isolation. Those factors can only hold out for so long in the face of Honduras' harsh economic realities and relentless population growth.

were untouched jungle. Unfortunately, they've been invaded in the past decade by a flood of land-hungry cattle ranchers from other parts of Honduras. In a move of questionable intelligence, the border of the reserve was set at the Río Paulaya itself, rather than the mountains on the western edge of the valley. So instead of encompassing the entire river valley, the reserve supposedly protects one side of the river but not the other. As no authorities patrol anywhere nearby, it's no surprise cattle ranchers have been hard at work hacking down the forest on both sides of the river. Although the forest hasn't completely disappeared yet, those who have hiked the Río Paulaya say it's a sad sight.

Unless you feel like seeing a forest disappear, the only reason to go into the Paulaya Valley is to visit the **Piedra Floreada petroglyphs.** These impressive rock etchings, located on the Río Kiniskisné, a tributary of the Río Paulaya, are described by Alison McKittrick in an Instituto Hondureño de Antropología e Historia (INAH) publication: several figures and geometric shapes are carved into two large rocks, and the rocks are surrounded by unexcavated mounds that may cover a pre-conquest settlement. Local cattle ranchers know of the site and will guide visitors there from the town of Sico, which can be reached by boat from Palacios.

A trail follows the Río Paulaya upriver into a wild area of Olancho, near Dulce Nombre de Culmí, where there are other petroglyph sites similar to the Piedra Floreada. Formerly a central trade and communication route between coastal and inland Indian tribes, this path was also used extensively by smugglers and raiders from the English-controlled Mosquitia on their way to Olancho during colonial times. Reportedly the route can be hiked in two or three days—see the Olancho section below for details.

BRUS LAGUNA

Originally established as the English outpost named Brewer's Lagoon, Brus Laguna is now a mainly Miskito settlement of about 5,000 inhabitants on the southern edge of the lagoon of the same name. Apart from experiencing this quirky little town of wooden shacks spread over the grassy savanna, there's not a great deal to do. Brus Laguna's main attractions are sport fish-

ing with a high-end outfit on Cannon Island in the lagoon, and jungle trips up the nearby Río Sigre with local guides, if you can find them.

Considering the high population of crocodiles, swimming in the lagoon is not recommended. Locals do it anyway, but everyone's got a story about someone they know who lost an appendage, so it hardly seems worth the chance. The mosquitoes and sand flies can be a plague, particularly in the rainy season.

The one cannon on the grassy field in the middle of town originally came from Cannon Island, a fort used by Miskito Indians and British settlers in conflicts against the Spanish.

Brus Laguna is legendary for its plentiful and huge—up to five feet long—**iguanas,** often seen carted around by locals with their legs tied behind their backs, an "iguana suitcase," so to speak. Iguana meat can form a substantial part of the local diet, especially if the harvest has been bad.

Practicalities

Official accommodations in town are limited to a few ultra-basic rooms run by the owner of the *pulpería* next to the docks, costing US$3.50, and a couple of slightly better ones run by the *pulpería* near the crossroads on the main street, for US$4.50. Elga Goff, who manages the Sosa airline office, also has four beds for rent. Nobody seems to be running any guided trips into the jungle these days, but you may be able to find a local guide through word of mouth. Flowing into the lagoon from the south, the upper reaches of the Río Sigre are lined with dense jungle.

There are no restaurants in Brus, so ask around for someone who can cook you a meal. Expect *plátano*, rice, beans, shrimp, iguana, or whatever else the latest boat brought in. Beer is technically illegal in town but can usually be found if you ask around discreetly.

The local Hondutel office, near the main intersection, is now equipped with a parabolic antenna link to the rest of the country.

Rollins and Sosa both fly to and from La Ceiba three times a week, charging US$48 one way. The *pulpería* at the docks sells Rollins tickets, while Elga Goff sells Sosa tickets from her store on the main street. Usually a pickup drives out to the airstrip to meet each flight—ask when you get a ticket.

Sami flies in daily except Sunday, charging US$24 to Belén (near Palacios) or Ahuas, and

US$27 to Puerto Lempira. The Alas de Soccoro mission plane comes in irregularly and generally charges US$15 to wherever the plane is going. For information on either, ask at the *pulpería* on the main street in the middle of town.

Lanchas from Brus across the lagoon and out to Barra Plátano cost about US$35 *viaje especial,* and it's rare to find a boat heading out there to hitch a ride on. An occasionally open canal crosses between the lagoon and the Río Plátano, and from there boats continue through other canals all the way to Palacios. It may also be possible to find a boatman willing to navigate the canals and waterways across the savanna to the Río Patuca. Either one of these trips would be expensive and subject to water levels in the canals.

The **MV *Captain Rinel*** usually pulls into the lagoon once a week and can take travelers eager for a tramp-freighter experience on the two-day run back to La Ceiba. Other boats occasionally come through on their way to Puerto Castilla, La Ceiba, or elsewhere.

Cannon Island

The finest sport fishing outfit in Honduras, if not all of the Caribbean, Cannon Island offers eight-night, seven-day fishing packages for US$2275 pp, double occupancy, or four-night, three-day trips for US$1490 pp, double occupancy. The price includes transport from San Pedro Sula, lodging in one of three wooden cabins on the mosquito-free island, excellent home-style cooking, and daily fishing trips aboard one of the lodge's six boats. The fishing excursions go to one of five rivers, the lagoon itself, or the open ocean in search of world-class snook, tarpon, snapper, barracuda, and the occasional shark, all catch-and-release. Guests are welcome to bring a favorite pole, but all equipment is provided. For information and reservations, call Pan Angling in the U.S. at (800) 533-4353, fax (317) 227-6803, or contact the resort at (504) 455-5460; e-mail: jdnovi@teleport.com, website: www.cannonisland.com.

RÍO PATUCA

The Río Patuca is the longest river that runs completely inside Honduras and the second largest in Central America after the nearby Río Coco, shared between Honduras and Nicaragua.

The Patuca's convoluted 500-km course winds from its headwaters in the mountains of the Olancho, El Paraíso, and Francisco Morazán departments, emptying out through the Mosquitia into the Caribbean. From the coast as far up as Wampusirpi, the broad Patuca is lined with a narrow gallery forest, interspersed with many Miskito villages and farms, and backed by grassy savanna extending east to Puerto Lempira and west to Brus Laguna. Farther south, toward the border of the department of Olancho, the river enters the rainforest, and the homeland of the Tawahka Indians. Numbering only about 1,000 souls living in a few villages on the banks of the Patuca, struggling to hold out against encroaching loggers and settlers from Olancho, the Tawahka recently celebrated a small victory, the creation of the Reserva de la Biosfera Tawahka Asangni, encompassing 233,142 hectares of supposedly protected jungle. The best place to go for guided river or hiking trips into the jungle is Krausirpe, the unofficial Tawahka capital. Although Wampusirpi is downstream of the jungle, surrounded by savanna and secondary forest, it's possible to hire boatmen to take you up nearby tributaries of the Patuca into the rainforest.

South of the Tawahka reserve and created on the same day is the new **Parque Nacional Río Patuca,** covering 375,584 hectares of jungle and mountains between the Río Patuca and the Río Coco. Beyond the park, the Río Patuca enters inhabited areas of Olancho, where immigrants have turned jungle into pasture.

Barra Patuca

At the mouth of the Río Patuca is the large Miskito town of Barra Patuca, with several stores and a couple of basic *hospedajes.* Several families will cook travelers a meal for a fee. Narrow, uncomfortable cargo boats run every day or two upstream 7-10 hours to Ahuas, or through the waterways to Brus Laguna in an hour or two. Likely as not you'll have to wait around a couple of days to find a boat with an open seat; expect to pay around US$10-15 to Ahuas, or US$5 to Brus. Finding boats east along the coast to Puerto Lempira or west to Palacios is much more difficult.

Ahuas

The largest town on the Río Patuca, Ahuas has a population of about 2,000, almost all Miskito,

Ahuas International Airport

spread out over the savanna and pine groves a couple of kilometers from the river. Missionaries have been hard at work at Ahuas, as evidenced by the several churches in town. There's not a lot of reason to come here, except that Ahuas is the town farthest upstream on the Patuca serviced by regular flights, and from here it's possible (with great patience) to catch boat rides upstream to Wampusirpi or into the Tawahka reserve.

An exploratory oil well was sunk near Ahuas in the 1970s, and the remnants of the derrick are still nearby. The extremely anomalous big-rig truck in the middle of town was floated up the river by the oil crews and left when the well was abandoned. A local got the semi cranked up again not long back, but there's nowhere to drive it except out to the oil rig and back again.

One family in town offers rooms in a wooden shack for US$2.50 a night, not far from the airstrip, and another family near the "hotel" regularly cooks meals for visitors for US$1. A couple of *pulperías* in town sell basic supplies. The mission hospital near the airstrip usually has a western doctor in residence and offers good emergency care.

Ahuas is the base for Alas de Socorro, the mission-sponsored emergency plane service run by Geoff Goff. He is usually happy to take on passengers for US$15 a ride to wherever he's going, but his schedule is unpredictable. If his services aren't needed elsewhere, he will also charter special flights, but that can be expensive. Sami flies to Ahuas every day except Sunday at irregular hours, charging US$26 to Palacios or Puerto Lempira. Reservations can be made at the hut next to the airstrip.

At Ahuas, the Patuca is a wide and impressive river, bordered by a narrow strip of jungle. Boats frequently head downriver from here to Barra Patuca (US$5, three and a half hours) or upriver to Wampusirpi (US$7, seven to eight hours). These narrow cargo/passenger boats are often packed and uncomfortable, so be prepared. *Viajes especiales* cost a great deal more.

Wampusirpi

Upriver from Ahuas is Wampusirpi, a former Tawahka town that in recent years has been taken over by Miskitos, many having fled the violence of the Contra war in the 1980s. Wampusirpi is surrounded by savanna and stands of Caribbean pine, with patches of gallery forest lining the nearby rivers. The local Spanish priest, Padre José, is usually happy to put up travelers for a nominal fee, and others in town also have simple rooms for rent. Basic meals can be arranged without too much difficulty, although there are no restaurants per se. It's best to come out this way prepared with a tent and food. The jungle-clad Río Uhra, a tributary of the Patuca on the west side not far downstream from Wampusirpi, makes for great one- to three-day explorations with a hired boatman. Upstream from Wampusirpi on the Patuca are the Miskito villages of, in order, Kurpa, Tukrun, and Pimienta.

THE CANOE BUILDERS OF THE RÍO PATUCA

On the banks of the Río Patuca, near the confluence of the Río Wampú in the heart of the Mosquitia jungles, are the ancestral lands of the Tawahka, one of the smallest ethnic groups in Honduras. A rainforest tribe thought to have migrated up from South America in the distant past, the Tawahka now number only about 1,000 souls in several riverside villages, the largest of which is Krausirpe.

Originally one of many related subtribes in the Mosquitia, the Tawahka fell under the sway of the newly born Miskito tribe in the 17th century. Well-armed and aggressive, the Miskitos came to control the Mosquitia region during the colonial era, demanding tribute from the Tawahka, and even inventing a derogatory term for them that is still used by Miskito and *ladinos* today: the Sumu.

Although they originally roamed over a much larger territory, centuries of pressure from the Miskito and, especially in the last two decades, *ladino colonos* (migrant farmers) has whittled down Tawahka territory to a fraction of its former size. The tribe now has access to barely enough land to maintain its traditional lifestyle of small-scale agriculture along the riverbanks combined with hunting and plant gathering in the rainforest.

Among their many talents, the Tawahka are renowned as superb builders of large canoes, and in the past frequently supplemented their income by selling 10-meter crafts, hollowed out of a single mahogany, to Miskitos on the coast or to *ladino* farmers upriver. In fact, it is thought the Tawahka first began making the large canoes at the behest of the Miskitos in the 19th century, as part of the tribute the tribe was forced to pay. These days, however, canoe builders are having an increasingly hard time finding suitable trees, as the valuable wood is coveted by the *colonos* busy hacking down what was the Tawahka's "canoe forest" near the Río Wampú. Tawahka are leery of venturing up the Wampú, or the nearby Cuyamel, for fear of running into gun-toting *colonos*.

Poor and uneducated as they are—many speak only faltering Spanish—the Tawahka have found it difficult to halt the steady invasion of aggressive *ladinos* who cut down their forest and start homestead farms and cattle ranches. In 1987, the tribe

created the Federación Indígena Tawahka de Honduras (FITH), which now works to protect Tawahka land and rights with other indigenous groups in Honduras and with international organizations. One victory for the newly organized Tawahka and their allies was the eventual cancellation of a proposed hydroelectric dam on the Río Patuca, which would have covered part of their lands in a reservoir.

More recently, after much pressure by the Tawahka, a new biosphere reserve was decreed by the Honduran government around their homelands. Created on 21 December 1999, the Reserva de la Biosfera Tawahka Asangni covers 233,142 hectares—much less than the Tawahka had hoped for, but at least a reprieve in their constant struggle to hold on to their lands.

KENDRA McSWEENEY

Tawahka men push a newly finished pipante *(dugout river canoe) out of the forest and down to the Río Patuca.*

Tawahka Region

Beyond Pimienta is Krausirpe, a riverside village that serves as the unofficial capital of the Tawahka. This is the center of the new Reserva de la Biosfera Tawahka Asangni, connecting the Río Plátano Biosphere Reserve to the Bosawas reserve in Nicaragua. The Tawahka, with some international help, pushed strongly for the reserve as a means to combat the constant incursions of *ladino* immigrants from Olancho.

With Tawahka guides, visitors can hike from Krausirpe to pre-conquest caves, petroglyphs, or into the jungle in any direction. The well-beaten Wankibila Trail cuts from near Krausirpe along the Río Sutawala valley, through a gap in the hills, and over to the Río Coco Valley and the town of Ahuasbila, where trucks to Puerto Lempira can be found. The trail takes a full day to hike (leave at dawn) and requires a guide (US$7.50 a day).

Beyond Krausirpe is the village of Krautara, and continuing up the Patuca into Olancho are the Tawahka settlements of Yapuwás, Kamakasna, and Wasparasní.

The most frequent way into the Tawahka region is by plane to Ahuas and from there by boat via Wampusirpi along the Río Patuca, or by flying directly in to Krausirpe by special flight.

Another route into the Tawahka region available to independent travelers (probably the least expensive all in all) is from Nueva Palestina, a cowboy town in Olancho on the upper part of the Río Patuca, reached by bus from Danlí. Boats and pilots can be hired in Nueva Palestina or on the river at Arenas Blancas, down one or two days to Krausirpe. Other, even less orthodox ways downstream from Olancho can be found, along the Río Cuyamel or Río Wampu, but this is dangerous territory indeed and not suitable for casual travelers.

PUERTO LEMPIRA

The capital of the Gracias a Dios department, and the largest population center in the Mosquitia with just under 10,000 people, Puerto Lempira is laid out in a grid of dirt roads running back from the southern shore of Laguna Caratasca. From the long dock right in front of Puerto Lempira, *lanchas* venture out to Miskito villages around the lagoon or along the connected waterways. While the region around Puerto Lempira is relatively expensive to get to (US$116 roundtrip to La Ceiba at last check) and not known for tourism, the more adventurous and unrushed traveler will find huge expanses of lagoons, savanna, riverside jungle, and windswept, deserted Caribbean beach to explore.

For most of its history an isolated little port in the farthest corner of the Mosquitia, Puerto Lempira experienced a boom in the 1980s, when it became the center of operations for the CIA-directed insurgency against the Sandinista government in Nicaragua. The U.S. spooks are long gone, and now this part of Mosquitia makes its living mainly from fishing, particularly lobster diving, a lucrative but dangerous profession that has left several hundred Miskito men crippled with the bends. Apart from fishing, most of the area's people eke out a living as small-scale farmers. Puerto Lempira also has a large population of *ladinos* (*indios,* as the Miskitos disparagingly call them), working in the many government offices in town.

A new entrant to the local economy, which makes use of the region's deserted beaches and coastline, is cocaine, smuggled in large quantities from Colombia north to the United States and elsewhere. Everyone in Puerto Lempira is happy to discuss who in town is involved, and it's easy to note the young men driving new pickup trucks, which were expensively shipped in and use gasoline twice as costly as in the rest of Honduras. How long this new trade will continue, and to what extent it will develop, remain to be seen. But the smuggling goes on at hidden airstrips and beaches very far from any settlement, so visitors run no risk in the trips around Puerto Lempira mentioned below and are only likely to run into suspicious characters if they go to the local disco.

Accommodations

The two-story **Hotel Flores** in the center of town is the "best" lodging in Puerto Lempira; rooms have a/c, cable TV, and private bathroom. Unfortunately, the rooms are also boxlike, the power is constantly cutting out, and the a/c is not very effective. An added drag is the extremely noisy generator in the back, on until 4 a.m. every night. All in all, the hotel is overpriced at US$20 s, US$30 d.

A new hotel was under construction at last check down by the dock, which may rival Hotel Flores as the place to be. The new owners are also named Flores—no relation.

On the opposite side of the street from the current Flores, down a couple of blocks toward the airport, is **Hospedaje Modelo** with simple but relatively clean wooden rooms with fans for US$7.50 s or d. Ask in the store opposite for information about rooms.

Hotelito Central on the second floor of a building on the main intersection in town has basic rooms for US$4 s or d, US$5.50 with fan, all with shared bathroom.

Food and Entertainment

On the north side of the shady *parque* is **Merendero Tropics,** the favorite place to eat in town among both locals with money and the few foreigners working in the area. The owner (who unfortunately may leave town in 2002) keeps the place very clean and serves simple but satisfying meals all day for US$2-3—breakfast, lunch, and dinner. She even has fresh orange juice and good pancakes for breakfast.

Next door is **Cafetería Central,** with decent burgers, chicken, beer, and soft drinks, open every day until 10 p.m.

Right next to the dock is **Lakun View,** a favorite spot for an afternoon beer, with a breezy porch and blaring music. Open daily until midnight. The happening disco in town is **Caratasca View,** on the shorefront a few blocks north of downtown. Festivities get going around 10 p.m. and last until 3 a.m., sometimes later.

The local boys usually get a pick-up basketball game going on the court behind the *parque* most afternoons an hour or so before sunset, if you feel like showing your moves.

Services

The Hondutel office, a couple of blocks north of the *parque,* is open Mon.-Fri. 7 a.m.-9 p.m. If it's not open, try the **Centro Comunitario,** which has phone service at the same prices, plus a few magazines and newspapers for sale. The owner, Chepe, is a friendly sort, happy to answer the questions of a foreign visitor. Open 7 a.m.-10 p.m. daily.

Banco Atlántida, in the same building as Hotel Flores, tel. 898-7580, will exchange U.S. dollars and traveler's checks for *lempiras,* as well as advance money on a Visa card. Nicaraguan money is not accepted—you have to get rid of your *córdobas* at Leimus. Open Mon.-Fri. 8-11:30 a.m. and 1:30-4 p.m., Saturday 8-11:30 a.m.

The Sosa office, tel. 898-7432, open Mon.-Fri. 6:30 a.m.-noon and 1-5 p.m., Saturday 6:30 a.m.-noon, can change dollars and traveler's checks at bad rates and has one of the few photocopy machines in town.

Migración is next to Hondutel, open Mon.-Fri. 8 a.m.-noon and 2-5 p.m., Saturday 8 a.m.-noon. They will happily extend visas for US$2, no hassle.

The **Mopawi headquarters,** tel. 898-7584, or in Tegucigalpa at tel. 235-8659, is on the edge of the lagoon, a few blocks south of the main dock. Formed in 1985 with the help of World Relief, the name derives from "Mosquitia Pawisa," which means Mosquitia Development in Miskito. The organization coordinates a variety of social and environmental projects in the region, and its workers are often excellent sources of information on the Mosquitia and its peoples. Mopawi operates a well-stocked store at its headquarters, selling all sorts of useful supplies and packaged food, as well as T-shirts and maps.

Getting There and Away

Both Sosa, with an office in town, tel. 898-7432, and Isleña, office at the airstrip, tel. 898-7443, fly to La Ceiba every morning except Sunday for US$58. Sami, office at the airstrip, tel. 898-7491, also flies between Puerto Lempira and Ahuas, Brus Laguna, and Belén (near Palacios) every day except Sunday.

The MV *Captain Rinel* pulls into the main dock usually once a week and will gladly take on the random traveler wanting to spend a few days on the high seas on the way back to La Ceiba for a negotiable fee.

Small *lanchas* are constantly zigging and zagging across the lagoon to various villages and usually charge US$1 a ride if you're going their way.

Around Laguna Caratasca

The expansive Laguna Caratasca, so big it develops good-sized waves, measures 66 km long and 14 km wide. Linked by waterways with the adjacent Tansin and Warunta lagoons, Caratasca is the center of a gigantic freshwater lagoon system across northeastern Mosquitia, fed by the Mocorón, Warunta, and Nakunta Rivers, among others. The wide lagoon entrance, Barra Caratasca, is directly opposite the lagoon from Puerto Lempira, visible on a clear day. Along the edges of this watery network live several thousand Miskito in lakefront communities varying in size from a couple of houses to towns of 2,000. Many of these picturesque villages are well worth visiting, to experience the long-lost feel of these isolated places and meet the local Miskitos, as well as to enjoy deserted Caribbean beaches and boat along the inland waterways looking for birds, manatees, monkeys, and other wildlife living in the mangroves and coastal jungles. If you were somehow able to get a sea kayak or light canoe out to Puerto Lempira, it would be the perfect vehicle for exploring these waterways. Heavier wooden *cayucos* might be found for rent in Puerto Lempira or a lakeside village, and you can certainly find boatmen willing to take you on trips of varying length in their motorized *lanchas.*

The lagoon is a paradise for **fishing,** stocked with world-class tarpon, snook, jack, grouper, and other fish; you'll need to bring your own tackle and hire a boat to take you out, as there are no tourist fishing facilities in Puerto Lempira (the closest are at Cannon Island, near Brus Laguna). The best fishing season is between May and July. Favored places to fish are at the outlets of lagoons into the open ocean, at either high or low tide, or where rivers flow into the south side of the lagoon. Snook and tarpon are favorite game.

One of the more attractive Miskito communities near Puerto Lempira is **Kaukira,** worth visiting if only for the seemingly endless Caribbean beach. A large town spread over a couple of kilometers on a narrow peninsula, with the ocean on one side and the lagoon on the other, Kaukira is easily reached by the frequent daily (except Sunday) *lanchas* cruising back and forth to Puerto Lempira. Boats usually leave Kaukira at 7 or 8 a.m. and depart Puerto Lempira for the return trip midmorning, charging US$4 for a fast boat or US$3 for a slower one. Getting a ride out in the afternoon is difficult—better to plan on staying the night, unless you want to pay US$35 or so for a *viaje especial* back to Puerto Lempira. Rooms and food are easy to come by

in Kaukira by asking around. The canal leading from the main lagoon to the smaller one behind Kaukira passes through extensive red and white mangroves—keep a close eye out for wildlife as you pass. There's a dirt airstrip in town, to which Sosa supposedly flies twice a week from La Ceiba (US$61), but service is irregular. The beach on the far side of town from the lagoon is unusually broad and, though scattered with driftwood and occasional bits of garbage cast up from the ocean, quite clean. The waves and currents might be too rough for less than confident swimmers. The calmest season for the ocean here, and everywhere in Mosquitia, is the February-June dry season.

On the north shore of Tansin Island (actually a peninsula), on the shore of Laguna Caratasca, **Palkaka** is a relaxed Miskito village with a small freshwater beach. Fishing in the lagoon nearby is plentiful, and the waterways to the west are full of different kinds of waterfowl, manatee, and other lagoon wildlife. As with Kaukira, boats leave most every day to Palkaka from the main dock in Puerto Lempira.

On the southeastern shore of the Laguna Tansin, and linked to Puerto Lempira by a 17-km dirt road leaving past the airstrip, is the Miskito village of **Mistruk,** with a clean freshwater beach on a corner of the lagoon. The beach sees a few visitors from Puerto Lempira on weekends, and quite a crowd during Holy Week, but is otherwise deserted. Locals will happily arrange boat trips along the lagoons and waterways to watch for birds, crocodiles, manatees, and other critters at a negotiable fee. A taxi from Puerto Lempira costs US$10 to Mistruk, or you can bicycle there in an hour or two if you can borrow or rent wheels. Hitching rides is possible, particularly in the morning, but finding a ride back in the afternoon might be problematic.

By Road South and East of Puerto Lempira

A dirt road winds southwest from Puerto Lempira past Mistruk through savanna and stands of pine to the villages of **Mocorón,** on the banks of the Río Mocorón about three hours from Puerto Lempira by pickup truck. The river, running northeast to Laguna Caratasca, basically forms the divide here between the savanna on the southeast side and the jungle on the northwest. Trips into the rainforest are possible from Mocorón, either on foot or by boat, and reliable sources say there are noteworthy caves and a couple of little-known pre-Columbian ruins in the vicinity. Beds are not difficult to find in Mocorón, but it's best to bring your own food.

The dirt road continues southwest past Mo-corón another two hours to **Rus Rus,** and an hour beyond to **Ahuasbila,** on the Río Coco. Ahuasbila, situated on a savanna right at the edge of the jungle, is 265 km and six to eight hours from Puerto Lempira. From here it's quite possible for the Huck Finn wannabe to either put in a raft you brought by plane and truck via Puerto Lempira or hire a boat and float down-stream several days to Leimus. Here you can get a truck back to Puerto Lempira, or continue on the river all the way down to the coast. Rafters can also put in upstream on the Río Coco in the department of El Paraíso and come out at Ahuasbila. The place to put in is **El Tablazo,** reached from Danlí to Arenales. From El Tabla-zo down to Ahuasbila would take several days, passing through class III-IV rapids not to be taken lightly. The first couple of days you'll float past grazing and farming country cut out of the forest, while the last couple of days are through mostly jungle, with a few Miskito villages on the Nicaraguan side of the river.

Between Mocorón and Rus Rus a road turns south to the Nicaraguan border at **Leimus,** where travelers can cross into Nicaragua. Hon-duras has opened a *migración* office at the bor-der, open 6 a.m.-10 p.m. daily; Nicaragua says it will soon, too, but it hasn't yet. Until it happens, travelers wanting to cross into Nicaragua this way are still left at the mercy of the reputedly very greedy Nicaraguan immigration officials in Puerto Cabezas, where they must register as having entered Nicaragua. Just so it's clear: crossing into Nicaragua is very easy, but get-ting your entrance stamp to that country is an-other matter. Passenger traffic only can cross the river at Leimus—there is no bridge or barge for wheeled vehicles to cross. I have heard no re-ports of travelers making this trip. If anyone has first-hand information, please let me know!

Usually one or two trucks a day go from Puer-to Lempira to Leimus, leaving in the early morn-ing for the three- to five-hour trip, charging US$5. At last check Evaristo López was running a truck to Leimus every day. Look for the truck at a small store a couple of blocks northeast of the square. Past Leimus, after crossing the Río Coco in boat, a road follows the river downstream to Waspam, and then turns inland to Puerto Cabezas. The road from Leimus to Waspam is terrible, so it's usually faster and more pleasant to take a boat, then continue to Puerto Cabezas from Waspam by truck.

Río Coco and Far Northeastern Mosquitia

A dozen or so Miskito villages line the Río Coco, mostly on the Nicaraguan side, between Leimus and the ocean. One large town is **Sawa,** known colloquially as *yul aikraa,* "dog-killer," in requiem for a local victim of the ferocious mosquitoes. The closest village to Cabo Gracias a Dios it-self is **Planghikira,** but nobody lives out on the blustery point itself. Canals head west from the Río Coco to the villages of **Irlaya** to **Raya,** and from there back to Laguna Caratasca. Thus one could, with patience, catch rides from Leimus downriver along the Río Coco, and return to Puerto Lempira via Raya and Kaukira.

Regarding **Laguna Apalka,** an apparently landlocked lagoon between the Río Coco and Laguna Caratasca, the locals have an interesting legend. Word has it that a British pirate ship was caught up in a fierce storm trying unsuccessful-ly to round the cape and ended up getting blown into the lagoon, where it sank. Some say the treasure was removed and buried nearby be-fore the ship sank, while others maintain it re-mains with the ship, which they claim can be seen from above through the clear waters. But malevolent spirits are said to guard the wreck, and all the divers who have swum down to in-vestigate never returned . . .

Off the Caribbean coast from Raya are several small coral cays, including **Bogas Cay,** the clos-est in, and **Savannah Cay,** farther out and larg-er. Jamaican fishermen are the only people on the cays, and they often come into Raya for sup-plies and can sometimes offer rides to vagabond adventurers. Be prepared with camping gear and plenty of food and water. The reef and water quality are reported to be excellent. A great many other cays, sand banks, and reefs are known to the fishermen of the Mosquitia coast, if you have the time and money to get out that way.

OLANCHO

INTRODUCTION

It is a broad valley, beautiful and amenable, but ringed on all sides by very high mountains, cut by deep rivers and dangerous canyons. The first who came this way was surely bored of their existence.

—PADRE JOSÉ ANTONIO GOICOECHEA,
MISSIONARY IN AGALTA IN 1802

The far-flung valleys, rugged mountains, and thick forests of Olancho are a sort of Honduran "Wild East," as it were, a wide open territory with immense expanses of wild country to explore. Known by its residents, only half in jest, as "La República Independiente de Olancho," this department has long maintained a Texas-style disdain for the central government and a firm belief in taking care of things themselves, thank you very much.

The self-reliant attitude of *olanchanos* arose during the colonial era, when pirates began raiding the north coast and cattle ranchers in the region found their outlet to the wider world cut off. The closest major marketplace was Guatemala City, at that time many long days away over rugged mountains, so *olanchanos* got used to doing without manufactured goods. Instead they developed self-sufficient haciendas where everything needed was made with the materials at hand. Wandering the back roads and trails across Olancho, intrepid travelers can still find plenty of old-style *ranchos* filled with handmade wooden furniture carved from mahogany, worked leather clothes, and other antiques. Honduran bargain-hunters have taken to visiting Olancho *ranchos* in recent years to buy up the antiques and resell them in shops in Valle de Ángeles or Tegucigalpa.

Because of their minimal communication with the outside world until the 20th century, the people of Olancho commonly use certain old Spanish turns of phrase and odd words, many from Andalusia and Extremadura, where a number of the Olancho colonists originated.

Another trait developed during the colonial era is the propensity of *olanchanos* to take justice into their own hands, seeking solutions to problems down the barrel of a gun, in a style not unlike the U.S. cowboys of a century ago. Residents nowadays claim their reputation for violence is much exaggerated, but it's still common to see tough-looking men walking around with guns stuck in their belts. As one resident commented dryly to a newspaper reporter, "The *olanchano* isn't violent, but you have to respect him."

The family feuds and crimes of passion are not directed at foreigners, and in fact *olanchanos* tend to be courtly and hospitable with outsiders, proud to show off the land they love so much. One safety issue for travelers is the increased incidence of highway holdups, particularly on the remote highway leading to La Unión and Parque Nacional La Muralla in western Olancho.

While Olancho is unquestionably a rough region, there have been no reports at all of foreigners being assaulted, even the many Peace Corps volunteers who live out in some of the wildest parts of Olancho for two years at a time. And the more adventurous travelers who do make it out to Olancho often find the department to be their favorite part of Honduras, offering unparalleled hiking opportunities at El Boquerón, near Juticalpa, or in the magnificent Parque Nacional Sierra de Agalta, ranked by many as the greatest natural area in the country outside of the Mosquitia. Intrepid visitors can also explore many ruin sites in Olancho, such as Dos Quebradas near El Boquerón or at the Cuevas de Talgua, dating from the region's dynamic but little-understood pre-Columbian cultures.

The Land

In a word: impressive. At 23,905 square km, Olancho is by far the largest of Honduras' 18 departments, covering one-fifth of the country's territory. Like much of Honduras, Olancho is criss-crossed by mountains—Sierra de Agalta, Sierra La Esperanza, Las Montañas del Patuca, La Cordillera Entre Ríos, and La Cordillera De Miscoso all cut through the department.

Unlike the rest of the country, however, these ranges are separated by broad valleys, covered by the rich pastureland that sustains the department's economic backbone, the cattle industry. Major valleys include the Catacamas (or Olancho), Agalta, Lepaguare, Azacualpa, and Amacuapa. Altitudes range from 400 meters on valley floors to a high point of 2,354 meters in the Sierra de Agalta.

Much of Olancho is blanketed either in grasslands or seemingly endless pine-forested mountains. On the higher reaches of some mountains in Olancho, most particularly Sierra de Agalta and La Muralla, are some of the densest, most extensive cloud forests in Central America. And in northern Olancho begin the tropical rainforests that continue down into Mosquitia.

The mountains of Olancho give birth to several major river systems. The Río Guayape, famed for its gold, joins with the Río Guayambre to form the mighty Patuca, Honduras' longest river, running through the Olancho plains into the jungles of Mosquitia before reaching the coast after a journey of some 500 km. Parallel to the Patuca, forming the border with Nicaragua, is the even longer Río Coco (also called the Río Segovia). And in northwestern Olancho are the headwaters of the Plátano, Paulaya, and Sico Rivers.

Because of its size, describing Olancho's climate in general terms is not easy. Rainfall in the department ranges between 80 and 260 cm per year on average, depending on the region. The southern valleys tend to be driest, while the wettest areas are the mountain forests to the north. The dry season is usually February to April. Temperatures in Olancho also vary wildly, mostly depending on altitude, but it's usually comfortable in most populated areas—warm in the day and cool at night. Bring warm, dry clothes if you plan to camp in the mountains.

History
Discoveries at the Cuevas de Talgua near Catacamas have led archaeologists to believe that a sedentary village culture lived in the plains of Olancho 1,000 years before Christ. Little is known about these early *olanchanos,* but evidence suggests the culture evolved on its own, rather than as an offshoot of the parallel cultures developing at that time in the Ulúa Valley. A great deal of investigation remains to be done in the countless unexcavated archeological sites in Olancho, many extremely impressive in size and complexity, to learn more about their builders.

One fact that may have accounted for the development of an organized society in pre-Columbian Olancho is the extraordinarily rich deposits of gold in the mountains and rivers of the region, much of which has yet to be worked to its full potential. It is said that the Aztecs of Mexico indicated to the gold-hungry Spanish conquistadors that this region was where they received much of their supply.

Whether in search of gold or for other reasons, it is indisputable that the conquistadors came di-

Vaqueros ride the trail in Parque Nacional Sierra de Agalta.

rectly to the Olancho region when they first arrived in Honduras. Many different indigenous tribes inhabited Olancho when they arrived, including Pech, Lenca, Tawahka-Sumu, Tolupan, and perhaps descendants of Nahuatl immigrants from Mexico, who later lost their original language and blended in with other groups. According to local legend, the Nahuatl arrived after a long journey from the north, fleeing a great drought. The name Olancho is thought to be a derivation of a Nahuatl word meaning "land of tule trees," which are plentiful in Olancho's forests.

The Spanish era in Olancho began in 1524, when Gil González Dávila, coming from the north coast, and Hernando de Soto, marching overland from Nicaragua, met in the Valle de Catacamas and promptly started a fight over who had the right to conquer Honduras. The internecine struggles continued for several years and prevented the Spanish from subduing the rebellious Pech, Tolupan, and Tawahka. Under the orders of Hernán Cortés, the first Spanish settlement in Olancho was founded in May 1526 in the Valle de Agalta. Named Villa de la Frontera de Cáceres, the town was quickly sacked by Spaniards opposed to Cortés, who then founded another settlement, Villa Hermosa, somewhere in the vicinity of Juticalpa. Villa Hermosa was in turn leveled

COYOL WINE

A traditional Olancho drink, seen more rarely these days as imported *aguardiente* and rum take over, coyol wine can be thought of as a cross between hard cider and champagne. Local Indians once made the wine by climbing up a coyol palm, hollowing out a hole under the bud, and sucking the sap out with a reed. The sap, which is strongest in March and April, in the middle of the dry season, ferments over the course of a few days or a week.

Nowadays, *olanchanos* can't be bothered climbing trees, so they generally just cut the whole thing down. A single tree can yield up to three gallons of wine. Olancho historian Jose Sarmiento, commenting on the early history of the wine, writes: "It is not known how the drink coming from the coyol palm was discovered, but the first who tried it can be called, with complete confidence, the first *olanchano*."

by a surprise attack by Indians the same year.

Having found gold in the rivers of Olancho, the Spaniards returned in force and stomped out the Indian revolt. By 1530 the town of San Jorge de Olancho had been established in the Valle de Olancho, near El Boquerón, and its inhabitants forced black slaves and Indians to work the surrounding rivers for gold, especially the Río Guayape. Not long after, colonists established the towns of Juticalpa and Catacamas, now the two major towns in Olancho.

Either due to cruel treatment by the Spanish or a generally independent spirit, the indigenous peoples of the province were in constant rebellion for the first two centuries after the Spanish arrived. They regularly fled from the gold works, attacked villages, and massacred missionaries. The security of the region was further weakened as the English gained power on the north coast. Their allies, the Miskitos, invaded Olancho by boat from the Patuca, Paulaya, or Sico Rivers in search of gold or Indian slaves to sell to the English.

When the Spanish regained the north coast and expelled the British at the end of the 18th century, Olancho enjoyed a couple of decades of relative peace, but the advent of independence brought renewed violence. Always protective of their right to manage their own affairs, *olanchanos* resented efforts by the new Liberal government to assert control through taxation and also disagreed with Liberal policies against the Church. In October 1828, beginning in the town of Gualaco, tensions broke out into open rebellion against the central government.

In 1829, war raged throughout Olancho, except in Juticalpa, which remained loyal to the government. Because the *olanchano* fighters employed hit-and-run tactics rather than open battles, Olancho historian Jose Sarmiento considers the rebellion the first example of modern guerrilla warfare in the Americas.

General Francisco Morazán himself came to Olancho in late 1829 to lead the government troops, and he managed to put an end to the rebellion with a feat of brave diplomacy. Between Juticalpa and San Francisco de la Paz, at that time a bastion of the rebels, is a stretch of windy road called Las Vueltas de Ocote. Knowing the general was on his way, the rebels arrayed their forces at Las Vueltas and waited in ambush. Morazán, aware the rebels were there, ordered his troops to halt just outside Las Vueltas, took off his sword, and walked into the hills alone and unarmed. The general clearly knew what sort of men he was facing. Deeply impressed with this display of personal bravery, the rebels allowed Morazán into their camp unharmed. The general asked them to explain why they were rebelling. Over the course of the hot afternoon of 21 January 1830, he hammered out an agreement to end the rebellion, conceding to Olancho a certain degree of self-government. Today a bust of Morazán, growing moldy in the elements, commemorates the event at the site.

Despite the settlement, many *olanchanos* continued to be unhappy with their new government, and for reasons still not entirely clear, a new, more widespread rebellion broke out in 1863. Conflicts this time had a markedly social character, pitting the lower class, small-scale *mestizo* ranchers and laborers against the wealthy *criollo* cattlemen.

The rebellion continued for two years, spreading into Yoro and threatening Trujillo, before it was put down with extreme brutality by President-General José María Medina, in a campaign known to this day in Olancho as "La Ahorcancina" ("The Hanging"). The heads of two rebel leaders, Bernabé Antuñez and Francisco Zavala, were stuck on pikes and left on a hillside overlooking Juticalpa for several years afterward, as a warning to any would-be rebels.

Whether from Medina's terror campaign or exhaustion after years of fratricidal war, Olancho settled into relative peace, resigned to remain part of Honduras. The 1980s saw a renewed surge of violence in Olancho, this time from the CIA-directed Contra War, part of which occurred along the long, wild border between Olancho and Nicaragua.

Although it has pockets of dire poverty, Olancho is thought of as one of the wealthier departments in Honduras, rich in fertile agricultural and grazing land, surrounded by dense forests, and with deposits of gold in many local rivers. In the rest of Honduras, *olanchano* is a slang term for someone who is lazy, because in olden times at least, the local inhabitants reputedly didn't have to work hard to get by.

Currently, Olancho makes its living through cattle-raising, logging (some legal, much not), and infrequently panning for gold. The occasional, wild-eyed foreign miner still wanders into the wilder reaches of the department hoping for a lucky strike.

JUTICALPA

The capital of Olancho, the Spaniards first established a small settlement in Juticalpa probably around 1530, on the site of a Tawahka Indian village near the then-capital of San Jorge de Olancho. Stone axes and arrowheads are still often found in town, particularly in the Belén neighborhood.

Situated at the southern end of the Valle de Catacamas 400 meters above sea level, Juticalpa's 87,600 residents make their living either working with the departmental government, cattle ranching, or as merchants for the surrounding area. Juticalpa is often a stop-off point on the way to Olancho from Tegucigalpa. It's a convenient place to take care of business and prepare for expeditions to the nearby Monumento Natural El Boquerón and Sierra de Agalta, or farther afield to Parque Nacional La Muralla and the Mosquitia.

Accommodations
The best hotel in downtown is the new **Hotel Honduras,** two blocks west of the square, tel. 885-1331, fax 885-1456, charging US$8 s or US$10 d for a modern room with fan, telephone, TV, and bathroom, a bit more for a/c.

On the same block is **Hotel Antuñez,** tel. 885-2250, a large building with an often sullen staff but a large selection of rooms at different prices, ranging from US$5 d for the most basic, with communal bathroom, to US$9 d for a decent upstairs single, to US$17 d with cable TV, refrigerator, and a bathroom inside. The hotel runs a cafeteria and has free purified water.

Hotel El Paso, on the road between the highway and the square, close to the bus station, tel. 885-2311, has 30 rooms around an inside courtyard with parking available. The clean, spacious rooms go for US$4 s or US$7 d, with bath and fan, or a bit more with cable TV—a good value. The rooms toward the back of the hotel tend to be quieter. The friendly owners also run a bakery.

Super lower-price digs can be found at **Hotel Reyes,** a small family-run hotel one block southwest of the square; US$2.50 s with a communal bathroom, US$4 s with private bath.

Far and away the best hotel in Juticalpa, and in all of Olancho for that matter, is **Hotel Villa San Andrés,** tel. and fax 885-2405, with eight spacious, very clean rooms with a/c, cable TV, and telephones in what looks like a large house, rather than a hotel, for US$30 s or d. This is a peaceful, lovely spot to stay, especially if you have your own wheels. It's located along the old road to Catacamas, near the main highway. Look for Discotec El Sesteo, then take the side road a couple hundred meters to the hotel. Taxis in town know the way.

Food and Entertainment

Juticalpa is not overflowing with creative cuisine—most restaurants focus heavily on beef. Apart from the restaurants below, meals in the many foodstalls in the local market are inexpensive, sanitary, and tasty. A couple of *baleada* ladies are usually out on the corner of the square opposite Banco Atlántida every night until at least 9 p.m.

One of the better upscale eateries in town, frequently recommended by locals, is **Restaurante La Fonda,** on the highway toward Tegucigalpa just past the Dippsa gas station on the right-hand side, coming from town. The menu is nothing outrageous—steaks, chicken, *pin-*

chos, etc.—but the food is well prepared and the portions are heaping. *Pinchos* are served with an appetizer of hot beans, cream, and chips served in an ingenious ceramic mini-oven called an *anafre.* Open daily 8 a.m.-9 p.m.; US$3-5 per plate. If you don't have your own wheels, take a taxi out from town and arrange to be picked up later.

Cafeteria Gypsy's, diagonally across from Hotel Antuñez downtown, has an inexpensive buffet three meals a day, with several different entrees to choose from. Open Mon.-Sat. 7 a.m.-9 p.m. A block north of the square is **Fat Burger,** open daily until midnight, with decent burgers (US$2-4) but—despite the name—better pizza (US$3-6).

A block behind the church is **Restaurante El Rancho,** serving *pinchos,* chicken, burgers, and sandwiches at benches and tables on a patio. Open Mon.-Sat. 8 a.m.-10 p.m.

If you'd like to try a little Honduran Chinese food, check out **Restaurante Asia** on the *parque* or **Restaurante Oriental,** a half-block south of the Catedral, with pretty much identical, large menus offering *chop suey, chaumin* (that would be chow mein), and fried rice dishes with a variety of ingredients for US$3-5. The two restaurants, both run by recent Chinese immigrants who barely speak Spanish, are open daily until 10 p.m.

Tropical Juices on the square whips up excellent fruit shakes and juices Mon.-Sat. until 10 p.m.

Disco Los Arcos, almost across the street

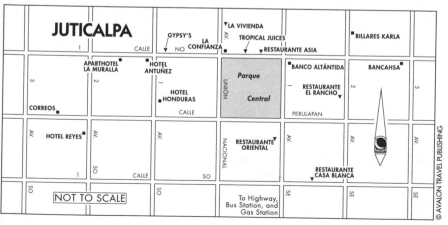

JUTICALPA USEFUL TELEPHONE NUMBERS

Police: 885-2028
Fire Department: 885-2910
Cruz Roja Ambulance: 885-2221

from Restaurante La Fonda on the highway out toward Tegucigalpa, has live merengue music Thurs.-Sun. 8 p.m.-2 a.m., entrance US$1.50. **Discotec El Sesteo,** by the old highway exit to Catacamas, is also reputed to be a good time. The discos in the center of town are not too safe.

For a game of pool and a few beers, **Billares Karla** is a near the square, past Banco Atlántida and to the left at the end of the block.

Services

Hondutel, open daily 7 a.m.-9 p.m., and the post office are both a half-block west of the park. Both Banco Atlántida and Bancahsa will change dollars, though not traveler's checks; both will also advance money on a Visa card. Banco Atlántida has a cash machine. Many stores in town will buy dollars for better rates than the banks, including **La Confianza** on the northwest corner of the square and **La Vivienda,** half a block away.

The Saturday market, set up by the old bridge leaving town to Catacamas, four blocks northeast of the *parque,* is a great place to wander around and check out local handicrafts and produce.

Getting There and Away

Juticalpa has two **bus stations,** a block away from one another on either side of the entrance road from the Tegucigalpa highway. Closest to the highway is the terminal for Aurora and Discovery, tel. 885-2237, which both run buses to Tegucigalpa nine times daily, local service (US$1.50, three hours), with three direct buses at 6 a.m., 9 a.m., and 2 p.m. (US$2.50, two hours).

Across the street and one block back toward town is the terminal for buses to Catacamas, with frequent buses between 8 a.m.-4 p.m. (US 75 cents); Gualaco, with two daily at 6 a.m. and 1 p.m. (US$1.30, two and a half hours); and San Esteban, with two buses daily, the last in early afternoon (US$2, three and a half hours).

One bus departs daily for Tocoa (US$3.50, seven hours), via Gualaco, San Esteban, and El Carbón, leaving at 5 a.m. from the Texaco gas station on the highway, near the bus stations.

The 192-km, two-lane highway to Tegucigalpa from Juticalpa is in good shape and can be driven in two hours. Catacamas is 41 km from Juticalpa, while the turnoff to San Francisco de la Paz, which leads eventually to the north coast via San Esteban, is 10 km northeast of Juticalpa on the Catacamas road. At last report, the main bridge leaving Juticalpa toward Catacamas was down, making traffic either go through the river (4WD only) or across the old bridge, from the back end of town. The bridge should be up by the end of 2000.

EL BOQUERÓN AND VICINITY

Between Juticalpa and Catacamas is Monumento Natural El Boquerón, a 4,000-hectare natural area covering two canyons and a mountain peak in the foothills of Sierra de Agalta, on the north side of the highway. Much of the surrounding area has been turned into pasture or farmland by local *campesinos,* but small patches of cloud forest and a healthy stretch of river-valley forest remain. The canyon is a fine place to take a day trip, but if you've got a couple of days consider camping and birdwatching up on the mountain or visiting the little-known pre-Columbian ruins site of Dos Quebradas.

Hiking Up the Canyon

The main canyon of El Boquerón, on the Río Olancho, has a very pleasant stretch of quiet forest with several swimming holes and plenty of opportunities for birdwatching. If you see a *campesino* nearby, you could ask him to show you the entrance to **Cueva de Tepescuintle,** with some impressive stalactites and stalagmites. In the 1940s an archaeologist found some evidence of pre-conquest habitation at the cave. To get to the canyon, get off the bus (or out of your car) where the Juticalpa-Catacamas highway crosses the Rio Olancho, then follow the dirt road upstream along the edge of the river, which angles roughly north-northwest. Paths follow the river on both sides into the canyon, but the east side seems a bit easier to follow, at least for the first part of the hike.

The forest within the canyon is generally intact, although some small patches have been cut down, especially farther up the canyon. Coming from the highway, the canyon at first seems to support a dry forest, with dense stands of middle-sized trees. But in the serene central section of the canyon one can feel the humidity increase, and the trees are much taller—up to 30 meters—and covered with bromeliads and other epiphyte plants. Begonias, bougainvillea, and a plethora of other flowering plants decorate the banks of the river.

About halfway up the three-and-a-half-km canyon, the path switches to the west side and climbs up the hillside into pastures before reaching the *aldea* of **La Avispa,** about a three-hour hike from the highway at an easy pace, with stops to look around. Here day-trippers will want to head back down along the canyon and out to the highway, while those with more time and the requisite gear can hike south up Cerro Agua Buena and back down to the Juticalpa highway, or continue on dirt roads west to the Dos Quebradas ruins.

Cerro Agua Buena

From La Avispa, ask villagers to point out the trail leading up to **Cerro Agua Buena** (1,433 meters), the mountain separating La Avispa from the Catacamas valley to the south. The trail climbs up steeply through coffee plantations, planted in the traditional style with lots of shade trees, then crosses a ridge top and continues down the far side. Crowning the mountain's summit, above and to the west of where the trail crosses the pass, is a small patch of cloud forest. The views from the ridge top across the valleys, both to the

---

THE DESTRUCTION OF SAN JORGE DE OLANCHO

Not far from the Catacamas-Juticalpa highway near the Río Olancho is the site of San Jorge de Olancho, the region's early capital, which was wiped out by a natural disaster of mysterious character in 1611. William Wells, a North American traveler who passed through Olancho in the 1850s, reports the following local legend of the town's destruction in his book, *Explorations and Adventures in Honduras:*

The great wealth of Olancho in olden times had centered at the ancient town, which was once a sort of local emporium of fashion and luxury. The owners of cattle estates resided there, and collected immense treasure by mining operations on the Upper Guayape, and by purchasing gold of the Indians. The inhabitants, however, were niggardly; and, although they had such quantities of gold that the women wore nuggets of it in their hair, they withheld their hordes even from the Church, and were consequently stricken with Divine Wrath. In one of the churches a golden statue of the Virgin had been ordered by ecclesiastical authority, but the people were slow with the necessary contributions. The body of the statue was completed, but there being an indifferent supply of gold for the crown, the sacred brows were enriched with a "corona de cuero" (a crown of hide). The padre of the church protested; but these infatuated wretches, unmindful of the wealth they were enjoying by the special favor of the Virgin, snapped their fingers in the face of this holy man! The infamous desecration of the Holy Mother was speedily avenged. While the population were collected in the church, the mountain broke forth with terrific violence, and in an hour the whole town was destroyed with showers of rocks, stones, and ashes. Many were killed, and the remainder fled affrightened out of the place. After the destruction, some few ventured back, but were seized with sudden sickness and died on the spot.

Locals claim the town was destroyed by a volcano, but since volcanic mountains do not exist in this part of Honduras, that seems unlikely. A massive landslide is a more logical explanation, especially considering the sheer cliff faces of El Boquerón, just behind the town's former location.

The survivors moved on to Olanchito in Yoro, bringing their patron saint, San Jorge, with them. The last vestiges of the old mining town have disappeared, but locals continue to turn up all sorts of early colonial artifacts in the fields between the highway and the mountain.

north and south, and up the Sierra de Agalta to the east, are magnificent from the hilltop, making it a fine place to camp (bring your water). And the many wild fruit trees at the upper edges of the coffee plantations attract hordes of different birds, as well as a great variety of small mammals, like *pizote, tepesquintle,* troops of monkeys, and even the occasional jaguar wandering down from Agalta. Bring your binoculars. Quetzals have even been spotted here, making it one of the lowest-elevation habitats for the bird.

From the ridge, the trail from La Avispa continues south down through the coffee fields to the hillside village of **Agua Buena**, where there is a good water source (hence the name), then downhill past El Bambú to the Juticalpa-Catacamas highway at Tempisque, near the Río Olancho bridge. The same hike is possible in the other direction as well, starting at Tempisque and crossing to La Avispa.

Dos Quebradas Ruins

In the Guacoca Valley, west of La Avispa toward the highway between Juticalpa and San Francisco de la Paz, is an extensive pre-Columbian ruins site, rarely visited by anyone besides the *campesinos* who live practically on top of the site. Dos Quebradas was only surveyed by archeologists once, in the 1930s, and little is known about its builders, other than they made lots of attractive pottery which is continually found all over the surrounding valley.

From the village of Guacoca, a couple of kilometers from La Avispa by dirt road, a side road turns north to Dos Quebradas, a small *aldea* a bit over a kilometer from Guacoca. Yet another side road branches off here to the east; a five-minute walk leads to a compound of several *ranchos* right in front the ruins. Ask permission from the owners of the house to walk through their fields to several mounds *(lomas),* 10-15 meters in height. On one, to the north side of the main structures, the original rocks encasing the dirt building are visible. Ask the residents of the nearby houses to show you a sizable monolith *(piedra grande)* in the adjacent field, which has fallen over on its side, and the nearby remnants of one of the many stone causeways *(caminos de piedra)* in the valley.

While you walk around this area, don't be afraid to stop and greet local families, who are

a fallen pre-Columbian monolith at Dos Quedabras ruins, Olancho

generally a friendly and hospitable bunch. If they invite you in, it's polite to sit on the porch for at least a few of minutes to say hello. Travelers who speak a modicum of Spanish may find themselves having interesting conversations about the region and the lives of its people, if they make the effort. And while you're there, take a look around at some of the fine old wooden furniture, farm implements, and worked leather saddles hanging around these humble but usually tidy *ranchos.*

From Dos Quebradas, it's an easy hour's walk west to the highway, and from there you can catch a ride to Juticalpa or San Francisco de la Paz.

CATACAMAS

A dusty town set against the base of the Sierra de Agalta, Catacamas is much like Juticalpa, only smaller, and is noteworthy mainly as a stop-off point for those looking to visit the Cuevas de Talgua (difficult to do these days) or take longer excursions to Sierra de Agalta or the Mosquitia.

The *parque,* a few hundred yards up from the highway, is dominated by a massive ceiba tree, which spreads generous shade across the square. A few blocks toward the mountains from the square is a stairway leading up to **Cerrito de la Cruz,** a small hill with a cross on top affording good views over Catacamas and the rest of the valley.

Accommodations

Half a block from the square, around the corner from the bus station, is **Hotel La Colina,** tel. 899-4488, offering clean whitewashed rooms for US$10 s or d with hot water, fan, and TV.

Two doors down is the less expensive but still comfortable **Hotel Oriental,** charging US$2.25 s for a basic cell, US$5 for a nicer room with double bed and bathroom, or US$8 d with cable TV also. All rooms have fans.

Rock-bottom digs are available at **Hospedaje San Jorge,** on the *parque,* with very basic rooms for US$1.75 s or US$3.50 d.

Food and Entertainment

A funky little joint with wooden benches a block from the park, **El Rinconcito Típico** has inexpensive burgers, chicken, steak, and *comida*

THE CAVE OF THE GLOWING SKULLS

Four kilometers from Catacamas, near the village of Guanaja by the banks of the Río Talgua, is the Cueva de Talgua, an extensive cavern long known and explored by adventurous locals and the odd spelunker. In April 1994, four cavers clambering through the cave made an incredible discovery that has rewritten the history of pre-Columbian Honduras.

Hondurans Jorge Yáñez and Desiderio Reyes and Americans Tim Berg and Greg Cabe were about 2,000 feet inside the cave when they noticed an opening in a limestone wall 10 meters off the cave floor. Yáñez and Reyes scaled the wall, peered into the opening, and saw a scene out of a science-fiction movie: hundreds of skulls and bones apparently made of crystal, glowing in the light of their headlamps.

Once word of the discovery got out, a team of archaeologists led by Dr. James Brady of George Washington University examined the cave and determined that the bones had been placed on the ledge some 3,000 years ago by a hitherto unknown Mesoamerican civilization. Over the millennia since their burial, the bones had become coated with calcite dripping from the cave roof, which both preserved the remains and lent them their unearthly appearance.

In an apparent ritual burial, the bones of some 200 people were carefully stripped of flesh, painted with a red ochre, and stacked in neat bundles along with pieces of ceramic and jade. As with many other Mesoamerican societies, caves were seen as entrances to the underworld, and the dead were evidently placed there to speed them on their journey to the next world. Additional exploration revealed a second cave nearby, called the Cave of the Spiders, holding more bones and with several pictographs on its walls. A third cave has since been found on a nearby mountainside.

Mounds above ground near the caves are believed to have been the villages of those buried in the caves. Little is known about these first *olanchanos,* other than they were relatively tall and healthy, and they seemed to have traded with other societies in the region, judging from the pottery found. The earliest positive date of bones is from 1400 B.C.

The Honduran government invested a chunk of money building tourist facilities in and around the cave in 1997 and 1998, but before they even had a chance to open, Hurricane Mitch trashed the lot of it. The caves have been closed since the hurricane, and most of the bones are now at IHAH offices in Tegucigalpa, to safeguard them from vandals. If you'd like to try to get into the cave, the best option is to take a taxi (US$4 or so) from Catacamas to Guanaja, and there start asking for the caretaker, who has the key to the gate across the cave mouth.

corriente. The old Wurlitzer jukebox is well stocked with great old and new *ranchero* tunes. Open daily for lunch and dinner.

The finest restaurant in town is the **As de Oro,** a half-block off the highway, just past the main entrance to town on the Dulce Nombre de Culmí side. Food is expensive at US$8 for a full meal or US$3.50 for burgers or sandwiches, but the chicken, steaks, fish, and (miracle of miracles!) vegetarian dishes are excellent and filling. The open-air patio, surrounded with plants, is a relaxing place to eat. Credit cards are accepted, if you feel like a splurge.

Buffet Ejecutivo on the southeast corner of the *parque* has very good and inexpensive buffet meals daily 7 a.m.-8 p.m. It's a great spot for breakfast.

Tropical Juices next to the movie theater, a couple of blocks uphill from the *parque,* serves juices and fruit shakes Mon.-Sat. 10 a.m.-10 p.m.

The **Cine Maya** runs a daily double feature, US$2.

Services
Banco Atlántida on the northwest corner of the *parque,* open Mon.-Fri. 8 a.m.-noon and 2-4 p.m., Saturdays 8-11 a.m., has a cash machine and can give cash advances on a Visa card, but does not exchange dollars. **Librería Julio Verne,** a block down from Banco Atlántida, exchanges dollars at a decent rate.

Hondutel, a block north and half a block east from the *parque,* is open daily 7 a.m.-8:30 p.m.

Getting There and Away
The Aurora/Discovery terminal, on the *parque,* tel. 899-4393, has nine regular buses to Tegucigalpa (US$2.25, four and a half hours) between 2:30 a.m. and 5 p.m. Four direct buses (with one stop at Juticalpa, US$3, three and a half hours) leave daily between 6 a.m. and 2:30 p.m.

Local buses to Juticalpa (US 75 cents, one hour) leave from in front of the terminal all day until 5 p.m.

Four buses a day drive between Catacamas and Dulce Nombre de Culmí (US$1, two and a half hours) the last one leaving at 3 p.m. Two of these buses continue past Culmí to Las Marías, in the frontier zone on the south side of the Río Plátano reserve. These buses, and others to areas north and east, leave from the market,

several blocks northeast of the *parque.*

Tegucigalpa is 232 km from Catacamas and can be driven in three to four hours on the well-maintained paved highway. Juticalpa is 41 km from Catacamas.

FROM OLANCHO INTO THE MOSQUITIA

Dulce Nombre de Culmí
A rough frontier town 50 km northeast of Catacamas in rolling pine forested hills, Culmí lies near the southern boundary of the Reserva de la Biosfera del Río Plátano. This is the southern entry into the Mosquitia for the hard-core adventurer (or suicidal fool, might say some) who wants to cross from Olancho through the jungle north to the Caribbean coast.

Formerly Culmí was a Pech mission settlement founded, along with Santa María del Carbón, by the Franciscan Manuel de Jesús Subirana in the mid-19th century. The icon of the Dulce Nombre given to the town by Subirana still rests in the more modern church in town and is widely revered throughout Olancho. Don't come by for the *feria* in early January, though, as you'd be sure to see one or two shootings a day amongst the drunken cowboys.

The Pech have long since departed Culmí to outlying villages like Agua Zarca, Vallecito and Pisijire, driven away by ranchers, loggers, and not a few *banditos* flooding in from other parts of Honduras, particularly the south. People in Culmí like to say that just about no one over age 20 in the area was actually born there, apart from the Pech.

The illegal logging under way north of Culmí, in both the buffer and core zones of the biosphere reserve, is prodigious. In late 1999, an army patrol swept through the area, confiscating large quantities of illegal wood but not making any arrests. There has been talk of setting up an army post at the crossroads just north of Culmí, where much of the illegal wood must come through, but, with so many powerful interests in both politics and the military benefiting from the logging, it has yet to materialize.

Facilities in Culmí are minimal. The only rooms in town are at **Hospedaje Kevin,** for US$1.75 s or US$3.50 d, and there are a couple of simple *comedores* nearby. Several *pulperías* sell basic supplies, but anyone planning an expedition should bring everything needed.

North from Culmí

Rough dirt roads head north from Culmí, leading to frontier villages and *ranchos* in the southernmost section of the Río Plátano reserve, and eventually leading to the headwaters of the Paulaya, Plátano, Aner, and Wampú Rivers, which empty out into the Mosquitia. Although this immense, unexplored region offers unbeatable opportunities for venturing into pristine rainforest and seeking out the numerous pre-Columbian ruins, it is a totally lawless area. Shootings are common. While foreigners are generally not targets, it's always possible to run across someone in particular need of money or just get caught in the crossfire. Which doesn't mean you can't go, always of course fully equipped for the jungle and with a guide (or guides) you can trust. It's definitely an "at your own risk" sort of place, not to be taken lightly. The Río Wampú region is particularly known to be unsafe. All in all, the best option for those possessed with a fierce desire to see this dangerous but truly incredible region is to pay for a guided trip. The best guide for the region is Jorge Salaverri of La Moskitia Eco-Aventuras, in La Ceiba.

Six km north of Culmí, the road forks three ways, all of which eventually meet back up and continue on to the town of Las Marías (not to be confused with the Las Marías on the Río Plátano near the Caribbean coast), roughly 40 km from Culmí. From Las Marías, mule trails continue into the jungle to the headwaters of the Río Plátano and down to the Mosquitia, through the heart of the biosphere, a two-week voyage of serious jungle and rafting adventure. At least one bus a day usually drives to Las Marías from Catacamas via Culmí. From Las Marías guides are essential to get to the headwaters. And don't consider rafting the river without someone who knows it, as there are plenty of fierce rapids, including the ominously named *subterráneo*.

Traveling from Culmí by truck and foot down the Río Paulaya Valley to Sico and Palacios in the Mosquitia is doable in three to five days on dirt roads and well-beaten trails, most of it through pastures and patches of farmland hacked out of the jungle. Either catch the occasional bus or look for trucks from Culmí to La Pimienta, which is reached from a turnoff to the northwest between Culmí and Las Marías. Beyond Pimienta the road crosses into the Paulaya valley and continues to La Loma en Medio, a village on the side of the river. From here trails continue downstream along the river to Sico, where you can either catch a boat to Palacios or a truck out to Tocoa. Best to cross the river by Loma en Medio, as crossing downstream is more difficult. All in all, as the valley is pretty much stripped of jungle, it doesn't seem worth making the effort to go that way, when other trips are available. There is talk of putting a road along this well-traveled route, which would open up the western side of the biosphere reserve to accelerated logging and deforestation.

The right-most of the three forks just north of Culmí leads to the village of Los Mangos, where a side road branches off to **La Llorana** and the source of the Río Wampú Those with their own rafts can put in at the river and continue down to the Patuca and on to the ocean. Here you can sometimes find locals to help build balsa rafts. Other dirt roads continue farther north past La Llorana to the headwaters of the **Río Aner.** In this region are the unexcavated ruins of unknown pre-conquest civilizations, including Las Crucitas, Marañones, Saguasón, and others.

It is out in this part of the jungle where **Ciudad Blanca** is said to exist, a fabled and possibly mythical pre-Columbian city of huge proportions out in the middle of the jungle. Since the early part of last century, various explorers have claimed to find the city, only to die in mysterious circumstances. To this day, modern-day Indiana Joneses regularly pop up in Honduras, scouting around to raise funds for an expedition to find the lost city. Reportedly the A&E cable channel is about to show a documentary of one such explorer. For any who should be bitten by the Ciudad Blanca bug, I repeat: the Río Wampú and Río Aner regions are dangerous, from both natural hazards like venomous snakes and other nasties, but more importantly from men with lots of weapons and few scruples about using them.

To the Río Patuca

Anyone who takes a close look at a map of Olancho will notice that the rivers beginning around Juticalpa and Catacamas eventually empty out into the Río Patuca, which flows through the Mosquitia rainforests on its way out to the Caribbean coast. At least two river trips are feasible, not including the dicey Río Wampú and Río Aner routes mentioned in the previous section.

The safest and easiest route is to go from Tegucigalpa via Danlí, in the El Paraíso department, out to Nueva Palestina in Olancho, near the Río Patuca. At least one bus a day runs all the way from Mercado Jacaleapa in Tegucigalpa out to Nueva Palestina, or you can switch buses in Danlí. Nueva Palestina is a fairly rough frontier town, although it's better than it used to be since liquor was banned. **Hotel La Estancia** has about the best rooms in town. From Nueva Palestina, a dirt road continues to Guineo, on the Río Patuca, and then downstream to Arenas Blancas, the closest good put-in point to Nueva Palestina. Finding a reliable boatman will require several hours of talking to people (Spanish is a must), either in Nueva Palestina or Arenas Blancas. Don't go with just anyone—make sure you find a guide who really knows the entire route down at least as far as Krausirpe, in the Tawahka zone. In fact, if you can find a Tawahka boatman who has come upriver on business, better still, as they know the river better than anyone. Rates are very negotiable, but it should be around US$100-150 for a two- or three-day trip to Krausirpe. An important aspect of the price calculation is to figure out the current gasoline price and how many gallons the trip will require. After passing first through a gorge known reassuringly as the *Portal del Infierno* (The Gates of Hell), the river winds several hours through secondary forest and grazing land before entering the primary forest. Many small Tawahka farms dot the riverbank, so to fully appreciate the forest you either need to get out of the boat and hike, or take the boat up smaller tributaries. Tell your boatman to turn off the motor and drift (river permitting) when going through the jungle, so as not to scare off the wildlife. All sorts of brilliantly colored toucans, macaws, parrots, and even the rare harpy eagle fly overhead, and plenty of small mammals like peccaries, armadillos, tapirs, and jaguarundis roam the riverbanks. Bring binoculars. From Krausirpe, either return to Nueva Palestina on the same boat (you'll have to pay for the boatman's gas to get back anyhow—unless your boatman is a Tawahka), or continue on

other boats down through Wampusirpi to Ahuas, with daily plane flights to Palacios and La Ceiba.

A more adventurous option by river from Olancho to the Río Patuca is along the **Río Cuyamel,** reached by a dirt road branching off the Catacamas-Culmí highway just beyond where the pavement ends, and continuing through the town of La Bacadia before reaching the Río Cuyamel. One bus a day drives from the Catacamas market to La Bacadia (hour and a half), and once a day a *baronesa* (truck rigged up with wooden bench seats) runs all the way out to the Cuyamel. Here you can continue by river, either in your own craft if so equipped, or in a balsawood raft if you can make one or find someone who knows how. Only those with well-developed river skills should consider going without a guide, and finding reliable guides out this way is not a simple task. Though not as bad as around Culmí, the area around Río Cuyamel is not the safest, with plenty of shady types hanging around with guns tucked in their belts. But if you can pull it off, the pristine jungles along the Cuyamel and down into the Río Patuca will be your reward.

SIERRA DE AGALTA AND VICINITY

Parque Nacional Sierra de Agalta
Over 60,000 hectares of mountain forest are protected in the spectacular Sierra de Agalta, and in its core zone the park contains the most extensive cloud forest remaining in Honduras, and possibly all of Central America. Because of its remote location, Agalta's forest does not get as many visitors as La Tigra or Celaque, but the people who see it rate it as one of the country's most incredible natural areas.

The range's isolation has been its savior— loggers have not yet cut into the heart of the forest, and, with luck and a lot of vigilance, they never will. Around its perimeter, Sierra de Agalta is blanketed by pine forest, which is currently under pressure from coffee plantations and loggers. Above the pines, moist tropical forests with liquidambar (sweet gum) trees dominate, gradually giving way to the epiphyte- and vine-covered cloud forest, at elevations between 1,700 and 2,000 meters. At the highest elevations grows a bizarre elfin or dwarf forest, created by high winds and heavy precipitation.

Here stunted, gnarled pine and oak trees between one and a half and five meters high, buffeted by continual high winds, are cloaked in mosses and lichen.

The forests of Sierra de Agalta are considered a sort of transitional ecosystem, similar to the mountain forests of Costa Rica, while Celaque and other cloud forests in western Honduras are more like those of Guatemala and southern Mexico. Over 400 species of birds have been identified in Sierra de Agalta, as well as a myriad of mammals rarely seen elsewhere in the country. Tapirs, sloths, ocelots, jaguars, and troops of howler, spider, and white-faced monkeys all reside in the park. And in contrast to other mountains, the wildlife here is not shy about showing itself—far from having to search for them, I was pursued and mercilessly pelted by a troop of irate spider monkeys while hiking in Agalta. Apart from its natural beauty and the rare flora and fauna it sustains, the Sierra de Agalta is a critical source of water for northeastern Honduras, forming the headwaters for the Patuca, Sico, and Paulaya Rivers.

The easiest access to Agalta is from Gualaco, in the Valle de Agalta, where a well-developed trail climbs **La Picucha,** the highest point in the range at 2,354 meters. Hikers can also cross lesser-known trails from the Catacamas-Culmí side over the mountains to the Gualaco-San Esteban side along at least three different routes, or explore a complex cave system and stunning series of waterfalls near Gualaco.

The topographical maps covering the park are 1:50,000 San Francisco de la Paz 2960 I, Catacamas 3060 IV, Dulce Nombre de Culmí 3061 II,

HIKING LA PICUCHA

Hiking up to the highest peak in the Sierra, La Picucha (2,345 m), ranks high on the list of the most rewarding outdoor adventures in Honduras, along with the Río Plátano rainforest. Sierra de Agalta is a thriving forest, fairly bursting with animal and plant life of dizzying variety. And the Picucha climb takes you through all the different ecosystems of the park, from the lower pine forests up through different stages of cloud forest, and out onto the dwarf forest across the summit. If you've got the time and energy (it's a steep, hard climb), the Picucha trail is not to be missed.

Many visitors will want to hire a guide in Gualaco. The amiable Ramón Veliz, a.k.a Monchito, is an excellent guide who knows the trail well and charges US$8 a day plus food. Intrepid hikers could hike to La Picucha without a guide, if you're confident of your orienteering skills. Or they could before Hurricane Mitch, anyway, which felled a great many trees on the steep slopes of Agalta, making the trail impassable all the way up to the peak. Cohdefor officials in Gualaco hope to get sufficient funds to send a chainsaw crew up to clean all the fallen trees, but the only real way to find out is to go to the Cohdefor office in Gualaco and ask, or talk to the local Peace Corps volunteers. If the Picucha trail is still closed, hikers still have several excellent trails to choose from throughout the Sierra.

Should the trail be open, drive north from Gualaco on the highway 10 km and look for a faded sign-post on the east side of the road, marking the entrance to a 4WD track heading into the pine forest. This dirt road continues about five km steadily uphill, the last two km progressively more steep and rough. The road may be impassable by vehicle in the rainy season.

Formerly the road ended at the trailhead, but now the road continues beyond the trail entrance a short way, making it necessary to look closely for the trail on the left side. It's possible to bushwhack up to the trail from the end of the road, but better to look for the proper entrance.

Once on the trail, walk up along a ridge for about 45 minutes, and keep a close eye out for a trail branching off to the right, leaving the ridge and traversing down across a hillside. This first stretch of hillside was badly damaged, very nearly wiped clean of trees, by Hurricane Mitch. If you miss the turn, the other trail will eventually join back up with the first, but it takes quite a bit longer.

From the trail junction, continue two to three hours along the hillside, then down into a narrow valley, across the small Quebrada Perezosa, up again over another ridge, and back down again to the larger Río del Sol. The trail zig-zags upstream along the Río del Sol, crossing over it several times, so expect to get your feet wet. It's not always easy to keep track of the trail with all the river crossings, but just keep poking around and you'll find it. Along the edge of the river you'll find a simple thatched and Valle de Agalta La Venta 3061 III.

Los Chorros de Babilonia

An excellent alternative to the Picucha climb is to hike up to the series of at least 10 waterfalls tumbling down the precipitous northwestern flanks of Agalta. The falls are clearly visible from the San Esteban highway, coming down the hill from Gualaco into the Valle de Agalta. Visitors can either spend a day hiking up to different falls from the village of El Ocotal, one km south of the highway, or spend one or more days camping out in the mountains above. The trail from El Ocotal (at 600 meters elevation) climbs right up the side of the mountain near the waterfalls, with several side trails cutting in to different falls. At the top is a plateau several kilometers square at 1200-1300 meters in altitude, known as **Los Planes de Babilonia,** covered with coffee plan-

tations planted among tall shade trees left from the original forest. With a river running right through the lush plateau, teeming with birdlife, this is a great spot to camp. Following the stream uphill to the south will take you across the plateau to the edge of the cloud forest, with a few small footpaths continuing farther up for forays into the forest. Take good care not to get lost. Across a low ridge on the east side of the plateau is another trail back down to the Valle de Agalta, via the **Río Chiquito,** which reputedly has a spectacular waterfall tucked into a narrow gorge and hidden from view from the highway below. For this trip, plan on getting a guide, and be prepared for a few days in the woods. Relatively experienced hikers can probably make it up to the waterfalls and plateau on their own, just by asking directions from local farmers. But if you

champa, which makes an excellent campsite for the first night out.

About 20 minutes from the campsite the trail arrives at **La Chorrera,** a lovely waterfall pouring around a large boulder. Just below the falls, the trail crosses the river a last time and heads straight up the mountainside. From the river, it's a four- to six-hour walk to the next campsite, high up on the mountain. The trail upward is very faint in places, with many trees fallen across it requiring circumnavigation. If in doubt, keep looking around for machete marks, and backtrack until you're sure of the trail. There's only one path, and it stays on a compass bearing roughly between 160 and 200 degrees the whole way, following the ridge upward. Above the river, the forest—first arid tropical forest closer to the river, then cloud forest higher up—is pristine and full of wildlife. Troops of howler and spider monkeys along with all manner of birdlife frequent the towering trees above the trail.

After about four hours the trail levels off somewhat on a high ridgeline; at this point start looking for the second camp. It's on the right side slightly below the trail, with a few flat spots to pitch tents and a couple of fire pits. A stream nearby provides water for most of the year, but if there's been very little rain it's best to bring water up from La Chorrera.

Above the second camp the trail winds its tangled, steep way up the ridgeline to the peak in one and a half to two hours. The vegetation here is so dense, most of the path seems to be more on root structures and branches than dirt. You'll also notice, about an hour above the camp, all the trees around

are remarkably short—this is the famous dwarf forest of Agalta, stunted pines and oaks, gnarled and twisted by the wind and soaking wet from the near-permanent clouds. Everything is covered with lichens, moss, and ferns.

Apart from being an odd and beautiful sight on its own, something out of a fairy tale, the short trees of the dwarf forest also allow visitors to admire truly stupendous views from La Picucha, across both the Catacamas and Agalta Valleys and over the mountains extending northward into the jungles of the Mosquitia. From La Picucha, a trail continues over to a nearby peak with a radio tower on it, a good area to hike around and explore the dwarf forest. No trail descends to the Catacamas side from La Picucha.

Take particular care returning from La Picucha back down to La Chorrera waterfall, especially between the second campsite and the river. It's much easier to get lost on the way down, as ridges branch off frequently in different directions. A wise hiker will bring a supply of colored string or plastic and tie off frequently when ascending, picking the tags up on the way down. From the highway to La Picucha it's a total elevation gain of 1,550 meters over a distance of roughly 10 kilometers. It's best to plan for at least two nights out—one at the *champa* at the river below, and another at the high campsite. It is possible to hike the peak at dawn from the second camp and then hike all the way out back to Gualaco in the same day, but it's quite a slog. Better to spend a third night at either one of the camps and allow more time to explore the higher reaches of the mountain.

don't want any problems and would like to learn a bit more about the forest and the region while you're at it, guides are available in Gualaco, and likely in El Ocotal as well, for around US$8 a day. Highway holdups have been reported at the bottom of the pass between Gualaco and San Esteban, where the road enters the Agalta Valley at a place called Pie de la Cuesta (Foot of the Hil). Most of the time the road is fine, but it's best to check in Gualaco for the current status. Once off the highway, though, hikers are quite safe, as the *banditos* are looking for wealthy cattle ranchers and merchants, not *campesinos,* so they stick to the roads and don't venture off into the hills.

Word has it that a small, 4.2-megawatt hydroelectric dam may be built in the future on the Río Babilonia, above the falls. It remains to be seen how this will affect the falls and the surrounding forest.

Hikes Across the Sierra

Intrepid hikers can choose from at least three fairly well established trails across the Sierra de Agalta, from the San Esteban-Gualaco side over to Dulce Nombre de Culmí and Catacamas, or vice versa. The first is navigable easily enough by solo hikers, while the other two are longer and more complicated, requiring a guide.

Northwest from Culmí, a well-beaten trail called **Sendero Malacate**, or the Malacate Trail, heads over a low pass in the Agalta range, coming out near San Esteban. The hike, through coffee plantations down lower and stretches of virgin pine and cloud forests at higher elevations, is a good option for an overnight hike. From the Culmí side, the trail begins at El Cerro, an *aldea* about an hour's walk or 20-minute truck ride up a dirt road north of Culmí. From El Cerro, the trail climbs steadily in a northwesterly direction up through coffee plantations to the pass at around 1200 meters. At the pass, the pine and broadleaf forest thickens into a patch of primary forest, before coming out into coffee plantations again on the San Esteban side. Below is the village of San Agustín, where a dirt road winds out to the highway near San Esteban in about an hour's walk. Camping on the higher reaches of the trail is safe, and the birdwatching is excellent. You won't be able to miss the three-wattled bellbird, which makes an incredible racket for such a small creature.

A second trail passing through more extensive intact forest crosses Sierra de Agalta from Vallecitos, a large village several kilometers northeast of Catacamas, over a 1,600-meter pass and down to Dos Ríos near San Esteban, a two- or three-day hike. This historic trail connected Catacamas to San Esteban in previous centuries, and it is clearly marked on the 1:250,000 Instituto Geográfico Nacional maps for the region, passing just to the east of Río Babilonia and Río Chiquito.

To get to the trailhead, either drive or take a bus from Catacamas toward Culmí, and turn northwest at San José del Río Tinto on a dirt road leading to Vallecitos, 12 km away. From Vallecitos, the trail winds steadily uphill through farmland and shady coffee plantations to the *casería* of Mata de Guineo, tucked into a small valley where three streams meet, a good place to spend the night. Beyond Mata de Guineo, the remarkably broad trail (from years of mule trains) heads into a dense stretch of cloud forest, continuing for several kilometers before coming out into pine forest on the Agalta side and droppping down to Dos Ríos, a kilometer from the San Esteban highway and 15 km from San Esteban. A small clearing in the forest along the trail beyond Mata de Guineo, but before coming out on the Agalta side, is a superb place to camp if you'd like to turn this into a two-night trip. This area is thriving with wild animals, of which birds are the most noticeable denizen. Hawks, bellbirds, quetzals, and countless other rare tropical species are common here. Although the trail is well trod, it's best to get a guide at least on the stretch between Vallecitos and Mata de Guineo, as several trails branch off and it's easy to take a wrong turn if no *campesino* happens to be around to ask.

A third trail, less frequently used and higher than the other two, begins in El Mormullo, a village six kilometers northwest of Catacamas, reached by bus, *jalón,* or foot in a couple of hours. Two kilometers beyond El Mormullo is Las Delicias, where the trail begins a steep climb up the side of the mountain. Crossing the pass at around 1800 meters, hikers are rewarded with a sizable stretch of superb cloud forest, full of wildlife, before descending to Linares, a village just southwest of Gualaco. Guides can be found in El Mormullo, Las Delicias, or Linares, a must for the two- to three-day hike.

JUTICALPA-SAN ESTEBAN HIGHWAY

Ten km from Juticalpa on the road to Cataca-mas, a dirt highway turns northwest through a gap in the hills, passing the towns of San Francisco de la Paz, Gualaco, and on to San Esteban before continuing down past El Carbón all the way to Tocoa and the north coast. The broad Gualaco and Agalta valleys along this route, flanked on their southeastern side by the wall of the Sierra de Agalta, are among the richest in central Honduras, supporting flocks of content-edly fat cattle and contentedly wealthy ranchers.

Gualaco

Settled in the early years of Olancho colonization, the logging and ranching town of Gualaco is a good base for anyone wanting to climb up the Picucha trail into the Sierra de Agalta. The small, dusty highway town has a couple of decent hotels and comedores, and places to buy basic packaged food for camping.

The 17th century **Iglesia de San Jerónimo** on one end of the wide, green parque is fronted by a whitewashed facade with sculpted pillars. The two church towers were rebuilt in 1994 in an unfortunately less than subtle style, but the building is worth a look nonetheless.

Hotel Calle Real on the road between the highway and the parque, has well-kept, simple concrete rooms around an interior parking lot for US$2 no bath, US$3 with bath. On the park is **Hotelito Central,** not as good but functional in a pinch, with similar prices.

Several comedores in town serve up a palat-able meal. **Comedor Sharon** on the highway is better than most, and the owners are friendly and glad to talk to visitors. It also has posters on the walls with photos and descriptions in English and Spanish about Sierra de Agalta and the Cuevas de Susmay, written by local Peace Corps volunteers.

Next to the gas station on the highway are the offices of **Grupo Ecológico de Olancho** and **Cohdefor,** where you can get information on the current state of the Picucha trail. Currently no maps are available, but GEO has a large, detailed topographical map on the wall, which has the La Picucha trail marked. The Cohdefor official

in charge of the park, Francisco Urbina, is extremely knowledgeable and a great source of information, and the local Peace Corps volunteers are helpful as well, but the rest of the Cohdefor workers won't be of much use to tourists.

The Trujillo-Tegucigalpa bus passes Gualaco each day in both directions, to Tegucigalpa (US$3.50) at around 9 or 9:30 and to Trujillo (US$3.50) in the early afternoon. The Juticalpa-Tocoa bus passes going to Tocoa in the early morning and to Juticalpa at around noon. One bus a day runs between Gualaco and Juticalpa (US$1.50), leaving early morning.

Near Gualaco

Foremost among the destinations of visitors to Gualaco will of course be the Picucha trail or the Río Babilonia waterfalls in Sierra de Agalta. But a couple of closer destinations make good day trips.

About an hour's walk from Gualaco are the **Cavernas de Susmay,** near the aldea of Jicalapa. The caves are a 15-minute walk beyond Jicalapa, at the base of the mountains—ask anyone to point the way. The bottommost cave, which has a bone-chillingly cold river running through it, has interesting stalactites and other formations. You have to wade and swim to get into the cave. About a half-hour in, you'll run into a large rock fall, which must be swum under to continue. Most sane folk, by now already numb from the cold water, will turn around here and return to the entrance.

Uphill from the first cave are two more, which have been roughly treated by local youth with spray paint. Farther up is supposedly at least one more cave, with intact formations. To find this more hidden cave, either ask around in Jicalapa for someone to show you, or better yet get ahold of Ramón Veliz (a.k.a. Monchito) in Gualaco, a local caving and hiking fanatic who is always more than happy to guide visitors to Susmay or other caves he knows in the area, for a negotiable fee.

An hour's walk from Gualaco toward the mountains on a dirt road is the aldea of **Magua,** an area teeming with all sorts of birds, including parrots and toucans. Come with binoculars.

San Esteban

At the northeastern end of the Valle de Agalta

HONDURAS' BLOODY FAMILY FEUD

Since the late 1980s, San Esteban has had the dubious distinction of being home to one of the longest-running and most violent family feuds in Central America. The Turcios and Nájeras families were once close friends. In 1987, however, they began feuding—some say it resulted from a dispute about land, others say it arose from a cockfight in the town square. Whatever the cause, the feud has taken more than 30 lives since it began. The families signed a public truce sponsored by the military on 2 June 1996. During the truce ceremony, the two families provided ample evidence of the spread of arms in Olancho, a situation no doubt encouraged in part by former Contra soldiers. Among the weapons relinquished at the ceremony were 13 AK-47s, a Mauser, and a 30-30 carbine.

As could be expected, each side kept a supply stashed away, and after a couple of quiet years the families were at it again. In 1999, on 15 May, José Galeas Turcios was shot dead, reputedly at the hands of Javier and Luis Nájera Martínez, who were captured. The fact that a Turcios is running for national Congress in the upcoming elections may inspire that family to hold off on avenging young José's murder—for the time being at least. But likely as not we haven't heard the last of the Turcios and the Nájeras.

tonio de Pacura, and ask around for Juan Antuñez, Chavelito, or anyone else who can serve as a guide for the six-hour horseback ride or hike to the site via the Montaña de Botadero to the village of Cayo Sierra, and then on to the ruins along the Río Naranjal. This route formed part of the old Camino Real to Trujillo in colonial times, and passes near the famed Minas de Tayaco, one of the first mines dug by the Spanish conquistadors. Parts of the trail, passing through the densest rainforest, are literally three meters deep, worn down by centuries of use.

Extensive, solid stone Los Encuentros, located in what is now a cow pasture, is merely the largest of literally dozens of ruins scattered throughout this wild region near the border of the Colón and Olancho Departments. Thought to have been built by the ancestors of the Pech, the ruins of Los Encuentros was used as a refuge and ritual site for the Indians at least until the early 1800s, and possibly later.

From Los Encuentros it is possible to hike out via the Río Sico to La Balsa in two days, passing through stretches of old growth jungle and pine forest, filled with wildlife and ruins.

According to satellite forest cover maps of Honduras, to the northwest of Los Encuentros is a huge stretch of virgin tropical forest, blanketing the mountains separating this part of Olancho from the Valle de Aguán around Tocoa. Hiking out here would be a serious proposition in wilderness adventure and should be contemplated only with a local guide hired around Pacura or in El Carbón.

El Carbón

On the highway between San Esteban and the coast, in the jungle-clad mountains near the border of the Olancho and Colón departments, is the village of Santa María del Carbón, usually just called El Carbón. It's one of the most traditional Pech communities left in Honduras. With the Peace Corps' help, a couple of small, humble huts were built for visitors, and a few local men can serve as guides into the nearby mountains.

After arriving in El Carbón, it's best to ask around for Linton Escobar, the main guide and really the only guide in town who is comfortable dealing with outsiders. A few of the other young guides are fairly friendly too, if you speak Spanish and make an effort to talk to them. One, Na-

lies the cattle town of San Esteban, founded in 1805 and named in honor of Padre Esteban Verdelete, martyred by Pech Indians in the early 1600s. Because of its reputation for violence (dating from colonial times, apparently), most people don't spend much time in San Esteban, although local Peace Corps volunteers claim it's actually not that bad a place. Beyond the gas station and few *comedores* on the highway, there's little reason to stop by, unless you're planning to hike across the mountains to Culmí.

Los Encuentros

West of San Esteban is Los Encuentros, a large pre-Columbian ruin possibly built by the ancestors of the Pech. To visit Los Encuentros, hitch a ride from San Esteban to the town of **San An-**

tividad, is also a *curandero* (healer) and knows more than most about the plants of the forest. Guides usually cost around US$7 per day. You can also ask for the local Peace Corps volunteer, *voluntario/voluntaria del Cuerpo de Paz,* who usually lives next to the visitors' huts and is invariably more than happy to help arrange guides and talk about the town and region. The simple but clean huts, built with mud walls in the traditional Pech style, rent for US$4 pp a night. Meals can be arranged, but it's best to come with your own food as well.

Any buses passing between Juticalpa and Tocoa or Trujillo can drop visitors at El Carbón. At last check three or four a day drove in each direction, but this seems to change frequently. The last bus in either direction usually passes El Carbón around 2 p.m.

To get to El Carbón from the north coast, the best bet is to go to Corocito, a turnoff on the Tocoa-Trujillo highway, and wait for the next bus heading to Olancho. The last passes around

A Pech craftsman shows off one of his wares—a traditional Pech drum

noon. Corocito is 50 kilometers from El Carbón on a dreadfully potholed dirt road. It's better, and safer, to wait at Corocito than in the unpleasant and not altogether safe roadside town of Bonito Oriental, a few km past Corocito on the road to El Carbón.

From Juticalpa, get a bus to Tocoa, Trujillo, or La Ceiba, or hitch from the turnoff on the Juticalpa-Catacamas road. If you're on a bus, be sure to let the driver know you want to get off at El Carbón, as the bus doesn't always stop there.

Near El Carbón

The surrounding **Sierra del Carbón,** a proposed protected area, is a northern extension of the Sierra de Agalta running from El Carbón northeast into the Mosquitia, home to extensive tropical jungles and pine and cloud forests within a day or two's hike from El Carbón.

Very few tourists come out this way, but Linton Escobar in El Carbón can guide a trip for you or find you another guide, all charging around US$7 per day. One favorite destination, set in a jungle-clad valley a few hours' hike from El Carbón is **La Cascada,** a gushing 80-meter waterfall on the Río Ojo de Agua, a tributary of the Río Sico. The hike from town leads through secondary forest, across fields, and into a steep, narrow valley blanketed by virgin jungle.

About an hour of slippery, treacherous hiking from the mouth of the valley brings you to **Lago de la Sirena,** a small lake at the base of the torrential falls, surrounded on three sides by lush hillsides. The lake is named for a spirit who allegedly protects the cuyamel fish. Those who catch cuyamel can expect an unpleasant visit from the Sirena in their dreams. For the full experience, take a swim out to a rock in the lake directly in front of the falls and feel the power of the blast. It literally takes your breath away. La Cascada can be visited in one long day, but the mouth of the canyon is a good spot to spend the night. If your Spanish is not up to interacting with the guide, you could try asking the local Peace Corps volunteer to come along and interpret.

Guides from El Carbón can take visitors on more adventurous treks up any of several peaks in the vicinity, including Cerro El Diablo, Cerro Jesús Cristo, and Cerro Alpes. From El Carbón the ecosystems change from pine forest to dense, broadleaf jungle, to cloud forest in the higher reaches, and even patches of elfin forest similar to that found on Sierra de Agalta mountaintops.

Near the village of **Agua Amarilla,** a few hours' hike from El Carbón, is a ruin of unknown origin covered with dense jungle, discovered in the mid-1990s. The large site, covering a couple of acres, is fronted by a large sloping wall, atop which are the remains of several structures and an altar.

LA MURALLA

In far western Olancho, near the border with Yoro, is the broad mountain range of La Muralla ("The Wall"), containing probably the most extensive untouched swath of cloud forest in the country outside of Sierra de Agalta. La Muralla National Park is particularly famous for birdwatching. It's a very unlucky or impatient visitor who doesn't get a glimpse of the renowned quetzal while at the park.

Unfortunately, due to the high incidence of armed robbery on the roads into La Unión both from the north coast and from Tegucigalpa, for the time being getting to La Muralla is a somewhat risky proposition. The worst stretch of road is between Salamá and La Unión, quaintly dubbed the "Corredor de la Muerte" by local newspapers, but the roads from La Unión down to Olanchito and over to Yoro are also risky. The bus currently running once a day from Tegucigalpa to La Unión is usually safe, but it has been hijacked in the past. If you've got a car, be sure to stop at Limones, then turn off the Juticalpa highway and ask the police or other drivers what the current situation is. You could consider doing what some locals do, hiring a policeman to literally ride shotgun with you to La Unión for a negotiable fee (maybe US$10). If this is your plan, go during the week, when more policemen are available at the Limones post, and get there early in the morning.

La Unión

A small logging town about 200 km each from Tegucigalpa and La Ceiba, set a couple of kilometers off the highway at an elevation of 800 meters, La Unión is the first stop for anyone going to visit La Muralla. Because of the current state of the road, the following information is not updated from 1996—take it for what you will.

Hotel La Muralla on the main street has bare rooms for US$2 s or US$4 d. Decent food is sold at **Merendero Mi Ranchito,** a concrete building with a thatched roof a couple of blocks toward the highway from the downtown park, as well as a couple of other *comedores.*

The **Cohdefor** office is helpful in arranging transport to La Muralla, and if a truck is going visitors are usually welcome to hop in. There's no gas station in town, but fuel is sold out of drums by various people—ask around.

Parque Nacional La Muralla

Covering 17,243 hectares between 900 and 2,064 meters, the park hosts forests ranging from pine on the lower fringes to pine mixed with liquidambar (sweet gum) at the middle elevations, to broadleaf cloud forest on the peaks. Thirty-seven mammal species have been spotted in the park, including jaguars, ocelots, white-faced and howler monkeys, and tapirs, as well as at least 150 bird species. Little biological investigation has taken place in the reserve, especially in the more remote reaches away from the visitors' center; it's likely other species will be identified.

La Muralla has a well-built visitors' center at 1,430 meters, offering three beds, displays on flora and fauna, and several detailed maps on the walls. Reservations for the beds (which are presently free of charge) are supposed to be made in the Cohdefor office in Tegucigalpa, tel. 223-0342 or 223-4796, though you may be able to arrange it in the La Unión office. Otherwise it's no problem to pitch a tent on the lawn out front. The trees in front of the visitors' center are great for birdwatching, especially in the early morning.

In the southwestern corner of the reserve a system of trails allows visitors to explore a section of the forest without a guide. The 3.7-km Pizote Trail makes a loop around a low peak, with several benches at strategic points to watch for birds. For the more ambitious, the 10-km Monte Escondido Trail descends into the Río Escondido Valley and up again into the higher reaches of the park. Getting to the lookout on Monte Escondido and back is a two-day trip, and a guide would be a good idea. The trees felled by Hurricane Mitch may still be blocking off this trail—ask at the Cohdefor office in La Unión.

Hikes deeper into the park, to the peaks of La Muralla (1,981 meters), Los Higuerales (1,985 meters), and Las Parras (2,064 meters), require guides and several days in the woods. Cohdefor can arrange guides for about US$7 per day, and permission is required to camp in the park.

The visitors' center is 14 km from La Unión, reached by a rough dirt road connecting La Unión to the village of El Díctamo farther west. Those without a car can walk from town three hours uphill through pine forest and coffee plantations, or try to hitch, although traffic is not frequent. The best option is to catch a ride with one of the Cohdefor trucks, which usually go to the park every day during the week. The topographical map covering the park is 1:50,000 La Unión 2861 II.

SOUTHERN HONDURAS

Although not much explored by the average tourist, there are, tucked away in the mountains and coastal plains of southern Honduras, a few hidden attractions worth seeking out, especially for those passing through on their way to Nicaragua or El Salvador. Highlights include the colonial mining towns of El Corpus and Yuscarán, the cigar factories of Danlí, the cloud-forested Sierra de la Botija, and the volcanic island of Amapala.

THE PACIFIC COAST

Honduras' Pacific coast is a scorchingly hot, dry plain facing the Golfo de Fonseca, which it shares with El Salvador and Nicaragua. Coastal beaches do exist, most notably at Cedeño near Choluteca, but they can't compare with those in nearby El Salvador or on Honduras' Caribbean coast. The region's struggling economy, one of the poorest in the country, is dominated by shrimp farming and cattle ranching.

Three major rivers—the Choluteca, Goascarán, and Nacaome—trisect the narrow Choluteca Plain. The country's only volcanoes are found here, the termination of the volcanic chain of the Colinas de Juacarán, beginning in El Salvador. Isla del Tigre (Amapala) is an example of one of these extinct volcanoes.

Much of the Pacific coastline is, or was, covered with mangrove swamps, but in recent years the growing shrimp-farming and cattle-ranching industries have severely threatened these fragile ecosystems. The **Bahía de Chismuyo** not far from the El Salvador border, is a protected area of mangroves in name, but shrimp farmers have been clamoring to be allowed to clear more land there. One of the country's most forceful environmental groups, the Committee for the Preservation of the Fauna and Flora of the Golfo de Fonseca (CODEFFAGOLF), wages an unending fight to halt the farmers' expansion.

SOUTHERN HONDURAS HIGHLIGHTS

- Visiting the colonial town of Yuscarán
- Touring a cigar factory in Danlí
- Admiring views over the Golfo de Fonseca from the volcanic peak of Isla del Tigre
- Hiking in the dry tropical forest and cloud forest of Sierra de la Botija, near San Marcos de Colón

---

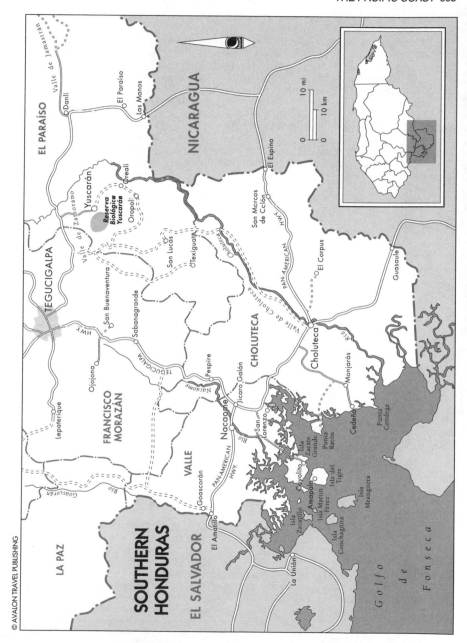

SOUTHERN HONDURAS

© AVALON TRAVEL PUBLISHING

The Choluteca Plain and surrounding hills have been heavily farmed for years, and the deforestation and massive use of pesticides and fertilizers combined to wreak havoc on the land. Desertification is advancing relentlessly in the south, and many *campesinos* have been forced to migrate to other parts of the country because the land is no longer arable.

One unavoidable fact about Choluteca is the heat. For much of the year, especially outside of the May-October rainy season, it is unbearably hot, often reaching temperatures as high as 40° C. Rainfall on the Pacific coast is not as intensive as on the Caribbean side, and the wet and dry seasons are much more clearly defined. The rains start in April or May and continue until November, while the remaining months are invariably cloudless.

CHOLUTECA

Although it's the fifth-largest city in Honduras, with about 100,000 residents, Choluteca feels more like an overgrown village. The colonial downtown area remains much as it was a few centuries ago, with its *parque central,* narrow cobblestone streets, and one-level, tile-roofed colonial buildings, most of which are in a sad state of disrepair.

The name Choluteca, which is thought to mean "broad valley," derives from the pre-conquest inhabitants of the region, the Chorotega Indians. The Chorotega, related to the Toltec, were relatively recent arrivals themselves, having migrated from Chiapas, Mexico, sometime before or around A.D. 1000.

The area around Choluteca was first explored by Andrés Niño, as part of a 1522 expedition led by Gil González Dávila up the west coast of Central America from Panama. Capt. Cristóbal de la Cueva founded Xérex de la Frontera— later called Choluteca—in 1541.

During colonial times Choluteca grew quickly, its economy driven by the active Pacific seaport and the rich mines of El Corpus, in the hills above Choluteca. The town was originally settled on the west side of the Río Choluteca, but after pirates sacked and torched the town in the 17th century, colonists relocated to the present site. Anyone interested in the history and legends of Choluteca and the region, and who read Spanish, should look for two books published in 1996, *Por Cuentas Aquí En Choluteca* and *Por Cuentas Aquí En El Corpus.* Also, Padre Jesús who works in the *casa cural* across from the Catedral is very knowledgeable on local history.

Local officials talk about restoring many of the colonial buildings downtown in an effort to boost the town's meager tourism potential, but they've yet to take action. The annual **Feria Patronal** of Choluteca, held 6-14 December, is reputed to be quite a bash, with lots of good food, music, dancing, and fireworks on the last night.

Orientation and Getting Around

Choluteca is essentially a one-story city, extending along dusty streets from the downtown square. It's built along the east bank of the Río Choluteca, and the highway to Tegucigalpa leaves Choluteca across an impressive-looking (but structurally questionable) suspension bridge.

The highway from Tegucigalpa, called the **Panamericana,** continues east bypassing downtown on its way to the Nicaraguan border. The city has two markets: the main, older one, **Mercado San Antonio,** is two blocks south of the square; the other, **Mercado Nuevo,** is six blocks farther south. Although Choluteca covers a lot of ground, most places of interest to travelers are within walking distance of the square in the northwest quadrant. One exception is the bus station, a dozen or so blocks southeast of the square. Taxis to the terminal and around town cost US 50 cents.

Sights

The **Catedral Inmaculada Concepción** on the square dates from at least 1643, the date on the baptismal font, but is thought to be older. The wood-paneled ceiling resembles the hull of a boat. In 1914 the facade was rebuilt to its present form.

Two blocks east of the cathedral is the older **Iglesia de La Merced,** also built at an unknown date but thought to have been erected in the middle or late 16th century. It features eye-catching twisted (Salomonic) columns on the outside. In colonial times the surrounding neighborhood housed the city's Indian and black population, who prayed at the church. The church is normally only open on Saturday.

The colonial building on the southwest corner of the square is the former home of famed native son José Cecilio del Valle (1777-1834). The building now houses the local library, but the Instituto Hondureño de Antropología e Historia (IHAH) has plans to rebuild it and turn it into a museum. The statue in the middle of the square is of Del Valle.

Accommodations
Of the less expensive hotels in town, **Hotel Santa Rosa,** tel. 882-0355, and **Hotel Bonsai,** tel. 882-2648, are both good values. The Santa Rosa, next to the old market, charges US$4 s or US$7.50 d for clean rooms—each with fan and

private bathroom—around a small courtyard, while the Bonsai, half a block south of the square, charges US$5.50 s or d for a room with fan and private bathroom, or US$10s or d for a newer room with a/c and TV.

One block south of the road leading out of town to the Panamericana is **Hotel Pacífico,** tel. 882-0838, and across the street is **Hotel Pacífico Anexo,** tel. 882-3249. The original charges US$7.50 s or US$10 d with private bathroom, more with a/c, while the slightly more rustic Anexo rents for US$5.50 s or US$7.50 d, more with a/c and TV.

For a bit more luxury at still reasonable prices, head to **Hotel Pierre,** one long block south of the

JOSÉ CECILIO DEL VALLE~PHILOSOPHER OF CENTRAL AMERICAN UNITY

Known among Hondurans as "El Sabio," or "The Wise One," José Cecilio del Valle is renowned as one of Central America's first great intellectuals, a sort of Thomas Jefferson to Francisco Morazán's George Washington. Del Valle was born on 22 November 1777 to a wealthy landowning family. As a youth he moved to Guatemala for his education, and at the age of 23 he graduated as a lawyer from the Universidad de San Carlos. At that time, the first calls for independence from Spain could be heard echoing through Central America, and Del Valle quickly plunged into the nascent movement with a passion, editing the pro-independence newspaper *El Amigo de la Patria* and leading the Partido Evolucionista.

When independence was officially declared on 15 September 1821, Del Valle was on the scene at the Palacio de Guatemala and was one of the writers of the Act of Independence. He initially opposed the annexation of Central America by Mexico under Iturbide but agreed to act as a deputy to the congress in Mexico. As a re-

lentless defender of the rights of Central America, Del Valle irritated Iturbide, who had him thrown in jail for six months. When the empire fell in 1824, Del Valle regained his freedom and was elected deputy in the new congress of the Central American Union.

Conservative Manuel Arce then appointed El Sabio as vice president, but he refused to accept the office, campaigning against the illegitimacy of Arce's regime. When Arce was overthrown in 1829, Del Valle competed against independence hero Francisco Morazán for the Central American presidency but lost. Del Valle finally won the 1834 elections but died before he could take office.

Throughout his career Del Valle was legendary for his intelligent and humanitarian proposals and his tireless efforts to unite the Americas. In 1822 he published a manifesto on his Pan-American beliefs, which ends with the words: "America from this moment will be my exclusive occupation— America by day when I write, by night when I think. The study most worthy of Americans is America."

square, tel. 882-0676. It is unremarkable, but air-conditioned rooms with TV and private bathroom rent for US$11 s, US$14 d.

The motel-style **Hotel La Fuente,** on the Panamericana between the bridge and the Boulevard, tel. 882-0263, fax 882-0273, has 40 clean, modern rooms—each with a/c, TV, and telephone—around a large pool for US$34 s or d. The hotel is convenient for those traveling through with a car and is popular with people in Choluteca on business.

By far the classiest and most expensive setup in town is **Hacienda Gualiqueme,** just across the suspension bridge on the highway toward Tegucigalpa, on the right side, tel. 882-2750, fax 882-3720. Rooms are spread across extensive grassy grounds, each with stained wood beams, tile floors, and high ceilings. Amenities include a/c, cable TV, direct-dial telephones, a good restaurant, pool, outdoor patio, spa, and a helpful staff. Rooms cost US$48 s, US$54 d, or US$66 suite. Less expensive packages are available for multi-day stays.

Food and Entertainment
Pizza King, a couple of doors down from Hotel Pierre, tel. 882-0676, makes respectable, inexpensive pizza as well as burgers and sandwiches. Open daily 10 a.m.-7 p.m., closed Sundays. **Pizza Capri,** around the corner, is also supposed to be good.

One of those classic general store-restaurants where everyone stops in to catch up on the local gossip, **Comedor Central** on the square is a good place for snacks, breakfasts, light meals, and beers. Open Mon.-Sat. 6 a.m.-10 p.m. and on Sunday afternoon.

Cafe Frosty, two blocks south of the square on 3 Calle, serves cheap, unexceptional breakfasts, *comida corriente,* snacks, and ice cream.

One of the best restaurants in town is **El Conquistador** on the Panamericana, tel. 882-3308, offering seating under a covered patio. The food can take a while, but it's worth the wait for the well-prepared seafood, steaks, beef stroganoff, soups, and sandwiches for US$3-6 per entree. Open daily 11 a.m. until all the customers are gone, usually around 10 or 11 p.m.

If you're up for a movie, head for one of the town's two theaters; **Cine Caribe** and **Cine Rex** are both near the market.

Services
Banco Atlántida will exchange dollars but not traveler's checks, while Bancahsa will exchange both. Correos, several blocks southeast of the square, has EMS fast-mail service. Next door is Hondutel, which receives faxes at tel. 882-0053.

Policlínica Ferguson, on 3 Calle and Av. Central, tel. 882-0281 or 882-0300, can help with basic health problems.

Getting There and Away
Astrasur has frequent buses between the main Choluteca terminal, a dozen blocks southeast of the square, and Mercado Mayoreo on Comayagüela (Tegucigalpa), US$2.25. Mi Esperanza, tel. 882-0841, offers the same service at the same price from a private terminal a couple of blocks north of the main terminal. Bonanza, tel. 882-0831, runs a regular local service to Tegucigalpa for US$1.65 and also has a direct *lujo* service four times a day for US$5, tel. 882-2712. Dandy, tel. 882-0204, runs eight regular buses a day to Tegucigalpa from the main Choluteca terminal.

Buses to Guasaule on the Nicaraguan border leave from the Mercado Nuevo daily every hour between 5 a.m. and 5 p.m., US$1. The buses invariably swing by the main terminal to pick up passengers before leaving town. It's an hour-and-a-half ride, and the bus drops passengers off right at the bridge over the border.

Buses leave the main terminal for San Marcos de Colón frequently between 4 a.m. and 6 p.m. for US 60 cents. From San Marcos you can continue on to the Nicaraguan border at El Espino. Buses also frequently leave the main terminal heading to El Amatillo at the Salvadoran border. All buses leaving from the terminal invariably take a spin through town to look for more passengers, so if you can't get to the terminal it's often possible to flag one down. Taxis to the terminal cost US 50 cents from the square.

CHOLUTECA USEFUL TELEPHONE NUMBERS

Police: 882-0951, 882-0966, or dial 199
Fire Department: 882-0503, or dial 198
Hospital: 882-0231

Buses to El Corpus leave regularly between 6:30 a.m. and 5 p.m. from the Mercado Nuevo, charging US 50 cents for the one-hour ride.

The main highways leaving Choluteca toward Guasaule (47 km), San Marcos de Colón (56 km), El Amatillo (85 km), and Tegucigalpa (142 km) are all paved and in relatively good condition.

CEDEÑO

The Pacific coast town of Cedeño is a low-budget Honduran beach getaway, a fairly seedy collection of worn wooden buildings lining a reasonably decent stretch of sand. The few restaurant/discos in town are usually packed on the weekends and deserted during the week. In spite of being on the protected gulf, waves can get fierce, depending on the tide and the season. Better, more isolated beaches than the one in town lie within walking distance, just a few minutes in either direction.

Practicalities
Of the few extremely minimal hotels in Cedeño, the best seems to be a concrete place next to Restaurante Miramar, charging US$4 s or d with fan and private bathroom. The Hotel Las Vegas and Hotel Cedeño are grim.

Restaurante Miramar has about the best food in town and turns into a hopping disco on weekends.

Four direct buses leave Cedeño daily for Tegucigalpa, the last in early afternoon, charging US$2.30. Buses frequently depart for Choluteca; US 50 cents. The last bus out of town to Choluteca leaves at 4:30 p.m.

The 34-km potholed road to the highway passes through sugar plantations and the dirt-poor town of Mojaras. Along the way are turnoffs to Punta Ratón and Puesta del Sol, where reportedly good beaches can be found if you can get a ride out there. The turnoff to Cedeño is five kilometers west of Choluteca on the highway to Tegucigalpa.

AMAPALA

The only town on the volcanic island of Isla del Tigre, Amapala was once Honduras' primary Pacific port, but it has long since been superseded by Puerto de Henecán near San Lorenzo. Amapala is now a decaying 19th-century relic, looking for a way to survive. The town boasts no obvious tourist attractions, apart from a couple of mediocre beaches nearby, though some travelers find the slightly surreal, lost-in-time feel of the place fascinating.

Andrés Niño first sighted Isla del Tigre in 1522, but the Spanish didn't settle there initially. Pirates used the island as a hideout until 1770, when the governor of San Miguel, El Salvador, ordered a town built. For a short time during the presidency of Marco Aurelio Soto, Amapala functioned as the capital of Honduras.

Although subject to the same heat as the Choluteca plain, the island is often graced by an ocean breeze, making the climate more hospitable. Isla del Tigre is six km in diameter, and the volcanic peak is 760 meters high. Until the early 1990s, a U.S. Drug Enforcement Agency (DEA) contingent staffed a base at the peak, but now it's deserted.

Practicalities
Right at the end of the dock is the only actual "hotel" in Amapala, such as it is; the **Pensión Internacional** offers ultra-basic but spacious rooms upstairs above a family's house; US$2 pp. The balcony makes a good spot to hang out and contemplate the bay.

El Faro Victoria next to the dock has decent burgers, fish, chicken, and other snacks for US$2-4 per meal. The friendly owner, who speaks a bit of English picked up from the U.S. officials who used to be stationed on the island, also rents out rooms for US$6. Open for lunch and dinner Fri.-Sun., dinner only Mon.-Thursday.

None of the banks in town exchange foreign currency. It's often a good idea to bring a lot of change as breaking big bills on the island can be a problem.

Boats across to Coyolito should be only US 50 cents for the 10-minute trip, when going with other passengers, but the boatmen will invariably try to charge you more. From the dock in Coyolito, buses leave to San Lorenzo every 90 minutes between 5:30 a.m. and 3 p.m.; US 50 cents.

The 31-km paved (but badly potholed) road to Coyolito turns off the Tegucigalpa highway two km west of San Lorenzo and passes shrimp farms and mangrove swamps on its way out to the dock.

Around the Island

A dirt road of roughly 15 km rings Isla del Tigre, so named for one of the island's long-extinct animal denizen. Many extremely poor *campesino* families live in simple huts along the road, scraping a living from little agricultural plots on the mountainside. From Amapala heading southwest (counterclockwise), about 20 minutes from town by foot and just past the Honduran military post, a dirt road turning inland leads to the top of the volcano, the site of the now deserted DEA base. The walk takes about two hours of hard hiking, and the views, especially in the early morning when the sky is clear, are superb.

About 45 minutes from Amapala on foot, not far past the mountain road, is **Playa Grande,** a swath of black sand facing El Salvador and lined with several fish restaurants. At the north end of the beach is La Cueva de la Sirena, an interesting red volcanic rock cave with two entrances, one on the ocean. Local legend has it Sir Francis Drake hid a stash of his ill-gotten booty here. A few houses are for rent at Playa Grande for a negotiable but not excessive amount, depending on the number of people in the group. Usually an entire house costs around US$15 for the night.

Another half-hour south on the main road is **Playa Negra,** where **Hotel Villa Playa Negra** sits on a hill above the beach. The 18 rooms set on a hillside above the beach, facing Isla Meanguera and the open ocean beyond, rent for US$24 d with fan or US$42 d with a/c. The restaurant has good food and a swimming pool. For reservations call the hotel's office in Tegucigalpa at 232-0632; the staff will pick you up at the dock in Amapala.

Continuing around from Playa Negra, there's not a lot to see along the road but a shrimp-packing plant and a few *campesino* settlements. Several beaches are reportedly accessible by trail from the road, including **Playa Brava,** which is said to have decent waves.

One bus circles the island each day, and there's some traffic in the morning—good for hitching rides—but in the afternoon it's usually deserted.

SAN LORENZO AND THE TEGUCIGALPA HIGHWAY

San Lorenzo

A hot, unattractive town of 17,000 on the gulf, San Lorenzo's main reasons for existence are nearby Puerto de Henecán, the country's third-largest port after Puerto Cortés and Puerto Castilla, and the shrimp-packing plants in town.

Should you be unfortunate enough to have to stop in San Lorenzo for the night, the waterfront **Hotel Miramar,** tel. 881-2039, fax 881-2106, offers by far the best accommodations in town. It's often patronized by visiting businesspeople and also has a restaurant. Air-conditioned rooms with two beds cost US$25 s or d with a/c and TV.

One block toward the water from the square is the far less expensive **Hotel Piasandu,** where rooms in a family's house rent for US$3 pp. Another cheapie is **Hotel Perla del Pacífico.**

Several restaurants beyond Hotel Miramar on the waterfront serve up decent seafood, and there are a few basic *comedores* in the center of town.

Both Banco Atlántida and Banco de Occidente will change dollars.

Buses running between Choluteca and El Amatillo pull into the town market. If you're looking to catch a Tegucigalpa bus, it's best to go out to the highway and flag down one coming from Choluteca.

Many casual travelers may end up in San Lorenzo in order to get a bus to Coyolito, where boats cross the bay to Amapala. The buses leave the town market daily every 90 minutes between 8:30 a.m. and 4:30 p.m.; US 50 cents.

Jicaro Galán

Jicaro Galán is little more than a few buildings at the junction of the Tegucigalpa highway and the Panamericana, which runs from El Salvador through Choluteca and on to Nicaragua. On the Tegucigalpa side of the junction is **El Oasis Colonial,** tel. 81-4007 or 895-4007, fax 895-4006, with motel-style air-conditioned rooms around a pool for US$39 d. Jicaro Galán is 43 km from Choluteca and 99 km from Tegucigalpa.

El Amatillo

A blastingly hot and unattractive border post in the midst of desolate hills, El Amatillo is a place to depart as quickly as possible. The border is open daily 6 a.m.-10 p.m. The nearest town in El Salvador is Santa Rosa de Lima, reached by frequent bus until late afternoon. Most buses to Tegucigalpa and Choluteca stop running after 4 p.m. If you do get stuck, there's **Hotel y Comedor Remar** near the Texaco station. El Amatillo is 42 km from Jicaro Galán on a paved two-lane highway.

Pespire
Set in a river valley just above the Choluteca plain, 82 km from Tegucigalpa, Pespire is a small, quiet colonial town with a lovely domed church and a historic two-story government building, both on the square.

Sabanagrande
Farther up into the hills is Sabanagrande, 42 km from Tegucigalpa, a town of 4,000. In precolonial times, the town was known as Apacunca, meaning "place with washing water" in Lenca. The Spaniards first settled the town in the late 18th century, as an extension of the mining

early morning in Pespire

boomtown Ojojona. The **Iglesia de Rosario** on the square has an elegant wooden roof and balcony. The best food in town is at **Comedor Los Tucanes,** on the highway. You'll notice lots of places advertising *rosquillas*—this is a crunchy bread snack eaten with coffee, for which the town is known. Buses to Tegucigalpa cost US 50 cents, and pass frequently on the highway.

EL CORPUS AND THE NICARAGUAN BORDER

El Corpus
A jaunt up the dusty roads to the colonial mining town of El Corpus is a worthwhile day trip while in southern Honduras, for the adventurous. During the colonial era the town became the center of one of the richest mining regions in the country, and some mines in the surrounding hills still operate. One old mine is located directly behind the church. No formal hotels or restaurants operate in the small town, but you can find inexpensive and basic food and lodging if you ask around.

The cobblestone streets and colonial architecture are reason enough to see El Corpus, but the surprisingly lush countryside all around the town adds to its feel of being an oasis in the hot, dry south. Many paths lead up into the hills, including to a viewpoint where you can see out over the Golfo de Fonseca, into Nicaragua, and sometimes as far as El Salvador. Two particularly good hikes are to **Cerro Calaire,** two or three hours away, or a longer hike via the *aldea* of Agua Fría to **Cerro Guanacaure.** From the top of Cerro Guanacaure, covered with a sort of dry tropical forest, hikers have great views over the volcanoes of Nicaragua and the Golfo de Fonseca. Agua Fría is about a three-hour hike from El Corpus, and the mountaintop is another hour or two farther. Locals will be happy to point the way.

The turnoff to El Corpus is from the new loop road between the exits to San Marcos Colón and to Guasaule. The bumpy dirt road to El Corpus is 15 kilometers long. Buses to Choluteca leave about every hour until mid-afternoon for the hour-long ride, charging US 50 cents.

Guasaule
A border town not much more attractive than El Amatillo on the Salvadoran side, Guasaule is

the easier and more popular of the two crossings into Nicaragua from Choluteca. Buses (US$1) drive frequently between Choluteca and Guasaule daily between 6 a.m. and 10 p.m., which is also the operating hours of the border offices. Direct buses to Tegucigalpa leave several times a day until early afternoon, charging US$2. Minibuses run directly between Guasaule and El Amatillo, US$3.50, for those just transiting through Honduras.

Should you be forced to spend the night in Guasaule, **Hotel Los Tres Hermanas,** the last building on the Honduran side, is not too bad. Across the street, decent food can be found at **Cafetería La Aurora.**

Just past town is the border bridge, over the Río Guasaule. Half a kilometer farther is the Nicaraguan border post, then another five kilometers is the town of Somotillo. From here other buses continue elsewhere inside Nicaragua.

SAN MARCOS DE COLÓN

San Marcos de Colón, a small town set at an elevation of 960 meters, is mainly visited by travelers on their way through to Nicaragua. The town itself is nothing to write home about, even though the climate is pleasant enough, but nearby, Sierra de la Botija harbors pristine streches of cloud forest and dry tropical forest, great for day trips or multi-day hikes.

Practicalities

Hotelito Mi Esperanza, two blocks off the square, tel. 888-3062, has clean, tile-floor rooms for US$3 s or d for one bed with shared bathroom, US$4.50 with private bathroom, US$8 for two beds.

On the highway back toward Choluteca, at Km 173, is **Hotel Monte Lorenza,** tel. 887-4819, a small rustic spot perched on the hillside with a great view of the gulf. It charges US$27-40 per cabin.

The best food in town is at **Restaurante Bonanza,** half a block up the hill from the back of the church, with an extensive menu including spaghetti, shrimp, *pinchos,* nachos, and, believe it or not, gyros, for US$1.50-5 per meal. Right near the bus station is **La Exquisita,** serving delicious *enchiladas* and tacos, and even pizza

on occasion. The owner manages a refuge of sorts in the Sierra de la Botija and is a good source of information on the region.

DeliFruit Garomar, one block off the square, has *licuados,* juices, *baleadas, comida corriente,* and burgers at low prices.

The Hondutel and Correos offices are next to the market. Banco Atlántida and Bancahorro both change dollars but no traveler's checks or *córdobas.*

Getting There and Away

Direct buses to Tegucigalpa from San Marcos leave from the Mi Esperanza terminal next to the market five times daily between 6 a.m. and 4:45 p.m., US$2. Buses to Choluteca leave frequently between 4:45 a.m. and 3:30 p.m., US 60 cents.

Colectivo taxis to the border at El Espino, 11 km away by paved road, cost US 50 cents, although drivers will often try to charge you more returning to town from the border. From San Marcos, the taxis leave from next to the market, right by the buses. A bus usually runs the route to the border from San Marcos at 10 a.m. and 1 p.m.

The border offices, infrequently used compared to Guasaule (much to the chagrin of the local officials), are open daily 8 a.m.-5 p.m.

Sierra de la Botija

This little-known forest mountain region near the border of Nicaragua is one of the great undiscovered treasures of southern Honduras. Much of the forest is pine and oak, while seven peaks above 1500 meters have patches of cloud forest on top. On the lower slopes descending into Nicaragua are patches of primary tropical dry forest, a rare find these days in Honduras. The highest elevation is 1735 meters. As of early 2000, the Honduran government is considering declaring the area a natural reserve covering around 10,000 hectares. The mountains here give birth to the Río Coco, Central America's longest river.

The forests of Sierra de la Botija are really excellent for spotting birds of all kinds, blue morpho butterflies, and several mammals (even a jaguar not long ago, though it seems to have moved on). White-faced monkeys are seen all over the forest. Several waterfalls are found in the sierra, including **La Cascada de la Mina,** near an old mine shaft, and **La Loma del Salto.**

In 2000, a Peace Corps volunteer was hard at work in the forest with a group of locals building an interpretive trail up to one of the cloud forest peaks, Cerro de Águila. Plenty of less well-trod trails criss-cross the forest. The owner of Restaurante La Exquisita in San Marcos runs a nature refuge called **Ojochal** in the mountains, with a stone cabin for visitors. Ask at her restaurant in San Marcos for details.

The best access to the mountains is via the village of **Duyusupo,** reached by twice-daily buses from San Marcos. From here locals will happily guide visitors anywhere they'd like to go in the park, including up Cerro de Águila or to the waterfalls. Another way in, closer to the source of the Río Coco, is taking the highway back toward Choluteca, and turning off to the *aldea* of **Comalí.** The Cohdefor office in San Marcos can supply more information on the park and may be able to help out with rides.

DEPARTMENT OF EL PARAÍSO

The rolling hills and broad plains of the El Paraíso department in southeastern Honduras have long been favored by Hondurans for their rich agricultural potential and mineral wealth. The valleys of Jamastrán and Moroceli are dotted with farms and cattle ranches, and the surrounding hills are filled with coffee plantations.

The climate in El Paraíso is generally temperate and comfortable, with most villages and towns located between 800 and 1,000 meters in elevation. Several major river systems are either born in or pass through El Paraíso, including the Río Choluteca, the Río Coco on the border with Nicaragua, and the Río Guayambre, one of the major tributaries of the Río Patuca. Adventurers can begin trips in the department of El Paraíso into Olancho and Gracias a Diós, along either the Patuca or Coco Rivers.

DANLÍ

A sizable city of 116,000, Danlí lies in the center of the Valle de Cuzcateca, which extends south to the town of El Paraíso, and is not far from the rich Valle de Jamastrán. Apart from the cigar industry in Danlí, cattle ranching and coffee production are the region's economic mainstays.

Sights
La Iglesia de la Inmaculada Concepción, on the main *parque central* and pleasingly flanked by palms and other trees, was built in the early 19th century at the end of the colonial era. Inside are five simple wood and gilt *retablos* (altarpieces). On the opposite side of the square is the

Museo del Cabildo, housed in a decrepit two-story building built in 1857. It features an odd assortment of pre-Columbian and colonial-era trinkets and an old caretaker who will happily tell you about them if your Spanish is up to it.

Danlí is home to a burgeoning cigar industry. A dozen or so factories operate in the vicinity of the city, including Honduran Cuban Cigars, Cuban Honduran Tobacco, Placencia Tobacco, Central American Cigar, Tabacalera Occidental, and Puros Indios. **Honduran Cuban Cigars,** tel. 883-2089, fax 883-2294, an excellent hand-rolling factory on the road leading from town to El Paraíso, gives tours of its factory with advance notice. It also has a store in Tegucigalpa.

The **Festival de Maiz,** held annually between 23 August and 1 September, is Danlí's major yearly party. Featured are music and dancing, and many different corn products for sale, including *chicha* (corn liquor), soups, *nacatamales, mantucas, atole* (a warm corn drink), and *totopostes.*

Because of the large cowboy population in and around Danlí, the town sports several saddle and leather shops, which can turn out good-quality products with several days' advance order.

Accommodations
Two inexpensive hotels, both next to the gas stations at the entrance from El Paraíso, are **Hotel Apolo,** tel. 893-2177, US$4 s and US$8 d with private bathroom, and the more run-down **Hotel Danlí** across the street, US$3.50 s with private bathroom.

Hotel La Esperanza, tel. 883-2106, also near the gas stations, has nicer rooms around a one-story interior courtyard for US$8 s, US$12 d with private bathroom and fan, or a bit more with a/c and cable TV. Parking is available.

On the highway bypassing Danlí between Tegucigalpa and El Paraíso is **Gran Hotel Granada,** tel. 883-2499, fax 883-2485, a one-story motel-style building favored by visiting businesspeople, with modern, comfortable rooms for US$22 pp with TV, hot water, and fans, or US$75 d for newer rooms with a/c. The hotel has a cafeteria and restaurant.

THE CIGAR CAPITAL OF HONDURAS

B ecause of its reliable climate, with an average temperature of 24° C (75° F) and an average 75% humidity, the region surrounding Danlí is considered a natural humidor, perfect for cigar production. Taking advantage of these ideal conditions are eight cigar factories, and more may be coming to capitalize on the boom in cigar smoking in the U.S. and Europe.

A few of the factories use mainly locally grown leaves to make a midrange, inexpensive cigar, while others blend leaves from Brazil, Panama, Costa Rica, the Dominican Republic, Nicaragua, and (believe it or not) Connecticut and Pennsylvania in the United States to create a hand-rolled, top-quality stogie, prized by connoisseurs and highly rated in *Cigar Aficionado* magazine.

Wherever the leaves were grown, when they first arrive at the factories, they are stacked in piles *(pilones)*, sprayed with water, and left to sit for several months. Because of a chemical reaction in the leaves, the *pilones* literally cook themselves, reaching temperatures of 45° C. Each factory has its own master in charge of the *pilones*, who decides when the leaves have been properly cured and are ready to roll. This idiosyncratic process is probably the most crucial in establishing a certain cigar's flavor—two factories can buy the same leaves at the same time and because they cure them differently, produce completely different-tasting cigars.

After leaving the *pilones*, workers remove the veins by hand from the leaves in a separate room, and the leaves are again sprayed and stacked. Rolling is accomplished in two stages: first the filler leaves, usually four of them, are rolled and cut to shape, and then put in a mold overnight. The next day the wrapper leaf—often an Ecuadoran Sumatra—is put on, and the cigar is moved into the humidor room for storage.

Because of the current rage of cigars in the United States and Europe, cigar factories are experiencing severe shortages in quality tobacco leaf, as the plant is notoriously tricky to grow properly. According to experts, to receive leaves for production now, a factory should have placed orders six years ago, thus none of the factories have enough tobacco to fill their bulging order sheets. Just about every cigar produced in Danlí has already been sold before even being rolled.

Almost all cigars rolled in Danlí are exported and are very difficult to come by in Honduras. Three places in Tegucigalpa to purchase Danlí cigars are Tobacco Road Tavern, Tabaco Fino, and Casa Havana. Cigars rolled at the Flor de Copán factory in Santa Rosa de Copán, of a somewhat lower grade, are available in many tourist gift shops. If you can arrange a tour with one of the factories around Danlí, you may be lucky enough to be allowed into the *bodega* to buy a box of your choice.

Honduran cigar rollers

Food

Of the several restaurants in the center of town, **Rincón Colonial,** tel. 883-3390, is about the best. A block north of the square, with patio seating, the restaurant offers a large menu of reasonably priced Honduran standards, like *anafre* (bean-dip appetizer, US$2), *pinchos* (US$4), or good sandwiches (US$3.50). Full meals with chicken, steamed pork, or beef served with baked potato, salad, and rice, go for US$5. Open Tues.-Sun. 11 a.m.-10 p.m.

Pepylus, one block north of the church, tel. 883-2103, has similar meals for similar prices, with tables in a quiet indoor courtyard. Open daily 8 a.m.-10 p.m.

Restaurante Kuan Ming, two blocks from the square on Calle Canal, tel. 883-2105, serves decent Cantonese food (or the Honduran version thereof, at least) for US$2-4 per meal. Open daily 9 a.m.-10 p.m.

On the main avenue between the square and the bus terminal is **Pollos La Cesta,** serving tasty chicken, as well as other *típico* meals, for not much money. Open daily 8 a.m.-4 p.m. and 5-11 p.m.

Licuados Gloria, next to Hotel Apolo, has *licuados,* juices, sweet breads, snacks, and inexpensive *comida corriente.*

Services

Bancahsa, Banco de Occidente, and Banco Atlántida all change dollars and sometimes traveler's checks. Hondutel and Correos are just off the park. The Correos offers EMS fast-mail service.

Getting There and Away

All buses leave Danlí from the central bus terminal near the exit of town toward Tegucigalpa. Discua, tel. 883-2217, and Emtra de Oriente both run buses every hour or so to Tegucigalpa. Buses run 5 a.m.-6 p.m., US$1.25 for the local service and US$2 for the express service. Frequent buses ply the route back and forth to El Paraíso for US 50 cents. Transportes Mi Empresa has four buses a day from Danlí to Nueva Palestina, where boats can be found down the nearby Río Patuca into the Mosquitia, US$2.25 for the three-and-a-half-hour ride.

Tegucigalpa is 93 km from Danlí by a well-maintained two-lane highway. Continuing past Danlí toward Nicaragua, the smooth paved road continues through El Paraíso to the Nicaraguan border at Las Manos, 30 km from Danlí.

EL PARAÍSO AND THE NICARAGUAN BORDER

A mid-sized town 18 km from Danlí at one end of the Valle de Cuzcateca, El Paraíso doesn't offer much beyond its proximity to the Nicaraguan border at Las Manos, 12 km up the road.

Should you need to spend the night in town, **Hotel Isis,** on the square, tel. 893-4251, has clean rooms for US$7 s or US$10 d with private bathroom, fan, and TV. The hotel also has a parking lot and a decent restaurant.

Banco Atlántida on the park will change U.S. dollars, but not traveler's checks or Nicaraguan *córdobas.* The best bet for changing to or from *córdobas* is at the border itself. The bank can advance cash on a Visa card.

A gas station at the highway junction in town can give you a last fill-up if you're on your way to the border.

Minibuses to the border leave every hour or so from the terminal until 4 p.m., charging US 25 cents. *Colectivo* taxis fitting four passengers will go for US$3.50.

Buses to Danlí leave frequently, charging US 50 cents. A few buses daily drive straight through from El Paraíso to Tegucigalpa for US$1.40.

Las Manos

The Nicaraguan-Honduran border at Las Manos is a collection of huts along the highway with a large gate across the middle, in the midst of green hills dotted with fields of coffee. Both the Honduran and Nicaraguan immigration and customs offices are open 8 a.m.-noon and 1:30-5 p.m.

Also at the border are a Hondutel office, *casa de cambio, comedor,* and *pulpería.* Buses continue into Nicaragua every hour or so from the border

---

DANLÍ TELEPHONE NUMBERS

Police: 883-2224, 883-2253, or dial 199
Fire Department: 883-2340, or dial 198
Cruz Roja Ambulance: 883-2295

until mid-afternoon. The entire trip from Teguci-galpa to the border can be accomplished in three hours by bus, if you don't have to wait long at El Paraíso for a bus to Las Manos. The last bus re-turns to El Paraíso from the border at 5 p.m.

YUSCARÁN

A charming colonial mining town, Yuscarán is a jumble of twisting cobblestone streets and tile-roofed plaster buildings perched on the edge of a mountain at an elevation of 850 meters. The town centers around an inviting square filled with trees and flowers. The climate is semitrop-ical and the surrounding area is pleasingly lush.

Silver ore was discovered in the mountains above Yuscarán in the late 17th or early 18th century, and by the 1740s a town had evolved, in the haphazard manner that characterizes many mining settlements. After hitting an early peak to-ward the end of the 18th century, the mines went into decline until the last decades of the 19th century, when there was a brief revival. Mining currently plays no role in the town's economy, but foreign mining companies regularly come through to take samples, reviving the hopes of the job-starved townsfolk.

Although only about 2,000 people live in Yus-carán, the town is the capital of the El Paraíso department. The best-known *aguardiente* liquor in Honduras is produced here at the **El Buen Gusto** factory. Tours are available, and visitors usually get a little bottle at the end.

Sights

Apart from the simple **Iglesia de San José** on the park, finished in 1768, the only sight of note in town is **Casa Fortín,** a family house built in 1850. The two-story house, declared a national monument, usually serves as the town muse-um but recently has not been in full operation. If it's closed, ask at nearby houses for the own-ers, who will let you in. Downstairs you'll find many mineral samples as well as mining and farming tools from the past century, while up-stairs is a *sala ambiental,* or environmental room, featuring a display on the flora and fauna of the mountain above town. The person in charge of the Casa, Oscar Lesama, is very knowledge-able about Yuscarán's history and surround-ings. He works with a local group that built a few trails in Monserrat and cleared out a couple of old mines for tourists to visit, but their efforts were un-fortunately wiped out by Hurricane Mitch. The mines will likely be cleared out again in the next year or two—ask Oscar.

After visiting Casa Fortín and the church, it's easy to spend an hour or two walking around the town admiring the rustic colonial architec-ture and cobbled streets.

Practicalities

A slightly eccentric Dutchman operates a hotel downhill from the center of town, with rooms with bunk beds and a shared bathroom going for US$8 a night, and private rooms for US$25. The unnamed hotel, tel. 892-7213, may soon have a cafeteria.

Yuscarán cityscape

A foreign couple owns a restored two-story building on the *parque* and reputedly rents rooms out for an unknown price. The owners were unfortunately away on vacation at last check, but one traveler who stayed there said the rooms were very nice and not too expensive. Families regularly rent out rooms to visitors, by the day, week, or month—just ask around.

Típicos Monserrat, just off the park, and the less expensive **Restaurant Filomena de Cortés** (the name of the owner) in an unmarked building across from the Banco de Occidente, both offer decent, inexpensive meals. **Comedor Lita,** almost opposite Casa Fortín, has similar fare, but the spacious dining room with a view out over town makes it a particularly nice spot to enjoy your meal.

Three buses a day drive the 68 km to Tegucigalpa, the last leaving at 2:30 p.m., charging US$1. The 17-km paved spur road to Yuscarán leaves the Danlí-Tegucigalpa highway between Km 47 and 48, at El Empalme.

Reserva Biológica Yuscarán

The highest parts of the mountains looming above town form a biological reserve covering 2,625 hectares. Peaks inside the reserve include El Volcán (1,991 meters), El Fogón (1,825 meters), and Monserrat (1,783 meters). From Yuscarán, take the road out toward the Tegucigalpa highway and look for a dirt road turning steeply up to the left (west) just outside of town, past a small *quebrada* (stream). The road winds precipitously up the mountainside seven km to the Hondutel radio tower atop Cerro Monserrat. Suitable for 4WD only, and unnervingly steep even with that, the road is walkable in a couple of hours. Totally exposed in places on the bare hillside, the road offers spectacular views east over the Río Choluteca Valley and into Nicaragua and south down to the Pacific Ocean.

The uppermost part of the mountain is covered by a modest cloud forest, some of it secondary growth. An easily spotted trail leaves the dirt road from just below the Hondutel radio tower and heads down into the forest, where you can look out for the many noisy birds living in the reserve. Visitors could pitch a tent easily enough either near the tower or in the woods below. Try to convince the Hondutel *vigilante* to let you into the compound on the mountaintop for the view across to the forest-covered peak of **El Volcán,** to the west.

A saddle, now cleared of its forest and used as pasture, connects Cerro Monserrat to the main section of the reserve around El Volcán. Beware of camping out in this pasture as the ticks are plentiful (I can personally vouch for that)—stick to the forest near the Hondutel tower. No trails appear to continue west from the saddle up into the forest toward El Volcán, though they may have just been blocked off by Hurricane Mitch. El Volcán is reportedly best accessed from the *aldeas* of La Granadilla and La Cidra, on the north side of the reserve. Take the road out of Yuscarán toward the highway, and look for a well-traveled gravel road turning left (west) three km from town. Off this road, which leads eventually to Güinope in the Valle de Zamorano, a side road turns off left (south) up toward El Volcán. The only trails out this way will be from local hunters.

Cerro Monserrat and the surrounding hills are perforated with dozens of old mines. Three mines close to Yuscarán were cleared out for visitors, but Hurricane Mitch unfortunately closed off the entrances again. A local group hopes to reopen them again soon.

Elsewhere Near Yuscarán

Two major sets of petroglyphs are located south of Yuscarán, one near the junction of the Río Oropolí and the Río Choluteca past the town of Oropolí, and the other near the village of Orealí, closer to Yuscarán. Along the banks of the Río Choluteca near Orealí are a series of swimmable hot springs. As the Río Choluteca here is downstream of Tegucigalpa, it would seem advisable not to take a cooling-off dip in the river, but the springs themselves are clean. Two buses daily drive between Yuscarán and Oropolí, and hitchhiking is not difficult.

Off the Tegucigalpa-Danlí highway, near the Yuscarán turnoff, is **Teupasenti,** a sizable market town for the many coffee growers in the area. Farther up this road will take you to the village of El Chile and the southern side of the **Reserva Biológica El Chile,** a small patch of cloud forest. Buses to Teupasenti leave Tegucigalpa's Mercado Jacaleapa twice a day, and truck *jalones* up to El Chile are not hard to find.

The town of **Moroceli,** also off the Tegucigalpa highway near Yuscarán, west of Teupasenti, has a large cigar factory right in the center of town, run by a Cuban expatriate who is reportedly happy to take visitors on a tour of his shop.

BOOKLIST

HISTORY

General History and Information

Acker, Alison. *Honduras: The Making of a Banana Republic.* Boston: South End Press, 1988. Acker's account of Honduran history is somewhat cursory, but the slim volume makes good reading.

Alvarado, Elvia. *Don't Be Afraid, Gringo: A Honduran Woman Speaks from the Heart.* New York: Harper and Row, 1989. An excellent and at times harrowing account of life as a poor peasant woman in rural Honduras.

Barry, Tom, and Kent Norsworthy. *Honduras: The Essential Guide to its Politics, Economy, Society and Environment.* Albuquerque, NM: Resource Center Press, 1994. A responsible though relentlessly critical general overview of present-day Honduran politics, society, and economics.

Chapman, Anne MacKaye. *Masters of Animals: Oral Traditions of the Tolupan Indians, Honduras.* Philadelphia: Gordon & Breach Science Publications, 1992.

Davidson, William V. *Historical Geography of the Bay Islands, Honduras: Anglo-Hispanic Conflict in the Western Caribbean.* Birmingham, AL: Southern University Press, 1979.

González, Nancie L. *Sojourners of the Caribbean. Ethnogenesis and Ethnohistory of the Garífuna.* Urbana, IL: University of Illinois Press, 1988.

Merrill, Tim L. *Honduras: A Country Study.* Washington, D.C.: U.S Government, 1995. Put out by the Department of the Army, this area handbook is freighted with some rather obvious built-in biases (the historical account of the Contra affair is laughable), but it is nonetheless a good source of general information on Honduras.

Peckenham, Nancy, and Annie Street, eds. *Honduras: Portrait of a Captive Nation.* New York: Praeger, 1985. This collection of essays covering Honduran history from colonial times to the mid-1980s ranges from obscure to extremely enlightening.

Yuscarán, Guillermo. *Gringos In Honduras: The Good, the Bad, and the Ugly.* Tegucigalpa: Nuevo Sol Publications, 1995. Otherwise known as William Lewis, Yuscarán has written several volumes of short stories about his adopted country, as well as two interesting short histories, one on foreigners who have lived in Honduras, and the second about Honduras' best-known painter (below).

Yuscarán, Guillermo. *Velásquez: The Man and His Art.* Tegucigalpa: Nuevo Sol Publications, 1994.

Colonial Era

Chamberlain, R.S. *The Conquest and Colonization of Honduras, 1502-1550.* Washington, D.C.: Carnegie Institute, 1957. Although dated, Chamberlain's book remains the only detailed, practically day-by-day account of Honduras' conquest.

Floyd, T.S. *The Anglo-Spanish Struggle for Mosquitia.* Albuquerque, NM: University of New Mexico Press, 1967. The book focuses on the centuries-long battle for the Caribbean coast between the English and the Spanish, a little-studied aspect of Central American colonial history.

Newson, Linda. *The Cost of Conquest: Indian Decline under Spanish Rule in Honduras.* Boulder, CO: Westview Press, 1986. Rather than trace the specific course of events in colonial Honduras, Newson relates the broad panorama of Honduras before, during, and after colonization to assess its impact on the region's indigenous populations.

The Banana Companies

Amaya Amador, Ramón. *Prisión Verde*. Tegucigalpa: Editorial Baktun, 1983, third edition. Although technically a novel, Amaya's famed (in Latin America) work provides an excellent though chilling account of life in a banana plantation from the point of view of a Honduran worker.

Karnes, Thomas L. *Tropical Enterprise: The Rise of the Standard Fruit and Steamship Company in Latin America*. Baton Rouge, LA: Louisiana State University Press, 1978.

Kepner, Charles David, Jr. and Jay Henry Soothill. *The Banana Empire: A Case Study of Economic Imperialism*. New York: Russell and Russell, 1935.

Langley, Lester and Thomas Schoonover. *The Banana Men: American Mercenaries and Entrepreneurs in Central America, 1880-1930*. Lexington, KY: University of Kentucky Press, 1995. Although the first chapter is numbingly theoretical, the rest of the book is a fascinating account of the wild characters involved in creating and running the Central American banana empires. Special attention is paid to Lee Christmas, a man who deserves a full-length feature film to do his story justice.

McCann, Thomas. *An American Company: The Tragedy of United Fruit*. New York: Crown Publishers, 1976.

The Soccer War

Anderson, Thomas. *The War of the Dispossessed: Honduras and El Salvador, 1969*. Lincoln: University of Nebraska Press, 1981.

Durham, William H. *Scarcity and Survival in Central America: Ecological Origins of the Soccer War*. Stanford, CA: Stanford University Press, 1979.

Honduras and the Central American Crisis

LaFeber, Walter. *Inevitable Revolutions*. New York: W.W. Norton, 1983. Not specifically about Honduras, LaFeber's classic work brilliantly traces the development of U.S. foreign policy in Central America and the revolutionary fermenting of the 1970s and '80s.

Schulz, Donald E. and Deborah Sundloff Schulz. *The United States, Honduras, and the Crisis in Central America*. Boulder, CO: Westview Press, 1994. Possibly the best book of Honduran history written in English—and maybe in any language—the Schulzes' book minutely traces the course of the country in the 1980s, with special emphasis on relations with the United States and the Contras. For anyone interested in understanding Honduras during that time and today as well, this extremely well-written, balanced, and occasionally very funny book is a must-read.

LITERATURE AND TRAVELOGUES

19th-Century Travelers

For some reason, Honduras seemed to attract foreign travelers with literary proclivities during the past century. Of the four books listed below, Stephens' is by far the most famous. Wells, a mining engineer sent to prospect in Honduras, wrote a lively account with a wealth of detailed observations, particularly regarding Olancho.

Cecil, Charles. *Honduras: A Land of Great Depth*. New York: Rand McNally, 1890.

Soltera, Maria. *A Lady's Ride Across Honduras*. Gainesville, FL: University of Florida Press, 1964.

Stephens, J.L. *Incidents of Travel in Central America, Chiapas, and Yucatán*. New York: Dover, 1969, two volumes. Originally published by Harper and Brothers, New York, 1841.

Wells, William. *Explorations and Adventures in Honduras*. New York: Harper, 1857.

Fiction

Henry, O. *Cabbages and Kings.* New York: Doubleday, Page and Co., 1904. Famed short story writer O. Henry (the pen name of William Sydney Porter) spent some time in Puerto Cortés and Trujillo around the turn of the century while on the run from U.S. authorities, who were pursuing him on charges of embezzlement. With the material gathered during his stay, he wrote this collection of stories.

Theroux, Paul. *The Mosquito Coast.* New York: Avon, 1982. This novel, along with the movie version starring Harrison Ford, has probably done more to put the Mosquitia region of northeastern Honduras on the map than anything else. Unfortunately, the site was apparently chosen by Theroux to represent the lowest state of humanity, and he shows little appreciation for anything Honduran.

Yuscarán, Guillermo. *Blue Pariah, Conociendo a la Gente Garífuna, Points of Light, Beyond Honduras, Northcoast Honduras, La Luz Hondureña.* Tegucigalpa: Nuevo Sol Publications. William Lewis, now known by his adopted name Guillermo Yuscarán, lives in Honduras, where he paints and writes short stories and novels. A born storyteller, Yuscarán has published several fiction and nonfiction books on Honduras. These can be found in several bookstores and more expensive hotels in Tegucigalpa, San Pedro Sula, Copán, the Bay Islands, and the north coast beach towns.

RECREATION AND TRAVEL

Collins, Sharon. *Diving and Snorkeling Guide to Roatán and Honduras' Bay Islands.* Houston: Pisces Books, 1997, second edition.

Garoutte, Cindy. *Diving the Bay Islands.* New York: AquaQuest Publications, 1995. AquaQuest line: (800) 933-8989, (516) 759-0476. Locust Valley, NY. Garoutte's book is obviously the product of much time spent diving in the islands. Her book provides an excellent overview to diving on all the main islands and is accompanied by some spectacular photos and useful dive-site locator maps.

Ford, Frank. *Living Well in Honduras: How to Relocate, Retire, and Increase Your Standard of Living.* Santa Fe, NM: John Muir Publications, 1998. A must-buy for anyone considering moving to Honduras, with helpful suggestions on places to live, legal matters, and more.

Kelly, Joyce. *An Archeological Guide to Northern Central America: Belize, Guatemala, Honduras, and El Salvador.* Norman, OK: University of Oklahoma Press, 1996.

Rhodes, Rick. *Honduras and the Bay Islands, A Mariner's Guide.* Heron Island Media, 1998. For boaters, this is the only guide available with detailed information on sailing and onshore practicalities. Comes with 19 nautical charts and 55 GPS waypoints for harbor entry.

Cruising Guide to the Honduras Bay Islands. Stamford, CT: Wescott Cove Publishing Co. This guide is unfortunately currently out of print, although the publishers say another edition can be expected in 2001. Call the publisher's office in Stamford, Connecticut at tel. (203) 322-0998.

NATURAL HISTORY

Mader, Ron and Jim Gollin. *Honduras: Adventures in Nature.* Santa Fe, NM: John Muir Publications, 1997. An overview of protected areas in Honduras, combining nuts and bolts travel practicalities with environmental information.

Forests

Carr, Archie. *High Jungles and Low.* Gainesville, FL: University of Florida Press, 1953. Well-known biologist Archie Carr spent several years in Honduras, most of it at the Escuela Agrícola Panamericana in the Valle de Zamorano. His account of this time combines plant and animal biology, particularly regarding the cloud forest and the tropical rainforest, with anecdotes and stories about local people. This well-written volume, obviously a labor of love, clearly shows the author's affection for Honduras and its people. Carr also wrote "Animal Habitats In Honduras," one of the best English-language essays on the subject, which appeared in *The Bulletin of the American Museum of Natural History,* 1950, volume 96.

Forsyth, Adrian and Ken Miyata. *Tropical Nature: Life and Death in the Rain Forests of Central and South America.* New York: Charles Scribner's Sons, 1984. Not specifically about Honduras, this book is nonetheless a good anecdotal overview of the workings of the rainforest ecosystem found in La Mosquitia, written for the general reader.

Kricher, John and Mark Plotkin. *A Neotropical Companion: An Introduction to the Animals, Plant, and Ecosystems of the New World tropics.* Princeton, NJ: Princeton University Press, 1997. Another good general study for nonspecialists, more thorough and less anecdotal than *Tropical Nature.*

Reef

Humann, Paul. *Reef Fish Identification, Reef Creature Identification,* and *Reef Coral Identification.* Jacksonville, FL: New World Publishing, Inc. This three-volume set, published, respectively, in 1989, 1992, and 1993, is considered the best available on Caribbean reef life. The volumes can be ordered through the publisher by calling (904) 737-6558.

Birds

No bird guide exists for Honduras alone, although bird man Mark Bonta (author of the special topic on birding in this book) will publish one soon. In the meantime, two good regional guides cover most of the species found in the country.

Howell, Steven and Sophie Webb. *A Guide to the Birds of Mexico and Northern Central America.* Oxford: Oxford University Press, 1995.

Ridgely, Robert and John A. Gwynne, Jr. *A Guide to the Birds of Panama, with Costa Rica, Nicaragua, and Honduras.* Princeton, NJ: Princeton University Press, 1989.

GLOSSARY

aguas calientes, aguas termales—hot or thermal waters, hot springs

alcalde—mayor

alfarda—an inclined plane of decorative stonework, an example of which can be seen at the Mayan ruins of El Puente

aguardiente—the favored Honduran poor-quality booze

artesanías—handicrafts

ayudante—helper, specifically a young man who helps the driver of a bus by seating passengers and collecting fares

baleada—a popular Honduran snack, made with a flour tortilla filled with beans, crumbly cheese, cream, and sometimes other ingredients, then grilled lightly

balneario—swimming hole or pool

bando—a spicy fish stew popular on the north coast and the Bay Islands

bistec—beef steak

billiar—pool, billiards

bodega—storeroom

busito—literally, little bus, frequently used in rural areas

camacha—a traditional Pech instrument similar to a maraca

campesino—peasant; usually a small-scale farmer

canícula—a brief dry spell in August during the middle of the rainy season

cantina—a low-priced bar (not always safe for women)

caoba—mahogany, the most prized wood in Honduras

caracol—literally, the shellfish conch, but also the nickname given to Bay Islanders by mainland residents

casa cural—the administration office of a church

caseta—toll building or place where admission is collected

cassava—a yucca dish made by the north coast Garífuna

cayuco—canoe

champa—a thatch-roofed hut with no walls

chichicaste—a stinging shrub found in Honduras

cipote—Honduran slang for a little kid

colones—Salvadoran currency

comida corriente—a set meal, usually the least expensive choice on a restaurant's menu

conejo—rabbit (often eaten in Honduras)

córdobas—Nicaraguan currency

criollo—a term used in colonial times to denote peoples of Spanish blood born in the Americas

cueva—cave

curandero—a healer using traditional indigenous spiritual techniques and herbal medications

desvio—turnoff, as from a highway onto another road (these are frequently given names in Honduras)

dugu—a Garífuna dance

encomienda—the colonial system of alloting Spaniards land and the right to tribute and labor from Indians living there

guisado—stew

hacienda—a partially or fully self-sufficient ranch (the department of Olancho is known for its haciendas)

indio—the name given to *ladinos* by Miskito, Tawahka, and Pech Indians

jalón—word used to ask for a ride, as in hitchhiking

jejenes—sand flies

junco—a type of palm native to the Santa Bárbara region, used to make baskets, hats, and other crafts

lancha—launch; small, motor-powered boat

libra—pound (the unit of weight)

licuado—a popular drink made by blending milk, sugar, and fruit

ladino—people of mixed Spanish and indigenous blood, comprising most of the population of Honduras

machuca—a Garífuna stew made with fish, banana, and coconut milk

manzana—a unit of land measurement equal to 0.7 hectares; also, an apple

mestizo—a person of mixed indigenous and European blood, a term commonly used in the colonial era but less so now

milpa—a small patch of farmland on which peasants grow beans, corn, and other vegetables, mainly for their own consumption rather than to sell

mondongo—tripe (intestine) soup

nacatamale—a cornmeal food boiled in banana leaves and stuffed with spiced meat and vegetables

nance—a small fruit, often sold on the street in bags as a snack

ocote—a type of pine tree common to the highlands of Honduras

olanchano—someone from the department of Olancho

pan de coco—coconut bread, a Garífuna specialty

panadería—bakery

papel de arroz—rice paper, or cigarette rolling paper

parque—park, usually the downtown square. Unlike many other Latin American countries, Hondurans do not use the word "plaza."

pastelito—a favorite Honduran snack consisting of a puff of dough filled with spiced beef and deep fried

patronatos—local organizations dedicated to preparing saint's day festivals. In Tegucigalpa and other cities, these groups have evolved into grassroots social organizations.

peatonal—pedestrian street

pinchos—a shish kebab-style meal with beef or chicken and vegetables served on a skewer

pipante—a dugout canoe propelled by poles, common in the Mosquitia

pisto—Honduran slang for cash or money

plato del día—plate of the day, an inexpensive set meal

plato típico—the Honduran national dish, which usually includes beef, fried plantain, rice, beans, a chunk of salty cheese, a dash of cream, and lots of tortillas

pulpería—a general store

punta—traditional Garífuna music, a modern version of which has become a popular Honduran dance music

pupusa—a thick tortilla filled with sausage and/or cheese, more common in El Salvador but also found in Honduras

quetzal—a legendarily beautiful bird living in the cloud forests

retablo—an altarpiece at a church. Many are gilded and intricately carved.

ron—rum

sacbé—an elevated Mayan roadway (one is visible at Copán)

salón de billiar—pool hall

sampedrano—a resident of San Pedro Sula

sopa de caracol—conch soup, frequently made with coconut milk

tajadas—fried bananas or plantains, eaten like chips

tapado—a fish, yucca, and coconut dish made by the Garífuna

tenpuca—a traditional Pech drum

terminal de buses—bus terminal

timbre—a type of stamp sold at banks for different amounts, sometimes required to renew a tourist card

torta—a sandwich

tostones—slang term for Honduran 50-cent pieces

tramitador—someone who helps deal with official paperwork

tranquilo—relaxed, sometimes said to another person as an admonition to relax

tránsito—the traffic police

tuk-tuk—a motorized canoe in the Mosquitia, so called for the noise it makes

túmulos—speed bumps

varas—a unit of land measurement equal to 838 square meters

viaje especial—a special trip, in a taxi or boat, which will cost more than a normal ride

vigilante—a guard

wabul—a traditional Miskito Indian drink made from bananas and coconut

zancudos—mosquitoes

zona viva—a district of a town or city known for its nightlife

SPANISH PHRASEBOOK

PRONUNCIATION GUIDE

Consonants

c   as **c** in **cat**, before **a**, **o**, or **u**; like **s** before **e** or **i**
d   as **d** in **dog**, except between vowels, then like **th** in **that**
g   before **e** or **i**, like the **ch** in Scottish **loch**; elsewhere like **g** in **get**
h   always silent
j   like the English **h** in **hotel**, but stronger
ll   like the **y** in **yellow**
ñ   like the **ni** in **onion**
r   always pronounced as strong **r**
rr   trilled **r**
v   similar to the **b** in **boy** (not as English **v**)
y   similar to English, but with a slight **j** sound. When y stands alone it is pronounced like the **e** in **me**.
z   like **s** in **same**
b, f, k, l, m, n, p, q, s, t, w, x as in English

Vowels

a   as in **father**, but shorter
e   as in **hen**
i   as in **machine**
o   as in **phone**
u   usually as in **rule**; when it follows a **q** the **u** is silent; when it follows an **h** or **g** its pronounced like **w**, except when it comes between **g** and **e** or **i**, when it's also silent

NUMBERS

0	*cero*	11	*once*	40	*cuarenta*
1	*uno* (masculine)	12	*doce*	50	*cincuenta*
1	*una* (feminine)	13	*trece*	60	*sesenta*
2	*dos*	14	*catorce*	70	*setenta*
3	*tres*	15	*quince*	80	*ochenta*
4	*cuatro*	16	*diez y seis*	90	*noventa*
5	*cinco*	17	*diez y siete*	100	*cien*
6	*seis*	18	*diez y ocho*	101	*ciento y uno*
7	*siete*	19	*diez y nueve*	200	*doscientos*
8	*ocho*	20	*veinte*	1,000	*mil*
9	*nueve*	21	*viente y uno*	10,000	*diez mil*
10	*diez*	30	*treinta*		

DAYS OF THE WEEK

Sunday — *domingo*
Monday — *lunes*
Tuesday — *martes*
Wednesday — *miércoles*
Thursday — *jueves*
Friday — *viernes*
Saturday — *sábado*

TIME

What time is it? — *¿Qué hora es?*
one o'clock — *la una*
two o'clock — *las dos*
at two o'clock — *a las dos*
ten past three — *las tres y diez*
six a.m. — *las seis de mañana*
six p.m. — *las seis de tarde*
today — *hoy*
tomorrow, morning
  — *mañana, la mañana*
yesterday — *ayer*
day — *día*
week — *semana*
month — *mes*
year — *año*
last night — *anoche*

USEFUL WORDS AND PHRASES

Hello. — *Hola.*
Good morning. — *Buenos días.*
Good afternoon. — *Buenas tardes.*
Good evening. — *Buenas noches.*
How are you? — *¿Cómo está?*
Fine. — *Muy bien.*
And you? — *¿Y usted?*
So-so. — *Más ó menos.*
Thank you. — *Gracias.*
Thank you very much. — *Muchas gracias.*
You're very kind. — *Muy amable.*
You're welcome; literally, "It's nothing."
  — *De nada.*
yes — *sí*
no — *no*
I don't know. — *Yo no sé.*
it's fine; okay — *está bien*
good; okay — *bueno*
please — *por favor*
Pleased to meet you. — *Mucho gusto.*
excuse me (physical) — *perdóneme*
excuse me (speech) — *discúlpeme*
I'm sorry. — *Lo siento.*
goodbye — *adiós*
see you later; literally, "until later"
  — *hasta luego*

more — *más*
less — *menos*
better — *mejor*
much — *mucho*
a little — *un poco*
large — *grande*
small — *pequeño*
quick — *rápido*
slowly — *despacio*
bad — *malo*
difficult — *difícil*
easy — *fácil*
He/She/It is gone; as in "She left," "He's
  gone" — *Ya se fue.*
I don't speak Spanish well.
  — *No hablo bien español.*
I don't understand. — *No entiendo.*
How do you say . . . in Spanish?
  — *¿Cómo se dice . . . en español?*
Do you understand English?
  — *¿Entiende el inglés?*
Is English spoken here? (Does anyone
  here speak English?)
  — *¿Se habla inglés aquí?*

TERMS OF ADDRESS

I — *yo*
you (formal) — *usted*
you (familiar) — *tú*
he/him — *él*
she/her — *ella*
we/us — *nosotros*
you (plural) — *vos*
they/them (all males or mixed gender)
  — *ellos*
they/them (all females) — *ellas*

Mr., sir — *señor*
Mrs., madam — *señora*
Miss, young lady — *señorita*
wife — *esposa*
husband — *marido* or *esposo*
friend — *amigo* (male), *amiga* (female)
sweetheart — *novio* (male), *novia* (female)
son, daughter — *hijo, hija*
brother, sister — *hermano, hermana*
father, mother — *padre, madre*

GETTING AROUND

Where is . . . ? — *¿Dónde está . . . ?*
How far is it to . . . ?
  — *¿A cuánto queda . . . ?*
from . . . to . . . — *de . . . a . . .*
highway — *la carretera*
road — *el camino*
street — *la calle*
block — *la cuadra*
kilometer — *kilómetro*

mile (commonly used near the
  U.S. border) — *milla*
north — *el norte*
south — *el sur*
west — *el oeste*
east — *el este*
straight ahead — *al derecho* or *adelante*
to the right — *a la derecha*
to the left — *a la izquierda*

ACCOMMODATIONS

Can I (we) see a room?
  — *¿Puedo (podemos) ver un cuarto?*
What is the rate? — *¿Cuál es el precio?*
a single room — *un cuarto sencillo*
a double room — *un cuarto doble*
key — *llave*
bathroom — *lavabo* or *baño*
hot water — *agua caliente*

cold water — *agua fría*
towel — *toalla*
soap — *jabón*
toilet paper — *papel higiénico*
air conditioning — *aire acondicionado*
fan — *ventilador*
blanket — *frazada* or *manta*

PUBLIC TRANSPORT

bus stop — *la parada del autobús*
main bus terminal
  — *terminal de buses*
railway station
  — *la estación de ferrocarril*
airport — *el aeropuerto*
ferry terminal
  — *la terminal del transbordador*

I want a ticket to . . .
  — *Quiero un boleto a . . .*
I want to get off at . . .
  — *Quiero bajar en . . .*
Here, please. — *Aquí, por favor.*
Where is this bus going?
  — *¿Adónde va este autobús?*
roundtrip — *ida y vuelta*
What do I owe? — *¿Cuánto le debo?*

DRIVING

Full, please (at gasoline station).
— *Lleno, por favor.*
My car is broken down.
— *Se me ha descompuesto el carro.*
I need a tow. — *Necesito un remolque.*
Is there a garage nearby?
— *¿Hay un garage cerca?*
Is the road passable with this car (truck)?
— *¿Puedo pasar con este carro
(esta troca)?*

With four-wheel drive?
— *¿Con doble tracción?*
It's not passable — *No hay paso.*
traffic light — *el semáfora*
traffic sign — *el señal*
gasoline (petrol) — *gasolina*
gasoline station — *gasolinera*
oil — *aceite*
water — *agua*
flat tire — *llanta desinflada*
tire repair shop — *llantera*

AUTO PARTS

fan belt — *banda de ventilador*
battery — *batería*
fuel (water) pump —
bomba de gasolina (agua)
spark plug — *bujía*
carburetor — *carburador*
distributor — *distribuidor*
axle — *eje*
clutch — *embrague*

gasket — *empaque, junta*
filter — *filtro*
brakes — *frenos*
tire — *llanta*
hose — *manguera*
starter — *marcha, arranque*
radiator — *radiador*
voltage regulator — *regulado de voltaje*

MAKING PURCHASES

I need . . . — *Necesito . . .*
I want . . . — *Deseo . . .* or *Quiero . . .*
I would like . . . (more polite)
— *Quisiera . . .*
How much does it cost? — *¿Cuánto cuesta?*
What's the exchange rate?
— *¿Cuál es el tipo de cambio?*

Can I see . . . ? — *¿Puedo ver . . . ?*
this one — *ésta/ésto*
expensive — *caro*
cheap — *barato*
cheaper — *más barato*
too much — *demasiado*

HEALTH

Help me please. — *Ayúdeme por favor.*
I am ill. — *Estoy enfermo.*
pain — *dolor*
fever — *fiebre*
stomache ache — *dolor de estómago*
vomiting — *vomitar*
diarrhea — *diarrea*

drugstore — *farmacia*
medicine — *medicina, remedio*
pill, tablet — *pastilla*
birth control pills — *pastillas
anticonceptivas*
condoms — *preservativos*

FOOD

menu — *lista, menú*	watermelon — *sandía*
glass — *vaso*	banana — *plátano*
fork — *tenedor*	apple — *manzana*
knife — *cuchillo*	orange — *naranja*
spoon — *cuchara, cucharita*	meat (without) — *carne (sin)*
napkin — *servilleta*	beef — *carne de res*
soft drink — *refresco*	chicken — *pollo*
coffee, cream — *café, crema*	fish — *pescado*
tea — *té*	shellfish — *mariscos*
sugar — *azúcar*	fried — *a la plancha*
purified water — *agua purificado*	roasted — *asado*
bottled carbonated water — *agua mineral*	barbecue, barbecued — *al carbón*
bottled uncarbonated water — *agua sin gas*	breakfast — *desayuno*
beer — *cerveza*	lunch — *almuerzo*
wine — *vino*	dinner (often eaten in late afternoon)
milk — *leche*	— *comida*
juice — *jugo*	dinner, or a late night snack — *cena*
eggs — *huevos*	the check — *la cuenta*
bread — *pan*	

VOS

In Honduras as well as several other Central and South American countries, the pronoun "*tú*" is not frequently heard, and it sounds to locals (especially out in the countryside) like a sophisticated affectation. More commonly used, and rarely taught to westerners in their Spanish classes, is "*vos*."

Essentially vos is used in the same instances as *tú*, that is, between two people who have a certain degree of casual familiarity or friendliness, in place of the more formal "*usted*." The *vos* form is derived from "*vosotros*," the second person plural (you all) still used in Spain. However, *vosotros* is not used in Latin America, even in places where *vos* is common.

For all tenses other than the present indicative, present subjunctive, and command forms, the vos form of the verb is exactly the same as *tú*. Hence: *tú andaste/vos andaste* (past tense), *tú andabas/vos andabas* (past imperfect), *tú andarás/vos andarás* (future), *tú andarías/vos andarías* (conditional).

In the present indicative, the conjugation is the same as with *tú*, but the last syllable is stressed

with an accent. The exception is with -ir verbs, in which the final "i" is retained, instead of changing to an "e." Hence: *tú andas/vos andás, tú comes/vos comés, tú escribes/vos escribís*.

In the present subjunctive, the same construction is followed as with the normal subjunctive, except the *vos* accent is retained. Hence: *tú andes/vos andés, tú comas/vos comás, tú escribas/vos escribás*.

In radical changing verbs like *tener, poder,* or *dormir*, the *vos* form does not change from vowel to dipthong *(tienes, puedes, duermes)* in the present subjunctive form. Hence: *vos tengás, vos podás, vos durmás*.

Vos commands are formed by simply dropping the final "r" on the infinitive and adding an accent over the last vowel. Hence: *vos andá, vos comé, vos escribí*. When using object pronouns with *vos*, "*te*" is still used. Hence: *Yo te lo escribí a vos*.

One common irregular *vos* form is "*sos*" for *ser* (to be). Also, because the conjugation would be bizarre, the verb "*ir*" is not used in the *vos* form. Instead use *andar: vos andás*.

INDEX

ARCHAEOLOGY/ARCHAEOLOGICAL SITES

CHURCHES/CATHEDRALS

MUSEUMS

SCUBA DIVING

CHRIS HUMPHREY BEGAN TRAVELING at the age of five, when he ventured across town to a friend's grandmother's house, and he's been at it ever since. Chris moved to Mexico City in 1994, where he began working as a journalist, first with an English-language newspaper and later as the politics reporter for Bridge Financial News. He has written freelance stories on business, travel, and politics in Latin America for a variety of publications, including *The Houston Chronicle, The San Francisco Chronicle, Latin Finance, Outside,* and *Summit.* In addition to writing the *Honduras Handbook,* Chris co-authored the first edition of Moon's *Mexico City Handbook* with Joe Cummings. When not staying up all night to meet deadlines, Chris spends time reading whatever book comes his way; listening to music at full volume; trying not get hurt playing rugby, mountain biking, and climbing; and doing his utmost to keep his decrepit vehicles on the road. He lives in Mexico City.

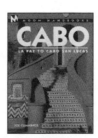

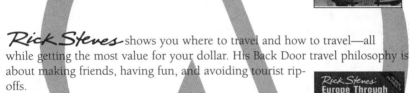
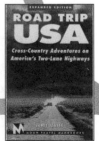

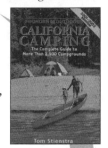

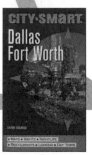

www.travelmatters.com

User-friendly, informative, and fun:
Because travel *matters.*

Visit our newly launched web site and explore the variety of titles and travel information available online, featuring an interactive *Road Trip USA* exhibit.

also check out:

www.ricksteves.com

The Rick Steves web site is bursting with information to boost your travel I.Q. and liven up your European adventure.

www.foghorn.com

Visit the Foghorn Outdoors web site for more information on the premier source of U.S. outdoor recreation guides.

www.moon.com

The Moon Handbooks web site offers interesting information and practical advice that ensure an extraordinary travel experience.

U.S.~METRIC CONVERSION

1 inch	=	2.54 centimeters (cm)
1 foot	=	.3048 meters (m)
1 yard	=	0.914 meters
1 mile	=	1.6093 kilometers (km)
1 km	=	.6214 miles
1 fathom	=	1.8288 m
1 chain	=	20.1168 m
1 furlong	=	201.168 m
1 acre	=	.4047 hectares
1 sq km	=	100 hectares
1 sq mile	=	2.59 square km
1 ounce	=	28.35 grams
1 pound	=	.4536 kilograms
1 short ton	=	.90718 metric ton
1 short ton	=	2000 pounds
1 long ton	=	1.016 metric tons
1 long ton	=	2240 pounds
1 metric ton	=	1000 kilograms
1 quart	=	.94635 liters
1 US gallon	=	3.7854 liters
1 Imperial gallon	=	4.5459 liters
1 nautical mile	=	1.852 km

To compute celsius temperatures, subtract 32 from Fahrenheit and divide by 1.8. To go the other way, multiply celsius by 1.8 and add 32.

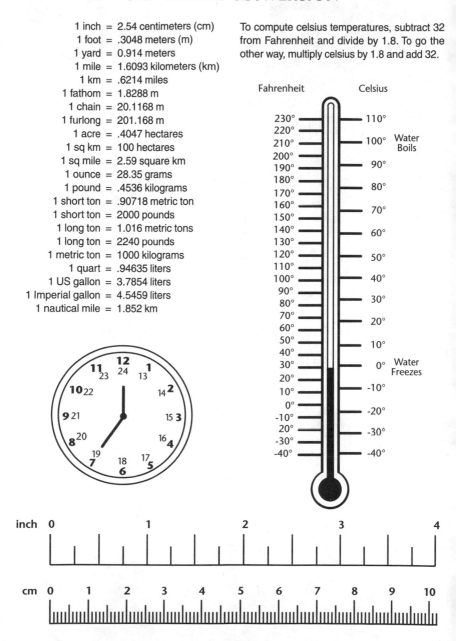

Will you have enough stories to tell your grandchildren?